MW00640138

ASIAN LAW SERIES

SCHOOL OF LAW

UNIVERSITY OF WASHINGTON

Number 3

The Asian Law Series was initiated with the cooperation of the University of Washington Press and the Institute for Comparative and Foreign Area Studies in 1969 in order to publish the results of several projects under way in Japanese, Chinese, and Korean law. The members of the editorial committee are: Herbert J. Ellison, Director of the Institute for Comparative and Foreign Area Studies; John O. Haley; and Dan Fenno Henderson, chairman.

1. *The Constitution of Japan: Its First Twenty Years, 1947–67*, edited by Dan Fenno Henderson

2. *Village "Contracts" in Tokugawa Japan,* by Dan Fenno Henderson

3. *Chinese Family Law and Social Change in Historical and Comparative Perspective,* edited by David C. Buxbaum

4. *Law and Politics in China's Foreign Trade,* edited by Victor H. Li

5. *Patent and Know-how Licensing in Japan and the United States,* edited by Teruo Doi and Warren L. Shattuck

6. *The Constitutional Case Law of Japan: Selected Supreme Court Decisions, 1961–70,* by Hiroshi Itoh and Lawrence Ward Beer

CHINESE FAMILY LAW AND SOCIAL CHANGE

in Historical and Comparative Perspective

Edited by
DAVID C. BUXBAUM

UNIVERSITY OF WASHINGTON PRESS
Seattle and London

Copyright © 1978 by the University of Washington Press
Printed in Hong Kong

All rights reserved. No portion of this publication may be reproduced or transmitted in any form or by any means, electronic or mechanical, including photocopying, recording, or any information storage or retrieval system, without permission in writing from the publisher.

Library of Congress Cataloging in Publication Data
Main entry under title:

Chinese family law and social change in historical and comparative perspective.

(Asian law series; 3)
"A collection of papers delivered (and discussed) at a conference sponsored by the University of Washington Law School in August 1968."
Includes index.
1. Domestic relations—China—History—Congresses. 2. Domestic relations—Taiwan—History—Congresses. 3. Domestic relations—Asia—History—Congresses. 4. Sociological jurisprudence—Congresses. I. Buxbaum, David C. II. Washington (State). University. School of Law. III. Series.
Law   301.42'0951   76-7781   ISBN 0-295-95448-5

Preface

The subject of "law and social change" has been frequently discussed in recent years by law scholars and social scientists. However, little research has been undertaken on the role of law as an instrument of social change in China, and theories about this process are generally unsubstantiated. Just how little has been done in this field becomes obvious when one realizes that rarely, if ever, have American law scholars and social scientists come together to discuss even a specific domestic area of law and related social institutions, although Americans have done more of this type of research than most Western scholars. Nevertheless, judges, legislators, and scholars in the United States still frequently assume that a judicial decision or passage of legislation is in itself invariably sufficient to bring about intended social change. Hopefully, comparative law scholars and social scientists with comparative interests have provided a lead in the research presented in this manuscript to those who restrict their scholarship to one jurisdiction.

Quite simply, in order to know why social change occurs and the role of law and other institutions therein—a subject of great importance throughout the world—it is necessary to evaluate change on the basis of field research and other detailed data. This truism, trite as it is, has yet to find its way into the minds of most law scholars and law makers dealing with problems of law and social change. This volume is a collection of papers delivered (and discussed) at a conference sponsored by the University of Washington Law School in August 1968. The contributors represented the disciplines of sociology, anthropology, and law, and came from Europe, Taiwan, and Japan, as well as from the United States. Because major research efforts had recently been devoted to the Chinese family and family law, it was felt that at conference time much new data would be available which would permit us to examine changes in the Chinese family and thereby an excellent opportunity would also be provided for an evaluation of the role that law played, if any, in bringing about such changes. In order to accomplish this we examined Chinese family and law in historical and comparative perspective, hoping thereby to clarify developments. We were most fortunate in our ability to bring together many of the best scholars in the world of both the family and family law to discuss this subject. Although there have been many unforeseen delays between the presentation of the original papers and publication of this volume, it is hoped that the overview of Chinese family law and social change presented here will be no less significant today than it was at the time the conference was held.

While I chaired and organized the conference, much of its initial impetus was provided by the Director of the Asian Law Program of the University of Washington, Dan Fenno Henderson, who saw its possibilities at an early date and helped to sponsor several of the major research projects that culminated in this meeting. In view of the very conservative and traditional bias of American law schools, few law scholars have exhibited both the imagination and courage required to sponsor a project such as this one. Certainly Professor Henderson in his own teaching and research and in his sponsorship of the research of others, has done much to take comparative law out of the realm of the esoteric and superficial and to bring it into the world of real scholarly endeavor. He has contributed in the same manner to the field of law and social change. He had the good fortune to be supported in his endeavors by an imaginative dean, Lehan K. Tunks, and a senior scholar of renown, Warren L. Shattuck.

To these scholars, and to all who helped in bringing this volume, I express my sincere thanks.

DAVID C. BUXBAUM

New York

September 1976

Contents

Chinese Family Law and Social Change
in Historical and
Comparative Perspective

Family Law and Social Change: A Theoretical Introduction

DAVID C. BUXBAUM

This introduction is an attempt to build a preliminary theory of the role of law in social change based only in small part upon data provided by the papers in this volume which deal primarily with China. The theory is offered to other scholars interested in the field for criticism and refinement so that we may be able to develop more sophisticated concepts for dealing with problems of law as an instrument of change, but is not offered as definitive theory.

TOWARD A THEORY OF THE RELATIONSHIP BETWEEN LAW AND SOCIAL CHANGE

The successful use of positive law as an instrument of social change is dependent upon many variables. Isolation of some of the more significant factors should permit a theoretical conception of the entire process.

Judicial-Political Power

Communications. In order to function as an instrument of change, legal institutions must be able to communicate their decisions to the population. Therefore, a good system of communications within the society is required. Aside from the ability to physically transmit information from one place to another, there must be political-legal communication with members of the populace. Education plays an important role in this area because it is obviously easier to transmit information rapidly to a literate population. On the other hand, even in traditional societies with low levels of literacy, there are relatively efficient means of transmitting legal information, particularly if there is a literary elite. Notice boards were used in both Japan[1] and China in

---

[1] *See* D. Henderson, *Promulgation of Tokugawa Statutes,* in TRADITIONAL AND MODERN LEGAL INSTITUTIONS IN ASIA AND AFRICA 9, at 19 (D. Buxbaum ed. 1967).

traditional times. Public readings[2] and lectures by gentry elite[3] are other means of spreading information. In modernizing societies such as China with increasing levels of literacy, radios and loudspeakers as well as frequent political meetings are utilized to communicate legal norms and decisions to the population.

Extent of judicial penetration. Aside from communications within the society, another major factor affecting the utilization of positive law to bring about social change is the degree to which the judiciary has penetrated the society.

The formal court system must be available at reasonable expense and distance from the numerous centers of population. It must also use language and law that are intelligible to the people of the community within which the court operates.[4] Even if there is no linguistic problem, rules that are imported from foreign soil and substantially vary from indigenous practice, may be misunderstood, resulting in indifference or hostility on the part of the populace to the formal judicial institutions.

In many modernizing nations the formal court system is staffed by a foreign-educated elite. The new judicial personnel, if educated outside their own nation or in foreign-type schools within their nation, must acquire knowledge of the social circumstances within which they administer law, if they are to be able to effectively administer justice. A jurist trained in England or the Soviet Union, although of Chinese ancestry, is not necessarily aware of the social circumstances in Singapore or China, within which he dispenses justice.

In most premodern societies, the law is largely administered by an informal court system. The clans, families, and guilds of traditional peasant society, or the tribal organizations of preliterate society, mediate most disputes.

If positive law is going to influence social practice in these societies, it must also be applied by the informal courts. It is necessary either to replace the

---

[2] *Id.* at 16.

[3] K. HSIAO, RURAL CHINA, IMPERIAL CONTROL IN THE NINETEENTH CENTURY 184 ff. (1960).

[4] *See* S. Ottenberg, *Local Government and the Law in Southern Nigeria,* in TRADITIONAL AND MODERN LEGAL INSTITUTIONS IN ASIA AND AFRICA 26, at 39 (D. Buxbaum ed. 1967), where he notes that the language of certain rules of council in Nigeria were ". . . detailed, complicated, in a second language, and foreign to many persons." This linguistic problem exists in many "former" colonial nations such as Singapore, Malaysia, India, and Hong Kong to name just a few. The problem is partially one of the colonial-trained elite having a vested interest in the colonial language and, furthermore, a problem of what language to use in multi-ethnic states with communal conflicts. Even dialects are important where, for example, in Taiwan, the police and judicial officials are often "mainlanders" who cannot communicate easily with the "Taiwanese." However, the problem of communication in Taiwan is not a serious one. There are also dialect problems in mainland China as seen by the deliberate transfer of southern cadre to the north, and vice versa.

informal courts (which generally emphasize conciliation) by other semi-formal institutions, as has been done in the People's Republic of China, or to politicize the existing traditional structure sufficiently to affect the norms used by these "courts" in their administration of justice.

Degree of judicial-political power available. In order to affect the norms used by the informal courts and to catalyze social change, the state must be favorably disposed toward the use of judicial-political power. The degree of power needed will vary with the size of the group affected by the law and with the degree to which the law deviates from traditional norms, thus creating a potential reaction of hostility or resistance.

Judicial-political power may be applied by propaganda-education methods. The dissemination of new norms may take place in schools and at political meetings as well as through the mass media and the theater. They may also be publicized by the use of show trials or mass meetings at which trials are discussed.

Another important aspect of judicial-political power is the application of coercion. The ability of the courts and other institutions to impose judicial sanctions upon violators of the new "legislation"[5] will noticeably affect compliance. Of course, there is no direct relationship between willingness and ability to apply sanctions, and the impact of "legislation" upon social practice. Excessive or misdirected sanctions may create additional hostility to an enactment.

Power of the Social Groups Affected

The effectiveness of positive law depends not only upon judicial-political power, but also upon the size of the groups affected and the extent to which they feel a benefit or detriment.

The size of the group affected by the new law naturally influences the ease with which a particular norm may be institutionalized. If there is a small alien landlord class which controls the land, it may be easy to redistribute this land to the peasant population. On the other hand, new laws that raise the social status of women in a traditionally patriarchal society are ordinarily difficult to institutionalize. The whole social structure, or a large part of it, may have to be altered in order to bring about the desired change.

In addition to the function of size, the power of the group affected is very important in determining its ability to resist new positive law. If a small landlord class controls local credit necessary to finance farmers until harvest time, it may well be difficult to effectively take their land from them, even if they are a small group. Similarly, if a relatively small group (such as the farm organizations in the United States) exerts important influence upon the

---

[5] "Legislation" by a legislative, administrative, or judicial body is included in this term.

political-legal institutions, it may be difficult to enact and/or enforce legislation
against it. A diminution in the real economic, political-legal, or social power
of a group may make it easier to affect them by new legislation.

A third related factor is the degree to which the group feels affected by
the "legislation" aimed at it. In many cases part of a group may regard a
particular law as bestowing a benefit, and another part may feel adversely
affected. If the group feels its very existence is endangered by new legislation,
it is more likely to resist it strenuously. If, on the other hand, the group feels
that while its interests are adversely affected, nevertheless it may survive,
while opposition on the other hand may bring destruction, the group affected
may then, as certain capitalists in China did in the 1950's, prefer to cooperate
with the regime and to abide by the new legislation even when it is partly
directed against them. The important factor here is not to what extent the
group actually is affected, but to what extent it feels itself affected. Furthermore, it is often difficult for a group actually threatened with destruction to
accept that fact, and if rationales are provided for by the lawmaker, the group
may grasp at them as many Jews did in Europe and many capitalists did
in China.

Values of the Society and the New Laws

The extent to which groups in the society believe they are affected by a
particular piece of legislation is in part dependent upon the values of the
society.

The traditional values of the modernizing society are important from at
least two points of view. The first is the degree to which traditional values
manifest receptivity to change. If the society's values are fairly rigid ones and
there is a low tolerance for perceived change, then any "legislation" may be
met with resistance. If, on the other hand, change was acceptable even in the
traditional value system, there would be less resistance to institutionalizing
new laws. We might expect therefore that in a Muslim country with fairly
strict religious laws and a high regard for the *Koran* and other religious
norms, it might, under most circumstances, be more difficult to effect change
than in a Muslim country in which the *adat* always played an important
role in law and in which the *adat* was subject to change, including perceived
change.

Traditional values permeate different societies in different ways and to
different degrees. Thus, a further factor in determining the susceptibility of
a particular society toward change would be the degree to which traditional
values continue to hold sway. This depends upon numerous factors such as
the impact of foreign ideas and institutions, the passage of time since the
downfall of the traditional political hierarchy, and the extent to which
economic and social changes deviating from traditional patterns have taken
place.

Finally, the extent to which traditional or existing values conflict with the new law will determine the extent to which "legislation" might find opposition within the society. If, for example, traditional values were always ambivalent about secondary wives and it was in fact possible for only a few wealthy citizens to take advantage of such an institution, then legislation to prohibit the taking of secondary wives might easily be enforced and might rapidly affect social behavior.

The other side of the coin is the extent to which the values of the new positive law conflict with traditional or existing values. The greater the degree of conflict with existing values, the more difficult one might expect it to be to change actual social practice.

Summary

We have talked of judicial-political power, of the power of the social group affected, and of the values of the society and the new laws as if each of these three factors could be discussed in isolation. Actually, they are all mutually dependent and interrelated. Furthermore, there are other factors—such as the degree of legitimacy of the regime, and the economic and social institutions that support the political-legal institutions—that we have only touched upon indirectly. Nevertheless, we have, hopefully, isolated some of the more important factors that determine the impact positive law may have on social change.

In order to test the above analysis, and to see whether it helps us to understand law and social change, we may examine it in light of some facts presented in this volume.

THE THEORY IN LIGHT OF REALITY

Judicial-Political Power

Communications. In traditional China levels of literacy were low and dialect barriers imposing. These limitations had a substantial effect upon legal administration, making it difficult to introduce new laws into the countryside.

In Taiwan, under Japanese rule, and in mainland China under the Communists, education has been stressed, as Tables 1 and 2 demonstrate. In Taiwan in 1899, there were 10,295 students in primary schools, exclusive of trade schools and others. By 1944, the enrollment figure had jumped to 932,525, more than 90 times greater than the number enrolled in 1899.[6] This increase is impressive even when compared to the population growth, which doubled between 1905 and 1943.[7]

---

[6] Taiwan Provincial Government, TAIWAN SHENG WU-SHIH-YI NIEN LAI T'UNG-CHI T'I-YAO (Essential Statistics of Fifty-one Years of the Province of Taiwan) 1212 (Taipei 1946).

[7] *Id.* at 76. There were 3,123,302 people in Taiwan in 1905 and 3,976,098 in 1923. In 1933, there were 5,060,507 and in 1943, 6,585,841.

TABLE 1

PRIMARY SCHOOL ENROLLMENT IN TAIWAN
UNDER JAPANESE RULE

Year	Enrollment
1899	10,295
1910	49,556
1923	238,574
1933	349,112
1938	544,946
1944	932,525

Similarly, in mainland China, the school enrollment for 1949 more than doubled by 1952 and more than tripled by 1959, when ninety million students were attending elementary schools.[8]

TABLE 2

PRIMARY SCHOOL ENROLLMENT
IN MAINLAND CHINA AFTER 1949

Year	Enrollment
1949	24,391,033
1952	49,999,944
1959	90,000,000

In traditional China, as noted above, dialect differences created additional communications problems. Since a magistrate was not permitted to serve in his own area, he might be unfamiliar with local dialects and local customary law. In mainland China, and to an even greater extent in Taiwan, emphasis upon Mandarin Chinese as the national dialect is helping to eliminate this problem.

China was and is a country of enormous size. A warrant for arrest often took many days if not weeks to reach a defendant by traditional methods of transportation. The result was that evidence was often difficult to acquire and warrants hard to serve.

On Taiwan the Japanese ". . . enlarged communications facilities; a thorough public network of roads, bridges, railway lines, telegraph and telephone installations, tunnels and mountain trails . . ." was constructed.[9] From the beginning of Japanese rule,[10] railways were pushed forward, so that by

---

[8] T. Chen, *Elementary Education in Communist China,* CHINA QUARTERLY 98, at 102 (April–June 1962).

[9] G. BARCLAY, COLONIAL DEVELOPMENT AND POPULATION IN TAIWAN 26 (1954).

[10] V. Lippit, *Development of Transportation in Communist China,* CHINA QUARTERLY 101 (July–Sept. 1966).

1910 there were over four hundred kilometers of operating lines in Taiwan, an increase of more than three hundred kilometers from 1900. By 1920 there were over six hundred kilometers of operating lines and by 1930 close to nine hundred. Evidently, physical communication was improved. In China, immediately after their conquest of the mainland, the Communists also stressed the importance of physical communications and did much after 1949 to make modern transportation readily available. With increased literacy, emphasis upon the national language, and improvement in physical communications, laws were obviously easier to propagate and enforce.

Extent of judicial penetration. In Ch'ing times the number of magistrates at the *chou* and *hsien* level (which was the lowest level court and had jurisdiction over civil cases) was, according to official figures, one for every 100,000 inhabitants in 1749, and one for every 250,000 in 1819.[11] Considering the size of the country and the limited communications, the government courts were not readily accessible to all.

On Taiwan, under Japanese control, the formal court system was extended,[12] and local organs of control such as the *pao-chia* were created on traditional models, though they employed modern instruments and techniques. The Japanese also institutionalized conciliation tribunals, as did the mainland Chinese after 1949, thereby formalizing certain traditional institutions. Various officials in Taiwan, such as the village mayor and the police, were utilized to conciliate and to administer the law. Thus, in both China and Taiwan (after 1895), important informal tribunals were penetrated by the government.

The Nationalist government had little opportunity to expand the formal judiciary and to penetrate the informal judiciary in the period between 1927 and the beginning of World War II. The formal courts were largely confined to the cities,[13] and much of the work of extension and modernization was in the planning stage. After the Republican government took over Taiwan, they accelerated the development of communications, education, and judicial institutionalization started by the Japanese. The Nationalist government, however, does not play as important a role in manipulating the informal tribunals as the Japanese did and the Communists do. However, acting through the police, local Kuomintang (KMT) officers, mayors, and a small

---

[11] HSIAO, *supra* note 3, at 5.

[12] Barclay, *supra* note 9, at 39.

[13] *See* J. ESCARRA, LE DROIT CHINOIS 414 (G. Browne transl. 1936). It was estimated that in 1932 there were "One Supreme Court, 59 Superior Tribunals, 203 local tribunals, 34 *hsien* tribunals . . ." in twenty-three provinces of China. Just by way of comparison there were about 1,500 district magistrates in Ch'ing times. Apparently, not all of these Nationalist tribunals had been modernized. It is obvious that very few districts *(hsien)* had local courts of the modern type. Also, see CHINA YEAR BOOK for relevant years.

number of conciliation tribunals, the government plays a moderate role in this important area of dispute resolution.

Degree of judicial-political power including propaganda utilized. As we have noted above, propaganda-education plays a part in effecting social change. For example, in Taiwan under Japanese occupation, and to a greater extent since 1945, adoption of a *t'ung-yang-hsi* (future daughter-in-law) and a *ca-bö-kan* (family maid) was strongly discouraged. Some encouragement was given to the free choice of a spouse.[14] In the mainland, on the other hand, propaganda relating to the marriage law, and thus against the two above types of adoption and in favor of the free choice of spouse, was very extensive, appearing in newspapers and radio programs, at show-trials, mass meetings, and in smaller group meetings. Women's associations became mass organizations, in part to propagate the marriage law, and a very heavy investment was made in the campaign to upset the traditional social order.[15]

The substantial use of the coercive power of the courts was most evident in Taiwan under Japanese rule, where substantive legal changes were generally moderate, and in China today, where the positive law envisioned fairly radical change. Neither in Taiwan under the Nationalists nor at an earlier period on the mainland under the KMT was the extensive coercive power of the state resorted to with any frequency for the purpose of bringing about rapid social change.

Power of Social Groups Affected

In order to examine the above postulates relevant to the power of the social group affected by new legislation, we will select several legal changes that have taken place in Taiwan since 1945 and make some comparative references to developments in mainland China.

Freedom to choose a spouse. We will first examine the size, power and degree to which the social groups felt affected in Taiwan after 1945 and in mainland China after 1950, by the law which gave individuals the right to choose their own spouse.

Certainly the social groups most directly affected by this law included not only the potential spouses but also their parents. Thus, a rather large segment of the population is affected. While it may be difficult to specifically assess the power of this group, insofar as marriageable children and their families do not necessarily identify with each other for social, political, or economic action, nevertheless, it would seem that those concerned would be quite

---

[14] Some of this is indirect; that is, through the newspaper publicity given to marriages of both Western and Chinese movie stars, and so on.

[15] *See* G. Massell, *Law as an Instrument of Revolutionary Change in a Traditional Milieu; The Case of Soviet Central Asia,* 2 LAW AND SOCIETY REV. 179 (Feb. 1968), for some interesting parallel notes regarding Soviet Central Asia.

powerful within the society, constituting as they do most of the post-puberty unmarried children and their parents. Furthermore, it is quite likely that most inhabitants of the rural areas felt affected by this regulation, although it may not have directly affected their marriage.

With regard to the relative power of the two groups involved, it would seem that in traditional rural Chinese society parents often controlled their children's primary source of sustenance. Therefore, their economic power, reinforced as it was by social pressure, ideology, and political-legal power, was quite strong. When alternate sources of employment became increasingly available and attractive to both children and their parents, and when the young became more mobile, the power of the parental group diminished. This is the present situation in both Taiwan and mainland China, although initially land reform had the effect of increasing the economic power of many parental groups.

It is possible to estimate the degree to which groups feel affected by various laws. In most circumstances today children prefer to choose their own husbands or wives. Parents, on the other hand, particularly when marriage involves locating in the home of either the husband's or the wife's family as it does in traditional Chinese society, naturally feel affected by the limitations on their power brought about by the new law. Such a diminution of authority is probably resented by the patriarchal hierarchy, irrespective of the locus of the marriage. Since marriages, particularly of sons, often cost parents a great deal of money and, in fact, may lead them into debt, they are unlikely to be too sanguine about having no choice over their children's mates. Therefore, we can expect most parents to feel strongly affected by this law.

Youngsters, particularly because schools and non-farm employment as well as increased communication give them more opportunity to be thrown toge'her, fall in "love" and are influenced by the ideology of the conjugal family, so that they are increasingly resentful of parental restrictions imposed upon them. Therefore, the hostility of a large social group, that is, parents, is partially offset by the favorable attitude of the younger generation. Nevertheless, the parental group is more powerful economically and socially if not politically.

Prohibition against the taking of secondary wives. The limitations on the taking of secondary wives, in Taiwan since 1945 and in mainland China since 1950, affected a much smaller group than those affected by the provision for free choice of spouse. The group of families willing to have their daughters become secondary wives was and is limited, and the number of men in traditional society economically able to afford more than one wife was not large. With improved economic circumstances, however, the number of men able to afford secondary wives grew. The natural desire to choose one's spouse also affected these matters since secondary wives were almost invariably chosen without much parental interference. On the other hand, if economic circumstances should improve sufficiently throughout the society, fewer women are likely to be available as secondary wives, although of course more than economics is involved in this institution.

The men who have the power to take secondary wives are better off economically, and thus relatively powerful within the society. The relationship of the power of the potential husband to that of the potential secondary wife is often, but not invariably, one in which the husband is much better off. Maids and employees form an important source of potential secondary wives.

Since Chinese society has always been somewhat ambivalent about the desirability of secondary wives, the restriction upon the taking of a secondary wife probably reinforces the negative aspects of this traditional attitude. On the other hand, many men who accumulate wealth undoubtedly feel that one of the benefits that should accrue to them is increased sexual freedom,[16] including the power to freely choose an additional wife, a concept reinforced by modern values.[17] Women who have been subject to a great deal of propaganda-education regarding this matter are more reluctant to become secondary[18] wives today.

Extensive political-legal pressure against marriages of this type exists in mainland China, and the law there strictly forbids such a marriage; thus, secondary wives are a rarity. Furthermore, individual economic circumstances have not improved sufficiently to permit much growth of this institution. Rationing affects government control over marriage by its ability to restrict the food supply. Where the prohibition is more flexible, as in Taiwan, the institution seemingly continues to grow, in part because of improved economic circumstances. Obviously, the men in Taiwan who are able to afford secondary wives are a small, though economically powerful, group that is growing in number. In mainland China only a very limited elite could potentially afford such a marriage, if it were not for political pressure and their ideological repugnance to the institution.

Right of married women to inherit property from their natal homes. Changes in inheritance law in Taiwan after 1945 and in mainland China since 1950, have given women who marry out of their natal homes power equal to their

---

[16] *See* N. Y. Times, Feb. 14, 1968, at 51. Tribal headmen in Kenya were reported opposed to restrictions upon polygamy, some feeling it amounts to Westernization of the law. Some people felt it should be allowed to pass away under the pressure of social and economic circumstances.

[17] Freedom to choose a spouse and restrictions on the number of spouses one may choose are two somewhat inconsistent modern concepts. This inconsistency is probably manifested by the fact that the older men able to choose a secondary wife did not choose their first wives themselves, while their children are more likely to have had a larger say in the choice of a spouse.

[18] For contrasting developments in the United States, *see* B. Merson, *Husbands with More Than One Wife*, 84 LADIES HOME JOURNAL 78 (June 1967). Mormons who secretly adhere to the injunction to take plural wives attach special ethical significance to this act.

brothers' to inherit property from such homes. The group affected by this regulation was larger than that affected by the restrictions upon secondary wives, but considerably smaller than that affected by the regulation granting the right to freely choose one's spouse. It included all women who had married out of their natal homes and whose families had heritable property. The latter qualification is a substantial one.

Generally, these women would not have much power in the society and particularly not much power relative to their brothers, since they no longer lived either in the natal home or, often, in the same locality. With the tremendous propaganda-education drive in mainland China, as well as the formation of politically active women's organizations, the power of these women increased, as did that of all women.

Since these married women are generally dependent upon the income of their husbands' homes, and ordinarily would not like to see his married sisters inherit property, they may not feel very strongly about the benefit provided by this law. Their brothers, on the other hand, who have to live in their natal home and make their living on the family farm, will undoubtedly feel a strong attachment to their property. As long as marriage remains patrilocal we may expect that relatively few married women will assert their rights to inherit property from their natal homes.

Limitation on the adoption of girls. The legal limits placed upon the adoption of *t'ung-yang-hsi* or *ca-bö-kan* in Taiwan and mainland China affect the girls themselves and the families wishing to adopt or to give female children for adoption. In parts of China there were substantial numbers of families who wished to enter such adoption relationships. The number was affected by economic circumstances, for with economic improvement, people were less concerned about the costs of raising a female child, of marrying off their sons in the future, or of hiring a maid.

The power of the affected group traditionally was limited to the poorer and less secure families and the adopted girls themselves, both groups with little independent power. The adopted girls' power has been enhanced, however, by the Women's Association, which gives them an agency to turn to for help in both Taiwan and mainland China. Furthermore, in both societies fairly extensive propaganda-education programs have been aimed at these girls, who thus have been elevated in power and self-consciousness. Resentment of this practice has therefore increased among the girls who often had some hostility to the situation, even in traditional society. Today, these girls feel affected by this new law in a real way and are aware that their power has been considerably enlarged. These factors, coupled with improved health and economic circumstances, have led to a very substantial reduction in the size of this institution in Taiwan and to a similar, more striking, reduction in mainland China.

Increased right of women to divorce. The increased legal power of women to initiate divorce proceedings affected those women who might potentially divorce and concomitantly circumscribed the power of their husbands. Furthermore, in the patrilocal-type marriage, the law limited the power of the husband's family, who traditionally had some control over divorce by their sons.

While divorce in Chinese society may have occurred more frequently than we have previously assumed, it probably was not a major social problem. Furthermore, there were strong ideological and social pressures against divorce. Nevertheless, there were various tensions within the family. The daughter-in-law both caused and bore the brunt of some of these tensions; therefore, she would most likely feel affected and pleased by her new power. The large number of divorces that occurred in Communist China shortly after the imposition of the Marriage Law, while undoubtedly catalyzed in no small part by government pressure, unquestionably were symptomatic of the feelings of a large group of women. When society guarantees the livelihood of the divorced wife, she is less fearful and has more impetus to take such a step. On the other hand, increased freedom in choosing one's spouse (but not the free choice of spouse) and improved economic circumstances, as well as more patrilocal or neolocal marriage patterns and restrictions upon *t'ung-yang-hsi* type marriages, all operate to make marriages more stable.[19] Therefore, potentially at least, divorce could become less important today than it was traditionally.

If we concentrate upon married women, their power, like that of adopted girls, is augmented both in Taiwan and on the mainland by the women's associations (although they have not received the same degree of concern in Taiwan).

In both societies, divorce is now frowned upon, and since there are still traditional restraints upon divorce, women may not think of themselves as being substantially affected by the new law.[20] Their husbands, on the other hand, may be more consciously aware of the increased power of their wives in that legal power coincides with propaganda-education support and with the creation of new political institutions, and thus husbands may be less prone to behave in a manner that might result in divorce proceedings. The women who

---

[19] N. Y. Times, Feb. 14, 1968, at 55. Mr. Alfred Aurbach, Clinical Professor of Psychiatry at the University of California's San Francisco Medical Center, said the prospects for a stable family life in the United States in the foreseeable future were dim, primarily because 40 percent of marriages were between teenagers, about half of these girls were pregnant at the time of the ceremony, and between 50 and 75 percent of these marriages will break up in a few years. Thus, teenage mothers will have to care for the children without their fathers, leading to poor identification and a potential for physical and mental illness.

[20] As noted above, women's right to institute divorce proceedings was traditionally more significant, particularly in certain marital types and circumstances, than has been believed.

may now potentially divorce probably do not constitute a very large group in either Taiwan or mainland China, but the indirect effects of their new rights are probably extensive. Despite the increased power of women to divorce, the increase in preferred marriage patterns in Taiwan helps to negate divorce possibilities, while the extensive freedom of children to choose their own spouses enhances it, since marriages that are based solely on the free choice of children are less stable than those where spouses were chosen by parents with the consent of the children.

Values of the Society and the New Law

It is also possible to discuss in somewhat more detail the traditional value system and the new law with reference to the aspects of family law analyzed above.

Freedom to Choose Spouse. In traditional ideology and law, there were prohibitions against a child choosing his own spouse. In a traditional rural milieu, where the farm was generally the primary source of income and where there were few alternate sources of sustenance, economic circumstances and important social institutions supported traditional ideological restrictions upon the right to choose a spouse. Furthermore, residence of a newly married couple was usually with the parents of either the bride or the groom. Therefore, the parents' power to choose a spouse for their child was strong and had substantial strength in rural areas of China.

By way of contrast, the law in Taiwan today is fairly specific in giving children freedom to choose a spouse, and the situation in mainland China is even clearer, since there is a positive injunction not to interfere with free marital choice; therefore conflicts with traditional values are quite direct.

Prohibitions against the taking of secondary wives. Traditional Chinese attitudes toward secondary wives for commoners were ambivalent. There were implicit and explicit concepts that held there was only one *ch'i* (primary wife) and that a secondary wife was truly secondary, although a wife nevertheless. Furthermore, there were ideological rationalizations about the taking of secondary wives that indicated one was not to be taken too readily. For example, one was justified in taking a secondary wife if one's primary wife bore no male heirs by a certain age. We have noted above, on the other hand, that possession of secondary wives was regarded as one of the accoutrements of wealth.

In Taiwan today the legal prohibition against the taking of a secondary wife is not very tightly drawn; however, on the mainland the law is quite strict. The conflict with traditional values is less striking with regard to changes in this area of the law than with regard to free choice of spouse, particularly in Taiwan.

Rights of married women to inherit from their natal homes. Traditionally, all sons were expected to share almost equally in their father's property and daughters had almost no rights thereto, particularly those daughters who married out of their natal homes. This was a strongly held value that made institutional sense, in that in ordinary circumstances the sons remained on the family land and retained the responsibility for the family sustenance and sacrifices.

The new law in Taiwan, while fairly clear in specifying that the married-out daughter is allowed to inherit, nevertheless contains provisions for waiver of this right. In the People's Republic of China, on the other hand, the administration of the law has varied and the provision has been loosely interpreted, so that there is less conflict with traditional values than might be expected.

Limitation on the adoption of girls. There were few significant traditional limitations on female adoptions, other than that a girl adopted as a *t'ung-yang-hsi* could not be of the same surname as the adopting home or have certain degrees of familial relationship with them. There was no positive injunction to adopt girls, but the adoption often filled the need for providing a posterity since boys were harder to adopt, at least in northern Taiwan, but easier to marry in.

The present law in Taiwan clearly prohibits adoption for purposes of a *t'ung-yang-hsi* marriage. However, a normal adoption of a female can be terminated, and once the girl is of age she can be married to a male of the household, thereby legally accomplishing the same purpose as a *t'ung-yang-hsi* adoption. Of course, according to law her husband would have to be freely chosen. On the mainland the law is very clear in prohibiting the *t'ung-yang-hsi* type of adoption.

The ideological attitudes toward adopting a girl vary in different parts of China, but nowhere was it considered an ideal situation. On the other hand there were strong pressures to provide for one's spiritual posterity and old age. Since adoption of a young girl often had these basic motives, there were substantial values involved in this traditional institution. The new restrictions in law conflict with the previous values, but only where there is a necessity to adopt girls because of economic or physical circumstances, and/or where the custom is extensively and widely practiced, will any serious dispute arise between the traditional values and the new law. The conflict is not a severe one in Taiwan because of economic improvement and better health.

Increased right of women to divorce. Women had little ideological or legal support that would permit them to initiate divorce proceedings, although since divorce by mutual consent was permitted by law, under favorable circumstances women could influence such a situation. Naturally, if the marriage was of the matrilocal type it was even easier for the woman to instigate such divorce proceedings. In fact, the ideology of the great tradition conflicted with the practice of the little tradition; women initiated divorce more often than previously believed, but nevertheless this was relatively infrequent.

The powers presently granted women permitting divorce initiative conflict with traditional values in both Taiwan and the People's Republic of China. In Taiwan, however, the social pressures against women going to court help restrict the possibilities of their taking advantage of this newly conferred power. In mainland China, aside from the initial encouragement of the courts and political institutions after the passage of the Marriage Law, it has now become difficult to obtain a judicial decree of divorce, and so the conflict with traditional values is not as severe as one might expect.

Summary

Differences Between Taiwan and Mainland China

We have noted the contrast between the degree to which the government in the People's Republic of China has been able to penetrate the legal institutions, including the informal institutions, with the situation in Taiwan where the informal institutions still remain largely outside direct government control, particularly when dealing with civil matters such as family law. Furthermore, the Communists have made more extensive use of propaganda-education in most fields and have been more willing to use coercion to obtain their desired ends.

In both areas communications are at a relatively high level for premodern societies, and education is relatively widespread. Of course, the older generation is largely unaffected by the formal system of education now available.

Law and Social Change

Freedom to choose spouse. We have seen that a large social group is affected by the law granting individuals the right to choose their spouses. However, the power of parents, whose legal authority over their children has been circumscribed, has been further diminished by new economic opportunities available outside the rural areas, though at an earlier period it was strengthened by land reform. An additional factor in Communist China which encourages the free choice of a spouse is that it presently costs little to have an ordinary wedding, which is the type the government prefers.

Although important traditional values were affected, despite the injunctions of the new law, actual change has been slow. Especially in Taiwan, where there is a dual revolution taking place, the cost of the traditional wedding and the frequency of patrilocal residence have helped to maintain traditional values. Nevertheless, changes are occurring, and the very concept of an arranged marriage has changed. Now children generally at least have rights of refusal as to a potential spouse chosen by their parents. With industrialization, which undermines the economic power of parents, high taxes on farmers, and Westernization, which affects the thinking of the younger generation, more changes are likely to occur. With increased modernization Chinese society is more likely to permit a greater number of "love" marriages.

On the mainland, despite the size of the social group affected, change seems to have taken place more rapidly. However, the *Lien Chiang* documents seem to indicate that the arranged marriage is still far from a thing of the past at least in parts of Fukien. Nevertheless, economic independence, the increased opportunities of those of marriageable age to meet, and the very powerful coercive arm of the state have all helped to restrict the role of parents as arrangers of marriages.

Prohibitions against the taking of secondary wives. We have noted that the group affected by the prohibitions against the taking of secondary wives is small, though relatively powerful. In Taiwan, their numbers have increased because of economic progress, which has not yet gone far enough to affect the availability of women. We further noted that traditional society was somewhat ambivalent about taking secondary wives. In Taiwan, where the legal prohibition is relatively weak, the institution has grown and probably flourishes to a degree unknown to the tradition, influenced in part by the new emphasis upon the desirability of selecting one's own spouse.

In the mainland, because increased national wealth has not led to disproportionately increased individual wealth and because the law has been very strict in its prohibitions and has used coercion extensively, the taking of secondary wives has been virtually eliminated. This was possible because of the limited size of the institution, the limitations of individual economic opportunities, increased sexual freedom, and ambivalent traditional attitudes, which permitted strict law enforcement and coercion to effectively put an end to this practice, at least for the time being. Furthermore, in Taiwan, the men affected were economically well-to-do and therefore powerful. In Communist China because of the lack of individual wealth and because those favoring such an institution belong to the nonpreferred classes, economic power has not played a role in affecting social practice or legal administration.

Right of married women to inherit property from their natal homes. A larger group was affected by granting married women power to inherit from their natal homes than by the law limiting the taking of secondary wives. The women have not been affected in as important a way, however, because they are still generally dependent upon their husband's home for economic support. Traditional values against this legal change were strong. Enforcing such a rule under present circumstances would have required a tremendous expenditure of political-legal energy. Furthermore, the Communists would have had to put emphasis not only upon women's rights but also upon private property to effectuate such a change.

The law in Communist China has been loosely interpreted and has not been strictly administered, because in the Chinese Communist system there is less private property to inherit. In Taiwan, the provision permitting waiver of these rights has opened an important loophole in the law. In fact, in both societies, few married women who reside in the husband's home inherit from their natal homes. With the growth of neolocal residence in the future there should be a shift in attitudes and values. Therefore, women should slowly attain this power to inherit in fact as well as in law.

Limitation on the adoption of girls. In Northern Taiwan and Southern Fukien the group affected by the limitation of the adoption of girls was fairly large. In other parts of China circumstances varied with locality. Usually the poor were involved in adopting *t'ung-yang-hsi,* so the power of the group was limited. In both Taiwan and mainland China, the development of women's associations has increased the power of adopted girls, as propaganda-education has enhanced their prestige. The law in Taiwan is not as strict in prohibiting this type of adoption as that of the mainland. On the other hand, in both societies, economic and health circumstances have improved so that there is less need for this type of adoption. Traditional ideological pressures did support the institution as a means of providing for sacrifices and old age, but contemporary political-legal power and propaganda-education have heavily opposed it, and in both Taiwan and the People's Republic of China, the *t'ung-yang-hsi* adoption is a dying institution which, barring economic depression, will pass out of existence in a few years.

Increased right of women to divorce. The group affected here was not a large one, for divorce had not been common traditionally and there were strong ideological pressures against it. The new laws were only important when the mainland government put tremendous coercive pressure upon families already under strain. With the stricter administration of divorce law in mainland China and with the requirement that the aggrieved wife file a complaint with the judiciary in Taiwan, divorce by litigation is not attractive. Divorce by mutual consent, however, remains the standard form of divorce. With increased freedom to choose one's spouse, an increase in preferred marriage patterns, and the later age at which marriage takes place in both societies, there should be little increase in divorce despite this provision, unless as is unlikely, complete freedom to choose a spouse devolves upon the children.

Conclusion

The relationship of positive law to social change is a complex one. It is dependent in large part upon the judicial power exercised, the power of the social groups affected, and the nature of both the traditional values and the new laws. We have seen that law, while only one factor in fostering change, nevertheless, under certain circumstances (such as the elimination of secondary wives in Communist China) plays a very important role. In contrast, the law granting married women the right to inherit from their natal homes has remained largely a fiction in both Taiwan and Communist China. The law permitting children freedom to choose a spouse has served to legitimate and enforce changes that were already occurring for multiple reasons, and thus children now generally have at least a right of refusal with regard to a potential spouse selected by their parents. In a similar manner, the law prohibiting the *t'ung-yang-hsi* type of adoption has helped to legitimate the support provided for these girls by the government and to catalyze some of the changes stimulated by economic circumstances so that in the near future, if there is no war or economic setback, this institution will disappear in both mainland China and Taiwan.

Thus, law plays many roles, catalyzing, legitimizing, stimulating, and at times even impeding social change. The manner of its implementation and the economic and social factors relevant to the desired changes will help to determine the effect of a particular piece of social legislation. Only through analysis of relevant social institutions can we foretell the likelihood of legal coercion effecting change.

PART I
MARRIAGE AND DIVORCE IN TRADITIONAL CHINA

Marriage and Divorce in Han China: A Glimpse at "Pre-Confucian" Society

JACK L. DULL

Much of the work by students of Chinese society has been based on the erroneous assumption that the values and sanctions contained in the Chinese classics were generally accepted and practiced in traditional (meaning Han through Ch'ing) Chinese society. Recent studies in Chinese scholarship, however, have raised grave doubts about the validity of such traditionally accepted ideas. This article is intended to be a continuation of that important trend in recent scholarship. The essence of the argument presented here is that marriage and divorce in the Han dynasty (or dynasties) do not correspond with the patterns of the commonly accepted norms of traditional China. In the realm of marriage, divorce, and remarriage, the picture of Han society that emerges is one that is much freer than, say, Ch'ing society.

In Han times there were very few adherents to the Confucian norms of marriage and divorce; indeed, there was considerable uncertainty about what the norms should be. However, by Later Han, and particularly during the latter half of that period, there were increasing demands for new laws that would reform society. There was, in a word, a rising demand for the kind of society that we usually think of as Confucian. The further evolution of those norms and their codification belong to the post-Han period, which is not dealt with in this paper. Thus, aside from what this paper tells us of Han marriage customs, it points to the post-Han (and probably pre-T'ang) period as one of the most important ones in the gradual elaboration and codification of the traditional Confucian family ideal.

The sources for this kind of study are, of course, severely limited in two respects. First, there is no large body of material from which to extract information; essentially the sources are limited to the *Shih-chi,* the *Han-shu* and the *Hou Han-shu.* Second, this material is generally concerned not with society at large but with the imperial clan and high officials. However, I think it safe to assume that the practices which emerged from this study were those prevalent in all levels of society; some of the cases do deal with nonofficial families, and they attest to the same social mores. One point that this study makes clear is that one cannot cite the classics in order to establish what the social norms were; to do so would be to repeat the erroneous assumptions referred to above. Nor can Han law be cited to show how men and women behaved. In the first place it is often dangerous to assume that custom actually corresponds with law. In the second place, one of the tentative conclusions offered in this study is not that Han marriage law has been lost, but that it did not exist; that is, there were no codified prohibitions against marrying someone of the same surname or of a different generation. And even when such laws were created in later dynasties, care should be taken about accepting them as mirror images of social behavior.

One other characteristic of the period should be noted, although there is little that can be done about it. A single empire in North China was a relatively new phenomenon when the Han began. Before the unification of 221 B.C., "China" consisted of many states, some of which perpetuated local customs that sharply distinguished them from others. Many of these local practices continued in the Han and, indeed, in later periods as well. Abundant details concerning such variations are not available, but the geographical descriptions of parts of the Han empire do indicate that there were significant customs common only to limited areas. For example, in Han China it was customary for the oldest daughter to marry before her sisters;[1] however, during the seventh century B.C. in the area of northeast China corresponding to the old state of Ch'i, Duke Hsiang was given to incestuous behavior, and his aunts and sisters did not marry. He then decreed that the oldest daughter in each family was not to marry; instead she was to look after the ancestral sacrifices. Pan Ku, the author of the history of the Former Han dynasty, then tells us: "Up to the present the people still observe this tradition." And he adds the lament: "Alas, can we not be cautious regarding the way by which the people are led!"[2] Several areas were known for the licentious behavior of their inhabitants. Thus, in the former state of Yen when a man had a guest in his house, the wife of the host spent the night with the guest.[3] The people of the area around Han-tan, one of the great metropolitan centers of Han China, were said to have placed a high value on bravery and strength, but they were unconcerned with licentious behavior.[4] Likewise, the area of the former state of Cheng,

---

[1] H. WANG, HOU HAN-SHU CHI-CHIH (The history of the Later Han dynasty with collected explications) ch. 84, 10b (1915) [hereafter cited as HHS].

[2] H. WANG, HAN-SHU PU-CHU (The history of the Han dynasty with supplementary annotations] ch. 28B2, 62b (1900) [hereafter cited as HS].

[3] HS ch. 28B2, 60b; also in Han Dynasty History Project series [hereafter cited as HDHP].

[4] HS ch. 28B2, 59b; also in HDHP.

noted for its "licentious music," still tolerated merrymaking assemblages of men and women in which they cavorted together.[5] Such loose behavior was a general reflection of other social mores that are strikingly non-Confucian. While some areas were known for their extravagant expenditures at weddings and funerals,[6] other sections of the country were generally deficient in ritual observances.[7] These observations by Pan Ku are in the category of general characteristics which are sometimes assigned to part of a former state or even to an entire pre-Ch'in state; while they must be accepted with great caution, in this case they should at least remind us that we are dealing with an empire that was far from being culturally integrated.

MARRIAGE AGE

If one believed that Han people took seriously the admonitions of the classical texts one would have to conclude that men and women married at a rather late age. According to the *Li-chi,* men married at thirty years of age and women at twenty.[8] The same figures were apparently agreed upon in the discussions in White Tiger Hall in the Later Han dynasty. At that time, the numbers thirty and twenty had a cosmic significance, for their sum of fifty was "the number of the Great Expansion, which begets the ten thousand things."[9] It might be expected that a cosmic interpretation of the marriage age would provide even more compelling reasons for adhering to that idea. However, even among the classical scholars of Later Han there was not unanimity regarding the application of these figures. The New Text School of Confucianism, which based its interpretations of the classics largely on cosmological speculations, argued for the position found in the White Tiger Hall discussions; however, the Old Text scholars (and it is important to note that the more authoritarian Old Text classics were not recognized in the Han) tried to prove that the ages of thirty and twenty applied only to commoners, whereas the ruler was supposed to be married by about age fifteen.[10] In fact,

---

[5] HS ch. 28B2, 57b; also in HDHP.

[6] HS ch. 28B2, 51b, 59b, 64b; all in HDHP.

[7] HS ch. 28B2, 60a; HDHP. By implication, before the administration of Han Yeh-shou in the reign of Emperor Hsüan (73–49 B.C.), Tung commandery had not placed much emphasis on ritual functions. HS ch. 28B2, 64b; HDHP.

[8] 1 J. LEGGE, LI-KI 65, 478, 479 (University Books reprint 1967).

[9] 1 T. S. TJAN, PO HU T'UNG: THE COMPREHENSIVE DISCUSSIONS IN WHITE TIGER HALL 245 (E. J. Brill 1949) [hereafter cited as TJAN].

[10] *See* a forthcoming article by me on the differences between the Old and New Text schools. This particular argument may be found in the collected fragments of S. Hsü, *Wu-ching i-i su-cheng* (Variant interpretations of the Five Classics with critical comments), in HUANG-CH'ING CHING-CHIEH (Classical exegetics of the Ch'ing dynasty) ch. 1249, 62b–63a (Juan Yuan ed. 1829).

there is no evidence from the Han dynasty that anyone (commoner, scholar, or emperor) felt bound by the classical admonitions for men to marry at thirty and women at twenty. Wang Ch'ung, the famous cynical and critical scholar of the first century A.D., asserted that this rule had never been applied in classical times and stated that it was not followed by his contemporaries.[11]

Generally, women of the Han dynasty married when they were in their teens, often in their early teens. Empress Ma of Emperor Ming was thirteen years old when she became his wife.[12] Emperor Hsüan's maternal grandmother was fourteen when she married Wang Keng-te.[13] Pan Chao, the noted authoress of the Later Han, married when she was fourteen, and Empress Hsü of Emperor Hsüan was fourteen or fifteen when she was betrothed to a man of the Ou-hou family who died before the marriage took place.[14] Huang Pa, who was to become a Prime Minister under Emperor Hsüan, was riding with a physiognomist who pointed out a rather plain looking girl of seventeen or eighteen and said that whoever she married would become a marquis. Huang found out who she was and married her.[15] Similarly, a daughter of Hsün Shuang was married when she was seventeen.[16] We do not know the age at which Cho Wen-chü first married, but she was a widow of seventeen years of age when she eloped with one of the greatest literary figures of Former Han, Ssu-ma Hsiang-ju.[17] The foregoing spectrum of ages is reflected (more or less) in imperial regulations according to which women chosen for the emperor's

---

[11] 1 A. FORKE, LUN-HENG 471–72 (2d ed. 1962). This passage is cited in S. YANG, HAN-TAI HUN-SANG LI SU K'AO (An examination of the marriage and mourning ritual customs of the Han dynasty) 28 (1933) [hereafter cited as YANG]. At this point, I wish to acknowledge a special appreciation for works by two scholars. Ch'ü T'ung-tsu has written a volume on Han social structure for the Han Dynasty History Project; I edited the volume and in the process learned a great deal about all aspects of Han society. Professor Ch'ü's interpretations of Chinese society are well known; as the reader will see, I do not share some of them, but this does not mean that I am any the less indebted to Ch'ü for his contributions. The second scholar who must be singled out is Yang Shu-ta. His work, cited above, is a very comprehensive compilation of materials concerning, for example, Han marriage customs. Indeed, he includes more cases than Ch'ü; however, Yang's work is little more than a compendium of quotations from Han sources. Rather than swell my footnotes with repeated references to Yang and Ch'ü, suffice it to say that most of the examples I cite can be found in their works; both works have been of inestimable value to me in writing this article.

[12] HHS ch. 10A, 7b–8a.

[13] HS ch. 97A, 20a.

[14] HHS ch. 84, 4b; N. SWANN, PAN CHAO: FOREMOST WOMAN SCHOLAR OF CHINA 82 (1932); HS ch. 97A, 22a.

[15] 1 A. FORKE, supra note 11, at 307.

[16] HHS ch. 84, 12a.

[17] YANG 27, quoting HSI-CHING TSA-CHI (Miscellaneous records from the Western Capitol).

harem were supposed to be at least thirteen but no more than twenty years old.[18]

There were, of course, exceptions on both ends of the scale. Liang Hung, a renowned recluse who had repeatedly declined marriage offers from powerful families, heard of a woman who was fat, ugly, dark, and strong enough to lift a stone mortar. Prospective husbands had been chosen for her, but she had refused to marry. On reaching the age of thirty, when her parents asked why she had not married, she replied that she had been waiting for a worthy man such as Liang. Liang heard of her comment and finally married her.[19] We need not accept her interpretation of the course of events, but there is little reason to doubt the statement about her age.

At the other extreme, several girls became empresses at very early ages. A daughter of Shang-kuan An was only six years old when she became the wife of Emperor Chao.[20] In another political marriage Ts'ao Ts'ao presented three daughters to the throne in A.D. 213; the youngest was so young that she was actually kept in her home until she was nineteen years old.[21] Only one case has been found of an unborn child being promised to someone; there too the motivation was political.[22]

Contrary to what might be expected, bachelorhood was apparently not uncommon in Han times. At least this is the situation suggested by one of the "Worthies" in the great debates on the salt and iron monopolies, for he argued that in antiquity a man had only one wife, whereas in his time (81 B.C.) some of the feudal lords had over one hundred wives and high officials had "tens" of mates. One of the results of this situation was that some men lived a life of debauchery and never married.[23] We have a case of an individual who refused to marry: Yang Ch'iao was a very handsome and talented man who caught Emperor Huan's eye. The Emperor issued a decree that Yang was to marry a princess. Yang objected strenuously to the order, and when the Emperor insisted, Yang starved himself to death.[24] The problem with this case is that we do not know whether Yang was already married; since in other cases in which the emperors tried to have a man marry one of their daughters

---

[18] HHS ch. 10A, 2b.

[19] HHS ch. 83, 8a.

[20] HS ch. 27A, 17b–18a.

[21] HHS ch. 10B, 13a. YANG 29, suggests that such practices were the antecedents of the institution of foster daughters-in-law *(t'ung-yang-hsi)*.

[22] HHS ch. 17, 19a.

[23] HUAN K'UAN, YEN-T'IEH-LUN (Discourses on salt and iron) 112–13 (Kuo-hsüeh chi-pen ts'ung-shu ed. 1956).

[24] HHS ch. 38, 11a, cited in S. Liu & C. Lou, *Han-tai chih hun-yin ch'i-hsiang* (Strange phenomena regarding marriage in the Han dynasty), 1 KUO-LI WU-HAN TA-HSÜEH WEN-CHE CHI-K'AN (National Wuhan University literature and philosophy quarterly) No. 1, at 276 (1930) [hereinafter cited as LIU & LOU].

(see below) we are told that the man was already married, I am inclined to believe in this case that Yang was single.

Men seem to have married at slightly higher ages than women. Emperors Ling and Hsien were both fifteen when they married;[25] Emperor Huan was sixteen, and so was one of Emperor Wu's sons.[26] Since these men were all members of the imperial family, it is possible that they married younger than most men. The evidence for this is weak at best; Chin Kuang-yen was eighteen when he married,[27] and presumably the recluse Liang Hung did not marry a woman much, if any, older than himself. Unfortunately, we do not have examples of other commoners.

At least one scholar-official was convinced that people married too young. Wang Chi argued that the high mortality rate of youngsters was due to the fact that men and women married and had children before they had learned enough about how to be parents. He urged Emperor Hsüan to create laws that would prevent such practices. The Emperor, however, thought that his admonitions were impracticable and took no action.[28]

Thus the evidence is quite clear that the classical literature did not influence social customs so far as the age at which people married is concerned. There is also no evidence to suggest that there were any Han laws relevant to this question. In spite of the presumed need to marry at ages thirty and twenty (for men and women respectively) in order to maintain cosmic harmony, social custom decreed much earlier marriages for both men and women.

Spouses Who Were Relatives and Spouses of Different Generations

The exclusive recognition of Confucianism in the reign of Emperor Wu in the Former Han dynasty did not mean that social mores suddenly began to conform to what we usually think of as Confucian tenets. The Confucianism that was predominant throughout the Han period was not the later Old Text orthodoxy of the *Chou-li* and the *Tso-chuan,* and it was markedly different from the even later Confucianism of the Sung and subsequent periods. The Old Text type of Confucianism, and particularly its post-Sung forms, placed the greatest emphasis on human relationships and especially on the family as the bulwark of a socio-political system that was highly authoritarian. The New Text Confucianism of the Han, while not devoid of concern with the family,

---

[25] HHS ch. 8, 1b, 4a, for Ling; HHS ch. 9, 6a, for Hsien.

[26] HHS ch. 7, 2b; HS ch. 63, 1b.

[27] YANG 26, citing a stele from HUNG KUA'S LI-SHIH (Explanations of the Li style of script).

[28] HS ch. 72, 6b–7b.

was focused more on cosmological questions. This helps to account for some of the "unusual" social phenomena of the Han.[29]

Ch'ü T'ung-tsu has shown that throughout much of Chinese history marriage between people of the same surname was opposed in the classical literature and that the law itself often forbade such a practice. However, he also points out that in spite of the admonitions and prohibitions such marriages were contracted.[30]

The very limited data from the Han period does not warrant strong conclusions with regard to this practice. The fact that we have only two cases of marriages of people of the same surname perhaps indicates that such marriages were rare. One case comes from the *T'ung-tien* and gives us only the barest possible facts: "In the Han, the sister of Empress Lü married Lü P'ing."[31] Since Empress Lü was a very unscrupulous woman and capable of the most unsavory acts in order to further her own political power and position, this one case is probably not to be relied upon for any argument.

The second example comes from the period near the end of Former Han when Wang Mang married a daughter of Wang Hsien.[32] However, Wang Mang, and apparently his contemporaries as well, thought of himself as a member of the Wang family of Yüan-ch'eng,[33] and of Wang Hsien as a member of the Wang family of Chi-nan; thus, although they had the same surname, they were clearly of different families, and this meant that they could marry. That the Wang family of Yüan-ch'eng was considered entirely separate from other Wang families may be seen from the following: Wang Mang based his claim to the throne, in part, on the fact that he was a descendant of the Yellow Emperor and of Emperor Shun of high antiquity. Five clans, with the surnames Yao, Kuei, Ch'en, T'ien, and Wang, descended from the same great figures. In A.D. 9 Wang Mang ordered that all members of those families were to be registered as members of the imperial (that is, his) house. And he then decreed: "'[members of] of the Wang family of Yüan-ch'eng are not permitted to intermarry [with members of the other four clans].'" Yen Shih-ku, in commenting on this passage, says that the prohibition did not apply to Wang

---

[29] LIU & LOU 260, where this idea is touched upon. This point is implicit in T. CH'Ü, LAW AND SOCIETY IN TRADITIONAL CHINA *passim* (Mouton & Co. 1961), but it is never developed there. The aspects of Chinese history dealing with intellectual history and social change are in need of a great deal of work; only after much effort will we be able to appreciate the relationship between the two.

[30] T. CH'Ü, *supra* note 29, at 91–94.

[31] Y. TU, T'UNG-TIEN (Comprehensive institutes) ch. 60, *Li* §20, 345 (Kuo-hsüeh chi-pen ts'ung-shu ed. in the Hsin-hsing shu-chü reprint).

[32] HS ch. 66, 7b–8a.

[33] HS ch. 99B, 5b–6a; 3 H. DUBS, HISTORY OF THE FORMER HAN DYNASTY 278–79 (1955) [hereinafter cited as HFHD].

families not from Yüan-ch'eng.[34] Or, in other words, those members of Wang families not from Yüan-ch'eng could marry members of any of the five specified clans, including the Wangs of Yüan-ch'eng. The principle, and it seems to be one which, as we see it here, Wang Mang extended to its fullest possible extent, is that clansmen who were descendants of a very remote ancestor were not allowed to marry even if they had different surnames, but people of the same surname who were not of the same clan could intermarry. The limited evidence leads to the conclusion that the later prohibitions against marriage of people of the same surname did not exist in Han.

Marriages between cousins were generally tolerated in Chinese history even when there were laws against it.[35] In Han times marriages between cross-cousins were quite common. During the reign of Emperor Wu when King Li of Ch'i, Liu Tz'u-ch'ang, succeeded his father, his mother, Queen Dowager Chi, arranged to have a daughter of her younger brother marry the new King. Thus King Li married his matrilateral cross-cousin. The reason the Queen Dowager arranged this marriage is also interesting: "she wished her family to double its favor [received at the hands of the royal family]."[36] The cross-cousin marriage was often employed as a means of strengthening the bonds between two families. In this case, unfortunately, there were drastic con-

---

[34] HS ch. 99B, 5b–6a. Note that my interpretation of this material differs from that of Dubs (HFHD 278–79, especially n.6.4). Dubs translates the key passage: " 'Let [the members of] the Wang clan from Yüan-ch'eng be ordered not to intermarry [among themselves], in order to distinguish [this clan] and to regulate relationships.' " It would make sense to render this "not to intermarry [among themselves]" only if that were already being done; however, there is no evidence to warrant this interpretation. Dubs' translation of this passage is based on Chou Shou-ch'ang's comment on it; Dubs freely translates (in n.6.4) Chou's remarks as follows: Wang Mang "had married the daughter of Wang Hsien who was of another Wang clan, and wanted to show that other members of the large groups of persons surnamed Wang could intermarry, yet also to make plain that he disapproved of the intermarriage of persons of the same surname. He was thus led to distinguish among those surnamed Wang." This interpretation is based implicitly on laws and presumed customs of periods of Chinese history much later than Han, but there is no reason to believe it is valid for Han. On the contrary, the context demands, as Yen Shih-ku saw it, that the intermarriage refers to the other clans. The object of the decree was not "to distinguish among those surnamed Wang," but to identify the Yüan-ch'eng Wangs with the descendants of the Yellow Emperor and to distinguish those Wangs as the only Wangs who could trace their descent from that Emperor. That Yen's interpretation is the correct one is further confirmed by the next entry in the HS test which records the enfeoffment of Ch'en Ch'ung and T'ien Feng; that is, the context is concerned with the descendants of the Yellow Emperor. It in no way suggests that Wang Mang "disapproved of the intermarriage of persons of the same surname."

[35] T. CH'Ü, supra note 29, at 95–96; H. FENG, THE CHINESE KINSHIP SYSTEM 43–44 (1948).

[36] HS ch. 38, 8b. YANG supra note 11, at 29 ff., was very helpful in preparing this section because of the diagrams.

sequences. The young King did not love the wife who had been chosen for him and had nothing to do with her. The Queen Dowager then sent her oldest daughter into the rear palace, not with the aim of having her get close to the King, but in order to manipulate affairs in the rear palace so that the King would give favorable treatment to his Queen. Instead, the King had illicit intercourse with his sister. During the reign of Emperor Wu, kings who committed offenses of this kind were harshly dealt with; the King committed suicide rather than face execution.

Another of the many examples of matrilateral cross-cousin marriage comes from the middle of the second century A.D. and concerns the family of Li Ying, a major political figure of the latter part of Han from the Ying-ch'uan commandery. Chung Chin, whose mother was the aunt of Li Ying, "was fond of study and admired antiquity; he was yielding in his mannerisms. He was the same age as [Li] Ying." Li Ying's grandfather observed that Chung Chin's character resembled that of members of his family and arranged for him to marry the sister of Li Ying; that is, Chung Chin married the daughter of his mother's brother.[37] This example is interesting because, in addition to the fact that it demonstrates matrilateral cross-cousin marriage, it shows that the grandfather felt it necessary to note that Chung Chin was the same age as Li Ying and, therefore, of the same generation as his wife. As we shall see, many Han dynasty marriages cut across generational lines; the inclusion of this statement here is perhaps indicative of changing trends due in part to the rising influence of the Old Text School of Confucianism.[38] It is also possible that this was a manifestation of a local custom. The material is simply not sufficient to reach a firm conclusion concerning either possibility.

Patrilateral cross-cousin marriages were not uncommon either. For example, Empress Dowager Lü of the founder of the Han dynasty wanted to make sure that she maintained a firm grip on affairs of state when Emperor Hui, Kao-tsu's successor, ascended the throne. She therefore arranged for the marriage of

[37] HHS ch. 62, 12a.

[38] Li Ying and his circle of friends were not orthodox (that is, New Text) Confucianists. Chang Chin came from a family which for generations had been experts in law (HHS ch. 62, 11b) and Li Ying's closest friends included Hsün Shu (HHS ch. 67, 7a) who was famous among Confucianists of the time because he refused to follow their New Text *(chang-chü)* Confucianism (HHS ch. 62, 1a). Hsün Shuang, one of Hsün Shu's outstanding sons and a friend of Li Ying, argued at great length for observances of funeral rituals which later became an accepted part of traditional Chinese custom; it is a further reflection on life at the time that the argument had to be made and, more importantly, that Hsün Shuang enjoyed only a very limited success (HHS ch. 62, 2b ff., 6b–7a). For another example of a similar relationship *see* HHS ch. 74B, 10b ff.: Liu Piao, a powerful warlord in the closing years of Later Han, chose for the wife of one of his sons, Tsung, a daughter of his second wife's brother. Thus Liu Tsung married his "step-cousin." This marriage also led to catastrophe, for it resulted in the alienation of Liu Piao from his favorite son Ch'i.

Emperor Hui and the daughter of Kao-tsu's sister.[39] Again, of the children of the King of Tai (the future Emperor Wen), a son became Emperor Ching, and a daughter known as the "older princess" married Ch'en Wu. When the future Emperor Wu, the son of Emperor Ching, was designated Heir Apparent, the Princess exercised her influence to have her daughter selected as Emperor Wu's wife and the daughter then became Empress Ch'en.[40] Thus, both Emperor Hui and Emperor Wu married their patrilateral cross-cousins.

Intermarriage between families was a fairly common feature of Han society. For example, "Cheng Ch'ung was originally from a great clan of Kao-mi. For generations [his family] had intermarried with the Wang family."[41] Of course, the most desirable intermarriage was with the imperial family for this gave great power, prestige, and wealth.[42] For four generations the Ch'ih family married into the imperial family; three males married imperial princesses, and one girl married a king (the son of Emperor Chang) who was her cross-cousin.[43] Similarly, the Tou family men provided husbands for three imperial princesses.[44] Members of the Fu family married three times into the imperial family, providing an Honorable Lady (the highest ranking concubine) for Emperor Shun, the Empress for Emperor Hsien, and the husband for one imperial princess.[45] As these examples suggest, intermarriage between a particular family and the imperial family was much more common in Later than in Former Han.

After the mourning system and the kinship system were fully developed and adopted either in law or by society, marriages between relatives of different generations were condemned as incestuous; these developments did not take place until after the Han dynasty,[46] however, and transgenerational marriages were fairly common in the Han. There are several cases of women marrying emperors of younger generations. For example, Ho Kuang, who was the actual head of government after the death of Emperor Wu in 87 B.C., had two female descendants who married emperors. One daughter married Shang-kuan An (another high political figure of the time), and from that union came the wife of Emperor Chao. Emperor Chao's brother's grandson was Emperor Hsüan who succeeded Emperor Chao to the throne. Emperor Hsüan

---

[39] HS ch. 97A, 5a.

[40] HS ch. 97A, 7a, 10b.

[41] HS ch. 77, 8b.

[42] This point is fully developed in Ch'ü's LAW AND SOCIETY IN TRADITIONAL CHINA.

[43] HHS ch. 19, 9a.

[44] HHS ch. 23, 9a.

[45] HHS ch. 26, 4a. Other examples are given in YANG 34–36: The Yin family provided an empress for Emperor Kuang-wu, the Empress for Emperor Ho, and a son who married an imperial princess (they were cousins). Two descendants of the Feng family and two of the Liang family married into the imperial family.

[46] H. FENG, *supra* note 35, at 24–25, 41, 43; T. CH'Ü, *supra* note 29, 94–95.

married another daughter of Ho Kuang; thus, strictly speaking, the Ho girl who married Emperor Hsüan was three generations older than he.[47] Similarly, Hsü Kuang-han and Hsü Yen-shou were brothers. Hsü Kuang-han had a daughter who became an Empress of Emperor Hsüan; later, Emperor Hsüan's grandson, Emperor Ch'eng, also had an Empress Hsü who was the daughter of Hsü Yen-shou's son, Chia. In other words, Emperor Ch'eng's Empress Hsü was of the same generation as his father.[48] Again, Liu Hsing, the King of Chung-shan, had no sons; consequently Emperor Ch'eng, the King's brother, said that since women of the Wei family had been fortunate in this respect he would arrange to have the King marry a younger daughter of Wei Tzu-hao. In effect, this girl was the King's aunt, for Emperor Yüan, the King's father, had another daughter of Wei Tzu-hao as his concubine.[49] Again in Former Han, Emperor Ai's Empress Fu was the cousin of his grandmother, Queen Dowager Fu of Emperor Yüan; that is, Empress Fu of Emperor Ai was his senior by one generation. Such marriages in Later Han were relatively rare. Emperor Ling's Empress Sung was a third generation descendant of Emperor Chang's Honorable Lady Sung, but Emperor Ling was a fourth generation descendant of Emperor Chang.[50]

Cases of men marrying women of a younger generation are less frequent, but there is sufficient evidence to show that this generational boundary was also crossed. Emperor Hui's Empress Chang was the daughter of Chang Ao who had married Emperor Hui's older sister; both Emperor Hui and the older sister were children of Empress Lü of Emperor Kao-tsu.[51] This is one of three marriages of members of the Lü family with members of the imperial family in which the imperial members married girls of a generation younger than themselves.[52] In Later Han, Emperor Huan married the daughter of his sister.[53]

All of the foregoing examples involve members of the imperial family; this evidence probably ought not to be interpreted to mean that there was one set of rules for them and another set for society in general. It is simply due to the

---

[47] HS ch. 97A, 17a, 17b, 18a, 23b, 24a.

[48] HS ch. 97A, 21b; HS ch. 97B, 1a; YANG 38–39, has provided the information needed to put these relationships together.

[49] HS ch. 97B, 21b. The Wei family's connections with the Imperial family went even further. Emperor Hsüan had a sister of Wei Tzu-hao as one of his concubines; so, in effect, when Emperor Yüan took one of Wei's daughters as his concubine he was taking his cousin into his harem.

[50] HHS ch. 10B, 8b. Also in Later Han, Emperor Shun took a daughter of Liang Shang as his empress and a sister of the same man as his concubine; thus he formed unions with two generations of women in the same family. HHS ch. 10B, 3a, cited by LIU & LOU 272.

[51] HS ch. 97A, 5a.

[52] YANG 40–41.

[53] HHS ch. 16, 21b–22a.

accidents of history that we have the kind of evidence that we do have. There
is, however, one case, tangentially related to the topic under discussion, which
indicates that transgenerational marriages occurred between other members
of society. It was not unusual in traditional China for a teacher to arrange a
marriage between his daughter and one of his students, but, as Liu and Lou
point out, it was not customary to reverse the generational relationship. In
Han times Ching Fang, an expert in the *I-ching,* had a student, Chang Po,
who married his daughter to Ching Fang.[54] The conclusion that can be drawn
from all this evidence is that people from all levels of society married relatives
of different generations. What we think of as the normal rules or taboos were
a function of a later era in Chinese history, one in which the mourning system
had been fully institutionalized and even codified.

Marriage Rites and Customs

Many essay writers of the Han and the historians of the period were not
favorably impressed with the level of morality that they saw around them.
Chung-ch'ang T'ung, a well-known writer of the closing years of the Han,
referred to wives "who in the morning cry for their good husbands and in
the evening marry another man."[55] Similarly, Wang Fu refers to widows with
"uncles who have no benevolence and brothers who have no righteousness;
some [of these relatives] are out to profit from the betrothal gifts, some of
them covet the [widows'] property, and some of them have selfish eyes on the
[widows'] children. Thus [such uncles and brothers] coerce them into returning home and deceive them into [re-] marrying."[56] General complaints such
as these reflect the views of a large part of society with regard to such questions
as women leaving their husbands and remarrying, or widows not remaining
loyal to their deceased husbands. These views suggest that in the eyes of
later Confucianists proper concern was not being given to the sanctity of the
marriage ritual and, indeed, that society in the Han dynasty was not bound
by quite the same moral values that we find in later generations in Chinese
history.

The historical records, particularly those for the Former Han, abound with
examples of various kinds of immoral behavior. To give a few examples: a
married daughter left her husband and returned home where she had illicit

[54] Liu & Lou 268–69, citing hs ch. 75, 10b.

[55] Chung-ch'ang T'ung, *Ch'ang-yen* (Glorious statements), in Kuo-han Ma, Yü-han
shan-fang chi-i-shu (Collected [fragments of] lost books in the Yü-han mountain
dwelling) ch. 66, 2, 2a (1883).

[56] F. Wang, Ch'ien-fu-lun (Discourses by a man in hiding) ch. 5, 138 (Ts'ung-shu
chi-ch'ing ed. 1937).

relations with a retainer (guest) of her father and perhaps also with a slave;[57] Shang-kuan An had sexual relations with his stepmother and his father's concubines and slaves;[58] Hsieh Hsüan, a widower, married a widowed imperial princess and after his death his son had illicit relations with the princess;[59] Liu Li, the King of Liang-huang, fell in love with and had sexual relations with his aunt;[60] Tung Yen was raised by an imperial princess, became her paramour, and finally married her.[61] Shang-fang Chin raped a man's wife, but he was still acceptable to a Grand Administrator, Chu Po, as an acting Prefect because Chu Po felt that human desires sometimes led men to act as Shang-fang Chin had done.[62]

Han thinkers were often convinced that men and women behaved in these ways because there was insufficient attention to propriety (that is, ritual behavior) or because the rites themselves were deficient, that is, neither clearly formulated nor adequately enforced. Thus, in the case given above of Tung Yen, he was charged on several grounds when he was indicated by Tung-fang Shuo: "[Tung] Yen, as a minister is privately (that is, illicitly) waiting upon the Princess; this is his first offense. He ruins the productivity of man and woman (apparently referring to the fact that the Princess was over fifty years old when Tung Yen, at age eighteen, became her paramour), throws into disorder the rites of marriage, and harms the royal institutions; this is his second offense." Tung Yen gives himself to the pursuit of various kinds of pleasures and "is the leader of licentiousness; this is his third offense."[63] The phrase "throws into disorder the rites of marriage" *(luan hun-yin chih li)* is somewhat of a problem if we attempt to understand it as a reference to a ritual system broadly applicable to all of society, for as we shall see, the rites were not very well developed. This statement does make sense when we consider it in conjunction with the next, namely, that the imperial regulations were being violated, for one of the Han regulations was that a princess could only marry a man who held a noble title, and noble titles were either inherited or granted for merit. This particular aspect of the imperial marriage rituals

---

[57] HS ch. 44, 14b–15a; *see also* 2 B. WATSON, RECORDS OF THE GRAND HISTORIAN, TRANSLATED FROM THE SHIH-CHI OF SSU-MA CH'IEN 388–89 (1961), for a slightly different version of this case.

[58] HS ch. 97A, 18a.

[59] HS ch. 83, 9a.

[60] HS ch. 47, 8a–9b.

[61] HS ch. 65, 10a–13a.

[62] HS ch. 83, 12a–b. Many other cases are available: Wei Ch'ing, a great general of Emperor Wu's reign, was born of an illicit union between his married father and a married slave; Wei's half sister had extramarital relations with several men (HS ch. 55, 2a–b, 7a). A Prefect had to handle a case in which a young man treated his stepmother like a wife; the young man was executed by the Prefect for this behavior (HS ch. 76, 20a).

[63] HS ch. 65, 12a–b.

was clearly being violated by Tung Yen. Incidentally, it might be noted in passing as a further comment on the mores of the period that, according to Pan Ku's history of the Former Han period, the Tung Yen case did not serve as a negative object lesson which would prevent such behavior in the future; instead, it began a trend that saw other court ladies following in the footsteps of this Princess.[64]

The interpretation of the foregoing case is based upon the assumption that when Tung-fang Shuo spoke of the marriage rites of the time he referred to rites with a narrow application. Those rites were supposedly practiced only by those members of society who held noble titles; they were not adhered to, or even applicable to, society as a whole. This interpretation is buttressed by Pan Ku's "Treatise on the Rules for Ceremonious Behaviour and on Music."[65] In effect, Pan Ku's essay is the record of requests during the Former Han for the creation and promulgation of rites and ceremonies that would be applicable to all of society. The outstanding thinkers of the period, such as Chia I, Tung Chung-shu, Wang Chi, and Liu Hsiang, all requested that the throne take such action, but they argued in vain. In still another context, Pan Ku criticizes the Confucianists of Former Han for adhering to a ritual system which "is mostly rules for the Son of Heaven, the feudal lords and the grandees. . . ."[66] Thus, according to Pan Ku and the men referred to above, the entire ritual system for Former Han was deficient in that it was not designed for universal application.

In Later Han the same problem continued to draw the attention of various scholars and officials.[67] However, in the later period, unlike the earlier one, serious attempts were repeatedly made to solve the problem through the compilation of various ritual works. Among the several collections of works having to do with ritual affairs, the record of the discussions in White Tiger Hall is probably the best known and the only one still extant.[68] However, the White Tiger Hall discussions were neither descriptive of Han rituals nor were they accepted as normative by a large group of scholars of the time who were identified with the Old Text School of Confucianism. Indeed, the evidence shows that within a few years after the discussions Emperor Chang himself, the ruler who had convened the conference, took steps to assist the Old Text scholars; thus he was instrumental in altering any norms, largely inspired by the New Text School, that may have been decided upon in the discussions.[69]

---

[64] HS ch. 65, 13a.

[65] HS ch. 22. Those parts of this chapter dealing with rites have been translated in 1 A. HULSEWÉ, REMNANTS OF HAN LAW 433–55 (1955).

[66] HS ch. 30, 13b, as quoted in 1 A. Hulsewé, supra note 65, at p. 454, n. 94.

[67] Pan Ku's remarks include all of Former and about the first half of Later Han.

[68] See TJAN, supra note 9.

[69] 1 TJAN 163; HHS ch. 36, 10a; and my forthcoming paper on the Old and New Text schools of Han Confucianism.

Probably about the same time that the White Tiger Hall convention was taking place, Cheng Chung composed a work called the *Hun-li* (The Marriage Ritual).[70] The *Hun-li* was already lost in early T'ang times when the bibliography in the *Sui-shu* was compiled; today we have only fragments of the work. The work was intended to be normative, not descriptive of Han practices. This is the view of Tu Yu, the author of the *T'ung-tien*,[71] and the *Chin-shu* also refers to Cheng's work as a piece of "ancient" practices.[72] Wang Kuo-han in the "Preface" to the fragments of the *Hun-li* follows the opinion of Tu Yu. Some scholars, however, have assumed that the work is an account of Han customs. Ku Huai-san and Yang Shu-ta both accept it in this way, but neither of them has bothered to question the place of the *Hun-li* in the literature of the time.[73] The general remarks about rites in Later Han as well as the specific examples from the same period argue convincingly that the work was not intended as a description of contemporary customs but was an attempt to fill the hiatus that Pan Ku and others had so often lamented.

At least one other attempt was made in Later Han to provide a comprehensive body of ritual. In A.D. 85 Emperor Chang, the same Emperor who just six years earlier had sought to unify the Confucian world in the discussions in White Tiger Hall, issued a decree in which he expressed an interest in the composition of a suitable body of ritual literature. Because of the opposition of some officials no immediate action was taken, but in A.D. 87 Ts'ao Pao was finally ordered to write a corpus of ritual for the Han. When Ts'ao's work was completed it consisted of 150 chapters *(chuan)* and covered everyone from the emperor down to the commoners and from capping and marriage to matters having to do with good and bad fortune. Unfortunately for Ts'ao, the opinions of his contemporaries on his work were so diverse and difficult to synthesize that Emperor Chang merely accepted the work without ordering an official evaluation and editing of it. The work never circulated although a part of it, with a commentary by Ts'ao Pao himself, was used in the capping ceremony for Emperor Ho in A.D. 91.[74] Later, in A.D. 101 Chang Fen suggested

---

[70] We do not know the date of the HUN-LI; Cheng Chung died in A.D. 83, and that is as close as we can come to dating the work. Cheng's biography (HHS ch. 36, 5a–6b) does not mention the HUN-LI, but Cheng and his father, Cheng Hsing, are well known as Old Text scholars who had considerable interest in rites and who both studied the CHOU-LI (Rites of Chou) and wrote on it. *See* Ma Kuo-han's prefatory remarks to *Chou-li : Cheng Ssu-nung chieh-chu* (Interpretative commentary by Minister of Agriculture Cheng to the Rites of Chou), in K. MA, *supra* note 55, at ch. 17. I see no reason to doubt that Cheng Chung wrote this piece on marriage ritual.

[71] Y. TU, *supra* note 31, at ch. 58, *Li* §18, 336.

[72] H. FANG, CHIN-SHU (History of Chin) 21, 21b (I-wen yin-shu kuan ed.).

[73] H. Ku, *Pu Hou-Han-shu i-wen-chih* (A supplementary treatise on literature of the history of the Later Han dynasty), in 2 ERH-SHIH-WU SHIH PU-PIEN (Supplements to the Twenty-five histories) 2143 (1936–37); YANG *passim*.

[74] HHS ch. 35, 7a–9a; HHS ch. 4, 4a.

to Emperor Ho that the work begun by Ts'ao should be completed, but, even though the Emperor approved of the idea, he did not promulgate the requisite command, and nothing was done.[75]

On a smaller scale Pan Chao's "Lessons for Women," probably written about A.D. 100, was intended to set forth some of the ritual guidelines for women. The humble and inferior role that she sets forth for the ideal woman indicates that she shared the authoritarian, Old Text ideas of her brother, Pan Ku. But, again, Pan Chao was not describing feminine life around her; she was trying to establish how it should be. And, like Ts'ao Pao, Pan Chao did not escape adverse criticism; her sister-in-law, Ts'ao Feng-sheng, "also was talented and gracious. She wrote a piece in which she contradicted [Pan Chao]; the text contains [points] worth observing."[76] Since the ideas expressed by Pan Chao were ultimately accepted as a part of the Confucian tradition and since her work was repeatedly republished,[77] it should not surprise us that a Ch'ing commentator could ask with regard to the statement concerning Ts'ao Feng-sheng, "How could [Pan Chao] be contradicted?"[78] But his statement should also remind us that we ought not to accept uncritically the views of those who do not see the dynamic social changes that occurred throughout the centuries of Chinese history.

The opposition encountered in Ts'ao Pao's attempts to formulate a *Han-li* (Rites of Han), as well as the opposition to Pan Chao's "Lessons for Women," are reflections of the divisions within the scholarly world of the time. And the continuing concern with the problem of ritual indicates very clearly that there was no widely accepted body of ritual which adequately covered such things as the marriage ritual. As Yüan Hung, the author of a history of Later Han, observed, many of the rituals of the time were already different from those of antiquity, and yet anyone discoursing on rituals had to base his arguments on (presumed) ancient practices which were not necessarily applicable in the new environment of the unified Han empire. The result was that there was a lack of unanimity as individuals of differing schools of thought each followed what he thought was appropriate.[79]

The formal wedding, according to the classics, was supposed to consist of six steps (seven if one includes the presentation of the bride at the ancestral

---

[75] HHS ch. 35, 5b–6a. For the broader context of Han Confucianism within which these reform efforts were made, *see* J. Dull, A Historical Introduction to the Apocryphal *(ch'an-wei)* Texts of the Han Dynasty, 1966 (unpublished dissertation, University of Washington).

[76] HHS ch. 84, 8a; I have modified slightly the translation in N. SWANN, *supra* note 14, at p. 41.

[77] W. HU, LI-TAI FU-NÜ CHU-TSO K'AO (An examination of the writings of women through the ages) 3 (1957); N. SWANN, *supra* note 14, at 57, 156.

[78] HHS ch. 84, 8a.

[79] Quoted in C. Yao, *Hou-Han I-wen-chih* (Treatise on literature of the history of the Later Han dynasty), in 2 ERH-SHIH-WU SHIH PU-PIEN, *supra* note 73, at 2362.

temple). These are mentioned in classical literature, they are adumbrated in a quotation, to be given shortly from the *Huai-nan-tzu,* and they were explained in the discussions in White Tiger Hall.[80] However, their inclusion in such works does not necessarily mean that they were a part of normal Han social behavior or even that they were practiced by the imperial officials and others in the upper strata of Chinese society of the time. The ensuing discussion follows the traditional pattern according to which a marriage was arranged and performed; I do this in spite of the foregoing remarks about Han ritual questions, not because all the "traditional" steps were followed in the Han, but because those steps provide a convenient way of treating the material. This treatment also allows us to see that some aspects of the "traditional" system were prevalent in the Han but that the system as a whole was not. Before taking up the six rituals it is necessary to comment on the matchmaker.

The matchmaker, according to the *Huai-nan-tzu,* was an indispensable institution: "As for [such practices as] getting a matchmaker and then joining in conversation, presenting the betrothal gifts, then taking a wife, at first avoiding and then meeting in person [the bride], it is not that these are not bothersome. However, the reason these rites cannot be changed is that they are the means for guarding against licentiousness."[81] In other words, men and women were not supposed to come into direct contact until their marriage was performed. Allowing free contact between them opened the door to socially unacceptable behavior.

The Han data do indicate that marriages were often arranged by parents, elders, or political superiors. Ch'en P'ing was poverty stricken when he reached marriageable age and too proud to marry a girl of the same economic status. However, he attracted the attention of a wealthy man, Chang Fu, whose granddaughter had lost five husbands when they had all died at a young age. In spite of the fact that the girl's father objected to her marriage with Ch'en, the will of the grandfather prevailed and the marriage was arranged.[82] The marriage of Chung Chin and his cousin of the Li family was arranged by the girl's grandfather.[83] The marriage of the founder of the Han dynasty, while he was still a low-placed official, was arranged by the father of the future Empress Lü over the protests of the girl's mother.[84] Usually, as in the case of Empress Lü, the parents of the young man or woman arranged the marriage. For example, Tai Liang, a very unconventional individual whose biography is in the chapter on recluses of the *Hou Han-shu,* had five talented daughters; "whenever he sought marriage [for one of them] she was immediately

---

[80] 1 J. STEELE, THE I-LI OR BOOK OF ETIQUETTE AND CEREMONIAL 18 ff. (1966 reprint); 1 TJAN 244–63.

[81] A. LIU, HUAI-NAN-TZU ch. 20, 635 (1959).

[82] HS ch. 40, 12a–b; 1 B. WATSON, *supra* note 57, at 152–53.

[83] HHS ch. 62, 12a.

[84] 1 HFHD 30–32.

accepted.''[85] A girl stopped an official on the road in order to plead for her father's release from prison and so impressed the official that he arranged for her to marry his son.[86] Kung-sun Tsan was a menial commandery official who impressed the commandery Grand Administrator with his good looks and ability as a speaker, and the Administrator married his daughter to him.[87] Again, Pao Hsüan so excelled as a student that his teacher arranged for Pao to marry his daughter.[88] There is one case that has a rare personal touch to it. The future Emperor Hsüan was raised part of his life as a commoner and part by eunuchs within the palace. When he reached eighteen years of age, Chang Ho, one of the eunuchs who had looked after him, heard that Hsü Kuang-han, a subordinate of the eunuch, had a daughter who had been engaged to a man who had died before the wedding could take place. Chang called in Hsü, plied him with wine, and, after Hsü was intoxicated, arranged for the marriage of the future Emperor with Hsü's daughter. Hsü's wife opposed this arrangement (probably because she was fearful of becoming identified with the imperial family which had recently been purged of some of its members), but Hsü made Chang the go-between and, because of a handsome betrothal gift, was able to carry through on the arrangements.[89]

At other times a person close to one of the parties, but not necessarily a relative, arranged for the marriage or, as in the following case, for the divorce and remarriage. Chang Erh, fleeing for his life, went to Wai-huang. A rich man of Wai-huang had a very beautiful daughter who was forced to serve her husband as if she were a slave. She fled from him and stayed with a retainer of her father. The retainer told her that if she wanted a worthy husband she should marry Chang Erh. When the girl approved of the idea, the retainer arranged for her separation from her husband and for her marriage to Chang.[90]

Thus, marriages arranged by the parents were a common feature of the Han period; however, that does not mean that the individual did not also have considerable latitude in picking a spouse. In fact, the Han-shih wai-chuan, a text more authoritative than the Huai-nan-tzu because it was an integral part of Confucianism, contained the idea that whereas the individual ordinarily did not arrange his own marriage, if his intentions were good this could be

---

[85] HHS ch. 83, 13a.

[86] CH'ANG CH'Ü, HUA-YANG KUO-CHIH (Gazetteer of Hua-yang) ch. 10B, 354 (1962) [hereinafter cited as HYKC].

[87] HHS ch. 73, 4a.

[88] HHS ch. 84, 1a–b; for other examples see YANG 6–8.

[89] HS ch. 59, 9b–10a; HS ch. 97A, 22a.

[90] HS ch. 32, 1a. There are some minor problems in this passage; for a slightly different rendering based on the Shih-chi version of the story, see 1 B. WATSON, supra note 57, at 171.

done.[91] Huang Pa, a prefectural policeman and later Prime Minister, was riding in a carriage with a physiognomist who assured Huang that a young girl they had just seen would become rich and honored. Huang "inquired about her and found out that she was the daughter of a shaman of the district. He took her as his wife and remained with her to death."[92] Of course, as in many of the preceding examples, we do not have all the details of the case; we do not know whether Huang Pa formally employed a go-between. It is fairly certain, however, that the choice at least was Huang's own.

In some cases the individual could express his preference in a negative way by refusing the mate whom his parents had selected. The fat, ugly, and muscular woman who married Liang Hung, according to her testimony, had refused previous mates selected by her parents because she wanted a man as worthy as Liang Hung.[93] Again, when Yüan Wei married Ma Lun, a daughter of the famous Old Text scholar Ma Jung, he asked: "Now your older sister is not yet married; is it permissible for you to go ahead?" He was told, "Your wife's older sister is [a woman of] superior conduct and distinctive profundity; she has not yet met a good mate. This does not seem to be despicable."[94] This suggests that the older sister had declined to accept mates who had been chosen for her or that she was looking for herself.

In other cases the choice was entirely up to the woman. An imperial princess, a sister of Emperor Wu, had lost her first husband; on the advice of her attendants she chose Wei Ch'ing as her husband, in spite of the fact that before his meteoric rise to power and prestige he had been an attendant in her household.[95] One of the most famous cases in Chinese history of a love-marriage concerns the wife of Ssu-ma Hsiang-ju who as a young widow left her father's home to elope with the talented poet.[96]

The evidence thus shows that many marriages, probably the majority, were arranged by older members of the family of the man or woman. It was generally felt that unmarried people ought not to be left to their own decisions about choosing a mate; personal choice presupposed personal contacts which ought to be avoided in order "to keep shame at a distance and to avoid debauchery."[97] In a few cases there is direct evidence of the institution of

---

[91] *J. Hightower,* HAN SHIH WAI CHUAN, HAN YING'S ILLUSTRATIONS OF THE DIDACTIC APPLICATION OF THE CLASSICS OF SONGS 40–41 (1952). *Cf.* T. CH'Ü, *supra* note 29, at 99: "In no sense was a marriage concerned with the personal wishes of the man and woman involved. . . ."

[92] HS ch. 89, 8b–9a. This was apparently a well-known marriage. 1 A. FORKE, *supra* note 11, at 307, takes the word *wu* (shaman) as a family name, but the HS text does not warrant that interpretation.

[93] HHS ch. 83, 8a.

[94] HHS ch. 84, 10b.

[95] HS ch. 55, 17a.

[96] HS ch. 57A, 1b–2b.

[97] 1 TJAN 244.

matchmaker, but in most examples that individual is lacking or it is suggested that the parents themselves perform that role. Of equal importance for an understanding of Han society is the fact that young men and women had opportunities to express their preferences, either by refusing the mates chosen for them or by personally choosing their spouses. This aspect of Han society will be further elaborated when we discuss divorce and remarriage in that period.

    Na-ts'ai, "the presentation of the choice [of the bride to the bride's parents],"[98] was the first of the six rituals carried out in the marriage ceremony. We have a very limited number of cases in which this term was used; they all involve unusual circumstances. Wang Mang wished to marry his daughter to the Emperor in order to solidify his own position; hence in A.D. 2 he submitted a memorial, a part of which reads: "I beg that the Five Classics be investigated and discussed in order to establish rites for [the imperial] marriage and to fix the principle of [the Emperor's] twelve women. . . ."[99] Although we cannot be sure of the details intended here, this statement strongly suggests, as has already been noted, that the ritual literature was not firmly established in the Han. Following a series of shrewd moves on the part of Wang Mang, the Grand Empress Dowager had to let the ministers select *(ts'ai)* Wang Mang's daughter. "The [Grand] Empress Dowager sent the Privy Treasurer [and others] to present the proposal [of marriage] and to interview the girl."[100] At that time, Wang Mang, as the bride's father, was presented with a leather cap and a plain lower garment in spite of the fact that according to several ritual texts he should have been given a goose.[101] Almost a century and a half later, in A.D. 148, when Liang Chi, the most powerful member of a domineering consort family, sought to strengthen his control over the throne, an official memorialized that the sister of Liang Chi should be the Empress of Emperor Huan and went on to suggest: "It would be fitting to prepare the ritual regulations and at the [appropriate] time submit the presents which would complete the wedding."[102] After an examination by the officials responsible for ritual matters, "they, thereupon, relied completely upon the precedent of Emperor Hsiao-hui (reigned 194–188 B.C.) when he had taken his Empress." The ritual for the "presentation of the choice" *(na-ts'ai)* included gifts of a wild goose, a perforated jade disc, carriages and horses, and silks.[103] Accord-

---

[98] The translation is a modification of that given in 3 HFHD 157 n. 9.3. For the other five terms, I follow his rendering. *Cf.* 1 TJAN 246.

[99] HFHD 154–55.

[100] *Id.,* 156–57. The phrase "[and others]" is my abbreviation of some of the material giving names of officials; other brackets are by Dubs.

[101] HS ch. 97B, 23a, has a slightly different version and refers to the gifts. The ritual gift (a goose) is noted in 1 J. STEELE, *supra* note 80, at 18; 1 TJAN 246.

[102] HHS ch. 10B, 5b–6a.

[103] *Id.*

ing to another history of the Later Han, the precedents followed included those of the marriage of Emperor Hui to Empress Dowager Lü's granddaughter and of Wang Mang's daughter to Emperor P'ing.[104] Although we are faced with a frustrating lack of details, both of these examples indicate that the *na-ts'ai* was probably not a normal procedure; instead, when there was some reason to make a wedding very special, it was then necessary to refer, not to the normal procedures by which the emperor took a wife (see below), but to equally special occasions as precedents. An obvious political ploy aimed at preventing the appearance of another consort family next to the throne was legitimatized by resorting to rituals that ordinarily were not followed.

The one case of a betrothal gift which does not involve the imperial family follows the same pattern. In the last decade of the Later Han, Ch'eng Ying at age nineteen had married a man named Wei, but before long her husband died. Wang Ch'ung wished to marry the girl and approached her uncle who said that the girl was determined not to remarry. Since Wang Ch'ung was a commandery official, Investigator of Transgressions, he appealed to his superior, the Grand Administrator of the commandery, to intercede for him. The Grand Administrator notified the officials of the prefecture in which the girl lived "to present her with a lamb and a wild goose, and to promulgate the order that the Grand Administrator was making these as betrothal gifts to her." Rather than accept them, the girl attempted suicide.[105] In this case the word for "betrothal gifts" is *p'in,* not *na-ts'ai;* however, the meaning is obviously the same. The principle seems to have been the same as in cases of the marriages of the emperors; an attempt was made to prevent effective opposition by recourse to supposedly hallowed ritualistic practices of an earlier day. The normal wedding probably did not include the ritual of *na-ts'ai.*

betrothal gift [handwritten margin note]

Wen-ming, "the request for the [girl's] given name," was the second of the six rituals in the elaborate marriage ceremony. I have not been able to find any use of this institution in a Han case. The term does appear in Cheng Chung's *Hun-li* where he says: "The request for the [girl's] given name means asking the girl's given name so they can return [to the man's ancestral temple] to divine about her."[106] However, Cheng's work is not based on current practices; it was an effort to establish certain practices. Yang Shu-ta, the twentieth-century scholar who has collected the most material on all aspects of marriage in the Han, thinks that *wen-ming* is implicit in the case of the wedding of Wang Mang's daughter. When officials were sent to "present the

---

[104] *See* Hui Tung's commentary to HHS ch. 10B, 5b–6a.

[105] HYKC ch. 10B, 356. The Grand Administrator was Li Yen who is mentioned in S. CHEN, SAN-KUO-CHIH (History of the Three Kingdoms) *Shu,* 10, 9a (I-wen yin-shu-kuan, ed.), and this provides the date.

[106] CHENG CHUNG, HUN-LI 1a (*see* note 70). All six terms are in Cheng's work; however, if there is any other information on the term, I do not call attention to his work.

proposal [of marriage] and to interview the girl," Yang argues, the interview was a means of carrying out the *wen-ming* ritual.[107] There is really no way of being certain that the rite was performed. We do know that when the officials returned from the interview they reported that the girl "has been imbued with virtue and culture and has a beautiful and fascinating appearance, so that it would be proper for her to continue the heavenly succession and uphold the [imperial] sacrifices."[108] This statement does not indicate that the *wen-ming* rite was performed. If anything it suggests another practice of at least Later Han times. Annually, in the eighth month, high court officials and a phy-siognomist were sent throughout the environs of the capital to look over the daughters of good families. Those who were beautiful and serious and who met the requirements of the physiognomist were taken back to the rear palace where they were sent through a selection process, and some then became members of the imperial harem.[109] The little evidence that we do have about the selection of Wang Mang's daughter suggests that the officials were performing the usual function for choosing a lady for the harem; there is nothing to show that the *wen-ming* ritual was actually a part of the process. After the officials made their report, divination was carried out, as Cheng Chung said it should be, but that belongs to the next step.

The third rite in the marriage ceremony was *na-chi*, "the presentation of the lucky [divination concerning the marriage]." Again, the only evidence of this rite being a part of Han marriage ceremony comes from the account of Wang Mang's daughter's marriage. After reporting on Wang Mang's daughter, forty-nine officials, including some of the highest of the empire, were sent to the ancestral temple of Emperor Kao-tsu to report the selection of the girl and to divine regarding the auspiciousness of the match. The responses to their questions were all favorable and this was duly reported.[110] But, again, the *Han-shu* does not tell us specifically that a rite known as *na-chi* was performed. And, in fact, at the time of divination the high ministers also selected the date for the wedding itself. According to the procedure to be followed for the "six rites" the date was not supposed to be fixed until after the presentation of the betrothal presents (the fourth rite).

---

[107] YANG 15. He says, "The historical text is somewhat incomplete" in spelling out all the precise steps.

[108] 3 HFHD 157–58. His "beautiful and fascinating appearance" *(yao t'iao)* was understood by Yen Shih-ku to mean "reserved and quiet." But the same term also meant seductive and bewitching; Dubs apparently was guided by this definition. *See* T. FU, LIEN-MIEN TZU-TIEN (A dictionary of binomial expressions) *yao-tiao,* definition 2 (1943). In view of the context, Yen is almost certainly correct. In spite of the high quality of Dubs' translation, one has to be careful about Dubs' interpretations, for he accepts Pan Ku's biases and the biases of those commentators who favor Pan's prejudices.

[109] HHS ch. 10A, 2b.

[110] HS ch. 97B, 23a; 3 HFHD 158.

The rite of *na-cheng*, "the presentation of the betrothal presents," was apparently universally practiced in the Han; it was the key feature of the marriage ceremony. The ritualists of the time looked upon the betrothal gift as a tool; we have already seen that a contributor to the *Huai-nan-tzu* admitted that the betrothal gift was a troublesome thing, but that it was worthwhile for it was one of the ways of preventing licentiousness.[111] The argument is expressed more clearly in the *Ta-tai Li*: "Whenever there is licentiousness, it is produced from men and women not being separated and from husband and wife lacking in righteousness. The offering of the betrothal gift in the marriage rite is whereby men and women are separated and what makes clear the righteousness of husband and wife. Therefore, if there are offenses of licentiousness, then adorn the marriage rites with the offering of betrothal gifts."[112] In other words, so long as betrothal gifts were required, men and women could not form marital unions on their own authority. Apparently the assumption was that the cost of the gifts precluded direct action by the young; they had to depend upon their parents for the gifts, and by extension the parents would also decide who was to be the wife of their son. Without the betrothal presents the marriage could not be legitimatized, or so the argument ran.

Several examples will demonstrate the importance of the betrothal gift. The impoverished Ch'en P'ing was willing to marry the granddaughter of the wealthy Chang Fu even though she had lost five husbands already. Since Ch'en P'ing had no money the girl's grandfather *loaned* him money for the betrothal gifts.[113] Again, Li Ku, who was to be one of the leading officials in the middle of the second century A.D., had a young subordinate who was a diligent student from a very poor family. When the young man was approaching his majority, Li was distressed that no marriage had yet been arranged for him and that neither friend nor relative was doing anything about it. Since, said Li Ku, "capping, marriage, and entering officialdom are not things done on one's own," he was prepared to adopt a paternal attitude, and he asked his other subordinates to contribute money so that the marriage rites could be carried out. He estimated that 20,000 to 30,000 cash would be enough

[111] HUAI-NAN-TZU ch. 20, 635.

[112] TA-TAI LI-CHI (The record of rites of the Elder Tai), *"Sheng-te-p'ien"* ("Flourishing virtue"), quoted from 1419 KU-CHIN T'U-SHU CHI-CH'ENG (A comprehensive collection of ancient and modern illustrations and documents) ch. 36 of the *I-li tien*, 5a (1884).

[113] HS ch. 40, 12a–b; 1 B. WATSON, supra note 57, at 152–53. In this case, *p'in* is used for betrothal gift, not *na-cheng*. We have already seen, in the case of Wang Ch'ung who had his Grand Administrator intercede so that he could marry a young widow, that *p'in* was also used when, more strictly, *na-ts'ai* was meant. *P'in* in Han times usually meant the *na-cheng; see, e.g.,* the statements in the biography of Wang Mang where gifts to him are called *p'in* but in another context the same gifts are termed *na-cheng*. 3 HFHD 162, 186, 187.

"to complete the wedding."[114] (Some idea of what this amounted to can be seen from the fact that a family of median means in the second century B.C. was worth 100,000 cash.)[115] Similarly, when Jen Yen became Grand Administrator of Chiu-chen (in what is now North Vietnam) he encountered people who were backwards economically, and he taught them agriculture. He found that they "had no rituals and laws pertaining to marriage" and "did not know the nature of the father and son [relationship] or the Way of husband and wife." He then ordered the Prefects under his jurisdiction to make the men of the area who were twenty to fifty years old marry women fifteen to forty. Those who lacked betrothal gifts for the ceremony were to be aided by local officials who were supposed to make part of their salaries available in order to aid them. Over two thousand people were married at the same time.[116] All three of these cases patently demonstrate that in the minds of many the betrothal gifts were an indispensable part of the marriage ceremony.

As several of the foregoing examples indicate, raising the money for the betrothal presents often presented a serious problem. One of the debaters in the *Discourses on Salt and Iron* alleged that ". . . patrimonies are wasted to provide sumptuous funerals, [and] dowries by the cartloads for marrying daughters. The rich strive to surpass one another; the poor, to catch up to the rich. The former deplete their capital; the latter resort to loans."[117] Although this passage does not refer specifically to betrothal gifts, the dowries were reciprocal, and it is difficult to imagine a large dowry without a large betrothal gift. Later, in the reign of Emperor Hsüan, Wang Chi complained that betrothal gifts and dowries were given "without restraint; thus the poor people cannot come up [to these standards] and therefore they do not raise their children."[118]

The institution of *na-cheng,* in view of its importance in a marriage and in view of the fact that the gift was often large, was easily abused. For example, when Wang Mang married his daughter to Emperor P'ing, the betrothal gift was first announced as being 200 million cash, but part of this was declined by Wang Mang. After a considerable amount of discussion, and after Wang's daughter had been married and had become Empress, the amount was finally fixed at 100 million cash.[119] After Wang Mang himself had assumed the

---

[114] F. Li, T'AI-P'ING YÜ-LAN ([Encyclopedia for] imperial perusal of the T'ai-p'ing era) ch. 541, 7b (Hsin-hsing shu-chü ed. 1959), quoted in YANG 18.

[115] I HFHD 272.

[116] HHS ch. 76, 4a.

[117] E. Gale, *et al., "Discourses on Salt and Iron,"* 65 JNCBRAS 109 (1934). I have slightly modified the literal translation on the basis of the text itself. K. HUAN, *supra* note 23, at 106.

[118] HS ch. 72, 7a.

[119] 3 HFHD 161, 184, 186, 190. The value of all the gifts amounted to more than this, for they included property and honors as well as cash.

emperorship he married a woman of the Shih family, and on that occasion the betrothal gifts bestowed by Wang included 300 million cash worth of gold as well as other things.[120] Liang Chi, one of the most unscrupulous members of any of the consort families to dominate the Later Han government, arranged to have his sister marry Emperor Huan. This was another case of unusual ritual preparations (which were attacked[121]), and the betrothal gift was twenty thousand catties of gold (that is, 200 million cash).[122] Even the non-Chinese were forced at times to comply with the concept of the sizable betrothal gift as when, in *ca.* 110 B.C., the Wu-sun were told that their chieftain could have a Chinese princess for a bride only after the presentation of a betrothal present of one thousand badly needed horses.[123]

Another form of abuse was to use the betrothal gift as a kind of bribe. In the middle of the first century B.C., Chang Po proved his loyalty to King Hsien of Huai-yang by noting that the King of Chao had sent men to him with a gift of thirty catties of gold; when Chang Po refused to accept it, the King of Chao then sent word that he wanted to marry Chang's daughter and was prepared to make a betrothal gift of two hundred catties of gold (two million cash). Chang again declined.[124] In another case the mother of the wife of the future Emperor Hsüan objected to the marriage arrangements made by her husband after the eunuch Chang Ho had gotten the husband drunk. The mother assented to the marriage only after the eunuch used his family wealth as a betrothal gift.[125] Tung Cho, one of the dictators in the closing years of Later Han, tried to convince a well-educated and beautiful widow that she should marry him. His betrothal gifts included carriages, horses, slaves, money, and silks. Although the gifts offered to the widow "filled the roads," she refused to be bought, as it were, and Tung had her killed.[126] Such practices, of course, do not characterize the *na-cheng* institution; they only show how it could be perverted.

In spite of the fact that the ritual texts do not specify reciprocity for the betrothal gifts and even though none of our cases explicitly indicate the practice of reciprocity, it is clear that the bride's family gave lavish wedding presents and that these were usually expected. The statements quoted above from the *Discourses on Salt and Iron* and from the memorial of Wang Chi both include references to large dowries. Wang Fu in his *Ch'ien-fu-lun,* written towards the end of Later Han, bemoans the competition between wealthy

---

[120] 3 HFHD 437–38.

[121] HHS ch. 63, 15b.

[122] HHS ch. 10B, 5b–6a. *See also* HHS ch. 10B, 13a, for the very expensive gifts to Ts'ao Ts'ao when he offered three daughters to the throne.

[123] HS ch. 96, 3b. Similar arrangements were made in 64 B.C.; *see* HS ch. 96, 6a–b.

[124] HS ch. 80, 2b.

[125] HS ch. 59, 9b–10a; HS ch. 97A, 22a.

[126] HHS ch. 84, 11b.

families as they send off their daughters with great shows of wealth and
sympathizes with the poor who feel ashamed that they cannot reach such
heights of expenditure.[127] Two sons of Ch'en Sheng married daughters of
rich families; "the female slave attendants numbered seven or eight and the
property given was of high value."[128] Tai Liang, an unorthodox individual
who was inclined to flout ritual, sent his five talented daughters off with
coarse garments, plain cotton blankets, bamboo hampers, and wooden shoes.
Obviously, he was not interested in competing with anyone, but still felt
compelled to follow at least some of the social niceties.[129] Some husbands who
did not have large estates were ashamed at the size of the dowries their wives
brought; thus, for example, Pao Hsüan had his wife take back to her father
the goods and servants she had brought when she married him.[130] This
became a celebrated case which was emulated by others.[131]

In sum, the fourth of the six rites of marriage, the *na-cheng,* was widely
practiced in the Han; in effect this rite, more than any other, was necessary
for the marriage. Without the presentation of the *na-cheng* gifts the marriage
was not completed.[132] The *na-cheng* was an occasion for "conspicuous
consumption" for the rich and a source of discomfiture for the poor. It was
also manipulable for political purposes and could easily become an ill-concealed
bribe.

The penultimate rite was the *ch'ing-ch'i,* "the request to fix a date [for the
marriage]." Yang Shu-ta has shown that among Han ritual specialists there
was a difference of opinion with regard to this particular rite. Cheng Chung's
Hun-li says that the term means "requesting a fortunate date on which to
welcome [the bride]." But Cheng Hsüan, the most important commentator
on the Confucian classics in Later Han, follows the *I-li* in that the date was
actually announced by the groom's family after the bride's father had declined
to pick a date.[133] We have two references to this rite for the Han period. The
first involves, again, the case of Wang Mang's daughter's marriage in which
high ministers of state were sent to the ancestral temple of the founder of the
Han dynasty to divine the date for the wedding.[134] The other instance comes
from the poem "A Peacock Flies to the Southeast."[135] In the first case the

---

[127] F. WANG, *supra* note 56, at ch. 3, 12.

[128] HYKC ch. 10C, 380.

[129] HHS ch. 83, 12b–13a.

[130] HHS ch. 84, 1b.

[131] HHS ch. 84, 10b.

[132] HHS ch. 10B, 6a.

[133] YANG 16, quoting Cheng Chung's HUN-LI and Cheng Hsüan's comment to the
I-LI.

[134] HS ch. 97B, 23a. There was a period of about one year between the divination
and the marriage; *see* 3 HFHD 158, 184.

[135] Quoted in YANG 17.

ministers were presumably acting on behalf of the groom's family, and in the latter case the groom's family chose the date; in neither case is the term *na-chi* itself used.

The final step in the six rites was *ch'in-ying,* "the [groom] in person fetching [the bride, bringing her to his ancestral home]." The ceremony is mentioned in the same two cases cited for the foregoing rite. Wang Mang's daughter was brought to the palace not by the Emperor in person but by high officials in a grand procession; they presumably were acting on behalf of Emperor P'ing who was only six years old at the time. In A.D. 23 when Wang Mang, then the ruler of his own dynasty, remarried, he personally met his bride, not at her home as ritual demanded, but at the steps of the palace.[136]

Although the traditional marriage was often thought of as a six-part cere-mony, there were two additional elements to it. The first was the wedding dinner; the second was the presentation of the bride at the groom's ancestral temple. As Dubs has shown there were two markedly different views concern-ing the marriage itself, views which are directly relevant to the marriage feast.[137] Scholars who were involved in formulating ritual ceremonies, the ideologues, argued, for example, in the *Han-shih wai-chuan:*

> The family of a woman who has been given in marriage does not extinguish the light for three nights: [this is because] they are thinking of the separation. The family [whose son] has taken a wife does not make music for three days: [this is because] they are thinking that he [soon] will succeed his father. . . . Sad thoughts for three days . . . are due to the feelings of the filial son.[138]

The gist of this is repeated in the White Tiger Hall records and then the text adds the explanation: the members of the family of the groom "feel sad at [the thought that] the father has grown feeble and old in the course of years and that [the time of his] being replaced [by the son] has arrived."[139] Thus, according to contemporary ritual literature the marriage itself was a solemn and, indeed, a saddening occasion without frivolity or gaiety.

In practice, however, the situation was very different. In 56 B.C., Emperor Hsüan enjoined local officials from " 'imposing prohibitions upon the common people when they give or take in marriage, so that they are not permitted to prepare feasts, to offer felicitations, or to summon each other together. In this way they have abolished the rites of proper conduct for the districts and villages and have caused the common people to be without any means of enjoyment. This is not the way in which to guide the common people' "[140] Obviously,

---

[136] 3 HFHD 438.

[137] 2 HFHD 249 n.19.4. My interpretation of the two views does not agree with his; Dubs speaks of two different customs, which at least for the Han is apparently incorrect.

[138] J. HIGHTOWER, *supra* note 91, at 72–73.

[139] 1 TJAN 249.

[140] 2 HFHD 248.

the social custom did not coincide with the staid admonitions given in the ritual texts. I cannot imagine that the officials addressed by Emperor Hsüan were attempting to enforce Confucian ritual, for Confucianism at that time was too "new"; furthermore, it was not the ritualistically oriented kind of Confucianism. Instead, the officials were enforcing a law that prohibited an assembly of more than three people even for such an occasion as a marriage dinner.[141] According to Chung-ch'ang T'ung, the parties to celebrate marriages frequently became orgies: "Today at wedding banquets, clubs are used in urging obscene tricks; wines are used in pursuit of lustful desires. Licentiousness is displayed among the broad masses; intimate personal matters are exposed among the relatives. Customs are defiled and usages perverted; licentiousness is produced and lecherousness is nurtured. Nothing is worse than this! It is impossible not to cut it off!"[142] Even allowing for hyperbole, this describes a situation far distant from the melancholy wedding prescribed in the ritual literature. To give one example, but without the sexual element, in 131 B.C. when T'ien Fen married (probably: remarried) he was Prime Minister; on the invitation of his sister, the Empress Dowager Wang, the guests for the banquet included "all of the nobles and members of the imperial family" who were invited to "offer their congratulations." The banquet became the scene of drunken arguments that had important political ramifications.[143] This particular part of the wedding ceremony seems to bear no similarity to the ritual pronouncements of what it should be.[144]

The final act in the marriage ceremony was supposed to be the presentation of the bride at the ancestral temple after three months of marriage. All available examples come from the records of the imperial house (that is, they deal only with empresses, not with commoners), and even then we do not have very many instances of this ceremony. Empress Shang-kuan married Emperor Chao in the third month of 83 B.C.; in the sixth month of that year

[141] 2 HFHD 249 n.19.4.

[142] YANG 23, quoting Chung-ch'ang T'ung's CH'ANG-YEN as quoted in CH'ÜN-SHU CHIH YAO.

[143] HS ch. 52, 9a–b; the quotations are from 2 B. WATSON, *supra* note 57, at 121 ff. For other examples which include puppets, singing, dancing, and so on, *see* YANG 22–24.

[144] There is a possible exception to this; as we might expect, it concerns Wang Mang. When he took a second wife in A.D. 23 shortly before his downfall, he "completed the ceremonies of the common [marriage] meal. . . ." (3 HFHD 438). The meal referred to was apparently according to the *I-li* which means that it was a severely simple, highly formalized, and sterile ceremony involving the bride and groom and attendants whose duty it was to place prescribed dishes in the proper order in the correct positions before the bride and groom (*see* J. STEELE, *supra* note 80, at 24–25). This meal is indicative of Wang Mang's growing fixation on ritual matters; by comparison, about 8 B.C. (that is, about thirty years earlier, long before Wang founded his own dynasty) when he arranged for the simultaneous weddings of his son and his nephew, "guests had filled his halls" (3 HFHD 128).

she was presented at the ancestral temple.[145] This does not necessarily mean that there was a three month period, but there may well have been. In the case of Wang Mang's daughter, her biography says that three months after she became Empress "she was presented at Kao [-tsu's] temple according to the rites."[146] In this case the full three month period was probably honored. In the middle of the second century A.D. Liang Chi's sister married Emperor Huan on the *k'ang-tzu* (twenty-second) of the sixth month and was presented at the ancestral temple on the *i-wei* (sixteenth) day of the eighth month.[147] This is actually less than two months. One might argue that three months are involved—the sixth, seventh, and eighth—but even that does not satisfy the reasoning behind the three-month period as given in the *Po-hu t'ung* discussions. There it is stated: "Three months [constitute] a season, [in which] the things have their [seasonal] completion, and the good and bad [qualities] of man can be known."[148]

We are thus left with a very mixed picture of the degree of adherence to the ritual prescriptions for the marriage ceremony. Some parts of the multifaceted ceremony were clearly practiced; this is particularly true of the betrothal presents. On the other hand, there is no evidence to show that the rite of requesting the girl's given name *(wen-ming)* was ever practiced in Han times. In other respects, such as the supposed solemnity of the marriage banquet, the social usage in no way reflected the lessons of the classical and ritual literature. Much of the evidence for some of the less common rites comes from the marriage of Wang Mang's daughter or Liang Chi's sister; it is to be noted that in both cases special attention was given to searching out precedents of the distant past which would justify the ceremonies adopted. In other words both of these cases, which provide so much of the evidence of this section, are atypical and ought not to be interpreted as reflections of popular custom or even imperial practice. Furthermore, in the case of Wang Mang's reliance on unusual rites the historian, Pan Ku, brings out these bits of evidence as a part of his case that Wang Mang was a conscious archaizer who manipulated rites and historical precedents from hoary antiquity for his own political benefit. To a lesser extent (and the material is not so full) the same was true of Liang Chi. The general impression then is that Han society was not strongly bound by "traditional" rites.[149] This impression is strengthened even more by the picture that emerges when we consider the evidence on divorces in the Han.

---

[145] 2 HFHD 157–58.

[146] HS ch. 97B, 23b.

[147] HHS ch. 10B, 6a; the specific dates come from the notes to this work provided by Hui Tung.

[148] 1 TJAN 250.

[149] Another possible research approach would be to look for references to the term *liu-li,* six rites. I have checked the indices to the *Shih-chi, Han-shu, Hou Han-shu,* and

DIVORCE

In view of what has been said already about marriages of people with the same surname, marriages of men and women of different generations, and the fact that Han society was not much bound or restrained by the ritual procedure of the classics, it should not come as a surprise that divorces by both men and women were prevalent characteristics of Han society; divorces did not have to be justified by reference to the "seven conditions" *(ch'i-ch'u)* under which a man could divorce his wife, nor was he prohibited from divorcing her because of the "three prohibitions according to which a husband could not expel his wife" *(san-pu-ch'u)*. There was little or no stigma attached to divorces either outside of those covered in the seven conditions or within those of the categories of the "three prohibitions."

Indeed, in the Han period divorce was generally accepted, whether initiated by the man or the woman. Early in the Later Han dynasty Feng Yen wrote: "Human nature [bestowed by] Heaven and Earth includes contentment and anger; the conjugal relation included the principles of separation and union."[150] Since this statement comes from a letter written by Feng to Jen Wu-ta informing Jen that Feng was divorcing Jen's sister, it is perhaps questionable to cite this as expressive of a general principle. However, other statements from the Han period evince the same idea. K'ung Kuang in the reign of Emperor Ch'eng, in arguing that the former wife of a man guilty of a heinous crime should no longer be made mutually responsible said that ordinarily father, mother, wife, and sons would be punished; "however, the Way of husband and wife is that if there is [mutual] faithfulness then there is togetherness, but without [mutual] faithfulness there is divorce." Since the accused man divorced his wife before the accusation, she should not be accountable for the crimes.[151] Even Pan Chao, the feminine moralist who was trying to teach women, for example, that they could not leave their husbands, had to admit that a satisfactory relationship depended upon the wife not rebuking her husband and the husband not beating his wife. "Should actual blows be dealt, how could the matrimonial relationship be preserved? Should sharp words be spoken, how could conjugal love exist? If love and the proper relationship both be destroyed, then husband and wife will be separated."[152]

P'ei-wen yün-fu and have found only one such reference: Ch'in Chia (flourished *circa* A.D. 150) in a poem to his wife wrote the lines, "Respect this new marriage/ So that the six rites are not forgotten." KU-WEN-YÜAN (Anthology of ancient literature) ch. 8, 10a–b (Ssu-pu Ts'ung-k'uan ed.). In view of the external evidence from other sources, we must assume that this is no more than a classical allusion, or that the poem itself actually dates from a later period.

[150] HHS ch. 28B, 12a, quoted in Hui Tung commentary.

[151] HS ch. 81, 16b–17a.

[152] HS ch. 84, 6a; I have slightly modified the translation in N. SWANN, *supra* note 14, at 86.

These quotations are all based on the assumption that divorce was a natural part of social customs; none of them indicate that the statements were made with the thought in mind of the "seven conditions" or the "three prohibitions." If the couple no longer loved each other or did not get along with each other, that is, if they were mutually incompatible, to use a modern term which would almost do justice to some of the foregoing passages, then a divorce was expected. It was not necessary to justify it on the basis of classical strictures.

And yet, in spite of statements such as the foregoing ones, there is a well established tradition that can best be presented in the following statement by Ch'ü T'ung-tsu: "For more than two thousand years disobedience to the husband's parents, barrenness, adultery, jealousy, incurable disease, loquacity, and theft were the traditional and lawful reasons for divorcing a wife."[153] As our cases from the Han will show, these reasons for divorce were rarely specifically cited, and, of equal importance, there were many divorces not covered by any of these categories. However, inasmuch as we are dealing with widely held views (and to facilitate handling the material), I will deal with the evidence relevant to each of the seven categories in the order in which they are quoted above. A critical review of the evidence will show that we are, again, not justified in complacently accepting statements of the classics as if they were descriptive of Chinese society throughout the imperial period. After treating the evidence cited for each of the seven reasons for divorce, we will look at additional divorce cases that do not fall within any of the seven grounds for separation.

"Disobedience to the girl's parents-in-law" or failing to serve them well is in many ways the counterpart of the filial piety expected of the son; for the wife to disobey her parents-in-law was the equivalent of the son lacking filial piety. In Han times two cases are often cited to exemplify this ground for divorce. During the first part of the first century A.D., Pao Yung served his stepmother in an extremely filial manner. One time, in the presence of his stepmother, Pao's "wife yelled at the dog and [Pao] Yung forthwith divorced her."[154] In the second case Chiang Shih was an exceptionally filial son and his wife followed his model, serving her mother-in-law in an outstandingly magnanimous manner. Chiang's mother was fond of water from a river six or seven *li* from the house. One time when Chiang's wife went after the water, her return was delayed by a storm. In the meantime Chiang's mother became

---

[153] T. Ch'ü, *supra* note 29, at 118. Yang Shu-ta, in spite of his exhaustive compilation of material from the Han on the subject of marriage and divorce, agrees with Ch'ü, whom he frequently cites. The same view is expressed in C. Tung, *Han-T'ang-shih "chi'i-ch'u" yen-chiu* (Research on the "seven grounds for divorce" in Han and T'ang times), in 1 WEN-SHIH HUI-K'AN (Journal of literature and history) No. 1, at 285–95 (March 1, 1935).

[154] HHS ch. 29, 5a. Cited in T. CH'Ü, *supra* note 29, at 120–21; YANG 46.

thirsty; "Chiang blamed [his wife] and expelled her."[155] There are several issues in these cases. First, it is not very realistic to cite the Pao Yung case as evidence of "disobedience to the wife's parents-in-law." By some stretch of the imagination the second case might fall into that category, at least as the category was interpreted to mean failure to serve the in-laws. But note that both husbands acted (so far as the evidence indicates) quickly and directly; neither of them justified the expulsion of his wife by reference to the supposedly customary grounds for divorce. They simply sent their wives off—that was their prerogative. Confirmation of the view comes from Po Chü-i the famous T'ang poet and official, who noted that simple displeasure on the part of the parents-in-law was adequate grounds for divorce; then he cited as precedents these two cases. With precedents such as these, he said, it was not necessary for the wife to be guilty of a major fault or transgression in order to justify a divorce.[156] (Technically, of course, he was not accurate in citing these cases since they indicate the son's, that is, the husband's, displeasure, not that of the parents-in-law.) The second issue in these cases is that the historian offered them as models of filial behavior. Pao Yung's biography is a eulogy to the man for his loyalty and filial piety. His stepmother was also treated in a biography among the model women.[157] The account of her life shows her also as the epitome of loyalty and as an ideal wife who served her own mother-in-law with great deference. Chiang Shih's wife was also accorded a place of honor among the women in the collective biography devoted to upholding the feminine ideal; even after being expelled from the household of Chiang Shih she lived with a neighbor and secretly helped to support the Chiang family. They finally found out about her unstinting efforts and took her back. Much of her biography is devoted to her husband, likewise an ideal young man and a superb, but low level, official. The point that the historian was trying to make was that these men divorced their wives because, as sons, they were such peerless models of Confucian conduct; it was this background that justified the divorces, not the failure of the wives to serve their in-laws. Neither of the sons referred to the "disobedience" of his wife, and, of course, neither of them saw his divorce within the framework of the "seven conditions for divorce."

"Barrenness" as an explicit failing that warranted the divorce of a wife is mentioned only once in the Han materials, and, in fact, there are not many references to divorce on this basis in Chinese history in general. This is probably, as Professor Ch'ü T'ung-tsu has suggested, due to the fact that it was believed that concubinage could provide the sons in case the wife could not.[158] This interpretation is implicit in the one Han case that we have:

---

[155] HHS ch. 84, 2a–b. Cited in T. CH'Ü, *supra* note 29, at 121; YANG 46–47.

[156] C. Tung, *supra* note 153, at 287.

[157] HHS ch. 84, 1a–b.

[158] T. CH'Ü, *supra* note 29, at 119.

"When [Ying] Shun was young he was a good friend of Hsü Ching. [Hsü] Ching's family was poor and his parents old. He had no sons. On behalf of [Hsü] Ching, [Ying Shun] sent off [Hsü's] wife and [arranged for him to be] married again."[159] The fact that Hsü's family was poor perhaps precluded his taking a concubine; hence, the necessity of divorce.

The situation with regard to "adultery" is unusual. We do not have any specific cases of it as grounds for divorce in the Han. However, we do have, as we have seen in many contexts already, general complaints about licentiousness and that often includes adultery. To add one more example at this point (see also the last section of this paper), Pan Ku in his treatise on law wrote: "Concerning . . . men and women committing adultery and incest, for all these the old punishments should be revived, constituting (all together) three thousand paragraphs."[160] These and other similar remarks suggest that morals were very "loose" in the Han; perhaps the ease with which one of a married couple could divorce the other helps to account for the lack of such cases in the Han. And, of course, Pan Ku's plea would not have been made if such offenses were fully covered in the laws.

"Jealousy," the fourth of the seven grounds for divorce, is mentioned several times in Han sources. Although we have none of the details, we are told by Pan Ku that the mother of Empress Yüan was divorced, by the first of her three husbands, for jealousy.[161] Feng Yen, whose statement about the character of matrimony was quoted at the beginning of this section, was first married to a woman who was "cruel and vindictive and who did not permit him to keep concubines."[162] One might ask why Fan Yeh, the historian, does not explicitly state jealousy as the reason for the divorce. The reason probably is that, as suggested by Feng's general comment, Feng did not base his divorce (actually: his first divorce) exclusively on jealousy; this point will be elaborated in a later context. Suffice it to say that a jealous wife could be expelled for little or no reason whatsoever. Jealousy was a legitimate cause in a period in which specific causes did not have to be given; however, the available evidence does not indicate that jealousy was thought of as one of only seven reasons for divorce. That is, although sufficient cause for divorce, jealousy was not considered in a context which recognized only seven such causes.

"Incurable disease" does not occur in a Han case.[163] Reference to it as a cause for divorce has been found in one of the many prognostication texts of

---

[159] YANG 46; T. CH'Ü, *supra* note 29, at 119; both cite the TUNG-KUAN HAN-CHI.

[160] 1 A. HULSEWÉ, *supra* note 65, at 349.

[161] HS ch. 98, at 2a.

[162] HHS ch. 28B, 12a–b.

[163] YANG 4, 51, considers the marriage of the Older Princess of Yang-hsin to Wei Ching to be an example of this, and if one takes uncritically the text of HS ch. 55, 17a, one comes to this conclusion. However, Wang Hsien-ch'ien and other commentators have convincingly put together sufficient data to show that the Princess's first husband,

the Later Han and post-Han period. The passage in question is prognosticatory lore based upon beliefs about horses: "Eating a white horse with a dark head will kill people. . . . Using the money gained from selling a horse to gain a wife will cause there to be many incurable diseases and the husband and wife will separate."[164] The text does not say that it is the wife who will have these diseases; as with many "good" predictions it is intentionally ambiguous. That leaves the possibility that either marriage partner could justify a divorce on the ground of incurable disease.[165] Actually, either could leave the other without any specific charge being made.

"Loquacity" was grounds for divorce in the Confucian tradition "because it caused discord among the relatives."[166] Under this rubric we have an example that apparently is based upon the classical literature: Li Ch'ung (flourished A.D. 106) was one of six sons living together in poverty with their mother. His wife said that they could not live in peace in such surroundings for very long, and, since she had some property of her own, she suggested that they leave his family. Li Ch'ung feigned acceptance and proposed a dinner at which their important step would be announced to friends and relatives. When all were drinking and eating, Li addressed his mother: "This wife is extremely lacking in proper conduct; she has urged me, Ch'ung, to separate from my mother and brothers. Her offense makes suitable driving her out!" He then abusively drove her out of the house, and the guests, deeply shocked at the proceedings, all departed.[167] Vague as it is, the context suggests strongly that Li Ch'ung was basing his remarks on the classical texts. The fact that Li Ch'ung later received an imperial summons to become an Erudite, the highest scholarly position in Han times, is additional, albeit weak and circumstantial, evidence that Li may have justified his action by recourse to the Confucian canon. It might also be added that Li did not conform to the standards of the Confucian gentleman in the manner in which he sent her off. As Shen Ch'in-han points out in the commentary to this passage, the *Po-hu t'ung-i* argues for a gentlemanly way of divorcing a woman so that she would not find it difficult to remarry. And there was even an appropriate ceremony

---

although so ill with an "incurable disease" that he left the capital for his marquisate, had died by the time Wei Ch'ing married the Princess. Yang, in his zeal to find evidence to fit this category, has disregarded most of the commentaries.

[164] C. Tung, *supra* note 153, at 290. The text is the LUNG-YÜ HO-T'U. There is no assurance that this is a Han period text and Tung's statement that these grounds for divorce come from records concerning merchants (apparently on the basis of the reference to a horse being sold) is purely gratuitous.

[165] It is interesting to note that if we do not accept the material summarized in note 163 *supra*, the Princess remarried because *he* had the illness. Perhaps these two weak pieces of evidence do suggest that either spouse could leave the other because of illness.

[166] T. CH'Ü, *supra* note 29, at 122.

[167] HHS ch. 81, 14b.

which was supposed to be followed in sending the former wife back to her family. Quite obviously, Li Ch'ung did not feel compelled to abide by such lessons.[168]

The second example of divorce allegedly on the grounds of loquacity comes from about the beginning of Former Han when Ch'en P'ing's brother's wife said that it was better to have no brother-in-law at all than to have one such as he. Ch'en P'ing's brother then chased her out.[169] Certainly her remarks would have created discord in the family (although it sounds as if it were already in evidence), and that could have been sufficient cause for divorce on the grounds of loquacity; however, the context does not lead the reader to believe that such a specific charge was in the mind of Ch'en's brother when the woman was sent off. The case of Li Ch'ung, however, does indicate that this charge probably was used, at least by an independent-minded Confucianist of the middle of Later Han.

The seventh ground for divorce was "theft." In view of the fact that theft of major proportions could reflect unfavorably on both husband and wife under most traditions, it is not surprising (or even necessarily Confucian) to find theft included in the list of offenses warranting separation of husband and wife. However, our evidence does not concern major cases of theft, but petty incidents. For example, K'uai T'ung told the story of a village wife who lost some meat at night; her mother-in-law became angry and chased her out.[170] This is certainly divorce, imposed by the mother-in-law, for theft, for the mother-in-law thought that she was losing meat from her own *wok*. But the case suggests the ease with which wives could be sent off, not that this village woman was adhering to Confucian doctrine. The second case is, however, within the Confucian mold. Wang Chi, who was punctilious in matters of form, found out that his wife had picked jujubes from the branch of the neighbor's tree which overhung her own yard and, because of that theft, he divorced her. The neighbors interceded and Wang Chi took her back. The historian concluded from the incident: "His stern ideals were of this kind."[171] Wang apparently believed that the pettiest theft warranted divorce, and we may assume that he thought he was living up to the letter of Confucianism by divorcing his wife.

Thus of the "seven conditions" for divorce, three cannot be exemplified by Han dynasty cases (disobedience to parents-in-law, adultery, and incurable disease). Of the remaining four categories we have Confucian examples, that

---

[168] *Id. See also* 2 TJAN 473; 1 TJAN 260–61. Li Ch'ung's behavior vis-à-vis his wife is fully consistent with other vignettes of his life, which is treated among the biographies of men famous for their independent action (*tu-hsing* biographies).

[169] HS ch. 40, 12a.

[170] HS ch. 45, 5b, cited in C. Tung, *supra* note 153, at 290.

[171] HS ch. 72, 7b.

is, divorces that were apparently justified by reference to Confucian morality, regarding only loquacity and theft (and perhaps the example of barrenness, but that is very uncertain). In sum, much of the evidence cited in order to establish the acceptance of the "seven conditions" in Han times does not, in fact, prove that point. At best, the relevant evidence leads one to conclude that while unusual individuals such as Wang Chi and Li Ch'ung would view the alleged offenses of their wives from the standpoint of Confucianism, most others did not. Furthermore, many of the divorces of the Han dynasty were in no way associated with any of the "seven conditions." That includes divorces initiated by men as well as by women; such divorces will now be dealt with in that order.

Husbands could divorce their wives on many grounds that were totally unrelated to the "seven conditions." Politics, social status, and economic concerns were all crucial factors not found among the "traditional" conditions; several examples of each of these are still to be found in the data from the Han. But before introducing them, I would like to return to Feng Yen who has been cited several times already. His case is noteworthy because it shows that whereas jealousy, as mentioned earlier, was a significant contributing factor in his divorce, he apparently felt that by itself his wife's jealousy did not warrant a divorce. Hence, it was necessary for him to detail conditions of their home life. Since his letter to his brother-in-law announcing his divorce affords us an opportunity to see into a troubled Han dynasty home and because it shows quite clearly that, in Feng's mind, jealousy alone was not sufficient grounds for a divorce, the letter is worth quoting extensively:

> Human nature [bestowed by] Heaven and Earth includes contentment and anger; the conjugal relation includes the principles of separation and union. According to the rites of the former sages, the scholar-official has a wife; although he respects her but little, he still wishes to surpass the limits [of normal endurance?]. As one becomes decrepit with age and the sunset of life comes in, he hates the [thought of her] entering the Yellow Springs. However, encountering jealousy, the Way of the family decays.
>
> As the mother of our five offspring she was still worthy of being in the family. [But] for five years, increasingly by the day and abundantly by the year, she has taken white to be black and wrong to be right. She fabricates things from one extreme to another and falsely gives rise to things from head to tail. When I was without an offense and free of crime, she vilified me in great clamor. Disorder has not been sent down by Heaven; it has been produced by my wife.
>
> The mind of the blue-fly does not pay attention to the state being destroyed; the feelings of the jealous do not shirk from destroying the individual. The cock-crow of the hen is what a family is apprehensive of. In ancient times it was a great calamity; in present times it has begun with me. In drinking and eating she goes beyond the [proper] proportions and has become an [Emperor] Chieh or Chou. Play of the bedroom is broadcast overseas. With staring eyes and gesturing hands she considers "there is" to be "there is not." Bitterness reaches up to azure heaven; poison flows in the five viscera. . . . On entering the door she goes to bed; our offspring are not taken care of. [Regarding] embroidery and weaving, our children have no [instruction in] women's tasks.

Our family is impoverished and without slaves; it is that of a poor man and wife. Therefore, when others see it, none are not sorrowful. Never have there been sympathetic favors. We have only one slave whom you, [Jen] Wu-ta, have seen. On her head there are no hairpins or ointments; her face is without rouge or powder. Her body is not hidden from view;[172] her hands and feet are covered with dirt. [My wife] shows no leniency regarding [the slave's] destitution; she does not take into consideration her feelings. She leaps up to the rafters, shouting loudly, and crying out as if entering Hades. [Even] the woman who sells candy cannot stand her attitude.

I have reckoned for a long time that I ought to divorce my wife. I kept in mind that the children were small and that the family had no other servants. I lamented the fact that Chiang and Pao (two of his children) would become slaves; I pitied them and was distressed. One matter after another soured my feelings. . . .

She was harsh and cruel to this slave who escaped death by a hair's breadth. For half a year, bloody pus flowed angrily. After the slave was injured, Chiang, throughout [the slave's incapacitation] pounded the grain and prepared the food; Pao also behaved rudely and got into trouble. They became very disheartened. Silk gauze and grain was scattered about [the house]; the winter clothing was not patched. She (my wife) sat upright fomenting disorder, and not one thread was strung.

Thus she lacks the wifely Way and she also lacks motherly deportment. In indignation I have seen her violations; in anger I have seen her cruelties. She relies upon severe commands as if she dwelled in Heaven. . . .

If I do not divorce this wife then the family will not be in repose. If I do not divorce this wife then the family will not be at peace. If I do not divorce this wife then good fortune will not be produced. If I do not divorce this wife then matters [of the household] will not be complete. I personally regret that I did not earlier, during the bloom of life, decide this myself. I have come [now] to the day when [my hair] hangs down white, when my family is impoverished, and when my person is poor. [He then says that he will cut himself off from family and friends and eke out a living as a hermit.][173]

Actually, Feng married again, but the second wife did not like his son Pao, who was twelve at the time of the first divorce, and tried to kill him. Feng said he had no alternative but to divorce his second wife too.[174] The point of his letter was not just that jealousy justified divorce, but that a nagging, domineering, jealous, cruel, and vindictive wife could not be tolerated, in spite of the fact that Feng had been married to her for a long time.

At times political wisdom seemed to demand that a man divorce his wife. Shortly after Emperor Hsüan came to the throne in 73 B.C., he began a purge of the once powerful Ho family which was plotting against the throne. Chin Shang, the son of Chin Mi-ti, had married the daughter of Ho Kuang when Chin and Ho were the highest ministers of state. Now that the Ho family (and those associated with it) were in danger, Chin Shang submitted a memorial in which he announced that he was divorcing his wife.[175] In another case,

---

[172] I am uncertain of the meaning here. Perhaps it means that she is not hidden in the husband's own quarters (or rooms of her own) or it should be interpreted to mean "not beguiling."

[173] HHS ch. 28B, 12b–13a is Hui Tung's commentary.

[174] HHS ch. 28B, 13a–b.

[175] HS ch. 68, 20b.

Huang Yün, a talented but unscrupulous young man, was already married
when he heard that the Minister of the Masses, Yüan Wei (in that office
during A.D. 172–176), had said that Huang would make an ideal husband for
his niece. When Huang told his wife that he was divorcing her, she requested
a banquet at which she could bid goodbye to her friends and relatives. When
the guests, over three hundred in number, were feasting and drinking, she
stood up, enumerated fifteen disgraceful acts that Huang had secretly committed, and then left. Huang thus lost his first wife and, because of his disgrace,
was not able to complete the union with Yüan Wei's niece.[176]

A major change in socioeconomic status was often accompanied by a change
of wife. In the early years of Later Han, Emperor Kuang-wu asked his
recently widowed sister, the Princess of Hu-yang, whom she would like to
marry among the officials at court. When she chose Sung Hung, the Emperor
called Sung before him and, with the Princess hidden behind a screen, quoted
a proverb and asked a question: " 'Becoming noble one changes one's friends;
becoming rich one changes one's wife.' Is that human nature?" Sung Hung
answered in kind: "Your servant has heard 'Friends of [the days of] poverty
cannot be forgotten; wives of [the days of] cheap food cannot be sent out of
the hall.' " The Emperor turned and said over his shoulder that the deal
would not go through.[177] The idea expressed in the proverb quoted by the
Emperor is behind the following: When, at the end of Han, Wang Yen was
enfeoffed because of his merit, his wife began to cry because now that Wang
"was rich and honored he would remarry."[178]

Concern with the family property was another cause for separation not
covered in the "seven conditions." Two cases from the Later Han period
show how this could happen (some of the data given earlier might be included
here; for example, Li Ch'ung's wife and Ch'en P'ing's sister-in-law were both
initially concerned with the family property, and it was that which led to their
divorces). Ju Tun and his wife lived together with his brothers; all of them
commonly owned the properties of his parents, which the wife of Ju Tun's
elder brother wanted to take over completely. At the urging of his wife, Ju

---

[176] HHS ch. 68, 5a.

[177] HHS ch. 26, 9a. *See also* Emperor Kuang-wu's remarks on HHS ch. 11, 14b, in
which he expresses surprise and pleasure that his high officers were not replacing their
wives with new ones. *Cf.* 1 TJAN 253–54, where in an apparent attempt to stop this
practice, the PO-HU T'UNG-I says that a great officer who has received a fief because
of merit may increase the number of his concubines, but he was not allowed "to enter
into a new marriage alliance with a large state, in order that he may not forget his
original principal wife."

[178] The *Tien-lun* (Discourse on institutes) of Emperor Wen of Wei in CH'ÜAN
SHANG-KU SAN-TAI CH'IN-HAN SAN-KUO LIU-CH'AO WEN. CH'ÜAN SAN-KUO WEN
(Complete [collection of] literature from antiquity, the Three Dynasties, the Ch'in
and Han Dynasties, the Three Kingdoms, and the Six Dynasties. Complete [collection
of] literature from the Three Kingdoms) ch. 8, 5a (Shih-chieh shu-chü ed.).

Tun surrendered his share of the fields, houses, and slaves, giving them all to his older brother while he and his wife went off on their own. When plowing, Ju Tun found a gold vessel which, again following his wife's suggestion, he gave to his older brother. When the older brother's wife heard of the arrival of Ju Tun and his wife, she thought they had come to borrow something and was very unhappy. However, when she found that they had come to present the valuable vessel, she "jumped about with joy." The older brother awoke to reality, immediately sent off his wife, and returned his brother's share of the family property.[179] In a similarly motivated case Cheng Hung was the bailiff of Ling-wen district. Among the people of the district there was a younger brother who had borrowed money from his older brother. The wife of the older brother demanded that the money be returned, and, when the younger brother did not do so, the wife went to Cheng Hung in order to bring charges against her brother-in-law. Rather than treat the affair as a criminal case, Cheng sold his shirt in order to pay back the older brother on behalf of the younger brother. When the older brother heard of this he was mortified. He bound himself and went to jail, thus saying in effect that he had criminally misbehaved. He also sent his wife away.[180] These cases lead us to conclude that a wife could be divorced simply because she was greedy.

Wives also left their husbands for a variety of reasons. Chung-ch'ang T'ung, as noted earlier, talks of wives who cry for one husband in the morning but who have married another man by the evening.[181] Admittedly, this is not without exaggeration, but nevertheless wives could desert their husbands with ease. We have already noted that Chang Erh married a woman who had left her husband and then stayed with a guest of her wealthy father.[182] Ch'en P'ing's great-grandson, Ch'en Ho, lost the fief that had originally been awarded to Ch'en P'ing for merit, because "he was convicted of making off with another man's wife. . . ."[183] And Chu Mai-ch'en, who was from a poor family, had a menial job as a firewood gatherer, but he was determined to improve his status and intoned his books as he carried wood along the road. His wife was ashamed of their economic status and sought to leave him. He tried to assure her that by the time he was fifty years old he would be a man of wealth with an honorable position. He went on to say that, since he was already over forty and she had suffered with him for so long, she should remain with him so that she could share the privileges that would come with his change in position. Her wrathful answer was: " 'People such as you die of starvation in a ditch; how can you ever have wealth and honors!' " And the text continues:

[179] HYKC ch. 10B, 342.

[180] YANG 48, citing K'UAI-CHI TIEN-LU fragments from the T'AI-P'ING YÜ-LAN.

[181] T. Chung-ch'ang, *supra* note 55, at ch. 2, 2a.

[182] HS ch. 32, 1a.

[183] 1 B. WATSON, *supra* note 57, at 167.

"He could not detain her and allowed her to go."[184] The age of Chu Mai-ch'en suggests that he may have been married to this woman for quite some time and that she had finally become fed up with his lack of progress; there was nothing to prevent her from leaving him in order to marry someone else (see below).

While marriages were frequently affairs between two individuals, they were often arranged by heads of families; the same can be said for divorces. In addition to the foregoing data showing divorces by either the husband or the wife, there are also data demonstrating that divorces were often initiated by parents, particularly the parents of the wife. As we might expect, such separations were often connected with political fortunes or at least with the exercise, or abusive exercise, of political power. Ma Yüan was one of the more important generals in the battles to restore the Han House, but after his death his family began to suffer an eclipse of power and prestige. To prevent a further erosion of their position, members of the Ma family arranged to have the youngest daughter of Ma Yüan enter the palace. In order to do this they had to break the marriage bonds between the girl and a son of the also predominant Tou family.[185] The Tou family in the first century A.D. committed many crimes against the individuals at all levels of society. One of their unsavory acts was the falsification of a decree from the Empress Dowager ordering Liu Hsü to divorce his wife so that she could marry Tou Mu.[186] For different reasons, Shih Tan, one of the highest ministers in the latter part of Former Han, had his daughter divorce Wang Chün because he did not like the political machinations of the Wang family.[187] We have already seen that Emperor Kuang-wu suggested to Sung Hung that Sung divorce his wife so that he could marry a member of the imperial family.[188] Had Sung been

---

[184] HS ch. 64A, 11a–b.

[185] HHS ch. 10A, 7b–8a. As Ch'ü T'ung-tsu demonstrates in his forthcoming book on Han social structure, this marriage was of crucial importance to the Ma family.

[186] HHS ch. 23, 9b.

[187] HS ch. 82, 2b–3a.

[188] We have another case much like this one: Tou Yüan was an Account Bearer, which means that he was sent by his Grand Administrator to carry the annual report to the capital, and there he and many other Account Bearers were received by the Emperor (on this office and the significance of audiences for these officials, see my forthcoming Local Government in the Han, vol. II of the Han Dynasty History Project series). Tou Yüan was so outstanding in this mass audience that the Emperor ordered him to marry a princess. When the audience was over, Tou's comrades ridiculed him, for he was already married. Before Tou had time to tell his wife of their imminent divorce, a decree arrived ordering him to prepare for the wedding. See YANG 49–50, quoting SAN-FU CHÜEH-LU fragment preserved in T'AI-P'ING YÜ-LAN ch. 389, 9b–10a.

I have not been able to identify Tou Yüan, and I do not know which emperor gave these orders; however, even if I could identify the man I have grave reservations about the validity of the account (although the principle involved is well substantiated by the

willing to leave the woman he married before his rise to high position, he could have married a princess.

Private individuals also arranged for the divorces of their children. Tsang Erh had two daughters while she was the wife of Wang Chung. One of them later married Chin Wang-sun and gave birth to a girl. When Tsang Erh consulted an oracle, she found that both of her daughters would be highly honored. Hence, overriding the strong opposition of the Chin family, she took back her daughter and arranged to have both of her girls enter the Heir Apparent's harem. The one who had been the wife of Chin was favored by the Heir Apparent and gave birth to the future Emperor Wu.[189] Parental

---

Sung Hung case). The problem with the account is that Han princesses had to marry marquises. This ruling was very objectionable to Han thinkers because this kind of marriage subjected the male to the female, for the son of this kind of union inherited his mother's fief. *See* 1 A. HULSEWÉ, *supra* note 65, at 449 n.67. A similar rule was also applied to men who married the daughters of kings; this led Fan Shu in the mid-first century to object to the marriage of the son of Shu's younger brother to a daughter, that is, a royal princess, of the King of Ch'u, for the son would then be compelled to leave his home and live in Ch'u. *See* HHS ch. 32, 4b.

There are some exceptions to this rule regarding the marriage of a princess: HHS ch. 10B, 14b–17a, lists imperial princesses; the marriages of thirteen are noted, and two of them married men who are not listed with noble titles. One, Han Kuang, married a princess in A.D. 39; I cannot identify him as a marquis. But it is possible that the fact that he was involved in a rebellious plot with King Yen of Huai-yang (see HHS 42, 16b), which led to his execution, has something to do with the case. That is, Han Kuang may have been a marquis for a very brief period, but his marquisate was not recorded because of his execution. There is a second possibility in his case: his office was *fu-ma tu-wei,* Chief Commandant of the Escorting Cavalry. This office was in command of the troops holding a secondary position among the emperor's personal troops, and this commandant was thus quite close to the emperor. Several members of the Ch'ih family held this position, and the Ch'ih family intermarried with the imperial family (*see* HHS ch. 19, 9a; *see also* 10a for Ch'ih Kuo, and 11a for Ch'ih Ping, both of whom held this position). In the immediate post-Han period this position was customarily held by the emperor's son-in-law and the title, originally that of a military office, came to mean imperial son-in-law. 12 T. MOROHASHI, DAIKANWA JITEN (Great Chinese and Japanese dictionary) (1955–59). Perhaps what we see in the Han Kuang case is the beginning of this change in meaning.

The second exception is Feng Shun. Since he was a middle son of seven he could not inherit his father's Marquisate Within the Passes *(kuan-nei hou)*. He did occupy one of the nine highest ministerial positions (Grand Harald, *ta-hung-lu*). Except for that position, I do not see how his marriage could have been justified.

These two exceptions were men of high position from well established families; perhaps that helps to account for their marriages to princesses. But the case of Tou Yüan does not fit any recognizable pattern; hence, my reservations about the evidence.

On the other hand, the princess who was first married to Ch'en Wu and who, after his death, made her former "adopted" child, Tung Yen, her paramour, had to appeal to Emperor Wu to have Tung showered with goods, favors, offices, and a marquisate so that she could marry him. HS ch. 65, 10a–13a.

[189] HS ch. 97, 8b–9a; 1 B. WATSON, *supra* note 57, at 386–87.

dissatisfaction with the son-in-law could also result in a divorce. Hsü Sheng was an irresponsible young man who spent much of his time gambling. His wife, Lü Jung, continuously sought to correct his behavior and transform him into a serious student. Lü Jung's father became increasingly impatient with Hsü Sheng and finally told his daughter that he wanted her to leave Hsü Sheng so that he could marry her to someone else. Lü Jung was, however, willing to accept "the fate she had met" and stayed with her husband.[190] Although the divorce did not take place, the principle is clear: a parent could arrange for the divorce of his child in order to arrange a more favorable match for her.

The concluding part of this section should deal with the "three prohibitions" under which a wife could not be divorced; however, there is no evidence that the term was applied in Han times, and certainly the data presented so far indicate that the institution of the "three prohibitions" could not have been shown much, if any, honor during that period.[191] The case that seems most relevant to this point is Feng Yen's. When he divorced his first wife, it is said that the people of the time "were disappointed" in him, probably because he and his wife were both old when he divorced her. However, there is no evidence to suggest that the "three prohibitions" were included in Han laws or that they were ever invoked to prevent a man from divorcing his wife.

REMARRIAGE

The custom of the Han period was for men and women who had divorced their spouses, or whose spouses had died, to remarry. There have already been many incidental references to this aspect of marriage customs in this paper; it remains now to draw some of them together. Divorced men and widowers customarily remarried. Pao Yung served his stepmother with great diligence; this shows that his father Pao Hsüan had remarried.[192] Fan Sheng, a well-known New Text Confucianist at the beginning of the Later Han period, expelled his wife from his house and was denounced by her. The denunciation led to his incarceration, but he was freed when one of his students interceded directly with the Emperor. In the course of his appeal, the student revealed that Fan had been married three times.[193] Conversely, Wang Chün, the son of Wang Chi, had reached the high office of Privy Treasurer when his wife died. His contemporaries were quite surprised that he did not take another wife.[194]

---

[190] HHS ch. 84, 10a.

[191] Reference to the "three prohibitions" was, of course, in the Han classics; see T. CH'Ü, supra note 29, at 118.

[192] HHS ch. 84, 1b.

[193] HHS ch. 36, 9a; HHS ch. 79A, 5b.

[194] HS ch. 72, 8b.

Women also remarried when they lost their matrimonial partners; however, the situation was not quite the same as with the men, for there was an ascending countercurrent of objection to women remarrying. We will deal with that after considering some of the evidence for what seems to have been the usual situation. In view of the later custom regarding women who had children, it is perhaps worthwhile to make a distinction between the remarriage of women who did not have children and of those who did. Wang Fu, in one of his complaints about life at the end of Later Han, wrote that "Nowadays she marries 'B' and without shame again [remarries], entering the 'A' family."[195] He apparently made no distinction, and much of the evidence on remarriage does not say whether the woman had any children at the time of her remarriage; in such cases I have assumed that she did not have children by her first husband. The mother of Empress Yüan married into three families. She was divorced by her first husband because of her jealousy, then she married Kou Pin, and finally she became the wife or concubine of Wang Chin.[196] The wife of Chu Mai-ch'en, who gave up hope of his success when at age forty he still sold wood for a living, left him and remarried.[197] The wife of the deposed Emperor Shao returned to her home after the death of the Emperor, and her father tried to arrange for her to marry someone else.[198] And certainly the record for remarriage in the Han must go to the wife of Ch'en P'ing, who had lost five husbands before she married him.[199] And finally, Tung Chung-shu felt that the childless widow could remarry (see Tung's statement quoted on page 68).

Even women with children remarried, though sometimes very reluctantly. Wang Fu again refers to a practice of his time: "Again, chaste widows, sometimes with sons and daughters already and with abundant wealth wish to maintain the ritual [admonitions] of one marriage and to carry to completion the principle of being buried together [with their husbands]." But, he goes on to say, such widows often have to cope with relatives who covet their property or their children.[200] The data substantiate Wang's general remark. Tsang Erh, the woman who forced one of her daughters to divorce Mr. Chin, had remarried after the death of her first husband even though she had children by that time.[201] Empress Teng of Emperor Huan was the daughter

---

[195] F. WANG, *supra* note 56, at ch. 5, 136.

[196] HS ch. 98, 2a

[197] HS ch. 64A, 13a. Later when Chu became a successful official he saw his former wife and her second husband preparing the streets for his arrival. Apparently she did not markedly improve her status with her second marriage; otherwise she would not have been serving corvée duty.

[198] HHS ch. 10B, 11a.

[199] HS ch. 40, 12a–b. Many other examples could be cited.

[200] F. WANG, *supra* note 56, at ch. 5, 138.

[201] HS ch. 97A, 8b–9a.

of a man named Teng Hsiang. When Teng died, his wife married Liang Chi, and for a while the daughter took the surname of Liang. Then, since that was opposed, she reverted to the surname of her father.[202] Again, a concubine of Emperor Yüan was born while her mother was married to a man named Fu; after Fu's death, her mother married a man named Cheng.[203] These two cases illustrate another practice of the time: children born of a man retained his surname even when their mother remarried. That remarriage of a woman with a child was not found too objectionable is perhaps best demonstrated in the case of Hsün Ts'ai. She was the daughter of one of the most outstanding scholars of Later Han, Hsün Shuang. She married at age seventeen; two years later she gave birth to a girl, and in the same year her husband died. Hsün Shuang betrothed her to a man whose wife had recently died and then had to trick his daughter into coming home in order to complete plans for her wedding.[204] Since a man of Hsün's stature in the scholarly and official world did not find it objectionable to arrange for the remarriage of his widowed daughter, we may assume that that was the general feeling of the time.

But if remarriage, even with children, was the customary practice in Han times, it must also be acknowledged that there were many who opposed the practice. The statement by Wang Fu quoted above shows that women who preferred to remain widows had a renowned supporter. But many cases show that women who had lost their husbands were subjected to intolerable pressures to remarry. Some could avoid remarriage with a simple refusal. Thus when Wang Mang, in spite of his lavish attention to ritual matters, tried to arrange a second marriage for his daughter, the widow of Emperor P'ing, she vigorously refused and Wang Mang dropped the matter.[205] Other widows had to take more drastic action; for some reason not known to me, the *Hua-yang kuo-chih* abounds with biographical sketches of exemplary widows who cut off a finger, slashed or cut off an ear, shaved their heads, or cut off their noses in order to show their determination not to remarry.[206] Still other women took the ultimate step. The best known example is the daughter of Hsün Shuang; although she went through the preliminary stages of her second

[202] HHS ch. 10B, 6b.

[203] HS ch. 97B, 16a–b.

[204] HHS ch. 84, 12a–b. For other examples of remarriage, see C. Tung, *Ts'ung Han tao Sung kua-fu tsai-chia hsi-su k'ao* (Research on the custom of remarriage of widows from the Han to the Sung dynasties), in 3 WEN-SHIH HSÜEH YEN-CHIU-SO YÜEH-K'AN (Monthly bulletin of the Research Institute for the Study of Literature and History) No. 1, at 193–213 (1934), which draws upon C. Wu, *Liang Han kua-fu tsai-chia chih-su* (The custom of remarriage of widows in the two Han dynasties), 37 CH'ING-HUA CHOU-K'AN (Ch'ing-hua weekly) Nos. 9–10, which I have not seen. See also the very full compilation of relevant materials in YANG 53–67.

[205] HS ch. 97B, 24a.

[206] HYKC ch. 10B, 340, 341, 355; ch. 10A, 312.

marriage, at first reluctantly and then with feigned pleasure, it was never consumated, for she hanged herself on her wedding day.[207] And again, the *Hua-yang kuo-chih* provides copious examples: widows starved themselves to death and stabbed themselves; other tried leaping into rivers or cutting their throats.[208] In spite of all this evidence (and of course that from the *Hua-yang kuo-chih* is limited to southwestern China), the prevailing custom was for the widow to remarry. This is further established by a statement from the dictator Tung Cho, who as Prime Minister from A.D. 189 to 192, tried to force the widow of Huang-fu Kuei to marry him. When she tried to argue her case against remarriage, he accused her of spreading "stern teachings . . . which will cause the customs of the world to be negated." And when she saw that her arguments were not helping her and denounced him, he killed her.[209]

As with many other aspects of life in the Han, the evidence on the question of remarriage presents us with a mixed picture. Undoubtedly the general practice was for divorcees and widows, with children or without, to remarry. But there was another practice, which seems to have been a growing tendency, and that was for the widow not to remarry. Toward the end of the dynasty there were respected scholars who gave their support to those women who preferred to remain loyal to the memory of their husbands, but certainly by the end of Han that view was far from the common one.

The Law, the Officials and Proposals for Change

When we shift our attention from Han marriage customs, and the rituals which almost negligibly influenced them, to the laws that governed marriage and interpersonal relations, we encounter a situation that is marked mostly by a lack of clarity and sharpness. The paucity of laws or legal guidelines is reflected in the conduct of the officials who were called upon to settle disputes between husband and wife or their respective families. One thing is clear, however; by the end of Later Han there were increasing demands for change, for fuller legislation, and for new social customs.

References to supposed laws dealing with marriage are not numerous, nor is it clear that there were in fact such laws in the Han.[210] We might start with a pre-Han law just to give some of the Ch'in background to the problem. In 211 B.C. a stele was erected in K'uai-chi by Ch'in Shih-huang-ti that in strong terms set forth prohibitions against a widow remarrying if she already had sons; furthermore, it stated that a husband who "becomes a wandering boar"

---

[207] HHS ch. 84, 12a–b.

[208] HYKC ch. 10A, 312, 313; ch. 10B, 341.

[209] HHS ch. 84, 11b–12a.

[210] It is most regrettable that Professor Hulsewé's second volume has not come out yet. He will bring to bear on this problem a great deal of background and a familiarity with the materials which this author lacks.

could be killed with impunity. It went on to say that men as well as women must adhere to high standards of righteousness and that a woman definitely could not desert her husband and remarry.[211] My review of the evidence for the Han indicates that there was no comparable legislation for that period. With the downfall of the Ch'in, this and its other laws were swept away; some of them were re-enacted, but either this one was not in the code or, if it was, it was disregarded.

Tung Chung-shu, the most famous Confucianist of the Han period, compiled a work known as *Decisions in Lawsuits According to the Principles of the Spring and Autumn Annals*,[212] from which one of the remaining fragments is relevant to our problem:

"A"'s husband "B" was going on a boat and when at sea they encountered a storm and the boat was sunk; he was drowned, [his body was lost,] and they were not able to bury him. Four months later, "A"'s mother "C" [arranged] to marry her [again]. What punishment ought to be meted out to "A"?
Some [might] say: "A"'s husband has died but not been buried [and] the law does not permit [re-]marriage, for it would be illicit to become the wife of another [under such circumstances]. She should be executed in the market place.
[Tung Chung-shu's] opinion: Your servant stupidly considers that the principle of the *Spring and Autumn Annals* is stated when it [says that] the wife was returned to Ch'i which means that when the husband dies without a son there is the Way (that is, the principle) of remarriage. The wife was not responsible for any conduct marked by perversity nor was she guilty of wilful licentiousness. She should be allowed to go on [to remarry].[213]

This would have us believe that a woman could not remarry until after her husband had been properly buried and that she could not remarry at all if she had had a child by her first husband. If there actually was such a law in Han times (and Tung's work may well be more normative than descriptive), then the last part of it was not enforced and there is no evidence either way concerning the first part of it.

There is a body of ancillary evidence which is useful at this point even though it is not directly relevant to our problem. It deals with incest and comparable offenses within the family and shows that even with regard to such behavior there were apparently no specific prohibitions, but that, nevertheless, decisions were reached by the court when such matters came to its attention.

Liu Ting-kuo, King of Yen, had illicit intercourse with his father's concubine who bore him a son; he also seized his younger brother's wife, made

---

[211] K. TAKIKAWA, SHIKI KAICHŪ KŌSHŌ 6, 63–64 (reprint of 1934 ed.); 2 E. CHAVANNES, MÉMOIRES HISTORIQUES 186–89 (1895–1905).

[212] 1 A. HULSEWÉ, supra note 65, at 51–52.

[213] T'AI-P'ING YÜ-LAN, supra note 114, at ch. 640, 8a, quoting Tung's CHÜEH-YÜ (Deciding cases); reference from C. Tung, supra note 204, at 193–94, who gives part of the text.

her his concubine, and, furthermore, had intercourse with her daughters. In 128 B.C. these acts came to the attention of the court; it referred them to the high ministers who found that the King had "behaved like a beast, thrown into disorder the human relationships, and offended against Heaven." They decided that he should be executed, and he committed suicide.[214] It is significant that the ministers who reached the decision did not refer to any part of the Han code.

In the following year the King of Ch'i was told by Chu-fu Yen that it was known that the King had committed incest with his sister. "The King felt that he could not escape; he feared that he would be likened to the King of Yen and sentenced to death. He killed himself."[215] This suggests that the case of the King of Yen was a precedent, either so far as the case itself was concerned or at least as indicating that the court would not tolerate such activity.

In the same year, 127 B.C., Liu Chien, who was the King of Chiang-tu and a sadistic pervert whose activities included gleefully watching people drown and attempting to breed palace women with sheep and dogs, also committed incest and was asked if he alone had not heard of the affairs of Yen and Ch'i.[216] Actually Liu Chien was not convicted of these crimes, due to a pardon, but he later killed himself when accused of plotting rebellion. His case, however, suggests the same conclusion as that of the King of Ch'i.

Liu K'uan, another King, was accused of having relations with his father's Queen, which "perverted human relationships," and he was also guilty of uttering imprecations against the emperor. He too committed suicide.[217] In this case, of course, it is impossible to separate one charge from the other.

In a slightly different kind of case, also in the reign of Emperor Wu, Ch'en Ho lost the fief that had been handed down in his family from the time of his great-grandfather, Ch'en P'ing, because he seized another man's wife. He was publicly executed and his family was deprived of the fief.[218]

In 73 B.C., Liu Ch'eng was convicted of killing a man, deprived of his fief, and sent back to his father's kingdom. There he committed incest with one of his father's concubines, and when the matter became known, he was publicly executed.[219]

With the exception of the last example, all of these cases occurred in the reign of Emperor Wu. One of the policies pursued throughout Emperor Wu's reign was the weakening of the feudal lords. On the slightest grounds they had their estates reduced or confiscated. The evidence here indicates that there

[214] HS ch. 35, 3b–4a; 1 B. WATSON, *supra* note 57, at 403, has a free translation.
[215] HS ch. 64A, 20a–b; 2 B. WATSON, *supra* note 57, at 237.
[216] HS ch. 53, 5a–b.
[217] HS ch. 44, 17a.
[218] HS ch. 40, 19b; 1 B. WATSON, *supra* note 57, at 167.
[219] HS ch. 63, 16a. I follow Wang Hsien-ch'ien in taking this man to be Liu Ch'ang instead of Liu Pao as the text says. Both were sons of the king.

was no attempt made to refer to specific laws in order to justify the legal action taken against these kings and marquises; admittedly, few societies condone incestuous behavior, but in this era it seems as if Emperor Wu were taking advantage of these offenses in order to weaken further the feudal lords.

Additional confirmation of this view comes from a case in which a step-mother complained to the Prefect Wang Tsun that her stepson treated her like a wife. He was jealous of her and beat her. Wang said: "The code has no law about [a man] treating his mother like a wife; that was something the sages could not bear to write about." He then treated it as a special case and had the stepson executed.[220] This occurred between 48 and 43 B.C., well after the cases during the reign of Emperor Wu. Again, the obvious: there was no law prohibiting this kind of behavior.

Later we have another case which, in spite of some ambiguities, leads to the same conclusion. In the period between 16 and 12 B.C., it was reported to the throne that King Li had harbored ill will against the consort family and that he had spoken evil words against the throne. An investigation proved that there was no substance to these charges, but it did reveal that the King had been involved in an incestuous relationship with his aunt. When the King first became interested in his aunt, he told Jen Pao, the aunt's husband (!), that he was fond of her and "wished to have her." Jen Pao warned the King: "The Princess is your aunt. The law is very strict." But the King shrugged off the warning and carried on an illicit relationship with her for several years. The question is: Was Jen Pao referring to the section of the Han code? Or was he drawing upon the precedents apparently established in the reign of Emperor Wu which may have had the force of law anyway?

An answer to these questions is suggested by Ku Yung. He did not refer to any law covering such offenses and, in fact, he argued as though there was no such law when he asserted that the proper activities of the ruler did not include spying on the private activities of people in the women's apartments or listening in on words spoken in the central chambers. He then suggested that the court had nothing to gain administratively or politically by charging the young King on the basis of the facts discovered. Furthermore, he added, it would not be wise to spread something like this throughout the empire. Ku's argument was effective; no action was ever taken against the King on these grounds.[221] This incident suggests, first, that the precedents established in the earlier cases did not provide compelling grounds for continuing action against such offenders and, second, that there were no laws specifically dealing with such offenses, although the court could act against such offenders on an *ad hoc* basis.

---

[220] HS ch. 76, 20a.
[221] HS ch. 47, 8a–9b.

If the Han code did not include provisions against such things as incest, perhaps it was because, as Wang Tsun suggested, the law-makers did not feel it necessary to incorporate such things into the laws. But, without clear-cut prohibitions against offenses of this nature, it seems unlikely that the code included laws concerning such things as the "seven conditions" for divorce[222] or the "three prohibitions." Certainly, there is no evidence that the "seven conditions" or the "three prohibitions" were a part of the Han code.

Local officials were often called upon to settle disputes involving women who had fled from one man to become the wife of another and to protect widows who were being forced to remarry. The manner in which these cases were handled also suggests that the Han code was lacking and probably devoid of laws regarding such matters. For example, a girl named Lo Kung was widowed at an early age and told her father that she would not remarry. On the father's instructions her groom-to-be went to the regional officials, one of whom ordered the subordinate prefectural officials to force her to return home. The girl then made a plea to the Regional Inspector himself who thought highly of her and sanctioned her appeal.[223] If we rule out extralegal local pressures (which is perhaps not warranted since the groom-to-be was probably a member of the well-known and powerful Ho family), we are almost led to conclude that the initial reaction of the officials was the customary one and that the Regional Inspector was allowing his personal feelings to interfere with normal procedure.

In a similar case, also undatable, a young widow, upon being forced by official and family pressure to return home to remarry, killed herself. The Grand Administrator of the commandery then executed the two men who were responsible for attempting to coerce her to return. This suggests, perhaps, that there was no legal ground on which she could refuse to remarry.[224] And we have earlier cited a case from the closing decade of the Han in which the Grand Administrator ordered prefectural officials to offer betrothal gifts to a young widow; thus, he gave official sponsorship for her remarriage.[225] A famous poetess of the last years of the Han warned her brothers, after she had lost her husband, that if they tried to compel her to remarry she would go to the officials and create a legal case (the nature of which is unspecified). However, she goes on to say that, if she does not succeed, she will commit suicide.[226] This case also points to the conclusion that not only were there no

---

[222] C. Tung, *supra* note 153, at 291, says that the *ch'i-ch'u* were in the Han code, but he provides not one piece of evidence in support of his statement.

[223] HYKC ch. 10A, 313.

[224] HYKC ch. 10B, 356–57.

[225] HYKC ch. 10B, 356.

[226] Tu Yü, NÜ-CHI (Records concerning women), quoted in T'AI-P'ING YÜ-LAN, *supra* note 114, at ch. 441, 8a–b. Again I express my appreciation to Yang Shu-ta, whose work contains this reference (YANG 55–56).

statutory prohibitions against remarriage, but that it could legitimately be expected.

The evidence already introduced in the section on remarriage of divorcees suggests that legally it was condoned. Wang Fu again offers a germane comment: "Nowadays she marries 'B' and without shame again [marries] and enters the 'A' family. The officials, examining the case, order that she remain in the family she has already entered (that is, with her second husband)."[227] Evidently, the first husband had no case (and, just as a reminder, this attitude concerning remarriage, and the apparent ease with which it was done, indicate again that the marriage rites had little relevance in Han society).

Many people in all levels of Han society were dissatisfied with the lack of attention to ritual and with the lack of laws governing divorce and remarriage, or the remarriage of widows. The Later Han was a period in which there were increasing demands for remedial legislation to prevent such practices. Even in Former Han there was some attention to these problems. Wang Chi, after complaining about people marrying too young and after pointing out that people were going to excesses in their betrothal gifts, suggested that good government was dependent on punishments (that is, clearly spelled out prohibitions in the laws) to prevent such behavior. However, Emperor Hsüan was unmoved by his proposals and nothing came of them.[228] One of the points that the *Po-hu t'ung-i* (A.D. 79) contains was an admonition that the man who became successful in political life ought not to divorce his wife in order to take a new one—presumably one from the same social group of which he was now a member.[229] Pan Ku, shortly before the end of the first century A.D., in his treatise on law, argued in favor of a lengthy law code that would bring to a stop the prevalent adultery and incest.[230] The strongest argument in favor of new laws comes from Wang Fu. He blames the officials for allowing women to flee their husbands to marry someone else. He asserts that the officials disregard completely that which would prevent such activities, namely, allowing and encouraging the chaste widow to remain just that and not allowing women to leave their husbands for other men. He says:

The former monarchs, on the basis of the contentment and anger [inherent] in human nature, with regard to what could not be brought to an end, established rituals and regulations and esteemed virtue and deference; with regard to what could be brought to an end, they set forth laws and prohibitions and made clear rewards and punishments. Nowadays, for selling in the marketplace to be without cheating or for marriage to be without mutual deceit is not something impossible to human nature. Hence nothing compares with establishing righteousness and following the law. . . .

---

[227] F. WANG, *supra* note 56, at ch. 5, 136.

[228] HS ch. 72, 6b–7a.

[229] 1 TJAN 253–54.

[230] 1 A. HULSEWÉ, *supra* note 65, at 349.

And the laws that he wanted to see were stern indeed. If a woman married into a second family, even if "she gave birth to ten sons and earned a hundred pardons," she and her second husband should have their heads shaved and be banished to a frontier prefecture. This, he suggests, will cut off licentiousness and disorder, "and then great peace will come."[231]

Demands for new laws were not the only way in which this trend was manifested. A woman who starved herself to death rather than succumb to her parents' pressure to remarry was immortalized by local officials who erected a stone monument in her honor.[232] Another woman who attempted to drown herself when confronted with the same opposition to her refusal to remarry was honored by having her picture hung in commandery head-quarters.[233]

Still another approach to the problem was to teach women a new mode of behavior. She was to learn to behave as the classics told her to behave: she was to be humble before her father and husband; she was to be loyal to one man; she was not to run off or even to remarry after her husband died. This is the gist of Pan Chao's "Lessons for Women."[234] And Pan Chao was not the only author of such admonitions. Cheng Chung's *Hun-li* was apparently an attempt to teach people to abide by the proper marriage rituals. Toward the end of Later Han, Ts'ai Yung and Hsün Shuang, two well-known scholars, wrote "lessons for women."

And yet, these moralists were not without their opponents. As we have already seen, a rebuttal was written to Pan Chao's work by her sister-in-law. Certainly Ku Yung, who said that the emperor really had no business knowing what was going on in the bedrooms of his subjects, would not have agreed with either Pan Ku or Wang Fu who wanted legislation to cover just such activities. What we see here is part of a larger debate that went on in Han times, a debate that to a large extent pitted the New Text scholars (in which group Ku Yung belongs) against the Old Text scholars (for example, Pan Ku). The New Texters would severely limit the role of the state in such personal matters; the Old Texters, on the other hand, sought to build a society that was one of "great peace"—a great peace imposed by the laws and rituals of their kind of Confucianism. The issue was never resolved during the Han; the full history of the codification of Confucianism is an account not yet written. It will depend upon much more work not only on Chinese society but also on Chinese intellectual history, for the Confucianism that was codified was not the Confucianism of the Han dynasty. For the Han itself, it can safely be said

[231] F. WANG, *supra* note 56, at ch. 5, 136–38.

[232] HYKC ch. 10A, 313.

[233] HYKC ch. 10B, 341. *See also* HYKC ch. 10B, 356, for two other examples of the same general kind.

[234] N. SWANN, *supra* note 14, at ch. 7.

that the rulers were not committed to the enforcement of the rules provided in the ritual literature, and they did not author an elaborate corpus of laws to provide full guidelines for social behavior. The more obvious things, such as incest, were not covered in the laws, but they were taken care of in a series of cases that dealt harshly with offenders, particularly offenders who were kings or marquises. It will sound trite, but it is not too far from the actual situation in Han to say that ritual did not extend to anyone, and that punishments only extended to the great officers.

Divorce in Traditional Chinese Law

TAI YEN-HUI

INTRODUCTION

The Nature of Traditional Divorce Law

Since ancient times, divorce has been the means for effective dissolution of a valid marriage. The marital relationship of a husband and wife is terminated from the time of the divorce onward; divorce is not retroactive. Under the present law, marriage and divorce are the private affairs of husband and wife, and in-law relationships are merely incidental effects. Therefore, causes for judicial divorce actions are all provided in connection with, and on an equal basis between, husband and wife.[1] Divorce by mutual consent is also recognized under the present law.

In traditional Chinese law, the purposes, nature, and effects of marriage were quite different from those of the present law, and consequently, the kinds, substance, and effects of divorce in the two systems are also different.[2] The traditional purpose of marriage was to benefit the family from the ancestors on down; the personal relationship between husband and wife was of secondary importance.[3] If a marriage were unable to achieve its objective, that

---

[1] The provision under art. 1052, Clause 4 of the CHINESE CIVIL CODE (1930) about a divorce based on the wife's maltreatment of the husband's lineal ascendants, or *vice versa*, which amounts to being unable to live together, is an exception. Also, judgments and theories have adopted an enlarged interpretation that maltreatment of a husband who is staying at the wife's family, and the wife's lineal ascendants also constitutes grounds for divorce. *See* TAI YEN-HUI, CHUNG-KUO CH'IN-SHU-FA (Chinese family law) 166 (4th ed. 1965).

[2] TAI YEN-HUI, CHUNG-KUO FA-CHIH-SHIH (A legal history of China) 219 (1966). The recognition of divorce by mutual consent under the CHINESE CIVIL CODE (1930) art. 1049, is based on traditional divorce law; there is, therefore no difference in the essence of divorce by mutual consent in both cases.

[3] N. NIIDA, SHINA MIBUNHŌSHI (A history of family law in China) 537 (1952); TAI, *supra* note 2, at 219, 222.

is, to benefit the family, then it could or even ought to be dissolved.[4] Thus,
in most cases, divorce causes were related to ancestors, parents, and members
of the family, particularly those on the husband's side. Marriage was arranged
according to the will of the sponsors, that is, the parents or grandparents;
their consent was also required for divorce. However, the will of the husband
was essential in a divorce case, and therefore parents or grandparents usually
did not compel their sons or grandsons to divorce their wives.[5]

Since marriage and divorce were primarily concerned with the family, a
wife maintained a residual marriage relationship with her husband's family
even after his death; divorce was also employed as a means of terminating this
residual relationship.[6] Divorce was in most cases initiated by the husband's
family, since the wife was in a subordinate position.

The Idea of Permitting Divorce

Under traditional law, marriage was regarded as artificial in nature, and an
affirmative position was adopted with regard to divorce. Since marriage was
the result of an agreement between two families, divorce might also be obtained
in the same manner.[7] The people in general have believed that a husband and
wife should divorce, if they are not harmonious.[8]

The Kinds of Divorce

Divorce could be divided into four types: (1) mutual consent; (2) the seven
conditions; (3) breaking the bond *(yi-chüeh)*; and (4) the wife's suit. The
traditional law emphasized the institutions of the Seven Conditions and
Breaking the Bond. Divorce by mutual consent was relatively simple, and
there were numerous cases, while divorce suits initiated by the wife were
rare. The Seven Conditions were civil in nature, and Breaking the Bond had
certain criminal aspects.

The institution of the Seven Conditions for divorce (with three limitations)
was first established in the Ch'un-Ch'iu or Spring and Autumn period

---

[4] N. NIIDA, *supra* note 3, at 674 ff.; T'AO HSI-SHENG, HUN-YIN YÜ CHIA-TSU
(Marriage and family) 49 (1934); T. HIGASHIGAWA, SHINA HŌSEISHI KENKYŪ (A study
on legal history in China) 331 (1926).

[5] TAI, *supra* note 2, at 240; RINJI TAIWAN KYŪKAN CHŌSAKAI (The Commission
for the Investigation of Old Laws and Customs in Formosa), TAIWAN SHIHŌ (The
private laws of Taiwan), Vol. 2, No. 2) 371 (1910).

[6] CHEN KU-YÜAN, CHUNG-KUO HUN-YIN-SHIH (A history of marriage in China) 236
(1966).

[7] CHOU MI, CH'I-TUNG YEH-YÜ (Unfounded talk) n.d.; T. H. CH'IEN, HUN-YI
(Marriage Ceremonies) n.d.

[8] T'ANG-LU SU-YI; (Commentaries on the T'ang Code); TAIWAN SHIHŌ FUROKU
SANKO SHO (Reference materials appended to the private laws of Taiwan) 321 (1910)
(hereinafter cited as "Shihō Sanko").

(722–484 B.C.) to impose limitations on the arbitrary ousting of wives. Divorce under the Seven Conditions did not require a suit before a competent officer, but the wife could contest the divorce before an officer if she had cause.

The institution of Breaking the Bond was already in existence in the Han period (206 B.C.–A.D. 220) and became more complete in the T'ang period (A.D. 618–906). Under the causes allowed by this institution, either spouse was allowed to compel the other to divorce through legal proceedings. Divorce under Breaking the Bond could also be compelled by a competent officer; failure to divorce in this case was punishable.

The effectiveness of the Seven Conditions decreased with time, while the causes for divorce under Breaking the Bond were increased. Traditional divorce law may be said to have developed from the concept of Breaking the Bond.

The Term "Divorce"

Traditionally, the concept of divorce has been expressed by the following terms: "to abandon" *(ch'i)*, "to oust" *(hsiu)*, "to send forth" *(ch'u)*, "to send away" *(fang)*, "to expel" *(chu)*, "to dismiss" *(ch'ih)*, "to discharge" *(ch'ien)*, and "to part" *(li)*, all meaning to divorce and terminate all relations with the wife.[9] Among the populace, "divorce" has in most cases been referred to as "to oust" *(hsiu)*, or "to abandon" and to "oust the wife" *(hsiu-ch'i)*, all originating from the meaning of "to terminate" *(chung-chih)*.[10] The expression "divorce document" *(hsiu-shu)* was also used in the *Ch'ing-Ming-Chi*,[11] and a further variation, "to terminate the marriage relationship" *(li-yüan)* has been used by the people in some regions (such as Taiwan) to mean "divorce."[12]

What may be considered equivalent to the term "divorce" within the meaning of the present law was described in traditional law as "to part" *(li or li-chih)* or "to part and separate" *(li-i)*, and the term now employed, *li-hun*, was not used, although it was in existence as early as the Nan-Pei dynasty (A.D. 420–477).[13] The term *"li-hun"* can also be found in a collection

---

[9] N. NIIDA, *supra* note 3, at 669.
[10] *Id.*
[11] The proverb of Pien-ching described in TUNG-HSIEN PI-LU (Records of the eastern district) says: Hou Kung-pu ousts his wife after his death. (Quoted in K. Chen, *supra* note 6, at 236.)
[12] SHIHŌ SANKŌ 316(3).
[13] As Professor Ch'en Ku-yüan points out: In the CHIN-SHU (The annals of the Chin dynasty) Hsing-fa-chi (Treatise on criminal law) there was a remark: "The Emperor permits divorce" (Chao t'ing li-hun). The term "Li-hun" was also used in the SHIH-SHUO HSIN-YÜ of the Liu-Sung period (circa 420–477) in Sung-Shu (The annals of the Sung dynasty by Shen Yüeh of Liang) in CHIU-TANG-SHU (The old annals of the T'ang dynasty) such as Wu-ti Pen-chi, and in the HSIN-T'ANG-SHU (The new annals of the T'ang dynasty), etc. Consequently, Professor Ch'en says: the term "Li-hun" was in existence at the latest by the time of the Northern and Southern Dynasties. K. Ch'en, *supra* note 6, at 235.

of judicial decisions in the Nan-Sung period (A.D. 1127–1229).[14] *"Li-hun"* was utilized as a standard term in the *First Draft Civil Code* (1908), and in the decisions and interpretations of the Supreme Court and its predecessor, the *Ta-li-yüan;* the present Civil Code followed that usage.

The Concept of "to Part and Separate" (li-i)

The concept of "to part and separate" *(li-i)* under traditional law was broader than that of "divorce" *(li-hun)* under the present law. It included the invalidation and dissolution of the betrothal, as well as annulment and divorce.

Marriage under traditional law referred to all family relationships arising out of marriage: those between the husband and wife; those between one of the spouses and the relatives of the other; and those between the relatives of the husband and the relatives of the wife.[15] Marriage could be divided into two steps; that is, the engagement (or betrothal) and the wedding. The parties concerned did not become spouses nor were the family relationships of kinship *(nei-ch'in),* that is, clan *(tsung-ch'in),* maternal relatives *(wai-ch'in),* and wife's relatives *(ch'i-ch'in),* completely formed, unless and until the marriage procedures had been completed.[16] However, family relationships somewhat similar to those just mentioned would exist even during the period of engagement. Engagement was a necessary procedure which, while not as significant as the wedding itself, had legal effects; under certain conditions an annulment of the engagement could be forced.[17]

Since the T'ang and Sung (A.D. 960–1126) periods, divorce and annulment have both been referred to as "to part and separate" *(li-i),* but there was a distinction between the two.[18] The present study will deal primarily with divorce.

The Criminal Aspects of Divorce

Under the traditional law, a divorce effected in violation of law was a criminal, as well as a civil, matter. The wife could not leave her husband without proper cause, and from the T'ang Code through the Revised Law of the Late Ch'ing period *(Ch'ing Hsien-Hsing-Lü),* there were provisions for

---

[14] MING-KUNG SHU-P'AN CH'ING-MING-CHI (Illustrious compilation of the decisions of famous judges) (reprinted 1964). (Hereinafter ILLUSTRIOUS COMPILATION) Hu-hun-men (Marriage Section), Tsa-lei (Miscellaneous).

[15] T. HIGASHIGAWA, *supra* note 4, at 344, states: "A marriage contract (that is an engagement) gives rise to familial relations." I use t'i-hun to distinguish the marriage contract under the present law from an engagement (ting-hun).

[16] TAI, *supra* note 2, at 234; also, the usage as a term of familial relations follows the usage in Art. 1317 of the *First Draft Civil Code* (the 3rd year of Hsüan-t'ung, 1912).

[17] T'ANG-LÜ (The T'ang Code) Hu-hun-lü (Laws of Household and Marriage).

[18] TAIWAN SHIHŌ, Vol. 2, 373; K. Ch'en, *supra* note 6, at 234; T. Higashigawa, *supra* note 4, at 337.

criminal sanctions against wives who did so. *T'ang Hu-Ling* (as adopted also in the Sung period in *Sung Hsing-T'ung*) contained provisions concerning the Seven Conditions, the Three Limitations, and Breaking the Bond. In both the T'ang Code and Sung law *(Sung Hsing-T'ung)* there were sanctions against divorcing a wife when she ought not to be divorced. On the civil side, the ousted wife was to be allowed to return and stay with the husband, and on the criminal law side the husband was to be punished. There were also provisions concerning sanctions against persons who failed to divorce when it was required by law under Breaking the Bond. During the Yüan period (A.D. 1280–1341), the same system (probably derived from the Chin Code) was adopted and put into practice, as recorded in the provisions of *Yüan Tien-Chang* and *T'ung-Chih T'iao-Ko*.

The household ordinances of the Ming dynasty (A.D. 1368–1662) provided only for the Seven Conditions and the Three Limitations, but did not refer to Breaking the Bond. The Ming Code, as did the T'ang Code, provided for punishment for divorcing a wife who ought not to be divorced and for failure to divorce on grounds arising from the provisions of Breaking the Bond. In the Ch'ing period (A.D. 1644–1911) there were no supplementary regulations, and the matters constituting the Seven Conditions and the Three Limitations were supplemented in the *Ch'ing-Lü Pen-Chu (Ch'u-Ch'i t'iao)*. Punishments for violations under Breaking the Bond were the same as those in the Ming Code. Under the Ming and Ch'ing Codes in the civil law provisions, it was specified that when a wife was divorced without legitimate reason, she should be permitted to return and restore marital relations with her husband. The basic principle consistently adopted by the old statutes to insure the observance of the laws was that an act of divorcing a wife who should not be divorced, or of failure to divorce a wife who should be divorced according to the law, were both punishable by criminal sanctions.

The Development of Divorce Law

Divorce law developed, along with the expansion of women's rights, as a result of the demand for justice, and in modern times along with the progress of women's education, and especially the development of the social and economic prerogatives of women.

The first stage permitted an unlimited abandoning of the wife (ousting the wife without any legitimate reason was possible). The second stage permitted ousting her only on the basis of proper legal grounds which occurred as early as the Ch'un-Ch'iu period, as provided by the Seven Conditions under the system of rites. It is difficult to determine the date when these rites were transformed into legal statutes, but there is no doubt that there were explicit provisions about the subject in the *T'ang Hu-Ling*. From then until the Ch'ing period, the statutes of every dynasty and period contained similar provisions. In the historical documents of the Han period, there were remarks about Breaking the Bond; whether the *lü* (formal or basic law) or *ling* (administrative regulations) of that period also contained provisions of this nature remains to be ascertained. In the T'ang period, the *lü* and *ling* began to regulate Breaking the Bond, which was a sufficiently abstract concept to allow the wife to sue the husband for divorce under its provisions.

In the Ming and Ch'ing periods, the grounds for Breaking the Bond provided in the *lü* were increased, the content modified, and the grounds upon which the wife might sue the husband for divorce also greatly increased. This may be identified as the third stage of development. However, the relative position of husband and wife under the divorce law remained unequal. After the establishment of the Republic, the fourth stage began. Owing to the influence of foreign legal systems (European, American, Japanese) during the latter part of the Ch'ing period, in the First Draft Civil Code (1908) the position of the wife in divorce law was substantially improved, even though the concept of inequality between men and women was by no means completely discarded. It was not until the Twentieth Year of the Republic (1931), when the family law part of the current Civil Code was promulgated, that the concept of equal rights between husband and wife was finally codified.[19] It should be kept in mind, however, that even though the development of the divorce law may be divided into four stages, the divorce system of a former stage usually continued to maintain its potentialities in later stages and also left its remnants in practice among the people. Even today, a husband may force his wife to divorce him and yet be able to employ the form of divorce by mutual consent. There are also cases in which there are grounds for divorce by the wife (for example, acts of adultery such as those committed when staying with a prostitute or maintaining a secondary wife) and yet some wives will not sue their husband for divorce, but will tolerate the situation. On the other hand, when adultery is committed by the wife, the husband ordinarily will not hesitate to divorce her (using either the form of mutual consent or that of divorce by judgment). At any one stage law cannot completely reflect reality, and we can best divide it into various stages according to the legal characteristics of the development in each stage. The present discussion will not follow the historical stages of development except within discussions of various types of divorce. We will analyze traditional divorce law according to the specific categories of divorce by mutual consent, the ousting of the wife, the Seven Conditions and Three Limitations, and Breaking the Bond, as well as divorce by the wife.

Despite all changes, traditional divorce law maintained roughly the same pattern from the Han through the Ch'ing periods, and the concepts and content of the Seven Conditions and Three Limitations and of the wife's suit

---

[19] Promulgated on December 26, the 19th Year of the Republic (1930), and entered into force on May 5, the 20th Year of the Republic (1931).

for divorce were relatively stable, so that division into time periods for purposes of discussion appears unnecessary. In contrast, the content and concept of Breaking the Bond, from which modern divorce law originated, were essentially changed during the period between the T'ang and Sung laws, and the Ming and Ch'ing laws, beginning with the Ming Household Ordinances and continuing through the *Ch'ing Lü-Li* and *Ch'ing Hsien-Hsing-Lü*. After the beginning of the Republic, the Ta-Li-Yüan, and later the Supreme Court, further expanded the applications of Breaking the Bond, until now the term is practically synonymous for "grounds for divorce by judicial decision." The judgments and interpretations rendered during the above twenty-year period, though in form based on the *Ch'ing Hsien-Hsing-Lü,* were in reality corrected and expanded by the general principles of law and thus established as legal rules. This law of judicial interpretation *(p'an-chüeh-fa)* continued to develop the older legal concepts, on the one hand, and accepted divorce concepts of modern law on the other, thus possessing the characteristics of a transitional law.

In China there has usually been a gap between custom and the written law; within the scope of divorce, customary law has been the more conservative. Since few people resort to formal courts for the settlement of civil disputes concerning personal affairs such as divorce, customary as well as written law must be considered in this article. The customs of the Ch'ing period will be emphasized.

DIVORCE BY MUTUAL CONSENT

Legal Regulations

Divorce by mutual consent was referred to as divorce by peaceful means *(ho-li)* in the T'ang Code. From the Chin dynasty (A.D. 1115–1234) through the Ch'ing, grounds were not required for divorce by mutual consent; a husband and wife who mutually agreed to divorce were not to be punished for divorcing without proper cause.[20]

The Actual Situation

Divorce by mutual consent was usually resorted to when the husband and wife did not get along well, when the wife did not get along well with her husband's parents, or when the husband's family was poor. However, there

---

[20] K. Chen, *supra* note 6, at 244; T'ANG-LÜ (The T'ang Code) and SUNG-HSING-T'UNG (Comprehensive Sung Criminal Laws) Hu-hun-lü (Laws of Household and Marriage), Yi-chüeh li-chih t'iao (Provisions Re: Breaking the Bond . . .); Chin-lü (The Chin Code) also invoked by Yüan-Tien-Chang Vol. 18, Hu-Pu 4, Board of Households); MING-LÜ (The Ming Code) and Ch'ing-lü (The Ch'ing Code), Hu-lü (Laws of Household), Hun-yin-men (Section on Marriage), Ch'u-ch'i t'iao (Provision for Divorcing a Wife), TAIWAN SHIHŌ Vol. 2, 370.

were cases in which the form of divorce by mutual consent was employed even though there were grounds for ousting the wife, for the wife to sue, or under Breaking the Bond.[21]

In reality, divorce by mutual consent was equivalent to divorce by unilateral intention.[22] Most cases were initiated by the husband, and the wife was forced to accept. Since men were regarded as superior to women, it was very rare for a wife to initiate a divorce action, for it was unlikely that it would be willingly accepted by her husband.[23]

When a husband and wife have agreed to divorce, the husband must then consult with his parents, obtain their consent, and have them negotiate with the wife's family. Since the parents could not completely ignore the feelings of the couple, they would generally not persist in refusing their consent.[24] The parents were only in a position to morally supervise the matter and had the power merely to check the divorce temporarily. In a few cases, divorce may have been initiated solely by the parents of the couple, but even in these circumstances, divorce could not be forced against the will of the couple involved.[25]

Customary Practices

Niida has mentioned two letters found in Tun-Huang before the Ch'ing period that refer to divorce by mutual consent. One letter referred to a couple who were on bad terms, and the other referred to a wife who did not get along well with her husband's relatives. In these cases, divorce was initiated by the husband's family; after the consent of their respective relatives has been obtained, the husband executed a document, gave it to the wife, and ousted her.[26]

In the Nan-Sung period a man who was unable to support his wife executed a document of divorce by mutual consent and allowed her to remarry in return for a certain amount of money.[27] Another man whose son-in-law has been missing for six years arranged for his daughter to be divorced by mutual consent rather than on the grounds of desertion. A document was executed and witnessed, and a certain amount of money was given to a proxy as a return of the engagement gift.[28]

---

[21] TAIWAN SHIHŌ, Vol. 2, 371.

[22] TAIWAN SHIHŌ, Vol. 2, 370; K. Chen, *supra* note 6, at 245; N. NIIDA, *supra* note 3, at 628.

[23] K. CHEN *supra* note 6, at 245.

[24] T. HIGASHIGAWA *supra* note 4, at 346.

[25] TAIWAN SHIHŌ, Vol. 2, 371; S. SHIGA, CHŪGOKU KAZOKUHŌ NO GENRI (Principles of family law in China), page 479 (1967).

[26] N. NIIDA, *supra* note 3, at 694.

[27] ILLUSTRIOUS COMPILATION, *supra* note 14. The Case of Yeh-szu and A-shao.

[28] ILLUSTRIOUS COMPILATION, the case of Lin Hsin-chung.

In the Yüan period a certain Liu Chih-yüan, who had married matrilocally, was forced by his brother-in-law to execute a divorce document. The document stated that Liu Chih-yüan was willing to divorce without coercion, because he had failed to worship his deceased parents-in-law and was unable to support his wife and children. It also stated that either party to the divorce would be liable to a fine, if he or she changed his or her mind later. A flower sign and the prints of Liu Chih-yüan's five fingers were affixed to the document.[29]

During the Ch'ing period divorce by mutual consent was the most commonly used form, although the causes ranged from disharmony and poverty to being unfilial to the parents-in-law or committing adultery.[30] In most cases of this nature, the wife's family would compensate the husband's family so that she could remarry; in others the husband would pay money to the wife's family. In some cases the wife's family would only pay money to the former husband if and when she became engaged to remarry.[31]

DIVORCING THE WIFE WITHOUT GROUNDS

In traditional times men were said to dominate women, who were expected to practice the three obediences *(san-ts'ung)*: namely, to obey father, husband, and son.[32] Moreover, in marriage the husband physically received the wife into his family, and in exchange the wife's family received a substantial marriage gift; thus marriage had the character of a purchase and sale. Consequently, the wife was allowed no freedom of choice in either marriage or divorce.

Divorcing a wife without grounds was a simple matter of the strong abandoning the weak. Even after grounds and limitations for divorce were established in the Rules of Propriety *(Li)*, they were not generally observed, and there were many instances of divorce without grounds.[33] In the Book of Odes *(Shih-Ching)* and in later periods, there were many poems and songs about divorced wives.[34]

However, many cases that appear to be divorce without grounds were simply instances of the husband's reluctance to make the grounds public. In

---

[29] N. NIIDA, *supra* note 3, at 692.

[30] TAIWAN SHIHŌ, Vol. 2, 370; SHIHŌ SANKO 317 ff.

[31] CHŪKAMINKOKU SHŪKAN CHŌSAROKU (A record of investigation of customs in the Republic of China) (hereinafter cited as SHŪKANROKU) (1943), 794, 805, 817, 853, 891.

[32] N. NIIDA, *supra* note 3, at 852 ff.

[33] N. NIIDA, TŌ SŌ HŌRITSU BUNSHO NO KENKYŪ (Research on the Legal Documents of the T'ang and Sung dynasties), 492 (1937) which cites many such cases.

[34] T. Y. CH'EN, CHUNG-KUO FU-NÜ SHENG-HUO SHIH (History of the livelihood of women in China) (1928) p. 36.

these cases a small incident would be used as an excuse for divorce so that the wife's remarriage would not be impeded.[35]

Since the time of the Sung dynasty it has been felt that on the one hand that divorcing a wife without grounds was a shameful act, while on the other hand, as noted above, arbitrary divorce was actually practiced. Although it was the general practice in Ch'ing times that legitimate grounds were necessary for divorce, there were still incidents of divorcing or even selling a wife or concubine on such pretexts as the husband's poverty, a tiny incident, or the husband's loss of interest because of a new lover.

Penalties were provided for divorce without grounds, but it was rare for the wife's family to bring such a case before the competent authorities.

SEVEN CONDITIONS AND THREE LIMITATIONS FOR DIVORCE

The system of Seven Conditions and Three Limitations for divorcing a wife was established by the Rules of Propriety *(Li)* in the Ch'un-Ch'iu period. A divorce law was thus created for the first time in traditional China. The Seven Conditions were restrictive grounds for divorcing the wife. A husband was entitled to divorce his wife on any one of the specified grounds, but he was not required to do so. If any of the Three Limitations applied, the wife could not be divorced. This system did not include concubines; because they had a more humble status, they could be divorced arbitrarily.[36]

The Seven Conditions and Three Limitations could be found in the classics as early as the Han period.[37] Whether these provisions were included in the Han Code and Ordinances *(Lü-Ling)* is uncertain. The earliest known and extant statute to include this system was the T'ang Code and Ordinances. It has subsequently been included in the *Yüan-Tien-Chang* of the Yüan dynasty, the *T'ung-Chih T'iao-Ko* also of the Yüan dynasty, the Ming Ordinances *(Ming-Ling)*, the Ming Code *(Ming-Lü)*, the Ch'ing Code and Statutes *(Ch'ing Lü-Li)*, and in the Revised Criminal Code of 1909 *(Ch'ing Hsien-Hsing Hsing-Lü)*.[38]

---

[35] CH'ING-LÜ CHI-CHU (Compiled commentaries on the Ch'ing Code), Hu-lü (Household Laws), Hun-yin men (Marriage Section), Ch'u-ch'i t'iao (Provisions for Divorcing a Wife); The Case of Tseng Ts'an, KUNG-TZU CHIA-YÜ (The Sayings of Confucius) Vol. 7, Ch'i-shih-erh ti-tzu chieh); in defense of Tseng Ts'an, PAI-HU-T'UNG (White Tiger Hall) (Vol. 2, No. 2, Chien Cheng).

[36] RYŌSHUGE (1961) (Vol. 10, Koryō 8, Shichishutsu jō).

[37] K'UNG-TZU CHIA-YÜ, *supra* note 35 (Vol. 6, Pen-ming chieh).

[38] Y'UAN-TIEN-CHANG (Yuan Code) Vol. 18, Hu-Pu 4 (Board of Households), MING-LING (Ming Ordinances), Hu-ling (Household Ordinances); MING-LÜ (Ming Code) Hu-lü (Laws of Household), Hung-yin men (Section on Marriage), Ch'u-ch'i t'iao (Provisions for Divorcing a Wife), CH'ING LÜ-LI (Established precedents and laws of the Ch'ing dynasty) (same provision as MING-LÜ); CH'ING HSIEN-HSING HSING-LÜ (Existing criminal laws of the Ch'ing dynasty) promulgated in the First Year of Hsuan-t'ung (1908) (same provision as MING-LÜ).

Although there were some differences in the terminology used for the Seven Conditions and Three Limitations in the various codes and ordinances, the basic meaning remained unchanged. Two different sequences were also used in listing the conditions and limitations. One sequence was used in *The Rites of the Great Tai, Ta-Tai-Li* of the Han dynasty, the *Sayings of Confucius, K'ung-Tzu-Chia-Yüi* of the Han and the Interpretation of K'ung of the Book of Rites *(Li-Chi K'ung-shu)* of the T'ang dynasty. The other sequence was used in the *Commentaries of Ho Hsiu* on the *Kung-Yang-Chuan* of the Han period, and the *Commentaries of Chia on the Book of Ceremonials, I-Li Chu Shu* of the T'ang dynasty and all codes and ordinances *(lü-ling)* and statutes *(li)* after the T'ang Ordinances *(T'ang-Ling)*. However, there seems to be no particular significance attached to these sequences.

The sequence used in the *Ta-Tai-Li* is as follows:[39]

1. The Seven Conditions:

   a. Being unfilial to the parents-in-law
   b. Having no son
   c. Adultery
   d. Jealousy
   e. Malignant disease
   f. Talking too much
   g. Stealing

2. The Three Limitations:

   a. If the wife has no place to return to.
   b. Having observed three years mourning for the parents-in-law.
   c. If the husband had been poor and humble at the time of marriage, and became rich and noble later.

The sequence used in *Kung-Yang-Chuan,* which has always been used since the T'ang Ordinances *(T'ang-Ling)*, is as follows:[40]

1. The Seven Conditions:

   a. Having no son
   b. Adultery and licentiousness
   c. Being unfilial to the parents-in-law (or failing to serve them with care)
   d. Talking too much
   e. Stealing
   f. Jealousy
   g. Malignant disease

---

[39] TA-TAI-LI (Book of Rites of elder Tai) Vol. 12, Pen-ming.

[40] KUNG-YANG-CHUAN, *Ho-Hsiu chu* (Kung-yang commentary; edited by Ho Hsiu) (the 27th year of Chuang-kung).

2. The Three Limitations:

    a. Having observed three years mourning for the parents-in-law.

    b. If the husband had been poor and humble at the time of marriage; and became rich and noble later.

    c. If the wife has no place to return to.

In the T'ang Ordinances *(T'ang-Ling)* adultery and malignant disease were not restricted by the Three Limitations. In the Ming Ordinances *(Ming-Ling)* and the Ch'ing Code *(Ch'ing-Lü)* adultery was not restricted. It may be that these grounds were considered too important for divorce to be prevented by the existence of any of the Three Limitations.

Failure to produce a son. Since continuation of the family was one of the primary purposes of marriage, failure to produce a son was considered a legitimate reason for divorcing a wife.[41] In the Han and Wei periods (A.D. 220–265) the duration of the marriage in these cases varied. One man, on reaching the age of thirty, wished to divorce his wife because they had no son.[42] The father and elder brother of another man, who had been married for five years without having a son, wished him to divorce and remarry.[43] Still another man divorced his wife on this ground after twenty years of marriage, because he favored another woman.[44]

Under T'ang law a wife could not be divorced for failure to produce a son until she had reached the age of fifty.[45] However, this provision does not always seem to have been applied. In one case a wife was divorced for failure to have a son after ten years of marriage.[46] The parents of one man wished him to divorce his wife on this ground after only three years of marriage.[47]

According to interpretations of Japan's *Yorōryō,* which was based on the T'ang Ordinances *(T'ang-Ling),* even if an heir were adopted, a wife could still be divorced on the ground that she had produced no natural son.[48] The wives of an emperor or a feudal lord, however, could not be divorced for

---

[41] WANG HUI, CH'I-CH'U YI (Discussions of the seven conditions for divorcing a wife), Chüan 12; H. T'AO, *supra* note 4, at 49.

[42] The case of Liang Shu-yü, TSO-CHUAN and K'UNG-TZU CHIA-YÜ, *supra* note 35.

[43] The case of Mu-tzu, Ts'ui Pao, KU-CHIN-CHU (Notes on the traditional and modern), Middle Chapters, No. 3, Music, n.d.

[44] Ts'ao Chih, a preface to miscellaneous poems relating to Liu Hsun's wife, Wang Sung; N. NIIDA, *supra* note 33, at 488 ff.; N. NIIDA, *supra* note 3, at 676 ff.; T'AI-P'ING YÜ-LAN (Imperial Compilation of the T'ai-p'ings), Vol. 521 Ch'u-Fu (Divorcing a wife).

[45] T'ANG-LING (T'ang Ordinances), T'ANG-LÜ SU-YI (Commentaries on the T'ang Code), HU-HUN-LÜ (Laws of Household and Marriage), CH'U-CH'I T'IAO (Provisions for Divorcing a Wife).

[46] CHANG CHI, CHANG SZU-YEH CHI (Collection of Imperial Tutor Chang [Chi]), Chapter 7, Yüeh-fu (Collection of Tunes), Li-fu (Divorcing a Wife).

[47] The case of T'ang, decided by Pai Chü-yi, CH'UAN-T'ANG-WEN.

[48] RYŌSHUGE, *supra* note 36 (Vol. 10, Koryō 8, Schichshutsu jō).

failure to produce a son. For them, there were only six conditions for divorce.[49]

Adultery. Divorce on the ground of adultery was allowed to protect the purity of the clan. This ground applied only to the wife and was not restricted by the Three Limitations. For the husband, only adultery with the wife's mother was considered a ground for divorce; this, however, was a criminal act which will be discussed later under the category of Breaking the Bond. The accepted interpretation of the term "adultery" was that it referred to completed acts only.[50]

Being unfilial to the parents-in-law. Another of the primary purposes of marriage was serving the parents-in-law. Failure to serve them with care was considered unfilial and thus flagrantly immoral. Therefore, it was natural to make such conduct a ground for divorce.

Being unfilial was a very abstract ground, and it was subject to ambiguous interpretations. In many cases simple displeasure on the part of the parents-in-law was sufficient cause for the daughter-in-law to be termed "unfilial."[51] In the late Han period one wife was divorced for being late in bringing water to her mother-in-law, and another was divorced for scolding a dog in front of her mother-in-law.[52] In the T'ang period another wife was also divorced for scolding a dog in front of her mother-in-law; however, Pai Chü-yi contended that a slip of the tongue did not constitute disrespect and that the husband should take back the wife.[53] A wife in the Ming period was divorced because she did not learn well and constantly argued with her mother-in-law.[54]

The term "parents-in-law" was a broad one that included the husband's grandparents as well as parents; it also included foster parents, the father's principal wife, and a stepmother, particularly during the T'ang period.[55] If a wife were disobedient or displeasing to any of these people, she could be divorced.

Talking too much. A wife who talked too much could be divorced, because she would cause discord among relatives. This included not only talking nonsense, but also saying anything that would disrupt the harmony of the family.

---

[49] K. CHEN, *supra* note 6, at 241.

[50] RYŌSHUGE, *supra* note 36.

[51] K. Y. CH'EN, CHUNG-KUO KU-TAI HUN-YIN SHIH (A history of marriage in traditional times in China) p. 46.

[52] HOU-HAN-SHU (Annals of the latter Han dynasty) *Chiang Shih chuan* (Biography of Chiang Shih).

[53] PAI CHÜ-YI, CH'UAN T'ANG-WEN, Vol. 673.

[54] *P'ai-an ching-ch'i,* Chapter 20; quoted in N. NIIDA, *supra* note 3, at 420; this same case with a slight difference in wording appears in CHIN-KU CH'I-KUAN (Traditional and Modern Strange and Wonderful Sights) (the 18th act) n.d.

[55] TAI YEN-HUI, T'ANG-LÜ T'UNG-LUN (Comprehensive Discussions of the T'ang Code) (1964) pp. 62, 460, 461.

In the Han period a wife was divorced on this ground for complaining that her husband's younger brother did not help with the family work.[56] Another Han wife was divorced for trying to persuade her husband to separate from his brothers.[57] A wife in the T'ang period was also divorced for trying to persuade her husband to separate from his brothers.[58]

Stealing. Theft committed by the wife was a ground for divorce, not only because it was immoral, but also because it damaged the reputation of the husband's family. The term "theft" included the theft of family property, as well as that of others and attempted theft.[59]

As long as the parents were alive, the younger members of the family, including daughters-in-law, could not have any private goods or private savings from family property; to do so was regarded as stealing the family property.[60] In the Warring States period a father once advised his daughter to have some savings after she married, because divorces were common; she was later divorced on the ground of theft, because her mother-in-law accused her of having too much private savings.[61] Another wife was divorced merely on the suspicion of stealing meat from her mother-in-law.[62]

Jealousy. Jealousy was a ground for divorce because it destroyed order and propriety in family life, especially between wives and concubines.[63] In the Han period a wife was divorced because her jealousy prohibited her husband from taking a concubine, who could have helped with the housework; as a result the children had to do the housekeeping themselves.[64]

Malignant disease. Malignant disease prohibited a wife from worshiping the ancestors with her husband; for this reason it constituted a ground for divorce. Under the T'ang Ordinances *(T'ang-Ling)* this ground was not restricted by the Three Limitations, but under the Ming Ordinances *(Ming-Ling)* it was so restricted. The term "malignant disease" was generally interpreted to mean leprosy or similar diseases.[65]

Development of the Seven Conditions

The Seven Conditions for divorcing a wife may be divided into two categories: those that involved personal responsibility, and those that did not.

---

[56] HAN-SHU, *Ch'en Ping chuan* (Biography of Ch'en Ping).

[57] HOU-HAN-SHU, *Li-Ch'ung chuan* (Biography of Li Ch'ung).

[58] The case of Liu Chün-liang in HSIN-T'ANG-SHU, *Hsiao-yu lieh-chuan* (Biographies of the Ranks of Filial Piety and Brotherly Harmony); N. NIIDA, *supra* note 3, at 678.

[59] HAN-SHU, *Wang Ch'i chuan* (Biography of Wang Ch'i).

[60] CHEN, *supra* note 51, at 46.

[61] HAN-FEI-TZU (The Book of Han Fei-tzu) (Shuo-lin); CHEN, *supra* note 51, at 46.

[62] HAN-SHU, *K'uai-t'ung chuan* (Biography of K'uai-t'ung).

[63] N. NIIDA, *supra* note 3, at 674.

[64] HOU-HAN-SHU, *Feng Yen chuan* (Biography of Feng Yen).

[65] RYŌSHUGE, *supra* note 36 (Vol. 9, Koryō, Mokumō jō) H. T'AO, *supra* note 4, at 49; TAI, *supra* note 1, p. 172.

There were five grounds involving personal responsibility: adultery, being unfilial to the parents-in-law, talking too much, stealing, and jealousy. The two that did not involve personal responsibility were failure to produce a son and malignant disease.

Liu Chi in the Ming period considered the grounds in the first category immoral acts, but objected to divorce on the grounds in the second category.[66] However, Wang Hui, also of the Ming period, considered the grounds in the first category as intolerable to men, and those in the second as intolerable to heaven.[67] Liu Chi's objection that a husband should not abandon his wife when she had encountered misfortune was based on humanitarianism and justice, while Wang Hui's interpretation was based on the traditional concept of marriage. Wang Hui also regarded the Three Limitations as sufficient protection for wives in this category, since both grounds were restricted by the Limitations in the Ming period. Li Tz'u-ming of the late Ch'ing period also contended that divorce for failure to produce a son was not unjust; since a wife could not be divorced on this ground until she was fifty years old, it was rare for her not to qualify for at least one of the Three Limitations.[68]

In customary practice the system of the Seven Conditions for divorce was rarely used to its full extent. During the Sung period divorce was considered scandalous, particularly by educated people, and social pressure usually prevented it.[69] If a husband and wife lost their affection for each other or failed to have sons, their family and close friends would usually persuade the husband to take a concubine rather than divorce.[70] Remarriage was also very expensive, and this reduced the number of divorces, especially among the poor.[71] It was also considered unlucky for anyone to execute a divorce document for someone else.[72]

After the Sung and Yüan periods the system of the Seven Conditions became a dead letter in judicial usage also.[73] Among the general populace the only grounds actually used were adultery, stealing, and being unfilial to the parents-in-law.[74] In these cases the effectiveness of the Three Limitations

---

[66] Liu Chi in Yü-Li-Tzu, CH'ENG-YI-PO WEN-CHI (Collected works of Liu Chi), Chüan 4, n.d.

[67] WANG HUI, CH'I-CH'U YI (Discussions of the Seven Conditions) n.d.

[68] LI TZ'U-MING, YÜEH-MAN-T'ANG JIH-CHI (Diary of Li Tz'u-ming) n.d.

[69] SZU-MA KUANG, HSÜN TZU-SUN WEN (An instruction to posterity) n.d.; CHAO FENG-CH'IEH, MIN-FA CH'IN-SHU-LUN (Discussions of Family Law in the Civil Code) (1945) p. 105.

[70] CHAO FENG-CH'IEH, *supra* note 69, p. 105; TAIWAN SHIHŌ, Vol. 2, 369.

[71] TAIWAN SHIHŌ, Vol. 2, 369; S. SHIGA, *supra* note 25, at 481.

[72] Li Ch'ang-ling, as quoted in T. Y. CH'EN, *supra* note 34, p. 144; N. NIIDA, *supra* note 3, at 106.

[73] K. CHEN, *supra* note 6, at 240, 242.

[74] TAIWAN SHIHŌ, Vol. 2, 378; S. SHIGA *supra* note 25, at 476.

was very weak, and it was almost impossible to restrict divorce by invoking them.[75]

The Three Limitations

Having observed mourning for the parents-in-law was one of the restrictions on divorce, because the husband owed a debt of gratitude to a wife who had done so.[76]

A husband who had been poor and humble when he married was restricted in divorcing his wife if he had become rich and noble later. It was considered a violation of the Rules of Propriety *(Li)* for a rich man to abandon a wife who had shared a time of poverty.[77]

Divorce was also restricted if the wife had no family to return to. Family in this sense was interpreted to mean the persons who could have presided over the marriage.[78] The persons who would have been qualified to preside over the marriage were: paternal and maternal grandparents, parents, paternal and maternal uncles, brothers, and maternal aunts and cousins.[79] However, the wife could not be sent back to maternal uncles, aunts, or cousins who did not live together nor own property together, even if they had presided over the marriage.[80]

Penalties for Illegal Divorce

Once the system of the Seven Conditions and Three Limitations had been provided, punishments for divorce without grounds were also initiated. Although there is no evidence of such punishments in the Han period, they were provided in subsequent times.

During the T'ang and Sung periods the penalty for divorcing a wife without grounds was imprisonment for one and one-half years; if there were grounds under the Seven Conditions, but one of the Three Limitations also applied, the penalty was one hundred blows; the divorce was also to be made void, and the wife was returned to her husband.[81]

Punishments for illegal divorce were made lighter during the Ming and Ch'ing periods. For divorce without grounds the penalty was eighty blows; for divorcing when one of the Three Limitations applied, the penalty was to be two degrees less; the divorce was to be voided, and the wife was to be returned.[82] However, the law against divorce without grounds was not strictly

---

[75] TAIWAN SHIHŌ, Vol. 2, 379.
[76] KUNG-YANG-CHUAN.
[77] RYŌSHUGE quoting HAN-SHU.
[78] RYŌSHUGE (Koryō 10, Shichishutsu jō).
[79] YŌRORYŌ (Koryō 10, Kajo jō).
[80] T'ANG-LING (T'ang Ordinances).
[81] T'ANG-LÜ and SUNG HSING-T'UNG in Hu-hun-lü; Ch'i wu ch'i-ch'u t'iao.
[82] MING-LÜ and CH'ING-LÜ (Hu-lü, Hun-yin-men, Ch'u-ch'i t'iao).

enforced. It was also rare for the wife's family to bring such cases to the attention of the competent authorities.[83]

BREAKING THE BOND

Traditionally, husband and wife were united by *yi*, the Bond of Righteousness; if an act violating this principle were committed, it constituted Breaking the Bond *(yi-chüeh)*.[84] The system of Breaking the Bond *(yi-chüeh)* designated certain situations in which divorce was compulsory; in these cases the competent officials were authorized to force the couple involved to divorce.[85] This system allowed for divorce in cases in which the husband was at fault without conflicting with the moral principle that the wife could not divorce the husband.[86] If the husband committed an act that constituted Breaking the Bond, the competent official rather than the wife would demand the divorce.

Breaking the Bond thus gave some relief to the wife. It was possible to increase the concrete causes included in such an abstract concept as Breaking the Bond, but it was impossible under the traditional concept of marriage to establish anything similar to the Seven Conditions in favor of the wife.

It is not known whether Breaking the Bond was included in the Rules of Propriety *(Li)*, but it was in existence as early as the Han period. The provisions for Breaking the Bond were probably included in the Han Code *(Lü)* or Ordinances *(Ling)*, but no definite evidence is available. The earliest extant statutes on Breaking the Bond are contained in the T'ang Code and Ordinances *(T'ang Lü Ling)*.

Grounds for Breaking the Bond

The only specific ground for Breaking the Bond that has been found in the Han period was killing of the wife's parents.[87]

During the T'ang and Sung periods the grounds were as follows:[88]

1. Acts committed by the husband:
   a. Beating the wife's parents or grandparents.
   b. Killing the wife's brothers, sisters, maternal grandparents, paternal uncles and their wives, and paternal aunts.
   c. Committing adultery with the wife's mother.

---

[83] TAIWAN SHIHŌ, Vol. 2, 376.

[84] T'ANG-LÜ SU-YI (Hu-hun, Yi-chueh li-chih t'iao); CH'ING-LÜ (Hu-lü Hun-yin-men, Ch'u-ch'i t'iao).

[85] TAIWAN SHIHŌ, Vol. 2, 376–377.

[86] TAI, *supra* note 2, at 239; S. SHIGA, *supra* note 25, at 478.

[87] PAI-HU-T'UNG, Chüan 4, No. 1, Chia Ch'u (Marrying a Wife).

[88] N. NIIDA, TŌREI SHŪI (Reconstruction of T'ang Ordinances) (1933) hereinafter TOREI SHŪI, p. 255.

2. Acts committed by the wife:

    a. Beating or cursing the husband's parents or grandparents.

    b. Beating or injuring the husband's grandparents, brothers, sisters, paternal uncles and their wives, and paternal aunts.

    c. Committing adultery with the husband's relatives who were within the five ranks of mourning *(szu-ma)*.

    d. Attempting to harm or kill the husband.

3. Acts committed by the close relatives of either the husband or wife: mutual killing between the paternal grandparents, parents, maternal grandparents, paternal uncles and their wives, paternal aunts, brothers, and sisters of both husband and wife.

All of these grounds were based on infringement of honor or bodily harm to relatives, besides the husband, whose original mourning dress was to be worn for one year *(ch'i-ch'in)* and those who were regarded as *ch'i-ch'in* in law although not actually as *ch'i-ch'in*.[89] The offenses that constituted Breaking the Bond when committed by the wife were less serious than those committed by the husband. The husband was thus still favored in this system of divorce. Beating or killing a concubine's relatives did not constitute Breaking the Bond by the husband, because a concubine's status was lower than that of a wife. However, an offense committed by a concubine against the husband's relatives constituted an even more serious crime than one committed by the wife.[90] A wife or concubine could also be divorced on grounds of Breaking the Board after the death of the husband.[91] All of the grounds for Breaking the Bond were applicable during the engagement period as well as after the marriage.[92] They were also applicable even when the crime involved had been pardoned.[93]

The term "beating" in these provisions included fighting between two people as well as unprovoked assault by one person or another.[94] The interpretation of "killing" included unintentional killing in a fight as well as murder.[95] "Attempting to harm the husband" included false accusation in addition to bodily harm.[96] "Cursing the husband's grandparents or parents"

---

[89] T'ANG-LÜ T'UNG-LUN, pp. 43 *et seq.* and pp. 463 *et seq.*

[90] RYŌSHŪGE, Vol. 10 (Koryō, Tsuma no Sohubo o naguru jo).

[91] RYŌSHŪGE *ibid.;* Taiwan Shihō, p. 376.

[92] TŌREI SHŪI, p. 255.

[93] *Id.*

[94] T'ANG-LÜ, Tou-sung-lü (Laws on Fighting and Litigation), Su-yi (Commentary), Huang-chia t'an-mien yi-shang ch'in t'iao (Provision on Imperial Relatives of Three Months Mourning and Above).

[95] T'ANG-LÜ, Ming-li lü (General Provisions and Established Precedents), Su-yi (Commentaries), Huang-t'ai-tzu-fei t'iao (Provisions on Concubines for Imperial Princes).

[96] RYŌSHŪGE, *supra* note 90.

could not be used as a ground for divorce unless the parents-in-law instituted action against the wife; if they did not complain, the offense was not a valid ground.[97]

At first the grounds for Breaking the Bond were probably limited to those enumerated above. An important step forward was made in divorce law when certain grounds favoring the wife were made by additions to the T'ang Code *(T'ang-Lü)* and by interpretations contained in the commentaries or the code *(Su-Yi)*. The new grounds for Breaking the Bond concerned acts committed by the husband as follows: (1) marrying one's wife or concubine to someone else, (2) selling one's wife as a slave, and (3) the husband, intending to influence officials, marries his wife or concubine to an official having jurisdiction over him to prevent legal action against him.[98]

By the Ming and Ch'ing periods the grounds for divorce under Breaking the Bond were increased still further. The Ming and Ch'ing codes were based on the laws of the Yüan period, which in turn were based on the old Chin code as well as the T'ang and Sung laws. Some of the additional grounds for Breaking the Bond in Yüan law were as follows:[99]

1. Acts committed by the husband or his parents:

   a. Accepting money or property in return for allowing the wife or concubine to be a prostitute.

   b. Compelling the wife or concubine to become a prostitute.

   c. Accepting money or property in return for marrying the wife to someone else.

   d. Maltreating the wife and accusing her of adultery because their relationship is not harmonious.

   e. Falsely accusing the wife's father of committing incest with her.

   f. Raping a stepdaughter or attempting to rape a stepson's wife.

   g. When the husband's father abuses his power by forcing or attempting to force his daughter-in-law to commit adultery with him.

   h. Beating or injuring the wife or concubine either without reasonable cause, or because the parents-in-law are not pleased with her.

2. Acts committed by the wife:

   a. Committing adultery for a second time.

   b. Committing adultery with the husband's brothers.

---

[97] T'ANG-Lü, Tou-sung-lü Ch'i-ch'ieh ou-li ku-fu fu-mu t'iao (Wife and Secondary Wives Beat and Curse Their Late Husbands' Parents); RYŌSHUGE, *ibid.*

[98] T'ANG-Lü, Hu-hun-lü, Ho-ch'ü jen-ch'i t'iao (Provisions on Harmonizing with and Marrying Another Person's Wife).

[99] YÜAN-SHIH (History of the Yuan dynasty), Hsing-fa-chih (Treatise on Ministry of Justice).

    c. Falsely accusing the father-in-law of having committed adultery with her by abusing his power, and thus causing the father-in-law to be tortured by the authorities.

    d. Conspiring with a lover and falsely obtaining a divorce under ground (1) (g) above.

    e. Falsely accusing the husband of committing a serious crime after having run away from his home and having been convicted therefor.

    f. Murdering a concubine's son.

Since the grounds for acts committed by the wife, with the exception of (2) (f), could have been construed under the Seven Conditions, the only new grounds for Breaking the Bond were actually for acts committed by the husband and/or his parents. Thus, the wife's position in divorce law was again improved.

The law of the Ming and Ch'ing dynasties was influenced by Yüan law. Besides the grounds for Breaking the Bond in the T''ang Code and Ordinances (*T'ang Lü Ling*) which were discussed above, there were added several grounds for Breaking the Bond, which we can divide into the criminal acts of the husband and his parents and grandparents:

1. Acts committed by the husband:

    a. Husband pledges his wife or concubine or rents them to another.

    b. Husband falsely claims that his wife or concubine are his sisters and married them to another.

    c. Husband allows his wife or concubine to commit adultery.

    d. Husband forces his wife or concubine to commit adultery.

    e. Husband sells his wife to another as a wife.

    f. Husband sells his wife to the man with which she committed adultery.

    g. Husband sells his wife or concubine to another as a slave.

    h. Husband marries his wife or concubine to an official having jurisdiction over him.

2. Acts committed by the husband's parents or grandparents:

    a. Husband's parents or grandparents allow or force his wife or concubine to commit adultery.

    b. Without reason beat the wife or concubine of the husband so that they are seriously injured.

Effects

The effects to be discussed in this section are those resulting from acts that constituted Breaking the Bond. The effects of a judgment granting divorce on the grounds of Breaking the Bond will be discussed later.

All acts that constituted grounds for Breaking the Bond were criminal acts, as well as grounds for compulsory divorce. The civil law effects of such an act were distinguished from the criminal effects. Even if the crime were pardoned, divorce was still required.[100]

A marriage was regarded as being legally terminated as soon as an act that constituted Breaking the Bond took place, even though the couple had not yet been separated.[101] If a husband committed a crime requiring banishment, the wife would ordinarily be banished with him; but if the crime also constituted Breaking the Bond, the couple were automatically divorced, and the wife was not banished with her husband. Divorce was not allowed under the Seven Conditions in these cases, because the grounds could be too easily falsified.[102]

In a case in the Sung period, a man charged his daughter-in-law with being unfilial, but upon investigation it was found that he had participated in the murder of her father. Since that crime had been pardoned, the daughter-in-law was at first declared guilty of being unfilial. However, upon review by a higher official, she was declared innocent since the father-in-law's crime had constituted Breaking the Bond. The marriage was regarded as having become legally invalid after the father-in-law's crime, and therefore, the daughter-in-law could not be charged with being unfilial.[103]

In cases in which a husband marries his wife to someone else, the civil effect was that both marriages were terminated. The first marriage was divorced because of Breaking the Bond, and the second was annulled.[104]

By the time of the Ming and Ch'ing codes the effect of compulsory divorce under Breaking the Bond had been modified to consider the intentions of the couple involved. Divorce was still compulsory on certain grounds, but it was optional on others. Some of the grounds on which divorce was optional were: (1) adultery committed by a wife or concubine through mutual consent or inducement; (2) the wife or concubine beats the husband; (3) the husband beats and injures the wife; (4) the wife's parents expel the son-in-law (who married matrilocally), and remarry their daughter to someone else.

Failure to Divorce

All grounds for Breaking the Bond were also criminal acts, and the competent official usually ordered a divorce upon conviction of one of the parties involved in the criminal offense. If the couple failed to divorce when so

---

[100] T'ang hu-ling, Yi-chüeh t'iao (Provision on Breaking the Bond).

[101] T'ang-lü su-yi, Ming-li-lü, Fan-liu ying-p'ei t'iao (Provision on Breaking the Law That Should be Punished by Banishment).

[102] *Id.*

[103] Chou Mi, Ch'i-tung yeh-yü (Unfounded talk), Vol. 8 (Sung dynasty, n.d.); N. Niida, *supra* note 3, at 684.

[104] T'ang-lü (Hu-hun-lü, Ho-ch'u jen-ch'i t'iao).

ordered, they were punished. Such failure to divorce was punished by imprisonment for one year in the T'ang and Sung periods.[105]

Only when there had been a judgment of divorce on the grounds of Breaking the Bond could punishment for failure to divorce be inflicted. There is no evidence to determine whether a competent official could take the initiative and render a judgment of divorce on grounds of Breaking the Bond, if the parties involved did not bring suit for the criminal offense.

When a couple failed to divorce when ordered to do so, the one responsible for the refusal was to be punished. If both husband and wife were unwilling to divorce, the one who took the initiative in refusing to divorce was to be considered the principal offender and the other the accomplice; the punishment for an accomplice was usually one degree less.[106]

In the Ming and Ch'ing periods the punishment for failure to divorce when divorce was required was eighty blows.[107] As in the T'ang and Sung periods, this offense referred only to cases in which a final judgment of divorce had been rendered.[108] The crimes which were grounds for Breaking the Bond and defiance of an official order for divorce were usually treated as though they had occurred at the same time; the guilty party received the heavier penalty of the two offenses.[109]

THE WIFE'S ARBITRARY DEPARTURE

From the Han through the Ch'ing periods it was not permissible for a wife to leave her husband of her own will; a husband was allowed to divorce his wife, but generally a wife was not allowed to divorce her husband.[110] Even if the husband had been convicted of a crime, such as stealing, he could not be divorced by his wife. (Divorce for offenses committed by the husband under Breaking the Bond was not regarded as divorce initiated by the wife.)

In the T'ang period punishment for a wife or concubine who arbitrarily left her husband was imprisonment for two years; if she had also remarried, the punishment was increased to three years imprisonment.[111] However, if the wife left temporarily in anger because of a dispute, it was not considered an arbitrary departure.

---

[105] T'ANG-LÜ SU-YI and SUNG-HSING-T'UNG Hu-hun-lü, Yi-chüeh li-chih t'iao (Breaking the Bond and Divorcing Therefrom).

[106] T'ANG-LÜ SU-YI; TAI, T'ANG-LÜ T'UNG-LUN, supra pp. 126, 377.

[107] MING-LÜ and CH'ING-LÜ (Hun-yin men, ch'u-ch'i t'iao).

[108] MING-LÜ CHI-CHIEH; TAIWAN SHIHŌ, 375.

[109] MING-LI-LÜ, Erh-tsui chü-fa yi chung-lun t'iao, and T'u-liu-jen yü fan-tsui t'iao.

[110] PAI-HU-T'UNG (Vol. 9, Chia-ch'u); CH'ING-LÜ, Chi-chieh, Hu-lü, Hun-yin-men, Ch'u-ch'i t'iao; CH'ING-LÜ, Chi-chu (Ch'ing Code, Official Commentary), Hu-lü, Hun-yin-men, Ch'u-ch'i t'iao.

[111] T'ANG-LÜ and SUNG-HSING-T'UNG, Hu-hun-lü, Yi-chüeh li-chih t'iao.

In cases of illegal remarriage sponsored by the wife's parents, the wife would be punished only for the crime of arbitrary departure, and her parents would be punished with the penalty for illegal remarriage. If the illegal remarriage were sponsored by a mourning relative in the closest degree, *(ch'i-ch'in)*, the *ch'i-ch'in* would be considered the principal offender and the wife as the abettor; the wife's penalty in such cases was reduced by one degree.

In Hou-Chou of Wu-Tai times (A.D. 907–960) there was a rescript issued on the crime of arbitrary departure in the Fifth Year of Hsien-Te, which preceded the Sung period. There were four differences between the *Hou-Chou Ch'ih* and the T'ang Code: (1) a distinction was made between a wife and a concubine, with punishment for the latter being one degree less; (2) the penalty for arbitrary departure was increased to imprisonment for three years, and the penalty for remarriage was increased to banishment for a distance of three thousand *li;* (3) the man who was married to the wife illegally received the same punishment as the wife, if he had had previous knowledge; punishment was reduced one degree if he only learned of it afterwards; and there was no punishment if he had had no knowledge of the wife's legal marriage; (4) annulment of the illegal marriage was stipulated. In the T'ang period even if the illegal marriage were pardoned, annulment was still required.[112]

During the Nan-Sung period if a wife left her husband arbitrarily and committed adultery, she was treated as though she had remarried illegally; if she had engaged in prostitution, the act was treated as though it were adultery, and it could not be pardoned; the man involved was not punished.[113]

In the Yüan period a wife who left her husband arbitrarily, even to become a nun, was to be sentenced sixty-seven blows and returned to her husband.[114]

The Ming and Ch'ing codes provided a penalty of one hundred blows for arbitrary departure, which is lighter than the T'ang Code. However, if the wife had remarried illegally, the penalty was death by hanging, which was much heavier than the T'ang Code.[115] According to the interpretation in the Ch'ing code, *Chi-Chu,* the penalty for illegal remarriage was more severe because of the malicious intention involved. In these cases simply maintaining an illegitimate relationship with a man was not considered remarriage; only a formal marriage violated the law.

---

[112] T'ANG-LÜ and SUNG HSING-T'UNG, Hu-hun-lü, Ch'ü t'ao-wang fu-nü t'iao (Provisions for Punishing a Man who Marries a Woman who Runs Away [from her husband]).

[113] NAN-SUNG (Southern Sung), Ch'ing-yüan, T'iao-fa Shih-lei (Classification of Legal Matters), Chüan 80, Tsa-men (Miscellaneous Section), Chu-se fan-chien (All Classes of the Crime of Illicit Sexual Relations).

[114] YÜAN-SHIH, Hsing-fa-chih (Treatise on Criminal Law), Hu-hun (Household and Marriage).

[115] MING-LÜ and CH'ING-LÜ, Hu-lü Hun-yin-men, Ch'u-ch'i t'iao.

If a husband had deserted his wife for a period less than that required for
a divorce and if the wife left his house without legal permission, the penalty
was eighty blows. If the wife also remarried illegally, the penalty was still only
one hundred blows in this case. The punishment for a concubine was two
degrees less. However, the husband's absence had to be for reasons falling
within the legal definition of desertion and not for reasons of business or
visits to relatives. In each case of this type the competent official was to
decide, according to the circumstances, whether to annul the second marriage
and return the wife to the first husband. If the circumstances warranted,
the second marriage could be validated.[116]

In ordinary cases of arbitrary departure or illegal remarriage, the husband
could decide whether to divorce the wife or allow her to return.

THE WIFE'S SUIT FOR DIVORCE

Disappearance, specific crimes, and serious maltreatment by the husband,
were the only grounds on which the wife was allowed to sue for divorce.

During the T'ang period if a man disappeared in the barbarian areas, it
was necessary for his wife to wait five years if they had children, or three years
if they did not, before she could sue for divorce and remarry. If a man had
deserted his family, his wife had to wait three years if they had children, or
two years if they did not.[117]

The waiting period in cases of disappearance or desertion in the Sung period
was six years. However, an Imperial rescript issued on the first month of 1014
(Seventh Year of Ta-Chung Hsiang-Fu), allowed a wife to sue for divorce
earlier if her husband had taken his properties with him when he deserted
and thus left her unable to support herself.[118] For a woman in the Nan-Sung
period whose husband had been banished and had not been heard from, the
waiting period was three years.[119]

A wife in the Yüan period who had been deserted for five years could
obtain a divorce without returning any of the marriage gifts.[120] During the

---

[116] CH'ING-LÜ, Chi-chu, Hu-lü, Hun-yin-men, Ch'u-chi t'iao.

[117] YORŌRYŌ, Koryō 10; N. NIIDA, supra note 3, at 707.

[118] Sung Dynasty, HSU TZU-CHIH T'UNG-CHIEN (CH'ANG-PIEN) (Supplemental
Lengthy Edition of the Tzu-Chih T'ung-Chien), Vol. 82, Chen-tsung, and Vol. 295
Shen-tsung, Twelfth Month, The First Year of Yüan-feng; N. NIIDA, supra note 3,
at 707.

[119] N. NIIDA, supra note 3, at 706; N. Niida, Seimeishu kokonmon no kenkyu, TŌHŌ
GAKUHŌ (Tokyo), Vol. 4, p. 147.

[120] T'UNG-CHIH T'IAO-KE (Comprehensive Institutes, Rules and Regulations), Chüan
4, Hu-ling, chia-ch'ü (Household Ordinances, Marriage), Second Month, The Eighth
Year of Chih-yüan.

Ming and Ch'ing periods a wife who had been deserted for three years could also obtain a divorce without returning any of the marriage gifts.[121]

The absence of a husband had to meet the following requirements to be termed desertion: (1) There had to be no legitimate reason for his absence. Being away to engage in trade or to visit relatives, even for several years, did not constitute desertion. (2) There had to have been no correspondence with him, and his whereabouts and whether he were alive or dead had to be unknown. (3) The wife had to be without any means of support.

In matrilocal marriages the marriage contract sometimes stipulated that absence of the son-in-law for sixty or one hundred days would be considered desertion, and the wife would automatically be free to remarry. However, these provisions were declared invalid, since they shortened the waiting period and stipulated prior conditions for divorce.[122]

There has been a similar custom in recent times in which a widow with small children marries a man who will stay in her home and cultivate her land. The marriage contract in these cases stipulates that, if the husband is lazy or a gambler, the wife can divorce him and remarry.[123] These contracts were also considered invalid.

If a husband did not support his family because of laziness, disability, or mental disease, the wife could not divorce him. She could seek support from relatives or return to her home temporarily, but she was required to return to her husband whenever he became willing to support her.[124] If a wife were denied food or clothing, she could consult with relatives or institute a suit to obtain food and clothes.[125]

The types of banishment that could be construed as desertion in the Sung period were cases in which a man had been given a death penalty, had been pardoned, and then been banished to a remote area, or cases in which a man had been convicted of some crime which had been listed in the household registrations, and put under control, and banished.[126] In both these types of banishments the wife was allowed to sue for divorce after a certain period of time.

[121] Ming hu-ling and Ch'ing-lü (Hu-lü, Hun-yin-men, Ch'u-ch'i t'iao, Fu-li).

[122] T'ung-chih t'iao-ke, Chüan 4, Hu-ling, chia-ch'ü.

[123] Shūkanroku, p. 812, the custom in Chiang-hsi Province, Tê-an hsien (Tê-an district).

[124] Shūkanroku, p. 767.

[125] Taiwan Kanshū Kenkyūkai (Research Society of Customs in Taiwan), Taiwan Kanshū Kiji (Reports on customs in Taiwan) (1904), Vol. 3, No. 12, p. 36.

[126] Li-tai hsing-fa k'ao (An examination of the criminal law of successive dynasties), Fen-k'ao 9 (Subdivision 9), contained in Shen Chi-yi hsien-sheng yi-shu (Chia-pien) (Works left by Sh'en Chi-yi); N. Niida, Chūgoku hōseishi kenkyū (Research on Chinese legal history) (1959–1967), Keihō (Criminal Law), p. 124.

METHODS OF DIVORCE

There is no doubt that divorces were usually initiated by the husband without the necessity of bringing the matter before a competent official. However, if the wife refused to accept the divorce and brought the matter before a competent official, the official would judge whether divorce was proper.[127]

When a man wished to divorce his wife, it was necessary for him to first obtain permission from his parents or grandparents.[128] If the grandparents or parents were no longer alive, the permission of other close *ch'i-ch'in* relatives of superior rank should be sought.[129] Only if no one in these categories existed could a man divorce his wife entirely on his own. If these relatives existed and their consent were not obtained, the divorce was not valid. However, if these relatives learned of the divorce afterwards but took no action for three months, they could no longer object.[130] This provision applied to all types of divorce.

When divorcing a wife, the husband was to prepare a document to that effect. The divorce document was to be cosigned by the husband's superior or other close relatives and neighbors. The fingerprints of those who could not write were to be affixed to the document.[131] Cosignatures simply certify the fact of divorce; they do not certify consent. However, if a cosigner were entitled to give consent, the signature would indicate that it had been given.

The divorce document was needed to remove the name of the divorced wife from the official household registration; it was not a requirement for the actual divorce.[132] In the Yüan period a divorce document was necessary to obtain a license from the authorities so that the wife could return to her own home and remarry.[133] The law prohibited the use of fingerprints in place of a document.[134] During the early Ch'ing period there was a regulation stating that divorces did not have to be reported unless there was a special situation that needed to be reviewed and settled.[135]

In the Ch'ing period it was customary for divorce documents to be executed. Among the lower and middle classes such a document would be given to the wife's family as evidence to prevent future disputes. However, the upper

---

[127] S. SHIGA, *supra* note 25, at 477.

[128] YORŌRYŌ (Vol. 10, Koryō, senyu jō); N. NIIDA, *supra* note 3, at 685.

[129] RYŌSHUGE (Vol. 10, Koryō, senyu jō).

[130] YORŌRYŌ (Koryō 10, Kajo kisai jō); N. NIIDA, *supra* note 3, at 685.

[131] YORŌRYŌ (Koryō 10, Scichishutsu jō).

[132] RYŌSHUGE (Koryō 10, Shichishutsu jō).

[133] YÜAN-TIEN-CHANG (18, Hu-pu (Board of Households) 4, Hsiu-ch'i (Divorce)).

[134] YÜAN-SHIH, Hsing-fa chih (Hu-hun).

[135] TA-CH'ING HUI-TIEN SHIH-LI (Established Precedents and Collected Institutes of the Great Ch'ing Dynasty), Chüan 756, Ch'u-chi t'iao.

classes did not like to make divorce documents; usually, the husband merely notified the wife's family and asked them to take her back.[136]

   There were three kinds of divorce documents: (1) a simple divorce document *(hsiu-shu)*; (2) a ransom document *(shu-shen-tzu)*; and (3) a document for the remarriage or sale of the wife *(chia-mai-tzu)*. Ransom documents were the most frequently used, with those for the remarriage or sale of the wife next.

   The simple divorce document *(hsiu-shu)* involved no exchange of money and was executed by the husband. It stated the reason for the divorce, that marital relations had been terminated, and that the wife was free to remarry. One document of this nature stated that a certain Chiang Te was divorcing his wife because of her many faults, but was unwilling to disclose them out of consideration for her. Chiang Te was willing to send her back to her own family and had no objection if she wished to remarry. A fingerprint was affixed to the document in place of a signature.[137] Similar documents were made in Taiwan during the Ch'ing period, stating the grounds for the divorce, that the wife was free to remarry, and that the document was executed to provide evidence of divorce in case an oral statement was not enough. Fingerprints were also affixed.[138]

   Fingerprints, palm prints, and footprints have been used on divorce documents since the Sung period.[139] The left palm print of the husband was usually used, and characters were written between the fingers to signify that both parties were willing and would not change their minds later.[140] The hand was primarily a symbol of trustworthiness, as well as a symbol for a person.[141]

   Ransom documents *(shu-shen-tzu)* were used for most divorces, regardless of the grounds involved. The method of ransoming was popular, because the husband could recover the marriage gift and the wife could be relieved of responsibility for the divorce. Ransom documents only stated that the husband and wife were not harmonious; the actual ground for the divorce was not mentioned. Only the fact that a certain sum of money had been paid and accepted would be clearly stated.

---

[136] KYŪKAN MONDŌ (Questions and Answers on Old Customs), in KANSHŪ KIJI, Vol. 2, No. 6, at 27.

[137] CHIN-KU CH'I-KUAN (Section 23, Chiang-hsing-ko chung-hui chen-chu-shan).

[138] SHIHŌ SANKŌ, Vol. 2, No. 1, at 315–316.

[139] N. NIIDA, *supra* note 29, at 419 *et seq.* Shukanroku, p. 714; N. NIIDA, *supra* note 71, at 335 *et. seq.*

[140] CH'ING-P'ING-SHAN-T'ANG HUA-PEN *(K'uai-tsui li ts'ui-lien chi)*, based on what is quoted in N. NIIDA, *supra* note 3, at 682; TAIWAN SHIHŌ, Vol. 1 *supra* note 5, at 182 *et seq.*

[141] N. NIIDA, *Min Shin jidai no hitouri oyobi hitojichi bunsho no kenkyū* (Research on documents re the sale and pawning of people in the Ch'ing and Ming dynasties), SHIGAKU ZASSHI (Journal of Historical Studies), Vol. 46, No. 6, at 81 *et seq.*

In cases of ransom the husband's family would first negotiate with the wife's family. Once the wife's family had consented to ransom her, the amount would usually be negotiated through a go-between. As soon as the husband had accepted the ransom money, he would execute a divorce document and give it to the wife's family. The document sometimes stated that the ransom money and the wife had been exchanged at the same time. The document also stated that marital relations had been terminated forever and sometimes specifically gave permission for the wife to remarry.[142]

The ransom document also gave certain guarantees. The husband guaranteed that he would not reclaim the wife and that, if there was any such trouble, the wife's family would not be responsible. There was a clause stating that there had been no coercion or abduction by the wife's family. There was often a clause stating that the wife's family would not be responsible if she died after her return to her family home. This meant that if the husband decided to dissolve the ransom contract, the wife's family would not be responsible if they could not return her.[143]

The return of the original marriage contract was usually not specified in ransom documents. However, in Hehlungchiang Province the wife was not allowed to remarry unless the husband's family returned the original marriage contract.[144]

Ransom contracts that specifically allowed the wife to remarry (shu-hui kai-chia-tzu) differed slightly from ordinary ransom contracts. A higher ransom price was usually paid and wishes for happiness, luck, prosperity, and innumerable sons and grandsons were included in the document.[145] In most cases the go-between would also give additional personal guarantees against any future trouble and would affix his fingerprint to the document.

Divorce documents contracting for the remarriage or sale of the wife by the husband (chia-mai-tzu), instead of returning her to her own family, were used when the wife had committed a serious offense such as adultery, or illegal remarriage. Sometimes, however, the wife was sold for remarriage because the husband's family was too poor, or because the couple did not get along well.[146]

Whenever a husband was going to negotiate the remarriage or sale of his wife, he would first ask the wife's family to ransom her. If the wife's family was unwilling, or unable, to ransom her, the husband would then proceed to

---

[142] N. NIIDA, supra note 29, at 114.

[143] N. NIIDA, supra note 140, Vol. 46, No. 5, at 49.

[144] Ch'ing-kang Hsien (Ch'ing-kang District), SHŪKANROKU, 660; Lan-hsi Hsien (Lan-hsi District), SHŪKANROKU, 647.

[145] SHIHŌ SANKŌ, 317; Kai-chia-tzu reported in SHIHŌ SANKŌ, Vol. 2, lower part, at 177.

[146] SHŪKANROKU, 853 and 959; SHIHŌ SANKŌ, Vol. 2, No. 2, at 177.

negotiate her remarriage, or sale. In these cases the consent of the wife usually had to be obtained.[147] The contract would be executed by the husband and signed by members of his family, the go-between, and witnesses; it was then given to the new husband. A print of the husband's left palm was usually affixed at the end of the document; the palm would be completely opened to show that the husband would not reconsider and try to reclaim his wife.[148] In these cases the marriage price or gift was accepted by the first husband; the wife's family received no part of it. The terms of guarantee were the same in these contracts as in ransom contracts, and the go-between was held responsible to the new husband.

When a widow wished to return to her own family or remarry, she first had to obtain what amounted to a divorce from her deceased husband's family. In most cases the widow's family would pay ransom, and a document of ordinary ransom or ransom for remarriage would be executed.[149] These ransom documents usually stated that the widow would have no claim on the deceased husband's property, and that any children she might have would not belong to the deceased husband's family.[150]

The remarriage or sale of a widow by the deceased husband's family was considered shameful in the Ch'ing period.[151] In such cases the marriage price would be shared by the widow's family and her deceased husband's family.[152] Divorce and remarriage documents of this nature were considered very unlucky, and the go-between would rarely use his real name when he executed one.[153] It was also necessary to give 2 or 3 percent of the marriage price to the town office to prevent the townspeople from extorting money from the wedding party with threats of stopping the marriage.[154]

However, according to Ch'ing law a widow was to be allowed to remarry freely. When she wished to remarry, her parents-in-law were to negotiate the matter and accept the marriage gift. If there was no one in the deceased husband's family qualified to preside over the remarriage, the widow's family was to do so. If any of the widow's family or the deceased husband's family made trouble, they were to be punished.[155] In some cases in which the widow's family presided over the remarriage they would accept all of the marriage gift.[156] In other cases the widow's family would preside over the

---

[147] KANSHŪ KIJI, Vol. 5, No. 6, at 38.
[148] KANSHŪ KIJI, Vol. 1, No. 9, at 48.
[149] SHŪKANROKU, 725, 731, and 751.
[150] SHIHŌ SANKŌ.
[151] T. Y. CHEN, *supra* note 34, 147.
[152] SHŪKANROKU, 738, 739, 777 and 785.
[153] SHŪKANROKU, 783.
[154] SHŪKANROKU, 752.
[155] SHŪKANROKU, 930.
[156] SHŪKANROKU, 645.

remarriage, but the marriage gift would go to the deceased husband's family.[157] The contracts for the remarriage or sale of a widow were the same as those for the remarriage or sale of a wife.

EFFECTS OF DIVORCE

Family Status

Divorce, of course, terminated the relationship between husband and wife, and between their respective families. However, the wife was still prohibited from marrying any of her former husband's close relatives. Such marriages were annulled, and punishments were inflicted according to the closeness of the relative involved.[158]

The relationship between children and their parents continued to exist after divorce.[159] Blood ties could not be terminated, regardless of the reason for divorce. A divorced wife also continued to be a mother-in-law to her children's spouses.[160]

The husband usually had custody of the children after divorce, although there was no law regulating custody. However, the wife could have custody through a special agreement, or under special circumstances such as the husband's inability to provide a proper home for them.[161]

If the wife were pregnant at the time of the divorce, the custody of the child could be disputed since the wife could remarry immediately after divorce.[162] Usually the custody of such a child would be determined by the mother's residence at the time of birth.[163] A child born before the mother's remarriage would belong to her family as a child born out of wedlock.[164] According to some views, however, a child born during the interval between divorce and remarriage should be adopted by the new husband.[165]

Property

The marriage gift. The custom of the marriage gift strongly resembled a purchase and sale, especially in the middle and lower classes.[166] Since the gift was taken from the husband's family property and exchanged for the bride,

---

[157] SHŪKANROKU, 899, 930, and 960.

[158] T'ANG-LÜ and SUNG-HSING T'UNG, Hu-hun-lü, wei t'an-mien ch'i chia-ch'u t'iao.

[159] T'ANG LÜ and SUNG-HSING-T'UNG SU-YI, Ming-li-lü, yi li ch'u-kuan t'iao.

[160] TOU-SUNG LÜ (Ch'i-ch'ieh ou-li ku-fu fu-mu t'iao).

[161] WEI-NAN WEN-CHI, Yi-chien-chih, and CH'ING-MING-CHI as quoted in N. NIIDA, BUNSHO, 496 et seq.

[162] TAIWAN SHIHŌ, Vol. 2, 385; KANSHŪ KIJI, Vol. 2, No. 12, at 30.

[163] N. NIIDA, supra note 71, at 196 and 352.

[164] TAIWAN SHIHŌ, Vol. 2, 386; KANSHŪ KIJI, Vol. 2, No. 12, at 34.

[165] S. SHIGA, supra note 25, at 502.

[166] TAIWAN SHIHŌ, Vol. 2, 296 et seq; N. NIIDA, supra note 3, at 633 et seq.

she could not be allowed to leave his family without some replacement of the original expenditure.[167] The marriage gift thus served as a sort of material evidence, and in cases of divorce its return would be demanded.[168] The ransom money paid to the husband's family in divorce cases was actually a return of a portion of the marriage gift.[169]

The dowry. The dowry *(chuang-lien* or *chia-chuang)* was generally considered as the property that the wife brought with her at the time of marriage, such as furniture, clothing, ornaments, servants, money, and land. The bride's family usually prepared a list of the dowry and delivered it to the groom's family; immovable property was listed in a separate document that stated whether ownership or only the right of use of the land had been given.[170] The dowry was not added to the husband's family property and could not be distributed during a family division of property.[171] The ownership of the dowry usually was retained by the wife, although the husband usually administered it.[172] There were some cases in which ownership of the dowry was transferred to the husband by special agreements, but this was not the accepted custom.

From the Han through the T'ang periods the dowry was to be returned if the wife were divorced.[173] Even children born to the serving maids whom the wife had brought with her at the time of her marriage were to be returned. From the Yüan through the Ch'ing periods, however, the law allowed the husband to retain the dowry when he divorced his wife; this also applied to widows who remarried.[174] In actual practice, however, the dowry was usually returned, and the law of the Ch'ing period was later changed to conform to custom.[175] The return of the dowry was required in cases of compulsory divorce, as well as divorce by mutual consent.[176]

Sometimes, when a wife with a son was divorced, she would take with her only part of the dowry and leave a part, such as immovable property, with the husband's family for the benefit of her son.[177] However, this was usually by

---

[167] S. SHIGA, *supra* note 25, at 514.

[168] TAI, CH'IN-SHU-FA, *supra* note 64; KANSHŪ KIJI, Vol. 3, No. 12, at 36.

[169] SHIHŌ SANKŌ, 316 *et seq.*

[170] TAIWAN SHIHŌ, Vol. 2, 354.

[171] S. SHIGA, *supra* note 25, at 513; N. NIIDA, *supra* note 3, at 663; Y. TAI, *Kinsei Shina oyobi Taiwan no kazoku kyōsansei* (The common family property system in modern China and Taiwan), 52, HOGAKU KYŌKAI ZASSHI, No. 11, 90.

[172] Y. TAI, *supra* note 171, at 90; Y. TAI, CH'IN-SHU-FA, *supra* note 64, p. 129 *et seq.*

[173] HAN-LÜ (Li-chi, Tsa-chi Hsia, Cheng Chu); YORŌRYŌ (Senyu jō).

[174] T'UNG-CHIH T'IAO-KE (Vol. 4 Hu-ling, chia-ch'u); N. NIIDA, *supra* note 33, at 498.

[175] TAIWAN SHIHŌ, Vol 2, p. 357 *et seq.*

[176] KANSHŪ KIJI, Vol. 4, No. 7, p. 26 (A custom practiced in the Taichung area of Taiwan).

[177] SHŪKANROKU, p. 826.

special agreement and was not a general custom. Dowry contracts customarily stated that certain property was given to the daughter to support her while she lived and to provide sacrifices for her after her death. Consequently, the dowry would naturally go with her if she were divorced.[178]

According to Dr. Shiga the disposal of the dowry depended upon the type of divorce. If the wife were divorced for adultery, the dowry did not have to be returned; if the husband were guilty of a crime, it should be returned; if the divorce were by mutual agreement, a settlement would be negotiated between the two families.[179] According to Dr. Niida the recent custom was to return the dowry.[180]

In some divorce cases the husband's family would withhold the dowry until the marriage gift was returned.[181] Usually the marriage gift was more valuable than the dowry.

The wife's private property. The wife's private property consisted of income from her own labor, gifts, and profits from her own lands. She was allowed to take these properties with her in cases of divorce or remarriage after being widowed.[182] As in the case of the dowry, the husband's family would sometimes withhold these properties until the marriage gift was returned.[183]

The husband's family property. The divorced wife naturally lost all claim to the husband's share of the family property. Even if she had been widowed, she had no claim to the deceased husband's property once she left his family to remarry or returned to her family's home.

Alimony. There have been few divorce cases in which alimony has been paid. In recent times, however, Dr. Shiga reports that a husband will pay alimony if he asks for the divorce; if the wife asks for the divorce, she will compensate the husband for the marriage expenses.[184]

In Shanhsi Province there was a special custom of paying compensation to the wife for spiritual damage *(che-hsiu-ch'ien)*, regardless of the reason for the divorce. If the wife were at fault, however, the amount of money paid would be small.

---

[178] S. SHIGA, GENRI, *supra* note 25, p. 529.

[179] N. NIIDA, KAZOKU, p. 350.

[180] TAIWAN SHIHŌ, Vol. 2, p. 359.

[181] SHŪKANROKU, p. 676; S. SHIGA, *supra* note 25, GENRI, p. 539; N. NIIDA, MIBUNHŌ, p. 663.

[182] TAIWAN SHIHŌ, Vol. 2, p. 366.

[183] S. SHIGA, GENRI, *supra* note 25, p. 530.

[184] SHŪKANROKU, p. 747.

PART II
PARTITION IN TRADITIONAL CHINA

Family Property and the Law
of Inheritance in Traditional China

SHŪZŌ SHIGA

Among the questions about the traditional institutions of the Chinese family
that have become occasions for dispute in the Japanese learned world are the
following: first, were father and son co-owners of household property; second,
were the women of the family co-owners of the household's property as well?
The late Professor Kaoru Nakata designated China's family system as family
communism *(kazoku kyōsan sei)*, holding that both the sons and the women
were members of the communistic group; that is, that they were partners in
the co-ownership of family property. His theory was adopted, in turn, by
Noboru Niida, Tai Yen-hui, and other scholars. The above-mentioned
dispute was further spun out when I voiced objections to this theory, in turn
invoking rebuttals from the late Professor Niida.[1]

---

[1] *Cf.* the following: K. Nakata, *Tōsō-jidai no kazoku kyōsansei* (Family communism
in T'ang and Sung times), in 3 K. NAKATA, HŌSEISHI RONSHŪ (Collected essays on
legal history) 1295 ff. (1943); N. NIIDA, SHINA MIBUNHŌSHI (History of family law in
China) (1942); Y. Tai, *Kinsei Shina oyobi Taiwan no kazoku kyōsansei* (Family communism in China and on Taiwan in recent times), 52 HŌGAKU KYŌKAI ZASSHI (Journal
of the jurisprudence association, the University of Tokyo) Nos. 10, 11 (1934); S. SHIGA,
CHŪGOKU KAZOKUHŌRON (Theory of Chinese family law) (1950); N. Niida, *Sōdai no
kasanhō ni okeru joshi no chii* (The position of women in the family property law of
the Sung), in N. NIIDA, CHŪGOKU HŌSEISHI KENKYŪ; DOREINŌDOHŌ KAZOKU SONRA-
KUHŌ (Studies in Chinese legal history; law of slave and serf, and family and village law)
365 ff. (1962); N. NIIDA, CHŪGOKU NO NŌSON KAZOKU (The Chinese rural family)
(1952); S. Shiga, *Chūgoku kazokuhō hokō* (Supplementary studies on Chinese family law),
67 and 68 KOKKA GAKKAI ZASSHI (Journal of the association of political and social
sciences, the University of Tokyo) Nos. 5, 9, 11; No. 7 (1953–55); N. Niida, *Kyū
Chūgoku shakai no nakama-shugi to kazoku* (The family and the notion of fellowship in
Old China), in N. NIIDA, CHŪGOKU HŌSEISHI KENKYŪ; DOREINŌDOHŌ KAZOKU
SONRAKUHŌ 393 ff. (1962).

My contention can be compressed into extremely simple terms. The term family communism is itself an ambiguous one, one not readily employable as a tool of analysis. One must, first of all, distingui.h the two concepts of common budget *(kyōzai; kung ts'ai)* and co-ownership *(kyōyū; kung yu)*. By common budget we mean a certain property belonging to more than one person in terms of its *economic function*. What is meant, in other words, is that the said property, in terms of its origin, has absorbed the labor and products of more than one person, while, in terms of its goal, it is intended to support more than one person. Co-ownership, on the other hand, refers to a property belonging to several persons in terms of *legal ownership*. To put the latter in yet other words, the possessors of rights over that property number more than one. If we now express ourselves in the light of this distinction of concepts, we must say that, while both the sons and the women are beyond any doubt members of the common budget group, the son never becomes a co-owner in partnership with his father, and the unmarried women never become co-owners at all. In Nakata's treatment, the word "communism" *(kyōsan)* is at times used in the sense of co-ownership and at times in the sense of common budget. Under a rubric called communism, the concepts of common budget and co-ownership, which are and should be distinct, have been merged. From this, in turn, has arisen a confusion in theory.

To express the same idea from a different point of view, Nakata was attempting to comprehend the rights of individual family members over household property entirely in terms of shares in common property. In the face of this I contend that the mere word "share" does not suffice as an analytical tool and that it is not possible to resolve this question completely without making use of several concepts belonging within the scope of inheritance law. I am prepared to go further and say that the question as to what sort of rights the several members of a family bore over the household property in relation to one another and the question as to how ancestral property in China devolved on descendants are, in reality, one and the same question.

Below, I intend first to furnish my own definition of the theoretical frame-work and the definitions of the fundamental concepts to which I subscribe, and then to set forth the concrete facts in minute detail, taking focus on the relationship between father and son, in order to prove that facts and theory coincide. In connection with the rights of the womenfolk over the household property, concrete facts are to be discussed on another occasion.

As material for clear presentation of the facts, I make use principally of the legislation throughout a succession of dynasties, of the juridical precedents recorded and handed down (the so-called *p'an yü*), and then, coming to more recent times, of the reports concerned with popular institutions, in particular the records of the interviews conducted by Japanese research groups in several villages of northern China during the Second World War.[2] As far as division into eras is concerned, there shall be no specific identification of time periods, with the mere proviso that the so-called feudal period preceding the unification of the empire by the first emperor of the Ch'in at the end of the third century B.C., must be given completely separate treatment. Traditional China is in that sense a handy phrase. In effect, however, and limited by the materials at hand, I have had in view principally the circumstances obtaining from the Sung era (that is, from the eleventh century A.D.) onward, most particularly during late Ch'ing and the early Republic, the point in time at which the modernization of China was just about to begin.[3]

I

The Common Budget System

Dr. Nakata, fixing his gaze on the peculiar meaning inherent in the Chinese expression "common living, common budget" *(t'ung chü kung ts'ai,* or in its common abbreviation, *t'ung chü* or *kung ts'ai),* argued that it was nothing other than one form of so-called family communism, examples of which are numerous among the world's peoples. Our first task is to analyze this term.

The expression *t'ung chü* is attested to have been in use as early as Han times and has been in frequent use from then till now in both legal and nonlegal writings, consistently expressing one legal idea. The histories tell us that Chang Shih-chih having served in an official capacity in the imperial capital for ten years without being promoted in rank and being anxious about imposing a financial burden on his elder brother, who dwelt at home in the *t'ung chü* group, entertained thoughts of tendering his resignation and going home.[4] In the *T'ang lü su i* (T'ang code with official commentary) will be found a passage saying that, "even if [under such-and-such circumstances] they continue to live in the same house, they are *i chü* [that is, not *t'ung chü*]."[5]

---

[2] CHŪGOKU NŌSON KANKŌ CHŌSA IINKAI (Committee on Chinese rural customs and practices), CHŪGOKU NŌSON KANKŌ CHŌSA (Research data on Chinese rural customs and practices) (Iwanami shoten 1952–58) [hereinafter cited as CNKC]. N. Niida was spokesman for the committee. Within this inquiry the portions dealing with the family were principally the responsibility of T. Uchida and T. Hayakawa.

[3] The present article is a summation in English of certain portions of chapters 1 and 2 of my recent work, CHŪGOKU KAZOKUHŌ NO GENRI (Basic principles of Chinese family law) (Sōbunsha 1967). Within this article as well, I have endeavored to corroborate my assertions with primary documentary evidence, but I urge the readers to consult the Japanese original where possible. The position of women is concretely dealt with in chapter 4 of that work.

[4] SSU-MA CH'IEN, SHIH CHI (Records of the historian) ch. 102, biography of Chang Shih-chih.

[5] T'ANG LÜ SU I (T'ang code with commentary), comment to art. 32 of *Tou sung* (On affray and suits).

Among the remarks of the peasants who answered the questions of the inquiry into customary institutions, there appears the expression of "living in separate houses while being *t'ung chü*."[6] Thus *t'ung chü* does not by any means signify living together physically in the same house.

The concept of *t'ung chü* contains three elements. The first of these, and the very core of the *t'ung chü* concept, is that the fruits of the labor of the several members go into a common account serving all of the members without exception. When all the members are farmers tilling the household soil, this expresses itself in joint cultivation of the land and joint reaping of the harvest. When some member of the family has a side income or when he lives apart and has a different occupation, it is his duty to place in the household account all clear profit accruing from these activities; that is, to hand it all over to the household accountant. The consumption of a part of the income as luxury for himself or for his wife and children, or the secret accumulation of one part of the income, is a violation of the rules, and close watch is kept by the head of the household and the other members of the family. This fact is pointed out in the writings of Olga Lang and Martin C. Yang[7] and is brought out with particular clarity in the above-mentioned records of interviews in northern China. In the villages covered by the inquiry, cases in which the household was maintained on farm income alone were, if anything, rare. From every village a considerable number of men had gone elsewhere to earn their living, having fixed employment in metropolitan areas and other outside places and coming home only to celebrate the New Year. It was not unusual for some to spend the prime of their working lives away from home. Even in such cases they would leave their wives and children in the village in most instances and would send their earnings not to their wives but to their fathers, grandfathers, or brothers, in short to the person who remained in the ancestral home and managed accounts for the whole family.

The second element of the *t'ung chü* concept is that the living expenses of all members are defrayed entirely from a common account. The household accountant remaining in the ancestral village pools all money sent in by persons who go out to do any but agricultural labor, using it all without distinction or discrimination to support the wives and children left behind in the village. All that is required is that a fair distribution be made on the assumption that expenses are expenses, without asking who earned how much. Especially important is fairness in the distribution of food, since collective cooking and eating constitute a central element of family life. The hearth, over which a portrait of the god of the hearth is installed, is the center and the symbol of the house. In order to divide the household, the hearth is

---

[6] 1 CNKC 296c.

[7] O. LANG, CHINESE FAMILY AND SOCIETY 158 (1949); M. YANG, A CHINESE VILLAGE; TAITOU, SHANTUNG PROVINCE 76, 234 (1945).

invariably built separately, while rooms need not be, and usually are not, newly added.[8] In the same way, clothing is also provided for jointly and distributed fairly. Those who go out to work have no choice but to be separate consumers, but all this means is that as a matter of convenience they are meeting their personal expenses, which in terms of their calculations are the expenses of their respective households, out of the money they earn at their place of work, money which likewise belongs entirely to their respective households. In theory they are not divorced from the relationship of the consumer community.

The third and last element is that surpluses left over from the joint account covering all living expenses of the type just mentioned are accumulated as common wealth for the good of all; that is, as household property. The favorite form of accumulating wealth, and the safest, was the acquisition of land. Land itself could then be a further source of income which, naturally enough, would be placed in a joint account. Then, when at some future date the household wealth was to be divided, it would be apportioned on a fixed scale determined by the status relationships of the several members of the family—the rule of thumb being equal division among brothers. There would be no stint in the share of a person who found himself unable to contribute anything to the household after leaving home or, even worse, who became a financial burden. Nor, as a rule, could a person who had made his fortune on the outside monopolize it. On this point, one may deduce from the following sets of question and answer exchanges, the clarity of people's sense of the rule:

I. (Q) When of three brothers, the youngest remains at home, while the eldest finds a job in Manchuria, must the latter, if he can, send home the money he has earned?

(A) He must. Otherwise he will be regarded as a feelingless scum.

(Q) Suppose the eldest brother has bought land in Manchuria. Then what?

(A) He must let his brothers know by post that he is going to buy land, or that he is investing his earnings in business, or whatever. Unless he does so, it can lead to a quarrel or even to a divided household. For that matter, the youngest brother may even go to Manchuria to inspect.

(Q) Suppose the brother has gone to T'ang-shan or to Peking to find work, and there bought some land.

(A) It is all right as long as he lets it be known by post that he has bought the land. If he does, it becomes the common property of the three brothers.

(Q) Even if he buys it without saying a word, eventually it becomes their property, does it not?

(A) If he bought it secretly and they know nothing about it, there is nothing they can do. If they learn about it, they will not let the matter rest.[9]

---

[8] A peasant says, "God of the hearth is the master of the household. In the absence thereof, the household is not established." 5 CNKC 458a.

[9] 5 CNKC 62bc.

II.   (Q)   If, for example, the youngest brother went to Manchuria to find work and sent home 200 *yüan,* with which land was bought, whose land would it be?
      (A)   The family's.
      (Q)   If the youngest brother splits off, can he not take the land with him, saying it is his?
      (A)   He cannot.[10]

III.   (Q)   Suppose there are three brothers, of whom the eldest is a hard worker and the youngest either a do-nothing or a minor. Suppose also that, before the household split, the father, with the money earned by the eldest, bought some land. Would he ever, as a special favor, give the land alone to the eldest?
      (A)   I have never heard of such a case.[11]

IV.   (Q)   If after the father's death the eldest brother earned an outside income, with which he bought land, while the youngest idles and does no work, must the eldest give him a share of the land he himself bought if and when the household splits?
      (A)   If it is land that he bought before the split, he will give him a share.
      (Q)   Suppose the youngest has caused the household a loss of property.
      (A)   It makes no difference.
      (Q)   In such cases, may the eldest say that he will give the youngest only a third, since the land was bought with money most of which he had earned himself?
      (A)   He may not. What he should do in that case is split the household sooner.
      (Q)   In a case like this one, will the eldest, with the father's consent, ever give the youngest only a third?
      (A)   The father will never agree to it.
      (Q)   Why not?
      (A)   This is Chinese custom.
      (Q)   A bad custom, surely. The more of an idler the youngest is, the more he gains by it, does he not?
      (A)   This is not the parents' fault. All that they can do in the eldest's regard is to split the household sooner.[12]

In sum, *t'ung chü kung ts'ai* was a joint account relationship that covered all the aspects of consumption and the maintenance of wealth; the fruits of the labor of all the members and the profits accruing from commonly owned wealth were treated as income, and all the members' living expenses, of which funeral costs for the dead constituted an important part, were paid out of it. If there were a surplus, it would be saved as common wealth, while if there were a deficit, the wealth would be eaten into and life thus maintained. The expression "household property" *(chia ch'an),* if it comes to that, was nothing other than a designation of wealth managed by such a joint account as has just been described. There is no feeling of landed property that should remain intact for generations in the expression "household property." Land did, to be sure, most commonly constitute the bulk of household property, but that

---

[10] 5 CNKC 65b.

[11] 5 CNKC 449a.

[12] 5 CNKC 459c.

very land could, depending on the household income and expenditures, be bought and sold with comparative nonchalance.[13] What this means, in other words, was that household property was, in essence, a fluid value that could be grasped quantitatively and that land was the safest accumulation device into which to convert it. Consequently, every time the joint account relationship itself was broken up, the land too could be parceled up in any way whatever.

Division of the Household Property

T'ung chü kung ts'ai is a relationship that comes into being of its own accord with no artificial prompting. The child at birth is automatically incorporated into the *t'ung chü kung ts'ai* relationship of the household into which it is born; the wife enters through marriage into a *t'ung chü kung ts'ai* relationship with her husband and, as a rule (in all cases, that is, except those of *chao hsü;* that is, matrilocal marriage), with his family. Yet, on the other hand, the *t'ung chü kung ts'ai* relationship is not one that is automatically dissolved. That is to say, the death of a member of the family—and this includes that of the father of the household—is no cause for the dissolution of a *kung ts'ai* relationship. Death means only that one person has left the common budget group; the relationship among the survivors remains just what it was. Also, even if one member of the family leaves the house in defiance of the wishes of the head of the household, the legal relationship of the common budget is not terminated by this mere fact.[14] To sever the common budget relationship, a clear-cut legal act, that is, a division of the household's property, is needed. If the property is just left to lie, the *t'ung chü kung ts'ai* relationship will continue for several generations and may eventuate in an extended family embracing several hundreds of members.[15]

---

[13] Yüan Ts'ai of the Sung period says, "There is no fixed destiny as to wealth and poverty, nor is there any fixed owner of fields and houses. If one has money, one buys; if one has none, one sells." YÜAN SHIH SHIH FAN (Teachings of Master Yüan about social life) ch. 3. Words to the same effect may be heard from the peasants themselves. *Cf.* 5 CNKC 104b.

[14] If this person has come home after a failure in life outside, the family head may not refuse to readmit him on the grounds that he left home entirely on his own initiative. *Cf.* 5 CNKC 64c.

[15] For surviving historical examples of this, *cf.* 3 K. NAKATA, *supra* note 1, at 1317; N. NIIDA, SHINA MIBUNHŌSHI 403 ff. (1942). For the report of an inquiry into one concrete example of this, dating to quite recent times, *cf.* T. Chikusa, *Dai kazoku* (The extended family), in 2 T. CHIKUSA, MANSHŪ KAZOKU-SEIDO NO KANSHŪ (The customs of Manchuria's family institutions) (1960). Note must be taken of the fact that it was not the extended family alone that was based on a set of principles peculiar to Chinese society. The principle of "common living, common budget" was one that governed all Chinese families, regardless of size of membership. Occasionally, it had the possibility of producing families with a large number of members.

However, in actual practice the brothers would usually, sooner or later, split up the household's property, and it was rare upon the deaths of all the brothers for the common budget relationship to survive among cousins. All the less common—an extremely rare exception, in fact—was a *t'ung chü* relationship lasting over several generations and becoming significant enough to be recorded in the histories. Consequently, the average figure for the number of persons in a single household from Han times to the present was roughly five or six, never swelling to enormous proportions.[16] "Division of household property" *(fen chia; kasan bunkatsu)* means a legal act whereby the actual wealth of the household is calculated, omitting no sum whether great or small, and divided among all; the joint account relationship that hitherto governed both income and expenditure is severed. Consequently, even in households having virtually no wealth to distribute, "division of household property" has great significance in the sense that it severs the joint account relationship.

The precise point in time when division of the household's property takes place is not fixed and has no direct connection with the death of the father of the household. It may be provided for by the parents during their own lifetime, or it may be attended to some time after their deaths. However, whenever the deed is done, it must be done simultaneously for all the brothers, or, if the brothers are all dead, for all the cousins.[17] It is not possible for them to achieve independence and then to split off one at a time. This applies even in cases in which there are brothers who are too young to be independent. At such times the parents, if they are alive, or, if not, one of the brothers, will take the youngsters in charge and rear them, managing their respective shares of the property in the role of guardian.

In effecting a division of household property, the procedure as a rule is to invite several outsiders of standing and consequence to be present; to discuss, in their presence and with the aid of suggestions from them, the manner of distributing the property; and, as a result of the decisions reached, to draw up a document. The document is executed in a number of copies equal to the number of the brothers, each of whom keeps one.[18] The execution of documents attesting to the distribution is a necessary condition for the division of household property, so much so that it is said that, "if there is no *tan*

---

[16] *Cf.* the following: T. Makino, *Kandai ni okeru kazoku no ōkisa* (The size of the family in Han times), and *Tōkei teki ni mita nisshi kazoku kōsei no hikaku* (A comparison of family structure in China and Japan, as seen statistically, both in T. MAKINO, SHINA KAZOKU KENKYŪ (A study of the Chinese family) 147 ff., 619 ff. (1944); N. NIIDA, *supra* note 15, at 329 ff.; P. HO, STUDIES ON THE POPULATION OF CHINA, 1368–1953, at 10, 56 (1956); W. EBERHARD, SOCIAL MOBILITY IN TRADITIONAL CHINA 153 n.2 (1962).

[17] 1 CNKC 241c, 276b; 4 CNKC 69bc; E. Hayashi, *Chūgoku nōka no kintō bunsan sōzoku no kenkyū* (A study of the inheritance of equal shares in Chinese peasant households), in TOKYO DAIGAKU SHAKAIGAKKAI (Sociology circle, Tokyo University), GENDAI SHAKAIGAKU NO SHOMONDAI (Problems of modern sociology) 67 (1949).

[18] 4 CNKC 81c; 3 CNKC 70a.

(document), the division of the household is null and void.''[19] Whenever the Chinese performed an important legal act, the means employed to establish the event and its content and to forestall all future disputes always consisted of two things, namely, the presence of a third party and preparation of a document; division of household property was no exception.

The mode of distributing the property was as follows: to the extent that this was possible, each piece of property would be assigned separately, and care would be taken not merely to distribute the whole in shares of equal value, but also to group it into consignments of approximately equal bulk. In addition to this, consignment would frequently be determined by lot. The consignment decided for each person would be minutely recorded in the form of a property register in the above-mentioned document of distribution.

Division of household property did not mean an instant change in the way of life whereby the brothers and their respective wives and children would live in a cluster around the same courtyard. The legal relationship binding them would, however, change completely. Needless to say, the individual does not become independent as a result of a division of household property. The greater collectivity, consisting of parents and brothers, would break up into several smaller collectivities, each consisting of a brother, as head, and his wife and children. Also, within each smaller collectivity the "common living, common budget" relationship is maintained. "Common living, common budget" was for the Chinese an absolute truth decreed by Fate herself. The possibility of a family life rooted in any principle other than this one never even occurred to them.

It is convenient to define a household *(chia)* in China as a group living a "common living, common budget" life. Even after dividing the household property, a common sense of being persons whose blood flows from the same ancestors remains. It also happens that those who can trace the male bloodline back to a common ancestor are regarded as a major group and that this group too is called a *chia*. However, in order to avoid confusion, it would be better to designate the latter by some such name as *tsu* or *tsung*. A "household" as defined here contains several married couples of the same generation. Each couple and its children constitute a lesser group, occupying certain fixed rooms within the household, which in turn is called *fang*. *Fang, chia,* and *tsu* are, so to speak, concentric concepts. Thus, division of household property means nothing other than the act whereby a *fang* establishes itself independently and becomes a *chia*.

Properties Not Belonging to Households

Under the family system just described, most property is preserved in the form of household property *(chia ch'an)*. This is not to say, however, that

[19] I CNKC 241b; also *cf.* I CNKC 229c; 3 CNKC 70b.

there were no other forms for the preservation of property. There are cases in which the *tsu* owns property. This consists of property that is exempted at the time of division and maintained in common ownership, as well as property contributed by those members of the *tsu* who have been successful. It was managed as a sort of foundation by representatives of the *tsu*. On the other hand, there are cases in which the *fang*, or even an individual, may keep property. While there were cases of accumulation of private property in defiance of the law, it is not to be forgotten that there were also cases acknowledged within the system.

First, anything acquired, not as the fruits of labor, but in return for nothing at all, becomes the personal property of the acquisitor. An example of this that has realistically important significance is the wife's dowry, which remains the property of the couple and which is never pooled with the household property belonging to a larger group that includes the husband's parents and brothers. This was a cardinal rule, unchanged throughout the ages. Also, though it was the fruit of labor, there was in Yüan times legislation acknowledging the pay earned in civil or military service as private property. This was not, however, regarded as an unchanging, self-evident rule as it was in the case of the wife's dowry.

Second, the duty to bring the fruits of their labor into the household budget was something not strictly required of the women. Since the women's profession was housework, to the extent that they did not shirk it unwarrantedly, whatever side income they earned in their spare time was considered their own individually. There were even cases in large families in which women were paid by their household heads for lending a hand in the harvest. It was particularly easy for unmarried women to come by opportunities to work and save a bit.

Of the two just mentioned, the former variety of personal property was, in fact, the property of the *fang*, and as the *fang* in the normal course of events proceeded to achieve independence as a household *(chia)*, its property merged with that of the newly formed household. In contrast to this, property of the latter variety must be regarded as purely personal property. And only women could own such personal property.[20]

The Concept of Single Unit as a Tool of Analysis

Now the conceptual content of the expression "common living, common budget" is as has just been stated, but it amounts to no more than that. In the conceptual content of the expression, co-ownership of household property is not included. To understand this, it should suffice to consider examples such as the following one. Let us imagine a household consisting of two brothers, *A* and *M;* *A's* three sons, *b, c,* and *d;* and *M's* son, *n* (leaving the

---

[20] On private property, *cf.* S. SHIGA, *supra* note 3, at ch. 5.

womenfolk out of consideration for the moment). These six surrender their several incomes in their entirety to the household fund and have all their expenses defrayed out of the same fund. For the distribution of food and clothing, each is counted as one. In other words, to the extent that they are all members of the "common living, common budget" group, there are no differences among the six. Nevertheless, in the event a division of property takes place within this household, the household's property will not be divided evenly among the six. Brothers *A* and *M* will divide the household property equally and will form two new households, each accompanied by his son(s). Then the father-son groups will maintain their own "common living, common budget" groups respectively. The division of the household property into two equal parts, in spite of the fact that *A's* household consists of four persons, while *M's* consists of only two, signifies that the household's property is owned jointly by two persons, *A* and *M*, and that *b, c, d,* and *n* are not included in the number of joint owners. That is to say, while the members of the *common property (kung ts'ai)* group number six, the household's property is *jointly owned* by only two of them. Also, when one considers the development subsequent to the parting of *A* and *M*, what one may expect is that each, becoming the single owner of the property obtained as his share, will proceed to construct a life of common property with his own son(s). In other words, there is no conceptual contradiction in the notion of "common living, common budget" under conditions of a single person's ownership.[21]

What I should like to do now is to introduce, as a tool for the clarification of the forms of the ownership of household property, the concept of the single unit in addition to that of the share. In the hypothetical case just cited, the relation between *A* and *M* is unquestionably one of sharing. However, it must be said that *b, c, d,* and *n* have no shares. Yet, in the event that *M* dies, the household property is then divided equally between *A* and *n*. On this point there is no ambiguity, whether in law or in customary practice.[22] Also, whereas *A* and *M* may each request a division of the household's property, *b, c,* and *d* may not as long as *A* is alive, nor do they have their own individual shares.[23] That is, *Abcd* and *Mn* each constitute a single unit holding one-half of the household property. Also, as long as the father is alive, the son might just as well not exist, for it is only with the father's death that he makes his appearance as a being who steps without further ado into the father's place. I call this the rule of the single father-son unit *(fushi ittai; fu tzu i t'i)*. It might be defined as a rule whereby during the father's lifetime the son's personality is absorbed into the father's, while after the latter's death his

---

[21] One thinks of the analogy of the family in ancient Rome, which maintained its economic unity under *patria potestas*.

[22] N. NIIDA, TŌRYŌ SHŪI (Remnants of the T'ang statutes) 245 (1933); 4 CNKC 81c.

[23] 1 CNKC 276a.

personality is extended into that of his son. Father and son are a continuum of the same personality, not two beings in mutual rivalry. It is only when there is more than one son that personality conflicts arise among them as brothers. Further, in relation to their father, each of them merges with him into a single unit. Consequently, in relation to one another they are equal. The principle of father and son as a single unit contains within itself that of the equality of brothers.

The position of the women, which a while ago we placed temporarily out of the scope of our consideration, can also be explained by the introduction of the concept of a single unit. Where the household's property is concerned, there is no such thing as a wife's individual share as distinct from that of her husband. On the other hand, when the husband dies without leaving a son, everything that used to belong to the husband goes in a body into the widow's custody. This I call the rule of husband and wife as a single unit *(fusai ittai; fu ch'i i t'i)*. It can be defined as a rule whereby during the husband's lifetime the wife's personality is absorbed into the husband's, while after the latter's death his personality is represented by the wife. Also, it is my opinion that among females the position of the unmarried woman may be explained as that of a person not bound to anyone in a single unit relationship; she is a dependent member of the family who is being temporarily fed until she marries.

Now I am not by any means introducing the concept of a single unit as an artificial contrivance. The expression characterizing father and son, or husband and wife, as a single unit (*i t'i*, literally, "one body") appears in the classics.[24] The awareness that the father-son and husband-wife relationships are the basic and most solid human relationships is expressed in the saying that "the father is the son's heaven, the husband the wife's"; it is also expressed in the specification that the obsequies of the *chan ts'ui,* the gravest of all mourning rites, should be observed by the son for his father and by the widow for her husband.[25] When I use the terms single father-son unit and single husband-wife unit, I am giving a definition from the point of view of jurisprudence to something which the Chinese have harbored as a concrete feeling without being able to define it analytically.

Professor Francis L. K. Hsu has created the term "father-son identification," explaining the relationship in terms of "whatever the one is the other is, and whatever the one has the other has."[26] My own thought of a father-son unit

---

[24] TU YU, T'UNG TIEN (Encyclopedia) ch. 167: "Although [the grandfather, the father, and the son are] three generations, they are united in one body." PAN KU, HAN SHU (History of the [former] Han dynasty) ch. 11 (Annals of Emperor Ai): "We hear that the husband and the wife are one body." I LI ([Book of] Ceremonials), *Sang fu* (mourning garments): "The father and the sons are one body. The husband and the wife are one body. The brothers are one body."

[25] *Cf.* I LI *supra* note 24.

[26] F. HSU, UNDER THE ANCESTORS' SHADOW 64 ff. (1949).

occurred to me independently of this, and my findings were published at virtually the same time as his.[27] By amazing coincidence, they point to an identical reality. If from the juridical point of view there exists between father and son what I call the father-son unit relationship regarding the possession of property rights, then there would have to be between father and son a relationship of the common enjoyment without discrimination of all advantages, both social and economic, over all property, whether tangible or intangible; in other words what Professor Hsu calls a "father-son identification."

Law of Inheritance : China and Japan Compared

It was the notion, expressive of the rule of the father-son unit, that the father's personality is carried on by the son—this was the underlying principle in China's inheritance law.

As a fact demonstrating in the most concise form possible the difference—a difference so great as, in effect, to amount to a confrontation—between traditional family institutions in China and Japan, one may point out that, whereas in Japan the notion of succeeding to the household (*ie o tsugu*) has at all times constituted the core of the inheritance law, in China such a notion never existed at all. While in Japan the verb indicating inheritance takes house (hold) (*ie*) as its direct object in an extremely natural construction, in Chinese there is no such expression, or, at the very least, it is not a common one. In Japan, house (*ie*) is not merely a collection of human beings, but a unit of social composition having its own peculiar goals and values. The household in its very name bore its share of the burden of the social division of labor. The person responsible at the present time for maintaining the above described social functions of the household is none other than the household head (*kachō*)—called *tōshu* in Edo times—and the succession of the new *kachō* to his predecessor was called *ie o sōzokusuru* (to continue the house). This could be brought about not only by the death of the former *kachō*, but by his retirement—institutionally called *inkyo*—as well. In the latter case the special phrase "to hand over the house" (*ie o yuzuru*) was used.

In China family or household (*chia*) meant a group of persons who, united by the male bloodline, shared their wealth. The components of a family were human beings and property, nothing more. The unit of the social division of labor was the individual, not the household. Individuals, however, would bring together and pool the properties and social advantages that they had acquired by working. Even in the family in the broader sense of the word, that is, in the *tsu*, there is a partial pooling through contributions and mutual aid, but in the family in the narrower sense, that is, in the household, there is a thoroughgoing pooling. This is what is meant by "common living, common

---

[27] *Cf.* S. SHIGA, CHŪGOKU KAZOKUHŌRON (Theory of Chinese family law) (1950).

budget." *Chia chang* (head of the household) means the oldest member of the earliest generation in the household. It signifies merely the first person in a naturally determined order of sequence and does not particularly signify a post to which a certain person is to be assigned. The one called *chia chang* according to the order of sequence is regarded as the person of prime responsibility charged with the household accounts. He is, however, given the circumstances, free to reassign the duties to some other appropriate person. The person charged with the household accounts is now *tang chia* (manager of the household), regardless of whether he is also the *chia chang*. Be that as it may, the terms *chia chang* and *tang chia* have nothing to do with the question of rights of ownership over household property. The question of rights of ownership is determined solely on the basis of the mutual status relationship between father and son, elder and younger brother, husband and wife, and the like; and the *chia chang* or *tang chia,* being a representative of the whole family, has no privileges where the ownership of household property is concerned. Consequently, their succession does not correspond to inheritance. Thus the household was to be divided, not inherited.

In both Japan and China it may possibly be said that little attempt was made to evaluate the individual as a being having a mission of inexchangeable individuality and possessing inviolable dignity; on the contrary, the constant attempt was to evaluate the individual as a component member of a family organization; in that sense both were societies, not of individuals, but of families. In a familistic society the laws of inheritance have grave significance. Under the circumstances the laws of inheritance do not see legacies purely and simply as property thrown away and requiring some sort of disposition, but rather, taking the maintenance of some continuing fundamental values as the central task, they seek to fix the mode of transmission and distribution of property as backing for this principle. In Japan, whatever the era, the element of succession by the eldest son was dominant, whether more or less, because the maintenance of each household as a unit of social composition over generations—one that could not tolerate excessive atomization—was regarded as the central task. What basic values, then, can the Chinese rule of equal division among brothers have been intended to maintain?

It seems that the crucial task of the inheritance law in China was to attempt to preserve intact, both socially and economically, the purely natural relationship in which the son was the prolongation or the extension of the life of his father.

Reference to father and son as a single body or substance *(i t'i)* has already been mentioned, but I should like now to call attention to the fact that father and son were also referred to as one breath *(i ch'i)* or the same breath *(t'ung ch'i)*. The word breath or vital vapor *(ch'i)* reflects all the more accurately the Chinese way of viewing nature. *Ch'i* signifies the male reproductive function and is counterposed to *p'ao* (placenta), which signifies the female reproductive function.[28] At the same time it refers to the formless life itself, which is extended through the male reproductive function to sons and grandsons. Father and son, so the expression goes, are "of divided form but of the same breath" *(fen hsing t'ung ch'i)*.[29] What this means is that, although they are two separate bodies, the life that pulsates in them both is identical. Every man's life is nothing other than an extension of the breath he received from his father. Consequently, brothers born to the same father are also of the same breath *(t'ung ch'i)*. By the mere use of the word *t'ung ch'i* the notion of 'brothers' is usually understood. The further extension of this relationship is the *tsu;* the view is that those of the same *tsu* are also of one and the same breath.[30] The following is a clear example of the mode of thinking just described.

> Though there are in the world those who slight brothers born to the same father of different mothers, and who favor brothers born to different fathers of the same mother, this must be branded a very serious error. Brothers born to the same father of different mothers are, to use a simile, like vegetables of the same seed planted some in an eastern field, some in a western one. Once they have budded, no one can say that they are not the same vegetables simply because they are growing in separate fields. Brothers born to different fathers of the same mother are like the seeds of two totally different vegetables planted together in the same field. Once they have budded, no one can call them the same simply because they are growing in the same field.[31]

In premodern China one similarity with old Roman law is worthy of note, namely, the maintenance of an agnatic family organization.[32] One difference, however, may never be forgotten, namely, that whereas in Rome the concept of blood relationship on the father's side *(agnatio)* was one having at its core the social element of *patria potestas,* in China the concept of *tsung* or *tsu* was one having at its base the natural element of the extension of life itself. The Chinese *tsung* had two rules: that "men and women of the same *tsung* may not marry," and that "one may not adopt a son from a different *tsung.*" In Rome, either these two rules did not exist, or, if they did, they died a very early death.

---

[28] A typical phrase would be: "Though some of the brothers and sisters may not be of the same 'placenta' (that is, though they may be born of different mothers), they were all born of the same 'breath.' " *Hsiao shun fu mu* (Filial piety regarding one's parents), in FAN HUNG, LIU YÜ YEN I (Lectures on the Six Edicts).

[29] LI YEN-SHOU, NAN SHIH (History of southern dynasties) ch. 15, biography of Fu Lung; TU YU, *supra* note 24, at ch. 167.

[30] In several clan genealogies such phrases as the following occur frequently: "The tributaries issuing from a common ancestor are parallel branches having the same breath." And, "Though in number of generations they may be far removed, they are all of the same breath."

[31] CH'EN HUNG-MOU, HSÜN SU I KUEI (Bequeathed teachings about social life) ch. 3 cites, *Wei Shu-tzu jih lu* (Diary of Wei Shu-tzu).

[32] G. JAMIESON, CHINESE FAMILY AND COMMERCIAL LAW 17 (1921).

These two rules are the institutional expression of the acknowledgment of blood ties only in the male line and of the sense of the bloodline as something that preserves its sameness in the male line forever.[33]

As a social and economic expression of the view of life-extension described above, the father's property, undergoing no change after his death, goes on to belong to the son, who is his *alter ego*. Since, if there are more sons than one, there is no difference among them in respect to the fact that they were all born with the father's breath and that the decisive element fixing their status is the absolute fact that they have all received their father's breath, they all occupy a perfectly equal position in relation to one another. Each and every son is in an absolute capacity the *alter ego* of his father. The transfer of property to the sons as a result of the father's death is a perfectly natural process, and there is almost no sense of it as a legal matter. There was never any interference of state power in this area, nor were there any words for the comprehension and expression of this as a legal matter.[34] Since father and sons had from the earliest times been persons following a "common living, common budget" way of life, the death of the father meant, in that context, only that there was one person less in the *kung ts'ai* group.

The sons' position, as described above, was on the other hand inextricably bound up with a duty to recognize their father as the source of their own existence, to surrender to their father all of the fruits of their own activities, and to submerge their own existences entirely into their father's. This is the concept of filial piety *(hsiao)*, which constitutes the core of China's morality. It takes the form during the father's lifetime of a prohibition against the sons saving the fruits of their labor as private possessions, as well as of a duty to serve and obey the father within a life pattern of "common living, common budget," while after his death it assumes the phase of a duty to sacrifice to his spirit. Because of the sacrifices, the relationship of a lifetime continues unbroken, and the food and clothing required by the deceased are furnished him symbolically, but beyond that the person in question is never allowed to

---

[33] If one were to attempt a classification of the provisions in the T'ang and Ming codes concerning prohibition of "incestuous" marriages, one would find that, from the male's point of view, the females whom he is forbidden to marry fall into four types: (1) persons of the same surname (particularly of the same *tsung*); (2) widows of members of the same *tsung;* (3) women of different generations of comparatively close kinship through the female bloodline or through marriage; and (4) sisters by the same mother though by different fathers. In the case of type three, the reason for the prohibition is not the closeness of kinship itself, but the difference in generations. Therefore, though marriage between first cousins of different clans *(piao hsiung ti tzu mei)* is not forbidden, marriage to second female cousins of one's mother *(tsai ts'ung i)* is. The only case in which kinship through the female bloodline is a cause for prohibiting marriage is that of type four.

[34] In the interviews, attempts to inquire into customary terms in this regard embarrassed the respondents. *Cf.* 4 CNKC 95b.

forget the fact that he is himself present as a continuation of his father. People are aware that their fathers are alive in their own persons. Thus is born, first of all, the duty to be circumspect with regard to one's own person and also with regard to life in general. There also results the duty to produce and rear descendants, to find marriage partners for them, and to save things to bequeathe to them. In one's descendants one sees one's own ancestors, and to those descendants one commits one's ancestors' lives as well as one's own. At the same time, one sees those ancestors first in the brothers who got those ancestors' *chi,* then in the clan *(t'ung tsu)* as a whole. From this is born a sense of clan solidarity.

In sum, then, a man lives in those who sacrifice to him, and his property is also inherited by those who sacrifice to him. The joint and simultaneous succession to sacrifices and property is indissoluble. This is the basic guideline of China's inheritance law.

The *Taiwan shihō* deals with succession to sacrifice and inheritance of property in two separate chapters, saying that only one person, normally the eldest son, is entitled to succession to sacrifices, while property must be equally divided among the heirs, and not explaining the relation between them.[35] As a matter of fact, it was in high Chinese antiquity (the Spring and Autumn era and earlier, that is, before 400 B.C.)—and, at that only among the feudal aristocracy—that the notion of monopolistic succession to sacrifices was the dominant one, for under Imperial rule it lost all real meaning, eventuating in a dimly vestigial phenomenon at best. The notion of monopolistic succession to sacrifices was tied to the inheritance of political power over the fief. Consequently, together with the dissolution of feudalism it lost its real groundwork. The dominant notion under Imperial rule was beyond any doubt the one that all sons are fully qualified (that is, obligated, but at the same time privileged) to sacrifice to their father, and, consequently, they perform the sacrificial ritual jointly. The rule of equal shares among brothers of the legacy of property was inextricably bound up with this. It was the steady increase over the generations of the collected assembly of sacrificial celebrants that constituted the real glory of the ancestors.

The difference between China and Japan in the fundamental notions of inheritance appears most obviously in the institution of adoption. In Japan the adopted son *(yōshi)* was a means for guaranteeing the household chief of the next generation. Consequently, as a general rule adoption of sons by persons other than a household chief was unthinkable. In the selection of an adopted son, the greatest importance was attached to his ability to maintain

---

[35] 2B RINJI TAIWAN KYŪKAN CHŌSAKAI (Temporary committee on research of customs and practices on Taiwan), TAIWAN SHIHŌ (Taiwan private law) 498 ff., esp. 506, 546 ff., esp. 561 (1910). It is also admitted by the authors of this work that the monopolistic succession to sacrifices, which they maintain is valid in theory, was in desuetude on Taiwan at that time. *Cf. ibid.,* at 499.

the household occupation; there were no severe restrictions apart from this. Not only when the head of the household had no son of his own, but even if he did, when there was doubt about his ability to maintain the household occupation, the succession could be given to an adopted son. The determination of a successor in Japan, as compared with the case in China, was far more subject to control by the circumstances of the moment. The reason for this is that the central task of Japan's inheritance law was the maintenance of the household as a social unit. In China, by contrast, a foster son had to be designated for any male who had reached a certain age without having a son, or for one who had died without leaving a son—unless he had died unmarried in his minority; due consideration was given to this, either by the person himself or by his entourage after his death, within the limits of possibility. The aim of the institution of adoption was to guarantee sacrificial celebrants to all human beings and thereby to guarantee eternal life to all. Thus the choice of foster sons was limited to persons of the same *tsu* and of the same generation as the son who might have been born. The sacrifices belonged to a relationship that could subsist only among persons who traced their lives to the same source, and the construction of a fiction in excess of these conditions was impossible.

In China, as traditional vocabulary having the sense of inheritance one may cite two characters, *chi* and *ch'eng,* as well as a variety of compound words having these as elements, most notably the word *ch'eng chi,* which combines the two. Also, the characters *hou* and *ssu* are used as words signifying heir. The verbs *chi* and *ch'eng* take three kinds of nouns as objects. First come the names of individuals, then nouns signifying property, and finally nouns signifying sacrifices. These three modes of expression do no more than seize on one and the same object from three different angles. Therefore, inheritance in China meant succession to a person (not to a household), and its concrete significance was that an inextricable effect of sacrificing to a man's spirit was the "universal succession" to that man's property. As a technical term indicating this mode of inheritance peculiar to Chinese society, I should like to use the word *ch'eng chi.*

In reality, Chinese words signifying inheritance, such as *ch'eng chi,* were almost constantly used with respect to foster sons. There was, in fact, even a tendency for the word itself to be interpreted so as to refer to the act of adoption.[36] The reason for this, too, is that as long as there was an actual son there was almost no sense of inheritance as a legal problem. All sons were automatically and as a matter of course heirs *(ch'eng chi jen)* of their father, and the question of who was to be designated the heir never arose. Conse-

---

[36] Cf. *ch'eng t'iao* and *ch'eng chi* in such dictionaries as Tz'u yuan, Tz'u hai, and Chung hua ta tz'u tien. Also, in spite of the fact that a true son has priority as heir *(ssu),* the word *ssu-tzu* indicates an adopted son.

quently, it was never a matter of verbalized discussion. As a technical term, I should like to use the word *ch'eng chi* to signify not the act of adoption itself, but rather the relationship settled by it.

The person qualified to inherit (in the sense of *ch'eng chi*) was primarily the son and secondarily an adopted son selected from the clan membership *(t'ung tsu)*. Apart from these, there was no person qualified to inherit. When such a successor can simply not be found for a deceased person, then the disposition of his legacy becomes a matter of issue. In the majority of cases the legacy is inherited by a daughter or daughters, if there are any. However, this is not *ch'eng chi*. In the light of the many documentary precedents in which there is a note of "no heir" *(wu ssu)* in spite of the presence of a daughter, it is evident that daughters are not included in the concept of *ch'eng chi*. It is also possible for a father to give part of his property to his daughter in dowry, or to give it to a young man of a different clan who is, in point of fact, an adopted son (called *i tzu,* as distinguished from a legally adopted son who is called *ssu tzu*). This too is not *ch'eng chi*. In a broad sense, among the processes by which property proceeds from ancestors to their descendants, it is necessary to make a distinction in one's thinking between the phenomenon of universal succession, that is, simultaneous inheritance of the total property, inextricably bound up with the sacrifices—this is what we mean by *ch'eng chi*—and the transmission of certain fixed property unrelated to the sacrifices. As a technical term referring to the latter, I should like to use the word "benefit" *(ch'eng shou)*, borrowing it from the draft of the late Ch'ing Civil Code.[37]

Women are not born to a position within the sacrificial relationship either as celebrants or as recipients. A daughter is not qualified to sacrifice to her father, nor is a woman who died unmarried qualified to receive sacrifices. A woman is united through marriage with her husband and sacrifices with him to his ancestors; together they receive the sacrificial offerings of their descendants. Eternal life through sacrifice is guaranteed to a woman through marriage. The role of the husband and wife as a single unit *(fusai ittai; fu ch'i i t'i)*, mentioned above, is nothing other than the socioeconomic expression of this.

II

Nakata understands the content of the concept of "common living, common budget" to include elements of *sōshu-teki kyōyū (Miteigentum zur gesamten Hand;* co-joint ownership). Consequently, according to him, the household property is always the joint holdings of the family as a whole, regardless of whether father and sons constitute the household or whether it is the brothers who make up the household after the father's death, and for the disposal of

---

[37] *Cf.* TA CH'ING MIN LÜ TS'AO AN (Draft of the civil code of the Great Ch'ing dynasty) art. 1468 (1911), as well as the explanation of the reason for it.

that property a consensus of all is necessary. However, since the father had the prerogative of absolute command where the sons were concerned, the authority he wielded as head of the household for the management of common property flowed into the authority of command he wielded as a father, and as a matter of practical reality, he was able to dispose freely of the household's property. This view was also adopted by Niida Noboru and Tai Yen-hui.[38]

Even before this, there was the following conclusion in the *Taiwan shihō*: "The household's property, as long as the *pater familias* [*kaso*] is alive, shall belong to him; after his death, it shall belong to his heirs; when there are two heirs or more, it shall belong to them in common [*gōyū; Miteigentum zur gesamten Hand*]."[39] Therefore, the various theories coincide in their interpretation of when the brothers constitute a household, while there are two concepts in mutual opposition as to the circumstances under which father and sons make up the household.

Of the two, the conceptual construct of the unity of father and sons *(fushi ittai)*, which is the view I hold, is closer to the concept in the *Taiwan shihō* and has the added advantage, in my belief, of being able to account for the assorted facts in a more unified and systematic manner. What I should like to do now is to set forth clearly the concrete facts and then to take up the question of the conceptual construct.

The Father's Authority Concerning the Disposition of Household Property

Sale of real estate. It goes without saying that without the father's permission the son could not sell the household's land at will. The father was the head of the household, and the important business of the household had to be managed by the head himself or in keeping with his instructions—as was only to be expected, as long as the household was a single unit; this rule had to be kept regardless of whether the head was the father or the elder of a lateral line. Yet it often happened that the ne'er-do-well son of a rich family, incited by a scoundrel hanger-on, would sell the household's land behind the back of the household's chief. In the face of this, the law provided that, if the household head disapproved, the transaction was to be null and void; the objects were to be returned; and the young ne'er-do-well, the buyer, and the mediator in the transaction were to be punished. For example, T'ang law prescribes as follows:

While the head of the household is alive (by which is meant living in a place no farther removed than 300 *li* and not separated from the place in question by a barrier), sons, grandsons, younger brothers, and nephews may neither pawn nor sell slaves, livestock, fields, houses, or any other property. (This also applies to loans where no pawn is involved.) When there is a need to pawn or sell, such action is permissible after obtain-

---

[38] *Cf.* the documents cited in note 1.
[39] 2B TAIWAN SHIHŌ (Taiwan private law) 549 ff. (1910).

ing a certificate of authorization from the local government office having jurisdiction over the area. When a pawn or a purchase is made at the will of the parties and in violation of the law, without consulting the head of the household concerned or the appropriate official, [the recipient] shall be ordered to restore the object of pawn or purchase to its original owner. The money paid shall be forfeited, and restitution shall not be made.[40]

In the verdicts *(p'an yü)* of the Southern Sung are to be found examples in which the sale by a son of his household's land without the father's permission (by forging his father's name and adding his own to the bill of sale) was declared null and void, and the objects were ordered to be returned.[41] There were also cases of the same thing in which uncle and nephew were involved instead of father and son.[42] Under the laws of the Southern Sung, the fixed practice was for the State to confiscate the money passed in the transaction.[43] However, as to the portion acquired and already consumed by the young offender, if the latter were the son of the household chief, he would be excused from restitution, while, if he were lateral kin to him, a corresponding amount would be deducted from the amount that would normally have accrued to him upon distribution of the household's property. The reason, as given in the text of the judgments, was that the son had no share in the household property as long as his father was alive.[44]

Now, could the father, who was the head of the household, sell the household's land at will or was the agreement of his sons necessary? Most of the scholars whose analyses of these matters stem from more or less personal experience of the social realities of Old China express the view that the father did not require the agreement of his sons in making his disposition.[45] Until

---

[40] N. NIIDA, *supra* note 22, at 853.

[41] HUANG KAN, MIEN-CHAI HSIEN-SHENG HUANG WEN-SU-KUNG WEN-CHI (The complete works of Huang Kan), Southern Sung edition, possession of Seikadō Bunko, Tokyo, ch. 39, 16a, *"Ch'en Hui-ch'ing su Kuo Liu-ch'ao-san shu t'ien"* (Ch'en Hui-ch'ing's suit against Kuo Liu-ch'ao-san for redeeming land).

[42] MING-KUNG SHU-P'AN CH'ING-MING-CHI (Illustrious compilation of the decisions of famous judges), Southern Sung edition, possession of Seikado Bunko, photographic reprint (1964) [hereinafter cited as CH'ING MING CHI with indications of page numbers of both the original and the reprint] 159b–328, *"Yeh wei fen erh ssu li ch'i tao mai"* (Before division of property, to privately establish a contract [is an] illegal sale).

[43] In addition to the references cited in notes 41 and 42, *cf.* HUANG KAN, *supra* note 41, at ch. 40, 5a, *"Ch'en Hsi-tien Shuai Wen-hsien cheng t'ien"* (Dispute over wet rice land of Ch'en Hsi-tien and Shuai Wen-hsien).

[44] This is incidentally mentioned in the case cited in note 42.

[45] *Cf.* G. JAMIESON, *supra* note 32, at 29; T. JERMIGAN, CHINA IN LAW AND COMMERCE 95 (1905); 2B TAIWAN SHIHŌ 549 ff. (1910); 2 T. CHIKUSA, MANSHŪ KAGOKU-SEIDO NO KANSHŪ 176 (1960). However, H. ŌYAMA, CHŪGOKUJIN NO KAZOKU SEIDO NO KENKYŪ (Study of the family institutions of the Chinese) 17 (1952) says, "The disposal of household property tends to be solely in the hands of fathers and grandfathers, as far as metropolitan areas are concerned, but in the countryside they may not dispose of it on their own initiative."

just before the Second World War, in fact, this was the standard view throughout Japanese scholarly circles as well.[46] However, after the war, Niida Noboru, drawing his conclusions from the aforesaid records of interviews conducted in northern Chinese villages, expressed the view that the peasants' sense of proper form on this question could not easily be comprehended, at least not in clear-cut terms. For, while in his view the authority in the household of the father-chief was so strongly felt as, in effect, to regard everything in the household, whether animate or inanimate, human or inhuman, as the father's possession, there were other cases in which the sense of common ownership of household property was so strongly in evidence that, if the father disposed of household property without his sons' approval, it was regarded as a fraudulent sale *(tao mai)*. There were also, according to him, local customs exhibiting a wide range of nuances between these two extremes.[47] All the same, it is hazardous to take this statement uncritically at face value— particularly that aspect of it that talks about restrictions on the father's authority. For Niida's line of reasoning has the following shortcomings:

1.   His reckoning in terms of nuance is based largely on an analysis of verbal expression; that is, on whether the peasant in answer to the question, "To whom does the household property belong?" answered "To father" or "To everyone." If the answer were "To father," this was regarded as a manifestation of the authority of the father-chief, while, if the answer was "To everyone," it was regarded as a manifestation of a sense of common ownership. As we shall explain later, such a pursuit of the question is a meaningless one.

2.   He lays stress on the fact that, when the father sells land, he *ordinarily* consults with his wife and children and gains their consent. There can be little doubt that this is true. However, what we are dealing with here are not sociological facts, but a conceptual construct in jurisprudence. What is important is whether the third party who got land in a sale from the father was completely secure in his possession, regardless of the consent or opposition of the sons. On this point the commentator is silent.

3.   He makes many material citations from records of question-and-answer exchanges with peasants, exchanges in which the subject was *chia chang* (head of the household) or *tang chia* (manager of the household). Now *chia chang* and *tang chia* are not limited to fathers but include uncles and brothers as well. To give the citations validity, one must single out those exchanges in which it is evident from the context that by *chia chang* or *tang chia* the father was meant. In this commentator's case, the choice was slovenly. For

---

[46] K. Nakata also placed the same construction on the facts by way of the conceptual construct of the confusion of the authority of command with the right of management of the household's property.

[47] *Cf.* N. NIIDA, CHŪGOKU NO NŌSON KAZOKU ch. 5 (1952); N. NIIDA, CHŪGOKU HŌSEISHI KENKYŪ; DOREINŌDOHŌ KAZOKU SONRAKUHŌ 369, 376 (1962).

example, the heading that there are cases in which the father's disposal of property is designated as a fraudulent sale is derived from the following exchange:

Q: May the *tang chia* sell his land without consulting anyone?
A: He may not. If he sells it without informing anyone, it constitutes "illicit purchase" and "fraudulent sale" *(tao mai tao mai)*. It is an action he may take only after giving due public notice.
Q: Whom must he consult?
A: If he has brothers, he must consult them. If not, he need only give public notice.
Q: By "public notice" *(kung k'ai)* what do you mean?
A: He must confer on the matter in such a way that all shall know about it.
Q: Who are "all"?
A: All persons within the household.[48]

As is clear from this exchange, the respondent in his thinking includes brothers under the term *tang chia*. The father is not at issue here. Although the former heading is repeatedly taken up in this commentator's writings, no other sources are given.

4. He stresses, giving concrete examples, that there are numerous cases in which the deed bears the signatures of both father and son. This is an undeniably important factual presentation, but however many joint signatures one may cite, in and of themselves they do not prove the necessity for joint signatures. For there is no material even hinting at the danger of trouble in the event that the document lacks a joint signature.

In sum, Niida has scarcely succeeded in concretely proving the nuances in local custom of which he speaks.

Now, on the points with which we are concerning ourselves, we have been able to find scant written evidence. Not only do the law codes down through the ages have no provisions for this sort of thing, but there are also no court cases to be found in which this point was directly at issue. In respect to cases in which one brother sold household land entirely on his own, there were laws decreeing that the other brothers could seek nullification of the sale,[49] and there were also judgments in which such nullification was actually ordered.[50]

---

[48] 5 CNKC 71C. NIIDA *supra* note 47 (1952) at 224.

[49] Southern Sung law specifies as follows: "In the event that, after the deaths of parents and grandparents, [one of the brothers] sells or hypothecates land and/or buildings which are common property and squanders the purchase price at his own pleasure, when the object in question has been divided up according to the law for the distribution of household property, [as much as should go to the other brothers] shall be restored, and the person who originally sold or hypothecated it shall be compelled to reimburse the purchase price. . . ." CH'ING MING CHI 92a–195, 181b–372.

[50] HUANG KAN, *supra* note 41, at ch. 40, 1a, *"Ch'en An-chieh, lun Ch'en An-kuo tao mai t'ien ti shih"* (Ch'en An-chieh complains against Ch'en An-kuo pertaining to illegal sale of realty).

In contrast to this, the negative data must be noted; where the father's acts of disposition are concerned, one finds no material of a comparable nature. Furthermore, in the decisions *(p'an yü)* positive expressions are to be found that indicate the assumption as a self-evident premise that the father is free to make whatever disposition he pleases. For example:

If the father, Yüan-heng, himself sold the land, what need was there for his son to sign the deed together with him? The notion that he would sell it jointly with his son is not above suspicion. . . .[51]

Setting aside, as a matter of course, that the grandfather or father may make of the household wealth whatever disposition he pleases, if any of the other elders is guilty of an unjust act, it is not against the law for the juniors, on this account, to petition for a division of the household property.[52]

This being the case, it is natural to conclude that the only reason this issue never became an object of legislation was that the father's right to dispose of household property was so self-evident that there was no need to provide for it, and that the reason it never became a matter of litigation is that there was no one so bereft of his senses as to dispute this. In the records of interviews in northern Chinese villages as well, where one of the brothers sells the household's land at his discretion, it is held that "the seller and the buyer shall be reported to the authorities . . . and the act shall be null and void, since it constitutes fraudulent sale," or that "the sale may be revoked,"[53] but there is not one case of such an expression issuing from the mouth of a peasant with respect to an act of disposition by the father. Not only this, but there is also the following exchange, which indicates most pronouncedly the difference between father and brothers:

Q: Is the household property the possession of the head of the household or of the whole household?

A: Of the whole.

Q: May the head dispose of the property of the whole household?

A: If he is the only surviving brother, he may, but, if he is one of two brothers or more, he must confer with the others.[54]

Q: [in a conversation having to do with borrowing and lending] May the head of the household do as he pleases in all matters?

A: If he is a parent, he may, but, if he is one of several brothers, he must confer with the others.[55]

---

[51] HUANG KAN, *supra* note 41, ch. 39, 16b.

[52] W. KUO, TA LI YÜAN P'AN CHÜEH LI CH'ÜAN SHU (Complete records of the decisions and precedents of the Supreme Court) 207 (1931), *San nien shang tzu* No. 616 (1914 Appeals case no. 616).

[53] 5 CNKC 62bc.

[54] 1 CNKC 270c.

[55] 1 CNKC 272a.

In a court in Talien under Japanese rule, experts reporting on Chinese customs stated unanimously that, "when the father disposes of household property, he need not get the consent of his sons."[56]

In conclusion it must be acknowledged that the traditional legal sense of the Chinese holds that the father's acts of disposition are perfectly valid even when he does not have his sons' consent.

Loans. As is generally known, there was in Chinese a very popular adage, which went to the following effect: "The father's debts the son must repay. For the son's debts the father is not responsible. *(Fu ch'ien chai tzu tang huan, tzu ch'ien chai fu pu chih.)*" Under the "common living, common budget" system, father and sons have no individual property; they live on a single property common to the household. The father's debts attach unconditionally to the obligations of the property of his household. Consequently, even after his father's death, the son, as long as he remains attached to the same household property—or, rather, because he has no other choice—must assume responsibility for their payment. As a matter of actual practice, this rule was enforced virtually without qualification. The peasant respondents said that the son must bear responsibility for all his father's debts, even those incurred from drinking and gambling.[57] Such an institution as the limited recognition of inheritance was unknown, nor were there any institutions corresponding to administrators of inheritance or executors of wills such as are provided for in Anglo-American law. Even during the father's lifetime it was also common when dividing the household property to distribute responsibility for the father's debts among the sons.[58]

Where the son's debts and obligations are concerned, it is necessary to consider them in terms of the circumstances. When the son has incurred a debt with the specific permission of his father or within the framework of his father's general approval, his father is naturally responsible. Also, even if there were no prior approval, if a debt had been incurred from a reasonable expense (as, for example, for reasonable living expenses away from home), the father had no choice but to approve it after the fact. Consequently, the applicability of the literary proverb quoted above is principally to cases in which the son has borrowed money to pay for his own amusement without his father's permission. The father was able to withhold payment on the ground that these were not expenses to be levied on the property of the household. On the other hand, apart from the household property, the son had no individual possessions that could be held as security for debts.

[56] *Cf.* KANTŌ-CHŌ NO HŌTEI NI ARAWARETARU SHINA NO MINJI KANSHŪ IHŌ (Report of Chinese civil customs appearing in the law courts of Kwantong area), being No. 165 MANTETSU CHŌSA SHIRYŌ (Research report of the Southern Manchurian Railway Company) 420 ff. (1934).

[57] 5 CNKC 453a; 1 CNKC 273a, 297a.

[58] 1 CNKC 273bc.

Consequently, the creditors were obliged to surrender their claims.[59] It was considered reprehensible to lend money secretly to the son of another household to help pay for his amusements, and there were, in fact, laws designed for the control of that very thing.[60] Since, however, the blind insistence by the father on his authority to withhold payment amounted to pushing his beloved son into a painful situation, the practical likelihood is that, more often than not, a solution was worked out by resort to some sort of compromise.

As a matter of theory, one may say that, just as the purchase and sale of land could take place legally only through the will of the father, so debts and obligations could be assumed by the household only if the father wished it.

When the head of the household is a lateral kinsman, other members of the family may object to obligations incurred by him. For example, in the report of the study *in situ* of the Soochow area in Kiangsu Province, there will be found an actual case in which the eldest of three brothers, who was head of the household, incurred some expenditures in connection with his activities as *pao chang* (head of the self-police force) and ran up a heap of debts. The brothers objected and effected a division of the household's property. While they divided equally the general run of debts and obligations, those incurred by the eldest in his capacity as *pao chang* they left to be levied on him alone.[61] Also, in households such as this one, if it should ever happen that one member of the family goes into debt on his own initiative and the head of the household refuses payment of his debts, the inevitable development would be in the direction of a division of the household's property.

The Father's Authority Concerning the Division of Household Property

The right to carry the division into actual effect. The law codes *(lü)* throughout the ages have forbidden the entry of children and/or grandchildren in registries different from the ancestral ones, where public law was concerned, and the division of the household's property, where private law was concerned, as long as the parents and grandparents were alive or until the mourning period was over after their deaths. While the former of the two, however, is absolutely forbidden, the latter is not included within the prohibition if the

---

[59] There were cases of secret loans to sons in which the death of the parents was decided on as the time for the liquidation of debts, and loans were accordingly made at exorbitant interest rates. *Cf.* YÜAN TIEN CHANG (Law and precedents under Yüan dynasty), Shen Chia-pen's reprint, ch. 27, 5a; CHUNG-HUA MIN-KUO SSU-FA HSING-CHENG-PU (Ministry of Justice, Republic of China), MIN-SHANG-SHIH HSI-KUAN TIAO-CH'A PAO-KAO-LU (Report of inquiry into civil and commercial customs) 784, 812, 821, 1037 (1930).

[60] *Cf.* N. NIIDA, *supra* note 22, at 853; YÜAN TIEN CHANG ch. 27, 4b.

[61] E. HAYASHI, *supra* note 17, at 75–78.

parents and grandparents order otherwise.[62] In other words, a consistent rule in the legislation was that, as long as the father was alive, division of the household's property could take place only in obedience to his wishes. Also, quite independently of the legislation, people in general regarded it, in terms of customary practice, as the thing to be expected.[63]

This stands in sharp contrast to the fact that, once the parents were dead, anyone could at any time petition for a division of household property as a matter of right.

Proportions of the division. In the division of household property, it is a known fact that equality among brothers was a hard and fast rule. In cases, however, in which the father himself effected the division in his own lifetime, was he subject to the same stipulation of equal division? This must be considered a dual question. The first of these is whether it was necessary to equalize the several shares of the brothers. The second is whether the father himself, as one member of the family, was bound by the rule of equal shares and hence entitled to no more than any one of his sons, or, even if not, entitled only to a rigidly fixed share. These are two quite separate questions and are not to be confused. To state our conclusions prematurely, the answer to the first question is in the affirmative, to the second in the negative.

The practice of leaving a portion of the property—in the majority of cases a fixed piece of land—for one's parents, under the title *yang lao* (for support of old age) or *yang shan* (support and care) was in vogue from ancient times. On the issue of what proportion of the property should be earmarked for *yang lao,* the legislation through the ages has not a word to say. In addition, in the inquiries into customary institutions, the peasants said in so many words that the proportion is not stipulated.

Q: When the son establishes a separate household, do the parents, as a rule, set aside their own property?

A: There is no fixed rule. For sometimes they give it all to the son. . . .

Q: If they do set some aside. . . .

A: That too is not fixed. There are times when it exceeds that of their son, there are times when the opposite is true. Though they may set aside any amount they please, in general they do not take too much. . . .

Q: May the parents reserve the entire property?

A: They may [as a matter of right], but usually they do not.

Q: Do the sons share what the parents leave?

A: It is shared equally by those who participate in the division of the household.[64]

---

[62] T'ANG LÜ SU I, art. 6 of *Hu hun* (On the family and marriage); TA CH'ING LÜ LI, art. 411 in Boulais's translation. G. BOULAIS, MANUEL DU CODE CHINOIS (1924). The latter provision is a repetition of one article in the Ming statutes.

[63] Note 56 *supra,* at 425; 4 CNKC 70a.

[64] 1 CNKC 242a.

The designation or non-designation of a certain amount of the property for *yang lao* purposes is, as has been seen, not a fixed thing, but at the other extreme it is possible to reserve the entire property for that purpose. Besides, the one who really decides these things is the father himself. One peasant who let his three sons form separate households said in answer to the inquiry[65] that he himself had decided the amount of land that was to support him in his old age *(yang lao ti)*; that he had no need to consult any mediators (that is, persons present when the property was divided); that he did not consult the opinions of his children; and that his children had no right to complain anyway.

From concrete examples and from answers to hypothetical questions, one sees that the property set aside for *yang lao* frequently amounted to far more than was distributed among the sons. Particularly when the total sum of the household's property is small, the proportion set aside for *yang lao* tends to be great with extreme cases being those of taking a slight property and "assigning it all to the parents as *yang lao ti,* letting the brothers go elsewhere to seek their livelihood."[66]

In sum, *yang lao* property is by nature property set aside in a quantity sufficient to support the parents in keeping with their wishes. As far as the division of the remainder among the sons is concerned, it was governed, as shall be shown below, by the rule of equality among brothers, and a flagrantly inequitable distribution would not be allowed even if the father wished it. Also, when the parents die, the *yang lao* property left behind once the funeral costs have been defrayed must be equally distributed. Among brothers, the rival claims to rights are virtually inviolable. However, these brothers possess no rights on which they can insist on their relationship as sons to their father.

Ejection. A father may bar from the house, any son, together with his wife, who is the cause of domestic discord. This is what appears in the reports of the inquiry into customary institutions under such names as *kan ch'u ch'ü* and *hung ch'u ch'ü* (to drive out or to expel). The life led by such an ejected son is known by such terms as *ling kuo* (to live apart) and *tan kuo* (to live alone).[67]

Division of a household *(fen chia)* is an act severing the legal relationship of "common living, common budget" and has nothing to do with the externally visible separation of dwellings; *ling kuo* is a word referring to a situation in which the externally visible features of daily life such as lodging, meals, and the like are maintained separately, while the legal relationship remains as it was.

---

[65] 5 CNKC 101ab.

[66] *Cf.* T. UCHIDA, CHŪGOKU NŌSON NO BUNKE SEIDO (The institution of the division of the household in Chinese rural communities) 286 ff. (Iwanami shoten 1956); S. SHIGA, *supra* note 3, at 177 ff.

[67] In this connection, *cf.* T. UCHIDA, CHŪGOKU NŌSON NO KAZOKU TO SHINKŌ (Family and belief in China's rural communities) 78 ff. (Kōbundō 1948).

Q: Is the word *fen chia,* then, not applied unless the property too is divided?
A: That is right.
Q: If they live in the same house and share their property. . . .
A: That is called *fen chia.*[68]

As can be seen from this, "division of the household" *(fen chia)* can take place while its members continue to live in the same house. On the other hand:

Q: How do *fen chia* and *ling kuo* differ?
A: The latter refers to living in a separate place while not splitting the household.
Q: Does the word *ling kuo* apply even when the parties share the same *yüan tzu* (compound)?
A: It does not. In the case of an identical *yüan tzu* (compound) the word is not used.[69]

Thus we see that a pattern of daily life in which the parties surround the same inner courtyard is not called *ling kuo.*

Q: In case of *kan ch'u ch'ü,* may the person subjected to it not live in the same village?
A: He may, but he may not go to his father's home.[70]

As may be seen from this, physical obstruction from the house in question constitutes the essential element of *kan ch'u ch'ü.* Consequently, *fen chia* is effected by brothers in unison, and it does not matter how young any of them happens to be. On the other hand, ejection is not carried out against a child who has not reached an age at which he can maintain himself separately, as can be seen in the expressions: "One does not eject small children," and "an unmarried person does not live separately *(ling kuo).*"[71] And there is, of course, no rule that it must be carried out by brothers simultaneously.

When ejecting a son, the father need give him nothing whatever, but as a matter of parental kindness it is not unheard-of for him to give some livestock and a bit of land as a means of self-support. In legal terms, the said property remains a part of the property of the household, having been no more than lent to the ejected son on a temporary basis and thus not becoming his possession.[72] The son may at best put it to profitable use, but he may not dispose of it.[73] If it comes to that, it is not only the property conferred on him by his household, but also that which the ejected son may have had the good fortune to acquire subsequently, which, in theory at least, never becomes his property but remains that of the household.

---

[68] I CNKC 229a.

[69] *Id.,* 269a.

[70] 3 CNKC 149b.

[71] I CNKC 283b, 269c.

[72] Consequently, there is nothing like the drawing up of documents to attest the act, as is the case in the division of a household.

[73] 4 CNKC 111c; I CNKC 272c.

Q: When that fellow [the ejected son] has made money and bought land elsewhere, whose property is it?

A: It should be the property of his father's household.[74]

Such was the respondent's view. This means that the legal relationship of *t'ung chü kung ts'ai* is temporarily interrupted, but not severed in a fundamental sense.

Consequently, even an ejected person may revert to his household at any time if he makes due apology.[75] Also, when the father dies, even an ejected son comes home for the funeral. He then either resumes life in the same household with the brothers who stayed behind or shares the household property with them. The distribution at such time is still made on a basis of equality, and no one is disadvantaged on the ground that he was ejected.

Q: Does an elder brother share property with a younger brother who has been living apart *(ling kuo)* or does he not?

A: If the parents die, he comes home and attends to their obsequies. When the obsequies and the mourning are over, there is an equal division of property.[76]

Many responses were in complete agreement with the above on this point.

Now this *kan ch'u ch'ü* is something that can be done by fathers and grandfathers to sons and grandsons, but elder brothers may not eject younger brothers, nor uncles nephews, after the death of the father or grandfather. This is the self-evident premise on which the remarks of the peasants were based, and a look at citations of concrete examples will reveal no exceptions. This is, among other things, a logical conclusion of the fact that the brothers have a right to demand division of household property of one another and that the father concentrates in his own hands the right to effect this division. When disharmony among lateral kinsmen living together *(t'ung chu)* becomes unbearable, division of household property must take place, and there can be no ejection.

The case of an only son. When there is only one son, the father and this son may not divide the household's property between them. It is not a question of whose will governs the division, but rather that division of a household's property between a father and an only son is absolutely unthinkable.

Q: Does it ever happen, when there is only one son, that the parents and his family divide the household [*sic*] between them?

A: Never.

---

[74] 4 CNKC 70a.

[75] 3 CNKC 149b; 5 CNKC 486 (the case of Yu Kuo-hsiang).

[76] 1 CNKC 269b.

Q: When the parents separate from their son's family, taking their *yang lao ti* with them, is that not division of the household *(fen chia)*?

A: It is not. When there is only one son the whole of the parents' lands inevitably remain as their property. Therefore if the parents live separately, it amounts to ejecting the son.[77]

That is what the peasants say. When the parents and their only son and his wife maintain separate households, this is the *kan ch'u ch'ü* and *ling kuo* mentioned above, but it is not *fen chia,* for it is not accompanied by any of the formalities that invariably attend *fen chia* such as the division of property in the presence of witnesses, the execution of documents, and the like. Concrete examples of this are to be found in the materials assembled by the inquiry, and the peasants' judgment of such cases was, "But it makes no difference whether they divide the household *(fen chia)* or not. For in case of such division between one parent and one child the child automatically inherits all the property on the death of the parent," or "It looks like *fen chia,* but is not in fact." As far as the number of households is concerned, it is counted as one, as before.[78] A look at the concrete examples furnished by the documents on division of household property will also reveal no cases of a father and a single son, but will show the presence of several brothers to be an iron-clad rule.

Restrictions on the Father's Authority

Right to inherit. The father may not bar his son or sons from inheritance. In this connection there is the following noteworthy case in the verdicts of the Southern Sung:

T'an Nien-hua had had by his former wife one son in addition to T'an Yu-chi. After his wife's death he married another woman, who brought with her a young boy named Li Tzu-ch'in. T'an Nien-hua treated Li Tzu-ch'in like his own son, and eventually became so partial to him that he had the wish to leave him all his property. He thereupon forged a bill of sale, which he signed himself, and which he forced T'an Yu-chi and his brother to sign, a document attesting to the sale of all the household land to Li Tzu-ch'in and thus forcing T'an Yu-chi and his brother off the land. After T'an Nien-hua's death, T'an Yu-chi and his brother appealed to the authorities for a redress of grievances. The authorities rendered a judgment pronouncing null and void the action taken by the father during his own lifetime as representing the "arbitrary will" *(ssu chih)* of T'an Nien-hua, quashing the forged bill of sale, and ordering the redistribution, on a basis of equality, of the household property among the three sons. To this is added the note that the inclusion of Li Tzu-ch'in on a basis of equality was a special act of grace, carried out in view of T'an Nien-hua's love for the young man.[79]

---

[77] *Id.,* 292a.

[78] 5 CNKC 472c, 473a; H. FEI, PEASANT LIFE IN CHINA 68 (1939).

[79] CH'ING MING CHI, 100a–211, *"Sui mu chia chih tzu t'u mou ch'in tzu chih yeh"* (A child who had been adopted by his mother's second husband deliberately planned [to take over] the property of [his foster father's] real sons).

The reason that, in the above case, T'an Yu-chi and his brother did not dare dispute this action during their father's lifetime was that the law granted the father absolute power of command and forbade under very severe pain any appeals by sons against their fathers. Hitherto, the theory has been that in the face of the father's power of command, accompanied as it was by prohibition of appeal, the sons had no recourse. Actually this is not so, for it is worthy of note that there was a recourse of appeal once the father was dead. The reason for the judgment is explained at great length, but at the core of the explanation is the allegation that, "if T'an Nien-ts'ao is allowed to have his way, then T'an Yu-chi and his brother will surely starve to death. If that is the case, then surely the spirits of the T'an clan will go eternally hungry." In other words, at the core of the judgment was the following line of reasoning: the persons qualified to sacrifice to the father and to all ancestors antecedent to him are, in this case, his blood sons alone; an adopted son from a different clan has no such qualifications. Inextricably associated with this is the fact that the father's property, all or at least the bulk of it, must be left to the blood sons, who were qualified to sacrifice to him. This is the time-hallowed rule, and any father's individual wish that flies in the face of this must be declared null and void.

The above is not based on the particular view harbored by a certain judge at a certain time, as can be seen from the following question-and-answer exchange appearing in the records:

Q: If the wife of the head of a household runs off with another man? . . .
A: The matter will be brought to law, and she will be declared unwanted [that is, divorced].
Q: In general, when the head of the household excludes a member of his family, must he do so through litigation?
A: Only in the case of a wife. As far as his children are concerned, however badly they may misbehave, they are his family and may not be excluded by recourse to law. . . .
Q: What action can be taken against a spendthrift?
A: There is no appropriate action. In fact, there is nothing that can be done. One may reprove him, but if he is deaf to the reproofs, one is simply helpless.[80]

Q: [Addressed some days later to the same person]: If a member of the family infringes on the prerogatives of the head of the household? . . .
A: The head warns and reproves him. As a last resort, he excludes him from the house.
Q: By what means?
A: The head excludes the person in question.
Q: What about the person so excluded?
A: He remains a member of the family.
Q: Is he simply driven out, then?
A: That is right.

---

[80] I CNKC 244a.

Q: Can he be deprived of membership in the family?
A: He cannot, not even by recourse to law.[81]

If a wife has been guilty of misconduct, she may be divorced by legal means, but a son may not be deprived of membership in the household, however he may have misbehaved. He may be driven from the physical premises of the house, which is what is meant by *kan ch'u ch'ü*, but as already stated, this brings about no change in the legal relationship. Ejected sons do not lose the rights of inheritance.[82]

This is not to say, of course, that a father could not, upon approval by a family council, banish forever or in extreme cases even kill a son who had perpetrated some foul deed in utter violation of human ethics.[83] This, however, has nothing to do with the laws of inheritance but must be understood, rather, as a privately executed punishment against criminals; it was something out of the ordinary, not something likely to occur by reason of mere disobedience to orders or out of fear that the person in question might fritter away a family fortune.

Also, under Ch'ing law, if parents or grandparents reported a child or grandchild to the authorities with a request for punishment on the grounds of defiance of parents *(ch'u fan)*, the authorities, without investigation and acting solely on the parents' complaint, would sentence the child to *fa ch'ien* (a form of banishment). However, if the parents were to request a pardon on an occasion of general amnesty, the pardon would be granted, and the child sent home. Also, once the parents were dead, if the accused had demonstrated true repentance at his place of banishment, the rule was to release him and send him home. In these cases he was not deprived of his right of inheritance.[84]

Changes in the equality rule. Until some time ago the universally accepted view of the scholarly community was as follows: when sons and grandsons divide the household property among themselves after the father's death, the share of each is rigidly fixed by law under the rule of equal shares among brothers, whereas, when the household's property is divided by the father during his own lifetime, the distribution of shares is determined entirely by

---

[81] *Id.,* 247a.
[82] F. Hsu, *supra* note 26, at 224. In Hsu's inquiry into the peasant communities of Yunnan Province, it is reported that in the area under investigation there has not yet been found credible proof of a case where a youngster was deprived of his inheritance rights.
[83] *Cf.* J. Kuwahara, Shina hōseishi ronsō (Essays on Chinese legal history) 7 (1935). If such a murder came to light, it was adjudged a crime in terms of state law. In the collected criminal cases of the Ch'ing there are several instances of this.
[84] Ta Ch'ing Lü li, *Tuan yü* (Imprisonment, judgment, and execution), *Yu ssu chüeh ch'iu teng ti* (Execution of judgment), sub-statute 12; *Ming li* (General provisions), *Ch'ang she so pu yüan* (Crimes to be excluded from general amnesties), sub-statutes 11 and 12.

the will of the father. However, as a result of the inquiry into customary practices in the agricultural communities of northern China, a social reality different from the above view was introduced into the scholarly community. The question must be divided into two, if it is to be properly studied. The view that has obtained hitherto is perfectly correct where it concerns the father's privilege of setting aside property to keep him in his old age. On the other hand, the said view must be amended insofar as it holds that the father was free to violate the rule of equal distribution where the sons' share too was concerned.

First of all, it was typical even of fathers not to distribute their property inequitably among their sons, as was learned from peasant responses too numerous to count. A look at concrete cases in documents dealing with division of household property will reveal the same.[85] Also, it was not uncommon for the father to have his sons draw lots.[86]

If that be the case, was it possible or was it not for a father, in admittedly exceptional cases, to distribute the property among his sons in a discriminatory way? On this point the following question-and-answer exchange is worthy of note:

Q: Is it possible to give 3 *mou* to the eldest son, 4 to the middle son, and 5 to the youngest, ignoring the objections of the eldest?

A: It is not possible where the land is concerned. The land may rise in price. At any rate, since it is something important, and since a third party present when the household is being divided *(fen chia)* will not accede to this, nor bear responsibility for it, this simply will not do. If it is a matter of a small sum of money, very well. If it is a matter of chickens or ducks, people's objections will not make an ounce of difference, but in the case of horses or pigs there can be no distribution in the teeth of complaints. If such is done, the third parties present will refuse to take responsibility. . . .

Q: When a *fen chia tan* is written, is the presence of a third party absolutely necessary?

A: It is.

Q: Is there any objection if that role is played by the head of the household, who is also the father of the person carrying out the *fen chia?*

A: There is. No member of the family will do.[87]

Since antiquity, it has been the usual practice for the Chinese, when performing important legal acts, to invite a third person to be present and then to decide on a course of action after a three-way conference with him. This third person was one who combined in himself many functions such as arranging terms acceptable to both parties, seeing them through to their conclusion, bearing witness to legal acts, and expected to act as mediator of disputes which might arise at some future time. On the occasion of division of the

---

[85] *Cf.* N. NIIDA, CHŪGOKU NO NŌSON KAZOKU 116 ff. (1952).

[86] *Cf.* T. UCHIDA, *supra* note 66, at 96 ff.

[87] I CNKC 297b.

household as well, a *chung jen* (mediator) must be invited from outside the family. Such a mediator, in the event of an inequitable distribution among brothers, makes no attempt to assume responsibility, so it is said. This means that the distribution of equal shares among brothers was institutionally guaranteed as the right of each and every brother through the intervention of a mediator.

If the father were unable to violate the rule of equal distribution among brothers (sons) even when dividing up the household property in his own lifetime, it stands to reason that he could not take the same action through a will. In the verdicts of Ming times will be found a precedent in which an official pronounced a will in which a father left his property at a ratio of 6 to 4 to an elder son (by his official wife, at that) and a younger son (by a concubine), respectively,[88] as a *luan ming* (that is, as a will not consonant with reasonable standards) and hence, null and void. In the records of interviews in northern China will be found numerous question-and-answer exchanges of the following import:

Q: If the father in his will orders that, when the division of property takes place, a larger share be given the younger brother, is his order obeyed?
A: It is not. The division must be equal.
Q: Is there then no need to obey the will to its letter?
A: None.[89]

Posthumous gifts. Not only wills that fly in the face of the equal share rule, but also those that leave a greater portion of the household property than they should to an outsider in spite of the presence of a son(s), are considered not to be binding. Among the verdicts of Southern Sung times a case is found in which a father on his deathbed ordered his wife and sons to give a fixed sum of money every year to his nephews. The widow carried out this order for several years but eventually stopped, and a dispute ensued. The judge decreed that even if the bequest were prescribed in a valid will, the widow and sons were not to be compelled to pay more, although they were also not to take retroactive steps to regain the money that they had voluntarily paid.[90] In the verdicts of the Ming as well, a bequest to a son-in-law from his father-in-law, in the light of the presence of a son born to a concubine of the father-in-law after the latter's death, was adjudged invalid and, regardless of the authenticity or spuriousness of the will presented in evidence, declared null and void as a matter of course.[91]

---

[88] Li Yü, Tzu chih hsin shu (Guide to governing, new text), ch. 14, *"Hsien p'an hei yüan shih"* (Governor's decision rescued grievance).

[89] 5 CNKC 457a. *Cf.* 1 CNKC 273a; 4 CNKC 83a.

[90] Ch'ing ming chi, 64a–139 *"Chu chih lun so i chu ch'ien"* (Nephews' suit [against their aunt] for providing money according to the [uncle's] will).

[91] Li, *supra* note 88, at ch. 14, *"Ch'ün hsiung chieh sha shih"* (Plunder and slaughter by a group of outlaws).

The common people's sense of the law was of a piece with this, for even after the Civil Code of the Republic of China had acknowledged the right to dispose of property in a will, the villagers, so it is said,[92] continued to hold the conviction that the sons have absolute rights where their deceased father's property is concerned.

In the light of the above, the only possible conclusion is that the latitude of wills and testaments within China's law of inheritance was extremely confined. Consequently, the very act of drawing up a will was extremely rare under ordinary circumstances. With the word "will" *(i chu)*, in fact, most people associate moralistic admonitions and/or legacies of words having to do with succession to business obligations.[93] As Francis L. K. Hsu says, the very concept of a legal will was alien to the Chinese mode of thinking.[94]

However, this is not to say that there were absolutely no cases in which a will could have a function in the legal sense. Such a case would be one, first of all, in which there was no son. Where the selection of a foster son *(ssu-tzu)* was concerned, if the wishes of the deceased were plainly known, due respect would be paid them. When there were neither sons nor widow and when the household was threatened with extinction as a result of the death of the person in question, a will took precedence over whatever the law might prescribe.[95] Second, resort to wills and testaments was most common when the wish was to be succeeded by a foster son, but at the same time to leave certain property to a daughter or to guarantee a surviving concubine a livelihood for the remainder of her days.[96] Bequests to such persons as daughters and concubines, who were not heirs but who did have a certain connection with the household, were recognized as valid as long as they did not markedly reduce the legacy of the heirs.

Therefore, within the framework of benefit *(ch'eng shou)* in the sense defined above, wills and testaments were able to exercise a certain function. However, the rules of inheritance *(ch'eng chi)* were unmoving and transcended the individual will of the deceased.

Gifts during one's lifetime. If one pursues the line of the three entries above to its logical conclusion, what naturally comes to mind are gifts made by the father during his own lifetime. If through the existence of a son the father's

---

[92] M. YANG, *supra* note 7, at 82.

[93] *Cf.* 1 CNKC 243c, 297c; 4 CNKC 96b.

[94] F. HSU, AMERICANS AND CHINESE 99 (1953); *cf.* G. JAMIESON, *supra* note 32, at 31 ff.

[95] T'ang law stipulated this most clearly. *Cf.* N. NIIDA, *supra* note 22, at 835.

[96] *Cf.* CH'ING MING CHI, 63a–137 *"Nü ho ch'eng fen"* (Daughters are to be given due portions in inheritance); 119a–249 *"Chi mu chiang yang lao t'ien i chu yü ch'in sheng nü"* (A stepmother wants to bequeath the land reserved for support of her old age to her daughter), both of which are cases of bequests to daughters. For bequests to concubines, *cf.* S. SHIGA, *supra* note 3, at 566.

freedom to bequeath was severely limited, is it not equally possible that not merely bequests but gifts in general were subject to the same sort of restrictions? Although they both amount to disposition of household property, for the purposes of this discussion a distinction must be made between disposal for a price in order to realize the exchange value of an object, and disposal gratis, which reduces the total value of the household property. The following provision from the T'ang code is worthy of note as material rich in hints from this point of view:

> If there be anyone who attempts to set a *pu ch'ü* (male client) or a *k'o nü* (female client) free, or to elevate a *nu pei* (slave) to the status of a *pu ch'ü* or a *k'o nü* or, for that matter, to set him or her absolutely free, this shall in every case be tolerated. In either case a certificate from the head of the household, countersigned by his eldest son and others, must be presented to the government office having jurisdiction, and due record made in the household registry.[97]

Nu pei, as well as *pu ch'ü* and *k'o nü,* were unfree persons belonging to private households—with the qualification that *pu ch'ü* were somewhat freer than *nu pei*—and were regarded as a sort of chattel, making up one portion of the household property. Manumitting them was an act depriving the household of one *nu pei* or *pu ch'ü* and through that deprivation endowing the *nu pei* and/or *pu ch'ü* with the gift of freedom, a sort of gratis disposition. It is worthy of note that, whereas there was no custom making validity of contracts contingent on countersignatures, to say nothing of any law demanding a son's countersignature on a certificate drawn up by his father for such matters as purchase and sale or hypothecation, in at least one concrete example the law did require it for an act analogous to the giving of a gift. Also, in the records of interviews in northern China, those respondents who in general affirmed the freedom of the father of a household in the disposition of household property gave negative answers to the specific question as to whether he could give such property away gratis.

Q: May the head of a household dispose of that household's property freely?
A: He may.
Q: May he give it away gratis?
A: He may not. His sons will not stand for it.[98]
Q: Whose property are the things in your house?
A: Mine.
Q: May you do with them anything you please?
A: I may.
Q: May you give them away?
A: I may not. Since they constitute property I got from my father, I must leave them to my sons.[99]

---

[97] N. NIIDA, *supra* note 22, at 261.

[98] 1 CNKC 297b.

[99] 5 CNKC 453a.

From this too it is evident that a fundamental distinction was recognized
between the freedom of the father of a household to dispose of something for
a price and the restrictions imposed on him where gratis disposition was
concerned. It is difficult to imagine that this sort of construction is of recent
origin. It would probably be as well to view the prescriptions of the T'ang
statutes cited above, where the special question of the manumission of slaves
was concerned, as a partial manifestation of the legal construction generally
placed upon gratis dispositions by the populace then as now.

Even so, the answers are not crystal clear when, granted that the construction placed upon the law as a rule of thumb was that even the father of a
household could not give away the household's property freely, the question
arises of the concrete ways in which the father's giving power was limited.
For example, could a son later nullify a gift that had been made without his
consent? All that can be said in the light of an overall view is that gifts, in
comparison with sales, constituted an uncertain legal act likely to give rise to
confusion. In connection with a gift, there was a tendency for the former
owner's attachment to not be completely severed. There might and probably
would be differences from case to case between legal right and practical
attachment, but either way there was a tendency for the giver or his wife and
descendants to continue to have some sort of say over the object long after it
had been given away.

In the verdicts of the Southern Sung, there is a case in which the husband
had given a bit of land to a maidservant during his lifetime, but after his death
the widow had entered a plea demanding its return.[100] In this particular case,
on the grounds that the maidservant had borne the husband a child and that
the piece of land was slight in relation to the household property as a whole,
the widow's plea was dismissed; but depending on the circumstances it is
conceivable that such a plea might be entertained or that sons or grandsons,
rather than the widow, might enter it.

Gifts that frequently became matters of issue were donations of land to
Buddhist monasteries *(ssu)* and Taoist temples *(miao)*. In a Ch'ing edict,
dated Yung-cheng 12 (1734), attention was called to the evil practice of
frequently selling off monastery lands secretly and in defiance of the law,
including the expression that "among the worthless monastic rabble of this
monastery and filially impious sons and grandsons [of the donors] there are
those who sell secretly."[101] The only reason that such illegal acts were possible
is that, where the donated object was concerned, the donor's say over it

---

[100] CH'ING MING CHI, 88a-187 *"Lo Ping nü shih Lai An su chu mu to ch'ü so po
t'ien ch'an"* (Lai An, a female servant of Lo Ping, complains against her mistress alleging
that the latter took away the realty which had been bequeathed to her).

[101] HU-NAN SHENG-LI CH'ENG-AN (Regulations and Precedents of Hu-nan Province)
ch. 4, 43b (1820).

persisted to the time of his sons and grandsons. Also, among the verdicts of Ch'ing times there is a case[102]—dismissed, to be sure—in which descendants of a donor, who had given some land to a Buddhist monastery seven hundred years before in Sung times, sought to get the land back and convert it into clan property *(tsu t'ien)*. The precedents of the supreme court of the early Republic acknowledge the existence of certain cases in which the donor of land to monasteries and temples could dispose of that land at will, and in which his right to do so was affirmed as a matter of customary law.[103]

Furthermore, there is rather widespread evidence of the practice of executing a formal bill of sale while fully intending to make an actual gift of the land; this act was presumably based on the intention of avoiding the appearance of gift-giving, which was an uncertain legal act that was likely to lead to confusion at a later date. Concrete examples of this are seen in the verdicts as early as the Southern Sung,[104] while, when we come down to more recent times, we see the following reported from Shang-wen-hsien in the Shantung Province:

When parents give farmland to their daughter, they invariably draw up a bill of sale, which they give to her husband or son. On reflection, it is evident that a certificate of a gift is not an accustomed thing in terms of the local practices. The feeling is that a bill of sale is more certain. Since it stems from the will of the person in question, it should be taken of course as valid.[105]

From Shan-yin-hsien in Shansi Province the following is reported:

There are occasionally persons who give land away because it is a nuisance to pay taxes on land of poor yield. On the deed, as a matter of form, the price of the cession is recorded, but in reality it is not collected. The reason for this too is that without money changing hands the document in question is not regarded as a contract.[106]

This means that there were regions where the people knew nothing of contracts binding as gifts. In the writings of the Reverend Pierre Hoang as well, it is stated that, while a certificate attesting to a gift *(ch'ien chü)* is helpful to the recipient, for future purposes it is safer to obtain a deed of unconditional sale *(chüeh mai ch'i)* with no money actually changing hands.[107]

---

[102] TUNG P'EI, JU TUNG P'AN YÜ (Decisions composed in the eastern area of the Ju River) ch. 1, *"Li Tso-ch'a teng ch'eng tz'u p'an"* (Decision on Li Tso-ch'a and others' complaints).

[103] W. KUO, *supra* note 52, at 37, *san nien shang tzu* No. 595 (1914 Appeals Case No. 595).

[104] *Cf.* note 79 *supra*.

[105] MIN-SHANG-SHIH HSI-KUAN TIAO-CH'A PAO-KAO-LU 241 (1930).

[106] *Id.*, 307.

[107] P. HOANG, NOTIONS TECHNIQUES SUR LA PROPRIÉTÉ EN CHINE (Technical comments on property in China), 10, No. 31 (1898).

Above, proceeding from the question of whether the father of a household may on his own authority give part of the household property to someone else, we have the uncertainty of the act of giving itself. This too is logical. Where the uncertainty of gift-giving is concerned, the agreement or opposition of a son is only a difference of degree, for after a son are to be expected numberless descendants, all of whom must give their consent once one speaks of "agreement." In sum, one possible interpretation is that, since gift-giving is an act in conflict with the rule of inheritance, which holds that the property of the ancestors must be transmitted down through the generations to male descendants, it could not easily escape the fate of uncertainty.

Theoretical Summation

Nakata's theory, which advocates the confusion of two capacities embodied in one person, the commanding authority as a father and the administrative authority as family head, has as its point of departure the a priori view that the element of *Miteigentum zur gesamten Hand* (co-joint ownership) is present in the conceptual content of "common living, common budget." This a priori premise must be taken up as a problem in its own right. If as a matter of fact the father could force the assent—or their countersignature as an expression thereof—of his sons to any transaction he wished, then the theory of confusion of capacities is clearly justified. The facts, however, are otherwise. With no inquiry into the sentiments of his sons, the father's dispositions were perfectly valid, and the position of those with whom the father conducted his transactions was a safe one, subject to no fear of creating problems at a later date. There was, in fact, a proverb saying, "What the father sells has nothing further to do with the son" *(fu mai tzu tuan)*.[108]

It is only when considering the father's authority to make dispositions in conjunction with the division of household property that one gets a satisfactory explanation. As long as he lived, whether the household's property was to be divided was up to the father to decide; even if the sons demanded a distribution, the father could refuse, and he could even expel from the household at his discretion a son who stubbornly insisted on his own independence. Also, in the event of a distribution, the amount of property that was to be kept in his own hands was a matter entirely up to the father. In other words, a division of household property during the father's lifetime was nothing other than an act of distributing to his sons of his own free will one portion of the household property that had been entirely his until then, and at the same time an act of conferring upon them the independence to thereafter treat their respective earnings as their own property. Through division of household property it was the sons, not the father, who had rights newly conferred upon them. All the father did in his own interest was to retain some of the rights

---

[108] CH'ING MING CHI, 164a–337.

he already had. Consequently, the certificate attesting to the distribution of household property had to be drawn up in several copies, one for each son. A certificate of distribution to be kept by the father was a thought that occurred to no one. The property kept by the father to maintain him in his old age was merely noted in the certificates of distribution given to the sons. If an object happened not to be specified, whether as something to be retained by the father or as something to be given to one of the sons, it was understood to be reserved for the father.[109] Besides, as is most clearly demonstrated by the fact that division of household property between a father and an only son was unthinkable, such division was in essence carried out among brothers and was not an institution for the purpose of regulating rival claims between father and sons.

In short, while among brothers who were sons of the same father there was a confrontation of mutually unassailable rights, between father and sons there was no such thing. The son had no rights in the face of his father, and the household property in its entirety was the possession of the father. Thus, it stands to reason that the father could dispose of it freely.

In the locutions found in the documents as well as in the responses in the interviews, expressions referring to the property of a household consisting of a father and sons as "the father's property" and as "everyone's property" are seen to be confused.[110] Both are perfectly reasonable expressions and perfectly consonant with commonly accepted views. The reason for this is that household property is a pooling of the fruits of the labor of all members of the household and the means of support of all. Seen from this point of view, it is "everyone's property." On the other hand, the one who has legal control over the household's property is the father. Seen from that point of view, it is "the father's property." Between the two expressions there is in reality not the least contradiction.

Yet there were some things that even the omnipotent father could not do. He could do none of the following: rob a son of his inheritance, curtail one son's share of the legacy in order to benefit another son, or reduce his sons' shares unjustly in order to make a bequest or confer a gift on some other person. In a word, the fact that the sons were the father's heirs *(ch'eng chi jen)* as well as the fact that they were all absolutely equal to one another in this capacity, was a rule of nature transcending the individual will of the father. This is connected with the fact that there was no one other than his sons whom a father could charge with the future obligation to sacrifice to his ancestors, an obligation that he currently bore. The rights of father and sons where household property was concerned kept their balance in the form of the

---

[109] *Cf.* 4 CNKC 69b; 1 CNKC 269; 5 CNKC 86b.

[110] *Cf.* N. NIIDA, *supra* note 15, at 441; N. NIIDA, *supra* note 85, at 221; S. SHIGA, *supra* note 3, at 208.

father's right of possession, which at the given moment extended to the whole
household property, and that of the sons' right to expect inheritance which
was no less total; neither stood, in any sense whatever, in a relationship of
shares to the other.

Succession to Ancestral Sacrifices and Adoption of Heirs to the Sacrifices:

AS SEEN FROM AN INQUIRY INTO CUSTOMARY INSTITUTIONS IN MANCHURIA

TATSUO CHIKUSA

The area of China known as Manchuria is the home of a motley conglome-ration of peoples. In Manchukuo times, 85 percent were Chinese, while the remainder were, in numerical order, Manchus, Koreans, Mongols, Japanese, Moslems, and White Russians.[1] Before the adoption of Manchukuo family law, I conducted, from 1939 to 1942, an inquiry into the institutions connected with the family systems of all the peoples resident in Manchuria with the exception of the Japanese. In the course of the inquiry I was dependent upon the collaboration of many individuals and agencies, but I went in person to the important places. As a result, I drew up a record of inquiries into institutional practices amounting to seven volumes of manuscript, eight or nine hundred pages in each volume. However, at war's end I lost five of those volumes. On the basis of the remaining two and with the addition of other manuscript material, I published a three-volume work entitled, *Manshū kazoku-seido no kanshū* (Customs of the Manchurian family system).[2] The present paper will attempt, on the basis of the fruits of the aforementioned inquiry, to make clear what sort of customary institutions obtained at the time in China's Manchuria. I will concern myself with three specific features: succession to ancestral sacrifices *(tsung-t'iao)*, adoption of a male heir from the same clan *(ssu-tzu)*, and adoption of a male heir from a different clan *(yang-tzu)*. Mention shall also be made occasionally of the customary institutions of the

---

[1] According to a provisional census carried out on October 1, 1940, the total popula-tion of Northeast (Manchuria) was about 43,200,000, of whom the Manchus numbered 2,680,000; the Chinese 36,870,000; the Mongols 1,070,000; the Moslems 190,000; the Japanese 820,000; the Koreans 1,450,000; other Manchus 50,000; and White Russians 70,000 (rounding off to the nearest 5,000).

[2] For details, *cf.* 1 T. CHIKUSA, MANSHŪ KAZOKU-SEIDO NO KANSHŪ (Customs of the Manchurian family system) preface (1960).

Japanese. Although the customs of the Mongols, Moslems, and White Russians in these regions have become slightly Sinicized through prolonged contact, mention of them is omitted because of the extreme cultural differences. The Manchus and Koreans also are omitted because of cultural variations.

At the time of the inquiry more than ten years had passed since the Republic of China enacted its revolutionary family law. The Republic's family law had been formulated in part on the basis of equality of the sexes in imitation of the legal institutions of Europe and America, and by rejecting family institutions of long standing. However, in China where the land was broad, education not widespread, and cultural penetration slow, the Republic's family law was so little heeded as to be virtually a dead letter. What largely remained in force were the family institutions of long before. Even in Japan, for fifty years following the enactment of a civil code in early Meiji times, customary institutions did not easily change nor did the social situation easily keep pace with the civil code. Family institutions, which have an intimate connection with manners and customs on the one hand, and moral and ethical principles on the other, do not change all that easily in response to legal reform and the alteration of political structure. In pre-modern China, a country in which the Communist revolution took place after the time under discussion, there are presumably points on which the said revolution exerted a considerable influence even on family institutions, but there is no ground for believing that all is different, at least in a general way, between the present and the time of my inquiry. In this sense, I believe that the inquiry may serve as a point of reference for studying the family institutions of contemporary China.

From a totally different point of view, it was thanks only to this inquiry into Chinese family institutions that we had the feeling for the first time that we understood Japanese family institutions. Some twelve hundred years ago Japan did import Chinese family institutions by way of the Taika reform, but we were all quite amazed at the unexpected proportion of institutions that we had imagined to be indigenous to Japan and that were, in fact, Chinese imports. Japan did not import the institution of the clan *(tsu)*, but the concept of household *(honke)* and division of household *(bunke)* does resemble it in some respects. The institution of family property *(chia-ch'an)* does not exist in Japan, but the property of the several members of a family is not so clearly distinguished as in countries in which individualism holds sway. Prohibition of marriage within the clan *(tsu)*, or among persons of different generations *(pei-fen)* did not exist in Japan, but remnants of a sort of master of matrimony *(chu-hun jen)* institution, whereby the parent concludes the betrothal as the representative of the child, survive to this day. The institution of concubinage existed in Japan even until early Meiji. The institution of establishing an heir for a deceased person *(shinshi)* when there was no son, and as a rule assigning this role to a member of the same clan *(dōzoku)*, existed until the end of the Tokugawa era (1603–1868). While there was no practice of adopting an heir for a deceased person, the revival of the abolished house *(haike)* and the extinct house *(zekke)* in the Meiji Civil Code was in the same spirit. The notion that succession to ancestral sacrifices is not divisible from inheritance of family property is related to the notion of succession to the headship of the house *(katoku sōzoku)* in Japan's Meiji Civil Code. In the background of the institutions of both countries the spirit of Confucianism, that is, the cult of the ancestors, was to work.

SUCCESSION TO ANCESTRAL SACRIFICES

The Institutions of Old China

The institution of succession to ancestral sacrifices *(tsung-t'iao)* is set forth in the *Chou li,* which specifies the distinction between a *ta-tsung* and *hsiao-tsung.* The mausoleum *(miao)* of the *ta-tsung,* unmoved for a hundred generations, was called *tsung,* while that of the *hsiao-tsung,* moved after five generations, was called *t'iao.* This was the original meaning of the disyllable *tsung-t'iao,*[3] and a *tsung-t'iao,* when all is said and done, is a shrine *(miao)* where one sacrifices to one's ancestors. Thus *tsung-t'iao* succession means inheritance of the status of officiant at ancestral sacrifices.

Since China's family institutions had stood by the principle of male heritage from antiquity, the successor to the sacrifices had to be a descendant in the male line. It was also felt that the ancestral spirits would not accept a sacrifice from a person of a different clan. There were three types of filial impiety; the gravest of the three was lack of issue, since this was tantamount to discontinuing the ancestral sacrifices. Thus, when there were no sons, a kinsman of the same clan would be adopted as a precaution against cutting off the bloodline.

The sequence of successors to the sacrifices. Among the common people the role of officiant at the sacrifices was not limited to the eldest son by the official wife, but could be held equally by all the male offspring *(chung tzu).* When a son established a separate household in which sacrifices were performed, there was no need to fix a rigid order of succession to these sacrifices. However, in cases where a single heir to the sacrificial office had to be determined in connection with succession to titles of nobility *(chueh-wei)* and the like, it was necessary to make the order of succession perfectly clear. For this there were two models. One was based on the principle of the lineage of the official wife, which meant that succession passed from the eldest son by the official wife to the eldest grandson, or, if he were not living, to other sons by the same mother, and then to sons by lesser wives. The other model was based on the principle of succession by generation *(pei-fen),* which meant that, regardless of whether there was a grandson in the line of the official wife, the eldest

---

[3] *Cf.* C. Hu, CHUNG KUO MIN FA CHI CH'ENG LUN (Inheritance under China's civil code) 7 (1945).

son by the official wife would be followed by a younger brother (the same generation), or in his absence by a grandson. Each of these two models were in vogue at different times.

Institutions of succession to sacrifices stood in a mutually complementary relationship to inheritance of fief and rank. Under the laws of the T'ang and Sung dynasties, the order and range of the selection of heirs was as follows: (1) eldest son by official wife *(ti chang-tzu)*; (2) eldest grandson descended of the official wife *(ti ch'u chang-sun)*; (3) younger brothers of (1); (4) sons by concubines *(shu-tzu)*; (5) younger brother of (2); (6) grandsons descended of concubines *(shu sun)*; and so on for the next two generations.

While there were some subsequent changes, the principle of adherence to the lineage of the official wife appears to have maintained itself. However, it was maintained only against a background of inheritance of fiefs and ranks, or of office and title. Among the common people, who had neither fief, rank, office, nor title, there was no need to adhere to this principle, nor does it in fact appear to have been consistently honored. The laws of succession to sacrifices in the codes of the Ming and the Ch'ing do no more than specify the sequence between those descended of official wives and those descended of concubines on the one hand, and between senior and junior *(chang-yu)* on the other. Adherence to the lineage of official wives is not specified, nor is there even a clear reference to it in the Ming code.[4]

According to the customary practices of the Chin (A.D. 936–944) in the case of sacrifices, unlike that of fiefs and ranks, if the eldest son by the official wife were not living, the succession as a rule would go to the younger brothers, and there was no institution in which grandsons descended of the official wife would take precedence over the eldest surviving son of the same wife.

Beginning with the Hsi-ning (1125–1168) era, the generation *(pei-fen)* principle in the matter of succession to sacrifices was enacted into law, and by the time of the promulgation of the *fu chih ling* in Southern Sung times, the order of succession was as follows: (1) eldest son by the official wife *(ti chang-tzu)*; (2) brothers of (1) whether descended by the same mother or not *(ti chang-tzu hsiung-ti)*; (3) eldest grandson descended of the official wife *(ti ch'u chang-sun)*; (4) younger brother of (3); (5) eldest grandsons descended of other wives *(chung chang-sun)*. In this way the heir to the sacrifices, who was determined on the generation *(pei-fen)* principle, came to be ranked legally alongside the heir to fief and title, who was determined by the lineage of the official wife. The codes of the Ming and Ch'ing may be interpreted in the light of either principle, as previously stated.

---

[4] *Cf.* N. NIIDA, SHINA MIBUNHŌSHI (History of status law in China) 491 (1942); 2 RINJI TAIWAN KYŪKAN CHŌSAKAI (Temporary committee on research of customs and practices on Taiwan), TAIWAN SHIHŌ (Taiwan private law) chüan 2, at 277 (1910) [hereinafter cited as TAIWAN SHIHŌ].

In China the head of the household, in the case of the same generation, is determined by age, while, in the case of different generations, a member of an older generation *(tsun-pei)* is preferred even to a grandson descended of an official wife. Consequently, if adherence to the lineage of the official wife is the rule, the successor to the sacrifices and the head of the household are not necessarily the same person, while if the generation principle is the guide, the successor to the sacrifices and the head of the household are, more often than not, identical.[5]

Heir to the sacrifices adopted from the same clan (ssu-tzu). If one had no sons, succession to the sacrifices could be conferred upon a kinsman from the same clan. This adopted heir *(ssu-tzu)* could be a nephew or even a second cousin so long as he corresponded to the generation of a son. If he did not correspond to the proper generation, the pattern of status within the family would be upset. The adoption of an heir from the same clan *(ssu-tzu)* will be explained in detail in the next chapter.

Combined successions (chien-t'iao). The rule of thumb for succession to ancestral sacrifices *(tsung-t'iao)* is one heir to one clan *tsung*. However, the law *(lü ling)* does permit an only son to be heir to two branches *(fang).* For example, if an elder brother had no sons while his younger brother had only one, the nephew would be heir simultaneously to both his father and his uncle. This is known as *chien-t'iao, tu tzu shuang-t'iao,* or, more popularly, *i chih liang pu chueh.*

This system came into being in order to prevent the discontinuation of ancestral sacrifices. The toleration of combined succession to senior and junior branches appears to have begun in Ch'ing times, specifically in the regulations *(t'iao ling)* of Ch'ien-lung 40. However, even in these, combined succession on the part of an only son was limited to the same clan *(tsung).*[6]

The relation of succession to the sacrifices and inheritance of official rank. In China there has been since antiquity a system of inheritance of official rank *(küan yuan hsi yin)* in addition to the system of succession to the sacrifices *(tsung-t'iao).* The law governing inheritance of official rank was a special law aimed at official functionaries whose positions and emoluments were hereditary. These two laws, having different goals, were independent of each other, and there was no need for them to coincide. That is to say, whereas *tsung-t'iao* succession was aimed at transmission of the *tsung* line in order to continue the ancestral sacrifices, the primary goal of succession to official rank was to enable sons, grandsons, younger brothers, and nephews to inherit in order to glorify ancestral achievements. Since the two laws had different goals, their specifications did not necessarily agree. However, succession to the sacrifices was to be guided by the order of inheritance of official rank.

---

[5] N. NIIDA, *supra* note 4, at 496.

[6] *Cf.* 2 TAIWAN SHIHŌ chüan 2, at 265.

The breakdown of the regulations regarding succession to the sacrifices. In this way succession to the sacrifices *(tsung-t'iao)* was intimately connected with inheritance of official ranks and emoluments, but together with the abandonment of feudal institutions and the disappearance of these forms of inheritance, the realistic need for clan laws *(tsung fa)* also disappeared. Furthermore, even in feudal times the *tsung fa* obtained only among royalty and the nobility and had nothing to do with the commonalty. Thus the basic unit of society in general was not the clan *(tsung)*, but the household *(chia)*. Ancestral sacrifices were managed in each individual household, and the terms *ta-tsung* and *hsiao-tsung* were obsolete.

Relation to Japan's institution of katoku sōzoku. After the Taika reform Japan adopted the institutions of the T'ang. Under the system of succession embodied in the laws enacted in Japan's T'ang derivative law *(ritsuryō)*, succession to the prerogatives of the head of a household was called keishi, and there was a regulation *(keishiryō)* dealing with it, while property inheritance was dealt with in the *(ōbunjō)* of the *(koryō)*. The former might be called the law of succession to the headship of a household *(keishi sōzoku hō)*; the latter, the law of property inheritance *(kei zaisan sōzoku hō)*. The former *(keishi sōzoku)* attaches the greatest importance to succession to the father's household; in other words, it was succession to ancestral sacrifices, as in the case of *tsung-t'iao* succession in China. Consequently, it was something different from Japan's ancient practice of succession to the family name *(kamei sōzoku)*.[7]

Katoku sōzoku in the Meiji Civil Code combined three things: succession to the family name *(kamei sōzoku)*, succession to ancestral sacrifices, and inheritance of property. Under the reform following World War II, succession to the family name and the sacrifices has been placed outside the law, relegated, so to speak, to the realm of individual morality. The legal specifications regarding succession were confined to inheritance of legacies, exactly as is the case with the section on inheritance in the Republican Civil Code of the 1930s in China.

Succession to the Sacrifices *(tsung-t'iao)* in Manchuria, *1939–42*

Let me now give an outline of the sort of customary practices that were in vogue at the time of my inquiry with regard to succession to ancestral sacrifices in Manchuria.[8]

---

[7] *Cf.* K. MAKI, NIPPON HŌSEI SHI (Japanese legal history) 1, 215 (1937); 1 K. NAKATA, HOSEI SHI RONSHŪ (Collected essays on legal history) 15 (1926).

[8] Where the Manchus are concerned, these findings are based on inquiries conducted in Kirin, Kaiping, Tsitsihar, and Shuang-ch'eng, as well as on 1 T. CHIKUSA, *supra* note 2, at 660 ff., 850 ff.

Where the Chinese are concerned, *cf.*, the inquiries at Kirin, Kaiping, and Tsitsihar (1 T. CHIKUSA, *supra* note 2, at 680 ff); the inquiry at Harbin (3 T. CHIKUSA, *supra* note 2, at 140 ff); and the inquiry at Yen-chi (3 T. CHIKUSA, *supra* note 2, at 561 ff).

Customs governing succession. Among the Chinese, the veneration of ancestors and the constant maintenance of sacrifices to them were matters of universal custom, and the institution of succession to the sacrifices *(tsung-t'iao)* was still in force. This fact was obvious from the adoption of heirs when one had no sons. Also, the successor to the sacrifices was invariably an heir to the property.

However, there were some who inherited the property without succeeding to the sacrifices. For example, there were cases in which the legator did not wish to designate a successor, but willed his property to a daughter or a nephew. This is known as *cho chi*, signifying the selection of an heir on the basis of character evaluation, and there are some who would argue that it is the nature of a testament, not an inheritance.

Successors to the sacrifices. In all areas investigated in Manchuria successors to the sacrifices were limited to males. The males take permanent charge of the sacrifices and worship the ancestors forever, while the females do not perform sacrifices in the households in which they were born. This is commonly known as "internal males and external females" *(nei nan wai nü)*. Consequently, the female cannot be a successor to the sacrifices. The Kaiping inquiry revealed that on the one day in the year on which sacrifices are performed to the ancestors *(sui shih fu la)*, participation of females who have married into other families is tolerated with reluctance. This having become the custom, women who have married into other families do not sacrifice in their own, and there are no married women who return to their maiden homes for this occasion. Also, the adoption of an heir *(ssu-tzu)* for a childless person takes place only for sons, not for daughters. Among the Koreans too, the successors to the ancestral sacrifices are limited to the males. Females generally marry into other families, and since a woman coming from another family always has a different clan name, it is the male alone who sacrifices.

Recent social organization regards the household *(chia)*, not the clan *(tsung)*, as the basic unit, and ancestral sacrifices are performed within the common clan *(tsung)*. When the members of a clan gather to sacrifice, the presiding officer is the clan chief who need not be a *tsung tzu*. The institution under which a *tsung tzu* presides over the sacrifices has ceased to exist, and the institutions of the household that sacrifices to ancestors one hundred generations back *(ta-tsung)* and the household that sacrifices only to ancestors no more than five generations back *(hsiao-tsung)* have also been discontinued. Consequently, from the inquiries in any area it is evident that nowadays the status of successor to the sacrifices is not confined to the eldest son by the official wife; if the eldest son has several brothers or half-brothers, any of them is qualified to succeed to the sacrifices. Only in the inquiry conducted among the Chinese at Yen-chi were the inquirers told that there could be only one successor, and that the sequence was the eldest son by the official wife followed by the eldest grandson descended of the official wife. However, this was merely a rote repetition of the content of the ancient canons, and there is some doubt as to whether it was actually the current practice.

Combined successions. Among the Chinese the practice of combined succession *(chien t'iao)* had general currency at the time of the inquiry.

Combined succession is usually resorted to between blood brothers when one of them has no son; among those answering the inquiry were some who said that these were the only cases (Kirin, Kaiping, and Tsitsihar). However, the cases observed were not limited to those of blood brothers, for it was felt that combined succession was permissible as long as the persons involved belonged to the same clan *(tsung)* and were of a generation *(pei-fen)* corresponding to that of brothers.

The most common form of combined succession is that uniting two branches but there was no unanimous agreement to the question of whether it was possible to unite three or more branches. Those who said it was not possible meant only that they did not know since actual cases were rare. The fact is, however, that there are cases of the union of three branches, and there is no reason that it cannot be done. In such cases it would probably be called *i chih san pu chüeh.*

The procedure for combined succession is usually the same as for adopted heirs *(ssu-tzu)*. Usually a document of adoption called *kuo-chi tan* is drawn up. However, all that is common to them is that the kin of both sides are assembled. In some cases the act of combined succession is publicized, and in others not.

In the case of combined succession, those who answered the inquiry at Harbin said that it is not usual to take a wife separately in each branch, while those at Tsitsihar, Kirin, Kaiping, and Shuang-ch'eng said that it is the more usual practice. Others (in Yen-chi) went so far as to say that combined succession consists of taking a wife separately in each branch. When two wives are taken, the father in each branch chooses the wife for that branch. From the point of view of monogamy, one of the wives should be a "wife," and the other a "concubine," but as far as customary practice is concerned, both are treated as wives; the same sort of marriage ceremony is conducted for both. The wife in the elder branch calls the father in the younger branch "uncle" *(shu fu)* or "younger brother of husband" *(shu shu)* and the mother *shen niang.* The wife in the younger branch calls the father in the elder branch "uncle" *(po fu)* (that is, older brother of husband) and the mother "aunt" *(po mu),* or in outlying localities *ta niang.*

When the real father and the foster father do not have separate households, the two wives occupy separate rooms. In the case of separate households, they live in different houses, and the husband frequents each house on certain fixed days.

When one of the wives dies, it is possible to take a new wife for the branch in question, but that is not done. Even when undertaking the care of her son, the property of the branch to which that son belongs is set aside, and care is taken to keep it separate.

Since combined succession is a device resorted to only when there is no prospect of the birth of a son, there are virtually no cases in which a son was thereafter born of either father. Yet, if one were born, does it or does it not mean that the adopted son does not succeed to the branch in which the birth took place? In other words, if a second son were born to the real father, does the first son (the combined heir) succeed only to the branch of his foster father; if a son were born to the foster father, is the combined succession thereby annulled? The answers to these questions vary. If there were no wife, the combined succession could probably be annulled. However, if it were not annulled, what happens? Also, if wives have been taken separately in each branch, the disposition of the wives becomes a problem in the event of annulment. Some persons answering the inquiry said that in cases involving wives in each branch, the combined succession was not annulled. However, when the real father has a second son, the continuation of the combined succession is unreasonable, and it suffices for the real father to send his daughter-in-law to the foster father's house. There were some who said that if the foster father has a son, the adopted heir does not lose his status and should receive an equal share of his foster father's legacy.

To which branch does a son succeed who is born to one who has succeeded to more than one branch *(chien-t'iao jen)?* In cases in which different wives have been taken for each branch, it is clear that the sons of each wife succeed to their respective branches. However, when there is only one wife, the situation to which all agreed is as follows:

1. When there is only one son, he combines both branches by *chien t'iao.*

2. When there are two sons, the elder succeeds to the senior branch, and the younger to the junior branch. Both of them never combine the two branches through *chien-t'iao.*

3. When there are three sons or more, the eldest succeeds to the senior branch, the second to the junior branch, and the third and all other younger sons to the original branch of their father.

The effects of succession. Ancestral sacrifices are carried on by the whole society, regardless of wealth or status. When there are several brothers, all sacrifice to the ancestors, and the one who officiates depends upon local custom. There are some cases in which the head of the household officiates, and others in which the eldest son in the senior line officiates. In a big family in Kirin, there was a person who owned a sacrificial field, and yearly by turns the several branches would preside.

The time and ritual of the sacrifices differ in accord with the people, the district, and the local beliefs. In all areas, they perform sacrifices on (1) the holiday known as *Ch'ing-ming chieh,* (2) the fifteenth of the seventh lunar month *(chung-yüan chieh)*, popularly known as *kuei chieh*), and (3) the first of the tenth lunar month, a day on which paper and cloth are burnt for the dead (popularly known as *sung han-i*). Apart from these, there are areas where sacrifices are regularly performed on the first and last of the year, or on the anniversaries of parents' and grandparents' deaths. There are also districts that sacrifice on specific occasions, such as a marriage, a succession, the division of a household, or when a person comes home who has been away for a long time and has long neglected his sacrifices. The ceremony is in every case a solemn one, but the manner of them varies from place to place.

The successor to the sacrifices inherits the grave, the burial utensils, and the like; manages the ceremony in which the coffin of the deceased is escorted to the burial ground and interred; and presides over the ancestral sacrifices. The successor to the sacrifices must also support the legator while the latter lives. In the event of division of the household, the eldest son may be given an extra portion of the property to help defray the expenses of the sacrifices, but this practice is no longer in general vogue.

The successor to the sacrifices *(tsung-t'iao)* inherits the ancestral tablet *(mu-chu* or *wei-p'ai)*, Buddhist icons, ancestral chapel, family tree, and sacrificial vessels of his ancestors; if there are sacrificial fields, he inherits them too. At Hai-ch'eng and Tsitsihar there were persons who owned household mausoleums *(chia miao)*, and at Mukden there were those who owned shrine property *(tz'u ch'an)*. However, the Northeast was an area only recently opened up, unlike China proper, and cases of ownership of household mausoleums and shrine chapels were extremely few.

The management of the ancestral hall *(tz'u t'ang)* is said by some to be in the hands of the senior branch, by others to be in the hands of persons of high generation *(pei-fen)* status. There are some again who say that it is attended to by powerful persons owning clan property, and others yet who say that it is done by persons appointed by the clan. In short, the accounts vary.

As to sacrificial vessels, inquiries into Chinese practices revealed that in cases where there are several brothers, the following persons are in charge:

1. The eldest usually takes charge.

2. Some who answered the inquiry said that, regardless of whether he were the elder or the younger, after a split in the household the one who remained in the original house was in charge. However, since in the event of division the assignment of real estate was most often determined by lot, there was no predicting who would remain in the old house.

3. There were cases in which charge would be taken by a person agreed upon by the brothers. If the eldest brother were a government official or long absent on business, the brothers might agree among themselves on a manager.

On the other hand, the inquiries conducted at Kirin and Kaiping revealed the following:

1. As long as the household was not divided, those living together would manage it in common.

2. Even if the household were divided, as long as they were still living together, charge would be taken by the person assigned the room in which the ancestral sacrifices were performed, regardless of whether he were the eldest or the youngest.

3. If the household were divided and they were living apart, charge would still be taken by the person assigned the room in which the ancestral sacrifices were performed, regardless of whether he were the eldest or the youngest.

Adoption of Heirs From the Same Clan and From Other Clans

The Institutions of Old China

Intralineage adoption. Among the cases of children who were reared by persons other than their parents, *kuo-fang-tzu* or *kuo-chi-tzu* were male children of the same clan who were adopted for the purpose of maintaining the sacrifices. These foster sons were also designated *ssu-tzu* and *chi-tzu* in the literary language. The difference between the terms *kuo-fang-tzu* and *kuo-chi-tzu* is not clear. Some say that a *kuo-chi-tzu* is a foster son from the same clan, adopted as heir to the sacrifices; others say that, on the contrary, *kuo-chi-tzu* are not confined to the same clan, while *kuo-fang-tzu* are limited to the same clan. However, it seems that both are used with about the same meaning and that there is no clearcut distinction between them.

The T'ang rules for the adoption of heirs to ancestral sacrifices *(kuo-fang-tzu; kuo-chi-tzu)* were as follows: (1) the foster parent had to be a male, (2) no one who had a son of his own could adopt an heir, (3) the adopted son had to be close kin to the foster parent and in the same clan (although this was not necessarily adhered to in all strictness), (4) the foster parent and child had to be in proper parent-child generations, and (5) the foster son could not be an only son (except in cases of combined succession). If a husband died without leaving a son or an adopted heir, it was felt that the widow was obliged to adopt an heir for the sake of her husband.

The *kuo-fang-tzu* or *kuo-chi-tzu* acquired through adoption a status identical to that of a son by the official wife. He entered, as a matter of course, into the household of his foster parents and severed his family ties with his own parents.

The T'ang code absolutely forbade the adoption of sons from other clans. Violators of this law could be sentenced to one year of penal labor; persons who gave their sons for such an adoption could be flogged fifty strokes.

Designation of heirs in the old codes. The system for designating heirs in the old codes was as follows:

The conditions for becoming a foster parent *(ssu-fu)* were:

1. One must have attained one's majority. This, however, did not apply to persons who died before the attainment of their majority, provided they fitted into one of the following categories:
    a. The person marries and dies.
    b. The fiancé dies after the betrothal, but before the marriage, and his fiancée enters his household and remains faithful to him, not marrying (a "woman who preserves her ideals").
    c. The person dies unmarried in battle.
    d. An only son dies prematurely, and there is no one in the clan of a generation appropriate to be his father's adopted heir.
2. One must be male. This is an absolute condition.
3. One must be married, except in cases (b), (c), and (d) above, as well as persons who died at the age of sixteen and above.
4. One must have no sons. The exceptions are persons to whom sons were born after they had adopted an heir, or those sons were missing but returned safe and sound after the adoption.

The conditions for becoming an adopted heir *(ssu-tzu)* were:

1. One must belong to the same clan.
2. One must be of an appropriate generation within the same kin group.
3. One must be male.
4. One must have brothers. The exception is the person who fulfills the requirements for combined succession.

The sequence of persons having the right to designate an heir was:

1. Legators.
2. "Women who preserve their ideals."
3. Senior blood kin in a direct line.
4. Family council.

When the first three designate the heir, as long as the person is of the appropriate generation, there is a free choice as to the worth and appeal of the person to be selected. However, when the choice is made by a family council, this latitude is not present.[9]

Comparison with the Institutions of Adoption in Old Japan

Japan inherited Chinese law including adoption laws through the Taika Reform. However, with the arrival of the Middle Ages the laws indigenous to Japan were to a certain extent revived and revised, and then revised once

---

[9] *Cf.* S. Shiga, Chūgoku kazoku hō no genri (Basic principles underlying Chinese family law) 311 ff. (1967); C. Hu, *supra* note 2, at 14.

again, presumably so as to match objective and subjective conditions. Consequently, while Japan's adoption laws differ on many points from Chinese institutions of adoption, the similarities are also numerous. The purposes of adoption in Japan as in China are the continuity of the household and the maintenance of ancestral sacrifices.

Middle antiquity. Since the institutions of adoption in middle antiquity had just been inherited from Chinese law, there are many points which are literal copies of that law. Adopted sons were allowed only for reasons of succession and only when there were no other male successors *(koryō)*. Also the adopted son had to be the appropriate generation. If one adopted a son from another clan, the punishment was penal labor for one year, while the person who was adopted would be flogged fifty strokes *(kokon ryō)*.[10]

The Middle Ages. The legal codes of the Middle Ages (from Kamakura until Tokugawa) added to the above by partially reviving and revising Japan's indigenous laws. The rules for the adoption of a male heir were identical with the Chinese except for the following: (1) if a son who had sons of his own died before his father, the potential intestate had to adopt his own grandson; (2) when the potential intestate had no direct descendants, it was customary for him to adopt a younger brother as a son; (3) when he had neither lineal descendants nor younger brothers, the potential intestate would adopt a nephew, a daughter's son, or a younger cousin.[11] Thus the Japanese revision of Chinese law did not limit adopted heirs to the same clan, did not adhere rigorously to the male line, and did not insist that the persons involved be of appropriate generations.

The Tokugawa era. Since in the Tokugawa era the households of the warrior class *(bushi kaikyū)* were constantly bound to, and dependent for their very lives on, the inheritance of feudal emoluments *(sehō seroku)*, their rules of adoption were not always the same as those of the commonalty. Among the adopted sons of the warrior class were those whose goal was succession to the status of household head *(katoku sōzoku)*. Adopted sons who were to become heads of the household were called *iseki sōroku no yōshi* or *katoku sōzoku no yōshi*, and to this corresponded what is commonly known as *muko-yōshi* or *jun'yōshi*, or even as *yōshi* without any qualifying prefix. Among adopted sons who were not to become heads of the household, the most important were the *bunchi haito no yōshi; bunchi haito* refers to the division of the father's feudal stipend *(chigyō)* to include the second and third sons. However, the law was later amended to make adoption for purposes other than succession to the household overseership impossible.

On the other hand, the fundamental rule throughout Tokugawa times, as far as application for adopted sons was concerned, was that the prospective

[10] *Cf.* K. MAKI, *supra* note 7, at 123.
[11] *Cf.* 1 K. NAKATA, *supra* note 7, at 290.

adopted son had to be chosen from the same clan and from among those of the closest possible blood relation. In the absence of these, one was permitted to seek an adopted son in another clan, but in these cases one was obliged to execute and submit a document stating that there was no appropriate candidate among persons properly qualified to be adopted.[12]

When the intestate died without having adopted a son during his own lifetime, his household, as far as feudal law was concerned, became extinct. Under medieval law in cases like this a family council could select from among the close kin of the deceased a successor to the position of headship of the house. Such a person was called *shigo yōshi*. This practice continued to be recognized even in Tokugawa times as far as ordinary law (*futso hō*; that is, the law in effect among commoners) was concerned, but it was not permitted under the feudal laws of the Shogunate. There were, however, cases in which an extinct household (*zekke*) of distinguished lineage and achievement was revived by the grace of a special command on the part of the sovereign. This revival of an extinct household was called *myōseki,* and the successor was called *myōseki sōzoku nin.* As far as mourning prerogatives were concerned, this successor was equivalent to an adopted son of the deceased. It is for this reason that he was called (*meiseki sōzoku no yōshi*). This was in the same spirit as the medieval (*shigo yōshi*), and coincides more or less with the Chinese law that sets up an heir for a deceased person. However, this type of adopted son did not necessarily have to be a member of the same clan as the deceased.[13]

Successors to the position of head of the household were most commonly adopted when there were no sons, but it was also possible to adopt a successor when the son was a minor or not equipped for the succession for some other reason. It was also possible to adopt a son-in-law and to groom him to be head of the household; such practice was called *muko-iseki,* or simply *iseki.* Commoners as well as warriors would adopt a younger brother, or a younger brother from the natal home of an adopted son, or even adopt a married couple (*fūfu yōshi*). However, the adoption of married couples was not recognized under feudal law. It was also possible to adopt a daughter as successor to the office of head of the household. These were phenomena which were simply not seen under Chinese laws of succession.

The Adoption of Heirs to the Sacrifices (ssu-tzu) in Manchuria, 1939–1942

The purposes for adopting an heir. The purposes for the adoption of an heir were (1) to maintain the ancestral sacrifices, (2) to bequeath property, and (3) to assure the adopting parents of support in their old age. However, the inquiries in all areas came to the conclusion that maintenance of the sacrifices was the primary aim.

---

[12] *Id.,* at 383.

[13] *Cf.* 1 K. NAKATA, *supra* note 7, at 534; K. MAKI, *supra* note 7, at 357.

The inquiry revealed that the adoption of an heir was possible even for a deceased person who had clearly expressed a wish not to have one. The ancestral sacrifices had to be maintained regardless of the wishes of the deceased. All those questioned in all areas agreed that when a person qualified to be a foster father dies, his wife, parents, and grandparents are obliged to adopt an heir for him.

Qualifications for foster parents. As in old China, heirs were adopted only for males who had no sons. To become a foster father, a person must have attained his majority—twenty years of age. However, in the following cases it was possible at the time of the inquiry to adopt an heir for a deceased person even if he were a minor when he died.[14]

1.   A married person who died without sons.

2.   A person who died after betrothal and whose fiancée has entered his household and remained unmarried. (There were actual cases of this in Yen-chi.)

3.   A person who died in battle before marriage. (However, those answering the Harbin inquiry said that, while such a stipulation might possibly have existed in previous times in order to encourage battlefield service, at the time in question there was no such custom in practice.)

4.   An only son who has died, when there is no person of the appropriate generation to become the father's heir.

5.   An only son who has died, when the only person qualified to become the father's heir cannot get on with the father or the mother.

It was also necessary for a foster father to be married. However, in the following cases the adoption of an heir was allowed for unmarried, deceased persons.[15]

1.   When a person in his majority has died. (However, according to the answers received at Yen-chi, if the person in his majority were an eldest son, he would be allowed an adopted heir unless he had many brothers. Since there would be inequities in the distribution of the property, the adoption of an heir in these cases would not be possible without the consent of the brothers.)

2.   When a person dies after betrothal, and whose fiancée enters his household and remains unmarried.

3.   When a person dies in battle before marriage. (However, in Harbin this was said to be impossible, while at Yen-chi it was said to require the brothers' consent.)

---

[14] This was acknowledged by the old codes and in the precedents set by the former *Ta-li-yüan* (Supreme court).

[15] *Ibid.*

4. When an only son dies, and there is no one in the same clan of the appropriate generation to become the adopted heir of the father.

5. When an only son dies, and when the only person qualified to be the adopted heir of the father cannot get on with the father or the mother.

As a rule, there is no adoption of an heir on the part of an unmarried male during his own lifetime. However, when for reasons of poverty, physical handicap, mental illness, and the like, there is no woman willing or fit to be a wife, then a single man may adopt an heir after he has reached a certain age.

Since married status was important in the establishment of an heir, men and women were sometimes married after their deaths *(ming hun)*. At Harbin the answer was given that in order to establish an heir for an unmarried, deceased person, it was necessary to perform a *ming hun*. All persons questioned knew of such cases, saying that in previous times the marriage of deceased persons had been regarded as important. One of the persons questioned had married his deceased son to a dead woman through the mediation of a go-between; the boy had been eighteen and the girl seventeen or eighteen. One person said that in his native village in Shantung, the daughter of his own younger sister had died and then had been married to a dead man. Another person answering the inquiry said that this practice was still going on in his native village in Chihli. Cases of it are also said to exist in Kirin, Kaiping, and Tsitsihar, and in small numbers at Yen-chi.

It sometimes happens that a marriage ceremony is conducted when a young man and a young woman who were betrothed have both died, but a marriage ceremony *(ming hun)* may also be conducted for a deceased man and woman who were unbetrothed.

The principal purpose for performing a marriage ceremony for deceased persons is to enable the establishment of an heir who will maintain the sacrifices. An unmarried, deceased minor cannot be buried in the family grave, but if a *ming hun* has been performed, he can be treated as a married adult; he can then be buried in the family grave, an heir can be adopted for him, and sacrifices can be offered to him. The unmarried, deceased woman is also benefited by the *ming hun* ceremony, since she cannot be included in the sacrifices of her natal family.

In the *ming hun* ritual the woman's coffin is unearthed first, and closely related pallbearers take it to the man's grave. Red paper is used to wrap the coffin on this occasion. Since the man is buried in a place removed from that of his ancestors, he is also disinterred and brought to his ancestral tombs. First a simple ceremony is performed, and the coffins of the man and woman are interred together; then a feast is held. The Harbin inquiry revealed that no marriage certificate is executed, but that words are pronounced to the following effect: "While they lived they did not marry, but now, since he has a bride, may the two live together in harmony." One person answering the inquiry said that, when a *ming hun* ceremony was conducted for the deceased daughter of his younger sister, a wooden tablet was made for her and brought into the house exactly as would have been done on the occasion of an ordinary marriage; the tablet was buried together with the coffin to the accompaniment of a prayer *(pai t'ang)* rite. At Kaiping the inquiry revealed that holes were bored in the coffins of the man and woman, and they were then buried across a bridge so that they could visit each other freely after death.

After the *ming hun* ceremony the families of the two parties became kin, just as if the principals had been married in their own lifetime.

The foster father must be older than the adopted heir, but there is no such stipulation for the foster mother. It was usual to avoid situations in which the foster mother was younger than the adopted heir, since the public tended to take a strange view of such a relationship. However, it was felt that the foster father could be younger than the adopted heir, as long as the foster father's generation status was above that of the adopted heir; that is, one could have an older nephew. When adopting an heir for a deceased person, the successor must be one generation lower than the deceased foster father.

There was no agreement on the question of whether it was possible to adopt an heir for a person who died as a Buddhist monk. At Tsitsihar it was said to be permissible to adopt an heir only if the person had been married before he became a monk. At Kirin, Yen-chi, Harbin, Hailar, and Wang-yeh-miao (Mongolia) it was said that the adoption of an heir for such a person was not permissible under any circumstances. At Kaiping in the household rules *(chia ch'eng)* of the Fan clan, a person who enters the Buddhist clergy merely has the fact plainly recorded under his name.

Qualifications for adopted heirs. The prospective candidate for adoption as heir to the sacrifices must be male since only males can maintain the sacrifices; he must also be a kinsman of the same clan *(tsung)* for the same reason.

However, if there were no eligible candidates in the same clan, the inquiry revealed that some felt that a kinsman of a different clan could be adopted as heir to the sacrifices (see Table 3). According to the household rules *(chia ch'eng)* of the Fan clan of Kaiping, adopted heirs of other clans are confined to kinsmen who may be entered in the clan register *(tsung p'u)*; however, since the son of the adopted heir would disturb the clan register, he is not entered therein. Those who answered the inquiry at Harbin felt that kinsmen from other clans could not be adopted as heirs to the sacrifices. However, the answer to the inquiry may have varied because of differences of opinion rather than because of differences in local custom.

A person who has no ties of kinship with the foster father may not be adopted as heir to the sacrifices. The admission of a wife's nephew to the succession in the absence of a kinsman of the same clan is alleged to be a makeshift rule applicable only in cases where there is no other choice. It may be regarded as indicative of the process whereby the old institution for adoption of heirs to the sacrifices was changing.

TABLE 3

ADOPTED HEIRS—ELIGIBILITY OF KINSMEN FROM OTHER CLANS

Relationship	Places	
	Kirin and Kaiping	Yen-chi
Son-in-law *(nü-hsü)*	No	No
Sister's son *(wai ching)*	Yes	Yes
Wife's brother's son *(ch'i Tieh)*	Yes	Yes
Wife's sister's son *(ch'i wai ching)*	No	Yes
Father's sister's grandson *(piao tieh ;* that is, *ku chiu tieh)*	Yes	Yes
Father's sister's daughter's son *(piao tieh)*	No	Yes
Mother's brother's grandson *(piao tieh)*	Yes	Yes
Mother's brother's daughter's son *(piao tieh)*	No	Yes
Mother's sister's grandson *(liang i tieh)*	Yes	Yes
Mother's sister's daughter's son *(liang i tieh)*	No	Yes

An adopted heir must be one generation below that of the foster father; that is, a generation equivalent to that of a son. There was no agreement during the inquiry, however, to the question of whether it was possible to adopt a person corresponding to a grandson without first adopting the person who corresponded to a son. At Kirin, Kaiping, and Tsitsihar this possibility was denied.

Both unborn persons and deceased persons could be adopted as heirs to the sacrifices if there were no other eligible candidates of an appropriate generation. Deceased persons were adopted as heirs so that their sons could in turn become heirs to the sacrifices of the foster family. Only at Kirin and Kaiping was the adoption of a deceased person as heir to the sacrifices alleged to be impossible.

From the ethical and legal points of view, an only son cannot become the adopted son of another and thus cut off the lineage of his own father. Combined succession may eliminate this problem.

It is impossible to adopt the eldest son of the senior line as heir to the sacrifices for the junior line. As a rule, the eldest son of the second line may not be the adopted heir for the third line or lower, but may be one for the senior line.

Procedures for the adoption of an heir to the sacrifices. The persons empowered to designate adopted heirs for deceased persons are as follows:

1. A fiancée who remains faithful to the deceased.
2. The deceased's concubine.
3. The deceased's parents or grandparents.
4. The deceased's brothers.
5. The head of the clan *(tsu)*.
6. A family council.

7. To these, some persons add the deceased's sisters, his daughters, his father's brothers and sisters, or his mother's brothers and sisters.

When there are several persons so empowered to designate an adopted heir, the majority of those answering the inquiry said that the order was the same as that listed above. There were, however, those who placed the deceased's parents or grandparents at the top of the list.

When a living person adopts an heir for himself, as a rule he considers the degree of kinship and relative age, but it is possible for him to select an heir on the basis of superior quality or affection as long as the heir meets the other requirements. However, when the choice of an heir is made for a deceased person, the guideline in all areas is degree of kinship and relative age, although some insist that the wishes of the deceased must be respected. It is not impossible for a person whom the deceased disliked in his lifetime to be designated as his heir, but as a matter of loyalty it is avoided as much as possible.

As a rule there is only one adopted heir, but it is possible to adopt two. This is usually done to eliminate jealousy over the property between two equally qualified candidates.

In all areas it is held permissible to designate an adopted heir in obedience to a will. For the most part this is done by word of mouth, transmitted by a small group of two or three kinsmen. After the death of the testator, his kin frequently dispute the identity of his intended heir and the succession to his property.

When a prospective foster father is about to adopt an heir, his choice must be approved by his wife, his parents, and his grandparents. For a widow to designate an adopted heir, it is felt that her choice must be approved by the parents and grandparents of her deceased husband.

Since the parent-child relationship with one's own parents is dissolved once one becomes an adopted heir, the contract of adoption is executed by the natural parents in most areas. If the prospective heir is of an appropriate age, his opinion is consulted. However, even if the prospective heir is an adult who executes the contract himself, the consent of his parents is felt to be required. If his parents are dead, the prospective heir executes the contract himself.

Certificates designating the adoption of an heir are usually drawn up. These certificates, called *kuo-chi tan, kuo-tzu tan,* and so forth, are done on red paper or cloth.

The matters contained in the certificates vary as follows:

1. The lateral relatives *(chih p'ai)* of the adopted heir's own father; the lateral relatives of his foster father; the name and age of the adopted heir; a statement to the effect that after the adoption he shall succeed to the sacrifices and the property of his foster father; clan *(tsung-tsu)* and other close kin; relatives and friends; the natural father and the foster father; the date (Tsitsihar, Kirin, and Kaiping).

2. The second type contains: (a) The name of the adopted heir; (b) He shall succeed to my sacrifices *(tsung-t'iao)* and be no different from a real son. My property shall all be his; (c) In the event of a dispute over the property, a go-between shall be the guarantor; (d) Not even my adopted heir may leave my house or squander my treasure in defiance of my will; (e) If there are any other conditions, they shall be written down and sent by the foster father to the adopted heir's house.[16]

At the adoption of an heir, there is usually a meeting of the kin and the signing and sealing of the certificate. When they cannot sign and seal, scribes usually write their names for them.

There is always a simple ceremony and a reception, except at Hailar where there is only a reception. The order is (1) a report to the ancestors, (2) the joining of the palms before one's parents and the performance of three kowtows, (3) presentation of oneself to all one's kin, and (4) invitation of guests. Apart from this the adopted heir's own parents sometimes caution him about how to behave himself after the adoption and admonish him to do his whole duty.

The effects of adoption. The relationships between an adopted heir and his foster parents and natural parents are as follows:

1. Since the adopted heir inherits the ancestral sacrifices, his relationship with his foster parents is the same as it would have been with his natural parents.

2. The adopted heir's relationship with his natural parents changes as follows:

   a. He loses the right of succession to the ancestral sacrifices and property of his natural parents.
   b. It is common for him to address his natural parents as uncle and aunt, although this is not always done.
   c. Upon the death of his natural parents, he mourns them for one year as persons whom one mourns in less than the usual way *(hsiang fu tzu)*.
   d. According to some, he no longer has a duty to support his natural parents.

The sons and daughters, whom the adopted heir may have had before the adoption, become the grandchildren of his foster parents. This practice is common to all peoples and places.

Dissolution of an adoption. An adoption is dissoluble by common agreement between the adopted heir and the foster parents. However, there is no agreement on the procedures for such a dissolution. Some say that a document must be prepared, while others say that it is sufficient to destroy the certificate of adoption.

---

[16] 3 T. CHIKUSA, *supra* note 2, at 121.

When a document of dissolution is prepared, it is necessary to record the circumstances of the severance, to declare the disavowal of the certificate of adoption, to have it witnessed by kin, and to inscribe the date. The destruction or burning of the certificate of adoption is said to take place in the presence of relatives and friends.

The grounds for renouncing an adopted heir and dissolving the adoption are not clear. In the opinions of some, the following circumstances will justify it:

1. When the adopted heir has been derelict in his duty toward his foster parents or grandparents, or guilty of grave discourtesy toward them.

2. When for no reason he has abandoned them.

3. When he has been sentenced to penal servitude.

4. When he has brought disgrace on the family name or has squandered the family fortune.

5. When for many years it has not been certain whether he is alive or dead.

6. When he disobeys his foster father.

7. When he takes opium.

8. When he steals the family's property and sells it.

There are some who deny the possibility of dissolution under grounds (3) and (5) through (8).

The grounds for renouncing foster parents are also not clear. However, a majority hold that dissolution is possible under the following circumstances:

1. When the foster parents have been derelict in their duty toward their adopted heir, or when they have heaped grave disgrace upon him.

2. When for no reason they have abandoned him.

There were also some who said that foster parents can be renounced when they have been sentenced to penal servitude.

The foster relationship cannot be unilaterally dissolved by the adopted heir for the mere reason that his natural parents have lost all their other sons. In this case the natural parents would adopt an heir for their deceased son, or they would have their natural son (who was given for adoption) combine successions for his deceased brother. However, if the foster parents agree, an adoption can, of course, be dissolved in these cases.

The grandparent-grandchild relationship between the adopted heir's children and the foster parents usually comes to an end as a consequence of the dissolution of the adoption. In these cases, the former adopted heir takes his children with him. However, he may choose to leave them with his former foster parents.

There was no agreement on the rights of a former adopted heir to the property which he may have received from his foster parents. There are some who hold that the goods received as gifts may be taken, while those inherited may not. On the other hand, there are some who hold that neither may be taken. There are still others who hold that both may be taken when the dissolution was at the instance of the foster parents, but not when it was at the instance of the adopted heir. There are yet others who hold that property is not involved since the adopted heir receives none during the lifetime of the foster father, and since no dissolution is possible after he inherits his foster father's wealth.

The Adoption of Heirs to the Sacrifices From Other Clans (yang-tzu) in Manchuria, 1939–1942

In China there are many foundling homes created for the philanthropic purpose of rearing abandoned children. At Mukden (Feng-t'ien, Shen-yang) I saw such a home, named T'ung-shan-t'ang, built on the contributions of philanthropic donors, which was caring for many abandoned children. I heard that there were many cases in which families without sons would adopt a son from the T'ung-shan-t'ang and rear him as their own. There were also cases in which married women without children would pass themselves off as pregnant by wrapping progressively larger cloths about their middle; they would then have themselves admitted to an obstetric clinic and have a nurse obtain a baby boy from the T'ung-shan-t'ang. At worst, there were cases of families who would exchange a newborn daughter at the T'ung-shan-t'ang for a son to be reared as their own. Consequently, when there was no son, the kin of the same clan would take care to see that these things did not happen.

In recently exploited areas in which there are few kin of the same clan, especially the Yen-chi area, there are many cases in which sons are adopted from other clans to succeed to the sacrifices and the household property, and to care for the foster parents in their old age. In this respect the original distinction between adopted sons of the same clan and those of another clan has vanished.

Qualifications for foster parents (yang ch'in). In general a person with a natural son or an adopted heir from the same clan *(ssu-tzu)* may also adopt a son from another clan *(yang-tzu)*. However, this was not acceptable in Tsitsihar, Kaiping, and Kirin, presumably because *ssu-tzu* and *yang-tzu* were regarded as identical.

Foster parents *(yang ch'in)* had to be married couples who were at least forty or fifty years old.

A deceased person could not become a foster parent *(yang ch'in)* in most cases. Where the practice was acceptable, the adopted son had to come from among the deceased person's kin. The persons qualified to effect the adoption were the same as those qualified to designate an adopted heir from the same clan *(ssu-tzu)*.

Qualifications for becoming a yang-tzu. The adopted son *(yang-tzu)* had to be one generation lower than the foster parents if he were kin to them. It was generally understood that the adopted son had to be younger than the foster parents.

An only child could not be adopted as a *yang-tzu*. However, there were cases of this in Harbin among poor persons without kin.

Procedures for adoption. Since adoption was usually effected during the infancy of the foster son *(yang-tzu)*, it was concluded by the foster parents and the real parents. If the foster son were an adult, his consent was needed, and he could be a party to the contract; but the consent of his real parents was still required if they were living.

A document was not necessary for the adoption of a son from another clan *(yang-tzu)*; it was enough for the foster parents to take the child home and rear him. If the foster son were an illegitimate child, a document was particularly not made, because it would disgrace the child.

If the child were adopted in exchange for money, a document was drawn up on red paper or cloth. It certified the amount of money exchanged, that the child would perpetually sever his ties with his natural parents, and that the natural parents would never interfere with the child. The document also recorded the names and ages of the foster parents, the natural parents and the child; the reasons for the adoption and the date were included. In Kirin, however, a verbal agreement was still considered sufficient, even when money was exchanged.

A ceremony in the presence of relatives was never held when a son from another clan *(yang-tzu)* was adopted. The foster parents usually tried to keep the fact from becoming generally known.

Dissolution of the adoption. The foster parents *(yang ch'in)* and the foster son *(yang-tzu)* could dissolve the adoption by common agreement. There was disagreement on the necessity for making a document in these cases. Some said that it was enough to destroy the original document of adoption. Others said that a simple announcement was sufficient. Still others declared that a document was necessary.

The justifiable grounds for a petition to dissolve the adoption of a *yang-tzu* were generally the same as those for dissolving the adoption of a *ssu-tzu*. However, less serious causes could be accepted in the case of a *yang-tzu*.

In general a foster son could not unilaterally dissolve adoption on the sole grounds that his natural parents had lost all their other sons, although there have been some cases in which this occurred. However, there were some who said that this could not be done if the foster son had been adopted at the age of six or less (Kirin).

The effects of dissolution of an adoption. The grandparent-grandchild relationship between the foster parents and the adopted son's children was usually nullified when the adoption was dissolved. However, if the foster son left his children in the foster parents' home, the relationship continued.

When an adoption was dissolved, the foster son no longer had any rights to the property of the foster parents. There was a difference of opinion, however, upon whether he could retain property he had received as a gift.

LEGISLATION ON SUCCESSION TO THE SACRIFICES
AND ADOPTED HEIRS

The Republican Law

In 1930 the Republic of China enacted and promulgated a section of the new Civil Code dealing with inheritance. This section took effect the following year, and under its provisions the rules governing succession to the sacrifices were abolished. The declared reasons for this action were as follows: (1) social conditions had changed; (2) heirs were being adopted regardless of clan; and (3) succession to the sacrifices did not allow equality of the sexes.

The new code allows adoption regardless of clan or sex, but it does not recognize the adoption of a living person for the sake of a deceased person. Also, the candidate for adoption must be of the appropriate generation (that is, that of a son or daughter) if he is a lateral blood relative within the eighth degree of kinship or a lateral relative by marriage within the fifth degree of kinship.

The Manchurian Law

Manchurian law also abolished the regulations for succession to the sacrifices and left it entirely up to personal morality. The requirements for adoption were also changed as follows: (1) both men and women, married or unmarried, could adopt heirs to property; (2) clan membership was not necessary and generation rank merely had to be lower than that of the foster parent; and (3) when a family council adopted an heir for a deceased person, he had to be a kinsman of the deceased.

This law of inheritance was promulgated in 1945, but it went out of effect as soon as the war ended.

The Japanese Law

As previously stated, Japan inherited the institutions of T'ang China through the Taika Reform. In a more recent period, the Meiji Civil Code adopted Western European institutions on a large scale, but the institutions of the household were powerful, and much importance was attached to succession to ancestral sacrifices and the maintenance of household continuity.

However, the Civil Code's section on inheritance was revised under the Allied occupation in 1947, and sweeping changes that affected all areas were introduced. Household institutions were abolished, and the rule of equality of the sexes was introduced consistently throughout the country. Succession to the sacrifices was left entirely to the individual conscience. The only stipulations were that the person to officiate at the ancestral sacrifices was to succeed according to custom to the sacrificial implements, the family registers *(keifu)*, and the tombs.[17]

If this new code is not to merely be a borrowed garment, it will be necessary to give the spirit of it general currency in the nation and at the same time to reform family life in keeping with it. This is the great task remaining for the future. The same may be said, we believe, for the reform of the Chinese institutions of succession to the sacrifices and the adoption of heirs to the sacrifices.

---

[17] *Cf.* JAPANESE CIVIL CODE art. 897.

Family Partition as Contractual Procedure in Taiwan:

A Case Study from South Taiwan[1]

MYRON L. COHEN

The process of family division among the Chinese merits close attention. The event, of course, is of crucial importance to those participating in it, for some of the closest social relationships undergo important changes, as do the economic situations of those involved. If the subject is approached with the aim of discerning those features of family partition which are replicated or of finding parallels in other contexts, a great deal of light may be shed on Chinese social structure and process in general. Furthermore, if family partition and related patterns are examined in a context in which there occurs a considerable amount of technological modernization, it is safe to say that, by noting the influence of the new developments on traditional patterns, we may learn much about the over-all locus and direction of social change.

These are the problems I hope to deal with here. The data I employ were gathered in southern Taiwan during sixteen months of fieldwork in 1964–65. In discussing my field investigation I will use certain place names rather frequently throughout this paper, so it would be best to supply the necessary descriptions and distinctions at the outset. Yen-liao is the name I give the village where I was based; its 705 residents (May 31, 1965) were the main object of my study. Yen-liao is in the Lung-tu region, which centers upon Lung-tu Town and includes several other hamlets of about the same size, as well as a scattering to more-or-less isolated farms. Lung-tu in turn is located in Mei-nung Chen (Township), where there are several other larger towns, including Mei-nung Town itself, and many hamlets. Mei-nung Chen, finally, forms an administrative subdivision of Kaohsiung Hsien (Country).

---

[1] Portions of this paper have been adapted for inclusion in M. Cohen, HOUSE UNITED, HOUSE DIVIDED: THE CHINESE FAMILY IN TAIWAN (1976).

Yen-liao is located in a rich agricultural region of south Taiwan where two rice crops and a variety of third crops are harvested annually. With respect to third crop cultivation, the entire Mei-nung region is distinguished from neighboring areas in that it is a center of tobacco production. Mei-nung is overwhelmingly populated by Hakka speakers, while in surrounding districts the predominant language is Hokkien. Although there has been much social change in Yen-liao, family organization in general, including the process by which families divide, has remained within a traditional framework. In Yen-liao economic and technological modernization has encouraged the maintenance of complex family structures, and the developmental sequence and economic organization of the family have also continued to follow traditional Chinese patterns; adherence to customary modes of family partition is, therefore, another element in the overall conservatism of domestic organization.[2]

I

The body of law and administrative practices in force in contemporary Taiwan affects the lives of the inhabitants of Yen-liao in a variety of ways. The laws must be dealt with and responded to, for they are enforceable; but in these responses the outlines of a vigorous system of customary practices may be seen, which gives little indication of changing under the present circumstances. To begin with a subject of practical concern to the fieldworker, there is the operation of the household and land registration systems; while yielding, among other things, invaluable demographic and land use data, the records do not truly reflect family composition or landownership patterns, which are still adjusted in accordance with customary procedure. Under the current system of registration the legal domestic unit is the household *(hu)*; household membership may be transferred, or a new household can be established. The household is the legal unit used to register Taiwan's population, and relevant taxes are levied against it. But household membership does not necessarily correspond to that of the traditional and still existing domestic unit, the *chia*. In Yen-liao, as of May 31, 1965, there were a total of eighty-four households registered, but the individuals contained therein were actually distributed among only sixty-eight *chia*.

It is, of course, to the *chia* that we must refer in order to examine the distribution of social and economic roles at the domestic level. And since it is the *chia* which, as a unit, is the major kind of property holder, we are confronted with the additional task of accounting for the strength of property relationships when these may have no legal existence in terms of the national legal system. Most of the Yen-liao plots are registered at the local land office in the names

---

[2] See M. Cohen, *supra,* for a detailed discussion of the subjects taken up in this paragraph.

of single individuals, although some, especially those used for residences, are registered jointly. The way in which land is registered is relevant to *chia* composition and ownership, but in no way do the records indicate that it is the *chia* as a unit which owns land and that the transmission of land across generations is associated with partition *(fen-chia)*.

The connection between the local system of property relationships and land registration practices can be seen at two points. The first is that *chia* land is indeed registered in the names of different *chia* members; a father, say, his sons and, sometimes, grandsons. After the father's death there will be the re-registration of his land in the name of one or more of his sons. Second, local practices are in conflict with contemporary inheritance laws which give sons and daughters equal rights to their father's property. This legal problem is resolved by having women sign away all claims when they marry or upon their father's death. Both procedures, distribution of land registration among male *chia* members and surrender by women of their rights to land, are by now quite standardized. In a sense they have become customary responses to the threat to traditional practices posed by a legal system that stresses individualism and equality of the sexes with respect to property.

I do not imply that the state-supported legal code is ineffectual. Quite the contrary, its effectiveness is demonstrated by the fact that many local practices survive only insofar as they are rendered legal. There have been several instances where legal claims that violated local customs were nevertheless pressed and resulted in court decisions favorable to the plaintiff. These cases, inheritance disputes, occurred shortly after Taiwan was restored to Chinese rule and concerned mainlander men married to local women, who were encouraged by their husbands to demand their share of the land registered in their deceased fathers' names. The defendants, of course, were the women's brothers, and they were forced to make cash settlements with their sisters. It was precisely disputes of this sort that either initiated or popularized the practice of demanding that the woman's inheritance rights be waived as a prior condition of marriage to a mainlander. The fact that this is now done is one manifestation of the continuing authority of the *chia*. The threat to customary practices originated in marriages contracted with men who at least initially were not involved in local social relationships. This indicates where we must turn to examine the forces supporting customary family structure and property relationships.

II

Yen-liao shares with much of rural and urban Taiwan traditionally derived patterns of social integration which exist side-by-side with newer institutions and practices. The innovations may be introduced by government action in the administrative, legal, and educational spheres, or they may result from technological and economic modernization not directly associated with government activity. The traditional elements will be dealt with first from the point of view of territorial integration, and then in reference to inter-group and inter-personal relationships.

Although Yen-liao does not coincide with any of the administrative subdivisions of Kaohsiung Hsien, its inhabitants emerge as a distinct grouping with respect to traditional patterns of organization. Within the larger Mei-nung region the term "Yen-liao" refers to a specific locale and its inhabitants and Yen-liao is one of several hamlets that, together with the town of Lung-tu, comprise a larger region in which the population is a sociologically demarcated group in many respects. The Lung-tu region was not an example of the standard marketing area described by Skinner,[3] although it might have fitted his description of the minor marketing area; in the past Lung-tu was oriented for purposes of marketing to Li-kang. A secondary orientation to the town of Ch'i-shan has steadily developed since the onset of Japanese rule, and its importance is now equal to, if not greater than that of Mei-nung Town, which also became a marketing center after the arrival of the Japanese. The inhabitants of the Lung-tu area are a maximal grouping in terms of face-to-face interaction; almost everyone in this region knows everyone else, not including children of elementary school age or younger. Administratively the Lung-tu region is at present divided into three administrative units *(li)*, though in Japanese times it formed one unit *(sho)*. But the institutions which provide foci of interaction for the population were established by neither the Japanese nor the present government. The people of the Lung-tu region define themselves most clearly in terms of the three temples they support and the regional religious celebrations in which they participate. In addition to many annual festivals, these include periodic religious festivals *(pai-pai,* the more accurate term for which is *chiao)*, and the Lung-tu population in fact forms a distinct grouping for the organization of religious festivals. As anyone who has been in Taiwan can testify, such religious activity is not confined to Lung-tu. In all the large cities, not to speak of the rural regions, there are recurrent religious festivals during which a district organizes itself on a massive scale for worship at the sponsoring temple and for a religious procession; the families living in the district must stock the food required to play generous host to many friends and relatives from wide areas of the island, who are feted for the duration of the festivities. The government views such events and their high cost with disfavor; some areas have been forced to reduce the frequency of their celebrations, while others have been made to abandon complex arrangements of rotational sponsorship in favor of consolidated festivals. Nevertheless, religious festivals are still held all over Taiwan, and most observers agree that they are growing

---

[3] G. Skinner, *Marketing and Social Structure in Rural China, Part I,* 24 J. ASIAN STUDIES 3–43 (1964).

in scope and cost. The dimensions a festival can attain are indicated by the following news item:

The largest single *pai-pai* that Taipei's Sungshan District has held in the past 49 years reached its climax yesterday. Informed estimates are that about 400,000 persons crowded into Sungshan to eat *pai-pai* [to eat off the tables of relatives and friends], 5,000 pigs were slaughtered, and NT$70,000,000 [US$1,750,000] squandered. . . .[4]

The religious content of the festival need not concern us here. What I want to emphasize is that these events offer dramatic testimony to the enduring strength of local systems of organization, which are able to carry out large scale mobilizations of manpower and economic resources. In 1965, for example, a large religious festival was held in a region several miles from Yen-liao. There, a population of over 40,000 was assessed NT$40 [US$1.00] per head to help defray costs. The political relevance of such events was highlighted at that time, when one of the region's most prominent personalities, an elected official of the provincial government and a Christian, was asked to play a key role in one of the religious ceremonies and quickly agreed.

The local systems which support religious festivals in Lung-tu are ongoing arrangements and are implicated in many additional aspects of social life. Festivals aside, the three temples in Lung-tu are the sites of frequent gatherings. Persons who desire political power within the area, or who seek to maintain and expand what influence they already have, use temples and temple-associated activities to widen their circle of friends and followers and to display in public their dedication to community undertakings. Needless to say, temples are not the only sites for such activities, but it is significant that all elected officials in Mei-nung Chen (and in many other parts of rural and urban Taiwan) are quite prominent in temple affairs. In this context there is an interplay between the power and authority derived from participating in state institutions, and that provided by occupying important positions in local organizations. The importance of the latter in social life is reinforced by the inclusion of men who are also part of the national government, while the support these men require to maintain their political position is in part provided precisely by their activity in these local organizations.

Patterns of interpersonal relationships in Yen-liao are still firmly within a traditional framework. The traditional modes of interaction did and at present still do allow considerable flexibility, yet at the same time these are restrained by what we might call "customary law," if this term is used in a sense general enough to cover a wide range of relationships. Within this general category there are two elements that seem especially crucial: the first is that social affiliations are aligned on the basis of a few criteria or orientations which may be manipulated in a variety of contexts; the second is that among the most

---

[4] *Lien ho pao,* (Taipei) Dec. 4, 1963.

strategic of these affiliations, including those involving economic relationships and transactions of more than ordinary magnitude, are those based upon contract.

The first point is simple enough and has been dealt with by many social scientists. I would only add here that, when we speak of "particularism," care must be taken to include all the important foci of affiliation and interaction: kinship, not only in the restricted sense of kindred, but in the broad sense of same surname as well; locale; language or dialect; age; school; and so forth. All of these criteria define populations whose members may interact on the basis of the shared quality; interpersonal relationships within any of these populations may have as a common feature nothing more than an orientation, in addition to those orientations which may align some members of this population with other populations. However, this orientation may be made the basis of instrumental relationships of many kinds, which are expressed as dyadic ties and through the formation of discrete groupings.

In amplification of the second point, it can be said that, while the common orientation upon which an instrumental relationship may be built need not change, the relationship itself may be created, modified through time, or terminated. Again, one can be born into a relationship above and beyond that implied by the common orientation itself, and this relationship may also be modified through time or terminated, while the common orientation remains. Such changes come about through contract.

Let me illustrate with a few examples. In Yen-liao the recruitment of labor for harvest or other work during the busiest part of the agricultural year is a serious matter. Available manpower is used almost to the limit, and arrangements have developed so that labor from over a wide area circulates and takes advantage of the small regional variations in onset of harvest or planting. Some of the Yen-liao men organize and lead teams composed of persons who come to work in the Yen-liao fields from other villages. The outside workers are usually recruited from villages where the Yen-liao organizer has kinsmen, most often from his wife's family. The Yen-liao man will ask his relatives (common orientation-"kinship") to hire men of their community (common orientation-"locality"); these men are then brought to Yen-liao where the organizer has already made arrangements with Yen-liao farmers requiring labor (common orientation-"locality"). Arrangements of this sort require contractual agreements at two points: between the organizer and the Yen-liao farmers using his team, and between the organizer (or his kinsmen) and the team members. The relationship between the organizer and his kinsmen is not contractual in this case, but it too can be modified through contract.

Farmers in Yen-liao also swap labor with each other under an arrangement known simply as "labor exchange" *(chiao-kung)*. This is a strict calculation of labor units, for the exchange involves equal amounts of labor at identical tasks (rice harvest, tobacco leaf sorting, etc.). If one family finds itself unable to supply the labor it owes another, a worker must be hired instead or, which is less preferable, the family to whom labor is owed must be paid the cash equivalent of the wage value of the labor performed. Here again is a form of contract where the common orientation is "locality." Now, the kinds of contractual relationships modifying the common "locality" orientation are too numerous to detail here, for this would involve a description of a substantial part of the economic life of the region, such as credit relationships with local stores, lending and borrowing small amounts of money, participation in rotating credit associations, and hiring laborers or craftsmen.

Contractual relationships are specific and differentially distributed; once a contract's terms have been met by both sides, the contractual element in the relationship ends, though some persons are obviously parties to more contracts than are others. Nevertheless, the "locality" orientation is associated with patterns of behavior that are not contractual and that may be considered the active components of the orientation itself. In terms of the "locality" orientation as applied to the entire Lung-tu region, there is the temple complex mentioned earlier, including participation in local festivals. "Locality" as Yen-liao includes in addition several kinds of cooperative and gift-exchange networks. One is known as "good and bad events" *(hao-shih huai-shih)*. For the ceremonies and feasts associated with weddings, birthday celebrations for the aged, and funerals, neighbors, if called upon, are expected to supply manpower to help the host family. The number of persons asked to render assistance for any occasion varies, of course, with the magnitude of the ceremony and the number of guests expected to attend the feast, so that while all families in Yen-liao are potentially liable to come to each other's assistance, an element of selectivity in fact enters into the picture. Nevertheless, there have been times in the past when mobilization of the villagers was almost complete, and any person in Yen-liao would agree that, if called upon by any other villager, he would respond. Gift-exchange networks operate in contexts such as the betrothal ceremony preceding marriage, at which time the groom's family presents the bride's side with large quantities of sweetcakes; these are distributed to categories of kinsmen and to neighbors as well. None of these gift-exchange networks takes in all of Yen-liao, but, since each is roughly concentric from the point of view of any individual family, the entire village is involved in an overlapping series of such exchange relationships.

The "locality" orientation also includes reference to the entire Mei-nung region. With a population nearing the 50,000 mark, Mei-nung Chen is not a community where all members are in a relationship of face-to-face interaction. But members of Mei-nung's economic, political, and social upper class do have this type of relationship, and they are involved in both state institutions and local relationships in a way which replicates the Lung-tu situation on a larger scale. For example, it was this group which helped organize the very large religious festival celebrated by all of Mei-nung in 1963. The area covered by the festival extended well beyond the Chen's administrative boundaries and was ceremonially integrated by having the temples in the region each send their chief deity to a central temple (in Mei-nung Chen, but not in the town); this was followed by a daylong procession covering most of the roads throughout the region. It is estimated that 10,000 persons participated in the march, while several times that many converged on the area and sat as guests at the tables of relatives and friends. Less spectacular but more frequent is the annual "second month opera" *(erh-yüeh hsi),* which takes place in Mei-nung Town and draws to the performance people from throughout the area, who also go to the carnival organized for the occasion. With respect to the region centering around Mei-nung Town, the "locality" orientation seems to coincide with Skinner's general description of the standard marketing area as a sociological unit,[5] in spite of the fact that some of the towns and hamlets in Mei-nung Chen are oriented toward Ch'i-shan for actual marketing.

The "kinship" orientation has many dimensions, with major differences between agnatic and cognatic kin. With agnatic kin, there is often an overlap between the "kinship" orientation and that of "locality." Most families in Yen-liao have as their neighbors close agnates who either share the same compound or live in adjacent or nearby compounds. Agnates in Yen-liao share many obligations and play specific ceremonial roles when one of their number marries or dies; also, such agnates are the first and most frequently called upon in the context of the cooperative arrangements described earlier. Agnates within Lung-tu have identical ceremonial obligations and are also invited to feasts. Agnates identified as such only on the basis of common surname are, within Yen-liao, somewhat more liable to render assistance; they may, for instance, be called in to help when a family is about to divide. The prohibition against marriage between persons with the same surname is still vigorously adhered to throughout Mei-nung; otherwise, the common surname "kinship" orientation does not seem to have, at present, an associated pattern of behavior that would distinguish it from the "locality" orientation as applied to Mei-nung as a whole.

The "kinship" orientation as it extends to cognatic relatives (through marriage and the maternal line) is the most important, for it is distinct from the "locality" orientation with regard to all regions; the cognatic "kinship" orientation may, in fact, actively affiliate persons scattered over wide areas of Taiwan. When this orientation does overlap with that of "locality," its content is perhaps more demanding and strategic than that of any other orientation beyond the domestic level. In addition to ceremonial obligations and reciprocal participation in weddings, funerals, and feasts given in the context of local celebrations, cognatic kinsmen are involved in a type of labor cooperation known simply as "help" (Mandarin, *pang-mang ;* Hakka, *t'en-chou*). This is an

---

[5] G. Skinner, *supra* note 3.

ongoing obligation to provide assistance whenever needed and in any context, and so is different from "labor exchange" and "good and bad events." For example, the "help" relationship between a family in Yen-liao and their kinsmen elsewhere in Lung-tu included, during one year, assistance in rebuilding the kitchen stove of the Yen-liao family, which in turn provided manpower needed to complete the refurbishing of the Lung-tu family's ancestral hall.

   In addition to "locality" and "kinship," there are other orientations of importance, all of which have implications for everyday behavior. However, if these are encompassed within the orientations already discussed, the result in most cases is simply a higher degree of interaction in a social context where interaction is already very substantial. For example, when the "peer group" orientation is combined with "locality" (Yen-liao, Lung-tu, Mei-nung) or with "kinship," interaction and mutual familiarity are greater than they would be if "peer group" were not an orientation shared in addition to the others. Thus, when an older person in Mei-nung meets one who is younger and unfamiliar, he will frequently identify him by asking, "Who is your father?" The obverse also obtains, as I found out when attempting to compile rather comprehensive genealogies. My informants, most of whom were middle-aged, were often unable to identify those of their cognatic kin who lived in other parts of Mei-nung and who were one or two generations younger than themselves; but their children had no trouble supplying me with the names I wanted. The same sort of relationship also exists between the orientations noted so far and others, such as "socioeconomic class" and "same school;" in appropriate contexts, the orientation of "language" is also important (Hakka as opposed to Hokkien or Mandarin).

   Within the Mei-nung region, persons with shared orientations may be divided into those personally acquainted with each other and those who are not. With respect to the former group, common orientations may be associated with the kinds of duties or cooperative relationships already described. As I tried to illustrate earlier, however, additional relationships may be initiated through contract, and this applies not only to "locality" as a prior orientation but to "kinship" as well. Among other things, agnatic and cognatic kin form partnerships, make joint investments, lend each other money, and join with nonkinsmen in forming rotating credit associations. Like many other contractual relationships, the rotating credit association is of short-term duration; after the final session, the erstwhile members of the association revert to patterns of interaction connected with the orientations they share in common and with whatever contractual ties that may still be operative. However, the rotating credit association is different from the other contractual relationships already mentioned in that it consists of a group of persons, rather than two individuals or social units, joined together in a common undertaking binding upon all participants. The use of the term "contract" in reference to such a situation may be a bit shaky, for more than two parties are involved. Within a

Chinese context, however, purely contractual agreements cannot be profitably distinguished from other forms of agreement which also add to the content of social relationships otherwise associated with shared orientations. In this paper, then, "contract" will be used with this more general meaning.

Long-term contractual ties can unite two or more persons, and the most enduring of such ties are those that lead to the formation or endowment of a common property. These, then, are corporate groups, and in the past they were found in great numbers and varieties throughout the Mei-nung region. Included were the "associations" *(hui)* formed for many different manifest purposes but in actuality quite similarly structured. There were, for example, many local shrine associations *(po-kung hui)* formed to maintain or refurbish local shrines *(po-kung)*; there were also associations organized to build bridges or keep them in good order, to improve river transportation, to establish or support schools, and so forth. All of these associations were instituted and organized in a similar fashion. A number of individuals would pool money for the purchase of land with contributions computed on a share basis. Income from the land was used to support the particular project sponsored by the association to subsidize a periodic feast for all association members, and, if there were a surplus, to provide members with dividends figured on the basis of shares (some members owned more than one). The members of these associations had "locality" as a common orientation, though some members might share additional orientations. Nevertheless, these orientations were also held by non-association members, so that the associations were new discrete social groupings formed through contract. Precisely the same situation was to be seen among those sharing the orientation of "kinship." Persons with the same surname formed land-based corporate groups with the number of shares held by each member determined by his original contribution. Dedicated to an ancestor remote enough to be common to all participants, groupings of this sort nevertheless excluded those who were not shareholders. Such corporate agnatic groups built ancestral temples *(tz'u-t'ang)*, held annual or biannual ceremonies of worship coupled with feasting, subsidized the educations of their brighter members, presented cash gifts to members over sixty, and distributed dividends (per share); in general, they fitted many of the specifications of "lineage" as that term has been used in reference to agnatic units in mainland China as well as Taiwan.[6] Yet, the Mei-nung groups also originated through contract.

Corporate groups, unlike other forms of contractual relationships, endure through time. The first members are united through contract, but their descendents inherit the shares. Membership thus grows larger, and the

---

[6] *Cf.* M. Freedman, LINEAGE ORGANIZATION IN SOUTHEASTERN CHINA (1958), and M. Freedman, CHINESE LINEAGE AND SOCIETY (1966) for mainland lineages; for Taiwan, see F. Ahern, THE CULT OF THE DEAD IN A CHINESE VILLAGE (1973), and B. Pasternak, KINSHIP AND COMMUNITY IN TWO CHINESE VILLAGES (1972).

maintenance of group integration depends at least in part on the fate of the common estate. Lineages or associations whose wealth increased in proportion to or in excess of membership growth remained strong; those whose estates remained constant or declined in value were unable to support the feasts and payments or to exercise the political power that would encourage members to assemble and interact with each other more than with others sharing the same orientation. The Japanese colonial authorities were very aware of the relationship between cohesive social groupings and their economic underpinnings, and especially during the latter part of their rule they encouraged, with a great deal of success, the dissolution of association and lineage estates and their distribution among the shareholders. The corporate estates that survived until the re-establishment of Chinese rule were for the most part broken up as a result of the Land Reform program instituted in the early 1950s. While these developments may be placed under the rubric of "modernization," insofar as that term includes the process whereby a government acquires increasingly efficient means for the exercise of power, they do not imply the weakening of the orientation by which the groupings were formed.

Contractual agreements may be made by persons who shared a common orientation but who were not previously acquainted; their shared orientation has instrumental significance in that it serves to align them, but it obviously does not include patterns of cooperation or common participation in local organizations. It is under such circumstances that one of the functions of the middleman or go-between can be seen. Such a person serves as a guarantor in many transactions, but often he is also an introducer. For purposes such as the sale of land, the middleman matches a buyer, with whom he is acquainted, with a seller who is also familiar to him. Buyer and seller both share orientations with the middleman which may include many forms of interaction, but neither buyer nor seller need necessarily share such an orientation with each other. Even though there is no prior acquaintance, a shared orientation between prospective buyer and seller may increase the likelihood of a successful transaction; i.e., if both are Hakka, or if both are from the Mei-nung area, or if they can discover some kinship link. In general, use of a go-between is one of the ways by which contractual relationships or transactions can be extended beyond the range of an individual's face-to-face contacts. In the formation of corporate groups, there need not be a middleman. Rather, there can be the process whereby individuals with overlapping but different circles of acquaintances are drawn together through mutual introduction and on the basis of a shared orientation. Thus, some of the lineages described earlier included members from widely scattered locales throughout the Hakka zone of settlement in south Taiwan, which covers a good portion of the present-day Hsien of Kaohsiung and Pingtung.

The people of Yen-liao participate in a local social system which in part derives from the traditions brought to Mei-nung by the first Chinese settlers, and in part results from the adjustment of these traditions to local circumstances. Many of the specific patterns of relationship are not applicable for persons from the Mei-nung area who are placed in a new social context. An obvious example would be that of labor exchange, which is not relevant to the requirements, say, of men who have moved to Taipei, even though they come from Yen-liao where their families continue to swap labor. Likewise, it is physically impossible for them to join in preparations for the religious events sponsored by the Lung-tu temples, unless they should choose to return home for the event and are able to do so. Thus, certain kinds of contractual and non-contractual interactions associated with some orientations are inappropriate under the changed circumstances. However, the orientations themselves are maintained and provide a context in which relationships, including those of contract, are aligned. In Taipei, the "locality" orientation draws together people from Yen-liao, Lung-tu, or all of Mei-nung, who interact with each other for a variety of instrumental purposes. This includes persons who knew each other at home, as well as those who never interacted on a face-to-face basis before coming to Taipei. But we have seen that even in the home environment persons in the latter category could initiate relationships on the basis of a shared orientation. People who interacted in terms of the "kinship" orientation in Mei-nung continue to do so in Taipei. Orientations associated with the changed circumstances may reinforce those already held in common and lead to heightened interaction and the formation of cohesive groups. So, for example, students from Mei-nung studying at different Taipei universities have organized themselves into a student association. On a larger scale, there are Hakka organizations based in Taipei and Kaohsiung that draw their membership from the two cities. The traditional orientations, maintained in cities and countryside, are not confined to people from Mei-nung. While the cities of Taiwan have properly been cited as centers of technological modernization, there is much evidence that the "kinship" orientation continues to serve as a focus for large-scale groupings in the form of clan associations,[7] and I would suspect that the staging of massive religious festivals is ample evidence of strong organization with reference to the "locality" orientation.

III

The preceding discussion concentrated upon three themes: general orientations, the substantive and non-contractual patterns of behavior associated with some but not all general orientations, and the role of contract in establishing relationships other than those associated with general orientations. The distinction between contract-based social relationships and those connected

---

[7] *Cf.* M. Fried, *Some Political Aspects of Clanship in a Modern Chinese City*, in POLITICAL ANTHROPOLOGY 285–300 (M. Swartz, et al., eds. 1966).

with a general orientation is crucial, not only for understanding broader patterns of social organization, but also with reference to family organization and partition. In general, families recruit wives (or, in some cases, husbands) through contractual agreements, and family partition also takes the form of a contractual alteration of social ties. Marriage as a form of contract will not be discussed here in detail. Suffice it to say that in Yen-liao marriage conforms to the general Chinese pattern; detailed negotiations among the two parties and the go-between precede the complex series of economic transactions that form part of the betrothal and marriage ceremonies.[8] Only after agreement has been reached is a religious specialist called upon to write the document that sets the date for each step of the ceremonial sequence culminating in marriage. Earlier in this paper, cognatic kinship was included as a general orientation rather than a contractual relationship. Strictly speaking, this is not so, for in the few cases in which divorce occurs, affinal ties are indeed severed. Divorce, incidentally, is an enormously complicated affair as well as one that is highly disapproved. Included is a financial settlement which involves disentangling, as it were, the many transfers of wealth incorporated into the wedding arrangements. Since divorce is quite rare, and since the kinship ties created by marriage endure beyond the life-span of the couple whose wedding initiated them, we may in general speak of marriage as creating a common orientation through contract.

In complex families (stem or joint), or in families that turn complex through a marriage, a man's taking a wife means that he is now jurally adult. Thus, while the marriage contract is between the two *chia,* each represented by its *chia-chang* (head of the *chia*), one result of marriage is that the new husband acquires the right to initiate contracts on his and his wife's behalf. As long as the new conjugal unit *(fang)* remains within the *chia,* the husband's new right is a potential one only, for the *chia* is recognized as the "legal person" in this respect (of course, I refer here to the traditional system). In another sense, however, marriage may be seen to change a man's relationship with the other jurally adult male members of his *chia* from one that is completely contained in a general orientation, to one that is also contractual. The existence of an option—whether to divide the *chia*—is a fact of life that is ever-present in the minds of the men who are members of joint families.

Elsewhere,[9] some of the factors encouraging or retarding the onset of family division have been dealt with; in this paper I refer only to the process itself. First, it can be noted that the anthropologist investigating Chinese family partition is indeed fortunate; in addition to the usual techniques of participant

[8] For an overall description of marriage practices in Yen-liao, *cf.,* M. Cohen, *Chinese Family Development and Economy in Yen-liao, Taiwan,* 1967 (unpublished doctoral dissertation, Columbia University).

[9] M. Cohen, *supra* notes 1, 2, 8.

observation and interviewing, he has at his disposal the documents that are drawn up at the conclusion of partition proceedings and that serve to permanently record details of the distribution of property and the allocation of responsibilities among the parties concerned. Although these documents must be used with caution, they are still an invaluable source of data; a selection of these documents, all from Yen-liao, has been appended to this paper and will be cited where relevant; they follow the same format and are basically identical to materials in the same category collected by different persons in widely separated areas of China.[10]

Family partition in Yen-liao follows the general and traditional Chinese pattern in that the foci of the proceedings are the male members of the *chia,* including those who may reside outside of Yen-liao but who nevertheless maintain their rights to the *chia* estate. The traditional principle that brothers have equal rights still holds. Depending upon the composition of the family about to divide, other considerations may also enter into the picture, so it is only when the *chia* consists of brothers, their wives, and children that a fairly straightforward division of the estate into equal shares may be observed. Greater genealogical complexity often adds to the complexity of the division process, for persons other than brothers do have claims of different sorts. First, there is the matter of the parents. Often, one or both may still be alive when the *chia* divides, and they must be taken into account. In general, sons when separated still retain collective responsibility for supporting parents and subsidizing their funerals. Although the father in principle has no direct right to a share of the estate, there are cases in which the father is nevertheless one of the parties to the division; he stands opposed to one of his sons, usually the eldest, and they must agree upon the distribution of *chia* holdings. Division Document A, which records one such agreement, is worthy of comment in several respects. First of all, from the document's title and preamble, it would appear that the division was initiated and ordered by the father. In actuality it was Te-lai, the eldest son, who agitated for separation to the point that communal living became intolerable for all concerned. Such a situation is not different from one in which one of several brothers demands division following the death of the parents. It is true that if a father is alive his consent must be obtained before the family can divide, and that sometimes he may initiate division himself; but precisely the same applies to brothers who are adult, that is, to brothers who have married. The maintenance of a joint family really involves balanced agreement among those men in the family who have the right to demand partition. In Document A, there are only three men in this category: A-t'ien, the father, and Te-lai and Kuang-t'ien, the eldest and second sons. Note, however, that the names of the third, fourth,

---

[10] *Cf.* R. F. Johnston, LION AND DRAGON IN NORTHERN CHINA (1910), p. 151, and Y. H. Lin, THE GOLDEN WING (1948), p. 125.

and fifth sons also appear; though having rights to shares of the estate, they were young and not yet married at the time of division, and so they did not have rights of partition and independent management. Document A, then, represents a case in which the father divides the estate with his eldest son in the name of his remaining sons, with the second of these indicated as the nominal representative of the second party to the division. This document details the distribution of property quite accurately; but it misrepresents the role of the father, not only as noted above, but also in that he seems to disappear from the picture, as it were, with the completion of division. A-t'ien in fact remained the family's head once the eldest son withdrew his portion of the estate.

The role played by the father in family partition proceedings is associated with his prior position in the family. If he has already retired as active family head, leaving the management of family life and finances to one of his sons, he will not take part in the separation proceedings as a *de facto* shareholder in opposition to other shareholders. The negotiations, rather, are confined to his sons, and the father's role is limited to perhaps demanding special considerations for himself and his wife and to participation in the overall adjudication of share allocations. Under such circumstances, the father's role more nearly resembles that of his wife; the sons agree to an arrangement whereby continued support of the parents is assured. Most commonly the parents (or the surviving parent) become what I call the "collective dependents" of the new families established by their sons. The sons undertake to distribute responsibility for their parents' support among themselves; the parents keep a room to themselves and eat in rotation, usually monthly, among their sons' families. Although the agreement to jointly support the parents is often noted in the division document, the technique of rotational board is usually left unstated.[11] The rotational technique is a standard one and is favored because, among other reasons, it leaves little room for any son not to live up to his commitment. Division documents serve to clarify and stipulate in detail arrangements that might otherwise be ambiguous; the specific means by which a general agreement is implemented need not be put in writing if it is not liable to future misinterpretation.

An alternative to rotational support of parents is an agreement whereby one son incorporates them into his household and receives compensation from the others. This may be in the form of stipulated payments[12] or through the assignment of additional land to the party undertaking to provide the parents with room and board. The latter arrangement is sometimes associated with the notion of the "eldest grandson's field" *(ch'ang-sun t'ien)*. The "eldest grandson's field" seemingly departs from the otherwise accepted idea that

---

[11] *Cf.* Document B in the *Appendix*.

[12] *Cf.* Document C in the *Appendix*.

all sons have equal rights to the estate, for it provides that the eldest son of the eldest son can obtain an additional share apart from those distributed among his father and uncles. To my knowledge, however, the "eldest grandson's field" is rarely if ever freely awarded, for the party receiving it assumes obligations not borne by the other parties to the division. Document D indicates that in one case a condition to the allocation of the "eldest grandson's field" was that the recipient undertake to be the sole support of his mother. The person who nominally receives this allocation is almost always still a member of his father's *chia,* and the land is actually an increment to the holdings of the *chia* as a whole. In Document D, then, the land is under the management of Wang-te, not his son Shao-hsiang. An "eldest grandson's field" is not demarcated unless all parties to the division agree, which almost inevitably assures that the recipient will also assume additional obligations.

Another consideration in the division of the estate relates to marriage. It is the sole responsibility of the *chia* to pay for the weddings of its members, and this responsibility can take the form of a claim upon the *chia* estate if the sons who are parties to the division have unmarried brothers or sisters. In Document E, this obligation is expressed in the form of an extra cash payment to one of three brothers, a widower planning to remarry. Money likewise is often set aside for a sister, who usually lives with one of her brothers during the period following partition but before her marriage.

Document F, which dates from an earlier period than those noted so far, is included mainly to illustrate how many of the different procedures and claims involved in partition may be invoked concurrently. There is the outcome of negotiations between father and eldest son phrased in the preamble as if it were the father's command; in clause three there is a claim on land for purposes of supporting a wedding; clauses four and five detail the utilization of property for father's support and funeral expenses. Obligations such as those due parents are not necessarily included in the texts of partition documents. These obligations are most likely to be put into writing when they are transformed into claims by one party against another; this represents a transaction through which the obligations shared by a group of brothers are borne by only some, who are compensated for assuming the additional responsibility. By the terms of Document F, then, Ting-jen is no longer bound to join in the support of his father, to subsidize his funeral, or to help pay for his younger brother's wedding. It can be seen, then, that even very fundamental ties between father and son can be modified through written agreement.

The different claims brought against the estate during partition proceedings may be categorized in terms of the distinction I have drawn between general orientations and contractual relationships. Support of parents and payments for weddings or funerals are obligations that are aspects of a general orientation; the way in which the obligations are to be met is negotiable, but they do not end through family partition. Mutual support as among brothers, through coordination of economic activities, pooling of income, and common exploitation of an estate is, on the other hand, a contractual relationship which may be terminated. In order for the partition process to begin, the agreement of all jurally adult males is required; this is usually forthcoming a short time after one of them has determined to divide, for the family is quickly plunged into endless quarrels; often it also begins to suffer economically, because some members may withdraw in part or entirely from family economic activities.

Thus, when the time for separation arrives, the position of brothers is usually one of confrontation and antagonism. Nevertheless, the process by which the *chia* estate is divided assures an equitable distribution of shares. After agreement to separate has been reached, members of certain other *chia* are requested to "convene a council" *(li hui)* and serve as "council members" *(li hui jen)*. One of the council members serves as the amanuensis *(tai pi jen,* or *i k'ou tai pi jen)*, who writes out the division settlement document. The purpose of the council is to both witness and mediate or arbitrate, as the case may be, the division of the *chia* estate. If *chia* members have informally agreed upon the main conditions of separation, the council serves as little more than a body of witnesses, perhaps smoothing out a few minor details. At the other extreme, strong disagreement within the *chia* forces the council to bring opposing parties together and hammer out a settlement. In any event, the council plays an important part in the partition process; a private matter is turned into a public one, and demands for disproportionately large shares of the estate or other uncompromising behavior may extend hard feelings, already existing within the *chia,* to outsiders. The council represents public pressures and assistance in expediting *chia* partition, and an analysis of council composition will indicate the nature of the pressures brought into play.

Between 1950 and 1963 there were nineteen cases of *chia* separation. Available division settlement documents allow an analysis of eleven partition councils, the membership of which ranged from two to seven councilors, for a total of forty-nine. Some persons participated in more than one council during this period, but for present purposes they are counted separately for each council. As indicated below, the majority of councilors had kinship ties with the *chia* seeking to divide (see Table 1).

TABLE 1

COMPOSITION OF ELEVEN PARTITION COUNCILS, 1950–63

Relationship to Partitioning Chia	Number
Close agnates	20
Same surname	14
Non-agnatic kinsmen	6
Others	9
Total	49

The term "close agnates" refers to persons related through a common ancestor only two, three, or four generations removed; most shared the same compound or complex of compounds with the family that invited them to act as councilors. The emphasis on the agnatic principle extends to those included under "same surname." In most of the division settlement documents, they are referred to as "lineage members" (*tsung, tsung-tsu, tsung-ch'in,* or *t'ung tsu,* terms also applied to close agnates). In one document (not included in the Appendix) the title "lineage head" *(tsu-chang)* is given a man who is prominent as the manager and religious leader of a nearby temple. The title is purely honorific; at the time neither he nor the *chia* concerned belonged to any lineage organized above the compound level. Nevertheless, the influence the man wields in local affairs is considerable. In fact, eight of the eleven councils contained men of more than ordinary weight in the affairs of Yen-liao and neighboring districts, and some were important throughout Mei-nung Chen. Men important in temples and religious life in general were included in two councils; in five others, one or another of two men active in Mei-nung Chen politics was to be found; three councils had as a member the head of Yen-liao's wealthiest family. Among members of the councils under consideration forty were from Yen-liao. Except for two close kinsmen, all the outsiders were within the category of influential persons.

Thus, when a *chia* separates it implicates in the process persons with whom it shares orientations, usually overlapping, of "kinship" and "locality," and influential persons are drawn in on the basis of one or both of these connections. When they are involved, these men of influence play the most active role in inventorying assets and liabilities, computing shares, and working out the text of the division settlement document. In fact, their expertise in such matters is one reason these men are in demand. From their point of view, participation in partition councils is a form of service falling within a wider category aimed at increasing obligations owed them by others. Councils that do not include prominent men contain villagers regarded as technical experts in the preparation of division settlement documents.

There are strategic reasons for the preponderance of agnates among the kinsmen serving as council members. The ties of a given agnate to men involved in *chia* partition are more nearly equal than those of affinal relatives. When brothers divide, this is obvious. Their father's brother, say, has equivalent genealogical connections to all of them, as do more distant agnates. When sons separate from their father, the situation is more complex. In the present sample, there are two such cases, and in each a father's brother was included in the council. Genealogically, at least, the ties between brothers are closer than those between uncles and nephews. However, persons with brothers and nephews about to separate usually are their immediate neighbors in the compound. The course of future day-to-day relationships and possibilities for cooperative activities can be influenced by the outcome of partition negotiations. Such close agnates are strongly motivated to see that as little hostility as possible is generated. While this might encourage them to absent themselves from partition proceedings entirely, they are actively sought out by the parties concerned. Of course, genealogically more distant agnates within a compound or complex of compounds will similarly have a strong interest in maintaining friendly ties with the new families.

The position of non-agnatic kin is quite different. The six who did attend partition proceedings in each instance were similarly related to all parties involved. In five cases the link was provided by matrilateral ties three to five generations removed. This tie was also present in the sixth case; here, however, the additional connection was that the council member concerned was also the brother, adopted out, of the three men who separated. In other contexts, such as at weddings, affines form an important category of kinsmen. During partition proceedings, however, they are strenuously avoided. A woman's close relatives are expected to give her husband strong support; the general belief is that their participation would exacerbate existing tensions and delay agreement.

The different connections implicated during partition serve to expedite the process. Failure to reach agreement not only reflects on the *chia* concerned but is also a rebuke administered to the council. Most persons are not willing to have social and economic ties with kinsmen, villagers, and men of influence qualified in this way. Therefore, they strive to arrive at a consensus. Furthermore, their desire to complete the division process often is reinforced by what may be the disfunctional state of the family economy at that point. As far as I have been able to determine, *chia* partition councils in Yen-liao have succeeded in every instance in obtaining agreement during the first session. Nevertheless, most partition sessions are marked by bitter altercations among *chia* members, and often will last until the early hours of the morning. In the larger Lung-tu area I know of one occasion, though there probably have been more, where several councils had to convene before settlement was reached. In this case, which required five council meetings, many council members refused to show up for the following sessions, and new ones had to be found. Finally, a specialist in legal matters was hired to preside; he succeeded in obtaining agreement at 4:00 A.M., for which he was awarded a sizable commission.

The partition proceedings, attended by the council and male adult *chia* members, take place during and following a meal in the dining room or ancestral hall of the unit about to divide. After the meal, the council makes a lost of all holdings and obtains agreement as to their value; debts, if any, are similarly reckoned. Assets and liabilities are then divided into lots of equal worth. Especially in the case of fields, each parcel is assigned a number against which the men draw. Where much non-agricultural property is involved, lots often are not drawn but are assigned through mutual agreement. Frequently, cash settlements are necessary to equalize the division. After the partition has been fully worked out, the details are recorded in division settlement documents, examples of which are included in the Appendix. These documents serve both as record and deed; they are affixed with the seals of the council members and the parties to the division, and each of the latter obtains one copy.

One possible result of *chia* partition is that the new units may divest themselves of all contractual obligations, so that interaction then falls entirely within the framework of their common "kinship" orientation. However, partition may also include the initiation of other forms of contractual ties. This can occur through the agreement of the parties concerned to set aside a portion of the estate as their common property. Under such circumstances, the division document becomes a positive contract detailing rights of cultivation and distribution of income. Estates set up in this way have as their manifest purpose the endowment of ancestor worship, and in actuality mark the formation of a corporate group similar to the lineages described earlier. In effect, shares are distributed equally among the original signers of the partition document, and their descendants are born into a contractual relationship.

Now the utilization of common orientations to draw into the partition proceedings persons who are not members of the *chia* is but one example of a general process that helps maintain the integrity of traditional contracts. Contract violation carries with it the possibility of compromising future contract-making ability, and it may also endanger non-contractual relationships.

Contracts initiated with face-to-face acquaintances to a large extent are supported simply by the awful consequences attendant upon their violation. Reneging on a labor exchange agreement or withdrawing from a rotating credit association could result in exclusion from future activities of the same sort, which for many farmers are critical in terms of their very livelihoods. Furthermore, aggrieved individuals may desist, and encourage others to desist, from the kinds of interaction and mutual assistance that, under ordinary circumstances, would be forthcoming simply in the context of common orientations. Violation of a contract involving a middle man puts the latter in a position of assuming full responsibility; he will, of course, exert as much pressure as possible to insure that the defaulting individual comes to mend his ways. If desperate enough, he may use all possible affiliations to threaten the party who has violated the agreement. But disputes over contracts rarely reach the point where the element of coercion is marked or even obvious. The pressures exerted to force compliance from a defaulter, or agreement where there are differences in interpretation, are usually applied in the form of mediators or arbitrators who seek to adjudicate the dispute. Yet the fact that third parties can be and are called in widens the social consequences of continued disagreement, so that even mediation must be seen as a form of contract enforcement.

IV

Although Yen-liao is rural, it by no means has been isolated from the modernizing forces that have been influencing Taiwan life. Many technological improvements have been incorporated into agricultural production, including the use of chemical fertilizer, power tillers, and so forth. More importantly, agriculture is overwhelmingly commercialized. The tobacco crop is completely under the control of the Taiwan Tobacco and Wine Monopoly Bureau, the exclusive purchaser, and farmers obtain more earnings from one crop of tobacco than from two of rice. In general, food produced and directly consumed on the farm forms only a small portion of the annual income of most families. This is especially true among those families that have been able to diversify into non-agricultural activities. Elsewhere[13] I have tried to show that, while diversification is a traditional tendency, Taiwan's modernization has led to an increase in the opportunities for such diversification and, through improved public health and medical technology, has assured the required manpower for most families.

Yen-liao's communication with the outside world has undergone distinct improvement. A five minute walk from Yen-liao takes one to a station where buses stop on their way to the main southern port city of Kaohsiung. Practically all families own radios, all have bicycles, and many have motorcycles as well. In terms of education, most men and some women who grew up during the Japanese period received six years of schooling. Since the re-establishment of Chinese rule, elementary school education has been compulsory for boys and girls, and a large portion of these children also manage to attend and complete the three-year junior middle school course.

Nevertheless, traditional modes of organization and orientation are maintained and, indeed, flourish. As of May 1965, the majority of Yen-liao's population were in fact members of joint families. The reasons for this boil down to the fact that technological modernization has given customary tendencies greater opportunities of realization. The same applies to social interaction in terms of the "kinship" and "locality" orientations. Improved methods of communication have widened the range of kinsmen with whom significant interaction is possible. "Help" relationships with kinsmen, for example, now join together persons scattered over wide areas of Mei-nung. Feasting at a kinsman's table during religious festivals or family celebrations is not as restricted by factors of distance as it was in the past. In fact, the increasing scope and extravagance of religious festivals all over Taiwan probably reflects a general extension of interaction with respect

---

[13] M. Cohen, *supra* note 1.

to the "kinship" orientation, and all this is occurring under the impact of technological modernization.

Obviously, there have also been many changes in social patterns. In evaluating these, however, a distinction must be drawn between what might be called strategic and non-strategic elements. At the most superficial level, it can be noted that the substitution of taxicabs for sedan chairs during weddings, or the growing popularity of permanents among women, cannot be seen to be of strategic significance, since the persons involved behave in traditional ways with respect to matters such as family life. Of greater importance, perhaps, is the fact that boys and girls must agree before their families can arrange marriage. However, the potential spouses are given an opportunity to see and evaluate each other in the context of a ceremony incorporated into the initial phases of the sequence culminating in marriage. The ceremony, which dates from the pre-Japanese traditional period, takes place even if the boy and girl had been acquainted before negotiations between their respective families and had, in fact, requested their parents to initiate the proceedings. Thus, between 28 February 1964 and 19 June 1965 there were marriages involving a boy or girl from Yen-liao, and six of these were the result of "free love"; in two the parents took the initiative, but the couple involved knew each other and approved before the first ceremonial meeting; while in the remaining marriages, approval was forthcoming only after the boy and girl had seen each other for the first time during the appropriate ceremony. Yet in all of these marriages the customary arrangements with respect to betrothal money and dowry were adhered to, and all of the newly married couples have been absorbed into the husband's *chia*. Marriages through "free love" have been part of the Yen-liao scene since the Japanese period; yet it is quite clear that strategic social relationships, those connected with the integrity of the *chia* as a corporate grouping geared to provide the subsistence of its members, have remained unchanged.

The distinction between strategic and non-strategic is of utility when one asks how the situation in contemporary Taiwan may inform us with respect to traditional China. Here, I can only offer a few suggestions based upon my interpretation of the Mei-nung data and general impressions of Taiwan as a whole. The contrasts at many points between national law and customary law indicate that the customary patterns must have been at least as self-supporting in the past as they are at present. When I say "self-supporting," I simply mean maintenance without recourse to specialized enforcement institutions. In fact, one might even ask if a good deal of what has been described as customary "law" might not be better dealt with simply as behavioral patterns or characteristics. For example, since contract was operative in family life itself as well as in the wider social setting, it seems pretty safe to say that the use of contract for instrumental purposes is a fundamental feature of Chinese behavior. An approach along these lines might help in explaining why so many of the Chinese who migrated to southeast Asia, and who generally were of peasant origin and not at all wealthy, managed to establish relatively comfortable positions for themselves in their host countries.

The connection between modernization and the traditional framework might be approached from yet another angle. Traditionally, contractual relationships would be formed in the context of general orientations which might or might not of themselves be associated with specific patterns of behavior. All this was quite consistent with a social structure that permitted and was indeed characterized by a relatively high degree of socioeconomic mobility and the absence of all but a few caste-like groupings, which in any event accounted for only a small proportion of the population. Furthermore, there was a comparatively high degree of occupational diversification, especially if it is kept in mind that even at the agricultural level widely divergent ecological zones were integrated within a unitary political, social, and economic system that was remarkably cohesive in pre-industrial terms. Although most men in China were poor, all were prepared to enter into new relationships and to manipulate their surroundings in an effort to better their lots. It is perhaps true, therefore, that the desire to exploit new opportunities was traditional, even though the opportunities were in fact limited. To the extent that modernization means the creation of new opportunities, it is not necessarily incompatible with traditional patterns of relationship, as can be seen today in Taiwan. But if a goal of national policy is to thoroughly revamp the traditional system of social relationships, then a simple reliance on the consequences of technological modernization may not do the trick at all. In fact, the planners might conclude that the only way to achieve this is to restructure economic arrangements so as to deprive contracts of their traditional utility, as is occurring in the People's Republic of China today.

APPENDIX

FAMILY DIVISION DOCUMENTS

(Note: all names have been changed, addresses omitted, and field registration numbers replaced with upper case letters)

DOCUMENT A

We all know it is a principle of nature that a large tree should grow many branches and a long river flow into many tributaries. Today, being your father and advanced in age I ask only that you brothers each establish your own household and plan for your future. I have invited here some of our agnatic and cognatic kinsmen *(tsu-ch'i)* to convene a council and set down the terms for the distribution of my land and other property. Each and every one of you must act in accordance with these terms and establish his own family and livelihood, so as to shed lustre on our ancestors. Such indeed is my most earnest wish. The details of the distribution are as follows:

1. Plot A, .7548 *chia* paddy land, covering the area bounded at the north by Lien-lai['s field], and extending all the way to the east and west, shall belong to Te-lai.

2. Plot B, .7127 hectares[14] of single [(rice) crop] land, extending from the boundary of Ping-ch'ang['s field] all the way to the two ridges to the north and south, shall belong to Te-lai.

3. The remaining land, after removing that given to Te-lai, shall belong to Kuang-t'ien, Sheng-t'ien, Chin-lai, and Feng-lai.

4. The tobacco house, drying chamber, the three rooms beneath it [that is, the entire tobacco house structure] and the vacant land extending for a distance of 1.2 *chang* [the Taiwanese *chang* equals 9.94 feet] from [the entire length] of the outside wall of the eastern room [of the tobacco house] shall belong to Te-lai.

5. The house in which we are currently living, [comprising] one veranda and one compound wing, belongs to Kuang-t'ien, Shen-t'ien, Chin-lai, and Feng-lai.

Everyone must adhere to the terms of the distribution established above. Since word of mouth is not dependable, two copies of this certificate of partition are hereby drawn up, and each [party] shall keep one copy as evidence for the future.

Min-kuo 54 [1965]/12/1

Distributor:	Father	Huang A-T''ien
Recipients:	Eldest son	Huang Te-lai
	Second son	Huang Kuang-t'ien
	Third son	Huang Sheng-t'ien
	Fourth son	Huang Chin-lai
	Fifth son	Huang Feng-lai
Councilors:	Huang Yu-lai	
	Huang Fa-lai	
Amenuensis:	Yeh Wang-hsing	
Postscript:	All five sons shall assume full and equal responsibility in paying all funeral expenses at the time of their father's death.	

Ratifiers of the Postscript:

Eldest son: Huang Te-lai

Representative of the other sons: Huang Kuang-t'ien

---

[14] "Plot B" was registered after the land offices dropped the Taiwanese *chia* as a measure of land area and began to use the hectare exclusively.

DOCUMENT B

In compliance with our mother's command we four brothers shall equally divide among ourselves all property inherited from our ancestors and all present property so that each of us may carry on his livelihood, enhance the prestige of the family, and shed lustre upon our ancestors. The complete details of the distribution of the family estate are as follows:

1. The right to separate residence [obtained by Hsin-feng]: The old shop by the dike and the plot on which it stands, within its recognized boundaries, shall belong to Hsin-feng. The tobacco house itself shall be jointly used by the four brothers, who shall also share equally the right to plant tobacco; the two lower level rooms of the tobacco house as well as property rights to the land on which it stands belong to Te-feng.

2. The two rooms at the west end of our original house and the four rooms at the southern end of our house by the road plus their foundation land belong to Hsi-hung; the four rooms at the eastern end (of the original house), the bamboo pig-pen at the northern corner of the road-side house and their foundation land belongs to Yüan-hung.

3. As compensation for construction expenses, the sum of NT$10,000 shall be removed from the common estate and given to Te-feng.

4. Hsi-hung, Te-feng, and Yüan-hung shall assume equal responsibility for full repayment of principal and interest of all our outstanding debts and taxes. Hsin-feng shall have nothing to do with these payments.

5. All four brothers shall assume full and joint responsibility for caring for their grandmother and mother, who are still living. They should pay for their living expenses, medical expenses, and for future funeral expenses. Moreover, the four brothers must take turns in making offerings to their ancestors.

6. Of our .73 *chia* plot of paddy land, .20 *chia* shall be given to Hsin-feng, and what remains shall be equally divided among Hsi-hung, Te-feng, and Yüan-hung; the .16 *chia* plot of paddy land shall be owned equally by Hsi-hung, Te-feng, and Yüan-hung. Also, cultivation rights to the .16 *chia* paddy land rented for 37.5 [per cent of the crop, the rate set by the Land Reform Laws] shall be given entirely to Hsin-feng.

7. Hsi-hung, Te-feng and Yüan-hung shall share equally cultivation rights to .6 *chia* of single-season public land at . . . which we rent, the .48 *chia* paddy field rented for 37.5 [per cent of the crop through Land Reform], and the .39 *chia* of redistributed land (through Land Reform).

8. From this day on, all four brothers shall take turns in descending order of birth in meeting the expenses of the annual celebration of their grandmother's and mother's birthdays.

In compliance with our mother's command, and with the assistance of a council convened by our agnatic kinsmen *(tsung-ch'in)* we brothers have arrived at the above terms of division. Four copies of the certificate of division have been made, and each of us shall keep one copy and forever abide by the terms agreed therein without dispute.

Mother: Ch'en A-chin

Brothers: Huang Hsin-feng
Huang Hsi-hung
Huang Te-feng
Huang Yüan-hung

Agnatic (lineage) Kin: Huang A-t'ien
(tsung-ch'in) Huang Yu-lai
Huang Lien-lai
Huang Fa-lai

Cognatic Kin: Yeh Wang-hsing
(kung-ch'in)

Amanuensis: Huang Ch'ing-yun

Min-kuo 47 [1958]/7/17

DOCUMENT C

We two brothers Fu Ch'ing-feng and Fu Ch'i-feng, the participants in this division of our family estate, often recall the admirable custom of nine generations living together handed down to us by Chiang Kung, and the loyal and fraternal spirit of the T'iens, who attempted to divide the *Ching* tree into three parts,[15] still remains fresh in our minds. However, the ancients have also reminded us that a large tree naturally forms many separate branches and that, as the years go by, a large family will ultimately divide into many separate households. Although we two brothers do not have the hearts of Kuan and Pao, we nevertheless still have the determination of Wu and Yüeh. Hence, we have agreed today to invite several councilors to convene and assist us in distributing our family estate. We sincerely hope that after partition each of us will do his best to build his future so as to bring glory to the family and promote the traditions handed down to us by our ancestors. The terms of the division are as follows:

[Clauses 1–7, detailing land distribution, are omitted.]
[Clauses 8–12, detailing distribution and construction of buildings, and distribution of farm tools, are omitted.]

---

[15] *Cf.* 28 CHUNG-WÊN TA TZ'U-TIEN (Chinese dictionary, unabridged) 149 (comp. by Chung-kuo wên-hua yen-chiu-so, 1968) for the meaning of this reference.

13. It is agreed that each party shall take turns at managing the [fish and water buffalo] pond in front of the old ancestral hall for a period of two years.

14. It is agreed that the $6,000 we have lent out shall be equally divided among us. However, the interest shall be given to our parents for their use. Moreover, the future funeral expenses of our parents shall be shared equally by both parties. (It must be further pointed out that Ch'ing-feng must donate 300 Taiwanese catties of rice each season to help support father. No objection to this agreement should be raised.)

[Clause 15 is omitted; describes distribution of the current year's crops as well as property not included in earlier clauses.]

16. Since word of mouth is not dependable, two copies of this division certificate have been drawn up, and each party shall keep one copy as evidence.

1953
Parties to
   the division: Fu Ch'ing-feng
                   Fu Ch'i-feng
Councilors: the head of the *li (li-chang)*, Yeh Wang-hsing
                   the head of the *lin (lin-chang)*, Huang Yu-lai
                   the *chen* representative, Liu Shuang-lin
                   lineage uncle *(tsu-shu)*, Fu Ting-wu
                   lineage younger brother *(tsu-ti)*, Fu An-feng
                   lineage younger brother *(tsu-ti)*, Fu Sheng-feng

DOCUMENT D

[Preamble omitted.]
[Clauses 1–3 omitted; they deal with distribution of land and buildings, and the settlement of outstanding debts.]

4. Plot A, .28 *chia,* shall be allocated to Shao-hsiang, the eldest son of Wang-te. (While mother is still living, the produce from this land shall constitute the source of her living expenses.)

5. All remaining household articles shall be placed in our mother's charge, and she will determine their proper allocation.

6. Equal rights to [unused] building ground shall be held by both parties. These properties may be divided in the future if necessary.

7. Since word of mouth is not dependable, two copies of this partition certificate have been drawn up, and each [party] shall keep one copy as evidence for the future.

Executors of
   Partition Certificate: Yeh Wang-te
                            Yeh Wang-ch'üan

Councilors: Yeh Wang-hsing
Liu Shuang-lin
Huang Ming-ch'ao
Yeh Wang-ch'ing
Yeh Wang-sheng
Yeh Shang-lin

Drawn up *Min-kuo* 44 [1955]/8/15 (civil calendar) 6/28 lunar calendar.

DOCUMENT E

In compliance with our parents' command, we three brothers shall each set up his own household and develop his own livelihood, so as to shed lustre upon our ancestors. The terms of the equal distribution of our entire family estate are as follows:

[Clauses 1–4 omitted; they deal with property distribution.]

[Clause 5 omitted, stipulates joint responsibilities to parents.]

6. It is a great misfortune that Ch'üan-jung has lost his beloved wife. In profound sorrow, his elder and younger brothers agree together to donate NT$6,000 to pay for his remarriage and related expenses.

[Clause 7 omitted; stipulates joint responsibility for payment of taxes.]

[Concluding paragraph omitted.]

Father: Yeh T'sai-yung

Mother: Kuo Fan-mei

Eldest brother: Yeh Kuo-shu

Second brother: Yeh Chüan-jung

Third brother: Yeh Po-pin

Agnatic (lineage) Kin: Yeh Wang-hsing
(tsung-ch'in)

Amanuensis: Huang Ch'ing-yün

Chung-hua 49 [1960] lunar interculary 6/3.

DOCUMENT F

I, Yeh Ch'ing-feng, the executor of this testament of partition, live at . . . , and have four sons, who are, in descending order of birth, Ting-jen, Ta-jen, Hsing-jen, and Ch'ang-jen. Knowing that a large tree will naturally divide into many branches and realizing further that this very same principle is also applicable to human life, I conclude that future conflicts could be avoided if I invite, while I am still alive, some of our kinsmen to come here and distribute, equally and as agreed upon, all the movable and non-movable property which

I bequeath [to my sons] forever. But after the final distribution, no one shall ever raise objections or cause any disturbances. It is for this purpose that I prepare this testament of partition; two copies have been drawn up to serve as proof for the future; one shall be kept by my eldest son Ting-jen, and the second by my three other sons, Ta-jen, Hsing-jen, and Ch'ang-jen. The details of the property division are as follows:

1. Plot A, .02 *chia,* paddy land, plot B, .265 *chia* paddy land, one share in the *Sheng-ting hui* [an association], and one share in the *Tien-hsüeh hui* [another association] shall forever belong to my eldest son Ting-jen.

2. Plot C, .395 *chia* paddy land, and plot D, .313 *chia* paddy land, shall be allotted to Ta-jen, Hsing-jen, Ch'ang-jen, and forever owned by them.

3. The .143 *chia* building ground and all buildings now located on plot E shall be set aside for the marriage expenses of Ting-jen, Hsing-jen, and Ch'ang-jen.

4. Plot F, .175 *chia* paddy land, and plot G, .19 *chia* paddy land, as well as all household effects, cattle, pigs, chickens, and so forth shall be used for paying up our present debt of approximately $1,000 and also for the living expenses and then the funeral of father, Yeh Ch'ing-feng.

5. Ting-jen, Ta-jen, Hsing-jen, and Ch'ang-jen shall share equally the interest [held by Yeh Ch'ing-feng] in the Yeh ancestral fields.

6. The land rented from Hsiao Yün-chin, comprising .88 *chia,* shall be allocated to Ting-jen for cultivation. He must pay the rent. Moreover, the security for this land, $210, and one share in the Trust Company, must be returned by Ting-jen to father, to pay for father's living expenses.

This testament of partition is hereby established.

Showa 14 [1939]/11/1

Executor
of testament of partition: Yeh Ch'ing-feng
Eldest son: Yeh Ting-jen
Second son: Yeh Ta-jen
Third son: Yeh Hsing-jen
Fourth son: Yeh Ch'ang-jen
Amanuensis: Yeh Kuei-jung
Councilors: Yeh Wang-hsing
               Lo Ting-ch'uan

Adjudication and Partition in the Tibetan Stam Family

MELVYN C. GOLDSTEIN

This paper examines one dimension of the interplay between the Tibetan legal system and the Tibetan corporate stem family. Specifically, it focuses on the relationship between a tendency for partition engendered by the ideal norms governing inheritance of land and particularistic aspects of the formal adjudicative process.

Since the data on which this paper is based were obtained through reconstruction interviewing, a brief statement of the sources and the methods by which they were elicited is in order. These data were collected during the course of a twenty-month field trip (December 1965–August 1967)[1] of which about seventeen months were spent in a Tibetan resettlement agricultural colony in Mysore, India.

Reconstruction research is obviously fraught with pitfalls, but these, I think, do not preclude the procurement of accurate data. One of the most serious of these dangers is the all too common tendency to extrapolate from the comments of a handful of "available" informants to the society in general, this being particularly true in complex societies like Tibet. A second basic problem concerns validating or determining the accuracy of informants' statements, especially differentiating the ideal from the behavioral patterns.

In order to cope with these and other problems, I focused the reconstruction aspects of my project on a small area in Tibet that was well represented in the Mysore settlement. The area eventually selected for intensive study was primarily the village complex of Samada *(sa mda')*[2] and secondarily the village

---

[1] The project was sponsored by the American Institute of Indian Studies.

[2] The transcription of Tibetan terms follows the system elaborated by T. Wylie, *A Standard System of Tibetan Transcription,* 22 HARV. J. ASIATIC STUDIES (1959).

of Chimdro *(chim 'brog)*. Both of these were in Gyantse district *(rgyal rtse)*, Tsang *(gtsang)* province.

There were about eighty persons from the Samada region in Mysore as well as a number of individuals from villages neighboring Samada, such as Gala *(Ka la)* and Khangmar *(Khang dmar)*. Contrary to popular opinion, the refugees did not consist predominantly of monks and aristocrats. They included persons from all the different social statuses, ascribed and achieved, high and low, clean and "un-clean."

The accuracy of the data collected was greatly facilitated by the presence of this relatively large sample. I was able to work in terms of specifics—specific families and incidents—and, crucially, was able to cross-check the remarks or opinions of one informant with others from the same and different intra-village social groups as well as with persons from neighboring villages. Finally, in addition to this intensive study of a narrow area, I also carried out general questionnaire interviewing of a sample representing the other areas in Tibet—together with a few in-depth interviews—so as to afford me some criteria for deciding the limits of generalization. For a number of reasons too involved to cite here, I decided to limit the scope of my generalizations to the heartland of political Tibet, Central Tibet.[3]

THE FAMILY[4]

Tibet was characterized by a well developed system of stratification. Although the political system was not really feudal, arable land was divided into manorial estates held by aristocratic families, religious corporations, and the central government. Typically, these estates not only comprised land but also a variety of types of attached serfs *(mi ser)*. The religious corporations and the aristocracy, together with a category of serfs, or landowning non-taxpayer, usually referred to as *tre-ba (khral pa)*,[5] characteristically possessed inheritable land. The latter two categories, moreover, were organized into corporate extended families which, as will be explained briefly below, fit into the category of stem family. In this short paper, I shall have to restrict the discussion to the family organization of the *tre-ba* serfs, particularly the *šung-gyu-ba (gzhung rgyugs pa)* or "government" *tre-ba* serfs.

The *šung-gyu-ba tre-ba*, although far outnumbered by the other main category of serfs, or non-landowning non-taxpayers, called *dü-jung (dud*

---

[3] Central Tibet is taken to include primarily the areas of *Dbus, Gtsang,* eastern *Stod* and secondarily the areas of *Dwags po, Lho Ka,* and *Kong po.*

[4] Many of the subjects which are only briefly touched on in this paper will be dealt with in detail in a monograph I am presently preparing on kinship, stratification, and politics in Tibet.

[5] Different areas often used different terms, *e.g., (khral mjal)* or *trong-ba (grong pa)*.

chung), were without question the dominant social, political, and economic stratum in village Tibet. In Samada, for example, there were only eight corporate *tre-ba* families, but approximately seventy-five, non-corporate nuclear *dü-jung* families. These eight families, however, hereditarily held all the land in Samada, the *dü-jung* existing as their dependent tenants.

Both the verbalized ideal and the actual behavioral pattern for the *tre-ba* saw the basic social unit as an agnatically oriented, named corporate, stem-type family. These named corporations were perpetuated preferably through agnatic links, but both fictive modes such as adoption and uterine links through daughters were permissible. The primary possession of these corporate families was land, which in many instances included both arable land and pasture land. Written title to this land was in the name of the corporate family, and so long as they fulfilled certain obligations, the *tre-ba* had the right to unilaterally, that is, without having to obtain even token permission, transmit this land to their progeny.[6] The nature of these obligations is indicated by the meaning of the term *tre-ba* which glosses as "one who does taxes" or "taxpayer." The land they held was considered the basis *(rten)* from which tax obligations in-kind *(lag 'don)* and in corvée service *('u lag, rta'u, khal ma)* were performed for their lord. Although taxes in-kind were theoretically fixed, the corvée taxes were open-ended, and together they comprised obligations of some considerable magnitude.

But whereas on the one hand the *tre-ba* had large tax responsibilities, on the other they had relatively large, permanent land resources affording them an economic base from which to obtain rapid economic success. The histories of the *tre-ba* families I was able to collect showed a high degree of economic fluctuation between generations with families moving from wealthy to impoverished and back again over the course of several generations. Certainly good fortune and capability were important variables, but the availability of manpower was also a significant factor and was repeatedly singled out by the verbal statements of informants, as well as the events in the case histories.

In relation to this, the *tre-ba* considered the intact perpetuation of their corporate lands of critical importance. So long as it remained so, the resources through which to achieve rapid economic mobility were available, even though at any given point the family might be impoverished. The nature of the norms governing inheritance, however, posed a potential threat to this intact perpetuation of the family's estate. The ideal norm stated that all males of the named corporate family have demand rights to a portion of the corporation's land. Therefore, although partition of the family land was perceived as disastrous, the ideal norms offered males just such an option. The reasons why such partition was not common will concern us in the rest of this paper.

---

[6] The complicated question of land tenure and inheritance will be discussed in the above-mentioned monograph.

THE MONOMARITAL PATTERN AND THE STEM FAMILY

There were several important factors that tended to override the right to partition afforded by the inheritance norms. One such factor concerned a monomarital marriage pattern, another the adjudicative process, and the third a pattern of downward mobility into the status of *chi-mi* ("common or collective man"). The *tre-ba*, as did the aristocracy, followed a "monomarital" principle in their marriage arrangements.

This "monomarital" principle or pattern can be defined as one whereby for each generation one and only one marriage should be made, the children of which are considered members of the family unit with full jural rights relative to their sex. Tibetans considered that situations with two conjugal families in a given generation were unstable and that in a situation such as Figure 1 structurally molded tensions and conflicts of interest between the conjugal families of X and Y would almost inevitably lead to partition between

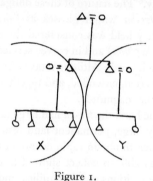

Figure 1.

the two units. Depending on the composition of the persons in the "marriageable" generation, as well as such factors as individual capabilities and personalities, the monomarital principle was employed to guarantee the

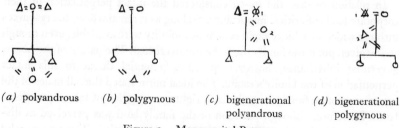

(a) polyandrous   (b) polygynous   (c) bigenerational   (d) bigenerational
                                        polyandrous   polygynous

Figure 2.   Monomarital Pattern.

establishment of only one jurally recognized marriage, this thereby minimizing one potential source of partition, namely the presence of two separate conjugal families on a given generation. In fact, in the several examples I obtained when two such conjugal families (within a single corporate family unit) were present on a single generation confirmation of this overt Tibetan belief was found since partition eventually occurred.

The four types of marriages cited in Figure 2 by no means exhaust the possibilities. In (a) the monomarital pattern operated by perpetuating the family via agnatic links yet establishing only one conjugal family. Example (b) often occurred when a family had no male children and brought in a bridegroom *(mag pa)* for their daughter(s). Example (c) also illustrates the monomarital principle. If the sons were of, or close to, marriageable age and the father was still relatively young, remarriage by him, followed by a separate marriage of the sons, would lead to the creation of heirs of two conjugal families. The bi-generational polyandrous marriage solved the sexual problems and lessened this potential source of conflict between the offspring of those concerned. The fourth example (d) is the reverse of this. In actuality, in Tibet any type of marriage was permitted so long as it did not involve individuals defined as within the parameters of exogamy.[7]

The effect of this monomarital principle on the structure of the family was that it led to the establishment of a unit that closely resembled a stem family. The stem family is commonly defined as a family in which the conjugal family of only one married child is linked with his natal family in a common household.[8] If we take the critical fact to be that the link must be through only one child, then obviously the Tibetan family we briefly described above cannot be regarded as a stem family since polyandous marriages are invariably contracted when more than one son is present. For example, in the reconstruction of the kinship system in Chimdro, I found that in the twenty-six examples of in-taking marriages reported for their nine *tre-ba* families, 60 percent were polygamous, but in each of the remaining 40 percent of the cases there was only one son present. If, however, we take the basic characteristic of the stem family to hinge not on the character of the linkage but rather on the fact that only one jurally recognized conjugal family is formed, then the Tibetan *tre-ba* family and others like it can be considered a type of stem family. In order to differentiate this type of stem family from those formed by such rules as primogeniture (e.g., Japan), I shall refer to the Tibetan variety as a monomarital stem family.

In terms of its organization, the dominant status in the monomarital stem family was that of family head or *abo (trong bey abo)*. Very briefly, the head

---

[7] Exogamy was defined at seven generations collaterally (or seven generations patrilaterally and five generations matrilaterally).

[8] G. Murdock, *Cognatic Forms of Social Organization,* in SOCIAL STRUCTURES IN SOUTHEAST ASIA 4 (G. Murdock ed. 1960); E. Johnson, *The Stem Family and its Extension in Present Day Japan,* 66 AM. ANTHROPOLOGIST 839 (1964); H. Befu, *Patrilineal Descent and Personal Kindred,* 65 AM. ANTHROPOLOGIST 1330 (1963); C. ZIMMERMAN &. M. FRAMPTON, FAMILY AND SOCIETY (1935).

had managerial rights over the property and resources of the unit. The head was always officially a male and usually the oldest male of the generation in power. However, it is clear that the head was not simply the eldest male. Accession to that position followed a developmental pattern. There was a point in the family's development when the incumbent head relinquished his control and retired, usually into a religious role for old people *(rgan chos)*. The new head normally was the eldest male of his generation, although transfer of authority sometimes occurred within a generation, e.g., elder brother to younger brother. The family head, knowing that he would be dependent in his old age on the head of the following generation, often attempted to manipulate the options available to him through the monomarital pattern so as to retain those of his children who would be most likely to cause no difficulty before, and to treat him well after, retirement.

There were then two critical points in the development of the family that were particularly susceptible to partition: the early period when the parental generation was trying to manipulate the human resources to their advantage, and the later point when the children's generation attempted to wrest authority from the incumbent head. A third important recurrent source of tension and potential partition occurred within a generation in polygamous marriages, particularly polyandrous ones. The problems and tensions related to two or three men sharing one wife cannot be discussed here, but it should suffice the show that (1) families in Tibet that did not have such inheritable land almost never contracted such a marriage, and (2) in India, these *tre-ba* adults and their children all marry monogamously. The only instance I found of polygamous marriage in Mysore was one sororal polygynous marriage that was a carry over from Tibet.

What then restrains male children from demanding their right to a share of land? Even though problems exist concerning marital relations, what keeps brothers together in one unit? These obviously are complex problems and all the relevant factors and possible alternatives cannot be examined here. However, in the remaining portion of this paper, I shall focus on one important factor restraining such activation of partition rights, viz., the adjudication system.

THE TIBETAN LEGAL SYSTEM

The Tibetan Central Government administered the polity by means of a network of provincial districts *(rdzong)*, each headed by one or more District Commissioners *(rdzong dpon)* selected by the government from among the permanent Lhasa based government bureaucracy, usually for terms of three years. The District Commissioner was the link between the center and the countryside. His responsibilities broadly consisted of collecting taxes, implementing government directives, formulating the particular needs and requirements of the district to the center, and, finally, adjudicating disputes and punishing criminals. Although the District Commissioner was the highest legal authority in his district, it is important to note that he had no law enforcement organization subordinate to him. The legal function he performed was fundamentally passive in nature. He did not initiate proceedings, and it was only when the participants to a dispute or the victims of a crime brought their case (or the criminal) before him that his authority to punish and render written decisions was activated.[9]

Although ancient legal texts and district edicts *(rtsa tshig)* existed, these were not consulted as the basis for settlements, and disputes should have been adjudicated according to relevant legal norms. Some of these "legal" norms were quite explicit. For example:

> *ra yod tsa ka zas dus*
> *ra med g.yas la zur dang*
> When horned animals are eating grass,
> hornless animals have to stay aside.

In other words, if for example a donkey was killed by a grazing yak, the owner of the donkey had no claim to compensation. In disputes brought before him, the District Commissioner should have rendered a decision after listening to both positions, after interrogating the disputants, and sometimes even after sending out investigators. These decisions were formal written documents called *tra-ma (khra ma)* which had to be signed by both parties to the dispute. If one of the parties felt the decision was unfair, he could refuse to sign *(khra log)* and appeal the decision to a higher authority (usually the Council of Ministers in Lhasa), although he did not have the option of simply ignoring the decision. Once a case was brought before the District Commissioner, he had the authority to use the legitimate force controlled by the Central Government to enforce his decisions, unless they were formally appealed. Since there were relatively clear-cut norms governing inheritance of land, the District Commissioners should have decided disputes on that basis, and, subsequently, procurement of partition of the corporate family's land should have been relatively simple. However, although the ideal pattern was characterized by such impartial, universalistic orientation, the actual operation of the adjudicative process deviated significantly from that ideal. How it did so, and how that deviation was relevant to partition will be discussed below.

First, there was a significant financial aspect to the initiation of litigation. The act of bringing a dispute before the District Commissioner entailed potentially a considerable expenditure of capital. The trip from the village

---

[9] I should mention that there were certain circumstances when the District Commissioner could in fact initiate action, but these were usually in special types of criminal cases and usually were of minor consequence.

to the district headquarters often took several days, and once there, there was no way to predict how quickly the case would be heard and, even more so, how quickly the adjudicator would render his verdict. Food and lodging as well as the loss of labor time at home could add up to a considerable expense. Tibetans in fact have a folk saying, which reflects this factor:

> yang na rku ma ma shor dgos
> yang na rku mjes ma zim dgos
> Either one should not lose to thieves or
> one should not catch them (because of the expenses involved).[10]

This financial factor in formal adjudication had another even more significant dimension. It was common practice for individuals invclved in disputes to present gifts of value privately to the adjudicator. Whereas these gifts were not outright bribes in the Western sense of the term, since they were neither solicited nor were they coterminous with any overt agreement between the giver and the adjudicator, nevertheless, their goal was to particularize the disputant-adjudicator relationship. The nature and size of these gifts varied in very complex ways with the nature and significance of the dispute. What is important to this paper, however, is simply that often both parties to the dispute entered into a pattern of competitive gift giving and that this magnified drastically the importance of financial resources in what ideally was a universalistic, formalized adjudication system.

But not only was a litigant likely to have to spend a considerable amount of money, there was also an element of uncertainty resulting from what I call the "reasonable settlement" pattern. Although the District Commissioner had the authority to unilaterally settle a dispute in favor of one or the other disputants, in many instances the adjudicator attempted rather to settle the dispute so as to preclude its being appealed to a higher authority. This pattern can be seen to result from the acceptance of gifts by the adjudicator, but it was also a consequence of intra-bureaucratic considerations. One of the main purposes of the position of District Commissioner was to diminish the quantity of minor disputes that might otherwise end up in Lhasa. It was, therefore, generally considered a reflection of the District Commissioner's lack of ability and incompetence if any number of disputes were appealed to Lhasa after he had adjudicated. The acquisition of such a pejorative reputation could seriously affect an official's subsequent appointments, and it was due also to this that the pattern of "reasonable settlement" existed. General awareness of this is illustrated by the following folk saying:

---

[10] This verse specifically related to criminal cases, and it should be noted that it not only referred to the financial aspect, but also to the danger that in the interrogationprocess the adjudicator might resort to whipping both the "plaintiff" and the "defendant" in order to determine prevarication.

> *ham pa ri tsam bshad na*
> *bden pa g.yag tsam thob yong*
> If you tell a lie as big as a mountain
> you'll obtain a truth as big as a yak.

In other words, a person who boldly lied might obtain more than he was entitled to, or than he would have obtained had he presented less fantastic demands. While this might or might not favor a particular individual wanting partition, it did add an element of uncertainty over and above the ideal norm. Even after a large outlay of money and forceful presentation of one's demands, the outcome was still somewhat dubious and, anyway, in the end could be appealed with a new round of even greater expenses.

The adjudication process was thus characterized on the one hand by a need for ready financial resources, and on the other by an element of ultimate uncertainty. It is not surprising, therefore, that the formal adjudication system was normally turned to only after all local attempts at mediation and reconciliation had failed to settle the matter. Moreover, it was generally the case that such disputes that reached the District Commissioner were between persons of the same social stratum, *i.e.,* between *tre-ba,* or if between *tre-ba* and *dü-jung,* between wealthy *dü-jung* and *tre-ba.* The formal adjudication system was generally not useful to the majority of poor persons in rural Tibet who depended more on asymmetrical dependency relationships with prominent *tre-ba* (or their lords) for protection of their rights.

It is clear, then, that the actual operation of the adjudication process was a major factor in restraining and limiting the enforcement of the ideal right concerning land. By imposing a potentially large, open-ended financial burden on litigants as well as an element of uncertainty, the initiation of litigation at this level was discouraged. Moreover, Tibetans clearly had a notion of opting to live in an unpleasant situation rather than turn to the formal adjudication system for satisfaction.[11] The idea of Pyrrhic victory was perceived. This does not mean that litigation over land never occurred, nor does it imply that the absence of frequent partition derives solely from the nature of the adjudication process. In fact, it is possible to show that certain types of persons in certain types of situations initiated litigation even though they were aware of the potential expenses. Nonetheless, in general, we may say that the particularistic aspects of the adjudicative process functioned to restrain partition litigation.

Let me now mention briefly one last important factor. We mentioned above that at various times, particularly in polyandrous or polygynous marriages, conflicts and tension arose. A wife favored one brother; a brother rejected a wife who desired him; a brother fell in love with another girl. However, in terms of the cases I collected, such situations did not usually end in partition, this being a relatively rare phenomenon. But, if litigation for partition were

---

[11] *Cf.* the verse on p. 212.

not perceived as a viable alternative, what happened in such instances if the tensions and anxieties became intense? Obviously, in some instances the individual simply tried to make the best of the bad situation. But for many, the solution was through descending to the status of *chi-mi (spyi mi)*.

Chi-mi literally translates as "common man," the common referring to the fact that the *chi-mi* were serfs of the village (*i.e.,* the *tre-ba* families) as a collective entity. *Chi-mi* were thus a type of *dü-jung* serf and as such had no hereditable land. While they were not tied to land, they did have to make a yearly payment to their Lord, the village, and, if needed, they could be sent to serve in the army as the village's representative (albeit with salary from the village). Other corvée obligations sometimes came into play, but they really do not concern us here since, generally, new *chi-mi* who had just voluntarily moved from the higher *tre-ba* status were somewhat differentially treated and tended not to get the unpleasant corvée obligations sometimes required of *chi-mi*.

If a conflict arose within a family and if the individual involved felt he did not want to or could not remain in the common household but yet either did not have the necessary resources or drive or even intelligence to attempt to activate his right to a share of the corporate land via litigation, he could ask for or accept a small settlement of such items as household goods, grain, and sometimes even a few heads of livestock. He would then enter the status of *chi-mi* (village) serf and thereby relinquish all rights to the remaining possessions of the corporate family. While this *chi-mi* status was ranked lower in prestige than the *tre-ba* one, the *chi-mi* were in many ways freer as individuals. They could marry whomever they desired, could work whenever and at whatever they felt like, and could go wherever they pleased. Moreover, while they were usually poorer than the *tre-ba* and without any voice in the decision-making process in the village, they also had none of the worries and responsibilities that the *tre-ba,* as a result of their heavy tax obligations, were burdened with. In all, the relative freedom and lack of responsibility provided sufficient incentive to make downward mobility into the status of *chi-mi* a viable alternative to litigation.

I have tried in this paper to briefly set out the manner in which the legal-adjudicative process in traditional Tibetan society affected change in the family structure by inhibiting and discouraging litigation relating to the activation of partitionary rights to land, and thereby supported the perpetuation intact of large, landholding corporate families. This, in turn, played an important role in stabilizing the general socioeconomic system characteristic of rural Tibet.

PART III
MARRIAGE AND DIVORCE IN TAIWAN

A Case Study of the Dynamics of Family Law and Social Change in Rural China

DAVID C. BUXBAUM

INTRODUCTION

The Varied Roles of Positive Law in Social Change

Marion Levy has suggested that modern industry needs universal criteria for employment of virtually all personnel. With reference to the particularistic inclinations of the traditional Chinese family, he has stated, ". . . modern industry and the 'traditional family' are mutually subversive."[1] Because such views have gained a measure of acceptance and as a result of the inclination of modernizing nations to adopt the external trappings of Western institutions[2] (as well as a desire to focus power in, and center the duties of loyalty upon, the central authorities), since the earliest part of the twentieth century, Chinese governments have attempted[3] to convert the traditional Chinese family into

---

[1] M. LEVY, THE FAMILY REVOLUTION IN MODERN CHINA 352 (1949).

[2] In part also motivated by a desire to rid China of the institution of extraterritoriality, a matter, however, that was primarily raised as a question of criminal law reform by Westerners.

[3] On January 29, 1901, the Empress Dowager, after having to flee from Western armies, appealed to the government officials for suggestions as to what way Western style reforms might be introduced. In response Liu K'ung-yi, Yuan Shih-k'ai, and Chang Chih-tung suggested legal reform among others in a series of memorials. M. MEIJER, THE INTRODUCTION OF MODERN CRIMINAL LAW IN CHINA 9, 10 (1950). In March 1902, Chinese ambassadors abroad were instructed to investigate the laws of the various countries, and experts on Western law (as well as those knowledgeable in Chinese law) were brought to the capital for consultation. In May 1904, the Law Codification Commission, *Fa-lü Pien-tsuan Kuan,* was established. Its work included translation of foreign codes (Id., 11). We may point to this action as the beginning of the reception of Western law. Naturally real legal reform did not begin until the establishment of the codification Commission, *Hsiu-ting fa-lü kuan,* in 1907 and the application of new legal concepts by the Supreme Court *(Ta-li-yüan)* after 1911.

the conjugal family,[4] and traditional marriage patterns into Western forms.[5] One of the clearest manifestations of such government policies can be seen in the promulgation and manner of enforcing laws relating to betrothal, marriage, divorce, adoption, and inheritance.

Legal change, however, does not automatically bring about social change, particularly in a premodern society. The effect of law on social institutions depends upon numerous variables. One important factor is the degree to which judicial-political power can be brought to bear on a particular conflict. This in turn depends upon physical communication, literacy, the extent to which the formal court system is available and intelligible to the populace, and the degree to which the informal courts have been penetrated by new leadership and new norms. Furthermore, the extent to which legal and administrative coercion and propaganda-education are available and are employed will also influence change, although not necessarily in the desired manner.

Another important factor in determining the effect of law upon social change is the power of the social groups affected. This will depend upon the size, strength, and degree to which the particular group feels affected, which, in turn, will depend upon existing traditional values and their relationship to the new law. Traditional attitudes towards change, the strength of any particular values, and the degree to which they conflict with the new

---

[4] "Ideally speaking the members of such a family unit are a father, a mother and non-adult children. . . . The members reckon solidarity more or less equally in terms of both the paternal and maternal lines of descent." 1 M. LEVY, MODERNIZATION AND THE STRUCTURE OF SOCIETIES 73–74 (1966). Levy refers to this type of family as the multilineal conjugal family, adopting Max Gluckman's term.

[5] This is not to suggest that the views of the various Chinese governments were in any way unreasonable, for as Levy notes: "One of the special characteristics of relatively modernized societies is their quite unusual type of family unit. Whatever the previous ideal family structure was, during the transition toward relative modernization, the ideals always change toward what anthropologists and sociologists call a *multilineal conjugal family* unless they already took that form." *Id.* While there is obviously a direct relationship between the conjugal family and certain marriage forms and practices, there is apparently not always such a relationship. For example, we might expect that arranged marriages would be uncommon with the development of the conjugal family, but at least according to government sources, ". . . of the one million marriages in Japan every year at least a third are arranged by parents with the help of go-betweens." Post Intelligencer (Seattle), Nov. 26, 1967, at 32. *See also* W. Yozo & M. Rheinstein, *The Family and the Law: The Individualistic Premise and Modern Japanese Family Law,* in LAW IN JAPAN 384, 393, 394 (A. von Mehren ed. 1963), where according to a survey taken before 1956, depending upon locality the parents' opinion varied in importance in the selection of a spouse. In Tokyo the parents would decide on their child's spouse in 15.9 percent of the cases, while in Okayama they would decide in 48.7 percent of the cases. In 42.5 percent of the cases in Tokyo and 38.4 percent of the cases in Okayama the decision would be made by consultation. Of course, this raises the question as to the extent of the development of the conjugal family in Japan.

law, will all help to determine the degree to which positive law can affect social change.

Of course, social change may occur independently of legal change. Conversely, the law may alter without noticeably affecting social behavior. As an example of the former, white—the color traditionally associated with death and funerals in China—has become in recent years the standard color for wedding gowns in parts of Taiwan.[6] Similarly, the sedan chair has been virtually replaced by the automobile in many areas of rural Taiwan as the usual means of transporting the bride to the home of the groom in ordinary patrilocal marriages.[7] The first of these changes is presumably associated with westernization; the availability of a new and more efficient means of transportation, accompanied by a loss of prestige of the traditional vehicle, largely accounts for the latter. Neither change is directly related to legal change.

On the other hand, some aspects of customary law, that is, unwritten law, have remained the same despite the passage of positive laws (by which I mean written laws) designed to bring about change. In both contemporary Kwangtung and Taiwan, despite legislation seemingly to the contrary,[8] it is rare for a woman who marries out of her natal home to inherit property from that household.[9] The customary law persists, in part, because the governments have not made strenuous efforts to change it and, in part, because under present circumstances such new practices probably are neither economically rational nor socially desirable.

However, forceful application of the positive law and use of effective criminal sanctions can seriously undermine customary law and effectuate social change. The present mainland government has, by use of a vigorous policy, managed to virtually eliminate the taking of secondary wives[10]—an institution

---

[6] Of course, the mere exposure to a Western style wedding dress and an association that such a dress was prestigious or desirable would not suffice to bring about change. The material to make the dress or a place from which to rent the dress would have to be available.

[7] Somewhat differently, however, the bicycle has largely replaced the sedan chair in present day rural Kwangtung for transportation of the bride, in large part as a result of government pressure.

[8] It should be noted that the provisions of the Marriage law in mainland China are not very specific with regard to intestate succession. Article 14, which forms the basis of the law, merely states that parents and children have the mutual right to inherit one another's property. However, from constitutional sources and other literature, it is clear that in principle at least the marriage law should certainly not be a bar to the power of daughters who have married out of their natal homes to inherit. In fact, however, the law is more ambiguous than Article 14 indicates, as shall be discussed later.

[9] Of course, there is only a limited amount of heritable property in the mainland today.

[10] *See* E. Westermarck, A. Short History of Marriage 1–2 (1926), for a definition of marriage, ". . . as a relation of one or more men to one or more women which is recognized by custom or law and involves certain rights and duties both . . . of the

that flourishes in Taiwan and continues to exist in other Chinese communities.[11] The success of the mainland government can in part be attributed to
the facts that secondary wives were not common traditionally and that there
was some ideological ambivalence about their desirability. Furthermore, it
was the wealthier citizens who availed themselves of this institution, and the
wealthy are now a disfavored class in the People's Republic of China. In
Taiwan, on the other hand, where the legal limitations on the taking of a
secondary wife are less clear and where enforcement depends largely upon the
filing of individual complaints, the institution of the secondary wife probably
flourishes as it never did in traditional China, where it was clearly sanctioned
by law.[12]

---

parties entering the union and . . . the children born of it." Westermarck further notes
that marriage ". . . always implies the right of sexual intercourse . . ."; ". . . is an
economic institution . . ." where the husband has the duty to support the wife and
children who in turn may have duties to work for him and, ". . . should be concluded
in accordance with the rules laid down by custom or law, . . ." Murdock suggests
polygyny exists when plural marriages are contemporaneous, all unions being
". . . genuine marriages, involving residential cohabitation and economic association
as well as sexual association." These ". . . unions must have the support of culture and
public opinion."

G. MURDOCK, SOCIAL STRUCTURE 26–27 (paperback ed. 1965). Murdock suggests
that concubinage "can . . . be distinguished from polygyny when it does not meet the
economic criterion of marriage . . ." *Id.*, 6–8. *See also* WEBSTER'S THIRD NEW INTER-
NATIONAL DICTIONARY 472 (unabr. 1961), which defines concubinage as cohabitation
of persons not legally married. This is a very unsatisfactory definition but would at least
relegate the pre-Republican *Ch'ieh* in Chinese society to the status of a secondary wife.
The status of the *yi t'ai t'ai* (secondary wife) subsequent to the 1931 Civil Code would
depend upon how one interpreted the positive law of Nationalist China and whether
one gave primary importance to positive or customary law. I would adopt a modified
view of both Westermarck and Murdock, suggesting that polygyny exists when plural
marriages are contemporaneous, all unions "being genuine marriages involving
residential cohabitation and economic . . . as well as sexual association." Those unions
furthermore must be permitted by customary or positive law. E. WESTERMARCK, *supra*,
at 231, notes that where polygyny exists: "The general rule is that one of the wives
holds a higher social position than the rest or is regarded as the principal wife; and in
most cases it is the first married wife to whom such distinction is assigned. . . ." This
would encompass the situation in China. There is a strong argument for calling the
women of these plural relations concubines. For the purposes of this paper, however,
I prefer the term secondary wife, recognizing the difference in status between the
primary and secondary wife.

[11] *See, e.g.,* D. Buxbaum, *Chinese Family Law in a Common Law Setting,* 25 J. ASIAN
STUDIES 630 ff., 640–42 (1966), which includes a discussion of the problems wrought
by applying the common law definition of marriage, found in the famous case of Hyde
v. Hyde [1866] L.R. 1 P & D 13, to various countries in the Commonwealth.

[12] However, the suppression of certain institutions may require the continued
vigilance of the authorities. The *t'ung-yang-hsi* marriage, for example, has been declared
"illegal" in both Taiwan and the mainland and is undoubtedly a dying institution.

Other changes occur under the umbrella of the law, which then serve to legitimate social alteration. For example, the law enacted in 1931 in China and carried to Taiwan in 1945, stipulating that children were to make betrothals of their own accord instead of having them arranged,[13] became partially effective only when economic circumstances changed. When factories and other alternate sources of employment began to attract the young, they were able to leave the family farms, gain a degree of economic and social independence, and more readily come into contact with potential spouses. At such times—which, in fact, in most parts of rural China was only recently—the law, first enacted more than thirty-five years ago, became something of a reality.[14] In mainland China the Communists have managed, in part, to "artificially" create a situation that results in fairly high mobility for an agricultural population. The *hsia-fang* policy, whereby cadre and others are sent to rural areas generally other than those of their origins,[15] and the practice of sending youngsters away from their locality for study and work, have contributed to some extent to freedom from the bonds of the agricultural community. The Communist system, furthermore, permits the young a certain amount of economic independence. The constant calling of meetings in mainland China and the employment of young women in many institutions contribute to the potentiality of contacts between members of the opposite sex. The Communists have also pressured parents not to interfere in their children's selection of spouses. In effect, the government policy on the mainland, coupled with industrialization, assists in bringing about changes similar to those in Taiwan. These changes take place in both areas under the aegis of the law.

Thus, we see the role of positive law under varied circumstances: social change occurring independently of law, law being ineffectual in bringing about social change, law playing a major role in stimulating social change, and law serving to legitimate change. The impact of law varies with governmental policy—particularly with the vigor of enforcement and the type of sanction applied—and with actual social, ideological, and economic conditions.

Nevertheless, the Lien-chiang documents seem to indicate that this institution still retains some tenacity in some areas in the mainland despite indications of fairly rigorous opposition by the government.

[13] CIVIL CODE (1931) Book IV, Chapter II, Article 972. Enacted also in the Marriage Law of the People's Republic of China in 1950, Chapter II, Article 3, which prohibits interference by third parties in arranging a marriage.

[14] Exposure to alternate types of marriage, universal education in both Taiwan and the mainland, and political drives such as that concerned with the Marriage Law in Communist China, all contributed to changing social conditions.

[15] *See* F. SCHURMANN, IDEOLOGY AND ORGANIZATION IN COMMUNIST CHINA 91, 182, 400, 464 (1966), for different aspects of the *hsia-fang* (send down to the villages) movement and for a brief discussion of the contrasting *hui-hsiang* (return to the village) policy whereby people were sent back to their native villages.

Obviously, law is an institution that can be used as an instrument of social change under certain conditions, but it is not socially meaningful unless it is related to actual social conditions. Thus, legislation cannot be an effective tool of social change[16] unless the society has relatively good communications, a reasonably high level of literacy, good and effective networks of political control, and a system of "courts" able to enforce its promulgations.[17] Only in modern societies does creative legislation become an efficient means for bringing about reasonably rapid social change.[18]

Although traditional China was much more "legalist" than we have previously believed,[19] the role of creative legislation, or positive law, was somewhat restricted. Traditional family law, particularly in the Ch'ing period, served to reinforce the rules of propriety *(li)*[20] and the customary law, while prohibiting those customs deemed obnoxious by the traditional morality or political hierarchy. When the Japanese occupied Taiwan, positive law initially played a role similar to its prior role in traditional society, but the Japanese gradually used the cases and administrative regulations, particularly the household register, to attempt to introduce changes in family relations. In mainland China the post-Ch'ing reforms and the Civil Code of 1931, as well as later court decisions, attempted to effect reform through the use of positive law enactments. Nevertheless, by and large, these laws served only to legitimate changes that were gradually taking place in the customary law and the social structure. But with the advent of the Communists in China a major forceful effort was made to use legislation as a positive weapon to bring about

---

[16] *See* D. Buxbaum, *Introduction,* 2 J. ASIAN & AFRICAN STUDIES 1–8 (1967).

[17] *See also* D. Henderson, *Promulgation of Tokugawa Statutes,* 2 J. ASIAN & AFRICAN STUDIES 9 ff. (1967), for a discussion of the problems involved in making legislation known to the populace in premodern Japan, a society with a comparatively high level of literacy.

[18] Henry Maine was one of the first to point this out. For a brief useful discussion of this topic, *see* J. STONE, THE PROVINCE AND FUNCTION OF LAW 456–63 (1961). *See also* 1 D. HENDERSON, CONCILIATION AND JAPANESE LAW 47–62 (1965), for an illuminating discussion of the role of law in premodern Japan and contrasts with modern concepts of law. Henderson refers to much of the adjudication which takes place outside of formal tribunals as "anthropological adjudication."

[19] This point was clarified by K. Hsiao, *Legalism and Autocracy in Traditional China,* TSING HUA JOURNAL OF CHINESE STUDIES 19, 108 ff. (1960). Hsiao points out that calling traditional China a "Confucian state" is misleading in so far as it ignores the role of legalism and fails to convey precisely the role of Confucianism. Ideally of course the Confucianists would rely upon moral suasion and rules of propriety rather than law to rule the populace. Although Confucius himself emphasized virtue *(te)* and the rules of propriety *(li),* he did not ignore the efficacy of law or punishments *(hsing). See* 1 K. HSIAO, CHUNG-KUO CHENG-CHIH SZU-HSIANG SHIH (History of Chinese political thoughts) 64 (reprint 1965).

[20] See particularly H. WILHELM, GESELLSCHAFT UND STAAT IN CHINA 49–59 (1960).

social change.[21] However, the tremendous energies exerted by the Chinese government to change social patterns, and particularly the movement to enforce the marriage law, may not be proportionately reflected in the results they have achieved—perhaps because, strangely enough, the Communists seem to underestimate the importance of economic change and industrialization which, once new ideas are received, provide the necessary environmental and social opportunities for new types of relationships.

The Growth of Government Intervention, the Weakening of Traditional Institutions, and the Decline in Contracts

The above discussion relates to the role of creative legislation and case law in bringing about change in family and marital patterns. There is another aspect of the law that should be briefly mentioned, that is, contract law. While marriage in China results in the creation of a new status, it has traditionally been preceded by a contract to marry. This contract was either oral or written. If it were an oral contract, the go-between, who invariably played a role in a Chinese marriage, served a very important function as witness to the negotiations and the final contractual agreement. If disputes arose about this most important contract, the go-between was a logical witness to the details of the agreement. Not infrequently, however, contracts to marry were, and still are, in written form. Traditionally, these contracts were written by literate members of the community, who were often professional scriveners especially trained for such work. They wrote not only marriage contracts, but also adoption contracts, agreements as to division of household property, and divorce agreements. The writing of divorce agreements was more difficult to arrange, however, because of the stigma attached to divorce and to all who assisted with the proceedings.

This area of contract law was influenced by positive law changes, particularly insofar as the parties would seldom contract in writing to do something the positive law prohibited. This became especially true when law courts began to play a greater role in the settlement of disputes and when administrative organizations began to interfere in family matters.

During the Japanese occupation of Taiwan, registration of marriages, adoptions, divorces, births, and deaths was required by law. While failure to register would not affect the validity of a marriage, it would subject one to administrative punishment. Since the household register was under the control of the police, who were quite strict, registration generally took place. The requirement of registration was not an innovation on the part of the Japanese colonial government in Taiwan, but rather a refinement and continuation of

---

[21] For a discussion of the Chinese Communist concept of law as an instrument of social upheaval and class warfare, *see* D. Buxbaum, *Preliminary Trends in the Development of the Criminal Law,* INT'L & COMPARATIVE L.Q. 1 (Jan. 1962).

practices that had existed during the Ch'ing dynasty.[22] The system was continued by the Nationalist government in Taiwan at the end of World War II and was reinstituted by the Communists in mainland China. While registration does not seem to have been a condition to entering a valid marriage either in Ch'ing times or under Japanese, Nationalist, or Communist law,[23] failure to register was penalized. Furthermore, the requirement of registration gave the government a greater role in determining marriage, adoption, and divorce patterns.

For example, it seems to have become difficult to register a secondary wife during the latter portion of the Japanese occupation in Taiwan despite the sanction of the positive law. It also became impossible to register a type of female adoption whereby the girl was adopted specifically to work as a servant in the adopting home. Adoptions of future brides (t'ung-yang-hsi) have been virtually illegal since 1931 under Nationalist and Communist rule. Furthermore, the Communists have made a point during registration of inquiring about the legality of the marriage and particularly about whether the spouses freely decided to enter the union. Registration of a marriage has become more significant in both mainland China and the Province of Taiwan.

The contract to marry, which was of utmost importance during the Ch'ing period, began to lose some of its significance in Taiwan as early as the Japanese period. Furthermore, under the Nationalists in Taiwan a wedding can, and in urban areas (although in proportionately few cases) more frequently does, take place in court. While marriage remains a civil contract that creates a status, the contractual element has recently become less important. We might facetiously say there has been a movement from contract to status; that is, the formal contractual aspects of the marital relationship have largely disappeared, while the creation of the status still remains, becoming in fact relatively more important. The government now plays a role in the creation of the status relationship, and secularization of the ceremony has accompanied this process of government interference.

At the same time institutions, such as the lineage (tsu) and the clan (t'ung-hsing-hui), which had played an important role both in the formation of marriages, adoptions, and so forth, and in the settlement of disputes that

---

[22] See K. HSIAO, RURAL CHINA: IMPERIAL CONTROL IN THE NINETEENTH CENTURY 573 (1960). See also the requirements of registration under the section Hu-lu (household regulation) in the Ch'ing Code. Registration during Ch'ing times was, except for a brief period, to be that of the entire household including females. It was connected with the pao-chia (self-police units) system which required plaques on the outer gate of homes listing the members of the household. The system of registration was inefficient and was aimed particularly at control for purposes of taxation and corvée duties, thus focusing on adult males.

[23] See M. Meijer, Specific Problems of Translation: Family Law, unpublished manuscript presented at conference on Chinese Communist Law, Bermuda, May 27–30, 1967, regarding the question of registration in mainland China.

arose from these relationships, were seriously weakened by a number of factors.[24] Deprivation of much of their landholdings, beginning in Japanese times in Taiwan and under the Communists in the mainland, has seriously affected the economic base and power of these organizations. Furthermore, the increased mobility of the population and the availability of alternative sources of employment outside the rural areas have made members of the lineage less dependent upon it for sustenance and thus less subject to its control.

With the passing of the gentry in China and the introduction of modern styles of government, the formal political leadership in the villages passed initially to appointed government functionaries. During the Japanese period (1895–1945) in Taiwan, the mayor of the village *(li-chang)*, who was selected by the government, performed a substantial amount of the conciliation and other dispute settlement work. He could, under extreme circumstances, call upon the police to back up his decision; therefore, his formal authority was imposing. In Taiwan the mayor is now an elected official. The result of this has been that even when the mayor's private status is high, he must be careful not to antagonize elements within the village if he wishes to be reelected. Furthermore, his decision does not carry the authority it once did. This is also true of those people who do not possess formal authority, but who undertake to conciliate disputes at the request of the parties. In Taiwan, therefore, the populace has turned to the courts with greater frequency for dispute settlement.

If the judges, however, feel the dispute to be too insignificant, they will ask that the parties attempt to conciliate it. The parties then turn to the police, party officials, higher ranking elected officials (for example, the head of the township), or the conciliation tribunals set up by the government, as well as family and village leaders, for conciliation purposes.

On the mainland, the Communists have made conciliation a major means of dispute settlement. The Women's Association, official conciliation tribunals, local cadre, and other government officials have come to play a major role in family dispute settlement. Conciliation in present day mainland China[25] is at times initiated by government institutions rather than by the parties concerned. This gives the government an opportunity to influence decisions and to disseminate ideology.

The result of turning to official leaders for dispute settlement in the family law area is that the official norms begin to play a more important role. Where the two conflict, the government official is more likely to rely upon positive law rather than customary law. This reliance is not invariable, however,

---

[24] *See* B. Gallin, *Mediation in Changing Chinese Society in Rural Taiwan,* 2 J. ASIAN & AFRICAN STUDIES 77–90 (1967). *See also* D. Buxbaum, *supra* note 16, at 5.

[25] *See* J. Cohen, *Chinese Mediation on the Eve of Modernization,* 2 J. ASIAN & AFRICAN STUDIES 54–76 (1967). *See also* D. Buxbaum, *supra* note 16, at 5 ff.

because, particularly in Taiwan, there is a social and political premium placed upon quick and relatively painless dispute settlement. Therefore, the officials, including the police, give substantial consideration to customary law. On the other hand, even when disputes are settled by informal leaders in Taiwan, the official norms, that is, the positive law, plays a greater role than they did previously in dispute settlement.

With the education of the young and their increased economic power and mobility, they are both more aware of the positive law and more willing to make use of it. One very important factor in the conciliation of almost all disputes is whether one has right on his side, which is often determined by reference to law and custom. Although customary law is still of primary significance in most rural cases, positive law can be brought in as an argument for one of the parties, if it conflicts with custom. For example, a child may insist that children now have independence to marry whom they please. While it is unlikely that there would be reference to the provisions of the law, in both Taiwan and mainland China an adopted girl, who had been instructed by the Women's Association, might well insist on her rights in order to marry whom she pleases. Therefore, positive law, which traditionally was of much less importance than customary law in the settlement of disputes, has become more important. The weakening of the traditional institutions that administered customary law, the greater interference of government in civil law matters, and the greater mobility of the population, have all contributed to this change. Nevertheless, customary law remains very important in Taiwan and, to a lesser extent, in the People's Republic of China.

The Relationship of Customary Law to Positive Law

This might be an appropriate time to discuss the terms "customary law" and "positive law."[26] For the purposes of this paper we shall use working definitions. "Positive law" shall be the law posited by either a legislative body or a court—the official written law. Since some of the rules and regulations concerning family matters were written down by lineage organizations[27] during the Ch'ing dynasty and occasionally were registered with the government, we have to decide what to do with this aspect of the "law." While such rules and regulations were written and often were modeled after the code, I think it best to refer to them as part of customary law, for they were not in fact official in the sense that there was no formal sanction for their breach.

---

[26] For an excellent discussion of a definition of law and its applicability to premodern and modern societies, see 1 D. HENDERSON, supra note 18, at 50–54. Henderson suggests that law "is a selected, hypothetical norm backed by a coercive sanction prescribed by the group."

[27] See H. W. Liu, THE TRADITIONAL CHINESE CLAN RULES 217 (1959), which indicates that several family law problems were common to the rules; e.g., inheritance and adoption of an heir, marriage matches, wife's role and conduct, remarriage of widows, adoption, secondary wives, and so on.

Customary law, therefore, would with the above exception be *ius non scriptum,* the unwritten law. There is some precedent for using this distinction in common law,[28] and it is most useful in Chinese law.[29]

In order to differentiate custom from customary law, we will have to define "law." For the purposes of this paper: "An order shall be called *law* where it is guaranteed by the likelihood that [physical or psychological] coercion, aiming at bringing about conduct in conformity with the order, or at avenging its violation, will be exercised by a staff of people especially holding themselves ready for this purpose."[30] It might be helpful to think of the difference between custom and customary law in terms of the question: When a dispute occurs, will the norm in question determine the rights and liabilities of the parties if the dispute is brought before a formal or informal tribunal?[31] Thus two factors are involved: the importance of the norm, that is, whether breach of it would give rise to a dispute subject to litigation or conciliation; and, if so, whether the "tribunal"[32] would apply the norm to adjudicate the rights and liabilities of the parties.

---

[28] *See* the Tanistry case in J. DAVIES, A REPORT OF CASES AND MATTERS LAW, RESOLVED AND ADJUDGED IN THE KINGS COURTS IN IRELAND 87 (1762), which says that custom ". . . is *jus non scriptum.*" For the best discussion I have seen on the relation of custom to law, *see* C. ALLEN, LAW IN THE MAKING especially 70 n, 1, 153–55 (7th ed. 1964). Allen says: "I do not think it is open to reasonable doubt that when a court accepts and applies a custom, it does so not in the belief that it is introducing a new rule into the law, but in the belief that it is declaring and applying what is already the law." *See also* M. GLUCKMAN, THE JUDICIAL PROCESS AMONG THE BAROTSE OF NORTHERN RHODESIA, especially 237 ff, 246 (1955).

[29] For a fuller discussion of customary law, *see* FAMILY LAW AND CUSTOMARY LAW IN ASIA xxxvi ff. (D. Buxbaum ed. 1968). It has been argued, with much reason, that customary law is quite important to litigation in common law jurisdictions and that such standards as "reasonable care," a "reasonably prudent man" and "mental cruelty" are in fact customary standards. *See* M. GLUCKMAN, POLITICS, LAW AND RITUAL IN TRIBAL SOCIETY 201 (1965). Customary law is also of some importance in jurisdictions which pride themselves for reliance upon a code. *See, e.g.,* the section on custom in R. DAVID & H. DE VRIES, THE FRENCH LEGAL SYSTEM (1958).

[30] MAX WEBER ON LAW IN ECONOMY AND SOCIETY lxiv (M. Rheinstein ed. 1954).

[31] *See* P. Bohannan, THE DIFFERING REALMS OF THE LAW, 67 AM. ANTHROPOLOGIST 34–37 (Dec. 1965). Bohannan suggests that law is a body of binding obligations "which has been reinstitutionalized within the legal institution so that society can continue to function in an orderly manner on the basis of the rules so maintained." The trouble with this definition is that unless "legal institutions" are defined very broadly, and even Bohannan's definition may not be broad enough, one can only call a rule "law" if it has been litigated or somehow promulgated, and neither of these strike me as necessary or useful in dealing with customary law in primitive or peasant society, or for that matter even in modern communities.

[32] P. Bohannan, *supra* note 31, whose definition of a legal institution is most useful. "A legal institution is one by means of which the people of a society settle disputes that arise between one another and counteract any gross and flagrant abuses of the rules . . . of at least some of the other institutions of society."

For example, while it was customary for the bride to cry when leaving her home to be taken to the home of the groom, her failure to do so could not give rise to a compensable or punitive action. In parts of southeastern China, however, if the bride was held out as a virgin and in fact was not, then the groom's family could litigate the matter in a formal or informal tribunal and would receive some form of satisfaction, ranging from compensation to rescission of the marriage contract. Similarly, it was customary in parts of China for the bride to throw a fan on the ground from the sedan chair as she left her parents' house, to manifest her intention to return. No cause of action could arise in any formal or informal tribunal if she failed to do so. If, however, the male did not provide a sedan chair, as was customary for the bride in the ideal patrilocal type marriage, and insisted she walk to his house, it is doubtful that the marriage would proceed. This could be brought before a "tribunal" which would adjudge the parties on the basis of customary law, which required a sedan chair. All this does not mean that the law did not exist until the litigation took place, because in fact there would be substantial psychological or social pressures upon the groom's family to provide a sedan chair. The failure to do so, barring some special circumstances, would be most unusual. Customary law already existed and influenced action before any dispute or litigation.

The Dual Revolution to Traditional and Modern Ideals

We have focused on the role of law in bringing about social change; obviously, however, law is only one factor in change. The traditional Chinese families ideal was the "extended" family, accenting ". . . the patrilineal line, and including as members of the family unit individuals of as many generations as have living representatives, the spouses of those in the main line who are mature, and the nonadult children of all the marital pairs."[33] The law in China has been modified so that the conjugal family has now become the legal ideal. While to some extent society is moving toward this new ideal, the direction of its development is not always straightforward.

In Taiwan, for example, during the Ch'ing dynasty and much of the Japanese occupation, there were various forms of marriage; for example, the

---

[33] 2 M. Levy, *supra* note 4, at 414. *See also* M. Freedman, Lineage Organization in Southeastern China 34–37 (1958), where it is noted that the family in China is the smallest unit of the lineage. "Several families make up a compound . . . [s]everal compounds make up a branch . . . [s]everal branches make up a sub-lineage . . . [and] [s]everal sub-lineages make up a lineage. . . ." Each of these groupings have a head. The family being the basic economic unit comprises "all relations in the paternal line who share a stove and prepare food together." Generally the "oldest man in the highest generation" heads the family. Compounds are reckoned by dwellings and families by stoves. The lineage is the Chinese *tsu* or *tsung-tsu*, sublineage is *fang*, branch is *chih*, compound is *hu*, and family is *chia*. Freedman takes this useful hierarchy from an article by Lin Yueh-hua which he translated. While Freedman finds fault with some of these definitions, they are nevertheless useful for our purposes.

t'ung-yang-hsi type, the matrilocal type, and what I call the "ideal patrilocal" type which traditional law and morality recognized as ideal. If families had sufficient income, they would almost invariably prefer to marry according to the standards of the ideal patrilocal form. However, because this form involved an exchange of gifts and expensive celebrations, it remained an unachievable ideal for many. Then, as economic circumstances in Taiwan improved, particularly after land reform and the injection of large amounts of foreign aid, more and more people were able to afford the ideal patrilocal form.

In the interim, however, the official ideal had changed. In order to save money, the governments in both Taiwan and mainland China preferred people to marry far less elaborately than tradition required. However, once they had achieved some economic self-sufficiency, the people, particularly in Taiwan, very often married in what was largely traditional form. There were some differences, however; on the marriage day the bride would frequently wear a white wedding dress with a red flower, rather than the reddish dress of tradition. Furthermore, even if the marriage were arranged, which is recently far from certain, the bride and groom would generally have had a chance to meet before the engagement and to at least indicate any violent disapproval they might have to the match. This was not as true traditionally. The very nature of the arranged marriage itself was changing. Thus, there is a dual revolution taking place: one toward the ideals of the tradition, and the other toward the modern ideals of the conjugal family which have been largely, but not completely, reflected in the positive law. While these dual tendencies feed on one another, they also conflict at some strategic points, and here law as well as other institutions will continue to play a significant role in mediating and directing this conflict and change.

Chinese Law and the International Revolution in Family Law

The social revolution in China and the legal changes that have both fore-shadowed and directed various parts of it are part of a world revolution. In many countries, including China, the modern civil law of Western Europe has provided the model for the legal changes that have occurred.[34] In other instances the common law has served as the modern legal model. Aside from the shift from polygamy to monogamy, there has generally been a change in the positive law, involving a ". . . mitigation or even complete abolition of the subjection of women to male domination."[35] There has also been a general

---

[34] *See* M. Rheinstein, *The Law of Family and Succession,* in CIVIL LAW IN THE MODERN WORLD 27 (A. Yiannopolus ed. 1965).

[35] *Id.* 31, 32. Rheinstein contrasts the CODE NAPOLEON (1804), which states: "The husband owes protection to his wife, the wife obedience to her husband," with the *Grundgesetz* (statutes) of the West German Republic (1945): "Men and women have equal rights"; to show how things have legally changed in Europe. Rheinstein further

lessening of the patriarchal power over children, which has been transformed into a public trust for the purpose of rearing children as responsible members of society. These legal changes are, of course, evidence of the social revolution that is taking place throughout much of the world.

While modern Western law has influenced legal developments in China and other Asian countries, it should be noted that in some ways traditional Chinese family law was more "progressive" than Western law. In the field of divorce, for example, there are only two western European countries that today permit divorce by mutual consent.[36] Chinese law has permitted this type of divorce for centuries, if not millennia. "Adoption was practically unavailable"[37] in the French law of 1804[38] and was legally unavailable in England until 1926. China has both permitted and practiced adoption for untold centuries.

The legal and social revolution that is taking place in family matters throughout the world has some common threads and tendencies. Nevertheless each country has its own historical patterns and means of resolving its problems.

A CASE STUDY OF FAMILY LAW AND SOCIAL CHANGE IN A RURAL VILLAGE IN TAIWAN

The Village

In order to gain some insight into how the law has actually affected social practice in China, we have chosen a small rural community in Taiwan as a basis for a case study of the relationship between family law and the family

---

suggests that: "The French pronouncement of 1804 not only stated an ideal but aptly described the reality of the overwhelming majority of families, not simply of France but of Europe and America also." The French law of 1804 paid respect to the "great family" and land descended only through the male line. As for the Basic Law code of Germany of 1949, Rheinstein feels that it too describes a reality, although perhaps somewhat less fully than the 1804 French law. It should be noted that the implementing legislation was not passed for some time in part because of the conservatism of the Christian-Democratic party, and the courts played an important role in bringing the law up to the standards of the *Grundgesetz* in Germany. A new law was finally enacted on June 18, 1957. The new law still retained certain paternal authority and was declared unconstitutional in 1959. French family law has been altered, particularly in 1938, 1942, and 1945, but is perhaps less egalitarian with regard to rights of spouses than German law.

[36] Belgium and Luxembourg. This concept was introduced by the Napoleonic Code. New York and California have moved in the direction of this concept recently.

[37] M. Rheinstein, *supra* note 34, at 33.

[38] Although the origins of adoption are found in Roman law, it disappeared in the Middle Ages, was reintroduced in 1792, and was permitted only for adoption of adults in 1804. *See* COMPARATIVE ANALYSIS OF ADOPTION LAWS, U.N. Doc. ST/SOA/30 (June 27, 1956).

during the past half-century. The village is located about fifty minutes by bus from Taipei, the major metropolitan center in Taiwan. The village is, and has been since late Ch'ing times, the center of five villages, having the only market street, public school (since early Japanese times), and police station. Access to the village from the major urban areas had been somewhat difficult, because it required crossing a narrow portion of the Tan-shui River. Until 1959 there was no good permanent bridge so that transportation to Taipei by the most direct route was difficult and often required the services of a professional boatman, who was continually available to take people across the river. One could, however, communicate with Taipei and other urban centers over a longer route without crossing the river. Now the public bus runs almost every daylight hour into Shu-lin and Taipei, as it has for some years. There is also a branch of the railroad, which runs somewhat less frequently into these urban centers.

The villagers are primarily rice farmers, although vegetables are also grown. In 1907, of those farms whose occupation we know of, forty-one men were classified as farmers and thirty-five as having other occupations in the household register. The laborers often worked in the mines and tea fields in the mountains near the village. In 1951, 166 men were farmers, while 59 were in non-farming occupations. To some extent, these figures are misleading, because often even those classified as having other occupations also farmed. In 1965, 144 men were listed as farmers and 140 as non-farmers. Many of the non-farmers were sons of a household having several brothers, some of whom farmed and some of whom worked in factories, mines, and so on. These sons at times helped with farm labor but were primarily occupied elsewhere. Some who had shops on the main street of the village also retained some farm land as they had in earlier years.[39] Most recently, factories have attracted the villagers with their wages and convenient location. An American-owned factory which paid good salaries and had good facilities was built about twelve minutes from the village by bus. Many of the younger members of the village were anxious to work there, and since I was an American, the villagers

---

[39] Some other pertinent facts about communications in the village are that the railroad came through a place near the village, starting in the mid-1920's. Before the river changed course few people went to Taipei as the main commercial metropolis—they went instead to Hsin Chuang, for it required a rather troublesome trip to get to Taipei —one went by boat and on foot. It would take one full day, that is, from early morning until evening, to get to Hsin Chuang. A road was built about forty years ago that permitted people to get to the train rather easily. Presently people go either to Shu-lin or to Taipei for their marketing and other needs, and transportation is quite convenient. While we know something of the history of the village, we are not precisely certain when it was first settled, although we do know that two hundred years ago there were settlers there, some of whom have descendants in the village today. For some interesting historical background of the area, *see* YING-KE HSIANG-T'U-CHIH (Local records of the rural area of Ying-ke) (Taipei 1934; in Japanese).

DAVID C. BUXBAUM

TABLE 1*

INTERVIEW DATA

YEAR	Ideal Type Mar-riage	Ideal Type Remar-riage (M / F)	Ideal Type Div-orce	Adopted Daughter Marrying Out Mar-riage	Adopted Daughter Marrying Out Remar-riage (M / F)	Adopted Daughter Marrying Out Div-orce	Adopted Daughter t'ung yang-hsi Mar-riage	Adopted Daughter t'ung yang-hsi Remar-riage (M / F)	Adopted Daughter t'ung yang-hsi Div-orce	Secondary Wives	Ordinary Type (M / F)	Adopted Daughter Type Mar-riage	Adopted Daughter Type Remar-riage (M / F)	Adopted Daughter Type Div-orce	Totals Mar-riage	Totals Remar-riage	Totals Div-orce	Long-term Extra-marital Relations
1899–1910	3			1			2					2			9			1
1911–15	2	/ 1		1			8	1 / 1				1			12	1		
1916–20	6	1* /		1	/ 1		4	1 / 1		1					14	1		1
1921–25	6		2	9		2	12	1 / 1	2	2		6		1	34	6	3	
1926–30	11	3* / 1*	1	6	/ 2	1	13	1 / 1		1		5	1		38	8	2	2
1931–34	10	1* / 1*		9		1	8			1	1	5			33	2	2	
1935–36	13	1 / 1		2			5			1				1	21	2		
1937–38	6	1 / 1		5		1	5		1	1		3			19	1	1	
1939–40	8	1 /		1			4								13	2		
1941–42	5			7			5			2		2			20			
1943–44	14	1* /		3	1 /	2	8	1 /	1			2	1	1	29	3	3	
1945–46	16	1* / 1*		3	/ 1		3		1	1		2		1	26	3	1	
1947–48	11	1 /		11	1 / 1	1	5	1 /	3	2		3			32	3	2	1
1949–50	12	1 /	1	11	1 / 1	2	8	/ 1				3			36	4	1	1
1951–52	14	1 /	1	6	1 /	4	1			1		3			24	2	3	
1953–54	14	1 / 1		6			3	/ 2	2			5	1 / 1		27	3		
1955–56	19	1 /		11			8		4	4		3	1 / 1		47	4	7	
1957–58	8	/	3	3			2		2	1		1	/ 1	1	18	2	4	
1959–60	15			10	1 /		2		2	2		4	/	1	31	2	1	
1961–62	15		1	6	/ 1		1	1 /	2	2		3			29	2	1	
1963–64	24	1* /		3			1		2	2		3	/ 2		33	3		
1965–66	28	1* / 1*	2	5	1 /		1		3	3	1	3		1	40	4	2	
TOTAL	**260**	**14 / 8**	**9**	**120**	**6 / 10**	**1**	**109**	**6 / 6**		**26**	**2**	**58**	**8 / 8**	**6**	**585**	**58**	**32**	**8**

* Data compiled from direct interviews with individual informants in one village in Taiwan. Presented according to date of marriage or beginning of long-term relationship. See text for description of types.

assumed that I could arrange such employment. In fact, because of the kindness of the manager of the factory, I was able to assist at least eight of the younger people to gain employment in the factory. This factory, newly constructed in 1966 and not quite completed in 1967, will have a major impact on the area. There are, of course, other factories, but none are as close or have as desirable a salary scale.

Patterns of Change in the Family

Two groups of statistical data pertaining to the village are available, and we will concentrate upon them. The first group of data is that compiled by the household records office of the township within which the village was located, and the second group consists of the results of my interviews. These two types of data are closely related but are not identical.

Within the household record data there are two divisions. The first division is that which we shall refer to as the official statistics for the village. These statistics vary somewhat from the household record statistics which I have tabulated. The variance is based upon the fact that I was interested in people who had an intimate connection with the village, even if they were not registered there. For example, some people actually lived in the village but had their household registration elsewhere. Some others lived quite close to the village, had children in the village, came to the village each day to shop and socialize, and served on various committees, but they were not registered in the village. I also included these people who interacted primarily with villagers in most of my tabulations. As a result, there is a disparity between my records and the official records, though this disparity is slight.

A greater disparity exists between my interview records and the household record data. The reason for this is obvious. I could not interview all the people who lived in the village during the past fifty or sixty years. Some had died, some had moved away, and some were untraceable. Furthermore, I have included people in these interviews who may actually live elsewhere, but who are intimately connected with the village; for example, by having family members there and by partaking of village life in some substantial way. Some of these people are registered as living there, and some are not. Although my interviews do not cover every marriage event that occurred in the village, and in this sense are less complete than the household record data, they do deal with subjects that are not covered in the household records data and are bountiful enough to show some changing patterns. Every present household in the village was interviewed, as were any others that were intimately connected with the village. With this in mind we will begin by looking at certain tables.

The ideal patrilocal marriage. If we look at Table 2 (from the household records),[40] we can see that the ideal patrilocal marriage has become more

---

[40] Unfortunately, since Japanese times the household records' official statistics have only classified marriages into two forms—matrilocal and patrilocal.

TABLE 2
MARRIAGE TYPE BY YEAR AND SEX

Year	Sex	Patri-local	Matri-local	T'ung-yang-hsi	Secondary wives	Others and unknown	Total
1907	M	52	11	41		13	117
	F	73	11	55		11	150
1913	M	40	14	55		12	121
	F	58	18	67		4	147
1951	M	96	13	40	2	25	176
	F	102	15	41		39	197
1956	M	125	19	42	6	35	227
	F	138	11	53	6	45	253
1964	M	170	14	33	2	34	253
	F	176	17	39	1	41	274
1965	M	182	16	34	2	33	267
	F	190	16	39		44	289
1966	M	171	16	40	4	35	266
	F	180	17	43	7	44	291

Classified Cases . . . 2613
Nonclassified Cases . . 415
TOTAL 3028

TABLE 3
PERCENTAGE CHANGE IN MARRIAGE TYPE, BY YEAR AND SEX

Year	Sex	Patri-local	Matri-local	T'ung-yang-hsi	Second-ary wives	Others and unknown	Total	Base number of cases
1907	M	44%	9%	35%	0%	11%	99%*	117
	F	49	7	37	0	7	100	150
1913	M	33	12	45	0	10	100	121
	F	39	12	46	0	3	100	147
1951	M	55	7	23	1	14	100	176
	F	52	8	21	0	20	101*	197
1956	M	55	8	19	3	15	100	227
	F	55	4	21	2	18	100	253
1964	M	67	6	13	1	13	100	253
	F	64	6	14	0†	15	99*	274
1965	M	68	6	13	1	12	100	267
	F	66	5	14	0	15	100	289
1966	M	64	6	15	2	13	100	266
	F	62	6	15	2	15	100	291

Classified Cases . . . 2613
Nonclassified Cases . . 415
TOTAL CASES STUDIED . . 3028

* Totals differ from 100% because of rounding off.
† Rounded off to 0%. Actually 0.36%.

Case Study of the Dynamics of Family Law in Rural China

common since 1907. In 1907, of the known types of marriages, half of the marriages were in non-ideal form. The data seriously under-represents the matrilocal *(chao-chui)* type marriage, because many of these were not registered as such. Nevertheless, it is obvious that if we select the year 1966, for example, only a little less than 16 percent of the 221 married men, whose type of marriage we know, had married in a non-ideal form (see Table 3). Since these figures are cumulative, the patterns are not representative of yearly changes.[41] Tables 1, 2, and 3, however, give us some idea of yearly changes. We can see that while the non-ideal marriages accounted for a large percentage of the marriages in the 1921–34 period (Table 4), thereafter, there has been

TABLE 4

NON-IDEAL MARRIAGES

Year	Total t'ung-yang-hsi marriages minus matrilocal style as per cent of all marriages	Total t'ung-yang-hsi marriages including matrilocal as per cent of all marriages	Per cent of all adopted daughters who marry out of their adopted homes	Per cent of all marriages involving adopted daughters	Total matrilocal marriages as per cent of all marriages	Total non-ideal marriages as per cent of all marriages
1899–1910	22.22	44.4	20.00	55.56	22.22	44.44
1911–15	66.67	75.00	10.00	83.33	8.33	75.00
1916–20	28.57	28.57	20.00	35.71	14.29	42.86
1921–25	35.29	52.94	33.33	79.41	20.58	55.88
1926–30	34.21	47.37	25.00	63.16	15.79	50.00
1931–34	25.00	40.63	40.91	61.11	18.75	47.35
1935–36	23.80	23.80	28.57	33.33	4.76	28.57
1937–38	26.32	42.11	38.46	68.42	15.78	42.11
1939–40	30.76	30.76	20.00	38.46	0.00	30.76
1941–42	25.00	35.00	50.00	70.00	10.00	35.00
1943–44	27.59	34.83	23.08	44.83	13.79	41.38
1945–46	11.54	23.08	33.33	34.62	11.54	23.08
1947–48	15.15	18.18	64.71	51.52	6.06	21.21
1949–50	22.22	30.56	50.00	61.11	13.89	36.11
1951–52	4.17	16.68	60.00	41.67	12.50	16.67
1953–54	11.11	22.22	50.00	44.44	14.81	25.93
1955–56	17.02	27.61	45.83	51.06	19.15	36.17
1957–58	11.11	27.78	37.50	44.44	22.22	33.33
1959–60	6.13	9.68	76.92	41.94	9.68	16.13
1961–62	3.45	17.25	54.55	37.93	20.69	24.14
1963–64	3.03	12.12	42.86	21.21	15.15	18.18
1965–66	2.50	10.00	55.56	22.50	15.00	17.50

[41] This village, which is perhaps typical of Northern Taiwan, is not necessarily typical of all Taiwan. In data kindly supplied to me by William Parish, based on marriages occurring in a village in Southern Taiwan in Annan *ch'ü* close to Tainan City, the percentage of *t'ung-yang-hsi* marriages seem substantially less. For example,

DAVID C. BUXBAUM

an uneven but steady decline in such marriages. At the same time the percentage of adopted daughters who married out of their adopted homes has increased (see Table 4). Coupled with this, the number of adoptions of girls is decreasing (see Table 5).

TABLE 5

ADOPTIONS BY SEX AND YEARS

Year	Female	Male	Total
1880–90	4	0	4
1891–95	5	2	7
1896–1900	12	0	12
1901–02	2	0	2
1903–04	12	1	13
1905–06	10	1	11
1907–08	11	0	11
1909–10	5	0	5
1911–15	20	0	20
1916–20	22	1	23
1921–25	36	1	37
1926–30	32	1	33
1931–34	39	1	40
1935–39	16	0	16
1937–38	8	0	8
1939–40	8	0	8
1941–42	12	0	12
1943–44	7	0	7
1945–46	6	0	6
1947–48	8	0	8
1949–50	4	0	4
1951–52	9	0	9
1953–54	3	1	4
1955–56	6	2	8
1957–58	5	0	5
1959–60	2	1	3
1961–62	4	2	6
1963–64	1	0	1
1965–66	2	1	3
TOTALS	311	15	326

in the 1913–17 period, of the forty-six tabulated cases only 15 percent involved *t'ung-yang-hsi*, while 11 percent were *chao-chui*. In early years, the percentage was even less. While 14 percent of the marriages in the 1933–37 period involved *t'ung-yang-hsi*, in the 1938–42 period, it seems to have dropped to 4 percent. The Tainan area is, of course, one of the oldest in Taiwan, and whether the proximity to this urban center may have influenced marriage patterns is difficult to say. The Parish data is based upon household records and is not cumulative as the preceding sets of data are. Based upon my interviews, the *t'ung-yang-hsi* marriages, excluding the matrilocal type, accounted for 25–30 percent of all marriages occurring from 1937 through 1942.

The ideal patrilocal marriage is also changing in other ways. For example, a larger percentage of the children are establishing their own residences. A dramatic change seems to have taken place at the end of the war in the 1947–48 period, when more than half of the couples married in this way established their own residences (see Table 6). Naturally, at that time some of the people in the village were returning from overseas, where they had been sent by the Japanese to assist as nurses or soldiers in prosecuting the war. This may account for the immediate rise. In the 1959–60 period, there is another dramatic jump—probably brought about by construction of the bridge which facilitated communications. Parents were less concerned about their children moving closer to the place where they worked, because means of communication was improved. Furthermore, in that period a number of houses in the village were destroyed by a typhoon, resulting in the construction of new individual dwelling units. Approximately 24 percent of the marriages in the

TABLE 6

RESIDENCE OF MARRIED COUPLE IN IDEAL PATRILOCAL TYPE
MARRIAGE (INCLUDING ADOPTED GIRL MARRYING OUT) BY YEAR AND TYPE

Year	Patrilocal	Neolocal	Matrilocal	Unknown	Total
1899–1910	4				4
1911–20	10				10
1921–25	12	1		2	15
1926–30	15	2			17
1931–34	15	3	1		19
1935–36	11	4			15
1937–38	10	1			11
1939–40	9				9
1941–42	7	3	1	1	12
1943–44	16	1			17
1945–46	17	1		1	19
1947–48	13	8		2	23
1949–50	21	2		1	24
LAND REFORM					
1951–52	11	5	1	3	20
1953–54	13	6		1	20
1955–56	24	3		3	30
1957–58	7	3		1	11
1959–60	11	12		2	25
1961–62	15	6			21
1963–64	21	4	1	1	27
1965–66	25	8	1		34

Number Classified . . . 365
Other (Unknown) . . . 18
TOTAL 383

last two years are neolocal in residence. Even this must be understood in the particular context within which village life takes place. Many of the men living neolocally actually live in the same compound as their parents, brothers, and sisters-in-law, but their livelihood and cooking are self-contained.

In calculating residence type we have used one year from the date of marriage as the basis upon which to calculate the residence of the couple, because young men may and often do return from urban localities to marry. They will marry at their parents' home and will remain there from a period of perhaps a few days until possibly after the first child is born. Subsequently, they return to their urban homes with their wives and children, if any. Thus, the real residence of the marriage cannot be determined until approximately one year after the marriage has occurred.

While the data are incomplete, it seems evident that neolocal residence has become much more common, particularly since 1947–48. Nevertheless, patrilocal residence remains the norm. It is obvious, however, that what we have called the ideal patrilocal type marriage is becoming neolocal in many cases; more evidence of the realities of the freedom given the couple by legal, economic, and social change is evidenced by this manifestation of the development of the conjugal family. The location of the marriage is less dependent upon ties of kinship.

A decrease in the *t'ung-yang-hsi* type of marriage and an increase in neolocal residence for the ideal patrilocal type and *t'ung-yang-hsi* marriage-out type has occurred, in part, because of land reform, improved economic conditions, and new social ideas and arrangements. Nevertheless, the legal change that decreased the power of the head of the household and increased that of the marrying couple, helped to legitimate changes that were occurring. In all probability it also stimulated the rapid decrease in the *t'ung-yang-hsi* type of marriage.

If we examine the preliminary tabulation of the household register statistics (which overestimates the number of married children living at their parents' home because those with urban residences do not always transfer their registration), the trend toward neolocal residence is confirmed. In 1907 there were sixty married and unmarried male children living at home, and twenty-one of them had their wives with them. Probably almost all married men lived at home and had their wives with them. Similarly, of the forty-four younger brothers of the head of the household living at home, twenty had their wives living with them. In 1951, however, of the 163 sons living at home, only 28 had wives living with them, and only 2 of the 22 younger brothers did. In 1965, only 35 of the 301 sons living at home had wives with them, and 8 of the 22 younger brothers did. This is in fact somewhat misleading, because while the records may show an individual household for some of the children, this could well be in form—registered for reasons of taxes, military service, and so on—and not necessarily indicative of social facts. The pull of tradition remains strong, but change is occurring.

The increase in the patrilocal style of marriage is, of course, part of the pattern of economic betterment which has improved the lives of the farmer since Japanese times, although these economic improvements have not been steady ones. It is also partly the result of the legal change that made the second most common type of marriage, that is, the *t'ung-yang-hsi* type, a violation of the law. More recently, this type of marriage is also somewhat difficult to arrange administratively because of the need to terminate the original adoption of the young lady before she can marry a son of the household.

Since 1945 the law has given children the power to select their own spouse. What impact has this had upon social practice? In fact, as we have noted, the decrease in *t'ung-yang-hsi* marriages, which are those almost entirely arranged by parents, to some extent reflect the fact that children are choosing their own spouses more frequently. If we examine those who married in the ideal patrilocal form, we find that the following preliminary statistics seem to reflect a growing opportunity to choose a spouse.

In the 1939–40 period there were nine ideal patrilocal marriages (see Table 1), three of which were entirely arranged by the parents. The children had no opportunity to see their prospective spouses before the betrothal, and they were not asked their opinion of the matter. Thus, in one-third of the marriages, the children had absolutely no say. Naturally, if we add the four *t'ung-yang-hsi* marriages to this, the percentage would be higher; that is, in seven of the thirteen marriages that occurred, the children had absolutely no say as to their mates. If we then jump to the 1947–48 period, which is a few years after the new law had been put into force, we find that in only one case out of twenty-two were the children who married in the ideal patrilocal form completely without an opportunity to see or to approve of their prospective spouses before betrothal. In four of these twenty-two cases, a go-between had arranged for the parties to see each other, and the parties had been asked their approval. It must be noted that usually when parents asked if their children approved, a child would either not answer or reply that if the parents wanted it that way, then it was all right. Either answer would be construed by the parents as agreement to the match. At the same time, everyone in the community would regard this as an arranged match, and the go-between would be called by the parents.

In the same 1947–48 period the go-between arranged a specific meeting between the boy and girl in five cases, and in two cases at least one partner secretly went to get a look at the other. The meetings arranged by the go-between involved a chance to meet once, but almost never a chance to talk together; thereafter, the children would be asked their opinion—they would usually express none—and the betrothal and marriage would be arranged. In four cases the spouses were neighbors before the arrangement, in one case they were schoolmates, and in another case they were related. Thus, in these six cases the children had a chance to meet before the betrothal, although in one case the children were not asked their opinions of the match.

Some very important trends became apparent in the post–1959 period. The first trend is that of giving the children a chance to see each other more than once and of allowing them to become at least slightly acquainted. For example, in any given year before 1961 there was no more than one marriage in which the children were allowed such freedom. In 1961–62, however, in four cases of the twenty-one ideal patrilocal style marriages, the prospective spouses were allowed to become acquainted and had a chance to go to a movie, shop together, take a walk together, and meet more than five times before giving their approval. In all these cases, these opportunities occurred only after the go-between had arranged an introduction, and these were also conceived of by the villagers as arranged marriages. But note one very important fact: the concept of an arranged marriage was beginning to change. Parents, bending to contemporary pressures and fearful of losing their children, had begun to allow them more freedom in determining their choice of a spouse.

Another trend is for the children to become acquainted before the match is made. In the 1965–66 period, of the thirty-four marriages that occurred, the families were neighbors in four cases, in three cases the children were co-workers, and in two cases classmates. The latter cases are of particular significance, that is, co-workers and classmates, because it is in such settings that children begin to select their own spouses. With increased higher education (and with more youngsters working in factories) children have a greater opportunity to meet a potential mate.

This is related to another trend; that is, for children to pick their own spouses and then obtain parental approval of the match. While such practice was negligible until 1959–60, during that two-year period in six cases out of twenty-five the children, together or individually, first raised the question of marriage to the prospective spouse they themselves had selected. In two additional cases—both adopted girls who married out of their adopted home—the parents were not even asked their consent. The latter circumstance is relatively rare in that it occurred in only seven instances since 1947 and in four of these adopted girls were involved.

Generally speaking, in cases in which the children raise the possibility of marriage, the parents' consent is asked and given. For example, while such a practice was negligible before 1959–60, during that two-year period it occurred in five cases, in eleven cases in the 1961–62 period (of twenty-one), in nine cases in the 1963–64 period (of twenty-seven), and in ten cases in the 1965–66 period (of thirty-three). Thus there is a definite trend to what is known in Taiwan as love marriages. Between one-third and one-half of the marriages since 1961 have been love marriages.

One factor which should be mentioned in this regard is the draft. It has affected marriage patterns, as has the opportunity for higher education. The effect has been twofold. In the first place, children who are affected by either or both of these institutions generally must leave their rural homes and go to live elsewhere, which gives them greater opportunity to meet prospective spouses. Furthermore, both have delayed the age at which people marry; therefore, the children are more mature and less likely to be as dependent upon their families.

The free choice of a spouse, made legitimate by law, has become more of a reality as a result of multiple factors. Most marriages, however, are still arranged, but the very concept of an arranged marriage has changed. While the positing of legislation itself has not brought about immediate change in social behavior, creative legislation, together with a host of other factors, has stimulated change in marriage patterns. In this area, where positive and customary laws have been in conflict, the customary law is beginning to change. Perhaps the general norm today would be: the parents would arrange an introduction; the children would be given a chance to see and approve of each other; and then the betrothal would be made. The *p'in-chin, chia-chuang,* betrothal, and wedding ceremony persist in somewhat modified traditional style.

Change is also occurring in marriage type since more marriages are becoming the ideal patrilocal type. More people now have the financial ability to afford such a wedding. There is, therefore, a dual revolution. The ideals of tradition are becoming a reality because people can afford the ideal traditional wedding, while at the same time (but more slowly), the ideals of a modified form of the conjugal family are becoming a reality.

T'ung-yang-hsi marriages. There has been a large drop in the number of adopted daughter-in-law *(t'ung-yang-hsi)* marriages. At one time it was quite common for people in the village to adopt girls as a matter of course; today the adoption of a girl is becoming rare (See Table 5). Therefore, the likelihood of the *t'ung-yang-hsi* style marriage decreases. For various reasons the *t'ung-yang-hsi* type marriage has been the least successful. In this village there have been 14 divorces in the *t'ung-yang-hsi* type marriage, out of a total of 109 marriages since 1899. Where the *t'ung-yang-hsi* married out of her adopted home, however, there has been only one divorce in 120 marriages since 1899. The only other comparable divorce rate is where the *t'ung-yang-hsi* marries a male into her adopted home. The reasons for the latter type of divorce differ, however.

With the decrease in adoption, the general lack of success of this marriage, which Arthur Wolf has attributed to psychological reasons as a result of the incest taboo, and with the advent of the law that gives children the power to marry a spouse of their choice, this institution is definitely on the decline. Furthermore, as noted above, it is more difficult to arrange such marriages because of legal and administrative complications.

Naturally, the primary advantage of this marriage type has been its lack of expense. For example, in the ideal patrilocal type marriage, betrothal money during the 1965–66 period for the average groom's family was between 6,000 and 9,000 new Taiwan (N.T.) dollars. It was not uncommon for cakes to cost another 5,000 N.T. dollars. At the wedding party it was common to have between four and twelve tables of guests, which would add another 1,200 to 3,600 N.T. dollars to the cost of the wedding. We omit the cost of the other presents and jewelry. Even if we accept the statistics of a report in Taiwan, indicating that a farm family earned, on the average, N.T. $33,088.60 per year of gross income,[42] marriage is a very expensive proposition. The average income of the people in the village in which I worked did not reach that level; thus the economic advantages of the *t'ung-yang-hsi* marriages are obvious.

The pressures against this type of marriage, however, are not only those suggested above. As we have noted, various organizations have taken an interest in the adopted girl, so much so that the people of the village claim that adopted girls are less obedient than girls who were born into the family. There have been complaints about the treatment of some adopted girls, although statistics covering 189,941 adoptions from 1956–58, inclusive, seem to indicate that only 18 per cent of the girls were living in bad economic circumstances or were mistreated. In 1960, of 93,550 girls, 53,578 were receiving primary schooling, and 4,544 were in junior high, high school, or college. Since many were not yet of school age, the figures hardly seem unreasonable. The data also seems to show that 1,595 were servants in their adopting homes.[43] Adopted girls were more frequently adopted by farmers and by families with average incomes. The three primary reasons girls were adopted were: because the adopting parents had no children, 51,732 cases; because they wanted a *t'ung-yang-hsi,* 17,188 cases; because they wanted a servant, 903 cases; for other reasons including those unknown, 23,026. Not as many people gave girls out for adoption solely because of poverty as one might expect,[44] but primarily because they had too many children, a finding which also, of course, has important economic overtones (see Table 7).

The Society for Protection of Adopted Children of the Province of Taiwan has handled various cases of mistreatment; of the 1,567 that were conciliated in 1960, for example, 99 concerned problems of marriage. Nevertheless, various regulations for the assistance of adopted girls were aimed at marriage. (While these statisticsare concerned primarily with adopted girls in general, we are here concerned with the *t'ung-yang-hsi.)*

---

[42] TAIWAN NUNG-CHIA CHI-CHANG PAO-KAO. (Report on rural households in Taiwan) (1965).

[43] H. Chang, TAIWAN SHENG TI YANG-NÜ WEN-T'I (Problems of adopted women in the Province of Taiwan), TAIWAN WEN-HSIEN 102 (Sept. 1963).

[44] *Id.,* 106.

TABLE 7

TOTAL ADOPTION OF GIRLS

| Year | Village Field Data | Household Records Office Data | |
		Village	Township
1926–30	32		
1931–34	39		
1935–36	16		
1937–38	8		
1939–40	8		
1941–42	12		
1943–44	7		
1953–54	3	1*	
1955–56	6	6*	
1957–58	3	1	76
1959–60	2	0	51
1961–62	4	4	53
1963–64	1	1	22
1965–66	2	0	10
TOTAL	145	13	212

* No designation as to sex.

The *t'ung-yang-hsi* also enjoys the benefits of those various institutions assisting in protecting adopted daughters. The Women's Association *(Fu-nü-hui)* helps to conciliate household problems and provides a place to turn to if a young lady feels she is being forced into a marriage she does not wish. We may expect that the ordinary *t'ung-yang-hsi* marriage will become a thing of the past, if economic circumstances remain relatively good and if the administrative institutions keep pressuring girls to marry as they choose.

The marriage contracts have remained virtually the same as they were in early Ch'ing times. Written contracts for patrilocal marriages are infrequent, but oral contracts are quite common. A *t'ung-yang-hsi* marrying her preselected spouse *(t'ou-tui)* is rare today, but it still occurs. Positive law and administrative action, coupled with good economic circumstances, are putting an end to this institution.

Matrilocal style marriages. As we have noted above, girls are most frequently adopted by people who have no children. Thereafter, a male is very often brought into the family through marriage. This type of marriage, like the ordinary *t'ung-yang-hsi* marriage, is fraught with difficulties, not because of psychological incest problems, but rather because of the situation of the male within the household. The husband is generally from a poor family, has no other opportunity to marry, and marries into a home which is generally not wealthy. He does not have the same status that he would have if he were to marry in his own home. Thus the male is generally ambivalent about his relationship to his wife's home. He may get on well with his wife, but not necessarily with his parents-in-law. He may hope to inherit their property, but may dislike his lack of status.

With increased health standards fewer people are completely without children. Nevertheless, situations of this type will probably continue to occur, and people will look to such a solution when they lack heirs.

This type of marriage has altered somewhat over the years. While in the past these marriages were generally arranged by the parents of the adopted girl without consultation with the children, since 1952 there has been an increased number of such marriages in which the bride and groom decide upon their own spouses. In the 1965–66 period, for example, of three such marriages all were arranged at the instance of the children. This seems to be the general trend, perhaps being one of the ways this institution retains some attraction for the couples concerned.

Written contracts for this type of marriage, as for all matrilocal marriages, are quite common, and the household record section retains printed forms which merely require the filling-in of blanks to complete the contract. If the parents have no children, the marriage contract often requires matrilocal residence for life.

There are problems with these contracts, which often give rise to disputes that require conciliation. At times the contract is terminated either by divorce or by the parties coming to some settlement whereby the couple is allowed to leave the home of the wife. Of three marriages of this type occurring in 1958, two resulted in leaving the bride's household as a result of bad relations. The percentages of departure from the girl's household are unusually high, but generally the pressures on this type of marriage are great, particularly since the wife may not have such close ties to her adopted home as she might to her natal home. (The latter ties might exercise some slight stabilizing influence upon the marriage.)

These marriages have remained somewhat constant, because they are predicated on necessity, at least from the point of view of the parents, who feel that they need someone to care for them in their old age, to *pai* for them, that is, to worship them when they die, and to take care of their funerals. This type of marriage will probably pass out of existence much more slowly than the ordinary *t'ung-yang-hsi* type.

From the legal point of view, if the children are given real power to choose their spouses, the marriage accords with the Civil Code. The only problem that remains is the social problem of the male's status in his wife's home—and this problem is likely to remain.

The ordinary type of matrilocal marriage is less common but slightly more stable than those involving an adopted daughter. At one time matrilocal marriages were quite common in Taiwan. For example, of the 31,058 marriages which took place among those domiciled in Taiwan (Taiwan *pen-chi*) in 1906, 22 per cent were matrilocal. This pattern continued and in 1911 approximately 26 per cent of the marriages were matrilocal. Thereafter, there is some decline in this type of marriage, and in 1925, for example, 16 per cent were matrilocal, or less than one-sixth of the total marriages among Taiwanese. There is a fairly sharp decrease after that; in 1943, only 6 percent of marriages were matrilocal.

There were a larger number of males than females in Taiwan, which may have been one factor affecting the type of marriage people entered. For example, in 1905 "there were more than 20 'surplus' males for every 100 females in the age group 15–19. . . ."[45] Furthermore, even today in the village in which I have done field research, there are more men than women. In 1965 there were 580 men and 410 women in the village. In the age group 20–24, there were 24 men and 35 women, in part because of the draft, but in the age group 25–29 there were 47 men and 35 women. Barclay notes that all but 2 per cent of the women and 9 or 10 per cent of the men over thirty years of age eventually married between 1905 and 1935.[46] Thus, to some extent, women were at a premium.

As we have noted, the ideal patrilocal marriage was quite expensive; the matrilocal type was thus more attractive to men without funds or family, or to families with too many sons. Nevertheless, the official statistics for matrilocal marriages consistently go down in Taiwan, although some are never registered (see Table 8). This is particularly true of the *chao-ju ch'u-ch'u* type

TABLE 8

REGISTERED MATRILOCAL MARRIAGES BY YEARS*

Year	Number of Matrilocal Marriages	Total Number of Marriages
1906	6,788	31,058
1911	7,394	36,486
1926	7,072	45,813
1943	2,988	48,156

* G. BARCLAY, *supra* note 45, at 229.

where the male has obligations to his wife's family which do not include full time residence at her home, except perhaps during brief periods. In many recent cases, certain patrilocal marriages that involve residence at the wife's home for a limited number of years have also not been registered. Perhaps

---

[45] G. BARCLAY COLONIAL DEVELOPMENT AND POPULATION IN TAIWAN 212 (1954).

[46] *Id.,* 211, 214. The Japanese census was supposed to record unregistered as well as registered marriages.

part of the decrease in number for Taiwan as a whole is a result of failure to register. The increased wealth of the populace also made the patrilocal ideal marriage much more common, and the increased fertility rate of the population and increased health standards gave rise to fewer instances of families without male children.

The *chao-chui* marriage discussed in this section, that is, the one not involving an adopted daughter, has remained an institution of some significance throughout the period under study. Nevertheless, it has been the least frequent of the major types of marriages, with the exception of that of secondary wives. To some extent, it has retained its viability by modifying some of its pre-requisites. While it always has included a number of marriages between the farmhand and the farmer's daughter that were not really arranged by the parents, recently the free selection of spouses seems to be most common. In the seventeen marriages of this type since 1949, three—an unusually high percentage—started with the couple first living together and afterward marrying.

Since the children have more opportunity to pick their own mates in this type of marriage, it does not violate the law. It is likely to continue as an institution until Chinese society changes quite radically, because it fulfills certain important social needs. At times this type of marriage requires matrilocal residence for a limited number of years, unlike the *t'ung-yang-hsi* type which is generally for life. Of the three matrilocal marriages made in 1965–66, two were for a limited period of years.

Secondary wives. The institution of secondary wives is growing in number, despite the legal restrictions placed upon it. It never has been very significant in the village, but it has occurred on occasion. Although one could legally take a secondary wife during the Japanese period (and it was done), it became difficult to register such a marriage during the later years of Japanese rule. It is now impossible to register such a marriage. The children of this relationship, however, can easily be made legitimate. Furthermore, few wives will make legal complaints against their husbands, even if they do take secondary wives. These marriages are also less likely to be co-residential today. The reason for an increase is the fact that more people can afford secondary wives, and these marriages generally take place among the well-to-do. At times they come about inadvertently.

Most of the few secondary wives taken by people in the village were taken by the very well-to-do; these people often had dual residences with one in an urban area. Some men even took two secondary wives. The secondary wives were almost all chosen by the husbands themselves, although not infrequently after an introduction by a go-between. In five of the twelve cases, the economic circumstances of the male's house were substantially better than the female's. In three cases the households were economically about the same, and in the remaining cases we are uncertain. In no case was the woman's house better off economically, at least to our knowledge. In all cases the primary wife's position was higher in the household, but the husband preferred the secondary wife. In at least four cases the wife's opinion was not asked.

This institution will probably continue to exist and flourish until equalitarian concepts further influence women's attitudes. The flourishing of this type of marriage, particularly in urban Taiwan, indicates that with increased economic resources, people will avail themselves of this traditional institution. However, this is not proof of the perseverance of traditional values. In the first place, it is less likely to be co-residential with a subsisting marriage, indicating that women are resistant to such unions. Furthermore, the increase in frequency is probably partly a result of the influence of the idea that one can choose one's own spouse. The older male generation, whose marriages were arranged, now wishes to enjoy the benefits of such an institution, and when it is economically feasible, they often do take a secondary wife.

Some changing attitudes in rural Taiwan. In order to determine some changes toward various aspects of customary law, besides the general interviews conducted about each marriage, a small survey was taken in which thirty-six different people, who for the most part were representative of the married strata of village life, were interviewed. The survey was biased in the sense that all people interviewed were married, and older people (over forty) were more heavily represented than younger ones. Men and women were almost equally represented.

One matter we interviewed about was whether people of the same surname were allowed to marry, since there is no legal impediment to marriage unless they are related. Furthermore, there are many opportunities to marry someone of the same surname, for in many villages like this a few surnames dominate and constitute the larger bulk of the population. In this village the surnames Lin and Ch'en were predominant; for example, in the eighth neighborhood *(lin)* all families had the surname Ch'en.

TABLE 9

SAME SURNAME MARRIAGES IN VILLAGE

Year	Male Total Marriages Existing	Same Surname Marriages	Percentage of Total Marriages with Same Surname
1965	267	3	1.1%
1964	252	3	1.2%
1956	216	2	0.9%
1951	172	1	0.6%
1907	119	0	0%

Even today, despite the fact that there are numerous possibilities for those of the same surname to marry, they rarely do so. Our interviews found only two instances of this. The household records, which exaggerate figures here, indicate that of the 267 males who were married in the village in 1965, only 3 at most married someone of the same surname (see Table 9). Generally speaking, people in the village resist this type of marriage. Therefore this norm, which was supported by Ch'ing positive law and by customary law, is still important in the village, despite the lack of positive law sanction.

This fact is confirmed by our survey. Of those queried twenty-three people felt that those of the same surname could not marry under any circumstances; seven others felt they could not marry under any circumstances unless they were of different races; four felt they could marry unless they were actually blood relations; two felt they could marry under any circumstances. Thus, the overwhelming majority were resistant to such a marriage; eleven felt there would be severe social criticism of such a marriage, while thirty-three felt there would be social criticism, though not necessarily severe. Only two felt such a marriage would not be recognized by customary law, and one felt it would not be recognized by positive law.

Twenty-five people felt that once such a marriage is made it should be maintained, but three felt that even if the couple had children they should divorce. Only one felt that, if there were no children, a divorce should take place. While the attitude toward this type of marriage seems to be resistant, although not overwhelmingly so, the attitude toward those marrying whose families have ancient hatreds is much more permissive, and many feel no criticism will result from the latter.

RELEVANT DEVELOPMENTS IN THE PEOPLE'S REPUBLIC OF CHINA

The Civil Code of 1931 was put into effect in those areas of China under the control of the Nationalist Government. In areas under Communist control, there was also an attempt to enact marriage laws.[47] However, in the 1930s and 1940s both of these governments were primarily concerned with problems other than family change. The Communists did not control large areas of China before the latter years of World War II and thus did not have the means to influence huge masses of people. The impact of the Nationalist law was primarily urban because of the lack of courts in rural China, but even the urban impact was limited. However, as we have previously discussed, new

---

[47] See M. MEIJER, MARRIAGE LAW AND POLICY IN THE CHINESE PEOPLE'S REPUBLIC (1971), which discusses these various regulations. See also M. VAN DER VALK, CONSERVATISM IN MODERN CHINESE FAMILY LAW (1956), for the regulations of the Shansi-Hopei-Ch'ahar Border Region in 1943. See also C. YANG, CHINESE COMMUNIST SOCIETY (1965).

ideas and economic circumstances were influencing social relationships throughout China. The real impact of family law change, particularly in rural mainland China, is largely a post-1949 phenomenon.

Family Law in the People's Republic of China

The marriage law. The Chinese Communist concept of family law is that it is a tool for the state to use to actively engender social change. The law and legal institutions are instruments of the state and are used by the state to educate, to perform propaganda functions, and to carry out political programs.[48] Having decided to alter marital relations, the government promulgated the Marriage Law on May 1, 1950, and then began to engage in political drives to enforce the law. An attempt was made to actively employ law and legal institutions to bring about social change. The government actively encouraged litigation and change.

The Communist law, in a declaration of principles in Article I, claimed to be based upon the concepts of marital freedom for the partners to the marriage, equality of rights between the partners, the principle of one wife and one husband, and the protection of the lawful interests of women and children.

Article 2 prohibited polygamy, the taking of secondary wives, the *t'ung-yang-hsi* relationship, and interference with the remarriages of widows. The law also prohibited anyone from availing himself of the marital relationship to extract gifts.

Limitations upon the arranged marriage were provided in Article 3, which states that marriage was to be based upon the complete willingness of the parties. Neither party was to use compulsion, and third parties were not permitted to interfere. The marriage was to be registered at the local government office by the parties themselves. Marriage certificates would be issued if, and only if, the marriage conformed to the provisions of the law.[49] Parents and children were mutually entitled to inherit one another's property.[50]

The law was thus a radical break with tradition, although it was a logical culmination of previous decisions by the Supreme Court and the Civil Code of the Nationalist government. The law left many problems untouched and was quite cryptic in style. There was no definition of marriage, of the forms it might take, or of the role of betrothal. The law practically defined the ideal conjugal family, but it did not indicate how it was to be brought about.

Early recognition of customary law. It was inconceivable that all of the changes envisioned by the law would come about in a short time. The government had to "show consideration for the customs of the masses. . . ."[51] The

---

[48] D. Buxbaum, *supra* note 16, at 1-3.

[49] MARRIAGE LAW (1950) art. 6.

[50] *Id.*, art. 14.

[51] M. van der Valk, *China,* in 5 LAW IN EASTERN EUROPE 297, 319-20, 326 (Z. Szirmai ed. 1961).

chao-chui type marriage and the right of descendants to inherit property for the ancestral cult were given legal sanctions. Furthermore, a somewhat ambiguous attitude was taken toward the right of girls to inherit property from their natal homes after they had married out of them.[52] It should be noted with regard to intestate succession that the provisions of the Marriage Law in mainland China are not very specific. Article 14, which forms the basis of the law, merely states that parents and children have mutual rights to inherit one another's property. However, from constitutional sources and other literature, it is clear that, in principle at least, the marriage law should certainly not be a bar to the power of daughters who have married out of their natal homes to inherit. Of course, there is only a limited amount of heritable property in China today.

Some of the literature recognized that according to the "custom of the masses" the girl who marries out of her natal home either does not inherit equally with other children or is not permitted to inherit at all. This "custom" is regarded as feudal and improper by the authors. Nevertheless, they suggest handling such matters of inheritance according to the particular facts. While they note that if the property has not yet been divided, there should be no distinction between married and unmarried women, nevertheless, at the time of division and after deliberation, one could suitably increase or decrease the amount of distribution, ostensibly for reasons based on the practical needs of the parties.[53]

Enforcement and interpretation of the law. Enforcement was not as radical as one might suppose,[54] although tremendous political energy was invested in bringing about change. Naturally, interpretation of various provisions changed with time and with the realities of the social situation.

Unlike the Nationalist law, the Communist regulations did not deal with betrothal, which traditionally was an essential procedure in constituting a

---

[52] *See* CHUNG-HUA JEN-MIN KUNG-HO KUO MIN-FA CHI-PEN WEN-T'I (Basic problems of the civil law of the People's Republic of China) 344 [hereinafter cited as Basic Problems in Civil Law]. *See* JOINT PUBLICATION RESEARCH SERVICE [hereinafter cited as JPRS]. Translation No. 4879, which translates this text. These materials recognize certain limitations upon the right of married daughters to inherit; for example, if they have been married for a very long time and the property has been inherited by others. *See also* SHIH HUA-PI, LÜEH-LUN WO KUO CHI-CH'ENG CHIH-TU TI CHI-KE CHI-PEN WEN-T'I (A discussion of several basic problems of the system of inheritance in our country) 26 (1957).

[53] *Ibid. See also* CHUNG-HUA JEN-MIN KUNG-HO KUO MIN-FA TS'AN-KAO TZU-LIAO 588, 589, 593 (Reference materials on the civil law of the People's Republic of China) [hereinafter cited as Ts'an K'ao Tzu-liao]. These materials again indicate that circumstances should be weighed in determining the share a married daughter should receive and that she can waive her rights to the estate of her natal home.

[54] *See* C. YANG, *supra* note 47, at 33, for a view of some of the changes which were supposed to have occurred.

marriage. The government recognized as late as 1963 that the betrothal was still customary in some areas of China.[55] The betrothal was held not to be an essential procedure for entering a marriage, according to the marriage law. The ordinary engagement was considered the personal affair of the husband and wife and was not protected by law. During registration of the marriage, it was held unnecessary to inquire whether the couple had been engaged. Obviously, specific performance of the betrothal was not permitted. Furthermore, an ordinary betrothal could be breached by one party by simply informing the other of the desire to terminate the relationship. The law did not protect the ordinary betrothal contract, and there was no legal compensation permitted for the non-breaching party. The ordinary betrothal had no legal consequences, and if it were arranged by the parents, the betrothal would violate the law and would be punishable.[56]

The law, however, did offer some protection to the betrothal of members of the military; if a woman wished to rescind a betrothal to a member of the military, her fiancée's consent had to be obtained.[57] The registering institution was instructed to explain and to help the woman understand the reasons for it; hopefully this would influence her to willingly maintain the relationship. If there were serious problems, however, after a thorough examination, the matter could be passed on to the higher level government office and eventually the betrothal could be rescinded.

The Communist law prohibited marriage from becoming a matter of bargain and sale. Emphasis was upon love and mutual attraction as important values in selecting a wife. Of course, the concept of the role of marriage in building the new socialist society was also stressed. With regard to the betrothal gifts, it was held necessary to differentiate between those that were sent voluntarily and those having the nature of a purchase and sale. There was no opposition in 1963 to the voluntary sending of gifts. The gifts connoting bargain and sale were generally those that parents, hoping to utilize the marriage to obtain property, forcefully employed their daughter to obtain. These, of course, were prohibited. Gifts that were freely given, not as a condition to the marriage but merely as an expression of the affection the couple felt for one another, were

---

[55] TSEN-YANG TSO HAO HUN-YIN TENG-CHI KUNG-TSO (How to do good marriage registration work) 33–34 (Nei-wu Pu Min-cheng Szu comp. 1963) [hereinafter cited as HUN-YIN TENG-CHI].

[56] *Id. See also* TS'AN K'AO TZU-LIAO 578. The government indicated in 1953 that if the parties themselves wish to enter into an engagement, they should be permitted to do so, provided that others had not forced them. If parents arranged for introductions and the couple agreed to the marriage, this was held to be within the law. *Kuang-ming jih-pao* (Peking) Feb. 3, 1953.

[57] The military became choice marriage prospects in recent years because of their extra rations and privileges.

permitted.[58] The organization registering marriages was ordered to interfere with the bargain and sale type of presents. The offending parties, generally considered to be the girl's parents, were to receive criticism and to be educated, so that they would recognize the error of their ways and correct their mistakes. However, if the children really wished to marry in the first place and if the girl's parents merely used this opportunity to insist upon presents, the registration office was not to interfere with the marriage. The office was first to permit the marriage and then to deal with the girl's household head *(chia-chang),* instructing him to either refuse or return the gifts.

The government objected to the use of the sedan chair *(hua-chiao),* the worship, and the wedding parties of the traditional ceremony, all customs which they felt connoted superstition and wasted money. They felt the new ceremony should eliminate the sedan chair and the worship, and should merely be an invitation to friends, relatives, and comrades to come over and talk, drink some tea, eat some candy and have a lively time. However, the personnel of the registration offices were not to lightly interfere with the wedding ceremony. They were to encourage the parties not to be wasteful, feudal or superstitious in undertaking their celebrations. The spirit of the revolution was expected to destroy the marriage customs remaining from the old society; somewhat like the virtue of the Confucian rules, it was to influence the people's conduct.[59] Physical interference was not recommended, at least not in 1963.

Communist law held the *t'ung-yang-hsi* form of marriage illegal. No adoptions of *t'ung-yang-hsi* were permitted. Girls who were adopted as *t'ung-yang-hsi* before the promulgation of the law, however, could return to their natal homes or select other spouses if they had not yet married. The adopting home was not to interfere in any way and was to continue to care for the girl until she married. She could, of course, decide to marry the male of the household who had been selected for her, if he agreed, but others were not to force her into doing so.[60] Furthermore, the adopting family could not reclaim the original betrothal presents or demand compensation for the cost of caring for the girl if she decided to return home or to marry someone else.[61]

---

[58] HUN-YIN TENG-CHI *supra* note 55, 35. *See also* HUN-YIN TENG-CHI 335–36, for a 1951 holding regarding *p'in-chin* and *p'in-li.* It was held that if the presents were voluntary gifts they need not be returned; however, if they were such as to cause the donor economic hardship and the donee had the capacity to return them, then depending upon circumstances the court may order a portion or all of the gifts returned.

[59] Of course the Communist ruler is quite a bit more active in spreading his "virtue" around than was the ideal Confucian ruler.

[60] TS'AN KAO TZU-LIAO 556–57. *See also* M. VAN DER VALK, *supra* note 47, at 87, for a translation of this material.

[61] *Ibid. See also* M. VAN DER VALK, *supra* note 47, at 82, for a similar 1951 explanation.

Social Change in the People's Republic of China

Pressures on the traditional system. The government in Peking made use not only of the courts, judicial and political personnel, and other organizations to implement the marriage law but also, as in Taiwan, of a women's association, *Fu-nü Lien-ho hui.* The earliest aspects of the movement in support of the marriage law emphasized that it was important for the various cadre to study the marriage law and to set examples for others.[62] There was an initial flurry of articles on the lack of legal effect of the betrothal. The early emphasis indicated that if the betrothal were rescinded, barring special circumstances there was no need to return the *p'in-chin* or *p'in-li* since they were gifts.[63] If there was a violation of the law and if the marriage was used as an opportunity to obtain involuntary gifts, then the gifts would be confiscated and the offending party could be punished.[64]

There were early complaints about the "feudal thought" of some of the cadres who refused to accept divorce cases brought by women and who charged such heavy fees that many people did not register their marriages.[65] There were large drives to publicize the law[66] and publicity committees were set up. Divorces began to increase,[67] and marriage and particularly divorce litigation became the most important type of civil litigation.[68]

Objections to marriage presents, large wedding parties,[69] go-betweens, and the use of the *pa-tzu*, which began in the early 1950s, could still be found quite often in the newspapers and magazines of 1964 and to some extent in 1965. Remnants of old feudal customs still existed in China in 1964, and it was felt that they should be destroyed.[70] The feeling that the ceremony should be particularly lively,[71] since one marries only once, was disputed. The sedan chair[72] and traditional *chia-chuang* were selected as examples of bad practices

---

[62] *E.g., see* Jen-min jih-pao (People's Daily) (Peking), Sept. 29 & Sept. 30, 1951.

[63] Shanghai chieh-fang jih-pao, July 20, 1952, at 1.

[64] *Id.* I am heavily indebted to Ezra Vogel for his very good as yet unpublished paper on the Chinese family that I made much use of in preparing this section.

[65] Jen-min Jih-pao (People's Daily) (Peking), Dec. 27, 1951.

[66] Ta-kung pao (Tien-chin), Feb. 2, 1953.

[67] Jen-min Jih-pao (Peking), April 17, 1950.

[68] Shanghai chieh-fang Jih-pao, July 19, 1951.

[69] *Pieh K'ai Sheng-mien ti Hun-li* (Do not undertake face-saving marriage ceremonies), Jen-min Jih-pao (Peking), Jan. 24, 1964.

[70] *P'o-ch'u chiu hsi-su, ch'uang-li hsin feng shang* (Destroy old customs and establish new trends), CHUNG-KUO CH'ING-NIEN (Chinese youth) 9 ff. (Feb. 1, 1964).

[71] *Pi-mi Chieh-hun Hsiao-i* (Small discussion of secret marriages), Hsin-min wan-pao (Shanghai), March 7, 1964.

[72] *Tzu-chi Tso-tao P'o-chia Ch'u* (Go to your betrothed's house yourself), Jen-min jih-pao (Peking), Apr. 6, 1964. There was also opposition to *li-ping* (ritual cakes). For example, *see Li-ping Li Shih Shem a-na* (What are ritual cakes), Yang-ch'eng wan-pao (Yang-ch'eng evening paper), Apr. 16, 1964.

in 1964.[73] Such objections to traditional customs can even be found in the 1966 literature, although with much less frequency,[74] perhaps because other matters began to dominate the news. However, even in the early stages of the Cultural Revolution, one can discern fragments of information concerning traditional family and marital institutions. For example, a Red Guard pamphlet, translated as "one Hundred Examples for Breaking the Old and Establishing the New," suggested in Article 41: "The feudal patriarchal system must be abolished, and nobody is allowed to beat or scold his children. The maltreatment of adopted children is not permitted. . . ." Article 73 states: "No wedding may ask for monetary gifts or be lavishly celebrated."[75] While these restatements of old slogans may not be an indication of social reality, certainly some statements of the Cultural Revolution have been directed, in part, at old customs and traditions. The official information seems to indicate that even in the 1970s the customary traditions had not been eradicated, despite the great efforts of the government. Interviews with refugees confirm this impression.[76]

Administration of the law and policy. Aside from the fact that certain traditional practices still exist, despite the major political drives that have been made by the Communists to change the marriage system, there are other developments that are parallel to those in Taiwan. The need for identity cards to process certain family law matters and the present necessity for registration, for a marriage certificate when registering a marriage, and for household records *(hu chi)* all exist in mainland China, just as they do in Taiwan. Many

---

[73] *Chia-chuang Feng Shang Jen-hsin* (The custom of trousseau still exists in people's minds), Jen-min Jih-pao (Peking), June 20, 1964.

[74] One can still see articles suggesting that there be no wedding party. *See Fu Tai-hui Pang-chu Cheng-tsung I-feng I-su* [The Women's Association assists the masses in changing their customs], Chung-kuo fu-nü [Chinese women], Jan. 1, 1966; no *chia-chuang (Ta Tso Te Wan-ch'uan Ho-ch'ing Ho-li* [He does things entirely rationally and in accord with circumstances], Hsin-min wan-pao Shanghai, Jan. 13, 1966); no go-between; no sedan chair; and so on (in an Inner Mongolian self-governing district), Hsin Chung-kuo-te hun-yin chih-tu [Marriage institutions of New China], CHUNG-KUO HSIN-WEN, March 10, 1966.

[75] SURVEY OF CHINA MAINLAND MAGAZINES [hereinafter cited as S.C.M.M.] No. 566 (Apr. 6, 1967), at 12, 17, 18.

[76] The interviews I conducted in Hong Kong were, of course, not comparable to those undertaken in Taiwan. I had little comparative data on any one marriage. There were no multiple sources for examination of the same event. I lacked the household records, and the reliability of the informant was always in question. Nevertheless, these interviews were valuable. The topic was one that most people had at least some information about. Certain patterns formed on the basis of interviews made unexplained deviations questionable. The interviewees were able to lend a new dimension to my research and to bring to life some of the written material. One problem with the interviews was that recent arrivals in Hong Kong tended to be younger men who had not yet married.

of these institutions are modern versions of the traditional *pao-chia* and public household records of the Ch'ing times. While they perform some of the same functions, they do so with much greater thoroughness, power, and effect. As in Taiwan, the registration system is also a check upon the administration of the law and has its impact upon practice.

Conciliation commissions have been established, but unlike those in Taiwan they play an important role in the administration of justice. The lineage system has suffered, not only because of the land reform, but also because it has been under direct attack by the government. A fundamental basis of the lineage and marriage system, the religious foundation, has been attacked by the government. The government, most anxious to insinuate itself into each dispute, moved quickly to set up institutions to handle matters that were formerly administered in part by family organizations. Aside from the conciliation tribunals, the Women's Association in the People's Republic of China plays a very important role in family disputes. Not passively awaiting the parties but charging into the fray at the drop of a rumor, this association has played an important role in raising the status of women and, in so doing, in spreading the ideology of the conjugal family.

On a more formal level, the *Min-cheng K'e* plays a role in handling civil disputes, as do the police officers to some extent. In the *ta-tui* below the commune, a representative of the Women's Association handles matters such as health problems, children's problems, and divorce. She is generally quite busy. In the commune the *Min-cheng Chu-li* representative of the *Min-cheng K'e* also handles civil disputes. During the early period, divorce was much encouraged, particularly for secondary wives. More recently, policy has changed, and divorces are now difficult to obtain. The government has also recently pushed hard to delay the age of marriage beyond the legal requirements.

In order to illustrate changes that have been occurring on the mainland, we will discuss some recent marriages. These marriages were far from being the most traditional, but nevertheless reflected some of the tradition. Naturally because most of the immigrants to Hong Kong were from areas in Kwangtung which were close enough to the coast to receive multiple influences, my interviews probably reflect more modern developments than would be expected in an investigation of the social situation in the interior.

Some typical marriages in mainland China. One of the more ideal marriages from the government's point of view occurred in 1961. The couple were both graduates of the same high school, where they met. They were both classified as middle peasants, and the girl worked in a bank. They lived in a city in Kwangtung with a population of about two million. Their homes were close to each other, and their parents were co-workers. They first raised the possibility of marriage with their parents. Both sets of parents agreed without hesitation; they became engaged and were married eight months later. No betrothal money was sent by the male, but the bride did bring a trousseau. It consisted of a *kuei-tzu*,[77] mosquito net, new clothes, and some jewelry. A car was rented to bring the girl to the boy's home. She wore a new pink dress on the wedding day, and both the girl's and boy's homes held parties. The boy's family had three tables of guests, and the girl's family had a party of a similar size.[78] Both the bride and groom were toasted by the guests with wine.

They registered the marriage, and both male and female had to affix their seals to the marriage certificate *(kai chang)*. Before doing so, they were asked if they were marrying forever, to which they both replied in the affirmative. (This practice was initiated when divorces became excessive, and the government in a reversal of policy decided to limit divorce.) The significance of the step which the parties are taking is emphasized by the registering official, rather than by the celebration and ritual that take place.

Although the contract to marry was once very important with the creation of the new status surrounded by ritual and great expense, it is now necessary to remind the parties of the significance of the marriage contract and their new status. By removing much of the ritual and the religious rites that surrounded the betrothal and marriage, the Party had helped to undermine their significance, and thus the marriage bonds were becoming frayed. Therefore, there was a need to emphasize the importance of the change in status. The contract to marry seems to have acquired much less importance on the mainland.

After the ceremony the couple described above lived at the boy's family home. This marriage of an educated couple with a favorable background seems fairly representative of its type during the past few years. There might have been a small amount of betrothal money, and a bicycle rather than a car might have been used to transport the girl, but other aspects seem rather ordinary. It probably approximates the contemporary official ideal, though it is tainted with certain traditional overtones.

The *chao-chui* marriage is still permitted by law in the mainland. In one case in 1961 in a rural village in Kwangtung, a *t'ung-yang-hsi* was living with her adopted parents. Her prospective husband had died and her own parents were dead. The foster mother of the prospective bride spoke to a young man she liked, regarding the prospects of marriage. The man had the same surname as the girl's adopted home.[79] The girl was twenty-five years old. She liked the young man and was agreeable to the match; the young man also agreed to the match. The girl's family had no other children, and he could help out in the household. The man paid no betrothal money, as he generally would not in the *t'ung-yang-hsi, chao-chui* type of marriage. He went to live at the girl's

---

[77] This is very traditional, as noted above.

[78] The cost of each table was said to be twenty *yüan,* and the income of the married couple was said to be about 300 *yüan* each per month, which would be quite high.

[79] But not the same surname as the bride, who originally at least had a different one. Traditionally having the same surname would be an advantage.

adopted family's home after the registration of the marriage. It seems that in the area in question there is less loss of prestige in a matrilocal marriage than there is in Taiwan. Generally speaking, in the mainland, the household records list the husband as head of the household, so that there are still patrilocal overtones to the official family structure, but the residence of the marriage is less significant.

In 1966 a twenty-six year old farmer married a farm girl; both were classified as poor peasants.[80] They were from different villages, but the same commune and the same *ta-tui*. They liked each other and, as was customary, went to talk with their fathers; both parents gave their consent. The couple were engaged for one year before the marriage. The girl wanted a small amount of money to make clothes, so the man's father sent one hundred *yüan*. The girl's family sent a trousseau consisting of a *kuei-tzu*, clothes, toothbrush, toothpaste, and perfume. In this locality the girl would usually request fifty to sixty *yüan*, but in this case more was requested. The government also issued an extra ration of cloth to make clothes and blankets, and the girl's family sent some beer to the groom's home. There was an engagement party at the girl's house in the evening. Friends of the couple were invited, and tea and candy were served. On the day of the marriage the bride went to the groom's home by bicycle. There was no red cloth decorating the bicycle, as would usually be the case. Firecrackers were set off along the way, and outside the groom's home colorful red strips of paper were hung, upon which wishes for a long life together and other appropriate sayings were written. This case could be called a love marriage with traditional overtones.

In another village in 1963 a man twenty-five years of age married a twenty-four year old girl. They lived in the man's home after the marriage. In this case a go-between played a new role. The groom gave the go-between ten *yüan* for making the introduction. The go-between knew the man and felt he was a good person. He spoke to him and said, "You have no girl friend, how would you like me to introduce you to one?" The man agreed. The go-between then went to the girl's home to arrange a meeting. The go-between told the heads of the respective households about this forthcoming meeting and something about the two families. Then, days after the introduction, the couple agreed to become engaged. An engagement ceremony was held six months before the wedding. There was a party at the girl's house to which three tables of guests were invited, which the prospective groom paid for. The parties registered the marriage on the day of the engagement, so that the government considered the marriage as established, although the parties only regarded it as an engagement. The marriage took place at the groom's home. The groom had given the girl some money to make clothes. At the wedding

---

[80] Without extended discussion at this time, suffice it to say that status plays an important role in Chinese society on the mainland.

party the groom's family invited seven tables of guests, including relatives, older members of the village, and friends. A bicycle decorated with red cloth was used to transport the bride to the groom's home. Before the wedding, the groom sent gifts of pork, wine, and rice to the bride's family. The groom's family had overseas Chinese relatives and so were presumably wealthier than most others in the area. The girl, in turn, sent a rooster, a hen, *kuei-tzu,* and a dressing table to the groom's house as a trousseau.

Some general trends. While my Hong Kong interviews were not subject to the same type of tabulation as those in Taiwan, the above cases were reasonably typical of at least the more modern style marriages. I have omitted some of the details, but quite obviously there has been change. The biggest change is that fewer of the marriages are arranged. I have statistics, which are at best very rough approximations of the percentage of arranged marriages in certain villages. The data indicate, however, that the larger percentage of marriages since 1958 are not arranged in a traditional manner.

Another noticeable fact about the marriages described above, even the one with the overseas Chinese relatives, is that they are rather simple affairs. There is little expenditure of money, primarily because people have less money to spend and also because the government objects to this type of expenditure. Finally, there is little religious worship. During the past year it was difficult even to buy incense sticks in China. What worship there was, was largely in private and in secret—at least in Kwangtung and Fukien. While the marriages I described above are of the more modern type, more traditional marriages do exist as the documents seem to confirm.

The well-known Lien-chiang Documents[81] claim that, despite the more than ten years of education in socialism, "old ideologies are still in evidence, showing up whenever the opportunity arises." Despite the fact that the Party has "taken direct action to oppose superstition and oppose money marriages, and in the past few years these old ideas have been partially eradicated . . . [nevertheless in the] last year, in the time of difficulty, money marriages, and superstitious practices such as fortune telling were again in evidence." The author notes that the tradition of several thousand years of "feudalism" and over one hundred years of "semi-feudalistic and semi-colonialist ideologies" are "deep-rooted and cannot be easily changed."[82]

---

[81] There are several versions of these documents. The draft English translation I refer to was made at Columbia University. I also have seen a microfilm copy of the documents as well as a less complete book entitled T'U-CHI FUKIEN LIEN-CHIANG LU-HUO FEI-FANG WEN-CHIEN HUI-PIEN (Compilation of Communist documents captured in the surprise attack on Lien-Chiang district in Fukien) (Taipei 1964).

[82] *Id.,* 36. The extravagance of giving parties was also attacked and incomplete statistics indicated 1,409 parties totaling 6,981 tables occurred since the beginning of the year. One cadre was said to have given a wedding party of thirty-four tables, at which he received gifts in excess of the cost of the party.

The survival of practices such as betrothal money is indicated in the report of the Ch'ang-sha brigade, which notes: "A girl can now be married off for 400 to 500 or 800 to 900 *yüan,* some even from 1,000 to 2,000 *yüan.*"[83]

Apparently, of the twelve women who were married or engaged in 1960, eleven were classified as having undertaken money marriages, and only one as having voluntarily married. Furthermore, two matchmakers and two *t'ung-yang-hsi* marriages were noted. The data are not clear, but there are obviously go-betweens and marriages with betrothal money.

Lien-chiang *hsien,* while on the coast, is somewhat isolated and the statistics may be rather special. It may very well be, however, that when the cadre relax their vigilance, traditional practices reassert themselves. We have more evidence of the continuation of arranged marriages, up to 1958.

While the Lien-chiang Documents deal with party reports pertaining to Lien-chiang *hsien* in Fukien, there is also another set of documents dealing with Pao-an *hsien* in Kwangtung, which give evidence that the patrilocal marriage is the usual form.[84] This receives some confirmation in a small book published in Peking in 1964;[85] while discussing the advantages of a willing and self-managed marriage, it notes that because the spouses' relations will be good, the parents of the husband will love their daughter-in-law as they do their son. The daughter-in-law, loving her husband, will also respect his parents. The implication is that they all were living together in the husband's family home.

While we have evidence of the tenacity of certain customary practices, all evidence seems to point to the virtual elimination of the institution of secondary wives. The secondary wife was not commonly seen in the villages of China and so legal and political pressures were more readily able to eliminate this institution, particularly since there was insufficient increase in usable income to permit the flourishing of this institution.

The dual revolution, one toward the traditional and the other toward the modern ideal, that is occurring in Taiwan has been short-circuited by the communists. While there are more people marrying in traditional ideal patrilocal style in Taiwan because the average farmer can now afford the resplendent wedding of the rules of propriety, the communists have attempted to put a halt to this aspect of the revolution. The economic priorities set by the government have called for the farmer to forego the pleasures of the present for the expected glory of the future. While in both Taiwan and

---

[83] *Id.,* 123. Individuals complained of this large expense. *See also* id., 155, for bad practices table in Ch'an-sha brigade, which includes such things as geomancers and fortune-tellers.

[84] 27 UNION RESEARCH SERVICE 111, 160 (1900). *See also* M. FREEDMAN, CHINESE LINEAGE AND SOCIETY 185, 186 (1966).

[85] CHOU CHIA-CH'ING, HUN-YIN FA CHIANG-HUA (Discussions of the marriage law) 29 (1964).

mainland China the *t'ung-yang-hsi* marriages and *chao-chui* marriages have decreased in importance and the ideal patrilocal type has become a norm, the communists have tried to jump over the natural evolution to the conjugal family. They have exerted political energies in an attempt to insure the fact that the conjugal family becomes the norm in the very near future, but with dependence upon patrilocal residence. This has required enormous political–legal effort and yet has achieved something less than total success. It also has caused the regime to lose some of its reservoir of public sympathy. Whether these energies might have been better directed elsewhere is difficult to say. The building of more factories, if possible, would certainly provide a more natural and less painful impetus to the development of the conjugal family than would the interference of the political cadre. The natural evolution to the conjugal family may be painful enough.

Positive law has served many functions in this historical development, not the least of which has been to legitimate change that was naturally occurring. It has also helped to undermine traditional norms and traditional customary law. Customary law has itself played a role by adapting to changing circumstances, particularly in Taiwan, but also on the mainland. Positive law has at times been used as a "weapon" to create and stimulate change. When it is used in the latter sense against a large social institution, it generally requires the expenditure of substantial political-legal energies to support the change, as we have witnessed in the United States.[86]

In the early stages of industrialization, it may make little difference if a given person's relative is employed rather than a third person, because both may be equally unskilled. Thus, the early rush to the conjugal ideal in the mainland may be unnecessary as well as disruptive. The relative prosperity of the 1970s and the decrease in the intensity of the cultural revolution seems to have encouraged a more relaxed attitude toward certain traditional marriage practices in the People's Republic of China.

In fact, the stability provided by a modified form of the traditional family, which may exist, for example, in Japan, may provide a stabilizing influence in societies undergoing rapid economic and political transformation, and such influence may do much to promote rather than inhibit economic development.

---

[86] W. GOODE, WORLD REVOLUTION AND FAMILY PATTERNS 369–70 (1963). Goode lists the pressures of industrialization upon the traditional family; *e.g.*, increased physical mobility, thus proportionately less contact with kin, class-differential social and/or economic mobility, urban and industrial agencies, the creation of the value in achievement rather than birth, specialization making it less likely that one can get a job for a kin, and so on.

Rural to Urban Migration in Taiwan: Its Impact on Chinese Family and Kinship*

BERNARD GALLIN[1]

Urbanization involves many changes not only in communities but also in people. The changes that take place in people involve their adaptation to a new kind of community, their association with unfamiliar institutions, and, sometimes, their acculturation to a new way of life. Yet, these changes need not, and perhaps most frequently do not, involve cultural change—the displacement of old cultural forms by the introduction of new ones. Rather, the changes brought about by urbanization require that conventional cultural institutions be adapted and modified by people to fit the new urban conditions.

* Two articles based on my more recent field work in 1969–1970 might be read for further development of the ideas and substantive content presented here. The articles are: "The Integration of Village Migrants in Taipei", in *The Chinese City Between Two Worlds,* edited by Mark Elvin and G. William Skinner; Stanford University Press, 1974 (with coauthor Rita S. Gallin); and "The Rural-Urban Migration of an Anthropologist in Taiwan", in *Anthropologists in Cities,* edited by George M. Foster and Robert V. Kemper; Boston: Little, Brown and Co., 1974 (with coauthor Rita S. Gallin).

[1] I am most grateful to my wife, Rita Schlesinger Gallin, who participated fully in both periods of field work, and who has done so much to help in the development and preparation of this paper. I also wish to thank my colleague, Professor Joseph Spielberg, for his many stimulating and theoretical insights, and Chen Chung-min, formerly a graduate student in anthropology at Michigan State University, who has assisted in the analysis of the field data and in the exploration of many of the ideas presented. The first field trip in 1956–58 was supported by a Ford Foundation Foreign Area Training Fellowship: the more recent field work in 1965–66 was supported by a Fulbright-Hays Research Grant and also by a research grant from the Asian Studies Center at Michigan State University. I am also indebted to the Institute of Ethnology, Academia Sinica, Taiwan, for its extremely valuable cooperation and for sponsoring me as a Research Fellow during 1965–66.

The urbanization of the peasant in Taiwan appears to be taking this course. These peasants are brought to the cities primarily by the economic and social pressures that result when a growing population tries to maintain itself on a stable, agricultural land base. As these migrants attempt to adjust to the new conditions of urban life, changes in their structural and behavioral patterns of life take place. But, as I shall show, these changes are the consequences of a socioeconomic adaptation to the particular conditions of the urban environment, not rejections of traditional values and behavior. Even in their new urban homes, these migrants maintain much of their traditional, rural, kinship relationships, and the persistence of the tie with home plays a significant role in maintaining the link with the home village and with fellow migrants. Thus, the changes in the Taiwanese peasants who migrate from their rural home to the city are not cultural changes of the kind so often seen from the viewpoint of the traditional folk-urban continuum or the acculturation approach, but rather socioeconomic adaptations by which the migrants eventually are absorbed into the urban way of life.

The data for this paper were collected during two periods of field work in Taiwan. The first, in 1957–58, was a study of Hsin Hsing—a rural agricultural village; the second, in 1965–66, consisted of a two-month re-study of the same village followed by a nine-month study in Taipei of Hsin Hsing people who have migrated to Taipei over the past twenty years.[2] The rural and urban area studies concern basically the same populations and therefore can be examined comparatively in terms of these populations' structural and behavioral differences.

HSIN HSING VILLAGE

Hsin Hsing village is a Hokkien agricultural community on the west-central coastal plain of Taiwan, approximately 130 miles from Taipei. The population of the village, as it has been officially recorded in the district public office, has remained relatively stable in total numbers over the last several years. In 1958 the village had a registered population of 609 people, who lived in 99 registered households (hu); in 1966, 612 people in 112 households were officially registered. The minimal growth in population, as actually recorded, is the result of emigration to Taiwan's urban areas, especially Taipei. In fact, of the 612 residents registered in Hsin Hsing in 1966, only 506 actually lived in the village. The rest were living in cities, particularly Taipei, to which they had emigrated.[3]

---

[2] The results of my earlier research are reported in B. GALLIN, HSIN HSING, TAIWAN: A CHINESE VILLAGE IN CHANGE (1966).

[3] See Tables 1 and 2.

TABLE 1

REGISTERED AND/OR RESIDENT POPULATION OF HSIN HSING VILLAGE, 1965–66

	Male	Female	Total
Number of persons registered and residing in Hsin Hsing	236	270	506
Number of persons registered in Hsin Hsing but living in Taipei	46	23	69
Number of persons registered in Hsin Hsing but living in other places (excluding Taipei) . .	25	12	37
Total number of persons registered in Hsin Hsing	307	305	612

TABLE 2

HSIN HSING MIGRANTS IN TAIPEI, 1965–66

	Male	Female	Total
Number of Hsin Hsing villagers registered and living in Taipei	96	96	192
Number of Hsin Hsing villagers registered in Hsin Hsing but living in Taipei	46	23	69
Total number of Hsin Hsing villagers living in Taipei	142	119	261

Almost all the people in the general area of Hsin Hsing are the descendants of Chinese immigrants who came from the coastal region of Fukien province (the Amoy area) in China during the late eighteenth century. Some 80 percent of the villagers have one of four surnames, and in many instances the majority of families who bear the same surname consider themselves part of the same localized lineage *(tsu)*. Member families within each lineage share a demonstrated common ancestor in the village itself. The village is multi-lineage, therefore, and each lineage is patrilineal and patrilocal. Almost all the members of the same lineage or of smaller, less well organized groups of patrilineally-related families live in their own separate neighborhood compounds in the village. Each family owns its own living quarters in the large house, usually has at least two or three rooms for itself, and, along with its patrilineally-related families, shares an ancestral worship room *(kung t'ing)* which houses the statues of gods and ancestral tablets of its kinship group. As the families grow through marriage and births, they usually add rooms to the existing house or build another house in the same compound. At the same time, as the kinship group grows in generational depth and expands in numbers and lineal subdivisions, each subdivision is likely to keep the separate tablets of its own immediate ancestors in a smaller room of its own quarters. All members of the several subdivisions of the kinship group usually still share the single ancestral worship room that houses the ancestral tablets of those ancestors whom they all have in common. (The larger ancestral worship room in a more formally organized lineage would usually take the form of an ancestral hall.)

The kinship organizations or lineages of Hsin Hsing have been relatively small and have only minor holdings of corporate lands. Thus, they have had only limited economic effectiveness. Nevertheless, they have functioned as significant sociopolitical motivating forces in the activities of the village and, in more limited instances, in the area. Until very recently the several important lineages of the village effectively organized and virtually controlled village elections and internal politics. The more powerful kinship organizations of the village successfully formed coalitions in an attempt to harmonize the activities and relationships of the village population. Families that were members of the large lineage organizations usually played more active and influential roles in village affairs. Kinship and political machinations, therefore, were strong bases for cooperation and solidarity, and the more powerful lineages generally controlled the political activities of the village. In addition, compound living arrangements, religion, and in many instances mutual interests in particular areas of agriculture and irrigation systems provided relatives with additional bases for a good deal of interaction.

In recent years, however, some of these bases for kin and lineage oriented solidarity have diminished. As a result of the Land Reform Program between 1949 and 1953, the lineages lost some of their corporate land holdings by expropriation, and even this limited economic source of solidarity was subverted. The Land Reform Program also made it difficult, or at least risky, to acquire larger land holdings. As a result, villagers now farm their land more intensively and plant more diversified crops (rather than the traditional staples of rice and sweet potatoes) in order to realize a greater profit from the land. When village farmers increase production of vegetables for cash crops, they become more and more involved in markets and turn outward away from village and lineage mates.

At the same time, the recent Land Consolidation Program (beginning in the early 1960s) has frequently eliminated a former basis for agricultural cooperation among lineage mates. The villagers' plots of land, both rented and owned, are almost a mile or two from the nucleated village and adjoin land operated by people from their own village as well as from other villages. In the past, because of the division and fractionalization of family land, lineage mates normally farmed many scattered adjacent plots. Under the Consolidation Program, however, the plots of individual farmers have been redistributed to provide each with a block or usually several blocks of land which are not necessarily adjacent to the plots of kinsmen; the new land location draws farmers into different cooperative relationships which also cross kin and village lines.

Kin and lineage based relations have also been further weakened in recent years by the activities of political factions from beyond the village and even the local area.[4] As the influence of these outside groups begins to penetrate into local village politics by drawing members from across lineage and village lines—thus splitting these groupings—the traditional political functions of lineages or lesser kinship organizations are undermined. As a result, villagers and members of such kinship organizations tend to look beyond their traditionally natural groupings and identifications.

The turning outward of villagers and kinsmen has also been stimulated by the general economic conditions in the area. The people of Hsin Hsing over the years have been among the poorer ones in the vicinity. Since the 1940s, and at least up through the mid-1950s, their situation had become increasingly acute as a result of an excess of population on the available land and a lack of economic opportunity in the local area. There has never been any significant local industry or job opportunities to absorb the excess labor in the Hsin Hsing area.[5] In addition, the village is not close to markets where cash crops such as vegetables can readily be sold or shipped to larger markets, and the land-holdings of the villagers are too small to tie up in the long term sugar production, which in Taiwan requires approximately eighteen months before the cane can be harvested and a profit realized.

HSIN HSING MIGRANTS IN TAIPEI

For many villagers, then, the solution to the lack of local economic opportunities since the late 1940s has been migration to urban areas.[6] By 1965–66,

---

[4] The recent development of local political factionalism in the Hsin Hsing area is discussed in B. Gallin, *Political Factionalism and Its Impact on Chinese Village Social Organization in Taiwan*, in LOCAL LEVEL POLITICS 377–400 (M. Swartz ed. 1968).

[5] The only local opportunities available to absorb excess labor existed before and during the second World War when the Japanese hired people to work on various military projects in the general area. Some Hsin Hsing villagers have pointed out that because of their small landholdings, even in those days, a number of the villagers took such jobs and thus developed the "habit" of considering temporary moves to other places to supplement family income. However, migration from the rural to urban areas seemed to have been rather unusual during the Japanese occupation.

[6] Only since the mid-1950s has still another alternative developed for supplemental income, *i.e.*, the growing and marketing of vegetables as a cash crop. This pursuit could become a serious possibility for the Hsin Hsing area villagers only when insecticides to eliminate some of the hazards of vegetable cultivation, and bicycles, which could be used to transport vegetables from the Hsin Hsing area to markets ten to twenty-five miles away, became more readily available. However, vegetable production and marketing have become a really significant alternative to migration for villagers only in the last five to six years. In the early 1960s, power tillers appeared in the area in some number. In addition to their use in cultivation, these tillers are used to haul carts of vegetables to markets as far away as Taichung, over twenty-five miles from Hsin Hsing. Several villagers who own power tillers and carts provide daily shipping services to markets; vegetable farmers are able to depend upon their services and thus receive a regular source of income.

as a result of over 20 years of migration, 261 Hsin Hsing people (including mates and children) actually resided in Taipei. They comprised 36 family units (2 joint, 5 stem, and 29 nuclear) for a total of 220 people; the remaining 41 Hsin Hsing migrants living in Taipei were individuals whose families resided in Hsin Hsing. Five of these 36 family units considered to be based in Taipei[7] have an additional 24 members still resident in Hsin Hsing, where these families maintain some land holdings. In fact, while most members of these 36 family units are actually now officially registered in Taipei, 13 of these families still have 50 of their members registered in Hsin Hsing.[8]

TABLE 3

MIGRANT UNITS: FAMILIES AND INDIVIDUALS IN TAIPEI
AND HSIN HSING, 1965-66

	Joint		Stem		Nuclear		Individual		Total	
	M	F	M	F	M	F	M	F	M	F
Hsin Hsing persons belonging to 77 migrant units and living in Taipei	8	8	20	15	83	86	31	10	142	119
Persons belonging to those 77 migrant units in Taipei and living in Hsin Hsing	0	0	0	0	13	11	78	83	91	94
Total number of persons involved in migration from Hsin Hsing to Taipei (living in both Hsin Hsing and Taipei)	8	8	20	15	96	97	109	93	233	213
Number of migrant units which have some members living in Hsin Hsing	0		0		5		41		—	—

For most villagers the initial move to the city, whether motivated by pure economic necessity or by the desire to diversify the family's economic activi-

---

[7] The term "Taipei based family unit" is used to describe a migrant family unit that includes the basic members (husband and wife) of a nuclear family and that is settled and living in Taipei. In some instances, even though members of such a family (children or an old parent) may reside in the village, the family is still considered a Taipei-based family unit.

When a migrant or several related migrants (from one family or *hu*) work and live in Taipei while most of the others in the family, including a husband or wife, are settled and living in Hsin Hsing, the family is called a Hsin Hsing or "village-based family unit"; the migrants of these families are placed in the catagory of "individuals."

[8] See Table 3. Since the Land Reform acts of 1949–53, in order to cultivate self-owned land legally, the tiller must actually reside in the area. As far as the villagers are concerned, without proof of residence they could be considered absentee owners whose land might be liable to expropriation in some future time. Therefore, they maintain

ties, is made to supplement the family's income from the land or from farm labor. Most Hsin Hsing migrants had land in the village at the time they moved to Taipei,[9] and all men moved initially without their wives or families.[10]

TABLE 4

Migrant Units with and without Landholdings in Hsin Hsing Village

	Joint	Stem	Nuclear	Individuals	Total number of units
Number of migrant units with land	2	2	15	12	31
1950					
Number of migrant units without land	0	2	4	2	8
Number of migrant units with land	2	2	19	13	36
1955					
Number of migrant units without land	0	2	7	3	12
Number of migrant units with land	2	3	19	20	44
1960					
Number of migrant units without land	0	2	9	7	18
Number of migrant units with land	2	3	19	34	58
1965					
Number of migrant units without land	0	2	10	7	19

Usually it has been the male head of a household or a grown son of a family who has gone to work and live in Taipei, and these men remit part of their earnings to their families in the village. At the outset, they frequently return to the village for planting and harvesting or to observe festivals or rituals. As time goes on, in most instances the family arranges for farm labor to take care of these agricultural activities, so that many men gradually reduce their trips

their village registration, believing this registration sufficient to constitute their proof of residence. In addition, the Land Reform Acts have made it difficult for a landlord to take land away from a tenant who is an actual tiller. Thus, a tenant who is working in Taipei safeguards his tenant rights by maintaining his registration in the village even while some relative is actually tilling his land for him.

[9] *See* Table 4.

[10] The first migrant came to Taipei to work in 1945, and each year up to and through 1965, village men continued to come to Taipei. The first female villager to come to Taipei to work did not arrive until 1956, and several more came only intermittently thereafter until 1965 when the largest single number of three arrived. Male villagers did not bring wives to Taipei until 1947 and then brought them only sporadically for the next few years. Since 1952–53, the flow of wives to Taipei has been fairly steady and in larger numbers.

to the village and limit their visits only to the most important ritual or festive occasions such as the village god's birthday, perhaps New Year's, or deaths and weddings.

Migrants usually do not return home to observe ancestor worship, nor do they worship in Taipei. Most migrants—whether they be individual urban dwellers or whole families—do not bring their ancestral tablets to Taipei. Instead, the tablets are normally left in the village where worship will be conducted on appropriate occasions by the patrilineal relatives. In only a very few instances do Hsin Hsing migrants participate actively in the worship of their ancestors. The frequency of visits to Hsin Hsing by migrants seems to be based primarily on the presence or absence of family connections or landholdings in the village. Visiting is also influenced by the kind of work or manner in which migrants earn a living in Taipei.

The majority of the villagers who migrate remain in the city[11] and eventually bring their families to live with them. Usually this move is made after a period of adjustment and settling in and after some kind of regular work is found by the men. Sometimes the decision to move to the city is made by the wives who become suspicious of their husbands' activities in the city, especially when the men fail to send money home regularly or when stories or gossip of their activities are carried back to the village by other migrants. In such cases, it is not unusual for the wife and younger children to go to Taipei, supposedly

---

[11] In past years only forty-five people, members of thirty-three family units, have returned permanently to live in the village after going to Taipei to work.

Some of these returned villagers first went to the city out of economic necessity. Since their return they have turned to vegetable production and marketing as an alternative to migration. The vegetables bring in a significant portion of their families' total income. All of these families have a sufficient family labor force at home to invest the great amount of time necessary for the growing of vegetables. Virtually none of these families now have members bringing in any significant additional income through outside work. Eighteen of the thirty-three returned Hsin Hsing-based family units are represented in this group.

A number of the returned villagers went to the city just to supplement the family income. They frequently were members of relatively large families—usually joint or stem—which had at least adequate landholdings to support their members. But in traditional style and as noted, in M. Cohen, *Variations in Complexity among Chinese Family Groups: The Impact of Modernization,* 29 TRANSACTIONS OF THE NEW YORK ACADEMY OF SCIENCES, Series II, 638–44 (1967), such families have sought to diversify their economic interests by sending a male member into the city in an attempt to bring additional income into the family till. Seven families of this type have not gone into vegetable production for cash, since they have enough land on which to live by growing rice and are unwilling to invest the time and effort to grow vegetables.

Three other families also had enough land at the time of the original migration and apparently were trying to diversify economically. Recently these families have made another attempt to diversify and again have sent either sons or other younger family members to work in Taipei. These families have not turned to the cultivation of cash crop vegetables, because they do not have enough family labor available in the village.

to cut down on family expenses by cooking and making a home for the man. On the average, the arrival of a wife, and perhaps others of the family, has been 6.8 years after the husband's arrival.

For many of the villagers who bring their families to the city, particularly those who might have left the village because they were dissatisfied with village life or openly preferred life in the city, the move soon becomes established as relatively permanent, and some men even sell off what little land they own.[12] In time, once they become rather settled in their Taipei work and especially after they bring their families to the city, these men and their families return to their village infrequently and then only on very special occasions. The trip home is expensive, and for most it would necessitate the loss of essential income from work.

Almost one-half of the men in Taipei work as unskilled or "coolie" type laborers and are spoken of by the villagers, including themselves, as having "gone to the city to be water buffalo."[13] On the other hand, migrants who have

---

The families of still a few other returnees who have some capital have started small businesses in the village in recent years as an alternative to migration or cash cropping. Even though they may have enough family labor available, financially well-off families usually do not like the heavy work of vegetable growing. Were they to hire laborers to cultivate their vegetable crops, they would realize only a small profit from the crop.

The remaining families containing returned migrants now have members who supplement the family income by working as hired laborers on the land, working in the nearby town of Lukang, or peddling produce or wares in the area. Three of these families have no land at all.

[12] Eight of the thirty-six Taipei-based families have sold all their land since their migration in order to meet critical economic needs. The majority of the migrants, however, retain their land in the village either for purposes of income or, in many cases, security, since the migrants sometimes derive little or no income from it. Nineteen Taipei-based families have arranged for a kinsman or a friend to tend their land in the village. These kinsmen retain most of, and in some instances all of, the proceeds from the land in return for their work. It is clear, therefore, that these nineteen families, although settled in Taipei, wish to be prepared for any contingency, such as the loss of jobs or the coming of another war. None of the heads of these families suggested that they were keeping the land because they themselves intended some day to return to live and work in the village. In fact, three of these families have sold off a portion of their land to build a house in Taipei, to buy a delivery cart engine, or to pay for the marriage of a son.

Regardless of whether the land is retained for purposes of income or security, however, none of the Taipei-based families sell their living quarters in the village, even when all their members live in Taipei and seldom return to the village. These rooms are simply sealed, used for storage rooms by the migrants or by relatives in the village, or loaned—normally without charge—to village relatives. A house, and land if it is considered to be ancestral (*i.e.,* land that has been inherited), seems to be retained for symbolic reasons: to sell an ancestral house or land would be evidence of the final breaking of ties with the ancestral home. In addition to the symbolic implications for the individual involved, it could bring some criticism from others.

[13] *See* Table 5.

prospered in business in Taipei are referred to by the villagers as "our overseas Chinese" since they frequently give large sums of money to help support village festive occasions. In general, the kinds of work village men do require that they frequently work at odd hours, often at night. Although their actual annual cash income and their standard of living in terms of food are higher than they were or could be in the village, nevertheless, almost every villager has greater rent, food, transportation, school, medical, and entertainment expenses in the city. A villager must work every day since his family's livelihood is completely dependent upon his day-to-day earnings. (See Table 5.)

TABLE 5

JOBS HELD BY HSIN HSING VILLAGE MIGRANTS
IN TAIPEI, 1965–66[14]

Job	Number Held
Vegetable cart drivers	30
Pedicab drivers	10
Peddlers	3
Merchants	9
Shop clerks	14
Factory workers	7
Gardeners, carpenters, etc.	10

The majority of the villagers in Taipei live either in the vicinity of the Central Market in Ch'eng Chung District or in another nearby area known as Wan Hua in the Shuang Yuan District. Both districts are two of the oldest areas of Taipei City and are inhabited heavily by Taiwanese. Both also house

[14] The heavy concentration of Hsin Hsing villagers in cart driving apparently is attributable to the migrants' early arrival in Taipei (from 1945 through 1952) at a time when the job market was still open and to the fact that cart driving is rather steady and secure work. The concentration is also a reflection of the aid the earlier cart drivers gave to their fellows who came to the city later. In a number of instances, later arrivals came to Taipei with the knowledge that they might obtain such a job.

The ten pedicab drivers all took up this work before 1959. The service kinds of jobs, therefore, were available and filled primarily in the early days of the rural to urban migration. On the other hand, the twenty-one jobs in factories and as clerks in shops have all been taken by villagers who came after 1960; the timing was a result of a greater willingness to send girls and young people to work in Taipei, an increase in factory jobs, and the lessening availability of lucrative service type jobs as the city became saturated with unskilled migrants.

Migrants who have become peddlers or especially merchants began coming to Taipei from the village immediately after the end of World War II in 1945 and have continued to come up to the present time.

large numbers of rural and urban migrants—undoubtedly because they are commercial areas that are centrally located near work areas, such as the Central Market, and have large numbers of dwellings that have been subdivided.

Most Hsin Hsing villagers live in residential concentrations and, in addition, in concentrations closely correlated with kinship relationships.[15] When possible, most villagers and kinsmen attempt to find living quarters very near each other. Although they do not necessarily live in immediate residential propinquity within their districts, they usually do live within easy visiting distance. The distances between their places of residence are primarily a result of the problems of securing living quarters in the city.

Migrants who live in other areas are usually families and individuals who are part of smaller kinship groupings in the village or are from non-related village families. A few of these "outlying" migrants are young individuals working in factories or as shop clerks, and they live in quarters furnished by their employers. But most of the migrants who do not live in the two central districts of heaviest villager concentration have either independent jobs or work in small businesses that are totally unrelated to those occupations in which so many of the other village migrants are involved. For example, none of these "outlying" migrants is either a cart driver or a businessman in the Central Market. Some of these migrants live and work with affinal relatives, city-acquired friends, or friends from their home area rather than with fellow villagers or kinsmen. Several actually share a house or some house facilities with others with whom they have a voluntary relationship rather than an obligatory one.

Seven of the Taipei-based families own their own houses of several rooms with facilities for cooking. However, the residences of most of the Taipei-based families and individual migrants consist only of a room or two, usually of a four-tatami mat size (approximately nine by nine feet). On the average, at least for Hsin Hsing migrants in Taipei, there are three people per room, but not infrequently there are six people sleeping in one room. Many families share cooking, washing, and toilet facilities (if present) with all the other families who live in the rented house. Within a particular house most families usually are not kinsmen or even from the same village or area; houses are scarce, and the migrants must rent what they can find.

COMPARISONS OF STRUCTURE AND BEHAVIOR

In order to manage under such new work and residence patterns, the migrants have had to adapt. The conditions of their new environment require behavior different from that to which they were accustomed in the village. For example, in the village agricultural economy, work is seasonal throughout

---

[15] *See* Table 6.

TABLE 6

DISTRIBUTION OF HSIN HSING KINSHIP GROUPS IN TAIPEI BY DISTRICT, 1965–66

	Huang	K'ang	Shen	Shih	Li	Wang	Others	Total
Total number of people living in Taipei	79 (100%)	47 (100%)	52 (100%)	37 (100%)	22 (100%)	13 (100%)	11 (100%)	261 (100%)
Number of people living in Ch'eng Chung	12 (15.2%)	10 (21.3%)	10 (19.3%)	25 (67.6%)	—	12 (92%)	—	69 (26.5%)
Number of people living in Shuang Yuan	48 (60.8%)	29 (61.7%)	40 (76.9%)	6 (16.2%)	22 (100%)	—	1 (9.9%)	146 (56.9%)
Number of people living in five other districts and suburbs	19 (24%)	8 (17%)	2 (3.8%)	6 (16.2%)	—	1 (8%)	10 (91.1%)	46 (17.6%)

the year with busy and slack periods; the peasant who farms his own land (owned or rented) is his own boss and usually does not depend on daily labor for his livelihood. Most often he can easily take a day off from his work on the land at the time of a death or for a festival. On a day-to-day basis, there is also limited economic competition between fellow villagers, and, in fact, a good deal of cooperation is required by the agricultural system in planting, harvesting, or handling irrigation problems.

Economic competition of a long-range type, however, does exist among villagers. There are always villagers wishing either to purchase or to rent additional land. Since the Land Reform Acts of 1949–53, this competition for land is usually among the smaller farmers; larger landowners hesitate to enlarge their holdings, for they fear that land again may be expropriated by the government. The competition for land to rent by farmers has been intensified by a continuing inability of peasants to obtain capital for land purchase. At the same time the Land Reform Acts have secured the rights of tenants to till the land and reduced the amount of land available for rental to a minimum. For the most part, though, competition between fellow villagers is more or less focused on gaining prestige within the social sphere or, for some, within the local political arena (which eventually may lead to economic gain). This competition for prestige, rather than for a living, is not an immediate economic matter.

In the city, on the other hand, competition for prestige among the migrants is limited. Villagers do participate in the informal political arena but not so much for social prestige as for economic power. The competition that exists between village migrants is usually within the economic sphere. And it is also within this sphere that much of the cooperation between migrants is engendered.

Although the possible opportunities for jobs and business may be considered almost unlimited in the city, nevertheless most villagers, particularly the family men, hold jobs in a small number of work categories or types of businesses. Large numbers of migrants work together or at the same kind of jobs in the Central Market. Such a situation can and does lead to both cooperation and, to some extent, competition in the struggle to earn increased income.

For example, the vegetable cart drivers in the Central Market of Taipei are organized into several groups. Most of the members of one such group are Hsin Hsing villagers, and many of these men are from particular Hsin Hsing village lineages.[16] (The concentration of villagers and related kinsmen within this group is based on continued contact among these people after their arrival

---

[16] Twenty-one of this group's members are Hsin Hsing migrants, and fifteen of the twenty-one are members of two Hsin Hsing kinship groups (ten Huangs and five Shens); the other six Hsin Hsing villagers are from three other kinship groups.

in Taipei.) Until the formation of this group in the early 1960s, many Hsin Hsing villagers and also villagers from neighboring areas frequently were in daily competition for the jobs that are so necessary on a day-to-day basis for carrying on life. The cart drivers' group, however, now regulates the assignment of jobs and wages. While the competition for work among men who provided the same service in the same areas was thus eliminated, a new problem in the men's relations was introduced by the new organization; men now complain and sometimes openly argue that some of their fellow workers—who receive the same wages as the others—manage to work less.

Competition is also evident in Taipei among some of the villagers who operate small vegetable stands as agents or who peddle vegetables or patent medicines. Although these men often have been brought into such businesses through the help of their fellow villagers or brothers, they frequently find themselves competing for each other's customers.

In addition to such sources of competition and possible conflict, and in spite of the cooperation possible between migrants on the basis of concentration of occupational groupings and associational memberships, there are a number of other factors that greatly affect the nature of the continued relationships of village migrants in the city. Because villagers in the city must work each day during prescribed hours, they have less freedom to participate in festivals or weddings or even to offer their services and physical assistance to relatives or fellow villagers at the time of a family death. Unlike the situation in the village, there is simply little, or at least far less, time available to cooperate and fraternize at will with their relatives.

Similarly, city residence patterns are far different from the institutionalized residence patterns in the village where patrilineally-related kinsmen live in small residence concentrations of their own compounds or large houses. In Taipei most villagers do not find housing as close to their lineage mates or even brothers as they might wish. Furthermore, life in the city provides the villager with his first opportunity to choose his place of residence, given, of course, certain conditions of availability and price. The new environmental situation provides the villager with the freedom and opportunity to escape from the close and involuntary relationships of kinship and village. Thus, eleven villagers, for reasons of either convenience or personal preferences, live closer to relatives of the female side (matrilateral or affinal) than to lineage relatives. Two of the families of sisters in Taipei even share a house. In the Hsin Hsing area such arrangements are virtually impossible, because marriage is patrilocal and usually between families living in different villages.

When the son in a migrant family marries under these new living conditions, he must usually find separate living quarters immediately, since it is unlikely that the expanded family can manage to live together in the small rented living quarters. In the village situation the marriage of a son normally brings an initial enlargement of the family in the same house, which, if necessary, is expanded in size. Even when the family divides, it continues to remain physically close through other bonds that make for the continued cooperation and solidarity of its members, such as through the agricultural process, ancestor worship, lineage relationships, and membership in and relationship with the larger lineage organization, as well as with the village community. In the city usually only the wealthier merchant migrants who can afford larger houses can hope to maintain joint families for any period of time after the marriage of their sons.

At the same time, the crowded living conditions in the city clearly affect a number of the villagers' behavioral patterns. One of the most immediate and obvious effects of the housing situation is the place in which migrant village women will give birth. In Hsin Hsing and other villages, where families normally have several rooms in their houses and therefore the possibility of privacy, all births take place within the home. No one goes to a hospital, which is usually not as conveniently located as in Taipei, nor does anyone go to a midwife's house to give birth. Going outside the home to give birth is not necessary as it usually is in the city. For the most part, regardless of how long they have been living in Taipei or how economically successful they have been, village migrants in Taipei apparently have not yet accepted the idea of giving birth to their children in a "formal" hospital. Twelve of the fifty-eight infants born to migrants in Taipei were born in the family's own quarters, and forty-six were born either in some kind of maternity home or in the room of a midwife in the city. Women usually stay in these facilities only between one and three days after giving birth.

The larger number of births taking place in specialized maternity homes is not simply a result of some form of urbanization or modernization that causes people to utilize modern health facilities. It is, rather, a result of a lack of a room in the home where a birth can take place in privacy. Thus, for virtually every migrant family living in a one-room dwelling (which usually did not include someone who could assist with the birth at home), the birth took place outside the home. On the other hand, for those families that had prospered economically in the city and had larger living quarters, most births took place within the privacy of their own quarters, frequently with either the help of a midwife or a member of the larger family to which they belonged.

The abrupt change in this housing pattern is no doubt likely to influence fertility rates among these rural migrants in Taipei. Although my data are insufficient for such an analysis, I expect that, given the crowded conditions and total lack of privacy plus the much greater availability of birth control information and facilities, fertility rates will decrease, as is suggested in the studies of other urban areas of the world. In Taipei, it is likely that the reasons for this decrease will be as much because of the lack of privacy and the purely biological consequences associated with high-tension, crowded living conditions, as the better communications of and facilities for birth control techniques.

The conditions of city living also affect the spending of the migrants, who must allocate greater amounts of their income to rent, food, clothing, and school costs for their children. Rent for a small room may be as high as NT$500 (US$12.50) per month, which may be one-quarter of the family's monthly income in the city. When villagers share cooking facilities with other people in the city house, to avoid any possible embarrassment, they may spend more on their daily food than they might otherwise do; their poverty is public, and they fear that people will laugh at them, if they do not eat reasonably well. Living in such close quarters is also obviously a factor in the villagers' efforts to dress better. On the other hand, migrants in Taipei may eat and dress better, not out of embarrassment and lack of privacy, but because of a greater daily availability of cash, easier access to food vendors and markets, and an escape from the necessity (in the village) of appearing thrifty in such matters as food and clothing.

But although their expenses are greater, the income of migrants is usually significantly higher than it would be in the village and is sufficient to cover the increased costs of living. Although villagers' incomes in the city might come from several sources—for example, when several family members work and contribute to the family coffer—their incomes in most instances are not sufficient to provide for very much savings. They must, therefore, borrow money when the need arises, but they do so usually from a well-to-do kinsman, friend, or from their employers. I found no village migrants who utilized any urban credit organization to obtain loans. Even though credit facilities are limited in the city for ordinary working-class people with minimum collateral, it seems likely that, even if public credit facilities were more readily available, the migrants probably would not use them. Whether by choice or necessity, most migrants borrow money from individuals or join the traditional money lending clubs. Usually, the people with whom they join in these money lending clubs are fellow villagers, kinsmen, fellow workers (so often also their fellow villagers), or at least other rural area people.

Borrowing, however, is not limited to times of need, and villagers may go into debt in an attempt to improve their condition. They may borrow money or use whatever savings they may have to buy a delivery cart so that they will not have to rent one, to buy a small engine for a cart so that they will not have to pedal, push, or pull it, or to finance a small business. As their economic condition improves, some villagers will save or borrow money in order to buy or build a house in the city. The money borrowed for such diverse reasons is normally paid back gradually out of the families' earnings. Among almost all the Hsin Hsing family units living in Taipei, however, such diverse reasons for saving or borrowing do not include that of buying agricultural land and returning to the village. In fact, eleven village migrants have actually sold all or part of their Hsin Hsing land in order to pay off debts or to use the money in Taipei.

A much clearer consequence of the crowded living conditions of the city can be noted in the effect on the villagers' religious and magical activities. Villagers who might want to transfer their ancestral tablets to the city so that they can worship regularly usually have no space available for them in their single room dwellings. "Certainly," one village man said, "our family could not be expected to sleep with our ancestors." In addition, even if space were available, a landlord usually does not permit his tenants to "invite" their ancestors' spirits into *his* house, because he fears that they may come into conflict with his own or any other ancestral spirits in the house. Consequently, not one Taipei based migrant family unit renting a house in the city has copied and moved its ancestral tablets from Hsin Hsing to Taipei. Many of these villagers believe that their responsibilities to ancestors continue to be fulfilled as long as someone, *i.e.,* their relatives in Hsin Hsing, is sacrificing for them. And a significant number of these families do send some money to their brothers or lineage cousins in Hsin Hsing to help pay the expenses of ancestor worship. In addition, if they still have their residences registered in the village, some are regularly assessed for the repair and maintenance of the family or lineage ancestral worship room.

This system of worship serves to maintain contact and relationships between migrants and their natal homes. Although most migrant families in Taipei consider the move from the village to the city a permanent one (at least in their lifetimes), they nevertheless still seem to view the village of their birth as their symbolic home. Most village migrants continue to maintain contacts with their natal village, fellow villagers, and fellow area people in Taipei. They even renovate or totally rebuild an unlived-in village house. The maintenance of such contacts, of course, may be attributable to a great degree to their inability to manage economically, socially, or psychologically without the help and relationships of familiar people.

Most villagers are extremely reluctant to sever ties with their homes. The apparent need to maintain the symbolic tie seems to be expressed in the attitude that Hsin Hsing villagers have regarding their ancestral tablets and the worship of their ancestors. The moving of the ancestral tablets from the village to the city symbolizes a severing of the tie with one's home. Thus, even those migrant families in Taipei who have their own homes are hesitant to copy and move their tablets from Hsin Hsing to Taipei. Only three of the seven families that own their own homes in Taipei have brought their tablets to the city. These three families who have moved their tablets to the city have several things in common. First, they are all relatively well established, both socially and economically, in Taipei. Second, none of these families has any immediate family (brothers) living in Hsin Hsing, and, in fact, two have brothers living in Taipei.[17] Third, of the three families who have copied and moved their tablets, all felt compelled (without being asked) to offer a justification for the transference of the tablets from the home village.

The head of one family who had transferred the family tablets explained that when he had been ill an ancestor had told him in a dream that he was sick because he did not personally worship his ancestors; therefore, he copied his tablets from Hsin Hsing and brought them to Taipei. Another family pointed out that since they had built a new house it was necessary to have their ancestral tablets present in order to have a proper new house-opening ceremony. (Apparently the presence of ancestral tablets was not considered necessary for the ceremony by any of the other families who also built their own houses in Taipei.) The third family explained that they had brought their tablets to Taipei so that they could have the proper ritual for their son's marriage in Taipei. (In most cases, villagers return to Hsin Hsing for the marriage ritual, since that is where the tablets are.)

Five other Taipei-based family units personally worship their ancestors in Taipei but do not have the tablets in Taipei at all. Each of these five families rents its living quarters and worships outdoors in front of a picture of the ancestor. Two of these families started to worship their ancestors in the city after being told by a shaman in Taipei that one of their close relatives was in trouble because they did not personally worship the ancestors.

Most Taipei-based villagers, therefore, are either unable or unwilling to worship ancestors personally in the city. For the first time, villagers have an excuse for not actively participating in ancestor worship. In addition, the frequent lack of proximity of living quarters to kinsmen and fellow villagers results in a decrease in social pressure to perform ancestor worship—a pressure that continues to play so important a role in its performance in the village. Migrants now have a justification for their limited or minimal participation in such a ritual.

Similarly, most migrant families in times of illness cannot bring curing shamans *(dang-ki)* into their Taipei homes; they simply lack a room in which rituals can be performed. It is true that Western-style medical practitioners with more advanced techniques are more readily available in the city than in the village, but there are also a great many shamans practicing in various parts of the city. Nevertheless, the need to pay the shaman in cash for each visit (which is not normally necessary in the rural area, since it is customary to call

---

[17] If any of these families did still have brothers living in the village, the copying and moving of the tablets would represent a very serious break with their family and natal home. One might say that the division or breaking up of a family can have three stages: (1) the division of the cooking; (2) the division of the property; and finally (3) the division of the tablets or, in other words, the worship of the ancestors. The final division is the most serious since it destroys one of the last significant sources of continued family unity even after the economic division has taken place.

in a shaman who is a fellow villager and therefore is not paid in cash for his services), plus the lessened village social pressure to call in a shaman, both seem to play a part in the decrease in the migrants' reliance on or use of shamans for curing purposes. This decrease represents another modification of strong tradition of the rural area and is indicative of the kinds of changes that are exhibited in the ritualistic behavior of migrants in the city.

DISCUSSION

The new environment of the city with its different residence and work patterns and the ensuing lessening of social pressure precipitates most of the change that occurs in the social structure in which the migrants participate and in the cultural behavior they exhibit; these alterations, at least initially, are not made by cultural transmission through contact with the urban population, nor are they a result of the rejection of traditional values.

In the city, villagers are allowed their first opportunity to limit their contact and relations with fellow Hsin Hsing people, relatives, and even brothers (both in the village and in Taipei). Migrants can select their own residential locations and economic forms of endeavor and are free to determine the degree to which they wish to participate in religious or other ritual activity. In the rural area, traditional social institutions and pressures prevent such free action and enforce virtually complete participation in all village and kinship oriented activities.

A few migrants have taken advantage of the possibility for anonymity and lack of community or lineage social control and have forged a new and freer life for themselves in the city. Most of the Hsin Hsing migrants, however, apparently still feel a need for the identification and security they derive from village fellows and especially lineage relatives in the home community. These migrants, then, have structured their lives, as much as the dissimilar city environment will allow, on the bases of these traditional and supportive relationships. The choice of these relationships as the most significant bases of their lives is voluntary. So, too, is the choice migrants make to maintain close ties with the home village. Direct linkages with the village, in and of themselves, foster and encourage relationships with fellow villagers and kinsmen who live in Taipei and influence the activities and behavior of the migrants.

The village migrants live and work in fairly heavy residential and occupational concentrations. There are outsiders—usually also migrants to Taipei and some few Taipei people—involved in the work or business activities with the Hsin Hsing migrants. Nevertheless, most migrants maintain their closest and most basic relationships and groupings with their fellow villagers and kinsmen. Social, economic, and occupational groups are organized by the migrants on these bases; for example money lending clubs, sworn brother groups, and the cart drivers' group include in their memberships a larger proportion of people from the home community. The cart drivers' group perhaps best exemplifies the advantages to be gained from organizing on such bases; it is an active and important force in the local political maneuvering that is necessary to help secure the cart drivers' jobs in the face of constant pressures from others to break their partial monopoly on this occupation.

Fellow villagers and kinsmen also join together socially, when possible, for festive occasions such as weddings. The new environment of the city, however, places severe limitations on the amount of socializing possible among migrants. Time and money often are limited. And, in addition, migrants say that they "are in the city to make money for their families, not to play." As a result, migrants in Taipei do not exhibit as much social cohesiveness as they did in the home community.

The migrants also do not exhibit any great sense of "larger-group" cohesiveness. Despite the great many Hsin Hsing villagers living in Taipei, nearly half the number actually living in Hsin Hsing itself, the migrants have not formed a village association. Nor have the small kinship groups, which have many members in Taipei as do some active lineage organizations in the rural area, formed any kinship associations. The most obvious explanation for this lack is the basic difference between the village and urban environments and the socioeconomic consequences of each.

In the village, for instance, but not in the city, an organization of villagers based on community identification or relatively formal organizations based on lineage are feasible. These organizations can exist and manage in the village because ritual and localized socioeconomic and political activities continue, for the most part, to regularly function as unifying forces for them. In the city, however, patrilineal or lineage relatives, and villagers generally, have more diversified interests and relationships—at least when compared with those they have in the village—and are unable to unify all the members and organize any operative socioeconomic and political manipulative force. (A group such as that of the cart drivers, while significant, includes neither all the Hsin Hsing villagers nor whole groups of fellow kinsmen, and its membership is not limited to people only from Hsin Hsing.)

As a result, although kinship and village based relationships continue to have significance for most villagers living in Taipei, they are limited to exchanges between individual kin-related and village-related families. They are not significant as the basis of membership in formal or informal kin or village organizations.

Formal associations that focus on kinship do exist in Taipei, however. But these broader based surname or clan associations are not necessarily based on strict or real kin relationships and generally serve as sources of identification, solidarity, and security only for people who have been socially and economically successful or, perhaps, have lived for a long time in the city. Large area associations also exist in the city, but they, too, operate only for the benefit of the more prosperous.

The concepts of kinship or localism as foci for orienting relations are not defunct in urban Taiwan. A particular form of kinship organization, that is, lineage, is defunct there; it simply does not suit the broad based, heterogeneous, large-scale society of the urban center. The new environment of the city influences and results in the modification not only of many cultural forms of behavior, but also of the rural form of the traditional lineage organization. Chinese urban life—even that of the emerging urban-industrial type as in Taipei—is not at all antithetical to kinship as a focus for socioeconomic and political organization and behavior. Rather, it is antithetical only to particular, non-functional forms but apparently not to clan associations in Taipei, as Fried[18] has recently pointed out. (It must be remembered, however, that a gradual functional decline in the lineage form of kinship organization is currently taking place even in rural Taiwan as it feels the impact of and becomes more involved in national life.[19])

Nevertheless, kin and village based relationships continue to be significant for migrants, even though in the city these relationships function only on an individual rather than a group level. They still provide some of the socioeconomic, political, and psychic security so often needed by the migrant in the city.

This desired and needed psychic security is also offered by the symbolic tie the migrant maintains with his natal home. Frequently, however, the perpetuation of this tie involves a loss of some economic security, for it may be maintained through financial privation; that is, when a migrant continues to keep land or a house which he does not use, but on which he must pay taxes. Nevertheless, for many of the migrants, to break the symbolic tie would leave them virtually isolated.

Finally, most of the rural to urban migrants from Hsin Hsing village cannot yet be considered urbanized. In fact, many of them are probably not even very far along in the process of being urbanized.

Although Taipei is a city that is rapidly industrializing, the majority of her migrants share in limited aspects of the new urban industrial complex in which they find themselves. Most of them work in unskilled and service type jobs and live in residential concentrations, just as they might if they were to live and work in a pre-industrial city. Other than taking advantage of the opportunity to enroll children in the public education system (as they do in the village area), and increasingly seeking the services of Western-style medical

---

[18] For a discussion of his research on clan organization in Taiwan *see* M. Fried, *Some Political Aspects of Clanship in a Modern Chinese City,* in Political Anthropology 285–300 (M. Swartz, *et al.,* eds. 1966).

[19] *See* B. Gallin, *supra* note 4.

practitioners, most migrants do not and in some cases cannot take advantage of the other services available in the urban center; for example, they make no use of credit facilities, wide organizational networks, or legal facilities.

Nevertheless, the new environmental arrangements of the city provide the migrant with alternatives that enable him to bring a new voluntarism into his behavior and his relationships. The new conditions of the urban setting both necessitate and make possible the modification and adaptation of many rural institutions such as family and kinship relationships; they do not necessitate rejection or replacement of rural institutions with urban-industrial type institutions. In Taiwan, then, the urban condition does not necessarily carry with it newly introduced cultural forms and values.

Modernization and Household Composition in Taiwan*

WILLIAM L. PARISH

The repeated observation that modernization is accompanied by the transformation of extended family systems into systems in which the nuclear family is the basic unit has led to the prediction that this change is inevitable.[1] Numerous aspects of modernization are said to be responsible for this change, but the exact role of each aspect is as yet unclear.

In this study I compare survey data from a village, an older city, and a new industrialized city in Taiwan to see whether the predicted changes in family complexity do in fact occur in these locations at different levels of modernization. Beyond that I examine how specific aspects of modernization are responsible for the observed variation among these three areas. The aspects of modernization most emphasized in this study are migration, inheritance of the means of livelihood, occupational mobility, and bureaucratization. Other

* I wish to thank the Bureau of International Educational and Cultural Affairs, Ministry of Education, of the Republic of China; the Tainan City Government; and the Kaohsiung City Government for their generous cooperation in this research. Also, I would like to thank my villager friend for the introduction to his village and David K. Jordan, who was studying the village at the same time, for his assistance.

The work was supported by a Carnegie Corporation grant through the London-Cornell Project at Cornell University and by National Science Foundation grant number GS-1473. Statements made are solely the responsibility of the writer.

[1] *See* examples in W. GOODE, WORLD REVOLUTION AND FAMILY PATTERNS (1963); J. Kahl, *Some Social Concomitants of Industrialization and Urbanization,* 18 HUMAN ORGANIZATION 65–69 (1959); G. FOSTER, TRADITIONAL CULTURES 31–34 (1962). For statements that the extended to nuclear change may not be rapid in all situations *see* M. Cohen, *Variations in Complexity among Chinese Family Groups: The Impact of Modernization,* in 29 TRANSACTIONS OF THE NEW YORK ACADEMY OF SCIENCES, Series II, 638–44 (1967); Joan Aldous, *Urbanization, the Extended Family, and Kinship Ties in West Africa,* 41 SOCIAL FORCES 6–11 (Oct. 1961).

factors studied, but somewhat less emphasized, are the loss of functions by
the family as the state takes over education, health care, and other welfare
facilities; changes in values through Western cultural contact such as emphasis
on increasing independence of the young, on the husband-wife relationship
and the love ethic, and on achievement and decisions on rational grounds
rather than the authority of elders; and changes in law.[2]

This ordering of variables is determined by the nature of the study—a
cross-sectional survey of differences within Taiwan in 1966–67. Since it is not
an historical study, some variation that is found primarily through time and
less across social groups at one time can not be studied in great detail. This
has the advantage of limiting the number of influences on the data and thus
simplifying the analysis, but it also has the disadvantage of preventing us from
making definitive statements about certain variables. In particular, the
cross-sectional analysis permits us to examine the influences of migration,
inheritance, occupational mobility, and bureaucratization of work organization
—variables that vary greatly among individuals within Taiwan today. On the
other hand, it limits our analysis of the effects of law, Western values, and
social welfare benefits. I will examine how these last three variables are related
to class differences, but it should be understood that these may vary less by
social class today than by time over the last fifty years. For example, Westernization of values may have decidedly promoted acceptability of household
division about equally among all groups in the society over the last fifty years,
yet it appears to promote little variation between social classes today. Nevertheless, a clearer delineation of the importance of the first group of variables
in explaining change in household composition should provide a better
understanding of how much variation remains to be explained by these latter
variables.

METHODOLOGY

The research is based on a survey of 487 married males in Tainan, a large
but relatively traditional city; 149 married males in Kaohsiung, a new and
growing industrial city; and 44 married males in a village of approximately
240 households. Males were interviewed in order to examine the effects of
working in larger and more complex organizations. Also, the sample was
limited to natives of Taiwan, so the effects of wartime migration of refugees
from the mainland of China would be excluded, and only the effects of internal
modernization included.

---

[2] For reviews of these various factors such as causes and consequences of family
change see M. LEVY, THE FAMILY REVOLUTION IN MODERN CHINA 273–366 (1949);
W. GOODE, supra note 1, at 1–26, 168–74, 366–80, and passim.; J. Kahl, supra note 1,
at 65–69; M. Zelditch, Jr., Cross Cultural Analysis of Family Structure, in HANDBOOK
OF MARRIAGE AND THE FAMILY 492–97 (H. Christensen ed. 1964); and further references
cited in the detailed discussion below.

Use of the household register in sampling permitted control over the population eventually interviewed. In the two cities an initial systematic sample was taken of the total population. This sample was then divided into twelve strata, and an equal number was sampled from each of the twelve strata in Tainan and from each of the six strata containing large industry employees in Kaohsiung.[3] It was this second sample that was eventually interviewed. Because of the greater homogeneity of population characteristics in the village, the sample selected there was much smaller and was not stratified. However, in order to interview only one male per household and still maintain probability sampling, households were first grouped by number of married males in each, and then a weighted number of households were selected from each size group to obtain the final sample of households.

City samples were stratified in order to provide a large number of cases in all categories when analyzing occupational status, length of residence, and size of work place. This was done by dividing the original sample according to whether the man was in a blue or white collar occupation; had lived in his present home three or fewer years, four to nineteen years, or twenty or more years; and had worked in a business with less than or more than fifty workers. Such stratification permitted me to carry the analysis further than an ordinary sample, in which some table cells are quickly depleted when controls are introduced for more than one variable. It is also superior to quota sampling in that it permitted me to maintain probability sampling and make estimates of total population characteristics.[4] These estimates of total population characteristics are referred to in the text as weighted estimates or weighted percentages. The reader is cautioned that only weighted estimates can be used to describe the total population or compare the total population with other populations. Unweighted tables should not be used for such purposes.

Field work was completed during the period July 1966, to September 1967. I spoke the official language, Mandarin, which could be used in interviews with educated persons; however, most interviews were conducted in the local dialect, Taiwanese. After the initial period of pretesting, college students and college graduates were hired to administer the approximately sixty-five minute interview to the total sample.

Characteristics of Each Study Area

Tainan City is an old city which served as the administrative center of Taiwan from the seventeenth into the nineteenth century. It is still relatively unindustrialized, with only a few large industries growing up on the outskirts

---

[3] This sampling procedure is discussed in L. Kish, Survey Sampling ch. 3 (1965). Kish would refer to this sample as a two stage sample with systematic sampling in the first stage and stratified selection (with equal allocation) in the second stage.

[4] *Id.*, 443-44.

of town which employ workers as much from rural areas as from the city. Its population has grown slowly. At the time of the first census in 1905 it had a population of 50,721; in 1940 it had a population of 139,827; and in 1966 the city proper had a population of 356,489.[5] Although the population is relatively large, probably 75 percent of it is contained in a dense core of no more than four square miles. In both cities it is only this dense core and not the surrounding rural area that was surveyed.

Kaohsiung City, about twenty-five miles to the south of Tainan, is an important port and a growing industrial center with some of the largest industries in Taiwan. It developed into a city much later than Tainan. Before 1920 Kaohsiung City was only a group of villages. By 1920 it had a population of 35,993; in 1940 it had a population of 124,924; and in 1966 the city proper had a population of 513,313.[6] It appears much more Western than Tainan because of its wide, planned thoroughfares, the abundance of new two or three story buildings along these thoroughfares, and the way it is spread out in contrast to the extreme compactness of Tainan. Another less sightly aspect of its recent development is the large blocks of crude shanty towns thrown up by rural migrants in search of city jobs.

The Village is on the agricultural plain to the north of Tainan City. It is about a ten minute walk from bus service which takes one into the nearby market town within five minutes, to Tainan in about forty minutes, and to another large town in a somewhat shorter time. It is also easy to bicycle to the market town or motorcycle to Tainan. A few villagers do such things as peddle fresh meat, cut hair, or run small retail stands in the Village; a few others work at clerical jobs in the nearby market town; and one or two commute to work in Tainan daily, but over 90 percent are busy full time or part time within the Village growing rice, sweet potatoes, sugar cane, and watermelons. The Village is somewhat large with a population of 1,668 in 1966, but this is not extremely large for the region. It is more homogeneous than most villages, with almost 75 percent sharing the same surname, but it is not organized within one lineage.

HOUSEHOLD COMPOSITION IN EACH STUDY AREA

The Village, Tainan City, and Kaohsiung City are progressively more modernized as measured by migration, dependence on agriculture, inheritance of occupations, and size of industry. The proportion of nuclear families

---

[5] By Tainan City proper I mean all precincts except the strictly rural precinct of An-nan. This smaller area is closer to the boundaries used in pre-World War II statistics, though it still includes slightly more rural area than earlier boundaries.

[6] By Kaohsiung City proper I mean all precincts except Tso-ying and Nan-tzu. The remaining precincts come closer to the pre-War area of the city than the present official administrative district, but still contain some rural areas not previously included.

should thus increase, and the proportion of extended or joint families should decrease, moving from Village to Tainan City to Kaohsiung City. This can be seen from the weighted distribution of various household types shown in Table 1. Definitions of the five household types shown in Table 1 are as follows:

1. Nuclear: A husband and wife pair possibly with unmarried children and unmarried siblings, but no other coresident kin. There was only one nuclear household that included unmarried siblings and no other kin; this household was in Tainan city. Only currently married men were interviewed, so no households with just the husband or just the wife alone are included.

2. Stem: A father or mother living together with only one married son or daughter. The married daughter is included to allow for situations in which a male heir has married into the family.

3. Fraternal joint: Two or more married brothers living together with no members of the parental generation present.

4. Paternal joint: One or both parents living together with two or more married sons.

5. Other: Households that do not fit types two through four, but which include other kin. Single individuals were not included in the study.

I will refer to non-nuclear households also—types two through five—as composite or complex households. The term extended household has been used in both a restricted sense to refer only to joint households and a looser sense to refer to both stem and joint households. Here I will use it in the looser sense.

The proportion of nuclear and composite households in each area does vary according to the predictions (see Table 1).[7] The number of nuclear households increases sharply from Village to Tainan to Kaohsiung. The major decline in composite families is in the proportion of joint families in the village as opposed to the two cities. This means that brothers are much more likely to live in the same house in the village than in either city. There is also a great decline in the proportion of households with coresident parents—that is in the proportion of paternal joint plus stem households—but the proportion of stem families alone varies little between each area.

------

[7] The cities are predicted to have more nuclear families than the village, only because they are more modernized in the sense of having more migration, industry, and occupational mobility and not because they are cities per se. Sjoberg claims that preindustrial cities have a larger proportion of extended families than preindustrial villages. G. SJOBERG, THE PREINDUSTRIAL CITY ch. 6 (1960).

TABLE 1

WEIGHTED PERCENTAGES OF HOUSEHOLD TYPES IN EACH SAMPLE AREA

| | | Household Type* | | | | | Number of Households |
	Nuclear	Stem	Fraternal Joint	Paternal Joint	Other	Total	
Village	18	25	14	43	0	100	(44)
Tainan	58	25	5	9	3	100	(358)†
Kaohsiung‡	79	15	0	2	4	100	(148)

 * See definition of household types in text. Household refers to a residential unit rather than a corporate economic or legal unit.

 † August and September Tainan interviews excluded questions on household composition and are, thus, excluded from household tables.

 ‡ In this and all following tables Kaohsiung City refers only to employees in factories employing 100 or more persons. However, because size of work place has little effect on kin relations, the situation of large industry employees may be fairly representative of the total population of Kaohsiung, which is also quite migratory.

In order to shorten the time of each interview and because I was not planning a detailed consideration of households at the time, respondents were only asked whether various kin lived in the same house. They were not asked whether they ate or cooked with these relatives, nor whether the household was still legally one or had been divided. Because of this the results here will show slightly more complex households than found in other studies. I believe the analysis still defensible, however, because the results will be roughly comparable—indicating the manner in which a more detailed investigation should be designed—and because the residential unit may be just as significant for some social phenomena as the more narrowly defined household. For example, that a child has a grandmother and aunts in the same house may be just as significant for the socialization of that child as having these same kin eat with and share a budget with the parents. Also, a brother in the same house may have almost as much effect on adult attitude formation as a brother sharing the same table and budget.

The extent to which the residential criterion overestimates the proportion of complex households—that is, stem and joint households—is seen when Table 1 and Table 2 are compared.[8] Each of the studies in Table 2, except

---

 [8] There are dangers in cross-sectional comparison of results within and between Tables 1 and 2. Normal sequences in the developmental cycle of extended families will produce a certain proportion of nuclear households at any one time. Therefore, finding a large or small proportion of nuclear households in a population without any further knowledge tells us little about the number of families that will pass through an extended stage once given the opportunity. The opportunity is not present for those families

the first and possibly the last, define the household as the corporate eating and budget unit. The first four studies in Table 2, all for rural areas, report much higher percentages of nuclear households and much lower percentages of complex households than found for the Village in Table 1. The Gallin study suffers from the use of government household register distinctions, which are frequently only approximate, but the Wang, Cohen, and Smythe studies use survey data to delineate as a household those eating together and sharing a common budget. This comparison of present study results with other studies shows that the use of the coresidence criterion alone grossly overstates the proportion of complex households in the Village compared to other definitions of the household.

TABLE 2*

PERCENTAGE OF FAMILY TYPES IN STUDIES FROM TAIWAN AND MAINLAND CHINA

	Nuclear	Stem	Joint	Single Person or Other	Total	Number of Families
Taiwan:						
Gallin, 1959	66	29	5	0	100	(99)
Wang, 1962	57	33	6	4	100	(105)
Cohen, 1965	44	24	32	0	100	(68)
Mainland China:						
Smythe: Rural, 1928–33	34	63		3	100	(2422)
Smythe: Urban, c. 1930	48	44		7	99	(2027)
Ch'iao, 1928–33	63	35		2	100	(37647)

* *Source :* B. GALLIN, HSIN HSING, TAIWAN 137–38 (1966); J. Wang, 篇補選簡中草 一青菲支 (The rural family on Taiwan: illustrated by a survey of two villages), 6 TAIPEI WEN HSIEN (Taipei Historical Journal) 32 (1963); M. Cohen, *Variations in Complexity Among Chinese Family Groups : The Impact of Modernization,* 29 TRANSACTIONS OF THE NEW YORK ACADEMY OF SCIENCES, SERIES II, 638–44 (March 1967); L. Smythe, *The Composition of the Chinese Family,* 5 CHIN-LING HSUEH-PAO (Nanking journal) No. 1, at Table 6 (1935); C. Ch'iao & C. Wang, *Jen-kou* (Population), in CHUNG-KUO CHING-CHI NIEN-CH'IEN (Chinese economic annual) Sec. 2, at B5 (3rd ed. 1936).

---

that do not produce male heirs or that lose the father before marriage of the sons. The opportunity to form an extended family is conditioned by death rates, ages at marriage, birth intervals, and total fertility. Since the three sample areas are approximately the same in the above respects, comparison among them is relatively safe. There is more danger in the comparison of areas at different levels of industrialization such as those these in Table 2. We await the development of a model that will permit control of areas extraneous factors.

See K. Morioka, *Life Cycle Patterns in Japan, China, and the United States,* 29 JOURNAL OF MARRIAGE AND THE FAMILY 595–606 (1967); H. Gould, *Lucknow Rickshawallas : The Social Organization of an Occupational Category,* 6 INTERNATIONAL JOURNAL OF COMPARATIVE SOCIOLOGY 37–45 (March 1965); M. Levy, Jr., *Aspects of the Analysis of Family Structure,* in ASPECTS OF THE ANALYSIS OF FAMILY STRUCTURE 1–63 (A. Coale *et al.,* eds. 1965).

On the other hand, comparison of the one urban area in Table 2 with Tainan and Kaohsiung indicates that the coresidence criterion may not seriously overestimate the proportion of economically and legally corporate households in the city. (The Smythe study, for example, actually reports a larger proportion of stem and joint families, 44 percent, than is found in Tainan, 39 percent, or Kaohsiung, 17 percent.) There are dangers in this comparison because of the difference in time and because Smythe sampled poorer areas of Nanking city, which at the time would be expected to have fewer complex households than other areas; however, there are additional reasons for thinking that the coresidence criterion will not cause serious overestimation of complex households in cities. Coresident brothers are more likely to have separate budgets and separate eating arrangements than a coresident father and son. Joint families, with coresident brothers, predominate in the Village; stem families, with a coresident father and son but no coresident brothers, are the predominant non-nuclear form in cities. Thus, it is likely that most urban non-nuclear households are corporate units. Since the coresidence criterion accords more with other definitions of the household in cities than in villages, only urban households have been used in the analysis of factors causing changes in household composition.

The last row of Table 2 by Ch'iao is also predominantly for rural areas, including sample districts over most of agricultural China. In spite of including the rural data used by Smythe, Ch'iao reports a large proportion of nuclear families—a proportion more similar to present day Taiwan percentages than to Smythe's results. One difficulty with Ch'iao's figures is that he does not say exactly how his household types are defined. I have tentatively placed them in the nuclear and the combined stem and joint categories, but he only terms his types "small" and "large." His figures are reported here only to caution about generalizing from Smythe's smaller sample until more information can be obtained on Ch'iao's figures for all of agricultural China.[9]

Another issue that must be considered concerns the influence of parents on the coresidence of brothers; if the existence of parents has a strong effect on whether brothers live together, then this must be controlled for in the tables that follow. The traditional pattern was for all brothers to live together until the father died; the pattern for living together while only the mother remained alive was less definite.[10] The number of households in the village sample is so small that the figures in Table 3 are unreliable; however, comparison of parts a, b, and c of the table indicates that in the Village the traditional pattern is followed. While the father is alive, no nuclear households are found; when

---

[9] Smythe's rural data are from four sample districts that were later included in Ch'iao's data from 100 sample districts. These data are all part of the study reported in J. BUCK, LAND UTILIZATION IN CHINA (1938).

[10] M. FREEDMAN, LINEAGE ORGANIZATION IN SOUTHEASTERN CHINA 21 (1958).

only the mother is alive, 14 percent of the households are nuclear; and when neither parent is alive, about 28 percent of the households are nuclear. In the urban areas, on the other hand, there is about the same or a smaller proportion of nuclear households present when only the mother is alive as when the father is alive.[11] As in the Village, the largest proportion of nuclear families is found when both parents are dead, but in both cities when either parent is alive, there is still a large proportion of households with sons living separately. This is seen when the total proportion of fraternal and paternal joint families in parts a, b, and c of Table 3 are compared. In Kaohsiung there are few joint families even when parents are alive, but in Tainan there is a drop from 17 or 20 percent, when at least one parent is alive, to 7 percent when neither parent is alive. Thus, the traditional preference for joint residence of sons, at least until the father dies, is followed less closely in the cities than in the Village. Nevertheless, in Tainan the presence or absence of parents does have some effect and must be controlled for in the tables that follow.

TABLE 3

WEIGHTED PERCENTAGES OF HOUSEHOLD TYPES IN EACH SAMPLE AREA WHEN
FATHER ALIVE, MOTHER ALONE ALIVE, OR NEITHER PARENT ALIVE*

	Nuclear	Stem	Fraternal Joint	Paternal Joint	Other	Total	Number of Households
a. Father alive							
Village	0[†]	22[†]	0[†]	78[†]	0[†]	100	(9)
Tainan	49	29	3	14	5	100	(138)
Kaohsiung	79	14	0	3	3	99	(68)
b. Mother alone alive							
Village	14	14	7	64	0	99	(14)
Tainan	45	36	2	18	0	101	(93)
Kaohsiung	70	22	0	4	4	100	(36)
c. Neither parent alive							
Village	32	0	21	47	0	100	(19)
Tainan	84	7	7	0	3	101	(109)
Kaohsiung	92	3	0	0	5	100	(38)

* Households of all respondents except those that married matrilocally.

† Percentages are based on a small number of households and are, therefore, only approximate.

[11] Since in urban areas the presence of the mother is just as important as that of the father, in urban tables below, I have controlled only for whether either parent is alive or both dead.

One further methodological issue concerns men who marry matrilocally.[12] Those marrying matrilocally will be affected differently by modernization than those marrying patrilocally or neolocally. The male marrying matrilocally necessarily migrates when he marries; therefore, tables analyzing the effect of migration on other forms of marriage would be misleading if matrilocal marriage respondents were included. The male marrying matrilocally generally does not inherit his father's property but rather takes over his father-in-law's property. To include him in tables relating inheritance of father's property and family relations would obscure the relationship. Because of these complications, they have been dropped from the analysis below.

During the interview we did not ask whether the respondent had married matrilocally, since most people would not like to say openly that they had so married. Matrilocal marriages were thus determined by examining whether the respondent lived with his wife's parents as opposed to his own parents or with his wife's siblings as opposed to his own siblings. Among those respondents on whom we have sufficient information to determine the type of marriage, 2 percent of the villagers, 5 percent of those in Tainan City, and 1 percent of those in Kaohsiung City had married matrilocally.[13] The small number of matrilocal marriages found in Kaohsiung may indicate that the procedure used underestimates the number of such marriages among the highly migrant. On the other hand, the Tainan City figure seems consistent with the 2 to 10 percent of matrilocal marriages in official vital statistics during the last thirty years when most of the respondents were getting married.[14]

MIGRATION

One major variable purported to be associated both with modernization and family change is migration. Better paying jobs in cities and increased pressure on the land, as a result of population growth associated with improved health measures, produce a movement from rural to urban areas. The ever larger number of professional, technical, and other white collar employees, who

---

[12] Matrilocal marriage is socially disapproved, and there is only a small number of such marriages today. In 1906, 21.8 percent of all Taiwanese marriages were matrilocal; in 1935, 9.8 percent; and in 1943, 6.2 percent. In 1966 only 1.9 percent of all marriages in Taiwan were matrilocal. T'AIWAN SHENG HSING-CHENG CHANG-KUAN, T'UNG-CHI SHIH, T'AIWAN WU-SHIH-I NIEN LAI T'UNG-CHI T'I-YAO (Fifty-one year summary of Taiwan statistics) Table 65 (1946). Republic of China, Taiwan Provincial Government, Department of Civil Affairs, 2 MONTHLY BULLETIN OF POPULATION REGISTRATION STATISTICS OF TAIWAN Table 6 (Feb. 1967).

[13] There was one person in the Village, forty-four persons in Tainan, and four in Kaohsiung for whom there was insufficient information to determine the type of marriage. These were included as non-matrilocal marriages.

[14] See note 13 supra.

frequently migrate between jobs, also produces more migration.[15] Further, since technical innovations are introduced more rapidly with industrialization, people frequently migrate from old jobs in outmoded fields to new jobs.

There are two types of migration within Taiwan that should be distinguished. One occurs when the male goes to the city to work while leaving his wife and children at home with his father's family. Extended families, when they exist in the village, are little affected by this type of migration. The second type of migration occurs when the husband takes his wife and children to the city where he is working. Unless the man moves his parents or brothers as well, a new nuclear family is formed in the city, and unless married brothers are left behind, any extended household in the village is dissolved.[16] The data below refer only to the second form of migration. Men living in the city without their families were not interviewed, since they tend to remain registered in their home village and cannot be located from the urban household register. Families of a few such absent men were found in the Village, but the men were not there to be interviewed. Also, in the discussion below, only moves between cities or village and city are considered migration. Moves within the same city or within the same village are not called migration.

There are three hypotheses implying a negative relationship between migration and the presence of extended households. One asserts that economic pressure causes people who would otherwise remain in extended families to move to another locale. This economic pressure may be lack of land, or job, or the desire to raise one's occupational status by taking a job in a new locality, particularly in an urban area. Such migration weakens extended families. When the move is from a rural area, there will usually remain some family members who continue to till the land. Also, it is unlikely that jobs for all members of an extended family can be found in one city at one time. Therefore, unless household division has already occurred, migration means a new nuclear family is established at the place of destination and at the point of origin, except where other married brothers are left behind. Migration of

---

[15] For data on the occupational distribution of migration *see* J. LANSING & E. MUELLER, THE GEOGRAPHIC MOBILITY OF LABOR 48 (1967). But also note that Bogue reports that exceptions to this occupational distribution of migration can be found. D. Bogue, *Internal Migration,* in THE STUDY OF POPULATION 504 (P. Hauser & O. Duncan eds. 1959).

[16] Not all migrants from the village to the city migrate out of stem or joint family units. That is, some were initially in nuclear families. Indeed one hypothesis is that those beginning in nuclear families are more likely to migrate than those in more complex families. The data in Tables 1 and 2 above show that if the coresidence criterion is used, most village households are stem or joint. However, if the economic or eating unit criterion is used, then in two of the three villages reported the majority of households are nuclear—though, possibly most individuals still live in the larger stem and joint households.

this type is one of the most frequently cited causes of the dissolution of extended families during modernization.[17]

This first hypothesis assumes that people want to live in an extended family and would do so if they could. A second hypothesis is that social relations within the extended family are often stressful and that some people will leave once they have a viable alternative. This alternative is provided by new jobs in the city. Migration then becomes an escape route for the person who wishes to form an independent nuclear family.[18] Migration thus does not result in the reluctant breakup of the extended family; rather, migration is the result of an attempt to form a nuclear family. Both hypotheses produce a negative relationship between migration and the proportion of extended families. Therefore, finding such a relationship will not allow us to choose between these two hypotheses. Moreover, migration may involve both these motivations at the same time; that is, migrants may be both eager to find a better paying job and somewhat happy to be out on their own away from other extended family members. Available evidence suggests that the economic motivation tends to be the more dominant one. Increasing population makes it more difficult to maintain a living off the land while, at the same time, urban jobs tend to pay more and to be more prestigious. The influence of these factors is seen both in the desire by fathers for some or all of their sons to take nonagricultural jobs and in the listing by migrants of economic considerations as the most important motivation in their move.[19] More refined research on motivations for migration in developing countries may help decide between these two

---

[17] *See* M. LEVY, *supra* note 2, at 313, 319; W. GOODE, *supra* note 1, at 369; R. DORE, CITY LIFE IN JAPAN 112-13 (1958); J. Kahl, *supra* note 1, at 59-61, 65-69; M. Nimkoff & R. Middleton, *Types of Family and Types of Economy,* 66 AMERICAN JOURNAL OF SOCIOLOGY, 215-25 (1960); W. MOORE, SOCIAL CHANGE 102 (1963); E. BURGESS & H. LOCKE, THE FAMILY 523-54 (1945).

[18] M. LEVY, *supra* note 2, at 313. Stress in the extended family appears most strongly in father-son competition, brother-brother competition, and mother-in-law/daughter-in-law hostility. *See* M. FREEDMAN, *supra* note 10, at 21-32; M. FREEDMAN, CHINESE LINEAGE AND SOCIETY 44-48 (1966); and, for a general account, W. GOODE, THE FAMILY 50-55 (1964).

[19] Evidence for fathers desiring some or all of their sons to go into nonagricultural occupations in Taiwan comes from informal discussion and from unpublished results of a study of villagers by the Joint Commission on Rural Reconstruction. In this study, 41 percent wanted all their sons to go into nonagricultural occupations, while 44 percent wanted at least one of their sons to go into a nonagricultural occupation. The predominant reasons given for such desires were the lack of land and the possibility of a higher standard of living in other occupations. I am grateful to Mr. T. L. Lin for this data. Published results appear in Y. C. TSUI & T. L. LIN, A STUDY OF RURAL LABOR MOBILITY IN RELATION TO INDUSTRIALIZATION AND URBANIZATION IN TAIWAN (Economic Digest Series No. 16, 1964).

Mr. Alden Speare reports on the basis of unpublished data for migrants in Taichung, Taiwan that economic motivation is cited more frequently than any other.

hypotheses, but the final answer will also depend on whether one views extended family relations as essentially benign or stressful.[20]

There is yet a third hypothesis implying a negative relationship between extended families and migration. This hypothesis is that extended families inhibit migration through either mutual affection or the authority of elders. Only those people not living in extended families migrate freely.[21] A counter proposition to this is that extended families promote migration by permitting trial migration. The person who is already married can go to the city by himself to try out various jobs, knowing that his wife and children will be safe in the village with the larger family. Even if the migrant is not yet married, having a family to fall back on can make him more willing to accept the risk of trying a new job in the city.[22] Data in this study are relevant to the first two hypotheses above, but not to these last two hypotheses. This is so because we have information only on household composition at the time of survey and after the time of migration. In order to test these hypotheses it would be necessary to have information on family structure before the time of migration. One could then observe whether those with strong extended family ties migrated as frequently, less than, or more than those without such ties.[23]

The first three hypotheses above suggest a strongly negative relationship between migration and extended families. There are, however, two other hypotheses stating that under certain conditions, migration may strengthen extended families rather than lead to their dissolution. The first of these says that some migration is motivated by the desire to rejoin kin already living in a different locale.[24] The second holds that even when economic motivation is uppermost in the decision to move, persons will tend to go where there is

---

[20] For an example of this difference in view compare the writings of Francis L. K. Hsu and Maurice Freedman. Their differences are summarized in M. FREEDMAN, *supra* note 18, at 155–59.

[21] T. Parsons, *The Kinship System of the Contemporary United States,* in ESSAYS IN SOCIOLOGICAL THEORY 191–92 (T. Parsons ed. 1954).

[22] This proposition was suggested to me by David K. Jordan. It is in accord with patterns observed in Taiwan and described in part by Gallin in this volume, in Africa as described by Solien de Gonzales, and in America as described by Tilly and Brown. N. Solien de Gonzales, *Family Organization in Five Types of Migratory Wage Labor,* 63 AMERICAN ANTHROPOLOGIST, 1264–81 (1961). C. Tilly & Cc. Brown, *On Uprooting, Kinship and the Auspices of Migration,* 8 INTERNATIONAL JOURNAL OF COMPARATIVE SOCIOLOGY 139–64 (Sept. 1967).

[23] One might ask, but receive a less accurate response, about intent to move; however, so few people said they planned to move during pretests that this question was dropped. Another way to find out about the effects of family ties on migration is to ask whether such considerations as leaving kin behind would hinder one's taking a better job in another city; however, this question was so difficult for respondents to answer in pretests that it too was dropped.

[24] *See* J. LANSING & E. MUELLER, *supra* note 15, at 126.

already a close kin or former extended family member.[25] Empirical studies show that even in the United States presence of kin in a particular city can condition one's moving to that city as opposed to some other city, that kin are important sources of information in making a move, and that kin help orient the mover once he gets to the new location. The aid of kin is greatest for those of the lower social class with ascriptive orientations.[26] From these data one can hypothesize that in Taiwan, where ascriptive orientations are still strong, members of the extended family and kin would be used in migration and, in particular, brothers would tend to follow one another to the same city. Although the initial effect of migration would be to separate members of the extended family, with the passage of time the extended family should tend to reform in the city.[27] To the extent that these two propositions are true, the negative relation between migration and extended families will be weakened; further, these will be a positive relation between the length of time migrants have been resident in a city and the proportion of extended families among these migrants.

In the analysis below migrants are defined as persons who reside in a city different from that where they grew up and nonmigrants are defined as persons who reside in the same city where they grew up. (The place where a person grew up is defined as the place where he lived from time of birth to age sixteen.) First, the effects of having moved away from the place where one grew up and, second, the effects of the length of stay in the present city of residence will be examined.

TABLE 4

PERCENTAGE OF HOUSEHOLD TYPE AND PLACE WHERE RESPONDENT GREW UP*

Household Type	Parents Alive		Parents Dead	
	Grew up In the City	Grew up Outside the City	Grew up In the City	Grew up Outside the City
Nuclear	31.2	75.8	82.3	90.8
Stem	44.5	13.5	5.1	3.1
Fraternal joint	2.5	2.8	8.9	0
Paternal joint	19.7	4.5	0	0
Other	1.9	3.4	3.8	6.2
Total	99.8	100.0	100.1	100.1
Number of households	(157)	(178)	(79)	(65)

* Households of urban respondents not marrying matrilocally.

---

[25] Id., 132, 224–32. C. Tilly & C. Brown, supra note 22.

[26] These data are ably summarized in C. Tilly & C. Brown, supra note 22.

[27] For data on this tendency in Africa see W. GOODE, supra note 1, at 190.

The relationship between place where one grew up and household composition is shown in Table 4. From the two left-hand columns we see that as long as one or more parents are alive there is a strong relationship between migration and household type. Those who grew up within the city live predominantly in stem and joint households, whereas those who grew up outside the city live predominantly in nuclear households. This indicates that city life by itself does not greatly reduce the propensity to live in stem or joint households but, rather, that the low proportion of city dwellers in complex households is to a great extent the result of migrants in the city who have left their kin behind. Whether this is the sole factor reducing the number of complex households in cities as opposed to the Village will be examined in greater detail below.

Before going on to these points, we should note the two right-hand columns of Table 4 show that when both parents are dead there is almost no difference between households of those growing up within and without the city. This is in accord with our previous observation from Table 3 that when neither parent is alive urban respondents do not live with brothers but alone. The strong negative relationship between migration and complex households that was predicted above is, then, found in Taiwan at least while parents are alive. As suggested above, whether one concludes from this relationship that economic incentives force people to migrate away from extended families, that persons who want to get away from the stresses of extended family life migrate, or that a combination of motives is involved in migration depends on external evidence. This evidence tends to favor the explanation that economic motivations are predominant. Whether migration is sufficient to explain all variation between village and city in household composition is examined further below.

One method of determining whether migration and the resulting physical separation accounts for all or most of the differences in household composition between village and city is to examine just those parents and brothers living in the same city or village. In this manner one considers only those kin with whom there is the immediate opportunity of living together.[28] In Table 5 when the percentage of all parents who are coresident is compared with the percentage of parents in the same city or village who are coresident, we see, first, that migration accounts for almost all variation between Tainan and Kaohsiung and, second, that migration accounts for almost half, but not all, of the variation between the Village and Tainan. This is seen most clearly in the second half of the table, which shows that when only those parents in the same city or village are included the difference between the Village and Tainan is reduced from 37 percent to 22 percent, while the difference between

---

[28] In these two cities almost all jobs in the city are within easy commuting distance. Therefore, two brothers with jobs on opposite ends of the city could live together without great hardship.

Tainan and Kaohsiung is reduced from 30 percent to 5 percent. The difference between urban areas is then almost completely because of variation in migration. The difference between rural and urban areas is also heavily influenced by migration, but a sizable difference still remains that must be explained by other factors such as those discussed below. Of course, the

TABLE 5

WEIGHTED PERCENTAGE OF PARENTS CORESIDENT IN EACH SAMPLE AREA*

	Percentage of All Parents Who are Coresident	Percentage of Parents in Same City or Village Who are Coresident
Village	87	91
	(23)†	(22)
Tainan	50	69
	(334)	(232)
Kaohsiung	20	64
	(111)	(34)
Village—Tainan: Percentage difference	37	22
Tainan—Kaohsiung: Percentage difference	30	5

* Parents of respondents not marrying matrilocally.

† Numbers in parentheses are total number of parents on which percentages to left and above are based.

difference here is only in the proportion of coresident parents. We know from above that the coresidence criterion overstates the proportion of economically and legally joint units more in villages than in cities. One quite possibly would find that once migration was controlled for there would be no difference between urban and rural areas in economic and legal ties between parents and adult children. This present table only shows that the opportunities for frequent interaction and sharing between parents and adult children is still higher in rural than urban areas even after the effects of migration are controlled. Other factors necessary to explain the remainder of this difference are examined in the next section.

A similar control for migration can be applied to figures for coresident brothers. When this is done, however, the percentage differences between village and city and between the two cities are not reduced but rather increased (see Table 6). The comparison between Tainan and Kaohsiung is not conclusive since the proportion of parents alive and in the same city—which influences the percentage of brothers who live together—is not the same for both places. In Tainan 56 percent of all respondents have parents alive and in the same city, but in Kaohsiung only 25 percent of all respondents have parents alive and in the same city. Were the proportion in Kaohsiung higher, the percentage of coresident brothers there might well be as high as in Tainan. On the other hand, since the percentage of respondents with parents alive and in the same city is quite similar in Tainan and the Village—56 percent and 65 percent—comparison between them is more conclusive. This comparison shows that migration, rather than creating a difference between rural and urban areas, has reduced the difference between these two areas. This is not because migration has no effect, but because it reduces the percentage of coresident brothers more in the Village than in Tainan. This is seen by comparing right- and left-hand columns in the top half of Table 6. For both the Village and Tainan when migration is controlled in the right-hand column, the percentage of coresident brothers is higher than when migration is not controlled in the left-hand column, but it is much higher in the Village than in Tainan. The reason for the greater effect in the Village is not that more

TABLE 6

WEIGHTED PERCENTAGE OF MARRIED BROTHERS CORESIDENT
IN EACH SAMPLE AREA*

	Percentage of All Brothers Who are Coresident	Percentage of Brothers in Same City or Village Who are Coresident
Village	40	73
	(75)†	(41)
Tainan	17	27
	(733)	(434)
Kaohsiung	4	9
	(212)	(73)
Village—Tainan: Percentage difference	23	46
Tainan—Kaohsiung: Percentage difference	13	18

* Married brothers of respondents not marrying matrilocally.
† Numbers in parentheses are total number of brothers on which percentages to left and above are based.

Village than Tainan brothers are living in other places—45 percent of Village brothers are outside the Village and 41 percent of Tainan brothers are outside the city—but, rather, that there is a greater propensity for brothers to be coresident when they are within the Village than within Tainan—73 percent of brothers within the Village are coresident, while only 27 percent of brothers within Tainan are coresident. Thus, migration only slightly reduces the proportion of coresident brothers in the city. It has a much greater effect on the Village with the result that it actually reduces rather than increases rural-urban differences. The explanation of the low percentage of coresident brothers in the city must be sought in factors other than migration. Some of these other sources are examined in the following sections.

Before looking at other sources of variation we should, however, consider whether the separating force of migration tends to be reduced over time as kin rejoin one another in the same city. It was noted above that Western studies show kin tend to follow one another to a new location; however, the strong negative relationship observed among urban respondents between growing up outside the city and complex households suggests that this tendency to rejoin kin in a new location can be no more than a very weak counter-trend. This is confirmed in Table 7, in which the residence of parents is compared with the number of years the migrant has lived in the city. From the first row in this table we see that the proportion of coresident parents does not increase regularly with length of time in the city. Yet, by observing the third row in the same table we see that the proportion of parents outside the city is higher for those who have been in the city less than twenty years than for those in the city twenty years or more. This means that while those who have been in the city twenty years or more have more opportunity to live with their parents, this opportunity is only slightly used. This is conditioned by a slight tendency for coresidence with those parents in the same city to decrease with age. Inspection of tables not shown here indicates that this tendency for coresidence with parents to decline with age applies to respondents growing up both within and without the city.

TABLE 7

Proximity of Parents by Respondent's Years of Residence in the City and Where Respondent Grew Up*

Percentage of Parents	Grew Up Outside the City: Year of Residence in the City					Grew Up in the City
	0–3	4–9	10–19	20–25	27+	
Coresident	27.8	15.5	12.5	28.6	23.8	66.5
In the same city	0.0	9.9	4.6	20.0	28.6	27.8
Elsewhere	72.2	74.6	83.0	51.4	47.6	5.7
Total	100.0	100.0	100.1	100.0	100.0	100.0
Number of parents	(18)	(71)	(88)	(35)	(21)	(212)

* Parents of urban respondents not marrying matrilocally. If both parents are living at the same address they are counted once. If both are living but are resident at different addresses they are counted separately. There are seventeen instances of parents living at separate addresses.

Tables for coresidence with brothers by length of time in the city were also inspected and found to follow a similar pattern. The proportion of married brothers inside the same city steadily increases, but the proportion of coresident brothers only slightly increases from 0 to 7 percent. The opportunity for coresidence with brothers increases even more steadily than for parents. Yet, as with parents, the opportunity is only slightly used.

In summary, those who leave a village, town, or other city in search of a better economic position, in an effort to get away from kin, or from a combination of these motives no longer have the opportunity that native residents of Tainan and Kaohsiung have to live with parents. Even though these migrants may eventually bring or be followed by their parents to Tainan or Kaohsiung, less than half of these parents will ever come; therefore, there is a strongly negative relationship between being a migrant to Tainan or Kaohsiung and living in a household with one's parents. That the low proportion of urban households with coresident parents is mostly a result of these migrants without parents in the city, can be seen by examining only those respondents with parents in the city. When this is done, the difference between the village and cities is cut in half; this indicates that the lower proportion of coresident parents in the city is not the result simply of unique conditions of city life, but at least equally of peculiar problems of the migrant who is not a native of the city and, thus, often less exposed than the native to "urban influences" throughout his life.

On the other hand coresidence with brothers in urban areas is only slightly affected by migration and more by aspects of urban life not yet examined. Those who migrate to Tainan or Kaohsiung do leave their brothers behind and are only slowly joined by these brothers in the city; however, even those who grow up in Tainan or Kaohsiung are only slightly more likely than migrants to have their brothers in the same house. The fact that natives of Tainan and Kaohsiung are much less likely than villagers to live with brothers cannot be attributed to migration or the reduced opportunity for coresidency with brothers. In fact, migration has just the opposite effect, reducing rather than increasing the difference between city and village. This is so not because more brothers migrate from the village than the city, but because those brothers outside the village had a greater propensity for coresidency than those outside the city.

INHERITANCE OF THE MEANS OF LIVELIHOOD

A second aspect of modernization frequently mentioned as responsible for family change is the decline in inheritance of the means of livelihood.[29] Inheritance of the means of livelihood occurs when a father passes on to his

---

[29] *See* M. Zelditch, *supra* note 2, at 492–97; M. Nimkoff & R. Middleton, *supra* note 17, at 215–25; M. Levy, *supra* note 2, at 321.

son a farm, cattle, a business, or in some professions a clientele. Professions increase with industrialization but do not offset the decrease in the number of farmers and independent businessmen.[30] If sons are not dependent on the father for their livelihood and do not spend long periods of time with him, it is predicted that they will act independently of their father and be inclined to move into a household by themselves.

Presently, in Taiwan very few urban residents have inherited occupations from their fathers. In the Village 80 percent of the respondents inherited their father's land, but in Tainan a weighted proportion of only 5 percent have inherited their occupation. Further, among Kaohsiung workers none have inherited their occupation. Because of the small number of urban respondents inheriting their means of livelihood, my analysis of this influence is somewhat tentative pending a larger sample of cases. Also, because of the small number of non-inheritors in the Village and the way Village inheritance is intermixed with such factors as nonmigration, I will discuss only the effects of inheritance in the city and not in the Village.

We see from the left-hand column of Table 8 that as long as one or more parents are alive and as long as no control for migration is introduced there is a definite relationship between inheritance and living in a composite household.

TABLE 8

PERCENTAGE OF COMPOSITE HOUSEHOLDS BY INHERITANCE
OF MEANS OF LIVELIHOOD*

Means of Livelihood	Parents Alive	Parents Alive and Respondent Grew Up in City
Inherited	83.3	83.3
	(12)†	(12)
Not inherited	43.5	66.9
	(322)	(144)

* Urban households of respondents not marrying matrilocally.

† Numbers in parentheses are the total number of households on which the percentages to the left and above are based.

The difference between inheritors and non-inheritors is large—40 percent—and, in spite of the small number of inheritors, statistically significant. However, when we control for migration in the right-hand column by examining only those growing up in the city, the relationship is reduced by more than

---

[30] The percentage of wage and salary earners in a society is positively correlated with the level of economic development of the society. See W. Moore, Change in Occupational Structures, in SOCIAL STRUCTURE AND MOBILITY IN ECONOMIC DEVELOPMENT 211 (N. Smelser & S. Lipset eds. 1966).

half. Again the number of inheriting households is so small that our conclusions are tentative, but it appears that nonmigrant inheritors are only slightly more likely to live in composite households than nonmigrants who have not inherited their occupation. This is even more so when the residence of parents alone is considered.

The left-hand columns of Table 9 also show that as long as no control for migration is introduced inheritance is mildly related to parents living in the same city and the same house. Forty percent of parents of non-inheritors live in the same house whereas 64 percent of parents of inheritors live in the same

TABLE 9

RESIDENCE OF PARENTS BY INHERITANCE OF MEANS OF LIVELIHOOD AND
WHERE RESPONDENT GREW UP*

Percentage of Parents in Each Place	All Parents: Means of Livelihood		Parents of Respondents Who Grew Up in City: Means of Livelihood	
	Not Inherited	Inherited	Not Inherited	Inherited
In the same house	40.3	64.3	66.3	66.7
Elsewhere in the same city	18.4	28.6	27.6	33.3
Outside the city	41.3	7.1	6.0	0.0
Total	100.0	100.0	99.9	100.0
Number of parents	(429)	(14)	(199)	(12)

* Parents of urban respondents not marrying matrilocally.

house. Also as above, when migration is controlled by examining only those parents of respondents growing up within the city, the relationship disappears. The right-hand column shows that there is no difference between these two groups of inheritors and non-inheritors.

These two tables, then, indicate the following: Persons who have migrated to the city, even more than other city dwellers, tend either to have had nothing to inherit or to have given up the opportunity to take over their father's land, store, or local clientele. Thus, very few migrants are inheritors. When this group, who tends not to inherit and not to have parents in the city, is excluded, we find that non-inheritors who do not migrate are just as likely as inheritors to live with parents. Therefore, in the city inheritance does not have the predicted effect of increasing parental control over children so that children will stay in the same house. If inheritance has any effect at all, it is only to keep sons who wish to inherit in the same city. These sons who stay in the same city are then more likely to live with parents than those who move to other places, though no more likely to do so than other sons who do not migrate out of the city.

On the other hand, even including the intermediate influence of migration, the relationship between inheritance and coresidence with married brothers is weak to nonexistent. Although only 11 percent of the 985 married brothers of non-inheriting respondents are coresident, still only 22 percent of the 32 brothers of inheriting respondents are coresident. This is not a significant difference.[31] The fact that one son inherits his father's business or occupation in an urban area does not make it very likely that his brother will have also inherited the business or occupation and be living in the same house.

In summary, inheritance of the means of livelihood is rare in Taiwan cities today and, thus, an insignificant force in keeping households together. From the small number of cases available here, it appears that inheritance will cause parents and children to live together more frequently, but the inheritance does not alter the relationship of those staying in the same city by making sons more subservient to fathers—it simply keeps sons in the same city. Non-inheriting sons who have stayed in the city are just as likely to live with parents as inheriting sons in the same city. At the same time, inheritance seems to have little or no effect on whether urban brothers live together. That one brother inherits his father's occupation does not mean that other brothers will also inherit the same occupation and stay in the same household to carry out that occupation. Inheritance of urban occupations, then, does not have as much unifying force for the total family as inheritance of farm land by villagers is reputed to have.

Occupational Mobility and Status Differences

A third aspect of modernization reputedly associated with household composition is occupational mobility. The hypothesized association between occupational mobility and the dissolution of extended households is stated in two different ways.[32] On the one hand, occupational mobility is seen as causing disruption of the extended family. It is predicted that with industrialization kin are more frequently found in different occupational statuses. The differing life styles and the unwillingness of those better off to contribute unequally to the maintenance of the family then cause the extended household to break

[31] As with parents, even this small difference disappears once we control for migration by examining only those respondents growing up in the city where they now reside.

[32] On arguments about whether vertical mobility increases with industrialization *see* G. Lenski, Power and Privilege 410–17 (1966); Social Structure and Mobility in Economic Development chs. 2, 6 (N. Smelser & S. Lipset eds. 1966); T. Fox & S. Miller, *Economic, Political and Social Determinants of Mobility,* 9 Acta Sociologica 76–93 (1965).

up.[33] On the other hand, it is argued that obligations to the extended family and other kin inhibit upward mobility.[34] Examples are given of situations such as businessmen being bankrupted by kin borrowing money which is never paid back, of incompetent kin being hired, and of persons refusing to take better paying and more prestigious jobs since any gains would go to kin and not themselves.

One exception to the argument that all kin attachment and upward mobility are antithetical is the situation in traditional China where those most upwardly mobile had the largest families and strongest lineages. Candidates in the examination system were dependent on kin for support in schooling, and kin, in turn, received extra wealth and prestige from the successful candidate. However, such a neat correspondence between upward mobility and family goals existed only with respect to the upper bureaucracy in traditional times.

More extensive criticisms of hypotheses of conflict between mobility and family ties include the following: Extended families may be used to organize business ventures that could not be sustained by one nuclear family alone.[35] Most mobility is between jobs differing only a slight degree in status; therefore it is seldom that father and son or siblings will be separated by large differences in life style, prestige, or economic standing.[36] In Taiwan many young adults do contribute heavily to their parents' support;[37] therefore, these people may spend money on their parents that would otherwise be invested in business. On the other hand, this later support of parents is frequently matched by an earlier heavy investment in education by the parents for the advancement of their children. Parents do glory in the advancement of their children, and it is unlikely that this success by their children could bring friction; rather, it should bring pride and great enjoyment of the children. Moreover, the advancement of the many salaried employees, whose promotion is determined by seniority and merit rather than reinvestment of profits, will be little influenced by the necessity to support their parents. However, differences in occupational status might put a greater strain on sibling relations. Indeed,

---

[33] D. Schneider & G. Homans, *Kinship Terminology and the American Kinship System*, 57 AMERICAN ANTHROPOLOGIST 1204 (1955); E. BURGESS & H. LOCKE, *supra* note 17, at 523–53; P. MARRIS, FAMILY AND SOCIAL CHANGE IN AN AFRICAN CITY 136–37 (1961). For a general review of the arguments *see* W. Goode, *Family and Mobility*, in CLASS, STATUS, AND POWER 600 (2d ed. R. Bendix & S. Lipset eds. 1966).

[34] *See* G. FOSTER, TRADITIONAL CULTURES 91–95 (1962); T. Parsons, *An Analytical Approach to the Theory of Social Stratification*, in ESSAYS IN SOCIOLOGICAL THEORY 78–79 (T. Parsons ed. 1954); T. Parsons, *supra* note 21, at 191–92; W. Goode, *supra* note 33, at 581–601.

[35] M. Cohen, *supra* note 1. For other exceptions from historical evidence *see* W. Goode, *supra* note 33.

[36] B. BARBER, SOCIAL STRATIFICATION 364–65 (1957).

[37] Marsh gives data on the proportion of adults helping their parents. R. Marsh, *The Taiwanese of Taipei*, 27 J. ASIAN STUDIES 572–75 (1968).

three or four persons did say they no longer had contact with a brother because they were a failure while their brother was a success. Overall, then, from informal evidence it seemed at the start of the analysis that parent-child relations would be little affected by occupational status discrepancies, while brother-brother relations would be somewhat more affected.

Consideration of occupational mobility also leads to the topic of simple class differences apart from any question of mobility. There are numerous influences on the extendedness of households in each class, but, overall, the situation tends to be reversed from what it was traditionally. Traditionally the higher class had more extended families than the lower class. The higher class, because of better food and more wives or concubines, produced more children who lived to adulthood; because of earlier marriage, they were more likely to have children married before the father died; more land and greater prestige made it advantageous for sons to stay at home; greater commitment to Confucian ideals made it more disgraceful to divide the extended family; and because their men had greater social ties outside the family, the men did not become committed to their wives against the greater family.[38] But many of these things have changed now. Because of better public health and more food for everyone, the lower classes as well as the higher classes have more sons growing to adulthood. Moreover, the higher classes migrate more often in pursuit of high status jobs, through higher education and other cultural contacts, adopt Western values more quickly, and are more cognizant of those parts of the law that promote independent families.[39]

Goode argues that a continuing force counter to the effects of changing law and values is the control over property, prestige, and jobs which the higher classes can wield over their sons in order to keep them attached to the larger family;[40] however, we have seen above that in cities there is little inheritance of occupation. Even where the potential for using this force exists, fathers may adopt Western values favoring independent nuclear families and thus not be willing to use such compulsion. It is doubtful, therefore, that this factor still has a noticeable influence on coresidence patterns.

Housing is another, but somewhat indeterminate, factor influencing present class differences. Higher classes have greater choice about whether they will share a house or not—if they desire, they can afford to buy separate houses and live apart or build one large house and live together. The housing situation of the urban lower classes in developing countries leads to further contradictory hypotheses. On the one hand, it is argued that even though they would prefer

---

[38] F. Hsu, *The Myth of Chinese Family Size*, 48 Am. J. Sociology 555–62 (1943). O. Lang, Chinese Family and Society 350 (1946). M. Freedman, *supra* note 10, at 20–30.

[39] The rationale for these hypotheses is discussed in greater detail below.

[40] W. Goode, *supra* note 1, at 371–72.

to live separately, they are forced to share the scarce and expensive houses in the city. On the other hand, it is argued that even though they would prefer to live together, they cannot afford a house in the city sufficiently large to contain everyone in the extended family.[41] Thus, it is impossible to predict the situation of lower classes in Taiwan cities. The situation is further complicated by some middle and upper status groups such as government officials, school teachers, other public employees, and even some large industry employees who receive housing as a part of their remuneration. This housing is more spacious than that of the lowest status groups but, except for high level officials, is designed for only one family. Additional kin can be and are included at times, but it is unlikely that this group of middle and high status employees will have many coresident kin. The indeterminateness of these various factors makes it impossible to say what influence, if any, housing will have.

A final factor possibly influencing class differences is the economic self-sufficiency of individuals in each status group. Here again upper status groups have greater freedom to act than low status groups. High status groups have higher income, greater income security, and greater ability to sustain themselves in emergencies. Lower status groups have less income, less income security, and less ability to sustain themselves in emergencies. Therefore, high status individuals can live independently if they want to, whereas low status groups must rely more on the larger family for economic support and security, regardless of their preferences. Should high status or both high and low status groups prefer to live separately because of positive values favoring such residence or because of attempts to escape strains in more complex families, this factor will lead to fewer complex families among the upper than among the lower strata. If both groups, or just the upper status group, want to live in large families, then this factor will have no effect.

Occupational status is measured on a four rank scale.[42] Examples of occupations at each rank are as follows:

---

[41] That scarce and expensive urban housing leads to sharing of space is suggested from observation of Zulu living patterns in Durban, South Africa. J. Kahl, *supra* note 1, at 67. The opposite prediction, that overcrowded housing causes extended families to disperse, comes from observation of other African cities. *See* W. GOODE, *supra* note 1, at 188–89.

[42] This ranking of occupational status was developed by first translating the Warner, Meeker, and Eells's occupational rating scale—W. WARNER, M. MEEKER, & K. EELLS, SOCIAL CLASS IN AMERICA 140–41 (1949). Research assistants were then asked to readjust the scale to local conditions by either lowering or raising the rank of certain occupations or by adding occupations that were not covered. The original scale consisted of seven ranks, but assistants in Taiwan found it very difficult to distinguish with accuracy among the top three ranks and the bottom two ranks in the original scale. Therefore, in this analysis the first three and last two ranks are collapsed to form the present ranks one and four.

1. Medical doctors, lawyers, teachers at the junior high level or above, government bureau heads, managers in large companies, owners of retail stores employing more than four or five persons, owners of factories, and bank clerks.

2. Other clerks, reporters, foremen, grade school teachers, owners of retail stores employing two or three people, farmers with more than 0.8 hectares of land.

3. Barbers, truck drivers, carpenters, retail store clerks, skilled factory workers, owners of small shops dependent primarily on family labor, policemen, farmers with 0.4 to 0.7 hectares of land, and those farmers for whom land area was unknown.

4. Semi-skilled and unskilled laborers, heavy manual laborers, and street pedlars.

The occupational rank of respondents is determined from their current job, the occupational rank of fathers is determined by the job they held longest. Occupational mobility is determined by comparing the respondent's and his father's occupational ranks. Those sharing rank one or two are classified as "both high"; those sharing rank three or four are classified as "both low"; those differing in rank are classified by whether the son's rank is higher or lower than that of his father.

This classification of occupational mobility is compared with the percentage of composite households in Table 10. In order to limit the effects of migration and compare a son's occupation with the occupation of only nonagricultural fathers, Table 10 is restricted to those respondents who grew up in their present city of residence. So as to limit the effects of whether a parent is alive or not, the table is further restricted to those respondents with at least one parent alive. The percentage differences in the table are quite small and, because of the small number of households in each row, not statistically significant—that is, differences this large frequently could be found by chance. However, since this same pattern is repeated below when the coresidence of a larger number of parents is considered, we have some confidence that the differences in this table represent actual, though small, trends in the total population. In the table, first note that the traditional situation with respect to class differences no longer holds. Rather, the consistently low status

---

This is a mixed scale reflecting a variety of criteria. For example, school teachers tend to be ranked high because of their prestige in the society even though their power and income are low. Government officials tend to be ranked high because of their power and prestige even though their income is low. Owners of large businesses tend to be ranked high because of their income even though their prestige is not particularly high.

The least certain aspect of the scale is the equating of agricultural and nonagricultural occupations. We have gotten by this problem in the tables below by including only those persons who live in a city and who lived there before age sixteen. That is, we have included only those whose own and father's occupations were generally nonagricultural.

households in row four are slightly more likely to be composite than the consistently high status households in row one. Second, note that occupational mobility or discrepancy in father's and son's status neither produces percentages greatly different from nonmobile father-son pairs nor consistently lowers the percentage of composite households. The upwardly mobile have a slightly larger proportion of composite households, whereas the downwardly mobile tend to have a smaller proportion; therefore, these differences cannot be attributed to occupational mobility in the usual simplistic manner of predicting that discrepancies in life style, economic position, and prestige lead to tensions and eventual dissolution of the larger family. Because of the small number of households in this table, I will present the table for coresidence of parents before discussing the implications of these findings.

TABLE 10

PERCENTAGE OF COMPOSITE HOUSEHOLDS BY FATHER AND SON'S
OCCUPATIONAL STATUS WHEN AT LEAST ONE PARENT IS ALIVE AND
RESPONDENT GREW UP IN THE CITY*

Respondent's Status Relative to Father's†	Percentage of Composite Households	Total Number of Households
Both high	63.7	(33)
Son 1 to 3 ranks higher	72.3	(47)
Son 1 to 3 ranks lower	61.5	(39)
Both low	75.0	(28)

* Urban households of respondents not marrying matrilocally.
† See text for definition of categories.

The percentage of coresident parents is compared with occupational mobility in Table 11. In order to eliminate the influences of migration and compare only nonagricultural fathers and sons, Table 11 is limited to parents of urban respondents growing up in the city. Further, in order to measure the factors of desire and obligation rather than just opportunity, the table is limited to parents in the same city as the respondent. From the table we see that the pattern of the household table is again repeated. As above, the differences are not extremely large, but the larger number of cases per row means the findings are statistically somewhat more significant. As above, the nonmobile high status pairs tend to have fewer coresident parents than the nonmobile low status pairs. Also, mobility does not have the predicted result of consistently separating parents and adult children. Rather the result of mobility depends on its direction. The upwardly mobile tend to have coresident parents

while the downwardly mobile tend not to.[43] How shall we then interpret
these trends?

TABLE 11

PERCENTAGE OF PARENTS IN THE CITY WHO ARE CORESIDENT BY FATHER'S
AND SON'S OCCUPATIONAL STATUS*

Respondent's Status Relative to Father's	Percentage of Parents Coresident	Total Number of Parents
Both high	61.4	(44)
Son 1 to 3 ranks higher	78.9	(66)
Son 1 to 3 ranks lower	61.4	(44)
Both low	77.8	(36)

* Parents of urban respondents who grew up in the present city and did not marry
matrilocally.

In the discussion of class differences in household composition above, six
factors were listed as possible causes of modern trends—namely, class
differentials in migration; Westernization of values; knowledge of law; control
over property, prestige, and jobs; housing; and economic security. How well
does each of these factors explain the findings in Tables 10 and 11? Some of
these factors may have minor effects that will tend to cancel one another out;
therefore, we will be limited to a search for major influences. Moreover, the
differences here are not large and the number of cases is small, but the topic
is worthy of preliminary speculation, which can be checked by larger samples
later on. The apparent influence of each of the six factors introduced above is
as follows.

Overall, migration is not related to occupational status. That is, about an
equal proportion in each status rank have grown up outside the present city
of residence. However, if we consider only those respondents growing up in
the present city of residence, then a few more high status father-son pairs have
been separated by migration than have low status pairs.[44] Yet the difference

---

[43] Because of the small number of cases in each category, the table is not presented
here, but examination of a table showing the effects of extreme disparity in status—two
to three ranks disparity—indicates that extremely upwardly mobile sons are even more
likely than those shown here to have coresident parents, while the extremely downwardly mobile are even less likely than those shown here to have coresident parents.
This somewhat strengthens our arguments below, but still requires confirmation with
a larger sample.

[44] This pattern occurs because rural to urban migrants tend to be of low status,
whereas urban to urban migrants tend to be of high status. Parents of respondents
growing up in the city are usually among the high status group migrating to other cities.

is small—8 to 9 percent—and insignificant. In any case, the influence of migration has been eliminated in the Table 11 above by examining only respondents who grew up within the city and whose parents are in the same city. The influence of migration is also limited in Table 10 by examining only those who grew up in the city, though a few households with parents outside the city are included. Even after the influence of migration is so controlled, there is still a difference in amount of coresidence between nonmobile high and low status father-son pairs and between upwardly and downwardly mobile pairs. Migration, then, is not necessary to explain the variation found in Table 11 nor likely to be important in the Table 10.

The influence of greater Westernization of values among high status persons is in partial, but not complete, accord with Tables 10 and 11. Through education, newspapers, magazines, and Western movies, high status fathers and sons should be more exposed to Western values of individual achievement rational decision making, equality of women, love marriage, husband-wife solidarity, and specific values in favor of independent nuclear families.[45] Thus the smaller percentage of coresident parents among nonmobile high status persons is consistent with the reputed influence of Western values.[46] Yet the variation between upwardly and downwardly mobile persons is not so easily explained by such value differences. Values of individual achievement and rational decision processes should make sons dissatisfied with the authority of their father. Values of female equality, love marriage, and husband-wife solidarity should make the young wife dissatisfied with dominance by the mother-in-law and also cause the son to side with his wife against the larger family. Accordingly, upper status children should be the least likely to have coresident parents, but just the opposite situation is observed—upwardly mobile sons with low status parents have more coresident parents than downwardly mobile sons with high status parents. For this observed pattern to be explained by the influence of Western values, we would need to presume that children's values remain unchanged while parent's values are rapidly transformed to those of the West. This is not plausible; therefore, Westernization of values cannot be a major influence on coresidence patterns.

The reputed effect of laws also encounters difficulties similar to those for Westernization of values. Supposedly higher status children should know the law better, and, consequently, higher status sons should demand the right to choose spouses who are not necessarily congenial to the larger family; young

---

[45] Besides being more likely to have a high education and to read more, high status persons are more likely to attend Western movies than Chinese movies. Among the few college students whom I asked, all said they never attend Chinese movies even though they go to Western movies fairly often.

[46] W. GOODE, *supra* note 1, at 18–22, 369–71; M. LEVY, *supra* note 2, at 284–86; R. DORE, *supra* note 17, at 115–16, 125–35, 157–88; M. NIMKOFF, COMPARATIVE FAMILY SYSTEMS 347–50 (1965).

wives should be independent because of their rights of divorce; and both should feel in general that his or her independence was justified.[47] As above, these predictions are not in accord with observed coresidence patterns among mobile sons. Upwardly mobile sons, instead of being separated from parents, have coresident parents 18 percent more often than downwardly mobile sons. Law, then, cannot be a predominant influence on status differences within Taiwan today.

Goode's proposition that higher class fathers have the control over property, prestige, and jobs necessary to keep their sons at home also does not hold. In fact the situation is just the opposite of his prediction. High status parents of high status and downwardly mobile sons are less likely to live with those sons than low status fathers of either nonmobile or upwardly mobile sons.

The explanations fitting these data best are scarcity of housing and the greater need of low status persons for mutual financial support. That is, low status fathers and sons are not able to afford separate housing, to buy separate household equipment such as furniture and cooking utensils, nor to sustain themselves in emergencies. They therefore tend to live together more than higher status parents and sons. Higher status persons can afford to live separately, and, additionally, some of them tend to have housing provided as a part of their pay. The higher proportion of coresident fathers among the upwardly mobile can be explained by the ability of high status sons to house and support their less well-to-do parents and by their social obligation to do so. The low percentage of coresident parents among downwardly mobile sons may be explained by two factors—one relatively straightforward; the other requiring an additional variable. First, downwardly mobile sons will not try to house and support their high status parents but will allow their brothers who have maintained a high status to do so. Second, although it is proper for parents to request aid from their adult sons, it is not proper for adult sons to request aid from parents. When I asked college students and recent graduates from whom they would get financial aid if in difficulty, they replied that their parents were the last persons they would go to. To do so would be very embarrassing. The cultural norm is that adult children support their

---

[47] For a discussion of how greater knowledge of the law is determined by the education of children and not the occupational status of fathers, *see* B. Kutschinsky, *Law and Education: Some Aspects of Scandinavian Studies into "The General Sense of Justice,"* 10 ACTA SOCIOLOGICA 24–26 (1967).

For a description of changes in Taiwan marriage and divorce laws that should have the above consequences, see Buxbaum's discussion of Taiwan in this volume. Note Buxbaum says changes in these laws have been made with the conjugal or nuclear family in mind.

For general statements of how new laws promote nuclear families, *see* R. DORE, *supra* note 17, at 117–20; M. NIMKOFF, *supra* note 46, at 57; W. GOODE, *supra* note 1, at *passim;* L. Baric, *Levels of Change in Yugoslav Kinship,* in SOCIAL ORGANIZATION 8–9 (M. Freedman ed. 1967).

parents and not the other way around as it tends to be in the West. A possible explanation of the low percentage of coresident parents with the downwardly mobile is, then, that financially unsuccessful sons are reluctant to be supported by their parents in a common household. Ability to house and support oneself and possibly one's parents, thus, seems to better fit the observed pattern of coresidence than any of the other variables above.

The analysis needs to be made somewhat more complex before this explanation can be complete, however.[48] Although many sons live separate from parents, only a small proportion of parents fail to live with at least one married son. Among parents of all Tainan respondents only 3 percent live with an unmarried son and 11 percent by themselves or with some relative other than their son. Among parents of Kaohsiung respondents these percentages are 11 percent and 12 percent.[49] If these figures were restricted to only parents of nonmigrant respondents, the percentages would be even lower. The implication of this is that parents who fail to live with the respondent do not generally live alone. Rather, they most frequently live with some other son, that is, with a brother of the respondent. Therefore, if this analysis is to be made more accurate, the number, residence, and occupational status of brothers should be considered as well. For example, respondents with brothers are more likely to have parents living separately with these brothers than those who have no brothers. Also, downwardly mobile sons with a brother remaining in a high status job are more likely to have parents living separately with this brother who can better support them, than a son with only a downwardly mobile brother. Other similar combinations could be suggested. Unfortunately, we do not have sufficient cases to check these more complex hypotheses. However, observation of brother ties alone can show the effect of comparative status of brothers and the need to include such considerations in an analysis of coresidence patterns.

The relation between the comparative occupational status of married brothers and their residence is shown in Table 12. Three points can be made from this table: migration separates high status brothers more often than low status brothers; occupational status discrepancy does not have the reputed effect of separating brothers; and predictions that high status kin will live together less frequently than low status kin are supported. First, although migration was partially controlled in this table by examining only those who grew up in the city, we see by observing column three—the percentage of brothers outside the city—that high status brothers are more likely to have

---

[48] Also, since the explanation offered here is economic, a purer ranking of income without prestige and power elements intermixed should be tried. If such a scale does not produce larger differences in coresidence by rank than the present scale, then something is wrong with the economic interpretation.

[49] These are weighted percentages.

moved out of the city than low status brothers. Specifically, among high status pairs 29 percent of the brothers are outside the city, whereas among low status pairs 10 percent of the brothers are outside the city. The mixed brother pairs in rows three and four are intermediate since they contain both high and low status brothers. This indicates, then, that among respondents who grew up in a city social status has some effect on coresidence through the intermediate variable of migration.

TABLE 12

RESIDENCE OF MARRIED BROTHERS BY OCCUPATIONAL STATUS
OF RESPONDENT AND BROTHER*

Respondent and Brother's Occupational Status†	Percentage of Brothers				Number of Brothers	Percentage of Brothers in the Same City Who are Coresident
	In the Same House	In the Same City	Outside the City	Total		
Both high	14.3	57.1	28.6	100	(70)	20.0 (50)‡
Both low	39.2	51.0	9.8	100	(51)	43.5 (46)
One rank disparity	24.6	55.3	20.2	100	(114)	30.8 (91)
2 or 3 rank disparity	20.0	65.0	15.0	100	(40)	23.6 (34)

* Married brothers of urban respondents growing up in the present city of residence, with parents alive in the city, and not marrying matrilocally.

† Occupational status is measured on a four rank scale. See text for definition of ranks. The amount of land farmed by farming brothers is unknown, hence all farming brothers are classified at rank three. However, since only brothers of respondents growing up in the city are included there should be few or no farming brothers in the table.

‡ Numbers in parentheses are total number of brothers on which percentages to left are based.

The second point to note from Table 12 is that mobility or discrepancy in status has no effect on whether brothers live together. I had in fact expected that such discrepancy in status would have a separating effect, particularly when brothers were separated in status by two or three ranks. This was because three or four respondents told us their siblings now ignored them because the respondent himself had fallen in status or had not kept up with their sibling's rise in status. Yet we see from Table 12 that regardless of whether migration effects are still included as in the far left-hand column, or excluded as in the far right-hand percentage column, brothers with disparate statuses are no less likely to live together than two high status brothers. This is so whether we consider those who are disparate by two or three ranks or those disparate only by one rank. Both groups fall approximately midway between the brother pairs that are "both high" and "both low." That is, these disparate pairs are intermediate, taking on some of the characteristics of both high status pairs and low status pairs. In sociological jargon, an additive model is sufficient to explain the situation of brothers with discrepant statuses; there is no need for a special explanation of strains due to differences in life style, economics, or prestige. If only those that were three ranks disparate were compared, it might have been found that discrepancy in status did have a general separating effect just as some of the respondents said. There are too few cases three ranks disparate to make the comparisons, but the fact that there are so few indicates that such an extreme disparity cannot have a widespread influence in the society. Thus, although three or four respondents report that social status differences have separated them and their brothers, in the total population such discrepancies generally do not have the effect of separating brothers.

The third thing we see from Table 12 is that high status brother pairs are less likely to live together than low status pairs. This is seen both in the far left-hand column, which includes some migration effects, and the far right-hand percentage column, which excludes migration effects. This is in accord with the parent-child pattern observed above. However, the lack of a differential upward and downward mobility pattern as found in parent-child relations prevents discrimination among the several hypotheses that predict high status persons in a modernizing society are less likely to live with kin than low status persons. That is, we cannot choose among the hypotheses that high status persons are less likely to live with kin because they have been exposed more to such general Western values as independence of the young or particular values favoring nuclear families; have better knowledge of law promoting free choice in marriage and the power of wives; and can more easily house and support themselves on their own. Nevertheless, the general pattern indicates that one should include a brother's occupational status when attempting to form a more general model of the forces that cause families to stay together or live apart.

In summary, occupational mobility and subsequent status discrepancy have neither a simple nor a very large effect on coresidence patterns. The effect depends both on the particular kin relation and the direction of mobility. In the parent-child relation, sons who are upwardly mobile relative to their father are slightly more likely to have coresident parents than downwardly mobile sons. This seems to be because upwardly mobile sons can afford to house and support their lower status parents while downwardly mobile sons are less able to do so. It also seems to be because it is culturally approved that sons support parents, but disapproved that parents support adult sons. On the other hand, discrepancy of occupational status between married brothers has no discernible effect on their coresidence. Brothers discrepant in status tend to fall midway between high and low status brother pairs in amount of coresidence, indicating that discrepant status means only that these brothers share some high status and some low status characteristics. Occupational mobility, then, does not have the strong effect frequently attributed to it. What effect it does have on parent-child relations is both slight and contradictory, depending on the direction of mobility.

Examination of status differences also indicates that Westernization of values and changes in law have no discernible effect on coresidence within each occupational status group. As predicted from these two factors, and opposed to the traditional situation, high status father-son and brother-brother pairs are slightly less likely to be coresident than low status pairs. However, the pattern of coresidence among mobile father-son pairs indicates that Westernization of values and changes in law do not have noticeable effects among status groups today. Rather, present day status differences in the city are better explained by the slight effect of high status migration and the greater ability of higher status persons to support themselves independently or, if need be, also support their low status parents. The long-run implication of this observation is that as income and income security increase and as people become less dependent on one another, then, there will be a slight decline in coresidence for all groups. This also tends to support those propositions which assert that with transfer of such functions as political protection, education, money lending, unemployment insurance, health care, and old age assistance from the family to public institutions the strength of the larger family will decline.[50] Another possible long-term influence of increasing income security and public welfare benefits in the city is that more migrants are willing to move their wives and children than before. Migration within Taiwan has always been high; the primary difference today may be simply that because of greater security in cities men stay longer in the city and more frequently move their wives and children rather than leaving them with the larger family in the village while they work temporarily in town. When this is done, the dissolution of extended families in the village is accelerated.

BUREAUCRATIZATION

A final aspect of modernization purportedly associated with household change is bureaucratization. Increasing size of work organizations during modernization tends to lead to selection and promotion on the basis of technical competence and to more impersonal relations within organizations. To use criteria other than technical competence in hiring and promotion would

---

[50] See W. GOODE, supra note 1, at 369; M. NIMKOFF, supra note 46, at 64-65, 360-61, 362-63; W. OGBURN & M. NIMKOFF, TECHNOLOGY AND THE CHANGING FAMILY 123-43 (1955).

endanger larger and larger capital investments.[51] Additionally, the applicant is less and less likely to have a kin or friendship tie with the person doing the appointing. It is hypothesized that when this is the case, kin can no longer be of help in getting jobs, and thus there will be less interaction with kin.[52] Secondly, it is hypothesized that the impersonality of social relations on the job carries over into all interactions off the job. Actually the suggested results of impersonality on the job have varied. Some predict that there is an increasing tendency to view personal relations from an instrumental point of view.[53] Yet it may be, "on the contrary, that the increase in the portion of the individual's interpersonal relationship which are depersonalized would cause him to emphasize the 'personalness,' the degree of affectuality, in those personal relations which remain to him."[54]

On the other hand, it is suggested that the particularism inherent in the extended family system will inhibit the development of the efficient bureaucracies needed in large industrial organizations.[55] In the present study only the first proposition, that large complex organizations weaken extended families, will be tested. That there already are large industrial organizations in Taiwan indicates that either extended families are relatively weak or that strong family ties are not an extremely serious limitation on the growth of such organizations.

Three indicators of degree of bureaucratization were used: number of employees at the place of work, total number of employees at the place of work and at all branch organizations, and number of levels of authority. Once migration is controlled none of these indicators are related to variation in household composition, coresidence of parents, or coresidence with married brothers.[56] An example of this lack of relation is shown in Table 13 where the number of employees at the place of work is cross tabulated with the percentage of composite households. All percentage differences in the table are small and, because of the small number of households in each category, statistically

---

[51] H. WILENSKY & C. LEBEAUX, INDUSTRIAL SOCIETY AND SOCIAL WELFARE 58–63, 95–97 (1958).

[52] M. LEVY, *supra* note 2, at 281, 317, 353–65; W. GOODE, *supra* note 1, at 369–70.

[53] K. MANNHEIM, MAN AND SOCIETY IN AN AGE OF RECONSTRUCTION 320–23 (1940); L. Wirth, *Urbanism as a Way of Life*, in CITIES AND SOCIETY 53–54 (P. Hatt & A. Reiss, Jr. eds. 1957).

[54] R. DORE, *supra* note 17, at 115. Some suggest that the nuclear family with its emphasis on emotionality, particularly in the husband-wife relationship, is better suited to providing emotional security when the world of work provides little. *See* W. GOODE, *supra* note 1, at 14.

[55] M. LEVY, *supra* note 2.

[56] The larger industries in this sample are predominantly in Kaohsiung, which has had more immigration than Tainan among all groups. Therefore, when migration is not controlled the large industry employees appear to have fewer coresident kin.

insignificant. The percentage of composite households for all groups but one is near 65 percent. The slightly higher percentage of 80 percent for those in organizations with a total of two to twenty employees may be only a statistical accident or may represent the frequency with which such organizations involve a father and son running a shop or factory with the help of several young, unskilled laborers. The pattern is repeated with the number of levels of authority where men in organizations with two levels of authority are slightly more likely to live in composite households than all other groups. Also, the pattern is seen for both number of employees and levels of authority when coresidence with parents is examined. But, again, these are very slight and statistically insignificant trends. Even if true, they do not fit the predicted pattern of a steady decline in the percentage of composite households with ever larger and more complex organizations. Within Taiwan today, then, increasing size and complexity of work organizations is not consistently related to a decline in complexity of households.

TABLE 13

PERCENTAGE OF COMPOSITE HOUSEHOLDS BY NUMBER OF
EMPLOYEES IN TOTAL WORK ORGANIZATION*

Number of Employees	Percentage of Composite Households	Number of Households
1	64.3	(28)
2–20	80.0	(45)
21–99	69.2	(26)
100–499	65.0	(20)
500 or more	63.7	(28)

* Urban households of respondents growing up within the city, with parents alive, and not marrying matrilocally.

SUMMARY

The relationships between four major aspects of modernization and change in household composition have been examined. Among the four—migration, inheritance, occupational mobility, and bureaucratization—migration is most closely related to variation in household composition. However, although closely related to declining coresidence with parents, migration is only slightly related to declining coresidence with brothers. There is, then, something to urban life other than migration that decreases coresidence of brothers.

In the two cities studied sons rarely inherit their means of livelihood from their father. In those few cases in which they do, inheritance is related to living with parents, but only because those who migrated forsook any opportunity to inherit or did not have anything to inherit initially. Non-inheriting sons who happen to stay in the same city are just as likely to live with parents as inheriting sons.

Occupational mobility and the resulting status discrepancy have neither the simple separating effect predicted nor a very large effect. The effect depends both on the particular kin involved and the direction of mobility. Upwardly mobile sons tend to house and support their parents, while downwardly mobile sons do not. This appears to be because, first, upwardly mobile sons can afford to support their parents while the downwardly mobile cannot and, second, it is culturally approved for adult children to support parents but disapproved for parents to support adult children. On the other hand, status discrepancy among brothers has no discernible effect at all. Discrepant brothers are simply intermediate between nondiscrepant high and low status pairs. Therefore, this aspect of modernization will not weaken household ties.

Bureaucratization also does not have the predicted effect of steadily reducing the proportion of complex households. The only noticeable trends are for those working alone to live slightly less frequently with parents, and those working in organizations with a total of two to twenty workers to live slightly more frequently with parents than the average person. This is opposite to the predicted tendency. Further, in organizations with more than twenty workers, increasing size does not lead to less coresidence with parents or brothers. There are no trends at all in brother residence by size of organization. Also, no relationship is found when coresidence by number of levels of authority is examined. Thus, this aspect of modernization also cannot explain any decline in coresidence.

Other than these four major variables, the influence of Westernization of values, changes in law, housing conditions, and need for economic support were examined by noting how well the predicted influences of each were in accord with observed occupational status differences. Differences in household composition by status are not large but lead to some significant speculations which can be checked by larger and more detailed investigations. Traditionally, high status persons were more likely to live in extended households than low status persons, but in Taiwan cities this situation has changed to a point where nonmobile, high status households are slightly less complex than low status ones. This situation is partly the result of improved health conditions which have allowed low status families to raise more sons to maturity. In urban areas it is also partly the result of higher out-migration of high status parents and brothers. But beyond these two factors it appears that low status families are forced to stay together by the need for housing and mutual economic support. This explanation is in better accord with the pattern of coresidence among mobile sons than explanations based on Westernization of values or changes in law. This explanation suggests, then, that as income security and welfare benefits increase with modernization, households will be slightly less likely to live together.

These conclusions apply primarily to differences observed among different groups within Taiwan today. If we were to observe changes in household composition in historical depth, we might want to weight these variables somewhat differently. For example, the observed propensity for upper status persons to live separate from parents and brothers when these are not in need of support may be the result of tensions always present in extended families, but it also may be the result of new values and laws that promote such division, whereas traditional values and laws did not. The observed status differences today indicate that Westernization of values and new laws are not having a major new impact in urban areas, but such changes may have helped set the stage for today's pattern. Otherwise, several of these factors may help promote migration—the variable most clearly related to decline in complexity of households. Changes in values and law may make persons more willing to leave their kin than before. Greater income security and welfare benefits may make persons willing to stay in the city longer and more willing to take their wives and children with them to the city.

In general, to understand those forces that separate parents and sons, we should look primarily at the causes and consequences of migration. To understand those forces that separate brothers, we should look less to migration and more to other forces such as changes in economic security, housing conditions, values, and law.

PART IV
MARRIAGE AND DIVORCE IN
THE PEOPLE'S REPUBLIC OF CHINA

Soviet Family Law and
Comparative Chinese Developments*

W. MÜLLER-FREIENFELS

THE SIGNIFICANCE OF COMMUNIST FAMILY LEGISLATION
IN RUSSIA AND CHINA

The formation of a new system of family law is a peculiar phenomenon. Considering the complexity of the matter and the constant collisions of the ideological, political, religious, and sociological postulates, which concern every individual and the community, one would perhaps think that further development of the family (that group commonly distinguished by peculiar stability) would be more easily promoted in a democratic way during calmer, reflective, and more balanced times in the life of a people. That would seem even more probable, if one follows the opinion of Karl Marx[1] that the legislator, just like a naturalist, must establish an objective law corresponding only to social conditions. To accomplish this, a certain stability and continuity should be needed, which are lacking during times of upheaval, although the class struggle asks for immediate revolutionary reactions.

Yet the reality of life reveals a different picture.[2] Frequently a reform of family law has been feasible only in times of political agitation. It prospered

---

* This paper was translated with the assistance of Robert J. Kapelke, a member of the Bar of the State of Colorado, who is presently continuing his studies in Freiburg, Germany, as a Foreign Fellow from the University of Chicago. I thank Dr. F. Müntzel, University of Bochum, for his help in translating Chinese texts, and Professor Shin'ichi Tohda, University of Hiroshima, for his help in translating Japanese texts.

This manuscript takes into consideration only legislation and literature appearing prior to 1969. The article was prepared at that time and there have been substantial delays in publication for which the author is in no way responsible.

[1] Karl Marx in 1 KARL MARX & FRIEDRICH ENGELS, WERKE 149 (East Berlin 1957). "The legislator must view himself as a naturalist. He does not make the laws, he does not invent them, he merely formulates them; he expresses the new laws of moral relationships in conscious positive laws." See Alice Tay Erh Soon and Eugene Kamenka in 5 QUADRANT 17ff., Melbourne 1960.

[2] Thus, Schwind remarks of Austria, "that an incisive regulation of this matter was always undertaken only in times of a non-democratic government leadership":

then, moreover, because it was borne in by the wave of revolutionary impetus.[3] Accordingly, it is no wonder that such social revolutionary movements as communism in Russia and China very soon turned to the task of re-creating the family law. It was especially important as a tool for these two modern social revolutions, because they wished to chop off radically and severely certain firmly rooted principles of their previous law. With this legislation as well as by other means, they sought to construct a changed world from the ground up in accordance with their specific concepts and value judgments.[4]

In Russia, scarcely two months after the October Revolution of 1917, the Bolsheviks began to reform the family law of Russia by issuing two decrees.[5] They acted without heed to the continuing civil war or to their in no way secure position. They thereby laid down the first principles for their new family policy. Nine months later the provisions of both of these decrees were significantly redeveloped and incorporated in a code.[6] Characteristically, this constituted the first codification of the Soviet state.[7]

In China, even during their war with the Nationalist Chinese (Kuomintang) in the thirties and forties, the communists were endeavoring to create a new marriage law in the regions they occupied, corresponding to their ideas. Thus,

---

Probleme des oesterreichischen Eherechts (Problems of Austrian marriage law), 3 EHE UND FAMILIE IM PRIVATEN UND ÖFFENTLICHEN RECHT, ZEITSCHRIFT FÜR DAS GESAMTE FAMILIENRECHT 14 (1956) [hereinafter cited as FamRZ].

[3] *See* Müller-Freinfels, *Legal Unification of Family Law*, 16 AM. J. COMP. L. 175 (1968).

[4] France, the world's first example of a modern social revolution, also very soon developed new family law provisions. *Cf.* M. Cruppi, LE DIVORCE PENDANT LA RÉVOLUTION (Divorce during the revolution), 1909 (thesis, Paris). *Cf.* further my contribution, *Zur Revolutionären Familiengesetzgebung, insbesondere zum Ehegesetz der Volksrepublik China von 1.5.1950* (On the revolutionary family law legislation esp. on the Marriage Law of the People's Republic of China of May 1, 1950), in 2 JUS PRIVATUM GENTIUM (*Festschrift für Max Rheinstein* [Publication honoring Max Rheinstein]) 843 ff. (1969).

[5] Decree of the VCIK (*Vserossijskij Central'nyj Ispolnitel'nyj Komitet*—All Russian Central Executive Committee) and SNK (*Soviet Narodnych Komissarov*—Assembly of People's Commissars) of the RSFSR of Dec. 18, 1917 *(Concerning Civil Marriage, the Children and the Administration of the Registry of Personal Status)*, in 1 DEKRETY VLASTI SOVETSKOJ (Decrees of the Soviet authority) 247–49 (1957); and of Dec. 19, 1917 *(Concerning divorce)*, in 1 DEKRETY VLASTI SOVETSKOJ 237–39 (1957). More specifically, *see* G. SVERDLOV, SOVETSKOE SEMEJNOE PRAVO (Soviet family law) 59 (Moscow 1958).

[6] *Kodeks zakonov RSFSR ob aktach grazdanskogo sostojanija, bračnom, semejnom i opekunskom prave* (Code of the RSFSR concerning personal status documents and the law of marriage, families, and guardianship—Family Law Code, 1918), in 3 DEKRETY VLASTI SOVETSKOJ 314–43 (1964). *Cf.* H. Freund, *Das Zivilrecht in der Sowjetunion* (Civil law in the Soviet Union), in 6 ZIVILGESETZE DER GEGENWART (Civil laws of the present) (K. Heinsheimer ed. 1927).

[7] H. Freund, *supra* note 6, at 15.

the first communist marital enactment was issued in Kiangsi, the Soviet Republic in China, on December 1, 1931 and was revised in 1934. In the years after the truce with the Kuomintang in 1937 and until 1943, marriage legislation sprang up in the various border areas of China.[8] These regulations were partly revised in the following years.[9] Finally, after the People's Government was formally constituted on October 1, 1949, it announced a new marriage statute,[10] ostensibly the final law. The Chinese marriage law of 1950, in addition to marital provisions, also contained regulations with respect to the status of legitimate and illegitimate children. In its arrangement, it already possessed some features of a family law codification.[11]

Thus the family law statute was, in China as in Russia, the first statute enacted by the communist government in the traditionally "private law" sphere,[12] although it is not really private law at all. As far as can be seen, it remains even today the only extensive statutory regulation in this area.[13]

As to the high estimation which the marriage law legislation enjoys in China, the familiar words of Mao Tse-tung from the year 1950 still apply today: "The Marriage law . . . is only next in importance to the Great Fundamental Law [the Constitution]."[14]

---

[8] The texts of the early communist marriage legislation in China are translated by M. MEIJER, *Early Communist Marriage Legislation in China,* in 6 CONTEMPORARY CHINA 84–102 (1962–64) (E. Kirby ed. 1968).

[9] S. Fu, *The New Marriage Law of Communist China,* in 1 CONTEMPORARY CHINA 116 ff. (E. Kirby ed. 1955); M. VAN DER VALK, CONSERVATISM IN MODERN CHINESE FAMILY LAW 68 ff. (1956).

[10] The Marriage Law of the People's Republic of China, April 13, 1950: *cf.* K. Bünger, *Das Ehegesetz der Volksrepublik* (The marriage law of the People's Republic), 16 RABELS ZEITSCHRIFT FÜR AUSLANDISCHES UND INTERNATIONALES PRIVATRECHT 112 (1951) [hereinafter cited as RabelsZ]; this article was also published in 1 CONTEMPORARY CHINA 121 ff. (E. Kirby ed. 1955). The text is also printed in C. YANG, CHINESE COMMUNIST SOCIETY: THE FAMILY AND THE VILLAGE (Part I: The Chinese Family in the Communist Revolution) 221 ff. (1965).

[11] M. VAN DER VALK, *supra* note 9, at 4, referring to Ch'en Shao-yü, Chairman of the Commission of Legislative Affairs, Report Concerning the Grounds for the Proceedings of the Drafting of the Marriage Law of the Chinese People's Republic.

[12] K. Bünger, *supra* note 10, at 113.

[13] The collective authorship of the book CHUNG-HUA JEN-MIN KUNG-HO-KUO MIN-FA CHI-PEN WENT'I (Fundamental questions of civil law in the People's Republic of China) 4, 111 (1958) is opposed to those conservative deviators who asserted, particularly at the time of the Hundred Flowers campaign of 1957, that China was a country without law and the little law left in China was not reliable and, therefore, the so-called six statutes of Nationalist China (which includes marriage and family law) should be reintroduced. To the contrary, according to the collective authorship, 747 provisions were enacted from 1949–57, not including the regulations issued on the local level. The "six statutes" could not be reenacted, because the law was to be a weapon of the class struggle.

[14] S. Fu, *supra* note 9, at 122.

The reasons for this urgent treatment of family law in the communist states are of a manifold nature. They go deeper than one tends to assume at first glance. Although it is too simple, one explanation is that both young communist states sought during the general legal void following the military dissolution of the old regime to get firmer ground under their feet by establishing the family law, which directly concerned every individual.[15] Indeed, in this field the general lack of order had its especially perceptible consequences. In Communist Russia the entire tsarist law was repealed, insofar as it was not compatible with the revolutionary conscience and legal sense.[16] In this regard, in Communist China the Peking People's Government of September 9, 1949 (even before being formally constituted on October 1, 1949) had set aside all existing statutes and ordinances of the National Government under Article 17 of the General Legal Guidelines of the Political People's Assembly (a sort of temporary constitution).[17] However, the obvious aberrations, which cropped up in various places,[18] would not by themselves have accomplished this first sparking of the legislative machine in the area of family law.

One can go further by observing that in Russia, and even more so in China in the period before the communist seizure of power, a more stringent and in part an even more oppressive coercion was exercised upon the inhabitants by the traditional, old-style family forms, although in both countries actions against the traditional pattern had been launched before the communists came into power. Essentially, the class, social and religious notions then being fought by the communists stood behind the traditional family system. For both countries Schurmann's remark on China's traditional elite seems to be valid: "The erosion of the social system deprived it of its status. All it had left was naked power and naked wealth."[19]

In Russia, tsarist family law[20] was dominated by the various religious faiths,

---

[15] W. Goode, The Family 1 ff. (1967).

[16] Cf. H. Klibanski, Die Gesetzgebung der Bolschewiki (The legislation of the Bolsheviks) 54 ff., 131 ff. (1920).

[17] K. Bünger, supra note 10, at 112.

[18] Cf. in this regard 5 A. Bergmann & M. Ferid (eds.), Internationales Ehe und Kindschaftsrecht (International marriage and child law), USSR, 11 (looseleaf collection 3d ed. 1965), quoting an example of a municipal decree issued in Vladimir in 1918, which declared that all unmarried girls over eighteen years of age as well as illegitimate children were "state property." An "Office of Free Love" was created, and compulsory prostitution for all unwed women was introduced.

[19] F. Schurmann, Ideology and Organization in Communist China 7 (1966).

[20] Cf. Swod sakonov grashdanskich (Civil Code) Bk. 1, arts. 1–382. See also H. Freund, supra note 6, at 4. Fr. K. Neubecker, Russisches und Orientalisches Eherecht (Russian marriage law) 10 ff. (1921); R. Gebhard, Russiches Familien-u. Eherecht (Russian family law and law of succession) 5 ff. (1910).

above all by the Greek-Orthodox Church.[21] It bore a class character.[22] The marriage contract and in particular divorce fell within the judicial competence of the church; only the effects of marriage were subject to civil law and secular jurisdiction.[23] Only the marriage law of the "True Believers" (that is, the members of the Greek-Orthodox Church) was coherently regulated, while for the rest a very splintered legal situation was standard. For all faiths the matrimonial age applied (for men eighteen years of age; for women sixteen—Articles 63 and 91 of the Civil Code), as well as the requirements of parental consent to the marriage and of freedom of decision on the part of the betrothed couple.[24] The divorce of a marriage entered into under the Greek-Orthodox rites was permitted in only a few specifically described cases:[25] proven adultery; impotency existing before the marriage; a penal sentence resulting in loss of class rights or exile to Siberia; a legal declaration presuming a missing spouse to be dead; and entry into a religious order.[26] Adultery, which was practically the only ground for divorce of any consequence, was not as a rule feasible for the spouse striving to get out of the marriage. Only proof by eyewitnesses was admitted, and from that requirement a whole occupational class of hired witnesses developed,[27] who either testified falsely or confirmed the committed, but unprovable, act of adultery. The class-structured character of the tsarist marriage law is clearly demonstrated by the fact that the man as head of the family transferred his rank and class rights to his wife, as well as his name, while conversely the woman who married a man below her station retained her class rights.[28] The class law was further applied to guardianships and trusteeships; as guardianship authorities there were a nobility guardianship,

---

[21] J. HAZARD & I. SHAPIRO, THE SOVIET LEGAL SYSTEM Pt. 3, at 99 (1962). "The church, the mosque and the synagogue dominated family life in pre-revolutionary Russia. . . . The family represented the major institution through which the traditions of the past were transmitted from generation to generation."

[22] The four classes in Russia consisted of the nobility, the clergy, the (urban) citizens, and the peasants. H. Freund, *supra* note 6, at 5.

[23] *See* J. MAGIDSON, DAS SOWJETISCHE EHERECHT UNTER BESONDERER BERÜCK-SICHTIGUNG DES EHEAUFLÖSUNGSRECHTS (The Soviet marriage law with particular consideration of the laws of the dissolution of marriage) 1 ff. (1931). FR. K. NEUBECKER, *supra* note 20, at 10 f.

[24] H. Freund, *supra* note 6, at 5.

[25] J. MAGIDSON, *supra* note 23, at 3; Florkowski, Das sowjetische Ehescheidungsrecht (The Soviet divorce law) 6 (1967) (thesis, Göttingen), for further references. R. GEBHARD, *supra* note 20, at 18.

[26] Catholics who wished to obtain a divorce often changed their faith and then returned to their religion after the divorce was completed. J. MAGIDSON, *supra* note 23, at 3.

[27] J. MAGIDSON, *supra* note 23, at 4. R. GEBHARD, *supra* note 20, at 19.

[28] H. Freund, *supra* note 6, at 5.

a clerical guardianship, and the municipal orphan's court, as well as the community assembly for the peasantry.

With the creation of the new family law, the Soviet government not only broke with all "bourgeois" traditions of tsardom and class dominion, but also totally cut the close ties with the church by the total secularization of marriage and family.

In China, indeed as early as the end of the twenties and in the thirties, comprehensive legislation patterned after European and particularly German-speaking legal spheres, partly from the Japanese point of view, was put into effect for a comparatively short period. This was, among other reasons, designed to counter any arguments that might eventually be raised by the numerous foreign states who maintained extraterritorial privileges in China on the basis of the so-called unequal treaties. Such arguments were to the effect that their countries' citizens would not be afforded adequate legal protection.[29] But this codification corresponded too little in its entire design, provisions, possibilities of execution, and structure to specific Chinese social conditions of that time. It lacked the potential to succeed. Its plan could not have been acceptable to any great extent to the majority of the people, quite apart from the fact that China's many internal and external conflicts at that time did not permit any actually successful reform of the statutes, considering the available forces.[30] Thus, in pre-communist China—apart from the individual large cities and the country's coastal provinces—the old traditional family forms in existence for about 2400 years were still being kept alive. They drew the individual within their supra-individual domain, as did family ties in almost no other country. The class rank of the individual was determined by that of his family; the family determined his education, and the family decided whom he must marry. The family was the basic unit of economic life; nearly all pursuits of agriculture, craftsmanship, trade, and industry were family pursuits.[31] Therefore, it was quite inevitable that this all-encompassing family "feudalistic" system[32] became the battle target of the communist attacks, "because it is the cornerstone of the old social order and the depository of old traditions, attitudes, loyalties, and cultural values that the communists identify with feudal society."[33]

---

[29] 1 A. BERGMANN & M. FERID, supra note 18, China 2.

[30] M. FREEDMAN, CHINESE FAMILY AND MARRIAGE IN SINGAPORE 175 (1957). "That these currents scarcely influenced the great mass of the population of China goes without saying."

[31] C. YANG, supra note 10, at 5.

[32] M. FREEDMAN, supra note 30, at 158. "Feudalism is a technical term of abuses in the vocabulary of Chinese communism and fulfills the function of . . . 'bourgeois of the West.'"

[33] T. CHEN, THE CHINESE COMMUNIST REGIME 261 (1967).

The family as product of the old feudal society should be eliminated. Besides this denigration of the old order, the positive motive of communism's message of salvation is at least as important in Russia and China. It is bound up with a radical reevaluation of the value system, as it is especially portrayed here in the counterbalancing of the authority of the man by giving the woman equal rights and in the setting aside of parental privileges in favor of a preference for youth. Moreover, systems of belief grounded on basic social and human values have been replaced by an ideology that expresses the values and goals of socio-political action and achievement.

Thus, a peculiar eschatology developed in the form of an ideal picture of a future communist society. In Soviet as in Chinese practice these concepts of the communist ideology have—under various hallmarks—a primary significance for the understanding and application of individual rules. Therefore, the legal form of the marriage patterned after the basic Marxist view is generally categorized as a "secularized-dogmatic marriage model."[34] The communist family statutes cannot be accurately comprehended at all without considering the missionary ideas behind them, since these also frequently prove to be guidelines for the application, expansion, and alteration of those statutes in new case law developments.[35] Also in this respect, the often repeated statement appears: "To overthrow a political power, it is always necessary first of all to create public opinion, to do work in the ideological sphere."[36]

Certainly, in relation to this official page of the law in the books the actually experienced reality of the family must not go unnoticed. This is especially true with respect to conditions in the rural areas, where the reform legislation, as Lenin had already emphasized for Russia in his time, "frequently remained only on paper."[37] Yet here one can only engage in very limited guesswork concerning these realities in Russia and especially in China. As far as my theme is concerned, this aspect remains somewhat in the background, for it is naturally the statutory provisions that primarily act as a gateway for the entry of new ideas into the legal order.

---

[34] O. BRUSIIN, ZUM EHESCHEIDUNGSPROBLEM (On the divorce problem) 17 ff. (1959).

[35] In those states having an "official moral version," the statute became the vehicle for preambles, program articles, principles, etc.: T. Raiser, *Sozialistisches Familienrecht zum neuen Familiengesetzbuch* (Socialistic family law of the new family code), 21 JURISTENZEITUNG 423 ff. (1966) [hereinafter cited as JZ], dealing with the new family code of the German Democratic Republic. *See also* M. Rheinstein, *How to Review a Festschrift*, 11 AM. J. COMP. LAW 639 (1962).

[36] C. Pao, *Indoctrination of the People's Liberation Army*, in SURVEY OF CHINA MAINLAND PRESS, American Consulate General, Hong Kong, No. 4176 (May 13, 1968).

[37] 28 V. LENIN, WERKE 176 (East Berlin 1959), with the observation that: "The influence of the clergy is responsible for this . . . this evil is more difficult to combat than the old legislation."

The communist ideas that are indispensable for an understanding of the Soviet family statutes are directly rooted in the orthodox principles of the theory of Marxism-Leninism. They go back to the origins of the communist teachings concerning the development of the family, since these were given, from the beginning on, as a primary component of the communist program.[38] At the same time, these communist ideas are based on the development of the family structure from the large clan family to the close-knit two-generation family, which had already developed in Western European mass society as a consequence of industrialization, urbanization, and increased technology. The development had still not penetrated the immense territory of Russia when the tsarist regime ended. In contrast, among the nomadic peoples—the Kirghiz, Uzbeks, and mountain tribes—the age-old customary law still prevailed with, for example, wife-robbery and sale, or polygamous marriages and the passing of the widow as part of the property assets of the deceased husband still in practice.[39] Here the new centralizing legislation in practice meant, above all, the prohibition of wife-robbery and sale, compulsory marriage, and polygamy. In view of all these circumstances one can confirm, with some reservations, at least some points made in Mackenroth's statement that ". . . basically by the bolshevik revolution a giant space has been readied for the Western European rural-bourgeois-urban-stamped two-generation family."[40]

In China the ideological revolutions, as they were already practiced in Soviet Russia, had to have more profound consequences with respect to the towering position of the family, based on three main factors connected to the cults of ancestry: preference for the male sex, strict ordering by generation, and veneration of age.[41] They were especially apparent: (1) in the wife's central tasks of bearing a son and acting as a servant for the personal welfare of her parents-in-law; (2) in the practical impossibility of the wife's obtaining a divorce (while the husband not only had such possibility, but could also bring into his house one or several women as co-wives or concubines); and (3) in the role of the wedding as a highpoint, not in the life of the young couple, but rather in the life of the husband's parents, who had by the arrangement of the youthful marriage accomplished one of the requisites of

---

[38] U. DROBNIG, IDEOLOGIE, RECHT UND WIRKLICHKEIT DER FAMILIE IN DER DDR (Ideology, law and reality of the family in the German Democratic Republic), VIII/2 JAHRBUCH FÜR OSTRECHT 158 (1967).

[39] On the Soviet efforts toward the ideal of the monogamous family as it was presented by Engels, see 2 R. DAVID & J. HAZARD, DROIT SOVIÉTIQUE (Soviet law) 326 (1954).

[40] G. MACKENROTH, BEVÖLKERUNGSLEHRE (Theory of population) 386 (1953). Going even further, M. Rheinstein, *supra* note 35, at 639, suggests: "Communism indeed is as much a part of Western civilization as Christianity. By the very process of adopting Communism, China has come to constitute a part of Western civilization."

[41] V. CHU, TA TA, TAN TAN, DIE WIRKLICHKEIT ROT-CHINAS, 162 ff. (German ed. 1964).

preserving the family clan. The family bore a hierarchical structure in which the eldest man of the eldest generation was the head of the family, having nearly unlimited power over the life and limb of the family members and being the sole administrator of the collective family assets. These principles, above all the veneration of age that Confucius had preached in his works,[42] were altogether "thrown overboard" by the communist teachings consisting of two major components, Marxism-Leninism as dogma and the thoughts of Mao Tse-tung as the motivating force. Their interrelation is described in the official version that the thoughts of Mao Tse-tung "unite the universal truths of Marxism-Leninism with the practice of revolution and construction in China."[43] This total reevaluation is unmistakably expressed in the words of Mao Tse-tung. In contrast to the former ideals, he sketched the principle goals of the Chinese Communists in the family law area:

> Protect the interests of the youth, women and children—provide assistance to young student refugees, help the youth and women to organize in order to participate on an equal footing in all work useful to the war effort and to social progress, ensure freedom of marriage and equality as between men and women, and give young people and children a useful education.[44]

THE DEVELOPMENT OF THE RUSSIAN AND CHINESE MARRIAGE AND CHILD LEGISLATION

The Classic Marxist Family Ideology

The need for a fundamental reform of marriage and child law was among the principal concerns of the socialist classicists. Ferdinand Lassalle had indicated in his letter written in the 1850s "concerning marriage": "We shall certainly have to stage a social revolution with regard to economic conditions; it is just as certain and necessary that we stage a revolution with regard to love, sexual life and morality."[45]

The communist family ideology is directly connected with the goals of the Communist Manifesto: ". . . formation of the Proletariat as a class, collapse of domination by the bourgeoisie, conquest of political power by the Proletariat."[46] The Communist Manifesto contrasts the bourgeois family and the proletariat family. While the bourgeoisie was said to have torn from the

---

[42] C. YANG, *supra* note 10, at 86,87.

[43] *Cf.* F. SCHURMANN, *supra* note 19, at 29.

[44] QUOTATIONS FROM CHAIRMAN MAO TSE-TUNG 296 (1966), cited from 3 SELECTED WORKS 288 (date?).

[45] FERDINAND LASSALLE, AUSGEWÄHLTE TEXTE (Selected writings) 27 (T. Ramm ed. 1962).

[46] 1 KARL MARX & FRIEDRICH ENGELS, AUSGEWÄHLTE SCHRIFTEN IN 2 BÄNDEN (Selected writings in 2 volumes) 35–36 (East Berlin 1955).

family relationship its veil of touching sentimentality and put it on a purely financial basis, the proletariat was said to be without property, and ". . . their relationship to wife and children therefore had nothing whatsoever in common with the bourgeois family relationship." "Only among the proletariat can sexual love be the basis of the husband and wife relationship." The conditions of life for the wife in the capitalist family were said to be comparable with those of the salaried factory worker. Thus Engels confirms that: "He [the husband] is the bourgeois in the family; the wife represents the proletariat,"[47] and it is stated in the Communist Manifesto that "the Bourgeois pictures his wife as a mere instrument of production."[48] Just as the proletariat is to liberate himself from his employer, so the wife is to free herself from the husband's domination by social revolution. With Mao Tse-tung this thought is expressed in the form that the wife is still oppressed by the husband's system of domination, wholly apart from the three systems of oppression affecting both men and women; namely, the political, religious, and clan systems.[49] Thus all four systems of oppression must be battled with equal vigor by the law.[50]

The classic Marxists take a broad approach in their substantiation. Thus Engels, who is most decisive on Communist family ideology, asserts that the husband created the institution of monogamy in order to be able to leave to his successors the assets that he acquired during his lifetime, for only the single marriage provides assurance that the wife's children will actually be his as well. Monogamy is, therefore, said to have been the first social form that was established for economic rather than natural reasons.[51] Through the division of duties in the marriage and family, by which the husband acquired all private property while the wife was to manage the household and rear the children, the wife was placed in an even more dependent position. In caring for her own existence and that of her children, she was forced to tolerate the

---

[47] F. Engels, *Der Ursprung der Familie, des Privateigentums und des Staates* (The origin of the family, of private ownership and of the state), in 2 BÜCHEREI DES MARXISMUS-LENINISMUS (Library of Marxism-Leninism) 74 (East Berlin 1953).

[48] 1 K. MARX & F. ENGELS, *supra* note 46, at 39.

[49] Mao Tse-tung, *Report on an Investigation of the Peasant Movement in Hunan* (March 1927), in QUOTATIONS FROM CHAIRMAN MAO TSE-TUNG 294 ff. (1966), cited from 1 SELECTED WORKS 44–46. "A man in China is usually subjected to the domination of three systems of authority—political authority, clan authority and religious authority. As for women, in addition to being dominated by these three systems of authority, they are also dominated by man (the authority of the husband). These four authorities—political, clan, religious and masculine—are the embodiment of the whole feudal-patriarchal ideology and system, and are the four thick ropes binding the Chinese people . . . the political authority of the landlords is the backbone of all the other systems of authority. With that overturned, the clan authority, the religious authority and the authority of the husband all began to totter. . . ."

[50] S. Fu, *supra* note 9, at 118.

[51] F. Engels, *supra* note 47, at 65.

marriage as a means of supplying her provisions;[52] that is, "the individual modern family is based upon the open or concealed domestic slavery of the wife."[53] The church, in alliance with the husband, made divorce even more difficult and thus practically prevented the wife from liberating herself from this plight. Like a prostitute, she had to endure a man she did not love, whereas the prostitute at least had the advantage of being able to refuse the sale of her embraces to one to whom she did not, for some reason, consent.[54]

With the channeling of the means of production into socialized ownership and the abolition of private ownership, the husband was to lose his economic interest in marriage and the family. At that point there would simply be no more acquired assets to devise or bequeath. Therefore, the wife could be integrated into the process of production and relieved of her traditional family tasks. The raising of the children and the management of the household would be taken over by society; central kitchens ("Central Food Preparation Institutions")[55] and washing establishments would discharge the tedious housework.[56] In this way the basic premises of full equality for the wife were to be created; she might, like the husband, learn an occupation, practice it, and become just as financially independent. In Engels' words: "Liberation of the wife [has] as its first precondition . . . the reintroduction of the entire female sex into public industry; . . . this again requires the removal of the single family's characteristic of being the economic unit of society."[57] Precisely formulated: the family, the burial ground for social progress, will die off in communist society. This is similarly expressed in the Communist Manifesto: "It is self-evident, that with the termination of the present conditions of production the resultant community ownership of wives, that is, official and unofficial prostitution (the bourgeois marriage) would disappear."[58] Some also cite Plato's statement supporting this thesis:[59] "The home and the family

---

[52] A. BEBEL, WOMAN AND SOCIALISM 106 (49th ed., not dated).

[53] F. Engels, *supra* note 47, at 73.

[54] A. BEBEL, *supra* note 52, at 118.

[55] A. BEBEL, *supra* note 52, at 430.

[56] Lenin has repeatedly emphasized these thoughts. He frequently underlines the importance of public food institutions, nurseries, and kindergartens, for these are actually suitable for liberating the wife. 29 V. LENIN, WERKE (419) (1961). In China the erection of people's kitchens, kindergartens, etc., was begun during the time of the "Great Leap": that is, in the years 1958–59. After this act of collectivization of the way of life at the end of 1959, reportedly 73 percent of the rural population affected utilized the people's kitchen—compare in detail M. BIEHL, DIE CHINESISCHE VOLKS-KOMMUNE IM "GROSSEN SPRUNG" UND DANACH (The Chinese People's communes in the "Great Leap" and since) 111 ff. (1965).

[57] F. Engels, *supra* note 47, at 74.

[58] K. Marx & F. Engels, *Kommunistisches Manifest* (Communist manifesto) (1848), in 4 KARL MARX & FRIEDRICH ENGELS, WERKE (Works) 478.

[59] S. Fu, *supra* note 9, at 118.

must also go, for in the family are the springs of all individualism. There must be community of possessions and community of wives. No one must know his offspring, just as no one must know his father or his mother. A generation will beget a generation."[60]

What ultimately remains for the classic Marxists is a marriage that is based upon mutual affection and individual sexual love, and is free of economic considerations. It continues to be moral only so long as the love endures. When the love dies for one of the spouses ("particularly with men the true length is always different") or when it is shoved aside by an even more passionate love, then "divorce is a benefit for both parties as for society."[61] In order to make this easier for the spouses, Engels in particular wants to "save the people from having to wade through the useless bog of a divorce process."[62]

By this, according to Engels, a new foundation of socialist society is attained. With the individual sexual love, a new moral yardstick arises for the valuation of sexual relations; it is not only asked: "Is he legitimate or illegitimate, but also: did he or did he not spring from a relationship of mutual love."[63] In contrast, the early Marx more strongly adhered to the interest of the family in preserving the marriage—an interest that ranked higher than the consenting intention of the spouses to sever their bonds.[64] Marx was of the opinion that one must speak not only "of the misfortune of spouses bound to one another against their will," but it is also to be considered "that almost every divorce would also be a family separation," and limits are thus placed on the arbitrary decision of the spouses. One must consider not the arbitrary whim of the spouses, but the "intention of the marriage," the moral substance of the relationship. Moral principles and rules, however, are, according to Marx, not the product of some unhistorical faculty of reason, but reflect the requirements of economic interests, of the process of production at given stages of social development. This corresponds to his belief in the possibility of an ultimate rationally planned society in which economic life would be rationally planned and relations between human beings in their practical everyday life would have assumed "the aspect of perfect intelligible and reasonable relations as between man and man and as between man and nature" (Karl Marx).

The Developments in Russia

The development of the Soviet Marriage and Child Law can be divided into three phases. It must certainly be noted in this regard that it has only

---

[60] 3 PLATO, THE REPUBLIC Book 5, at 136 (Jowett ed. date?).

[61] Compare all of these points in F. Engels, *supra* note 47, at 82.

[62] *Ibid.*

[63] *Ibid,* at 77.

[64] K. Marx (1842), *supra* note 1, at 148.

been since February 25, 1947, that the federal legislature has possessed the competency to "establish the basis for the legislation on marriage and family."[65] Consequently, there previously were only the individual state regulations of the fifteen union republics. Among them, the code of the largest and most densely populated republic, the RSFSR (Russian Socialist Federated Soviet Republic), was of prevailing importance.[66]

First phase (1917–1936). The first period of development commences with the December Decrees of 1917 and the Family Code of 1918 of the RSFSR. Their texts were rather cautious. But during the following years, public opinion and the courts were motivated more and more by political agitation, propaganda, and other means in a more radical pursuance of the ideological aims. The apex of the first period was reached with the 1927 Family Code of the RSFSR, which faded out in the mid-thirties. The Russian soldiers returning home from the First World War above all tried for some time to collectivize everything in the form of a "commune." In their view, not only should the enterprises and particularly agriculture be socialized, but also all personal matters such as eating, drinking, cooking, housing, and women. Bad experiences resulted from the attempt, and in the Russian program of collectivization an important decision was made against the communes and in favor of the "artel". Indeed, in the Program of the Communist Party that was ratified by the eighth session of the Russian Communist Party in 1919, the creation of "Production Agrarian Communes," as a completely voluntary union of farmers for the management of the common greater economic unit was already foreseen. "Consumption Communes and their associations in the supply co-operatives of the consumers, as well as purely Social Communes (Commune Houses)" were also projected. These were to take the place of the household economy, which oppressed the wife and was extremely unproductive.

Lenin also then wrote in the first draft of his article "The Immediate Challenges of the Soviet Power": "Each factory, each artel and agrarian enterprise, each village, that now comes into the new system of cultivation of the soil by application of the statute on socialization of the land, is now an

---

[65] Compare Article 14, Paragraph 23 of the Constitution of the USSR—Amendment based on Article 2 of the *Statute on the Amendment and Supplementation of the Text of the Constitution of the USSR,* VEDOMOSTI VERCHOVNOGO SOVETA, SSSR (Bulletin of the Supreme Soviet of the USSR) No. 8 (Feb. 25, 1947).

[66] The code of the RSFSR *(Kodeks zakonov o brake, sem'e i opeke—SU RSFSR),* 1926. No. 82, st. 612—[hereinafter cited as Family Law Code of 1927] was adopted by several of the Union republics; the Kirghiz SSR, the Kazakh SSR, and the Baltic states of Lithuania, Latvia, and Estonia. *Cf.* G. Sverdlov, *Das Eherecht der Union des Sozialistischen Sowjetrepubliken* (The Marriage Law of the USSR), in 1 LESKE & LOEWENFELD, DAS EHERECHT DER EUROPAISCHEN UND DER AUSSEREUROPAISCHEN STAATEN (The marriage law of the European and non-European countries) 574 (1965). It is important to note that the later amendments of these codes were independent of the RSFSR code, so that the versions are now different.

independent commune in the sense of the principles of the Soviet power, with internal division of labor."[67] But for inevitable practical reasons the realization of these postulates was at that time postponed by the Soviet government until the distant future. At first there would be the socialist structure, and only in the future, when a high standard of industrialization of the country and a surplus of goods were attained, could the form of Communism be adopted. Thereby, at least for the time being, the family basically remained a self-contained unit.[68] It further functioned as a unit in a spiritual and material respect, because it assured the solidarity of its members and at the same time served as the center for consumption. Each collective *(kolkhoz)* farmer maintained his own family homestead and administered his own consumer budget. Only the means of production were socialized. On the other hand, the consumer economy, including the home, basically remained outside the collectivization.

The family law claims of Engels that were directly adopted in the program of the Bolshevik Party and the effort to realize these radical postulates constituted the starting points for the legal formulations on marriage and children. These epochs of family legislation thereby assumed the character of a legislative battle campaign waged against the traditional forms, the "bourgeois marriage," the existing authorities, and religious fetters. The family law at that time was not to mirror existing conditions, but was rather to form and develop the social standards. Secularization of the marriage, equality of the woman, increased integration of the woman into the productive process, and a retreat from the traditional state preference accorded the marital status were in this sense its primary characteristics.

At first the clerical registry offices were transformed into civil authorities.[69] Only the marriage taking place in the registry office was given legal effect.[70] The banns were abolished; the marital impediments were reduced to a few;[71] the provision that the statutory domicile of the wife always remain that of the husband was abolished; after 1924 the spouses were no longer obliged to have a common family name; the right to a claim for resumption of consortium was

---

[67] *Der Mensch in der Kommune* (Man in the commune) (quoted from *Nowyj mir* Moscow, No. 7, 1960), 12 OST-PROBLEME 653 (1960).

[68] "No Soviet author has envisaged complete submersion of the family in such community enterprises as those that emerged in China during its commune phase in the late 1950's." J. HAZARD & I. SHAPIRO, *supra* note 21, at Pt. 3, 102.

[69] This extremely complicated process did not terminate until 1925. *Cf.* H. Freund, *supra* note 6, at 11.

[70] *Cf.* RSFSR Family Law Code of 1918, *supra* note 6, at Art. 52 *et seq.*

[71] Lack of sufficient marital age (for men it was 18 and for women 16), Art. 66; Mental illness, Art. 67; existence of a previous marriage, Art. 68; affinity within the first degree (even if illegitimate); and total and half consanguinity, Art. 69.

no longer acknowledged; and every spouse had the right to live apart at any time (Article 104, Family Code of 1918).

The turning away from the traditional marital principles appeared most clearly in the basic changes of the divorce law. In conformity with Engels' thesis that only a marriage founded on love was moral, the Family Code of 1918 left it up to the desires of the spouses as to whether to dissolve their marriage or not. Consequently, the Code of 1918 no longer contained any specific grounds for divorce. Divorce, like marriage, was viewed as a "private matter for each individual."[72] With respect to divorce, which was considered a "bilateral private law contract between two equal parties,"[73] the only distinction drawn was that for a divorce that was mutually consented to, a registry office was competent, while a divorce sought by only one spouse was within the competency of a court.

Even this limited state intervention was diminished. In order to further deliver into the hands of the spouses the fate of their marriage as a personal affair, the state retreated even further and renounced all interference with divorce. Yet libertine tendencies were not completely freed. Lenin was among those who opposed the views in some circles that the termination of private ownership would lead to the abandonment of monogamy.[74] Lenin followed the early Marx rather than Engels in emphasizing the social element of love: "there are two partners and a third, new life can spring forth."[75] In Lenin's opinion, the "glass of water" theory, by which satisfaction of the sexual urge was viewed as being as simple and irrelevant as drinking a glass of water, was "completely non-Marxist and, in addition, anti-social."[76] He stressed: "as a

---

[72] Similarly, A. BEBEL, *supra* note 52, at 434, already noted: "My intercourse with a person of another sex is as much my personal affair as my eating, drinking, sleeping and dressing."

[73] P. GIDULJANOV, KODEKS ZAKONOV O BRAKE, SEMJE I OPEKI S POSTATEJ NYMI KOMMEN-TARIJAMI (Code of laws on marriage, family and guardianship with commentary) 29 (1927).

[74] *Cf.* excerpts from the writings of Mme. Kollontai in: R. SCHLESINGER, THE FAMILY IN THE USSR 69, 72 ff. (1949). In contrast to that, "Communist China's literary history never included concerted attack upon the legal family or marriage as an institution. The 'free love' theme or 'glass of water' theory of sex has never enjoyed literary vogue as it did in the Soviet literature of the 1920's. As is well known, a generally puritanical tone is maintained in Communist China's fiction." AI-LI S. CHIN, MODERN CHINESE FICTION AND FAMILY RELATIONS 45 (1966).

[75] Lenin added: "Therein is concealed a social interest, an obligation arises toward the collective group." C. Zetkin, *Erinnerungen an Lenin* (Recollections of Lenin), cited in A. Pergament, *Die Ehe* (the marriage) in 2 SOWJETISCHES ZIVILRECHT (Soviet private law) 457 (S. Bratus ed., German translation 1953).

[76] *Cf.* C. ZETKIN, AUSGEWÄHLTE REDEN UND SCHRIFTEN (Selected speeches and writings) 139–40 (1960).

communist I have not the slightest sympathy for the glass of water theory, even if it bears the attractive slogan: 'freedom of love.' "

On the whole, marriage still had a certain special legal status. Yet the secularized marriage law was further "de-nationalized," particularly because the trend of Marxist-Leninist legal theory[77] at that time was moving in the direction of a certain legal nihilism.[78] The Family Code of the RSFSR of 1926, like most of the family codes of the union republics (but with the exception, for instance, of the Ukraine), abolished mandatory civil marriage and judicial, as well as civil registry, divorce. While the Family Code of 1918 made the official act of registering the marriage essential to its validity, henceforth it was only to have an evidentiary function.[79] The marriage only came into existence with the consenting intentions of the betrothed couple. The old maxim *"consensus facit nuptias"* was again honored under new aspects,[80] and in practice even implied declarations of consent were viewed as adequate. The Family Code (Art. 12) contained definite criteria for proving the existence of the marriage: common habitation, common financial management, appearance of legitimacy to third persons, mutual support, common rearing of the children, and so on. Registered and de facto marriages were thus accorded equal value.[81] Nevertheless, there were small differences; for example, only partners to a registered marriage could consent to select a common family name (Art. 7).

The married couple was likewise free to register the informal divorce, which could be unilateral and implied from one's conduct. According to the prevailing view, even a registered marriage could be divorced without registration of

---

[77] Accordingly, the task of the law (and the state) was to assure the economic interests of the ruling class. With the distinction of class difference it loses (as does the state) its function and is sentenced to die off. In its place arise the norms of the communist ethic and organizational-technical instructions, *cf., e.g.*, the introduction of the penal law decree "On the leading principles of penal law of the RSFSR" of December 12, 1919 (SU RSFSR 1919, No. 66, Art. 590): The Proletariate (after the institution of communism) was to "also destroy the organized power of the state and the law, as a state function." In theory the claim was supported with the assertion that law in capitalist society had already attained its apex and was no longer capable of progress; 2 D. LOEBER, OSTEUROPA (Eastern Europe) 170 ff. (1952).

[78] See A. Wyschinski, *Über einige Fragen der Theorie des Staates und des Rechts* (On several questions of state and legal theory), in 36. BEIHEFT ZUR "SOWJETWISSEN-SCHAFT" (36th Supplement to "Sowjetwissenschaft") 111 (1953).

[79] See J. MAGIDSON, *supra* note 23, at 11; H. Freund, *supra* note 6, at 17.

[80] G. Soloweitschik, *Das Eherecht der Russischen Sozialistischen Föderativen Sowjetrepublik unter besonderer Berücksichtigung seiner Stellung im internationalen Privatrecht* (The marriage law of the Russian Socialist Federative Soviet Republic with particular consideration of its position in the international law of conflicts), at 18 (thesis, Leipzig 1931).

[81] G. SVERDLOV, *supra* note 5, at 74 ff.; G. Soloweitschik, *supra* note 80, at 23.

the dissolution.[82] Therefore, many a spouse did not know whether he or she was still married or already divorced de facto.[83] Indeed, several marriages could be in existence at the same time. The practice found its own solution by viewing, as a rule, the entry into a new matrimonial union by one spouse as an automatic dissolution of the old marriage.

In child law, particularly, the pedagogical and economic duties of the family were reduced. The illegitimate and legitimate children were treated equally. If the woman had had intercourse with several men during the time in question then originally all of the potential fathers had to provide a share of the support, while later only one of them had this duty.[84] In his "Textbook on Marriage and Family Law" the jurist Brandenburgskij characterized the likely development at the time as follows:

> We are unmistakably on the road to cooperative rearing of children with social welfare for them at state expenses. If we are still maintaining the duty of mutual support within the family, this is happening only because the state cannot yet replace the family in this respect. At the present time the state is not yet in a position to have at its disposal the necessary means and conditions. In the course of time the family will disappear and be replaced by the state organization of community upbringing and social welfare.[85]

This marks the continuation and increase of a tendency toward further loss of function for the family, along with the explicit intention to abolish the family as an institution and the replacement of the two-generation family by the one-generation institution. The relationship might perhaps even be limited in time and would in any case require a separation of the children.[86] As practical measures to attain this goal, kindergartens, children's homes, and

---

[82] Yet there were several lower courts which took the position that a registered marriage was dissoluble only by following the forms for registered marriages. *Cf.* Judgment of the Sup. Ct. RSFSR, Sud. Prak. RSFSR 1920/20 p. 8. *See also* A. BILINSKY, DAS SOWJETISCHE EHERECHT (The Soviet marriage law) 21 ff., 86 ff. (1961).

[83] E. Florkowski, *Das sowjetische Ehescheidungsrecht* (The Soviet divorce law), at 40 (thesis, Gottingen 1967).

[84] *Cf.* H. BAHRO, DAS KINDSCHAFTSRECHT IN DER UNION DER SOZIALISTISCHEN SOWJETREPUBLIKEN (Child law in the Union of Socialist Soviet Republics) 25, 27 (1966).

[85] J. BRANDENBURGSKIJ, KURS PO SEMEJNO-BRACNOMU PRAVU (Lectures on family and marriage law) 20 ff. (1928).

[86] Batkis, *Die Sexualrevolution in Russland* (The sexual revolution in Russia), in 4 BEITRÄGE ZUM SEXUALPROBLEM (Selections on the sexual problem) 5–6 (Teilhaber ed. 1925). "The Soviet law is subject to the law of development, just as all the rest of the social institutions. But the Soviet law of today is the law of a temporary period; it goes its way, destroying remnants and thus laying the groundwork for the future, and it is at the same time a reflection of the present situation. This situation does not permit the young society to regulate the course of the entire material life, with respect to the caring for all citizens and the rearing of all children."

community kitchens were established and scattered throughout the entire country.[87]

Second phase (1936–1953). The second epoch of Soviet marriage law again begins cautiously in the first instance with the Family Protection Statute of 1936, for which public sentiment was aroused by Stalin's highly publicized visit with his old mother. After years of intensive propaganda about its main ideas it reached its climax with the Union Decree of 1944, which must be seen in connection with the deep-cutting consequences of the war. In particular, it again tied the marriage contract to state cooperation, no longer recognized the previous freedom of divorce, and sharply distinguished between illegitimate and legitimate children. From the fifties on (Stalin's death being on March 5, 1953), the way was then paved for a certain withdrawal, and thus for the transition to the third epoch.

The main steps were the following. In the middle of the thirties, there developed a change of view on important points of the family law. There were basic claims that remained intact such as the equality and occupational employment of women, as well as the relieving of the marriage of certain family duties. Yet the increasing demand that the foundations of the socialist marriage and family be strengthened led to the state's stronger reliance on the law for these purposes. The former conception, that the family was sentenced to die off, was revised as an erroneous interpretation of Marxist doctrine.[88] Rather, it was to be a matter of creating the "higher type family,[89] the socialist family."

At the same time there grew a general conviction in Soviet legal theory that the creative power of law for society should be utilized more effectively.[90] In response to these thoughts the Family Protection Statute went to battle against frivolous conduct with respect to the family and the marital duties.[91] Yet nothing was changed in the substantive marriage law. It still allowed the existence of the de facto wedding, as well as the de facto divorce. Also, the statute introduced no statutory divorce grounds but adhered theoretically to the principle of unlimited freedom of divorce. Nevertheless, the legislator prevented a flood of divorces with the divorce procedural law. According to the new provisions, at the time of the divorce proceeding both spouses had

---

[87] G. MACKENROTH, *supra* note 40, at 380–81.

[88] *Cf.* G. SVERDLOV, *supra* note 5, at 34 ff.

[89] A. Pergament, *supra* note 75, at 461.

[90] *See* A. Wyschinski, *supra* note 78, at 38 ff.

[91] Ordinance of the CIK and SNK SSSR of June 27, 1936 "On the prohibition of abortion, the increase of material support for the woman in childbirth; the establishment of state aid for families with many children; for nurseries, and for Kindergartens; the increase of penal liability for breach of the duty of support and on several amendments in the divorce legislation." (Family Protection Statute), in Family Law Code of 1927 (official ed. 1961), at 41–42 (excerpt).

to be attempting to bring about a reconciliation. But the appearance of only one spouse did not prevent the civil registrar from registering the divorce.[92] If the marriage were severed, the civil registrar had to record the divorce on the passes of both parties.[93] Behind this provision there were completely practical consequences[94] in view of the frequent use of the pass in daily life. It particularly made it more difficult for a spouse to conceal his divorce at the time of remarriage. Even more incisive was the drastic increase in the registration fee for divorce;[95] it proved to be quite an effective means of combating divorce. Under the new provisions it was also no longer possible for a registered marriage to be dissolved by a de facto divorce. To this extent the divorce registration had a constitutive significance.

This Family Protection Statute of 1936 contained for divorce law in the judgment of Rabinovic, no more than "single temporary, all in all timid steps on the road to combating arbitrariness."[96] On the other hand the Union Decree of July 8, 1944,[97] during the height of the war brought about the official radical change in family law. It must above all be viewed as an act of expediency of the population policy in order to make up for the losses in the Second World War. In contrast to the Family code of 1927 it contained three fundamental innovations: (1) it introduced compulsory civil marriage; (2) it abandoned the principle of freedom of divorce[98] and established the state divorce monopoly with the introduction of a three-stage procedure with a mandatory reconciliation proceeding before the People's Court; and (3) it

---

[92] F. Florkowski, *supra* note 83, at 61.

[93] Family Law Code of 1927, Art. 140 (May 10, 1937).

[94] A. BILINSKY, *supra* note 82, at 85.

[95] It was determined by the number of divorces, and amounted to 50 rubles for the first, 150 rubles for the second, and 300 rubles for each additional divorce. *Cf.* Family Protection Statute, Art. 28, *supra* note 91.

[96] N. Rabinovic, *Semejnoe pravo* (Family law), in SOROK BET SOVETSKOGO PRAVA, 1917–57 (Forty years of Soviet law, 1917–57) Pt. 2, 278 (L. Sargorodskij ed. 1957); cited in E. Florkowski, *supra* note 83, at 62.

[97] Decree of the Praesidium of the Supreme Soviet of the USSR of July 8, 1944: "On the expansion of state aid for pregnant women, for mothers with several children and for mothers who are alone, the strengthening of the protection of the mother-child relationship, the introduction of the honorary title 'Mother Heroine,' and the establishment of the order of 'Glorious Mothers' and the medals called 'maternity medals.' " (VVS SSSR 1944, No. 37).

[98] For a straightforward account, *see* A. Pergament, *O. kodifikacii respublikanskogo zakonodatel'stva o brake, sem'e i opeke* (On the codification of the Republic legislation on marriage, family, and guardianship), in NAUCNAJA SESSIJA POSVJASCENNAJA VOPROSAM KODIFIKACII SOVETSKOGO RESPUBLIKANSKOGO ZAKANODATEL'STVA (Scientific conference on problems of Soviet Republic legislation) 76 (1957): "It is incorrect to say that the existing law preserves the principle of freedom of divorce."

abolished paternity actions and brought about an essential difference between the legal status of legitimate and illegitimate children.

Under Article 19 of the decree of 1944 only the registered marriage was endowed with marital rights and duties. It was also to be registered on the passes individuals had to carry (Art. 22). One who was living in a de facto marriage could have it registered by declaring the length of its duration (Art. 19 II). From that time on divorce could basically be granted only in a public judicial proceeding (Art. 23). The competency of the civil registries to grant divorces was thus removed. The commencement of divorce proceedings, moreover, had to be published in the local newspaper at the expense of the party seeking the divorce (Art. 24c). The divorce proceeding itself now consisted of three sections comprised of two judicial proceedings and one administrative proceeding before the civil registrar. Following a recitation of the facts, there was at first a reconciliation proceeding under the influence of the court; there was no atonement process without judges. This was held before the People's (City) Court, the court of first instance in the Soviet Union. If this proceeding were unsuccessful, then the People's Court could not render a decision, and the proceeding went up to a higher court—the regional, country, district, or municipal court, or the Supreme Court of a Union or Autonomous Republic (Art. 25 para. 3). Such a court repeated the efforts toward reconciliation and permitted the divorce only when it was deemed necessary in view of the breakdown of the family (Art. 26). Here the public frequently participated in the proceedings.[99]

The divorce judgment still possessed no constitutive effect. The couple did not become divorced until the day the civil registrar registered the divorce and recorded it on the identification papers on the basis of the pertinent judicial decision. The civil registrar received on this occasion, from one or both spouses, a considerable fee (Art. 27).

The decree of 1944 established no individual divorce grounds either exhaustively or suggestively. The directives issued by the full Supreme Court of the USSR on September 16, 1949,[100] gave the courts some indications with the general advice that: "The court should only grant a divorce when the divorce complaint is filed for serious and established causes, when maintaining the marriage intact would contravene the principles of the communist ethic,

---

[99] *See* A. Pergament, *supra* note 75, at 473: "The Soviet public will not pass over such occurrences in silence. . . . Soviet society cannot help but indict the unworthy members. . . ."

[100] Official Designation: *Postanovlenie Plenuma Verchovnogo Suda SSSR No. 12/8/Y or 16.9.1949g. "O sudebnoj praktike po delam o restorženii braka"* (Directives of the Plenary Supreme Court of the USSR No. 12/8/Y of September 16, 1949: "On the judicial practice in matters of divorce"), in KODEKS ZAKONOW O BRAKE, SEMJE I OPJEKJE (Code of laws on marriage, family and guardianship) 90 ff. (official ed. 1961).

and when the normal requisites of living together and rearing children are not present."[101]

As to children born outside of a registered marriage, Article 20 of the decree of July 8, 1944, repealed the former right of the mother to file a claim for a paternal determination. The father of such a child was from then on basically not obligated to provide support for the child—a regulation that cannot be looked at without considering the great surplus of females resulting from the war. Yet the fathers who had actually paid support before July 8, 1944, were by the prevailing case law still obligated to continue the support. The mother who was not living in a registered marriage could place the child in a state home or receive monthly support aid (amounting to at least 5 rubles).

Third phase (1953 to 1968). Since about the middle fifties the transition of Soviet family law has moved toward a third phase. During the Stalinist era the provisions of the Union Decree of 1944 were in practice not openly discussed or criticized, although with the growing up of the post-war generation the population problems were viewed in a different light. Theory and practice were, in the typical fashion of that time, merely working out the advantages of this "Stalinist" family law. After Stalin's death on March 5, 1953, however, a freer and more fundamental discussion and evaluation of the prevailing family law system gradually began.[102] Reform initiatives on a broader foundation set in after the 20th Party Day of the Communist Party of the Soviet Union in February 1956. The reform movements even made reference to sociological investigations, which for a long time had been rejected as "western" and "bourgeois."[103] The Party Day ushered in de-stalinization and gave new impetus to the entire legal policy under the motto "work, learn and live communist!" They sought explicitly to overcome overly strict dogmatic legal concepts in order to more efficiently accomplish measures for preserving marriages, to prevent conduct inimical to society, and perhaps also to strengthen somewhat the citizens' interest in the law.[104] The reason given for this was that the principles of the socialist ideology had been increasingly accomplished with the growing consciousness of the citizens. In this connection and in direct regard to the competency of the union that had existed since February 1947, a new codification was demanded. In the coming Family code, those principles

---

[101] *Cf*. the German translation in H. Kotbe, *Zum Problem der Scheidung aus beiderseitigem Einverständnis* (On the problem of divorce by mutual consent), 4 NEUE JUSTIZ 339 (1950).

[102] Among them are included, *e.g.*, B. Antimov & A. Pergament, *Nužny li izmenenija v porjadke rastorženija braka?* (Are amendments in the divorce ordinance needed?), SOCIALISTICESKAJA ZAKONNOST (The socialist rule of law) No. 9, at 24 ff. (1954).

[103] *Cf*. especially A. CHARCEV, BRAK I SEM'JA V SSSR (Marriage and the family in the USSR) (1964).

[104] *Cf*. especially D. Loeber, *Die sowjetische Rechtsreform von 1958* (The Soviet law reform of 1958), 9 OSTEUROPA 355 ff. (1959).

that had in the meantime been developed in the case law were also to be partly adopted. It was thus that the wide freedom of judicial discretion, for instance, in the law of marital property and support, was to become a bit more specifically defined. The division of marital property consisted basically of a division into halves of the property acquired during the marriage, rather than leaving equitable division to the judge.

Yet the emphasis was not placed upon individual questions; rather the focus was generally on the socialistic type of marriage and family life. The reform views in the discussions concentrated upon the new order for the two branches of family law most deeply affected by the Stalin Union Decree of 1944; namely, the dismal status of the illegitimate child, who could be totally ignored by his father, and the increased difficulties of obtaining a divorce[105] —although the latter had been already somewhat ameliorated in practice by the case law.[106]

In the law of illegitimacy the material distress of the children stood in the foreground; the possibilities of participation by the father had not been exhausted, and state aid, both in its amount and duration, was viewed as unsatisfactory.[107] It was felt to be a contradiction of the principle of equality of men and women that (apart from the state aid) only the mother had to provide support for the child. The prohibition against paternity suits was viewed as a violation of communist morality. Numerous proposals on reforming the law of illegitimacy were made—from a claim against the putative father for support upon voluntary acknowledgment and judicial determination of paternity, to a complete equality of status of legitimate and illegitimate children in the manner of the Soviet Union legislation before 1942.

In divorce law the principles indeed remained: "In socialist society divorce cannot be left to the discretion of the spouses.[108] Criticism set in against the ceremonious, piecemeal nature of the procedure and the discriminatory side effects occasioned by divorce, especially the publication in the local press. These demands proved to be so pressing that the Praesidium of the Supreme Soviet of the USSR on December 10, 1965,[109] in spite of the far-reaching

[105] See G. Sverdlov, Die Entwicklung des sowjetischen Familienrechts seit der Oktober-revolution (The development of Soviet Family Law since the October Revolution), 11 NEUE JUSTIZ 686 (1957).

[106] Note, for example, the legal practice by which a father who was not in the personal register might still be required to provide support in a case where the events of the war prevented a timely determination of paternity. Cf. also Family Law Code of 1927, Art. 42 III.

[107] H. BAHRO, supra note 84, at 135, for further references.

[108] A. Pergament, supra note 75, at 470.

[109] Official designation: Postanovlenie No. 13 Plenuma Verchovnogo Suda SSSR ot 29.12.1965g. "O primenenii sudami Ukaza Prezidiuma Verchovnogo Soveta SSSR ot 10.12.1965g. O nekotorom izmenii porjadka rassmotrenija v sudach del o rastorženii braka"

preparatory work on the new Family Code, nevertheless issued a decree that effected an ameliorative partial reform. It simplified the divorce procedure and attempted to improve the possible sanctions against overly hasty divorces. The divorce trial decision was referred to the Rayon (municipal) People's Court, and the provisions requiring publication of the announcement of the commencement of a divorce proceeding were abandoned.[110]

Moreover, further warning was given of the danger that a statutorily fixed list of divorce grounds might incline the courts toward granting divorces too readily.[111] For this purpose, as well as for the purpose of not limiting a thorough judicial examination, the previous blanket nature of the divorce trial was maintained. There was also adherence to the provision that the divorce court must simultaneously regulate all of the legal relations of the parties that are directly touched by the termination of the marriage (division of the children, the assets, regulation of support, names, and so on).[112]

In a new thrust, it was deemed that the special forces of the work and home life be also mobilized toward a solution of marital and family conflicts.[113] The parties alone were not viewed as capable of deciding all by themselves whether

---

(Directive No. 13 of the Plenary Supreme Court of the USSR of December 29, 1965: "On the judicial application of the decree of the Praesidium of the Supreme Soviet of the USSR of December 10, 1965, on several amendments of the procedural system in divorce matters"), SOWJETSKAJA JUSTIZJA (Soviet justice) No. 3, at 32 (1966).

[110] *Cf.* paras. 1, 3 of the decree, *supra* note 109.

[111] *See* especially G. Sverdlov, *O razvode* (Concerning divorce), SOVETSKOE GOSUDARSTVO I PRAVO (Soviet state and law) [hereinafter cited as SGIP] No. 12, at 55 (1958). According to Giebel, *Ehescheidungen in der Sowjetunion* (Divorce in USSR), 21 DAS STANDESAMT (The registry office) 208 (1968), referring to the Soviet Statistical Monthly, in the year 1960 out of a population of 208,826,650 there were 270,200 divorces; in 1963 out of a population of 219,755,000 there were 291,500 divorces; and in 1965 out of a population of 229,000,000 there were 360,400 divorces and 1,992,000 weddings. More exact details are available for the individual Union republics. Thus for the Uzbekian republic, whose population in 1939 was about 6,334,000 and in 1956 about 7,313,000, the following statistics apply: 1939 = 52,700 weddings and 9,617 divorces; 1946 = 48,400 weddings and 653 divorces; 1950 = 64,100 weddings and 673 divorces; 1953 = 65,100 weddings and 780 divorces; 1956 = 81,600 weddings and 1,272 divorces. A. CHARCEV, BRAK I SEMJA V SSSR (Marriage and the family in the USSR) 168 (1964).

[112] Article 25 contained in the decree of December 10, 1965, *supra* note 109, the following version: The *Rayon* (Municipal) People's Court was to ascertain the motives behind the divorce application and to take measures toward reconciliation of the marriage. The *Rayon* (Municipal) People's Court can, by postponing the matter, set a period for reconciliation. If no reconciliation of the spouses results, and if the court concludes that a further cohabitation of the spouses and maintenance of the family have become impossible, the *Rayon* (People's) Court can issue a decision on divorce of the marriage.

[113] *See* J. Hazard, *Le Droit soviétique et le dépérissement de l'état* (Soviet law and the decay of the state), 8 TRAVAUX ET CONFÉRENCES 80 (Faculté de droit de Bruxelles 1960).

they should be divorced or live together in the future. As a means for this assistance of the people, more reference was made to social acknowledgment and social condemnation. The forces of the collective community at the place of work and neighborhood were to take joint responsibility, not only in the reconciliation of the spouses and the recitation of the facts, but also to judge, independently of the jury, individual contested issues such as the awarding of the home and support obligations. It is evident that in this way certain features of life in a responsible community were created in which everyone depended upon the collective opinion of the members of the community. Nevertheless, there may be differences between sections or states of the USSR about the degree of this "social participation." The psychological risks of subjecting the individual to such manipulation are obvious—even without open discussion of this element.

The actual statutory reform in family law belonging to this third phase of development was made by the fundamental legislation of June 27, 1968.[114] It went into effect on October 1, 1968. With this legislative work accomplished after long public discussion, the central government for the first time completely fulfilled the competency established on February 25, 1947, for the determination of principles for the legislation on marriage and family.[115] This statute regulates the substantive family law quite extensively. At first glance it would appear that the republics are intended to be left only with details of procedural law. That is even more true because the Soviet legislator considers that his standards in family law are always subject in a controlling sense to the ever-developing and in detail unpredictable influence of the official social ethic. Because provisions must always remain open for new and unforeseen developments, the rules contained in the legislative work of June 27, 1968, were not filled in too specifically. Necessary space was afforded for expansion,

---

[114] Cf. the USSR statute on the ratification of the new legislation of the USSR and the Union Republics on marriage and family, of June 27, 1968 [hereinafter cited as Family Law Code of 1968]: *Zakon sojusa sovietskich socialisticeskich republik oc utwershdenii osnow zakonodatelstwa sojusa SSR i sojusnych republic o brake i semje,* Pravda (Moscow), June 28, 1968, at 1.

[115] Since by virtue of Art. 14, para. 21 of the Constitution of the USSR of 1936 the legislature already possessed the legislative competency for civil law, the establishment of competency in 1947 was understood by many as an official confirmation of the interpretation that the family law might not be a part of the civil law, but rather constitute an independent branch of the law. In particular, a practical consequence of this doctrine is a less hesitant acknowledgment of the preemptory nature of the family law. As to the points of contention, *see* G. Sverdlov, *supra* note 5, at 22 ff; A Pergament, *supra* note 75, at 434; D. Loeber, Eherecht der Sowjetunion (Marriage law in the Soviet Union) (Thesis, Marburg 1950), at 32 ff; E. NIZSALOVSZKY, ORDER OF THE FAMILY 102 ff. (1968). Recently, Ioffe again views the family law as a part of the civil law. *Cf.* O. S. IOFFE, SOVETSKOE GRAZDANSKOE PRAVO (Soviet civil law) 38, 41 (1967).

adaptations, and even new solutions. There is no catalogue of legal grounds of divorce.

In its individual solutions, the statute of June 27, 1968, deviates substantially from the reform provisions since the Stalinist era. The draft printed in *Izvestia* on April 10, 1968, basically still followed that issued on December 10, 1965, for example, on divorce law. The only significant new provision was that the husband could not seek a divorce from the wife during her pregnancy or for one year after the birth of the child—a provision already known in the Communist Marriage Law in China since 1943. In contrast, the June 27 Statute made notable modifications. Article 14 facilitated divorce practice, but also left open possibilities for restrictions. All of this shows how controversial the regulations probably were right up to the last moment before issuance. There is so far no monopoly of views on family policies in Soviet Russia.

Divorce by consent[116] is again permitted when there are no minor children of the marriage.[117] As it was after 1927, the agencies of registration can again pronounce the divorce by mutual consent after a period of three months from the time of the parties' application. The agencies for registration of civil status also process the dissolution of marriage for those persons who are legally recognized as missing, legally recognized as incompetent as a result of mental illness or feeblemindedness, or sentenced for the commission of a crime for a term of not less than three years.

On the other hand, in disputed cases dissolution of marriage is conducted through a court, which is obligated to undertake measures toward reconciliation. Thereby, depending upon the judicial climate, a significant restriction of divorce might result. Also, in deciding whether there exists actual consent on the part of the spouses, different results might occur, depending upon the required standards of proof for showing consent. Moreover, the controlling issue for the court is still, as before, whether further cohabitation of the spouses and the preservation of the family have become impossible. The new

---

[116] *See* E. Egurskaja, *Normy zakonov o brake i sem j nuzdajutsja v izmenenii* (The statutory provisions on marriage and family are in need of change), Socialisticeskaja zakannost (The socialist rule of law) No. 1, at 31–33 (1965). This was publicly discussed in Literaturnaja Gazeta (Moscow), Dec. 25, 1965, at 2. The judicial practice is said to have revealed that in 85 percent of the cases both marital partners had consented to the divorce. Only 10 percent of the divorce complaints were dismissed by the courts.

[117] Similar proposals were already contained in Art. 225 of the draft on civil procedure in the Mold. SSR and in the draft of a family code of USSR. *See* V. Davydov, *Obsuždenie proektov Gk i Gpk Moedavskoj SSR* (Discussion of the draft of the private law code and the civil procedure law of the Mold. SSR), SGIP No. 6, at 134 ff. (1963); U. Ibragimov, Ob osmovnyeh položenijach proekta bracno-semejnogo kodeksa Uzbekskoj SSR (Basic principles of the draft of the marriage and family code of the UZBEK SSR), Izvestija of the Uzbek SSR, Academy of Sciences, Social Sciences Series, No. 5, at 37 ff. (Tashkent 1959).

statute adheres to the principle of marital breakdown, which by the prevailing view was consonant with the new development toward the ripened socialism. Finally, the statute of 1968 added as a last paragraph of Article 14: "A spouse, who changed his last name for another upon entering into marriage, shall have the right to continue to be named with this last name, or on his request to have his antenuptial name restored."

In the law of illegitimacy the paternity claim is again allowed. The statutory provision regulating the investigation of fathers of illegitimate children now reads in its expanded (in comparison with the original text) version: "In establishing paternity, the court takes into account cohabitation and the maintenance of a common household by the children's mother and the respondent before the child's birth or joint rearing or support of the child or evidence reliably confirming the recognition by the defendant of paternity." (Article 16, para. 4). The establishment of paternity by the court, as well as the voluntary recognition of paternity, results in the duty to pay child support to the same extent as the father would have to pay in a divorce affecting children born in wedlock.

All in all, with the new statute the pendulum is swinging away from the statutory restrictions imposed by Stalin at the height of the war. Obviously, the modern sociological investigations of marriage and family have played a role in its unhurried conception. Significant results were also accomplished by the numerous discussions in which opinions at various points of the spectrum found their expression. But the importance of the extra-legal factors in bringing about change must be kept in mind. The whole complex has to be seen under the educational implications of the Soviet campaign for *obshchestvennost* which may be freely rendered as "social will."

The Developments in China

The development of communist family law in China should not be viewed only from the background of traditional Chinese family law, which basically meant security more for the "extended family" or the clan than for the individual.[118] Moreover, in traditional society there had been a particular collectivism that was very strict within its limits. "Virtually every Chinese was thoroughly experienced in the benefits, problems, and adjustments of cooperative and associational life as a result of membership in small-scale social units."[119] Developments in Communist China must be examined in connection

---

[118] *Cf.* O. LANG, CHINESE FAMILY AND SOCIETY (1946); M. LEVY, JR., THE FAMILY REVOLUTION IN MODERN CHINA (1949). M. BIEHL, *supra* note 56, at 116, asserts with slight overstatement "that old China was a federal state of millions of autonomous clans, whose legal relationships among one another were governed by negotiation. The state was in many a place and at many a time only the echo of an echo."

[119] J. TOWNSEND, POLITICAL PARTICIPATION IN COMMUNIST CHINA 19 (1967).

with other prior or contemporaneous starts in the direction of reform of traditional Chinese family law; on the other hand, there must be consideration of the ideological goals that had been pursued and the practical experiences that had resulted from family law reforms undertaken in other countries, especially Russia. Finally, the family revolution in China is the work of at least half a century. It began at the turn of the twentieth century and was completed by the Communists. About the year 1921 the Communist Party of China was founded mainly by a group of young Chinese intellectuals attracted by the scientific character of Marxism and its international features which offered a means of compensating for the damaged national feelings.

Non-Communist reform effort up to 1949. Until the time of the Communist take-over in China in 1949 the erosion of traditional family patterns by the modern reform movement in the family law sphere had already passed through three stages during the last half century,[120] proving "the connection between modernism, nationalism and marriage reform."[121] The first reform efforts were observable a short time before the republican revolution of 1911, stimulated by relations with Europe. They led to no concrete results during the imperial period, but the elimination of the old examination system, the growth of modern schools, the improvements in communication and transportation, and the process of industrialization and urbanization pushed the development further on. In the following republican period and until the seizure of authority by the Kuomintang in 1928, the critical young urban intellectuals in particular demanded that the old family system be dissolved, that free marital choice by the spouses be introduced, and that equality of man and woman be pushed forward. These currents were precipitated, in part only, in new statutory drafts;[122] life in rural China persisted in the old forms. The third phase started with the power seizure by the Kuomintang in 1928 in which young Western-influenced intellectuals entered government positions. Influenced by them, the current in political life in China was so strongly in favor of marital freedom, the possibility of divorce by the wife, as well as the husband, and equality of man and wife, that all of these principles were adopted in the family law of the 1931 Civil Code of the Kuomintang.[123] This was done frequently by way of reception of numerous foreign legal provisions, often from the Japanese point of view, principally those of the Central European

---

[120] K. Bünger, *Die Rezeption des europaischen Rechts in China* (The reception of the European law in China), in BEITRÄGE ZUR RECHTSFORSCHUNG (Articles on legal research) 166–68 (E. Wolff ed. 1950) (special printing of RABELSZ).

[121] F. SCHURMANN, *supra* note 19, at xxxiv ff., 114 ff.

[122] C. YANG, *supra* note 10, at 14–15; J. Bünger, *supra* note 120, at 171 ff.

[123] *E.g.,* Arts. 972 1052, Civil Code of the Republic of China of 1931.

legal sphere and particularly those of Swiss law.[124] This new family law brought such important legal innovations for Chinese conditions as the principle of matrimonial freedom for the spouses, the prohibition against prearranged marriages during childhood, the prohibition against polygamy, and the end of discrimination against marriage by widows. Nevertheless, in practice this code was enforced merely to a very limited extent and with varying degrees of success.[125] The government also failed here to organize the masses in support of its objectives. Frequently it was asserted that the Code was designed more to remove the excrescences and abuses of a system that was still felt not to be bad in itself. It was rarely applied outside the cities of China. Therefore, the family structure in China, particularly in the rural areas, still remained widely untouched, although the thrust of the new family law was directly aimed at the dominant role of the family unit. Still, the spreading destruction of the old family structure caused by the encroachment of Western ideas was already observable.[126] The position of the traditional elite was already undermined when the act of class destruction was directed against it by the Communists.

Communist reforms up to 1949. The family policy conceptions of the Chinese Communists were placed in the foreground ostensibly because of the omnipresent opposition to them that was being exercised by the traditional elite and the nouveau riche peasants. On the other hand, they had to acquire a central importance in the framework of revolutionary reconstruction as one of the primary means for a new regulation of relationships in the communist sense, besides other more instrumental considerations such as serving production activity. Their direction was naturally influenced by the Marxist ideological goals of the neighboring Soviet Union without there ever being an actual identity of goals. But Soviet Russia delivered at that time a strategy of successful mass revolution and the arms and advisors to help carry it out. Moreover, Communism offered possibilities of a semi-religious ideology, which—although developed on foreign grounds (like Buddhism)—established connections to the people similar to the traditional reciprocal relation of religion and philosophy.[127]

This difference in goals has its historical explanation. While in Russia the battle against the tsardom had been waged by a purely urban group with

---

[124] According to Bünger, the Soviet Russian Family Law of 1918–22, in addition to the Japanese, Swiss, and German codes, was among the foreign codes that were particularly considered in the drafting of the Private Code of 1929–31. K. BÜNGER, ZIVIL UND HANDELSGESETZBUCH VON CHINA (Private and commercial code of China) 22 (1934).

[125] K. Bünger, *supra* note 10, at 115.

[126] K. Bünger, *supra* note 120, at 183 ff.

[127] W. BAUER, CHINAS VERGANGENHEIT ALS TRAUMA UND VORBILD (Facts and fantasies of China's past) 55 (1968).

predominantly intellectual accents (not a true mass organization until the eve of the Revolution itself), the Chinese Communists, especially the fashion-setting communists of the Republic of Turchi (Kiangsi Province), the Great March, and the Republic of Yenan (Shensi Province), were in part sons of peasants. "The leaders of Communist organization during the Yenan period were the poor young peasants of the villages who centuries earlier had been recruited into defense brigades or roamed the hills as rebels."[128] In the twenty years of the guerrilla war they had moved exclusively in a rustic world. They had lost their ties with the village societal system. They had assumed a collective style of living on a new plain (working, eating, learning, playing, and sleeping communally) in which the material and living community of the small groups had more real importance than the Marxist socialization of the means of production. Men with such a past came into numerous functionary positions and so it was obvious that they would attempt to further promote this way of living with the aid of ideological euphemisms. The economic conditions of the enormous population (90 percent rural) urged a gradual assimilation of city and country, while on the other hand the freeing and rationalizing of produc-tive resources to promote industrialization made their way. Thus, family reforms began simultaneously with land reforms in the early days of the Communist Chinese areas.[129]

Two years after the marriage regulation of the Chinese-Soviet Republic of December 1, 1931, at the Second Congress of the All-China Soviets at Juichin on January 22, 1934, Mao Tse-tung made a report on the experience of the Soviet movement in China. Under the heading "Marriage under the Soviets," he stated:

To free women from the barbarous marriage system handed down over thousands of years the Chinese Soviets as early as November, 1931, proclaimed the equality of men and women in marriage, with a new set of regulations declaring complete liberty of marriage and divorce, abolishing the sale of women as wives, and forbidding child marriage; provisions that have been enforced throughout the Soviet territory. As a rule a man of twenty may marry a girl of eighteen by registration at the Soviet office, provided he is free from dangerous disease. Lineal descendants from the same grand-father cannot, however, marry each other within five generations. Divorce may be granted by the Soviets if either of the parties to the marriage insists on it.

This liberation of women from the feudal marriage fetters is made possible only under the democratic dictatorship of the workers and peasants. . . . Men and women, especially the latter, must have political liberty first of all, and also some measure of economic liberty as a guarantee for free marriage. Women, more oppressed than men by the feudal marriage system, have been given more protection in the matter of marriage, and the burdens arising from divorce are placed for the most part on the men.

---

[128] F. SCHURMANN, *supra* note 19, at xii.

[129] M. Meijer, *supra* note 8, at 84 ff.

Children are of vital importance to the Revolution. They are, we may say, the new revolutionists, who must be protected. The Soviets recognize illegitimate children and give them protection under the Soviet law.[130]

Later on, after the truce with the Kuomintang in 1937, the early Chinese Soviets began to compromise with the family regulations of the National Government. Their legislation in the various border towns represents a rapprochement with the Civil Code of the Republic of China of 1931. Thus, Article 1 of the marriage regulations of the border area of Shansi, Ch'ahar, and Hopei states: "These regulations are based on the spirit of the legislation in the Book of Family of the Civil Law of the Republic of China, and are adapted to the circumstances prevailing in the Border Area."

In particular, the divorce grounds of Article 15 of this statute largely corresponded to those of Article 1052 of the Civil Code of the Republic of China (Kuomintang), and the marital prohibitions of Articles 7 and 8 corresponded to those of Articles 983, 976, and 1052 of this code.[131] In this period before their actual take-over of power, the Chinese communists did not strictly insist upon strongly pressing their ultimate goals, but rather adapted their measures in a pragmatic, flexible way to the possibilities presented. But when the united front against Japan collapsed at the end of the war, the Communists and the National Government separated and the civil war began. The marriage regulation of the Chinese Soviet Republic of December 1, 1931 and of April 8, 1934 (the so-called Kiangsi Period) now served as the basis of the Party policy.

Developments in the People's Republic of China; reform efforts after the Communist power seizure. After seizure of power in 1949, the Communist regime of Mao Tse-tung found itself emerging from the narrow conditions of the Yenan period and burdened with the fate of all of China. Thus the early years of the People's Republic of China saw a strenuous effort to consolidate the regime's mass base. In the beginning the Party fell back partly on the experiences and formulas of its Soviet mentor. Soviet Marxism could serve as a reservoir of revolutionary ideas on which the Chinese Communists could draw when they began to rule under the sign of a permanent revolution. Thus, after 1949 the Chinese Communists tried first, to a certain degree, to create in the family law field a second Soviet Union on Chinese soil. Nevertheless, they soon sought their own way with doses of inventiveness, multilateral tactics, and extremely alert pragmatism mixed with portions of a transcendental Marxism. They were also pushed along by the peculiar realities of the hard everyday life in China. Altogether, the Chinese who had become committed to the Communist side proved their renewed shyness of pyrrhic ideological victories and instead confirmed their art of applying theory only when it

---

[130] Cited in S. Fu, *supra* note 9, at 116.
[131] M. VAN DER VALK, *supra* note 9, at 68 ff.

promised success. Outwardly, they were especially anxious to avoid any association with Western "capitalistic" ideas.

The following Communist attack on the traditional Chinese family system, designed to win over and mobilize the masses for the Party's ideals, took place by use of the legislative competency of the ever-present modern state, which shoved aside subjection to the clan elders. The Chinese legalism of this time went two ways. It introduced the land reform that removed the rural land-holders, especially the newly emerging rich peasants who were the strongest supporters of the traditional family system. It was directed toward a class evolution of Chinese society. Thus, the Agrarian Reform Law of 1950 provided for people's tribunals, which determined the class status of individuals in rural areas with the help of local organs of government and Agrarian Reform Committees. But one month before the issuance of the Land Reform Law on June 2, 1950, which caused a national movement, another legalistic step was taken. The new Marriage Law of the Chinese People's Republic was enacted after preparation that lasted about a year and a half. Considering the persistency of the old rigid family system—its main features being about twenty-four hundred years old—the upheaval envisioned by the marriage law as it was pushed through by the Communists, in many cases without a prolonged transition, could not be carried out without the use of political pressure of all kinds.

Fighting the feudal marriage system meant fighting feudal and bourgeois thought. This political aim made marriage problems turn into thought problems for the transformation of society. The marriage law was therefore created as a weapon in the political battle, designed to destroy the old order. Although at first sight it may appear to be an overthrowing new formation in relation to the Kuomintang Code, it contained all the possibilities for radical enforcement. Inherently revolutionary in its conception, it became progressively more revolutionary in its application. From the first it systematically rejected China's historical past; in the style of an election manifesto it promoted the principles of free choice of spouse, equality of women, and the preference for child welfare and the little family as against the strict hierarchy of the "large family" dominated by the elders. By its liberation of women, it succeeded in the final destruction of the authority of the *pater familias,* which depended mainly on the suppression of women.[132]

The years 1950–53 were governed by the drive for female emancipation, while the later years, especially the last years before the Great Leap Forward (1956–57), were characterized by a legalistic emphasis on family relations. In this legalistic revolutionary opposition to historical patterns, there were evident parallels to Russian family legislation, which did not, however, affect

---

[132] F. SCHURMANN, *supra* note 19, at 7: "If the Communists have succeeded in anything, it has been in bringing women fully into public life."

such a nearly all-encompassing and deep-rooted family system. This antitraditional attitude, and even more its radical enforcement is in contrast to most family laws of other nations, which are characterized by the settling of various historical levels, the ascertainment of which presupposes general historical value theory analysis. Like the Soviet Russian statutes at the beginning of the first and second phases of development, the Chinese Family Law also contains a revolutionary upheaval in family law, though not in an overt way. It proceeds from the position that in the course of time its goals for development will be accomplished more radically and perfectly by other means.

After this legalistic period the introduction of the People's Commune (*Jen-min kung-she*, literally People's Community Unit) followed in the Marxist-Maoist spirit. This was the third aspect of the "Great Leap Forward" of the early winter in 1957: "The people's commune as a cell of the socialistic society." The People's Communes bore many features of the war communism of the Yenan period as it had become idealized in the meantime. Conceptions of an impending realization of the ideal communist society were seized upon as a first step into the better age. It was, according to W. Pennell, "A fantastic and yet fascinating experiment of a group of revolutionary ideologists whose . . . will and purpose surpassed not only their own immediate mentors who bowed to Lenin but all who have gone before them in all parts of the world."[133] Such things as "gratis distribution" of life's necessities were included, which were glorified by recollections of the simple equality of the war communism of the Yenan period. It was thus that, overtaking the ideological leadership of Moscow, the road to an immediate further collectivization of the way of life was paved in the direction of greater, more comprehensive, and more complex cells of the new society and in an ever more determined revolutionary fashion in accordance with the watchwords, "Party Struggle."

The economic system played a primary role as a motivational factor in the creation of the People's Communes as a new form of social organization, which meant primarily a radical transformation of traditional work organization. The dynamic centralized mobilization of labor resources, particularly of women, under time pressure for the formation of economic capital was undoubtedly an essential goal. A further purpose—in the customary jargon—was the transition from socialist collective ownership to general socialist people's

---

[133] W. Pennell, on HENRY Y. LETHBRIDGE, THE PEASANT AND THE COMMUNES (1962), in CURRENT SCENE DEVELOPMENTS IN MAINLAND CHINA No. 9, at 3 (1963). Compare certain parallels in the history of the Jesuit communes in Paraguay during the middle ages. A. SEPP, REISEBESCHREIBUNG (Travelogue) (1967); A. KOBLER, DER CHRISTLICHE KOMMUNISMUS IN DEN REDUKTIONEN VON PARAGUAY (Christian communism in the reservations of Paraguay) (1877); E. GOTHEIN, DER CHRISTLICH-SOCIALE STAAT DER JESUITEN IN PARAGUAY (The Christian social state of the Jesuits in Paraguay) (1883); F. SCHMIDT, DER CHRISTLICH-SOCIALE STAAT DER JESUITEN IN PARAGUAY (The Christian social state of the Jesuits in Paraguay) (1913).

ownership[134] by the transformation of all collective farms into rural communes. Yet the frenzy of the functionaries of the people's communes reached even further. It sometimes included a rather cold collectivization of one's life. Accompanied by tones of ideological ecstasy, such establishments (also known in the West) as people's kitchens, kindergartens, nurseries, and residence settlements were perfected and made obligatory in such a way that the essential functions of the family would immediately disappear. Yet the family was not to lose all of its functions as a social unit.[135] All totalitarian regimes have the inherent inclination to place the goals of governing above all others. But on the other hand, the legal family or marriage as an institution has survived all attacks. Thus again the question remains: Shall the liberties of the "little family," if the occasion presents itself, be revoked according to Engels' doctrine of the destruction of the family with the goal of entering the era of familyless communism.

An exact formulation of this can hardly be established. In the fundamental so-called Wuchang Resolution at the December 10, 1958, session of the Central Committee of the Communist Party on management of the People's Communes, the dogmatic position was defined more or less in agreement with the Soviet Russian attitude that "it [will] still be a long road to the goals of a mighty surplus of social products and a great facilitation of work. . . . Without all of these can be no talk of entering into a higher developmental stage of human society."[136] In the directives issued on this it was still stated: "In building new living quarters it must be seen that the houses are suitable for the man and wife, elders and children of each family to live together." And "The parents have to determine whether the children will also spend the night in the nursery, and they can take the children home at any time if it is convenient for them."[137]

But the ideological attempts to amalgamate state and society are nevertheless not forgotten. Some pressures in restricting the "little family" have continued. Perhaps it cannot be decided, therefore, with full certainty that the family in China will not at some future time have to disappear, although until now "basically the regime did not see the usefulness of trying to destroy that almost inaccessible core of Chinese socialist organization."[138] Moreover it would be erroneous to consider the Party's utopianism during the initial

---

[134] W. Tscherwenkow, *Narodnie Komunc* v. *Kitaje* (The people's communes in China), in Rabotnitschesko delo (Sofia), Jan. 15, 1959; slightly abridged and reprinted in 11 OST-PROBLEME 84 (1959).

[135] C. YANG, *supra* note 10, at 19. "Even under the people's commune, the family remains the basic social unit, though vastly reduced in its functions."

[136] M. BIEHL, *supra* note 56, at 43.

[137] New China News Agency (Peking), Dec. 18, 1958 (Current Background No. 542, Dec. 29, 1958), quoted in German in M. BIEHL, *supra* note 118, at 112.

[138] F. SCHURMANN, *supra* note 19, at 471.

period of communization as representative of its policies thereafter. The Party retreated considerably from its first impassioned drive for collectivization, and by 1960 very different emphases appeared[139] such as getting women back into the home, dramatized by the "back to the home village" movement launched in 1961, and moral education of the younger generation. According to Ai-li S. Chin:

> All these major policies point to a consolidation of the family and greater respect for the older generation. . . . Story content regarding kinship, marriage and the family in the post-1962 period is decidedly different from the earlier years. There is now an unmistakable note on the solidarity of the nuclear family, revival of wider kinship ties, respect for the older generation in general and for father's authority is particular. . . .[140]

Thus, Schurmann could even state "that the marriage law, which was a major problem in the early 1950s, has disappeared entirely from public concern in Communist China."[141]

The Marriage Law of 1950. The enactment on May 1, 1950, of the marriage law of the People's Republic of China represents a landmark in the development of Chinese family law. For the communist leaders of China, their ideological postulates as well as their previous experiences, including the foregoing communistic marriage legislation, were in a general sense primary forces in their development.[142] At the time of enacting the marriage law of 1950 the participants in the codification boasted expressly that they were adhering to the fundamental marital principles of December 1, 1931, bearing Mao Tse-tung's signature, and that they were supported not only by the actual Chinese experiences gathered in the cities and in the countryside and by the co-work of numerous corps (particularly the Chinese women's organization), but also by the classic Marxists, the marriage statute of the Soviet Kiangsi Zone and other, earlier liberated regions, and the marital statutes of the USSR, the East European People's Democracy, and the Korean People's Democracy. The draft was revised by the Government Administration, by Mao himself, and by the Democratic Women's Association. In this regard, at the 7th meeting of the Central People's Government Council on April 14, 1950, the chairman of the Law Compilation Committee, Ch'en Shao-yü, explained with pride each detail: "In order to link practice with theory in the

---

[139] In May, 1959, the Chinese Communists abolished the Ministries of Justice and Supervision, following a Soviet Russian action by three years. *Cf.* D. Buxbaum, *Preliminary Trends in the Development of the Legal Institutions of Communist China and the Nature of the Criminal Law,* INT'L. AND COMPARATIVE LAW QUARTERLY 1 (Jan. 1962), reprinted in GOVERNMENT OF CHINA 317 (G. San ed. 1966).

[140] A. CHIN, *supra* note 74, at 40.

[141] F. SCHURMANN, *supra* note 19, at 182.

[142] *See* generally, A. Stahnke, *The Background and Evolution of Party Policy on the Drafting of Legal Codes in Communist China,* 15 AM. J. COMP. L. 506 ff. (1967).

process of studying and drafting the Marriage Law, the Council learned from the important theories of Marx, Engels, Lenin, Stalin and Mao Tse-tung."[143] Moreover, he pictured it as also incorporating the experience of Soviet Russia and the Satellite States:

> In addition, for the sake of learning from the experiences of Soviet Russia, South East Europe and the Korean People's Democratic State, the latest editions of the Soviet Law of Marriage, the Family, and Guardianship were translated and published for reference. Moreover, books, articles and pamphlets on these themes from the same countries were studied.[144]

This was in accordance with the general attitude of the Chinese Communists of that time. "They translated thousands of Soviet writings on every conceivable subject. They modeled their entire institutional structure on that of the Soviet Union."[145] But the direct reference to the "latest editions of the Soviet Law of Marriage, the Family, and Guardianship," which at that time manifested the position of the second Stalinist epoch at its high point, also led to the public declaration by Teng Ying-chao, vice-president of the Federation of the Democratic Women of China and wife of Chou En-lai:

> On the other hand, our statute is not completely identified with the marriage laws now in effect in the Soviet Union. The Soviet Union is a country which is already in the stage of socialism, where man and woman are on a completely equal level in political, economic and cultural realms and also in education, as well as in the conditions of labor and the diverse aspects of social activity. The Soviet Union has already rejected the old system of marriage and introduced a new one, in order to practice marital freedom to the letter.
> This is precisely the reason why the Soviet Union in retaining the principle of freedom of divorce, introduced in 1944 a new procedure for divorce, which provides that the divorce cases be adjudicated by a court in public session and that a special tax be imposed on divorce. Beyond this, the Soviet Union limited the possibility of repeated divorces. The goal of these measures is the protection of the marriage and family from frivolity and lack of responsibility, and to encourage the public to found healthy and stable families. Why do we not adopt the Soviet system immediately? Because we are going through a *transitional period,* we must actively construct a completely new marriage system. We are forced, nevertheless, to first abolish the old system. We have before us the mission to assure full marital freedom to the people, to deal a decisive blow to the old marriage system, and to battle for the creation of new families. Consequently the marriage Law of the People's Republic of China is a matrimonial law of the New Democracy, which corresponds to the conditions of our country and the need of the hour.[146]

---

[143] Cited in S. Fu, *supra* note 9, at 119.

[144] *Id.*

[145] F. SCHURMANN, *supra* note 19, at 40.

[146] Teng Ying-chao, *La Loi sur le mariage de la république populaire de China* (On the marriage law of the People's Republic of China), quoted in English in S. Fu, *supra* note 9, at 120.

From this explanation it is clear on the one hand that the Chinese Family Law bears features of its model, the Russian statute. Yet it also presents others clearly stamped as creative provisions of Communist Chinese family policy, which are in many respects oriented to Chinese custom and indigenous usage.[147] In particular, personal experiences are not to be excluded from Mao's statements. His critique of traditional matchmaking practices discloses a sort of personal irritation that suggests that personal experiences by the young Mao in his own family played a considerable role.[148] Thus, the Marriage Law of 1950 was in no way strictly dependent upon Marxist doctrines or the Soviet Russian legislation—although not only in ideological belief, but also in practical aspects, the Soviets were the great model in the early fifties, in contrast to the closer relationship between the Chinese Marriage Law of 1931 and the Swiss Private Law Code.

On the other hand, the Chinese Marriage Law of 1950 matches the flexible and open character of the Russian law, which appears predestined for application under changing conditions. Indeed, as has been more than adequately demonstrated in the meantime, it leaves room for the most varied interpretations and supplementations according to the political and social commands of the hour. This flexibility and open-endedness is something new in Chinese legal development, which has known written law in the family law area for two and a half thousand years and as a code system country has always been aware of the advantages of issuing clear legal provisions. The lack of clarity of the statute led during the following period to substantial difficulties. And since there was no body of case law, those responsible for the administration of justice directed numerous questions to the Ministry of Justice concerning details of the application of the law. In this way a series of questions and answers, and interpretations and commentaries came to be published, which then in turn also had the force of law. In addition, the previously issued private code of the Kuomintang, with its reception of Swiss law, was an especially precise and exactly formulated statute. So this open-endedness and imprecision of the marriage law of 1950 is intended for, and is also justified by, the "revolutionary transition period."[149] This was especially true because the Chinese Communists even in their legalistic period did not hold that law was

---

[147] S. Fu, *supra* note 9, at 119, asserts that these components "are curiously confused"; whereupon he also points out "that the New Law distinctly adopts and continues the spirit of the chapter on Marriage in the Civil Code of the [Nationalist] Republic. . . ."

[148] R. Witke, *Mao Tse-tung, Women and Suicide in the May Fourth Era,* THE CHINA QUARTERLY No. 31, at 128 ff. (July–Sept. 1967).

[149] *See* CHUNG-HUA JEN-MIN KUNG-HO-KUO MIN-FA CHI-PEN WENT'I (Fundamental questions of civil law in the People's Republic of China) 12 ff. (1958) (composed by a collective authorship of the civil law department of the central school for juristic cadres, Peking) (1958) 19 et seq.

omnipotent. The political decision of the Party, therefore, must in no way be expressed in new statutory provisions. The call of the conservative revanchist for speedier proclamation of statutes for the most important legal areas was said to spring frequently from the desire to hinder, with the help of these statutes, the Chinese people's fulfillment of their revolutionary task.

Already this attitude makes it understandable why intensive propaganda and education campaigns were organized to press for effective application of the statute at the time the marriage law went into force and afterwards.[150] A long campaign of enforcement followed. Direct actions by organizations and officials outside the formal legal system were undertaken. The women's organizations, especially, carried out a variety of mass influences with many techniques to teach and discuss the official policy and to encourage participation in various kinds of parades and rallies. All of these nonjudicial possibilities —agitation and propaganda media—were utilized. Such a procedure coincided in a certain respect with basically quite different but long-existing attitudes in China. Historically the Chinese have generally tended to favor non-judicial methods of settling disputes, while the Western liberal has been steeped in a tradition that venerates law.[151] "The legalist doctrine of the traditional Chinese political order was a pragmatic corollary while the ideal of *rule* by moral example and instruction remained the primary principle of good government."

The Chinese communists apparently view the marriage statute more as a symbol, banner, or model, rather than finding in it a regulatory scheme that would determine concrete individual decisions in a painfully exact fashion, independent of the favorable or unfavorable character of the prevailing conditions. That view has certain parallels with the interpretation of the laws in Russia, insofar as these are to be applied more as guidelines in the courts of lower instance to lead them in their sovereign decision, than as binding norms that are to be peremptorily applied to the individual case. It is also no accident that in accordance with old communist doctrine the separation of the legislation and execution of laws is basically not practiced in this country.

Even where the Chinese marriage law establishes unambiguous, definite provisions, it does not mean that they are adhered to in practice. It was quite impossible in such a short time to enforce all the new regulations in a country like China. Consideration had to be shown by the government for the customs of the masses. With regard to the actual circumstances, it was not strictly insisted, for example, that every marriage had to be registered in order to be valid.[152] Also not every subsisting concubinage and bigamous marriage was

---

[150] S. Fu, *supra* note 9, at 132.

[151] A. Stahnke, *supra* note 142, at 509; S. Lubman, *Mao and Mediation,* 55 CALIFORNIA LAW REVIEW 1284 ff. (1967).

[152] *Cf.* M. VAN DER VALK, *supra* note 9, at 88 (Question 9).

dissolved. It was up to the factual situation, acting on the motto "no complaint, no trial."[153] Beyond that, each undesirable determination was gladly shoved aside with the rationalization that it contained pure formalism. This played a dominant role, especially in trials by people's assemblies, since these also served as schools of political education.[154] Finally, the jurisdiction of the ordinary courts in family matters may decline. As it was already shown in Russian family law, so also in China the use of such devices (founded on the intimate involvement of the Party with society) as comrades' courts and reconciliation committees in Russia may reduce the need for regular legal organs and exact legal codes as well, although the Chinese Comrades' Courts have probably never fulfilled real judiciary functions. The "mass line," which has in China been a continuing feature of communist-organized philosophy since Yenan times, is the counterpart of the Russian educational measures under the so-called social will and has been even more effective. "It is impossible to settle some family affairs without resorting to the mass line" is a typical phrase recently used in a discussion on "How I Educate My Children."[155] Thus there are, for instance, several hundred so-called neighborhood conciliation committees in all the larger cities of China elected by the population that elect the other organs of social organizations. It may be of special interest that, according to Woodsworth, "In some communities the conciliation committees are elected by the local trade union, university staff, etc. if the community consists of one occupational group." And Woodsworth adds:

> Conciliation is seen not only as a means of resolving the disputes between the parties themselves. Conciliation procedures are considered one of the means of public education to the new standards of personal morality and the new social relationships and responsibilities of the People's Republic of China. In this setting the conciliation procedures are a much more significant mechanism . . . than are the regular Courts.[156]

A DETAILED COMPARISON OF THE FAMILY STATUTES OF SOVIET RUSSIA AND OF THE PEOPLE'S REPUBLIC OF CHINA

System and Form of the Marriage Laws

First of all, it should be emphasized that in China, as well as in Russia, the marriage and child law is codified, not as part of a comprehensive civil law code (as is usually the case in countries with a codified law, and as it was both

---

[153] M. VAN DER VALK, *supra* note 9, at 82 (Problem 2), 86 (Question 1).

[154] *Cf.* SURVEY OF CHINA MAINLAND PRESS, American Consulate General, Hong Kong 4153/9 (April 4, 1968).

[155] *See* L. M. Gudoshnikov, in U.S. Joint Publication Research Service, No. 1, at note 16, p. 9 (1968).

[156] K. Woodsworth, *Family Law and Resolution of Domestic Disputes in the People's Republic of China,* 13 McGILL LAW JOURNAL 177 (1967).

in China and Russia before the communist seizure of power), but as a special law. This is connected with the communist governments' policy of highlighting the family law as a prominent weapon in the class struggle and revolutionary transformation. It harmonizes with the prevailing doctrine in both countries that family law is not included within the civil law sphere.[157] This doctrine is more in tune with the concept of a communist legal system, insofar as it is better suited to ignore the autonomous will of the individual, while forming his family relationship in conformity with communist morals, than is the individualistic arrangement of the family law within a civil law code.[158]

The Soviet Russian and People's Chinese family statutes are strikingly brief in comparison with the family law provisions within the general "private law" codes of Western tradition. In the French Civil Code the first Book, "Des personnes," consists of Articles 7–515 without the marital property law, which is to be found in Article 1400 ff; in the German Civil Code the fourth Book, "Family Law", encompasses sections 1298–1921 (apart from the provisions of the German Civil Code, there are also the 80 paragraphs of the Marriage statute [Statute no. 16 of the Control Council of Germany], which partially replaces provisions of the Civil Code); in the Swiss Private Law Code, "Family Law" fills Articles 90 to 456; and the fourth Book of the Private Law Code enacted by the Chinese Nationalist Government in 1930 contains 170 paragraphs on family law. In contrast, the Soviet Russian codification of statutes on Marriage, Family, and Guardianship of the RSFSR contains altogether ninety-four substantive legal articles (the rest of the provisions are of a procedural nature), and the Chinese Marriage Law of May 1, 1950, contains not more than twenty-seven articles in total, including the individual statutory principles for the entire law of inheritance (Articles 12 and 14).

Furthermore, the Chinese Marriage Law (in contrast to the Soviet Russian Marriage and Family Law) even includes penal law provisions; for example, Article 13 III provides: "Infanticide by drowning and similar criminal acts are strictly prohibited." This relates to the forbidden but nevertheless not quite abolished custom of killing newly born girls, mostly for economic reasons. Article 26 states: "In the case where interference with the freedom of marriage has caused death or injury, the person guilty of such interference shall bear criminal responsibility before the law." Thus, a provision already

---

[157] For Russia, *cf.* note 115 *supra;* for China, note 149 *supra* at 16, 53. The distinction between private law and public law is not made by the communist doctrine according to Lenin's statement: "We do not recognize anything that is private." *See* W. MÜLLER-FREIENFELS, EHE UND RECHT (Marriage and law) 95 (1962): E. NIZSALOVSZKY, ORDER OF THE FAMILY 102 (1968).

[158] Also in western literature the arrangement of family law in the category of "social law" is pursued as a tendency of anti-individualism. *Cf.* 1 O. GIERKE, DEUTSCHES PRIVATRECHT (German private law) 27 (1895); H. LEHMANN, DEUTSCHES FAMILIENRECHT 3 ff. (2d ed. 1948).

contained in the law of the imperial period was repeated, which connects with the Chinese view of suicide as a traditional form of protest in times of extreme distress, particularly for women.

The provision just mentioned concerning drowning or "similar" criminal acts is also illustrative of further characteristics of both Soviet Russian and Chinese statutes: their symbolic importance, their nature as a general framework, their indefiniteness, and their failure to decide individual concrete conflict questions. They reduce the pure judicial element and prefer a simplification of the statute even where sharply divergent interests ought to be coordinated by establishing preferences. In place of graduated regulations there are frequently catch-all provisions that give the courts discretion for determining an individual case. This is connected to a different conception of the judge's law-making power and even his general function. While, for example, divorce in the West, at least originally, has primarily been a ruling on the objective right of the plaintiff to get a divorce, the decision on the divorce suit becomes a genuinely creative act, when it is placed within the discretion of the court, as in Soviet or Chinese divorce law, or when this discretion is hidden behind a general catch-all provision.

Besides the scarcity of details in the provisions, the propagandistic didacticism of both statutes is striking. They provide tenets of a social-ethical nature that not only regulate possible conflicts, but above all emphatically guide and educate one toward the moral life in the sense of the communist future. This applied especially to the verbose general provisions of the Chinese marriage law. In both statutes the characteristic feature of the communist state, which views itself as educator and indeed guardian of the people, is expressed. The foremost magisterial duty of the state is to hammer the moral and ideological principles of communism into each individual.

At the same time, the communist state secures for itself the means to accomplish its acute, special political goals by enacting these general provisions for the common welfare. Since the socialist-communist state does not view itself as static, but rather seeks in accordance with the principles of historical materialism to align its legal position with the changes in the conditions of production, modification in statutory interpretation and application follows even more naturally. In this way, too, they can take as a central point the class struggle as it is reflected in matrimonial and family troubles. Only this legislative fashion harmonizes with its "spirit of permanent social revolution" and upholds the instrumental valuation of the law in communist ideology as a product of class struggle and class contradiction. For in this respect, "Whatever best advances the cause of the dominant class is suitable in legal policy, and since the Party has a monopoly on determining what is proper, its freedom in manipulating the legal organs and the statutes is theoretically unlimited."[159]

---

[159] A. Stahnke, *supra* note 142, at 508.

While there are indeed extensive parallel emphases in the systematic construction of both statutes, no strict all-encompassing conformity exists. Certainly, even the individual family codes of the Union republics, which are substantively quite consistent, show differences in their systematic sequence and construction. Thus, the Family Law of the Ukraine begins with provisions on the family, followed by guardianship and curatorship, and marriage is first treated in Part 3. On the other hand, the Family Code of the RSFSR of 1927 consists of four parts: first, marriage; second, the relationship between children, parents, and other relatives; third, guardianship and curatorship; and fourth, the registration of legal status and the law of conflict of laws. The new code of the USSR also retains this system of classification. The Chinese code is arranged in eight chapters, as follows: general principles; contracting of marriage; rights and duties of husband and wife; relations between parents and children; divorce; support and education of children after divorce; property and maintenance of divorce; and by-laws. Both proceed similarly, clearly providing that the family is constituted by the contracting of marriage intended by the bride and groom themselves (in contrast to the wedding as a family act of the clan). It is also expressed, especially in Chinese law, that the relations between parents and children should be comprehended as a consequence of the marriage relationship and should, therefore, along with the status of illegitimate children, be regulated in the Marriage Law. However, in contrast to the parallel Russian statute, the Chinese marriage law does not regulate guardianship and relatives, and indeed the name "family law" was perhaps, therefore, avoided in the Chinese legislation.

Marriage Law in Detail

Character and function of marriage. It is no accident that the new Soviet Russian Marriage and Family Code of 1968 emphasizes the family as a whole, while the Chinese Marriage Law of 1950 focuses above all on the marriage. For with the "victory of socialism," which was said to have "essentially already been realized" in the Soviet Union, the requisites for the creation of a "new socialist family" have been fulfilled according to the present Soviet view.[160] On the other hand, the Chinese interpretation advocating abolition of the family is closer to the view espoused by Russia in the first years following the October Revolution and by Engels and other communist theorists. The special susceptibility of the marriage to ideology is revealed with particular clarity.

Thus, it is stated at the beginning of the new Soviet Russian statute defining the aims of Soviet legislation on marriage and family[161] that its purpose is a

---

[160] R. Schlesinger, *The Family in the USSR,* in INTERNATIONAL LIBRARY OF SOCIOLOGY 324 (1949).

[161] Pravda (Moscow), June 28, 1968.

further consolidation of the Soviet family, based on the principles of the communist morals. The individual provisions, whose significance is not to be overrated, follow. The family relationship is to be erected upon a voluntary union between husband and wife, a deep love, comradeship, and a heeding of all members of the family, free from material values. The education of the children of the family is to consist of loyalty to the nation and to the building-up of communism, and they are to be trained to play an active part in the construction of the communist society; the detrimental traditions and customs of the past are finally to be set aside, and the sense of duty toward the family is to be developed.

In contrast, the Chinese Marriage Law is more concerned about the relationship between spouses. It begins negatively in Article 1 with the statement: "The compulsive feudal marriage system where the man is privileged but the woman is enslaved and where the children's interests are ignored is abolished. The new democratic marriage system, based on free choice of partners, monogamy, equal rights for both sexes and protection of the lawful interests of women and children, has been put into effect." Articles 1 and 8 then state positively: "Husband and wife are companions for mutual support and shall enjoy equal status in the home." They are "in duty bound to love, respect, assist, and look after each other, to live in harmony, to engage in production, to bring up and to educate the children, and to strive jointly for the happiness and the welfare of the family and for the building up of a new society." Also striking in this regard are the materialistic terms of the Chinese statute. While Article 1001 of the earlier Private Law Code spoke of the cohabitation of the spouses, the statute now mentions companionship as essential for earning common support and places in the center the duty to work for the benefit of production. From this is derived conversely, in the interest of production, a duty of the spouses not to quarrel, for "we cannot imagine that a couple not living together harmoniously, constantly wrangling and quarreling, could at the worksite in face of the people, perform their duties well and discharge their work without the slightest impairment."[162]

In contrast, the statutory listing of marital obligations in the Chinese Marriage Law of 1950 lacks any express mention of the marital duty of loyalty and the duty toward a joint life. Inthis connection Liu Ching-fan, vice-president of the central representative assembly of the movement for execution of the marriage law, stated[163] that free sexual relations between

---

[162] Hung T'ien-shou, *Meaning and Execution of Marriage Registration,* in Hsin-wen jih-pao (Shanghai), Dec. 21, 1952.

[163] Liu Ching-fan, vice-president of the Central Representative Assembly of the Movement toward Execution of the Marriage Law, stated, "The execution of the marriage law is an important task before us for the People's government at all stages and for the population of the entire country." Jen-min jih-pao (Peking), March 20, 1953; CH'IN T'I, TSU-KUO, 800 ff. (1966); *cf.* also V. CHU, *supra* note 41, at 169 ff.

husband and wife should not be the object of investigations or compulsory measures.

Family protection emphasized in the Soviet Russian marriage law and the connected encouragement of the family are in harmony with the turn toward a strong, positive official valuation of the family (after the first phase of development) and with the ideas of the program of the Communist Party of the Soviet Union,[164] which says that even when communism is achieved the family necessarily will continue to exist.[165] Therefore, during the first phase of development of Soviet family law, the private nature of the relationship of de facto marriage was emphasized—a relationship not to be directed by the state and concerning only the two partners.[166] Consequently, Soviet Russian marriage law lacks, as far as can be seen, any approaches toward state consent for marriages of Soviet citizens; an approach that would have resulted in a directive marriage policy.

Therefore, even today in the Soviet Union, marriage is propagandized as the ideal of human associations, while the situation of the unmarried person, standing alone, is disqualified as "unnatural" and "abnormal" from his own standpoint as well as from that of society. His status is seen as unsatisfactory "from the most varied of aspects—moral-psychological, economic, legal, etc."[167] Finally, this propaganda again today utilizes the old assumption that marriage and family exercise a conservative and stabilizing influence. The Soviet Russian families, therefore, raise a youth who unconditionally accepts the established regime. In the sense of these premises, then, stable marriages in Russia today form an essential factor in raising faithful communists.

Accordingly, the state in Soviet Russia today is essentially concerned with increasing the number of registered marriages. Statistics indicate that in Russia in 1913 there were 9.2 weddings per 1000 inhabitants, in 1925 there were 9.8, and in 1964 there were 12.1.[168] In this sense, Soviet Russia today favors registered marriages in other ways, too. Location of weddings in

---

[164] The constitutions of all peoples' democracies contain statements on the state protection of marriage and family.

[165] *Cf.* A. Chartschew, *Ehe und Familie in der Sowjetunion* (Marriage and family in the Soviet Union), 19 NEUE JUSTIZ 256 (1965). "Thus the program breaks once and for all with the bourgeois legend that communists are enemies of the family; it reconfirms that only communism is truly dedicated to the best moral traditions of the people."

[166] D. Loeber, *supra* note 115, at 8.

[167] B. Gruschin, *Slušaetsja delo o razvode.* . . . *O tak nazyvaemych "legkomys-lennich brakach"* (Discussion of the divorce problem. . . . Concerning the so-called "lightly considered marriages"), in MOLODAJA GWARDIJA No. 6/7 (Moscow 1964), extracts in German in 16 OST-PROBLEME 600 (1964). *Cf.* note 197.

[168] A. Chartschew, *supra* note 165, at 257. The sociologist Chartschew was contented to ascertain that: "These figures demonstrate above all that the civil registration of marriage has gained moral authority and that the number of so-called unregistered marriages has decreased, although they still have a certain circulation."

somewhat splendid, artistically furnished wedding palaces is encouraged, as are festivities and preference of married persons in the allotment of housing and bonuses.

On the other hand, it is reported from China that in practice it is becoming more difficult to marry. For example, Chu asserts that the marriage law of 1950 has significantly impeded the road to marriage, while clearing the way for getting out of marriage. This is true in certain respects, although the Constitution of the Chinese People's Republic of May, 1954, states (Article 96 II) that "the state protects marriage and the family."[169] Hindrances to marriage are introduced in the form of special consent requirements for the registration by local authorities, above all for the ideological political purposes of accomplishing social change and making it more real. In this respect, members of the working class should not have unions with the offspring of the old capitalist class. "Real love cannot exist between a feudalistic and a progressive person". The revolutionary is to subordinate his passions to the revolution.[170] Quite generally, it may be noted that the prospective marriage partner should have the right ideological attitude and an adequate performance capacity for production.[171] Moreover, at the time of registration of the marriage, it should be affirmed that the marital candidates are basically prepared and educated, ideologically as well as occupationally, before entering into marriage.[172]

While these reports indicate that registration also serves as a requirement for the formation of "lawful marriages" (cf. also Art. 6, Marriage Law) in China, it does not, like Russia, have state supported standards of furthering registration of marriage such as the location of the ceremony in a wedding palace and festive celebrations. In contrast, there was propaganda in China against greater wedding celebrations, among other reasons, to counteract the ever-existing rituals and feudal customs such as the giving of wedding presents as disguised bridal rewards for money marriages. In the Soviet Union today the community obligations of the marriage are dogmatically emphasized. Accordingly, under the influence of stabilization tendencies, there was an abandonment of the view of marriage that was taken in the first phase of

---

[169] CONSTITUTION OF THE PEOPLE'S REPUBLIC OF CHINA OF 1954 (English ed., Peking, 1954).

[170] Pei-ching kung-jen jih-pao (Peking), April 14, 1966; Nan-fang jih-pao (Canton), Feb. 13, 1952.

[171] Che-Chiang jih-pao (Che Kiang), March 11, 1952; Hsin-wen jih-pao (Shanghai), Dec. 21, 1952.

[172] Hung T'ien-shou, supra note 162, agitates against "those youths who seek a marriage partner only for their appearance and passion, instead of asking about their character and their valuable capacities of production. Such marriages are irregular; such youths must be carefully influenced educationally, their thoughts penetrated and they must not be afforded registration of marriage."

development—that marriage was the personal matter of the spouses. The marital relationship must, according to the present opinion, be regulated by the state.[173] Thus, in public opinion in the Soviet Union the family is viewed as the smallest cell of the state and at the same time as the bearer of the socialist-communist society.[174] Therefore, it is supposedly justified, as Sverdlov observes, for the state to actively influence marriage relationships.[175] At the same time it follows, according to Mrs. Pergament, that the state protects only the marriage it recognizes and views the marriage that has no social utility as senseless and, therefore, unworthy of being preserved.[176] Moreover, it is characteristic of both the Russian and Chinese legislation that they recognize monogamy as the only form of marriage, though not in the sense of the present Russian law that only the registered marriage creates rights and duties. In view of the fact that in Russia and China, as "in all known societies, the ratio of males to females at birth is slightly in excess of unity," the possibility of one man's legally having plural spouses at the same time, which would deprive another man maritally, would create a minority group, a development that is not consistent with Communistic ideals.[177] They attack every form of robbery or sale marriage, as well as bigamy or the taking of a concubine. Equal rights for husband and wife, freedom of marriage, freedom of divorce, monogamy, equal status of legitimate and illegitimate children, and separation of church and state are the principles which they have theoretically adhered to from the beginning to the present. However, they cannot be viewed absolutely, because they contradict each other in single consequences for borderline cases. The principles have in the meantime, of course, as has been shown, undergone in part a significant change in their content. Through the power of the state standing behind them and in view of the giant area they cover, they display a strong melting process in the direction of the postulates they have developed. The coercive elimination of tribal customs in the melting pot of the Soviet Union has many parallels in the "democratic centralism" of the People's Republic of China. Still, reference should be made in this connection to the last article of the Chinese Marriage Law (Article 27) which reads:

This law shall come into force from the date of its promulgation. In regions inhabited by national minorities, the Military and Political Council of the Administrative Area of the provincial people's government may enact certain modification of supplementary articles in conformity with the actual conditions prevailing among national minorities

---

[173] D. Loeber, *supra* note 115, at 13.

[174] *Cf.* A. Pergament, *supra* note 75, at 457, with reference to Lenin.

[175] G. Sverdlov, *supra* note 105, at 685.

[176] A. Pergament, *supra* note 98, at 79.

[177] *Cf.* 2 M. Levy, Jr., Modernization and the Structure of Societies 426 ff. (1966).

in regard to marriage. But such measures must be submitted to the Government Administration Council for ratification before enforcement.

Betrothal. The betrothal as a family law institution is not expressly regulated in the individual family codes of the union republics of the USSR.[178] Yet, similar to the religious wedding ceremony, it is not thereby denied, but rather merely stamped as a personal affair of the partners. This attitude is also retained by the new Family Code of the USSR of 1968.

In the future, parties contemplating marriage will no longer be able to attain their goal immediately. Article 9, section 4 provides now that the wedding can only take place at least one month after filing an application with the registry of civil status.[179] Thus, the old period of public notice is again being honored. The legislator thereby sets a period of deliberation for the intended spouses and creates a certain compensation for the engagement period, which, among other things, is to prevent a too hasty decision to marry. The permissible but not expressly regulated betrothal established no family law relationships. It can have financial consequences under Russian law,[180] when the betrothed have made matching agreements with regard to marriage; these are determined by the general provisions.[181]

The Chinese Marriage Law of 1950, similar to and indeed even influenced by its model in the Russian statutes, also contains no provisions on the engagement, although betrothal had long had a much greater significance in China than in Russia. The Chinese Marriage Law is in contrast to the detailed, if not always fortunate, regulation in Articles 972–979 of the Chinese Private Law Code of 1930. The silence in today's Chinese Marriage Law might forbid only particular connected family law consequences, but would not forbid the observance of the forms for betrothal (or for breaking an engagement) established in the classical Chinese law (such as voluntary giving of presents and written contract). Nevertheless, the breach of an engagement with a member of the military seems to receive a special legal treatment by inter-

---

[178] On the other hand, the undertaking of an engagement is regulated in the new Family Code of the East German Democratic Republic of December 20, 1965 as a mere acknowledgment provision, without attaching any family law consequences to it.

[179] In individual cases the period can be shortened by the legislation of the Union republics.

[180] G. Luther, *Verlöbnis* (Betrothal), in 7 RECHTSVERGLEICHENDES HANDWÖRTERBUCH (Handbook of comparative law) 205 (F. Schlegelberger ed. 1939); no duty to pay damages even in the case of unauthorized breach of the engagement. However, he cited D. Kauschansky, *Das europäische Eherecht* (European marriage law), 40 NIEMEYERS ZEITSCHRIFT FÜR INTERNATIONALES RECHT (Niemeyer's Journal of international law) (T. Niemeyer ed.) (1929), who assumes a duty to pay damages for the individual case, for equitable reasons based on the general provision of para. 406, Soviet Russian private law code of 1923.

[181] *Cf.* G. Sverdlov, *supra* note 66, at 581.

pretation of Article 19. The silence in the statute on the question of the engagement has in no sense been undisputed in Russia during the discussions on the Marriage and Family Law of 1968. It was proposed that the "old, but noble ritual of engagement" be reintroduced and, beyond that on a trial basis, that a one-half year engagement period be introduced in Wilna and Minsk, in order to give the young couple enough time to consider how they will live tomorrow and the day after.[182] The continued antipathy in China and Russia toward regulating betrothal statutorily might be connected with the fact that by "bourgeois interpretation" engagement also serves to create the material foundation for the future marriage. That is, it displayed, above all, a financial significance. In China even more, the founding of marriage in the opposed traditional forms was executed by the family by way of a completely different type of betrothal contract. Significantly, in Russia value was placed on the fact that most marriages were entered into after a period of acquaintance between partners of considerably longer than one year,[183] so that basically the value of the engagement period is again recognized.

Age of marriage. Statutory determination of a certain age for marriage can serve negatively as a weapon against traditional customs and norms such as the custom of engagement during childhood practiced in ancient China. It can, on the other hand, be established positively—although at most with only limited practical effects—as a means to attain certain family policy goals such as influencing the birthrate. In Russia Article 5 of the Family Code of the RSFSR of 1927 basically established the age of marital capacity at eighteen years for both men and women.[184] The age of marital capacity and private law's age of majority were thus the same. The relatively low age limit was also established to hinder extra-marital relations. At the same time, possibilities of parentally arranged marriages of minors were reduced. The Family Code of 1968 retains the former marriage age. It now uniformly permits the Union republics to reduce the marriage age statutorily by two years. Therefore, it did not follow the demand raised by many Soviet jurists in discussions on the draft of the new family code that the marriage age be raised to twenty-one years to assure a greater maturity on the part of marriage partners.

---

[182] *See* I. Kasjukov & A. Mendeleev, *Nužen li talant sem'janinu?* (Must one be talented for family life?), in NEDELJA No. 12 (Moscow 1967); extracts in German from 19 OST-PROBLEME 449, 450 (1967).

[183] A. Chartschew, *supra* note 165, at 257: "In less than a fifth of all marriages there exists the suspicion that the partners did not really know each other before marrying."

[184] For women it can be reduced by one year (Family Law Code of 1927, with amendments of April 6, 1928—Su RS FSR 1928, No. 47, Pos. 355—and of February 28, 1930—Su RSFSR 1930, No. 12, Pos. 146); in the Ukrainian, Moldavian, Aserbaijan, and Armenian Republics the women already have marriage capacity at age 16. *Cf., e.g.,* Family Law Code of the UKR. SSR Art. 109 comment. In the White Ruthenian SSR the marriage age can be reduced by two years for men and women (Family Law Code of the Byelorcissian SSR, Art. 4).

In China, on the other hand, according to Article 4 of the Family Law, the man must be twenty and woman eighteen in order to marry. With respect to the Private Law Code of 1930, the marriage age was increased by two years. Population considerations might have played a part in this, for in China, unlike Russia where the birthrate has fallen from 44 children per 1000 inhabitants in 1926 to only 18 children per 1000 inhabitants in 1966,[185] the population increase constitutes a cardinal problem. The political propaganda even enjoins young Chinese men not to marry, if possible, before age thirty, and young women not before twenty-five.[186] Finally, another reason behind this regulation (which is inconsistent with the usual preference for youth) is the goal of decreasing the influence of the parents on marriage. Such an influence is naturally stronger with the lower marriage age in which the children are still economically and personally dependent upon their parental home.[187] There exists a divergence here between Western and old Chinese rules in the calculation of years. According to the old Chinese fashion, the age of a person is calculated by the number of New Year Days he has experienced since his birth and not according to the number of complete years he has actually lived. If the possibility of counting in the old Chinese way is not excluded by the wording of the statute, though, it is at least apparent that the Communist authorities prefer the Western method, in accordance with their efforts to raise the marriage age.[188] In this sense there is also a realization of the trend toward checking the immeasurable population increase in China, characterized by a favoring of birth control and abortion, as well as the encouragement of late marriage.

Impediments to marriage. It is evident that the numerical reduction of statutory impediments to marriage observable in modern law has been particularly marked in the marriage statutes of the communist states. The general reasons for the diminution of impediments are stronger in Russia and China than in any other country. They reflect not only the schism of church and state, but in general the emancipation of the individual from the firm grip exercised in the past by a very complex social system. Both Russian and Chinese marriage laws have from the outset simply abolished the majority of traditional marriage interdictions that existed in their countries before the communist revolutions. However, while Russia today strictly adheres to the principle that only the registered marriage creates rights and duties, China does not completely exclude the possibility of allowing individual rights and duties to arise from a non-registered marriage. Thus, in such cases, some

---

[185] N. Y. Times, Aug. 28, 1968 (Weekly Review), at 5.

[186] *Cf.* T. CHEN, *supra* note 33, at 263.

[187] *Cf.* C. YANG, *supra* note 10, at 42.

[188] M. VAN DER VALK, *supra* note 9, at 88 (Question 8); M. van der Valk, *The Registration of Marriage in the CPR,* 16 MONUMENTA SERICA 348 (1957).

impediments to marriage in China actually prove to be only impediments to registration.

The following can be said of the remaining marital impediments. The laws of both countries prohibit matrimony where one of the intended partners is already married. Yet bigamy as an impediment to marriage had only the effect of a temporary postponement in the RSFSR, for from the time of the 1926 Family Code until the great revision of family law in 1944 there was no allowance for annullment[189] of prohibited marriages.[190] In the meantime, however, not only did the courts permit annullment claims, but they broadly applied penal law[191] sanctions against bigamy and polygamy. To this extent, the Soviet Union emphatically carried out the principle of monogamous marriage even in its Asiatic regions.[192] The Marriage Law of the Chinese People's Republic likewise professes the principle of monogamy by the fundamental provision in Article 2.

The Russian law further prohibits marriage in the case of mental deficiency or illness. In the RSFSR this prohibition requires prior determination in a special incompetency proceeding. Going even further than the model in this respect, the Chinese Marriage Law in Article 6 forbids marriage if the person lacks sexual capacity by virtue of some congenital disability or has a serious illness such as venereal disease, mental illness, leprosy, or other illness with which a person should not, according to medical opinion, enter into marriage. But while the Russian law specifies in detail who is to diagnose this malady and in which proceeding, these questions remain completely open in Chinese law. Precisely therein lies a problem in China which admits of no simple solution. In addition there is the ominous statutory designation of "other diseases" which are to be deemed equivalent to mental illness. What falls under this category? Apparently in this case too the Chinese legislator did not intend to create a more binding scheme.

Finally, Russian law prohibits marriage between close relatives; that is, when the parties concerned are in a direct line, or are full or half brothers or sisters. The formerly assumed equality of status between adopted persons and natural relatives has now been rendered unnecessary, insofar as the Family Code of 1968 now prohibits marriage between the adopting and adopted persons.

The Chinese Marriage Law of 1950, agreeing with the Russian law, forbids marriage between relatives in the direct line or between full or half brothers

---

[189] The annullment of a marriage basically has retroactive effect, although the children remain legitimate. A Pergament, *supra* note 75, at 478.

[190] In justifying this result, it was then pointed out that the contracting of marriage was outside of the competency of the legislature and could not be declared legally invalid by a state pronouncement. D. Loeber, *supra* note 115, at 53.

[191] Criminal Code of the RSFSR 1960–63, Art. 235.

[192] Noteworthy in this regard is the Mongolian Constitution Art. 93, §2 (1940).

and sisters. At that time, however, the Chairman of the Chinese Law Compilation Committee pointed out: "From the examples furnished by the modern Russian people, who do not prohibit marriage between collateral relatives, it has been proved that there is no harmful hereditary influence by blood."[193] Yet Article 5, paragraph 2 of the Chinese Marriage Law still recognizes the prohibition of marriage between collateral blood relatives within five generations. It goes one step further than the 1931 code in increasing the range of relatives within which marriage is permitted. This provision, which is a noteworthy concession, in spite of its minimal marriage restrictions, to the old customs[194] otherwise strictly opposed as being feudal and reactionary, might have decreasing practical significance. Perhaps the aims of avoiding sexual intercourse within the family clan and of counteracting nearer personal ties within the family have favored this restriction.

The Russian law impediments to marriage regained their full effectiveness in practice in the second period, with the introduction throughout of marriage registration as a constitutive requirement for marriage. Thus, the Family Code of the RSFSR contains no provisions on the consequences of violating the marriage prohibitions, because until 1944 the registration still had merely declaratory significance. This was first explained in detail in the directives of the Supreme Court of the USSR on September 16, 1949.

Requirements of the wedding. Originally in Russia, according to the principle of freedom of marriage, the free decision of the parties constituted marriage. Freedom of marriage thereby meant that the choice should be that of the partners, independent of any consent by third parties or of economic considerations. When marriage registration was retained after 1918, its retention was rationalized by asserting that the requirement remained in deference to those segments of the population who associated entry into marriage with the fulfillment of certain formalities. It was feared that the abolition of obligatory marriage registration might at that time have led to an increase in church weddings.

---

[193] S. Fu, *supra* note 9, at 128. Fu gives the following dialogue from the Propagandists' Handbook of the Marriage Law: "Question: If I and my mother's younger sister cherish an affection for each other, may we get married?—Answer: If the parties love each other and are willing to get married, marriage may be permitted. If you are ridiculed or interfered with by someone, that is the remnant of the feudal ideology—you may lodge a protest against that person."

[194] Indeed, it is pointed out in the literature that "in Chinese society, all marriages within the fifth degree of consanguinity are prohibited as a general rule . . . [are] considered shameful and disgusting by the broad masses of the people in China," whereas "a marriage between relatives within the fifth degree is not prohibited in Soviet Russia." Consequently, Fu asserts: "Close study reveals the astonishing fact that it is not a question of Chinese custom, but actually of Russian custom!" S. Fu, *supra* note 9, at 127.

During the second period—a period aimed at the consolidation of marriage and family—the de facto marriage of the twenties (formerly the expression of the new way of life) was countered, and obligatory marriage registration was reintroduced. State intervention took place in this area and in that of judicial divorce. By requiring the registration of marriage, the state implied its sanction of marital relations. Even today, Article 9, paragraph 3 of the Family Law still continues to emphasize the idea that only the registered marriage can produce legal effects. This was to leave no possible exceptions that might favor a resurgence of de facto marriages.

In introducing the civil marriage system, the marriage legislation in China followed the Soviet Russian marriage registration system ". . . already taken up by the Communists in the first regulations after the revolution. To be sure, this registration system did not remain unchanged in the following period, but rather was carried out with varying contents. This was especially true with respect to the central question, whether only the registered marriage produces marital rights and duties." Just as the Bolsheviks sought in their time to supplant the role of the church by adopting state registration of marriages, so the Chinese communists intended to remove marriage from the hands of the family. Family authority had to yield to the authority of the state. The traditional Chinese family being in a way its own church was expected to collapse if parental arrangement was impeded. The registration act also presented the possibility of propagating the government's ideas and pressing for their execution. So stated the preamble to the ordinance on the procedure for marriage registration of May 20, 1955. Announced on June 1, 1955, the preamble decreed:

> The purposes of the compulsory registration of marriages, divorces or remarriages are [according to the preamble to the ordinance] the protection of free choice of marital partner from the duties and whims of third parties, the protection of monogamy from concubinage, as well as the protection of the marital partners and their off-spring. Further, the obligatory registration of marriage is to avoid premature marriage, or remarriage between persons for whom there exists a marital prohibition or some other statutory impediment.

The Chinese communists had before them Soviet Russia's experiences with de facto marriage, where formal registration was left to the voluntary discretion of the marital partners for reasons of degovernmentalization of marriage. At the time the Chinese communists developed their revolutionary legislation in Kiangsi (in the Soviet Republic of China), codes were still in force in Russia that recognized the de facto marriage. But at the time of the passage of the China Marriage Law of 1950, the tide had already been turned in Russia, and the change toward recognition of only the *registered* marriage had taken place. The tendency toward degovernmentalizing the marriage was never as radically promoted by the Chinese communists as by their Russian counterparts. They, therefore, never pushed the ideological thesis of marriage as a personal matter so far as to unanimously recognize de facto marriages. The Chinese Marriage Law did not on the other hand also need to emphasize the registration requirement even as strongly as does the present Russian Marriage Law. Article 6 of the Chinese Marriage Law of 1950 merely says: "In order to contract a marriage, both the man and the woman shall register in person with the people's government of the subdistrict or village in which they reside." Thus it avoids a clear answer to the question of whether the registration is an indispensable condition for a valid marriage. This omission is not only characteristic of the lack of interest of the Chinese legislator in creating the most precise legal decisions possible, but also throws a light on the special position of the Chinese legislator, which is in no way to be identified with the situation of the Russian legislator. In Russian law at that time, strong forces aimed at taking marriage out of the hands of the government stood behind the recognition of the de facto marriage. In China, particularly with the marriage registration, a strong influence of the state is consciously built into the marriage law. The marriage registration appears here as a primary means of the Chinese regime of promoting the revolution according to its precepts, while the purpose of marriage registration in Russia was really, above all, "to register civil status." The Chinese legislator did not have to combat disagreement such as had later appeared in Russia as a consequence of the extensively practiced de facto marriage, which was sought to be eliminated by the tightening up of the marriage registration. The legislator's principal interest was by no means in the removal of negative consequences of concealed marriages, but rather was aimed most of all at the political indoctrination of the Chinese people. Therefore, the marriage registration was not designed primarily to prevent secret marriages, but rather to serve the execution of the law with the realization of the new marriage ideal and the concomitant broader social transformation. For the Chinese legislator an essential significance was attached to the decision of the civil status official; the latter had to carefully scrutinize the individual case. The engaged couple had to appear before him in person and could in no case, as for example in Japanese law, discharge the registration applications solely in writing. Thus, the provision was adopted in the Chinese Marriage Law that "if the marriage is not found to be in conformity with the provisions of this Law, registration shall not be granted" (Art. 6 II et seq.).

It does not follow from this, however, that in China only the registered marriage produces rights and duties, as is the case where there is a provision intended to afford validity only to registered marriages by the exclusion of informal marriages. The reason is that the beneficiaries of a void marriage, which was not registered for political reasons, also might well be the politically suspect personalities to whom the marriage registration has been denied; they might benefit in that they would perhaps not have to pay their marital partner support, although they had in fact lived together for years. Because of the voidness of the marriage the politically suspect partner might in this way be considerably better off in the long run, than the politically reliable person living in real wedlock, who accordingly has no possibilities of circumventing the duties of support. To this extent it is completely within the scope of the legal-political goals of the Chinese legislator that even the partner in an unregistered marriage should not be left free of obligations but, rather, that care be taken that he at least not be placed in a better position than the partner in a registered marriage. In this sense the contracting of an unregistered marriage represents in Chinese law something thoroughly undesirable, the violation of a legal mandate; however, the adequate sanction for this does not appear to be simply the denial of all legal effects. Rather, the unregistered marriage is basically still a marriage, and the child who is born of an unregistered marriage is deemed legitimate.[195]

Article 6 of the Registration Ordinance provides proof of the fact that the Chinese legislator is not primarily concerned with the notification or publication of marriages. According to that article, registration of divorce becomes superfluous when the spouses possess a judicial divorce certificate; so the register by no means provides a complete picture of the course of marriages. As to this "the Communist authorities have admitted expressly as valid unregistered marriages contracted before March 1953 if there have been actually factual relations of husband and wife."[196] This Chinese interpretation of the goals of marriage registration is in greater conflict with the traditional notions of marriage than are the Russian views. Perhaps it is for this very reason that the Chinese Communists so vigorously pursued the execution of the marriage registration, as it was thus interpreted. In their practical way, the Chinese did not hesitate to exhaust all the practical possibilities that marriage registration offered for carrying out their political purposes. It thus states in paragraphs 2–4 of the procedural ordinance of May 20, 1955:

> Both marital partners must appear personally before the competent registration authority and there fill out a marriage application form seeking registration. The form is filled out by a registration official on the basis of the oral statements of the parties, when the latter are not in the position to complete the form themselves.
> The registration officials are to examine the applications scrupulously, to clarify any ambiguities by questioning the applicants, and, as far as necessary, to conduct inquiries and require evidence. It is, nevertheless, expressly prohibited that the marriage be intentionally delayed by unnecessary inquiries.

---

[195] N. Niida, *Chūka Jinmin Kyōwakoku Koninhō* (Marriage law of the People's Republic of China), in 1 SHIN HIKAKU KONINHŌ (A comparison of laws relating to marriage and divorce) 39 (K. Miyazaki ed. 1960); N. Niida, *Chūgoku no jinmin minshushugi kakumei to kazoku* (People's democratic revolution and family law in China), in 1 KAZOKUMONDAI TO KAZOKUHŌ (Family problems and family) 218 ff. (A. Nakagawa, et als. eds. 1958).

[196] M. VAN DER VALK, *supra* note 9, at 88 (Question 9); *see also* M. van der Valk, *supra* note 188, at 350.

After the registration official has adequately explained the provisions of the Marriage Law and its marriage prohibitions, and has assured himself that the statutory requirements for marriage are all present, the recordation of the marriage is to be undertaken and a marriage certificate to this effect is to be presented to both parties. If the statutory requirements for marriage are not met, the registration is to be refused, with an explanation of the reasons.

Beyond this, registration officials in China apparently direct regular and emphatic questions to the marriage partners, asking, for example, whether they intend to found a lifelong marital union. Such a question stresses the enduring character of marriage *expressis verbis*.[197] (The statute does not expressly require this question by the officials.) The Chinese are thereby in line with Soviet Russia, which has emphasized marriage as a "bond for the entire lifetime" since the first phase of development.[198]

The following provisions of the Chinese Marriage Registration Ordinance express quite clearly and unambiguously the intention of the government in requiring marriage registration.

Paragraph 8—Duties of the Marriage Partners:
The spouses [parties] are obligated to make truthful registration applications. In the event that the registration authority determines that the parties are intentionally concealing circumstances which violate the Marriage Law, it [the authority] is to challenge this and admonish the parties [literally "educate"]. In serious cases the registration authority must petition the competent "People's" Court to proceed in accordance with the statutory provisions.
Paragraph 9—Duties of the Registration Officials:
The registration officials are obligated to follow with a strict sense of responsibility the provisions of the Marriage Law and the Ordinance on the Procedure for Marriage Registration, and to perform good work. They are forbidden to intervene in the freedom of marital decision [marriage freedom], to seek bribes from the parties or to demand other unlawful acts.[199]

When the Marriage Law came out in 1950, the view prevailed that a valid marriage needs registration. But in the meantime the opposite opinion has dominated, strengthened by the official view of the legislative commission that the non-registered marriage is unlawful but valid.[200]

Effects of marriage. In compliance with the principle of equal rights of spouses, marital regulations that include unequal treatment of a marriage partner are not provided in the Soviet Russian and People's Chinese statutes.

---

[197] B. Gruschin, *supra* note 167, on the present polemic in Soviet Russia against the principle (reportedly) propagated by many young people at the time of marriage—"if it doesn't work, we'll separate again."

[198] *Cf.* 1. V. GSOVSKI, SOVIET CIVIL LAW 129 (1948–49).

[199] 1 A. Bergmann & M. Ferid *supra* note 18, China, 40.

[200] N. Niida, *Shūkyō ni kankeinaki koninhō ; Chūgoku koninhō no kihonmondai* (Law of marriage without any religious influence; fundamental problems of new Chinese marriage law), 18 KIKAKUHŌ KENKYŪ (Comparative law journal) 49 ff. (April 1959).

Provisions on the statutory domicile of the wife with her husband, on a right of the husband to decide the children's education, or on a limitation of the occupational activity of the wife cannot therefore appear. There is no detailed regulation on the general financial consequences of marriage, for that would have an excessively materialistic character and accordingly would arouse a predominantly economic impression. It is this impression which the Soviet family law particularly seeks to avoid for the marriage it regulates as the "proletarian civil marriage with love." Also avoided are all statements on rights and duties of the spouses in the framework of the marital life union. In this context too, it abides with its general declaratory statements on marriage. The Soviet Russian as well as the People's Chinese statutes have but a few paragraphs dealing with the effects of marriage (China has four articles altogether). It is quite evident that the paragraphs are mostly designed to counter the ever existent ideas of dominance by the husband. The aim is the elimination of the old order. All duties during marriage are overwhelmed by the duty to fight for Communism, so that a legal specification of rights could weaken this main purpose.

The question of family name is also regulated. Since a statute requiring that the husband's name be taken would be a violation of the principle of equality, the spouses have the possibility of choosing the family name, and the choice applies for the duration of the marriage. Indirectly, this might lead to a gradual reduction of too common names.

According to Article 7 of the Family Code of the RSFSR of 1927, the spouses may jointly select the name of the husband or of the wife, but may also retain premarital names. This provision is carried over into Article 11 of the Family Code of 1968.[201] Article 11 of the Chinese Marriage Law says simply: "Each of the spouses has the right to take his own family name."[202] Since only the right of the spouses is mentioned, a common family name will also be permissible, as it already was under Article 1000 of the Private Law Code of 1930.[203] But the choice of the names has lost its old predominant significance of determining to which family the spouses and their children belong and whose ancestors they worship.

---

[201] In the draft of the new Family code, there was also foreseen, as a third variant, the combination of both premarital names as a common family name. Izvestia (Moscow) April 10, 1968, at 4.

[202] With this provision the political employment of the wife is facilitated; if she had made a name for herself politically before the marriage, she would thus have the possibility of retaining it. CH'IN T'I, *supra* note 163, at 800–807. Since there are no express provisions in Chinese law with respect to the family names of children, according to M. AOYAMA, KINDAI KAZOKUHŌ NO KENKYŪ (The modern family law) 174 (2d ed. 1967).

[203] *Cf.* K. Bünger, *supra* note 10, at 115. The spouses can also put the name of the other before their own. *Cf.* HUN-YIN FA CHI CH'I YU-KUAN WEN-CHIEN (The family law and connected documents), cited in CH'IN T'I, *supra* note 163, at 800–807.

Both spouses are free in their choice of employment and profession according to Article 9 of the Family Code of the RSFSR of 1927. Apparently the
statute presumes that both spouses are employed and leaves no doubt as to
the social and political desirability of this circumstance. When one spouse
changes his place of domicile, the other need not follow. This is expressly
stated in the new Family Code of 1968 (see Article 11, Section 4). However,
the Chinese Marriage Law (Article 9) establishes only freedom of occupation,
apparently viewing the question of independent domicile as self-evident.
Therefore, it does not regulate change of domicile, although for instance, the
question of the matrimonial residence and the possibility of its change played
an important role in the traditional Chinese society with its numerous forms
of marriage contracts. The Chinese Law emphasizes the freedom of each
spouse to participate in the social movements.[204]

Marital property law. The statutory regulation of marital property in both
the Soviet Russia and the People's Republic of China—as societies not based
upon private ownership—consists only of a clear expression that legislation
should merely be granted a secluded role in this area. Thus, the Family Code
of the RSFSR of 1927 treats marital property in all of two paragraphs
(10 and 13), and the new Family Code of the USSR of 1968 devotes only one
paragraph (12) to the subject, although in substance it contains somewhat more
than the earlier two paragraphs. The Chinese Marriage Law is also content
with a single article, limited to the single gem-like sentence: "Both husband
and wife shall have equal rights in the possession and management of family
property" (Article 10). Additionally, there is, however, a property regulation
in detail for divorce cases (Articles 23 and 24).

This position is based on the nature of "proletarian civil marriage with love"
(Lenin) and the anti-capitalistic attitude of the legislator. The capitalistic
system is said to be in open contrast in that it strives for propertied, rich
bourgeois families and law drafters, for whom the statutory property law
scheme is a quite central desire. To be sure, communism has not always
viewed marital property law as so unimportant. The pro-communist propaganda in China before the power takeover immediately seized upon the
distribution of assets in the traditional family as a primary point of attack and
envisioned the equal division between husband and wife as its revolutionary
goal. One of the main aims of the land reform in China was to give the woman
a certain economic independence by granting her some rights to land, insofar
as this is consistent with communist ideology. In the meantime, however, the
equality of rights in this respect has lost significance, because the pertinent

---

[204] A marital duty of living together has consciously not been adopted in order not to
prevent the employment of the spouses at different places of production. CH'IN T'I,
supra note 160, at 800–807. M. AOYAMA, *supra* note 202, at 173, presumes the genesis
of a new type of marriage, deviating from the former type, on the basis of the provision
that the spouses can freely choose an occupation and do not have to live together.

rights are reduced by the socialization of China. At the same time, they could add in this way some important sanctions for its effectiveness. After the 1957 collectivization of the Chinese farms into agricultural producers' cooperatives and the socialization of urban private business into joint state-private concerns, as well as the replacement of the cooperatives by people's communes in 1958, there no longer remained much room for it.[205] "The individual or the family no longer owns land, business enterprise, or any other significant means of production, and private property is reduced mainly to personal articles, with private ownership of houses in serious doubt."[206]

Peking's more extensive advancement of collectivization, in contrast to the Moscow government, matches the more radical approach of the Chinese Marriage Law to marital property compared to the Soviet Russian provisions. The starting point for both legislative works is clearly the principle of legal equality in the framework of the socialistic economic and social order. The valuation of the wife's work in the household and in raising the children on a par with the husband's professional work and with earning the family's livelihood is beyond question for both laws. (This is now expressly covered in Article 12 of the Soviet Russian Family Law of 1968.) The consequences which the two legal systems attach to this, however, are not uniform.

Both legal systems are now consistent[207] in assuming assets to be owned in common by the spouses, and this takes the form of joint ownership after they have both adhered to the idea of separate ownership of property in former stages of their developments. But already in the composition of these common assets there is a different assumption, even though there are not many criteria for this in the tests of the statutes. In Soviet Russia community property above all consists of assets acquired by the spouses *during* marriage through their own work (Article 12, Family Law of the USSR of 1968; Article 125, Family Law Ukr. SSR; Article 10, Family Law RSFSR of 1927). The premarital assets of each spouse, on the other hand, remain his own personal property (Article 12, Family Law of the USSR of 1968). His separate property comprehends not only the substitutes of his premarital assets, but also those acquired by gift or *causa mortis;* every acquisition specially attributed to one spouse (thus, for example, copyrights and awards for unique special personal accomplishment, such as the Lenin Award [not, however, bonuses from the

---

[205] S. LEC, NEUE UNFRISIERTE GEDANKEN (New untrimmed thoughts) 36 (1964): "Equality of rights in times of no rights, that's what."

[206] C. YANG, *supra* note 10, at 143; M. AOYAMA, *supra* note 202, at 158 ff. There may be some important changes since then, but no exact evidence of this is available to me.

[207] The former legislation of the Soviet Union had favored the regime of separate property to sustain the principle of the spouses' economic freedom. (*Cf.* Art. 105, Family Law Code of 1918 (*supra* note 6). But soon judicial practice had made several exceptions in favor of the community G. SVERDLOV, *supra* note 5, at 169.

wage fund for performance under work quotas]);[208] every savings account asset in his name, even when the asset is derived from joint work; the specific objects for the personal use of one spouse, again regardless of from whose means they come; and legal claims of one spouse such as the claim for wages (upon payment, however, the wages automatically become community property). If one spouse disposes of an object belonging to the community assets, the consent of the partner is presumed in the interest of protecting commerce.[209] This partner can produce countervailing evidence resulting in the transaction's nullification by proving that the lack of consent was known or should have been known by the other party. There are exceptions in the case of conveying a house, which requires the written consent of the marriage partner, and in disposing of motor vehicles.

In contrast, according to the leading interpretation in China, the premarital assets of both spouses and those acquired by gift or inheritance also fall basically within the definition of community property. The Russian system, in which there exist three funds of separately owned assets, was not adopted.[210] Moreover, the Chinese laws lack the subtle distinctions of the Russian law which are connected with the relatively strong emphasis on personal ownership interests. China, instead, places more stress on the idea of collectivization, since its property law is governed by the concepts of community onwership. The Russian solution appears to be based more on a system of separate owner- ship modified by notions of equalization of surplus. Behind this divergence is the long-standing fundamental difference of opinion generally existing in communist legal theory. One side[211] asserts that the principle of community ownership will be accomplished through progressive development toward socialism and will also extend to the pre-marriage assets. The opposing side[212] contends that community ownership applies only in the transitional period during which many women are not yet assimilated into the production process; they further assert that only the principle of pure separate ownership is consistent with the socialist society in which all women are themselves employed.

The provisions in Russian and Chinese law are also different with regard to asset distribution following termination of the marital ownership. According to Article 12 III of the Soviet Fundamental Family Law, in the future each spouse is to receive basically half of the common assets, unless the individual

---

[208] A. Hastrich, *Zum Ehegüterrecht der RSFSR* (On marital property law of the RSFSR), 7 OSTEUROPARECHT 260 ff. (1961).

[209] *But see* the divergent "cow-decision" of the Bulletin of the Highest Court, RSFSR, 1966–67.

[210] K. Bünger, *supra* note 10, at 116.

[211] *See* A. Hastrich, *supra* note 208, at 259.

[212] H. Nathan, *Gedanken zum sozialistischen Güterrecht* (Thoughts on the socialist marital property law), 12 NEUE JUSTIZ 120 ff. (1958).

case presents special interests of minor children or one of the spouses demands a different distribution. The Chinese law has rules only for distribution of assets following divorce. It provides that the wife's premarital assets are to be returned, while the husband's assets remain in the estate.[213] This favoring of the wife continues in Article 23, which provides that when the spouses fail to come to an agreement, the court distributes the assets, proceeding from the concrete circumstances of the family assets and considering "the interests of the wife and child or children and the principle of benefiting the development of production." Finally, Article 24 states that the husband must discharge debts arising from the spouses' ordinary living expenses that have not been covered by the community assets. The violation of the equality principle inherent in this provision was rationalized in the official explanation of the statute from 1953, which stated that under the present conditions in China the economic strength of the female party is weaker than that of the male. If, however, in an individual case the wife is in a better financial position, she has to pay the debts that the husband incurred during their marriage.[214]

This Chinese "interpretation" again demonstrates with particular clarity the different fundamental interpretation of legal norms in the socialist state from that in the non-socialist constitutional state.[215] While the constitutional state is cogently concerned with the concrete realization of fixed *abstract* norms of conduct, the socialist state logically does not presuppose any binding abstract rules at all, as indeed it acknowledges no subjective private rights. Instead of the separate legislation and application of laws, the legal ideas of the socialist state can be directly realized through concrete orders. In this sense it does not appear to the Chinese jurists to be a violation of the legal system when the judge deviates from the rules of the substantive law in order to reach a "just" solution in accordance with the plan and notions of the state. On the contrary, he is thus fulfilling his function as an administrative official; he gives orders that need not always be issued in application of "binding" pre-existent abstract rules.

Finally, both laws do not sanction marriage contracts contradicting these rules. In China the reason already seems to be that there is no marriage contract affecting property known to Chinese law at all.[216] In Russia such contracts would contradict the official principle that socialism does not provide any lawful opportunity for the spouses to pursue a course of private economy at variance with the prevailing matrimonial regime, since the aspects of the family with regard to the rights of property bring about an order suiting

---

[213] K. Bünger, *supra* note 10, at 116.

[214] *Cf.* M. VAN DER VALK, *supra* note 9, at 89-90 (Question 16).

[215] *See* especially W. BURCKHARDT, METHODE UND SYSTEME DES RECHTS (Methods and systems of the law) 219 ff. (1936).

[216] K. Woodsworth, *supra* note 156, at 172.

best the conditions in the life of working people taking part in social production. Here, family law is not private law. Thus, to this extent private autonomy does not exist.

Divorce law. The doctrinal position of the socialist state on the rule of law interprets the issuance of concrete orders (which are not of themselves either legal formulation or legal application), instead of the formulation in abstract statements and their application, to be no violation of the system.

Legal formulation and legal application are no longer necessarily separated, because it is not necessary that there be abstract rules of law. The legal ideas can also be directly realized in concrete orders. The legislation of the socialist state need not exist as a special function, because state orders need not always be founded upon pre-existent norms. . . . Whether these orders are issued generally and abstractly, or specifically and concretely is merely a question of expediency.[217]

An understanding of this distinction is particularly necessary to comprehend the divorce laws of Soviet Russia and the People's Republic of China. Although they have no rule of law as such, still they need substantive and procedural divorce law requirements in order to preserve the principle of monogamy. Only from this point of view can one accurately coordinate the many-sided decrees, guidelines, and directives[218] with the actual statutory provisions. All of these pronouncements serve to inject exact meaning into the catch-all provisions. Only thus can the peculiarity of the legislative technique of Soviet Russia and of the People's Republic of China be correctly evaluated.

Explanatory notes are added to the individual statutory articles of the marriage and family codification and constitute component parts of the statutes, which in practice display a very important significance, partially surpassing that of the statutory provisions. It is in these statutes that basically every norm issued from an authorized place is binding, because the division of powers here is only a formality.

Therefore, it is only a superficial distinction—not at all challenging the prominence of the divorce regulation—when one considers that the 1927 Russian Family Code contains only five provisions and that the new statute of 1968 devotes but a single provision to divorce law, while on the other hand the Chinese marriage law assigns more than a third of its articles (nine of twenty-five) to divorce law.[219]

---

[217] W. BURCKHARDT, *supra* note 215, at 219.

[218] Especially significant, for example, are the Union Decree of July 8, 1944, (*supra* note 97) and the Directives of the Plenary Supreme Court of the USSR of September 16, 1949 (*supra* note 100).

[219] This is particularly emphasized in C. YANG, *supra* note 10, at 68, who points out that the subject of divorce received more elaborate attention than any other subject in the Marriage Law.

In addition to the judgment of these divorce rules, careful account must also be taken of the changing financial burden (registration fees) and of the moral pressure exercised upon the individual spouse not to divorce and upon the judges not to allow divorce.

The filling in of the catch-all provisions of the divorce law must be seen in the context of the state's almighty position in China and Soviet Russia. While other states also have such provisions, they are generally filled by the judicial branch and reflect the varied personalities of the judges, who are independent of the political executive and free within the bounds of their discretion. However, in Soviet Russia and China the distance between divergent judgments is (theoretically) smaller, insofar as ideology in the party line possesses a much stronger force of penetration, occupying what might even be called a monopolistic position. The emphasis on the contrast to religion and the traditional family pattern is especially important for both, apparently from the fear that opposition to the state marriage policy might come from religious sectors. Thus, it can be said of both legal systems: "The discretion of state officials has a different meaning here than in the non-totalitarian regime." In case, for example, "the stability of the marriage is assigned a basic importance by the regime, then the regime can effectively influence and continually control the discretion of state officials through appropriate channels."[220]

The history of divorce law in Soviet Russia and China confirms, clearly parallel to their means of "struggle," the practical effects of this contrast. It demonstrates at the same time, however, (despite theoretical adherence to the principle of divorce freedom) how quickly and radically the position of the communist state can change in this regard. The Russians explain this by saying that the theory itself must be developed, while the Chinese call it development of new thought on the basis of unchanging theoretical doctrine.

Immediately following the October Revolution, the Soviet government sought to realize divorce freedom as a corollary to marital freedom (Decree of December 16, 1917) without more closely examining the compatibility of this principle with its other fundamental claims. In particular, they did not deal in detail with the question of how far this principle agreed with the realities of life and emphasized the doctrine of equality of husband and wife in the function of rearing small children.[221] In any case, the guilt principle was not decisive.

The revolutionary swing, which systematically cast away the historical past as well as the solutions of the contemporary bourgeoisie, dominated everything. The Soviet Russian law sought, after an initial and somewhat cautious legislative step in the first phase of development, to attain the developmental goal of divorce freedom, with radical consequences. Accordingly, the mere

---

[220] O. BRUSIIN, *supra* note 34, at 69.

[221] *But see* Art. 14, §4, Family Law Code of 1968, *supra* note 114.

desire of one spouse to dissolve the marriage sufficed for divorce; no special grounds were required. Such a divorce proceeding took place before the local court. However, when there was intent to divorce by both parties, the divorce was granted as a pure formality by the civil registrar.

The Family Code of 1924 then abolished the judicial divorce procedure and transferred divorce to the sole competence of the civil registrars. Although the courts were given sole jurisdiction during the restrictive phase of development, the Fundamental Family Law of 1968 again returned, if to a limited extent, to the old concept of divided authority. Consensual divorce, which today presupposes that the spouses have no minor children, is permitted (Art. 14, iv) before the civil registrars. Divorce intended by only one party, as noted above, comes before the local courts. Today the court must attempt reconciliation of the parties before it can determine that further cohabitation and preservation of the family have become impossible (Article 14).

Doubtful again today is the old fundamental question of whether the dissolution of the marriage is first accomplished with the registration of the final divorce decree at the civil registry office. In favor of this, one can note that the position of the civil registrar in the realm of divorce law has been elevated, and it is therefore improbable that he has been deprived of the prerogatives that he has long possessed. To be sure, however, the draft of Article 14, paragraphs 2 and 3 tends to go against this conclusion: "During the lifetime of the spouses a marriage can, upon petition of one of or both of them, be dissolved *(raztorgnut)* by way of divorce *(putem razvoda)*. The dissolution *(rastorženie)* of the marriage is accomplished judicially. . . ." Under the previous statutory terminology of the Family Code of the RSFSR only the "divorce" and not the "dissolution" devolved upon the court. The certification of the "dissolution" of the marriage through divorce was issued by the civil registrar. It is thus conceivable that according to the code, the "dissolution" of the marriage really comes about when the divorce decree becomes final. In the literature no position has been taken yet on this question. One must therefore simply wait until the courts express an opinion, or until a final explanation is presented in the approaching revision of the family codes.

This Soviet Russian divorce procedure with its two varying paths for consensual and non-consensual divorce, as well as the legally constitutive effect, was obviously a model for China's legislation. The Chinese Marriage Law provides (apparently following the Soviet Russian regulation in the family code of 1918, re-adopted in the Family Law of 1968 after contrary regulation in the 1944 decree): "In the case where divorce is desired by both the husband and wife, both parties shall register with the subdistrict people's government in order to obtain a certificate of divorce."[222] Consensual divorce, as in Russia, is handled by the administrative authority. The authority must, in accordance

---

[222] Art. 17, §2, Chinese Marriage Law.

with the statute, examine whether "appropriate measures have been taken for the care of children and property." If, on the other hand, only one spouse desires the divorce, he can petition the district people's government for a reconciliation proceeding.

> If such mediation fails, it shall without delay refer the case to the county or municipal people's court for decision. The district people's government shall not attempt to prevent or to obstruct either party from appealing to the county or municipal people's court. In dealing with a divorce case, the county or municipal people's court must, in the first instance, try to bring about a reconciliation between the parties. In case such mediation fails, the court shall render a verdict without delay.[223]

A court order is required for contested divorces. These court orders in divorce cases are one of the main signs of activity of the law courts in China. The fact that most of the descriptions we have of civil trials after 1957 involve divorce cases shows, moreover, that the main area left to the courts since then has been divorce.

According to Aoyama and Niida,[224] the Chinese requirement of a settlement effort before the actual divorce proceeding goes back to the Soviet government decree of 1944, with which Stalin carried out his slowed-down notions of family policy. That may possibly be literally true. However, the reference to the Soviet model can in no event conceal what great and quite specific significance the mediation procedure has long had in China and the very considerable extent to which the Chinese Communists, with their engrained pragmatism, made use of this traditional measure after revamping its meaning. Thus Stanley Lubman[225] claims: "Before the Communists gained power, mediation had been the primary mode of dispute settlement for thousands of years in traditional China. . . ." Also "since 1949, the Chinese Communists have continued to extol mediation and claim to use it far more extensively than adjudication in settling disputes. . . ." To be sure, "the Communists have substantially altered the traditional mode of mediation [and] have incorporated mediation into their effort to reorder Chinese society and mobilize mass support to implement Party policies." In this sense the mediation, politically utilized for supporting the "mass line," became a transformed institution to which the name "mediation" can no longer accurately be applied, for the political "mediators" in reality "decide rather than mediate disputes. . . ."[226]

---

[223] Art. 17, §3, Chinese Marriage Law.

[224] M. AOYAMA, *supra* note 202, at 179; N. Niida, *Chūka Jinmin Kyōwakoku koninho* (Marriage law of the People's Republic of China), in 1 SHIN HIKAKU KONINHŌ 87 ff. (1960).

[225] S. Lubman, *supra* note 151, at 1286 ff.

[226] *Ibid.*, 1338.

Primary dispute suppression occurs when resolution of the parties' differences is submerged in the mediator's application of abstract principles, stressing non-contentiousness and mutual assistance for the sake of national unity, collective living, and increased production. Thus, spouses who themselves cannot reconcile their sexual life with their hours of work are told by a judge that they cannot obtain a divorce, but are given no reason or alternative solution because national economic needs override their own.[227]

From this viewpoint it appears that the Soviet Union influences China less than the other way around; China is the forerunner of Russia. Horkheimer even suggests, quite generally, that the development in China, much more so than that in Russia, might also be the precursor for the West. He asserts, proceeding from the Chinese events:

. . . that the period of individualism, unreasonable today, is to some extent discontinued; that friendship between individuals, measured by the rise in collectivism, becomes subordinate; further the totally assimilated pragmatism, the motives of pure expediency manifested in each word of the Chinese leader—all of that is on the horizon of the West, as much as one tries to close one's eyes to it.[228]

In the substantive Chinese divorce law, to be sure, the postulate of freedom of divorce still dominates as "the necessary means for the abolishment of the old feudal marriage system, for the emancipation of the wife, who was humiliated under the feudal control, for the increase of happiness of the People and finally for the heightening of production force."[229] Already the marriage regulations of the Chinese Soviet Republic of 1931 guaranteed: "Freedom of divorce is established." In the manner of regulating the divorce grounds, the people's Republic of China also follows the Soviet example to a certain extent. The Russian marriage laws are characterized by non-assignment of specific substantive divorce grounds. They thus avoid being forced to grant a divorce whenever a specific ground is presented in the claim. Even the divorce-limiting Union decree of 1944 only instructed the courts that they were to determine the motives behind the divorce petition, while the upper court was to decide whether the marriage should be dissolved. Yet the decree did not specifically define which measures this court was to apply, but rather left such a decision to the discretion of the court. Some clues to the manner in which the courts exercise this discretion are provided by the 96–97 percent divorce-granting judgments and the 3–4 percent divorce denials. Certainly these statistics fail to consider the preceding "social influence" on the spouses yielded by the collective community's prescription of how marriage and family

---

[227] *Ibid.*, 1347.

[228] M. Horkheimer, *Die Zukunft der Ehe* (The future of marriage), in KRISE DER EHE? (Crisis of marriage?) 217 (1966).

[229] M. AOYAMA, *supra* note 202, at 175, quoting the explanatory preamble to the Marriage Bill.

should be run. Similarly, Article 17 of the Chinese Marriage Law only provides that in the event the attempted judicial conciliation is unsuccessful, the court must render a decision. Again, nothing is said of the decisional yardsticks to be applied by the court. According to Woodsworth's observation in China, in cases where only one party desires the divorce, the machinery of conciliation is a mandatory part of the legal proceedings, and he quotes a statement by Lo Chia-ting, vice-president of the Shanghai Higher People's Court, on the principles by which such a neighborhood conciliation committee should be guided in its work: "Firstly, to distinguish what is right from what is wrong; secondly, to seek harmony and unity in the family; and thirdly, to seek to benefit production and socialist construction."[230]

Chinese divorce freedom was as radically propagandized in the beginning as it had been in Russia in the first years after the Revolution. Thus Ch'en Shao-yü, a leading communist who took an active part in drafting the Marriage Law, explains: "In the new Democratic Society legal protection for freedom of divorce, just as the legal protection for freedom of marriage, serves as a necessary means to oppose and to abolish the old feudalistic marriage institution. It will give physical and mental emancipation to men and women who have been forced to suffer under the old marriage institution and enable them to insist upon divorce."[231] The marriages concluded under the old system had therefore to be transformed into "new democratic" marriages, where the women should not only be dealt with "as a piece of merchandise."

To be sure, in China's past, divorce by mutual agreement had theoretically been permitted for ages,[232] and in fact only the husband had been able to obtain divorce. But the past had been systematically rejected by the new government. To this extent the actual thrust of the revolutionary Chinese divorce scheme was especially aimed at remedying the wife's inability to obtain a divorce.[233] The motive is again evident; after their having long been disregarded, women would be won over as champions of the social revolution.

Official explanations in 1953 of the Chinese Marriage Law of 1950 are concerned in more detail with the handling of divorce. They insist on the breakdown principle without referring to the question of guilt.[234] To question

---

[230] K. Woodsworth, *supra* note 156, at 175.

[231] Quoted in C. YANG, *supra* note 10, at 63.

[232] K. Bünger, *supra* note 10, at 116.

[233] So, the relatively low divorce rates under the traditional system do not prove great family harmony. Family tensions were as a rule suppressed and shifted to the back of the wife who had to make this sacrifice for the family. *Cf.* C. YANG, *supra* note 10, at 67.

[234] Siu Kia-pei, *La Réforme du Droit du Mariage en Chine Communiste* (The reform of the marriage law in communist China), 8 REVUE INTERNATIONALE DE DROIT COMPARÉ (International review of comparative law) 577 (1956).

14, "Where one party insists upon divorce shall then a verdict of divorce be rendered?" the official answer reads: "The people's court shall grant the divorce if one party insists upon it and the mediation is without effect and the relations of husband and wife cannot be maintained. But if the facts prove that both parties have not yet reached the point that they really cannot continue to live together, they may also not grant the divorce."

This information demonstrates again that in their marriage law the Chinese, proceeding more pragmatically than the Russians who earlier drew conclusions from dogmatic notions, were in no way restricted. The possibilities of opinionated interpretation of the reconciliation provisions[235] in the evaluation of factual questions such as "cannot be maintained" encompass a very broad field. Thus, the official attitude toward divorce in China has passed through several different phases, as has the Russian line. From a very liberal starting point, a more stringent attitude was adopted. After the encouragement, discouragement soon followed. This development is also shown in the French divorce legislation after the grand revolution, which introduced divorce into the French legislation, by the law of September 20, 1792, which was a logical consequence of the secularization of marriage.[236]

Nevertheless, the Chinese Marriage Law describes two specific cases in which spouses of especially privileged persons cannot unilaterally demand a divorce. Thus, the spouse of an active member of the revolutionary army can only obtain a divorce with the consent of the other (Article 19). Soldiers receive this status privilege as "thanks for the sacrifice which they make to the security of the country and the new society, and in order to encourage them in battle."[237] Likewise, a husband cannot seek a unilateral divorce from his wife during her pregnancy or within a year following the birth of the child (Article 18). Under special circumstances, however, the People's Court can make an exception and grant the husband a divorce. A similar provision to this regulation in the Chinese Marriage Law is to be found now in the new Russian Family Law of 1968. This parallel also exists to the extent that both statutes fail to answer the following doubtful question: Should this objection also be considered when a husband seeking divorce alleges as the cause an act of adultery on the part of the wife, resulting in the birth of a child who is presently under one year old? The whole offers the interesting proof that

---

[235] C. YANG, *supra* note 10, at 81, citing a report concerning opposition to divorce.

[236] G. Thibault-Laurent, La Première Introduction du Divorce en France sous la Révolution et l'Empire (The first introduction of divorce in France under the Revolution and the Empire), 1938 (thesis, Montpellier).

[237] Bureau of the Legal Department of the Province Government of Hunan, *To strictly protect the marriage of the soldiers of the revolutionary army, in accordance with the law of the State*, Hsin Hu-nan pao (Hunan), Nov. 5, 1955; quoted in CH'IN T'I *supra* note 163.

certain Chinese family law provisions are assimilated by Russia, as well as the other way around, although the total influence of the one upon the other should certainly not be overrated.

Death of a spouse and divorce are the only types of termination of a marriage which are recognized in Chinese marriage law. It does not recognize voidable marriages of other types of termination.

Among the consequences of divorce, the cost regulation in Russia and China is significantly different from that customarily adopted in non-communist states. Primarily, especially in Russia during the second phase and in Romania today, the costs have been used as a means to repress divorce. According to the USSR decree of June 27, 1936, the costs were: 50 Rubles for the first divorce, 150 Rubles for the second divorce, and 300 Rubles for the third divorce (Art. 27). According to the decree of July 8, 1947, the court had to fix the costs between 500 and 2000 Rubles (1960: 50 and 200 Rubles new currency). Also in the People's Republic of China, the cost of divorce proceedings and marriage counseling today seem to be of little practical importance. In Soviet Russia and in the People's Republic of China the principle that the spouse who is responsible for the breach has to bear the divorce costs is unknown. Rather, the financial position of both spouses is the controlling factor. The allocation of costs based on the financial position is determined by the court's discretion.

Also, as to the question of maintenance, both the Russian statutes and the Chinese Marriage Law are mainly little concerned with the question of fault or responsibility. Basically, a divorced person—whether husband or wife—had no claim whatsoever on his former partner. Only when he has difficulty supporting or maintaining himself must the former partner render assistance to him, unless the needy person has already remarried (Article 25, Chinese Marriage Law). Unlike the majority of statutes of the individual Soviet Russian republics (compare Article 15, Family Code, RSFSR), the Chinese law does not in this regard require an ability to pay on the part of the obligated spouse (Article 25, Marriage Law). It also does not place a time limit on the duty to support the unfortunate party, as did most of the Soviet republics whose periods varied between one and three years. But this does not mean that China does not bear in mind the influence of this rule upon the production process, nor that the Chinese legislator does not share the fear of the Soviet Russian legislator of 1926 that divorce might be abused for financial speculation. The latter erected the time barrier so that unilateral divorce would not be used for the enjoyment of a temporally unlimited annuity. With this duty, which practically goes so far as to counter easy divorce, the Chinese statute (although not the Russian law) chiefly burdens the husband, as it expressly urges the courts in this discretionary decision to consider "the interests of the wife and the child or children, and the principle of benefiting the development

of production" (Article 23).[238] From the standpoint of the influence of the
Chinese Marriage Law upon the Russian provisions, the rearrangement of
Article 13 of the Russian Fundamental Family Law of 1968 should be mentioned. According to that article, the support claim which is fixed during the
marriage is not limited only to cases of sickness, disability, and old age, but
can now also be based upon pregnancy and the existence of a child under one
year of age.[239] Another new Russian provision is that the support claim
judicially fixed during the duration of the marriage continues to have effect
following divorce. Finally, completely new for the Russian law is the provision
that a divorced spouse can be judicially granted a support claim against the
other, when he is needy, but not yet incapable of working. This applies for
the case of an old spouse (fifty-five year old men, fifty year old women) who
cannot, after a long marriage, be expected to become employed, when he
will be enjoying a pension within five years.

Parent and Child

General principles. The move toward improving the position of minors,
particularly with respect to their independence from the family, is now much
further developed in both the Soviet Russian and Chinese parent-child law.
(There was already an expression of this tendency in the marriage law; for
example, in both countries' statutory emphasis upon the freedom of the minor
in marrying.) The primary general doctrine is that of the principle of child
welfare. Thus, in Russia the Preamble to the Family Code of 1927 encourages
the protection of the interests of the child, and Article 33 of this code provides
that parental rights are only to be exercised in the interests of the children.
(Article 18 IV of the new Fundamental Family Law of 1968 requires less
pointedly that the exercise of the parental rights should not violate the interests
of the child.) Article 1 of the Chinese Marriage Law systematically and sharply
rebukes the former marriage system, which "ignores the children's interests,"
and promises in its new people's democratic marriage system, "protection of
the lawful interests of women and children."

Certainly the "welfare of the child" is, as Brusiin[240] points out, quite
generally an "emotional parade argument." It is found more or less in all
modern child laws in the East and West. It is always a matter of what is
understood by this, for it certainly does not of itself contain any definitively
ascertainable criteria. Therefore, in this field, just as little affinity can be found
between Chinese and Russian laws as in the invocation of equal rights of both

---

[238] But it appears very doubtful that this maintenance provision of the marriage code
can be read as Yang reads it, as "an unmistakable sign of communist policy" in favor
of the family "as a social institution." C. YANG, *supra* note 10, at 19.

[239] *Cf.* Art. 18 of the Chinese Marriage Law of May 1, 1950.

[240] O. BRUSIIN, *supra* note 34, at note 80, p. 106.

sexes or the equal status of legitimate and illegitimate children; these points are also pursued today in many non-communist codifications.

Only the individual regulations explain the meaning of the principle of child welfare. The Chinese legislator, however, did not have many provisions in the Family Law for child law. In contrast to the Soviet family laws of 1927 and 1968 which regulate parent-child law in detail, the Chinese legislator apparently saw no advantage in this, all the more so since this problem had found many different solutions in the past. Rather, he left the further development up to practice, which (impelled by such postulates of marriage law as equality of the spouses, and by further revolutionary establishments, especially the people's communes) could in no way avoid the task. Possibly their reluctance to formulate child laws might have been reinforced in the beginning by the earlier experience with the Chinese Private Law Code of 1930, whose more detailed provisions on child law were barely applied by the courts at the time.[241]

Position of the parents. Public child-rearing was already demanded in Point 10 of the Communist Manifesto of 1847.[242] After its seizure of power, the Soviet government pursued the task of realizing this demand. The program of the Communist International[243] provided that society was to begin undertaking child care even during the transitional period.

Lenin reported at the beginning of the twenties that the "transfer to society of the child-rearing functions of the household" was already being accomplished.[244] Institutions such as nurseries, kindergartens, and trade schools were founded for the accomplishment of social child care. But since the Soviet state, after the October Revolution, did not have sufficient financial means to bring about an adequate realization of this demanding task, it had to content itself with a transitional solution. The rearing of children was assigned to the parents as authorized agents of the state, "temporarily, as it was thought at that time."[245] Accordingly, Article 71 of the Family Code of 1927 designated the parents as guardians of their children, from which it was concluded that they were assigned the rearing of the children.[246]

From the middle of the thirties on, this ideological approach was disavowed especially because the investigations of the educator Marenko from 1930 to 1935 demonstrated the importance of child-rearing in the family during the child's first years of life, when his attitudes and feelings were molded. In the following

---

[241] K. Bünger, *supra* note 10, at 117.

[242] 1 K. MARX & F. ENGELS, *supra* note 46, at 43 (Communist Manifesto); *Cf. also* F. Engels, *supra* note 47, at 75.

[243] Adopted by the Sixth World Congress in 1928.

[244] C. ZETKIN, ERINNERUNGEN AN LENIN (Recollections of Lenin), quoted in R. SCHLESINGER, *supra* note 74, at 79.

[245] H. BAHRO, *supra* note 84, at 53.

[246] *Cf. id.,* at 54.

period, communist child-rearing was thought to be best guaranteed by the natural influence of the parents.[247] For this purpose child-rearing was then declared to be the noblest duty of the family. The natural ties between parents and children were acknowledged, and parental love was praised as "the most natural of all human feelings."[248] At the same time, the parent's responsibility to society in child-rearing was sharply pronounced in the statute. While Article 41 of the Family Code of 1927 still merely said that the parents had to prepare their children for a "socially useful activity," the parents' obligation to society was strengthened with their entry into the primary child-rearing role. The precedence of social duties was as unquestionable as the classification of child-rearing as a social duty. So today Article 18, paragraph 3 of the new Fundamental Family Law especially obligates the parents to raise their children in the spirit and by the moral principles of communism. If they do not satisfy this obligation, or if their rearing otherwise has a detrimental effect upon the children, then their parental rights can be denied, or their children can be taken away from them (Articles 33, 46, Family code of 1927; Article 19 of the Family Law of 1968). Thus, likewise, today in the USSR the function and responsibility of child-rearing do not at all rest exclusively with the parents. Their role competes with the urgent educational claims of the state and the communist party. The rights and duties of the parents are derived from the legal position of the guardian and the curator. Until the child's fourteenth year, the parents are his statutory representatives, like guardians. From age fifteen to age eighteen, the parents' legal position corresponds to that of a custodian with all of the resulting consequences. The child attains his majority upon completion of his eighteenth year.[249] Finally, in the interest of the economy the rearing of the children is neither to harm nor altogether to cripple the production power of the parents.

The present picture of child-rearing in the People's Republic of China is dominated even more by the encompassing activity of the kindergartens, nurseries, schools, and youth organizations.[250] The social undertaking of child-rearing is said by one scholar to have already progressed so far that in 1959 around 70 percent of the infants in the rural areas of the country made use of state child institutions.[251] A further direct extension of these institutions

---

[247] See A. Pergament, *Das sowjetische Familienrecht* (Soviet family law), in DIE SOWJETUNION HEUTE (The Soviet Union today) pt. 16, at 14 (1959); similarly, see Family Law Code of 1968, *supra* note 114, Preamble.

[248] See A. Pergament, *supra* note 247, at pt. 17, at 14; G. SVERDLOV, OCHRANA INTERESOV DETEJ V SOVETSKOM SEMEJNOM I GRAJDANSKOM PRAVE (The protection of the interests of children in the Soviet family and civil law) 13 ff. (Moscow 1955).

[249] Civil Code of the RSFSR, 1964, Arts. 13, 14.

[250] Cf. T. Chen, *supra* note 33, at 265.

[251] M. BIEHL, *supra* note 56, at 112.

is being attempted; the schools are to be transformed into boarding schools, and the nurseries are also to take in infants overnight.[252]

Providing the ideological foundation for this were such writings as the "Party resolution on questions in regard to the people's communes" of December 10, 1958 in the Wuchang Conference of the Central Committee of the Chinese Communist Party.[253] It stated that these institutions must be so well managed that in every case a better revolutionary upbringing than could be given in the family will be guaranteed the child so that the parents thus will gladly place their children in such homes. Even though the Party Resolution of 1958 leaves the parents free to decide whether they want their children raised by the state, the demands of their work and social obligation (such as attending indoctrination classes) or the participation in public amusements induce them to assign their children to state institutions.[254] In the People's Republic of China man lives, works, and rests in organization.[255] According to Hung Tung-wen this corresponds to the natural course of things. The role of the family in child-rearing recedes more and more; the children belong to the state, and placing them in homes is a blessing for them.

This development is completely consistent with the statutory regulation of child law in the Chinese Marriage Law. In view of the dominant position of the state in child-rearing, the regulation in Article 13 of the Marriage Law, unlike the corresponding Soviet provisions, is no longer very surprising. This article lacks any statement that child education is to take place in the spirit of communism and that the children must be prepared for a socially useful activity. Because the legislator apparently proceeds from the presumption that the children primarily devolve to the care of the state, the Chinese statute, again in contrast to the Russian one, contains no provisions for taking the child away from the parents or depriving the parents of their parental rights.

The reasons for this adherence by the People's Republic of China to goals which the Soviet Union has long since abandoned are of the most varied nature. To a great extent practical considerations underlie this attitude. China today, more than Russia, is directed toward a better allocation of manpower. In contrast again to the USSR, China is still in the stage of economic construction. Women must still be liberated from household management and child-rearing in order to make them available for the production process. While in the Soviet Union today parental duties are discharged by a generation that

---

[252] *See* Liu Shao-ch'i, in EXTRACTS FROM CHINA MAINLAND MAGAZINES No. 149, Dec. 1, 1958, at 42.

[253] New China News Agency (Peking), Dec. 18, 1958, in Current Background, No. 542, Dec. 29, 1958.

[254] *Cf.* C. YANG, *supra* note 10, at 170; M. BIEHL, *supra* note 56, at 116; *cf. also* Kung Tung-wen, *On the Collective Way of Life,* in CHUNG-KUO CH'ING-NIEN (China's Youth) No. 9 (1960), cited in M. BIEHL, *supra* note 56, at 117.

[255] F. SCHURMANN, *supra* note 19, at 11.

has been molded in the spirit of communism for more than fifty years, the generation of parents in China (because of the notably short term of the communist regime) is not yet placed in the same ideological confidence. For the government, therefore, this is another reason for the state's role in child-rearing. This applies even more so because of China's heritage of an independently existing family, which was much less integrated into the state than was the case in Russia. In this respect the Chinese people's government must today be more concerned than the Soviet government with protecting itself from the past and assuring that its own ideas attain and retain reality.

In view of these discrepancies between the Russian and Chinese ideas of child law, it is still noteworthy that in present day Russia there are some voices raised in favor of the same goals pursued by the Chinese People's communes. The venerable Soviet philosopher Strumilin[256] suggested in 1960 that for the purpose of communist education each child should be separated from his parents immediately after birth and placed in the care of the state institutions (nurseries, children's homes, boarding schools). Even if the feelings of the parents are highly valued, the fate of the children should not be surrendered to them. The society principally should assume the collective responsibility for children, while the family should only be entrusted with a minimal share. Such a small family role would not be "detrimental" to the children. "The family more and more dwindles away [then] to that which is under all of the circumstances the most constant—namely the marital or even extra-marital, (so long as it is tied by the bonds of love) inseparable family couple."[257]

Support of the children. In conformity with the state's assumption of the child-rearing role, the support of children should also devolve upon the state.[258] Therefore, the Soviet Family Code of the RSFSR of 1918 provided that the maintenance duty of parents falls away "to the extent that children are supported by the state."[259] Since the Soviet state after the war did not see itself in a position to fulfill these obligations, this burden was temporarily left to rest upon the family. Accordingly, the Family Code of the RSFSR of 1927 no longer accepted the above-mentioned provision on the maintenance duty of the state. Simultaneously with the new orientation of the Soviet family policy, child maintenance was transformed into an obligation to be primarily

---

[256] J. HAZARD & I. SHAPIRO, *supra* note 21, at pt. 3, 102.

[257] S. Strunilin, *Rabocij byt i kommunizm* (The everyday life of the worker and communism), NOWYJ MIR No. 7, at 203 ff. (1960), summarized in German in 12 OST-PROBLEME 651 ff. (1960).

[258] 1 K. MARX & F. ENGELS, *supra* note 46, at 43 (Communist Manifesto); F. Engels, *supra* note 47, at 75.

[259] Art. 161 comment, Family Law Code of 1918.

fulfilled by the parents.[260] So, today, both parents are primarily obligated by Articles 42 and 48 of the Family Code to support minor children, as well as those who are of age but incapable of working.

The Chinese Marriage Law of 1950 recognizes only the duty of the parents[261] "to rear and to educate" the children. There is no mention in the Marriage law of an obligation on the part of the state. Unlike the Soviet Russian provisions, there are no specific conditions attached to the child's support claim. While in the case of illegitimate children, the duty of the father is statutorily limited up to the child's eighteenth birthday (Article 15, paragraph 4), for legitimate children the only time limitation lies in the use of the word "rear."[262]

The Chinese Marriage Law contains only very fragmentary, undogmatic provisions on these points, while the Soviet Russian laws offer very detailed solutions, which reveal the dogmatic main points. These solutions appear not to have had a highly significant influence upon the Chinese legislator.

Support of the parents. According to Article 49 of the Soviet Russian Family Code, children must support their parents who are needy and incapable of working. The scope of the maintenance duty is determined by the financial position of the parties. Article 52 of the Family Code obligated children proportionally for the support, so that even when only one child is sued, the financial status of the remaining children is also to be considered. Nevertheless, the court might also specify a joint liability on the part of the children.[263] Today, Article 20, paragraph 2 of the new Family Code makes it clear that children can be absolved from the duty of maintenance, if the parents have neglected their parental duties.

Article 13, paragraph 1, sentence 2 of the Chinese Marriage Law obligated children to support and assist their parents. The duty of support is owed to those persons who actually performed the functions of parents. If it is concluded by connecting "support" and "assist" that the maintenance duty only applies when the parents are indigent, then the statutory position would to this extent correspond to the legal situation in Soviet Russia.

Position of the illegitimate child. Equality for legitimate and illegitimate children is among the fundamental postulates of Marxism.[264] This dictate is

---

[260] The brief No. 104 (RSFSR) of June 12, 1926 (source in H. BAHRO, *supra* note 84, at 290) is characteristic; it expressly says that in deciding upon an adoption the unburdening of the state household is also to be considered.

[261] In contrast, Art. 1084 of the Chinese Private Law of 1930 mentioned the right and duty of the parents to protect and educate the children. K. BÜNGER, ZIVIL UND HANDELSGESETZBUCH VON CHINA (Private law and commercial code of China) 259 (1934).

[262] *See* K. Bünger, *supra* note 10, at 118.

[263] Brief No. 104 (RSFSR) of June 12, 1926 (source in H. BAHRO, *supra* note 84, at 290).

[264] 1 K. MARX & F. ENGELS, *supra* note 46, at 43 (Communist Manifesto); F. Engels, *supra* note 47, at 75.

to be accomplished by public care and rearing of all children, which avoids the difficulties traditionally found in the family system. The Soviet Russian legislation after the October Revolution immediately adopted the principle of equality for legitimate and illegitimate children. Indeed this was realized by affording all children equal rights with regard to the parents.[265] Natural descent, not marriage, became the foundation of the family. Consanguinity alone established a parent-child relationship without the children's legal status being affected by whether their parents were married.

This legal situation was radically altered by the Union decree of July 8, 1944, on the "Promotion of large families." The natural descent principle was restricted; a paternal relationship could only be established by the additional feature of marriage of the father with the mother. The illegitimate child had no more connections to his father and was viewed as neither related to him nor having any maintenance claim against him; between them neither rights nor duties were established.[266] Beyond this, the mother was denied the right to bring a paternity suit.[267] Although the mother indeed received state financial aid, it amounted to less than half of the maintenance that a father of a legitimate child had to pay[268] and ran only until the child was twelve years old.[269] Article 4 of the Decree granted the unmarried mother the option of placing the child in a state nursery at no expense.

After Stalin's death criticism was leveled against the 1944 Soviet law on illegitimacy, a law that is to be considered in connection with the events of the war and the associated population and family policy considerations, as well as with the social, economic, and personal convictions of the individual political bodies of that time. Discrimination against the illegitimate child was censured not only as a violation of the principle of equal treatment, but also as a breach of the principle of equality between the sexes and the communist ethic, especially because the state financial aid was very low. The Family Code of 1968 in response to this criticism returned to the principles applying before 1944 such as the natural descent principle, tempered, however, by experiences acquired in the meantime[270] and by new tendencies (Article 16).

---

[265] Family Law Code of 1918, Art. 144, made all of the possible fathers obligated to provide maintenance.

[266] Only by later marriage with the mother and acknowledgment of his paternity could the father still establish a paternal relationship: Family Law Code of 1927, Art. 28.

[267] Now, Family Law Code of 1927, Art. 29, amended by Art. 20 of the Union decree of July 8, 1944 (*supra* note 97).

[268] A. Pergament, *Pravovoe položenie vnebračnych detej dolžno byt' izmeneno* (The legal status of illegitimate children shall be changed), 9 SGIP 67 (1956).

[269] USSR Decree of July 8, 1944, *supra* note 97, at Art. 3, para. 2.

[270] When Article 16 of the Family Law Code of 1968 (*supra* note 114) in treating the paternity claim considers among other things whether the husband has managed a common household with the mother, or raised and supported the child, the thoughts of

The Chinese Marriage Law of 1950 is connected to the old Marxist postulates, for it establishes as a maxim the equality of legitimate and illegitimate children. Proceeding from its revolutionary thesis, it first had to win the support of the previously slighted children, and for this reason limitations of the basic principle such as those in Soviet Russia were not considered. Admittedly, the degree of this discrimination against illegitimate children in pre-revolutionary China had never been as striking as in Russia before the revolution. It is also true that until then the general acceptance of illegitimate children into the maternal family community in China never permitted the kinds of denial of status inflicted upon the unwed mother in the West.

The development in China since that time does not present, as far as can be seen, any statements advocating limitations on the equality of illegitimate children such as Russia has had until now. On the contrary, institutions such as the people's communes and movements such as the propaganda and indoctrination-waged campaigns to educate children in the communist way, have brought about the opposite effect. The Marriage Law with its general provisions erects no barriers against illegitimate children. Characteristic of its openness is its important (especially for the conditions of life in China) solution of the difficult question of determination of paternity: The mere testimony of the mother "or of another person" suffices to establish a maintenance claim against the putative father (Article 15, paragraph 2). Moreover, the emphasis of the Chinese statute, as its name already indicates, is on marriage and not so much on family (in contrast to the marriage resting on blood descent). Thus, the idea of weakening the family relations by improving the status of the illegitimate children is not beyond this attitude. The provisions of Article 15 make the position of the illegitimate child equal to that of the legitimate child after divorce. According to Article 13, the general provisions of the law are also applicable to the relationships between adoptive parents and their adopted children. Thus, adoptive children and illegitimate children enjoy the same protection.

Position of the children after divorce. Under present-day Soviet Russian law the divorce court has to determine in its divorce judgment which spouse should have custody of the children, as well as who has to provide child support and in what amount (Article 22). The problem of how to determine the welfare of the child in the individual case has to be solved by judicial decisions.[271] On this point the comments polemically stress the difference from law in bourgeois countries, where it is said that parents decide upon the children just as they do upon the individual property items. This implies

---

the prior case law on Article 42 of the Family Law Code of 1927 are being continued. In this way the practice had sought to ameliorate some of the particular harshness of the earlier provisions.

[271] A. Pergament, *supra* note 75, at 473 ff., 483.

that a decision on the suitability of a partner's character depends primarily upon his political reliability.

Similarly, in China the welfare of the children after divorce is the decisive factor, and, as in Russia, the scale may be tipped in favor of political considerations. The Chinese Marriage Law, however, differs from the Russian in its individual provisions on the custody of the children. The biological consideration that a child must remain with the mother while being nursed might have been an acceptable reason for the enactment of the corresponding provision in Article 20, paragraph 3, in favor of the mother. The Chinese Marriage Law in leaving the question of care and maintenance primarily to the agreement of the parents, adopted the Russian provision as it was before the Decree of July 8, 1944, and not as it is today. Article 21 might have arisen more for reasons of publicity than from considerations of legal necessity. This article expressly provides that an agreed upon or judicially determined amount of support or education does not prejudice a claim by the children for an increase in that amount. Moreover, in spite of its adherence to the principle of equality of the parents, the statute betrays in these provisions a concession to the female party. For example, it is still expressly provided that the husband who is (apparently alone) obligated to pay has to bear either all or a part of the costs of the necessary everyday expenses and of the education of the child, who remains in the custody of the mother (Article 22). The law provides for no payment duty on the part of the mother in cases where the father takes custody of the child. The basis for this difference was the generally weak economic position of the women, but the division of costs can otherwise be regulated so as to correspond to the economic situation of the wife. Other important questions such as the representation of the child or the visitation rights of the other parent are, on the other hand, not touched by the statute.

Guardianship and custodianship. During the early period following the October Revolution in the Soviet Union the strong emphasis upon the state's child-rearing influence at the expense of the parents was paralleled by a close coupling of guardianship and custodianship with the state authorities.[272] The state organs or social organizations directly exercised (without the interposition of an individual guardian or custodian) the function of caring for persons who were incompetent or only partially competent. With the Family Code of 1927 the principle of direct guardianship by the state or social organizations was loosened (Article 74). Still it remains true that a child in a children's institution acquires no particular guardian, but rather in these cases, which frequently occur in practice, the state institution itself is the child's guardian or custodian.

In addition, Soviet Russian law (decree of the RSFSR of September 2, 1925) has recognized the institution of foster parenthood. The possibility thus

---

[272] H. BAHRO, *supra* note 84, at 155 ff.

arises of placing parentless, particularly neglected, children in a family for a time by agreement. According to the currently prevailing ideology, "the combination of social upbringing in nurseries, kindergartens and schools with the upbringing in the Soviet worker family creates the best conditions for forming the personality of the child."[273] The agreement with the foster parents for the placing of these children, aged five months to fourteen years, is made in the rural areas by the chairman of the village soviet and in the cities by the municipal departments of public instruction. The minor enters into no family law relationships with the foster parents, *"puisque celui dont il dépend est en réalité l'organisme qui a passé à son sujet le contrat avec son patron."*[274]

In the People's Republic of China, because of the lack of a civil law code, there is no statutory regulation of guardianship. That was already the case in the Republic of China. The notion of guardianship is used in the broadest sense to signify the state managed care of incompetent persons or those having limited competency. Today, in the People's Republic[275] the legal institute of custodianship is viewed as unnecessary.[276] Altogether, the public law treatment of guardianship in contemporary China appears, even in the absence of statutory principles, to follow in certain respects rules not contrary to those existing before the revolution. Yet this only applies as long as the measures taken by the people's communes do not again interfere with practice.

---

[273] A. Pergament, *supra* note 75, at 503 ff.

[274] 2 R. DAVID & J. HAZARD, *supra* note 39, at 312.

[275] K. BÜNGER, *supra* note 261, at 87. This differs from the earlier view in China.

[276] 1 A. Bergmann & M. Ferid, *supra* note 18, China, 34.

Family Law and Social Mobilization in Soviet Central Asia: Some Comparisons with the People's Republic of China*

GREGORY J. MASSELL

It is surely a truism that law cannot be conceived of as an absolutely autonomous strategic instrument of rapid social change.[1] This should be all the more apparent in the case of family law, because it concerns sexual and generational roles and rights involving intimately and immediately sacred, as against secular, aspects of life, and thus consummatory rather than instrumental values.[2] At the same time, the extraordinary proliferation of variables confronting a political analyst and an aspiring social engineer alike, and the uncertainties about cause and effect in the social process, tend to place sharp

* This paper is a by-product of a general inquiry into the problems of strategy in engineered social revolution. I am engaged in this inquiry with the support of a Faculty Research Grant of the City University of New York, and wish to express my appreciation to the City University for helping make this enterprise possible.

[1] I have discussed this problem at some length in *Law as an Instrument of Revolutionary Change in a Traditional Milieu: The Case of Soviet Central Asia*, 2 LAW AND SOCIETY REVIEW 179–228 (Feb. 1968). I have also dealt with these issues in far greater detail in THE SURROGATE PROLETARIAT: MOSLEM WOMEN AND REVOLUTIONARY STRATEGIES IN SOVIET CENTRAL ASIA, 1919–29 (Princeton, N.J., 1974). For some complementary, as well as different views, and an excellent general review of the literature on law and social change, see L. Friedman & J. Ladinsky, Law as an Instrument of Incremental Social Change, Sept. 8, 1967 (paper read at the Annual Meeting of the American Political Science Association, Chicago, Ill.).

[2] I have attempted a preliminary systematic comparison of the role and impact of family law and other instruments and strategies of social engineering in: The Vulnerability of Islamic Society to Revolutionary Social Engineering: Soviet Central Asia, November 15, 1968 (paper read at the Plenary Session of the Annual Meeting of the Middle East Studies Association, Austin, Texas).

Some relevant discussions from a number of vantage points may be found in K. BOULDING, THE IMPACT OF THE SOCIAL SCIENCES, especially 78–101 (1966); A. Rose, *The Use of Law to Induce Social Change*, in 6 TRANSACTIONS OF THE THIRD WORLD

limits on our powers of generalization and prediction in this realm. Not surprisingly, both theories and strategies of social change (and of the role of law in such change) have so far been approached, by and large, with skepticim and caution—at least in the West.[3]

The Soviet Union and Communist China certainly mark a sharp departure in this respect. A deliberate quest was made here for strategies and tactics of holistic social engineering with a scope, intensity, and speed that are probably without precedent in history. By the same token, law was deliberately used as an instrument of revolutionary transformation. To be sure, Soviet and Chinese communists have never been content to rely on law alone to achieve desired ends and have tended to view the judicial process as one among many catalysts of change and, in some cases, as a distinctly subsidiary one. Yet it is precisely in the sphere of family law that some of the most telling reflections are found of communist attitudes to social change and of the responses on the part of communist elites to the imperatives, opportunities, and problems of social engineering.[4]

In this context, the notes that follow are intended to deal quite briefly, even schematically where possible, with a few sharply delimited questions. How can we compare and contrast the uses of family law in social change in Soviet Central Asia and Communist China? How can one account for the parallels and divergencies in the two models of legal engineering? In turn, what can such a preliminary comparative perspective tell us about the factors that determine the role (and the success or failure) of law and extrajudicial mechanisms as instruments of social mobilization and revolutionary change in modernizing nations?

CONGRESS OF SOCIOLOGY 52–63 (1956); Y. Dror, *Law and Social Change.* 33 TULANE LAW REVIEW 787–802 (1959); E. SCHUR, LAW AND SOCIETY: A SOCIOLOGICAL VIEW especially chs. 3–4 (1968); M. BERGER, EQUALITY BY STATUTE (rev. ed. 1967). The most comprehensive collation of some of Max Weber's explicit or implicit approaches to this problem may be found in MAX WEBER ON LAW IN ECONOMY AND SOCIETY (M. Rheinstein ed. 1966).

[3] For some recent reviews of the literature, *see, e.g.,* W. MOORE, SOCIAL CHANGE (1963); THE PLANNING OF CHANGE (rev. ed. W. Bennis, *et al.* eds. 1968). *Cf.* G. ALMOND & G. POWELL, COMPARATIVE POLITICS: A DEVELOPMENTAL APPROACH especially ch. 11 (1966).

[4] For some representative general studies of the role of law in the USSR, *see* H. BERMAN, JUSTICE IN THE USSR (1963); J. HAZARD, LAW AND SOCIAL CHANGE IN THE USSR (1953); G. GUINS, SOVIET LAW AND SOVIET SOCIETY (1954); K. GRZYBOWSKI, SOVIET LEGAL INSTITUTIONS (1952). *Cf.* H. GEIGER, THE FAMILY IN SOVIET RUSSIA (1968); PROSPECTS FOR SOVIET SOCIETY especially chs. 5, 14 (A. Kassof ed. 1968).

The papers from the conference on which this book is based are the most recent and comprehensive review of the evolution and role of family law in traditional and modern China. See the proceedings of the Conference on the Role of Law in Modernizing Nations: Chinese Family Law and Social Change, held at the University of Washington Law School, Seattle, August 1968.

No attempt is made here to construct an all-inclusive paradigm of the confrontation, by way of judicial and extrajudicial manipulation of family relations, between revolutionary and modernizing elites on the one hand and a cluster of Asian traditional societies on the other. Nor can much attention be devoted to specific nuances, actions, and interactions in the evolution of family law and of the judicial process in general in the two regions.[5] Instead, a preliminary balance sheet of the characteristic (and predominant) orientations of Soviet and Chinese communist elites toward the imperatives of legal engineering, and their perceptions of desirable responses to the attendant opportunities and problems will be drawn up. Such an evaluation is necessarily a tentative one; it is based primarily on a comparison of Soviet and Chinese experience in the first two decades of communist rule in the respective milieus —circa 1917–37 in the former case and circa 1949–69 in the latter.

EMPHASES AND AIMS OF LEGAL ENGINEERING: SOME PARALLELS BETWEEN CENTRAL ASIAN AND CHINESE MODELS

It hardly needs to be emphasized that in confronting the tasks of social engineering in their respective milieus Soviet and Chinese communists had a commonly shared pool of orientations toward ideology, politics, economics, culture, and social relations. In the realm of family relations—as in other respects—Marxism provided an apocalyptic vision of the future and a clear-cut normative vision of sexual and generational equality accompanying ultimate social harmony and individual self-realization. In Leninism, communist elites had an ideological weapon that combined a strong voluntaristic and teleological bias with equally strong organizational, interventionist, and manipulative dispositions. In effect, Lenin proposed to achieve consciously what Marx had expected to come about, by and large, spontaneously. Thus, the bolshevik amalgam of Marxism-Leninism implied a deliberate and concerted effort to induce (or accelerate) and manage the fundamental transformation of most aspects of human existence. We are dealing, then, in both cases with avowedly radical and authoritarian auspices of (and guidelines for) a holistic revolutionary effort. Such an effort reflected an activistic disposition to travel an unprecedented developmental distance on autonomously chosen routes at an extremely rapid pace, toward operational objectives forcibly imposed from above. It also reflected an instrumental disposition to search for optimum techniques and instruments useful in the controlled mobilization of human and material resources for purposes envisioned by the regime.

Such dispositions found a clear expression in Soviet and Communist Chinese views of law, including family law. In both views law was designed,

---

[5] The contributions by Buxbaum, Meijer, and Müller-Freienfels, in particular, to the Conference on the Role of Law in Modernizing Nations have dealt quite comprehensively with this subject.

first of all, to destroy the antecedent social order and life-style; afterwards it was expected to ensure human discipline in building an industrial system, to ensure the security of the Party-State administering this system, and to serve as a standard and means for building a communist society. Accordingly, just as communist political preoccupations stressed disciplined organization, so did early judicial perspectives emphasize detailed rule-making and codification, as well as heavy politicization of the judicial process. Even if there were doubts in Chinese communist ranks on this account—especially during the Yenan period of the 1930s—they were outweighed by the perceived need to emulate the Soviet model of a successful communist takeover.[6]

There was here, however, at least one subtle variation of emphasis, one that tended to distinguish the overall Soviet judicial model from the specifically Central Asian one. Early Soviet legislation concerning family relations, while embodying a number of Marxian postulates, was designed within, and by and large for, European Russia. Most important, in many spheres (such as cohabitation and divorce, as well as female and generational roles and rights in the familial and societal context) Soviet family law was designed to formalize and legitimize, at least as much as to encourage, a normative and behavioral revolution that was already well under way in the Russian milieu. In the case of Soviet Central Asia, however, it became apparent in fairly short order that sociocultural realities called for special ways of approaching the problem of revolutionary transformation. This was not merely a question of devising different laws for a different milieu. It meant, above all, the endowment of Soviet judicial institutions in Central Asia with functions that were rather more specialized than in Russia, functions that were far broader in scope, more significant and autonomous in expected impact, and more sharply focused toward social destruction and reconstruction. Paradoxically, it was precisely this variation between the all-Soviet and Central Asian judicial models that helped to make the parallels between Central Asian and Communist Chinese cases especially pronounced. In effect, it may be said that the Chinese communist elites could find the experience of the Turko-Iranian and Moslem societies of Central Asia more relevant in their consideration of the substance, role, and implications of legal engineering than the experience of the predominantly Slavic and Christian milieu of European Russia.

The differences between Central Asia and China as potential revolutionary arenas were, of course, profound. Most obviously, Moslem religious civilization differed greatly from the Buddhist, Confucian, and Taoist spiritual underpinnings of Chinese civilization. Moslem legal culture differed in many

---

[6] One of the most useful and comprehensive attempts to date to compare overall Soviet and Chinese revolutionary experience may be found in SOVIET AND CHINESE COMMUNISM: SIMILARITIES AND DIFFERENCES (D. Treadgold ed. 1967); for a comparison of some aspects of the judicial process, *see* especially pt. 3.

ways from China's. Likewise, China's historical development as a state, anchored as it was in a long established and rather sophisticated sense of ethno-cultural identity, contrasted sharply with the pluralistic and highly fragmented universe of Central Asia, where ethnicity never served as a dominant and binding factor and never provided the basis for an overarching political society. There were all too many other contrasts between the two settings, including different stages of economic development and urbanization at the time of the revolutionary experiment, and different tribal and village components of the rural milieu—variations that a sociologist of law and a political sociologist must surely take into consideration when gauging the potentialities and limits of law in comparative perspective.[7]

Yet, both in objective terms and—perhaps most important—in the subjective view of the two sets of elites, some similarities were striking. Given the strategic relevance of these similarities to communist imagination, it is probably a safe guess that they were of decisive significance for the action schemes that were ultimately adopted by both sides. I have in mind three sets of basic societal features characterizing both milieus: (1) the predominance of rural traditionalist orientations at the grassroots; (2) the organization of local societies around kinship units in relatively self-sufficient communities, by and large along patriarchal, patrilineal, and patrilocal lines; and (3) the relatively high degree of institutionalized dichotomy in status positions in society, where the most tangible aspects of inferiority and segregation were being enforced along sexual and generational lines.

It is hardly a coincidence, then, that communist moves and expectations in the sphere of family law in both Central Asia and China concentrated on the manipulation of, specifically, sexual and generational tensions as potentially powerful solvents of traditional social systems.[8] Communist expectations centered on the use of what I have called elsewhere strategic leverage, to be exercised in part by a surrogate proletariat[9]—in a milieu where a real proletariat (in Marxist terms) was not conspicuously present.

---

[7] Needless to say, limitations of space and the specific focus of this analysis do not permit a reasoned consideration of this matter in this context. Yet there is perhaps a saving grace here, at least for the limited purposes of the present argument; while the differences in milieu were indeed profound, a shared normative and operational bias on the part of both elites permitted them, at least initially, to under-emphasize the contrasts in the societal arenas confronting them and to stress instead the uniformity of political vision and schemes of action that were at their command.

[8] For a preliminary examination of bolshevik reasoning and actions on this account in the Central Asian context, see G. Massell, supra notes 1,2. The substantive material in the text that follows is based almost entirely on Russian sources, cited and discussed in the above studies. Due to limitations of space, specific references to these sources have been omitted here in the text.

[9] See especially my book, THE SURROGATE PROLETARIAT, supra note 1.

In both cases, one of the crucial targets of revolutionary action was the patriarchal family. The family was assumed to be the hub of traditional authority relations, the cornerstone of traditional secrecy and solidarity, and the primordial model of ascribed status positions that discriminate sharply between females and males, and the young and old. It is in this sense that traditional Central Asian and Chinese families were seen as vital carriers of "feudal-patriarchal" ideology. To strike at such a family meant to attack what was presumably the nerve center of an entire way of life. It meant to cut the bonds tying human beings to a pervasive pattern of values, beliefs, and relationships and by doing so not only to undermine the most important institutions of a status quo, but also to release individual human commitments and energies from an established matrix, and to make them available for large-scale mobilization and recruitment by new political elites. In this sense, communist perception of relevant imperatives, means, and ends may be said to have operated within a spectrum from ideological to instrumental considerations, from revolutionary idealism to cold political pragmatism, and from an individualistic stress on personal identity and self-assertion to a collective emphasis on political participation and economic achievement. In sum, just as the destruction of the traditional family system was expected to be crucially significant in the destruction of the old socio-cultural order, so was the activation of women and youth considered a highly efficient, even explosive, means of making traditional families and communities vulnerable to disintegration.

The details of communist egalitarian and emancipatory legislation in both regions are too well known to require elaboration here. Suffice it to say that the action schemes with respect to family relations in general, and female and generational roles in particular, reveal remarkable similarities. In the period between 1917 and 1927 in Central Asia and in the 1949–59 decade in China (reflected already in the insurgent legislation of the early 1930s in rebel-held territories), a series of judicial decisions were promulgated. These decisions proscribed religious and/or customary or informal tribunals, laws, and modes of adjudication and replaced them with a secular, uniform, centralized, bureaucratic, and hierarchical system of courts and with secular, egalitarian, uniform, and written codes of statutory laws. In the process, women and youth were endowed with unprecedented roles and rights. The catalog of proscribed acts included bride-price, child-marriage, forced marriage, arranged marriage, marriage by abduction, polygamy (or concubinage), and levirate, as well as mistreatment of children and wives. In addition, a number of constitutional guarantees, contravening the very core of religious and/or customary proscriptions, were designed to assure the new rights of women and youth: equal rights to initiate divorce; the right to equal witness in court; and the right to full-fledged participation in public life, including general education, professional training, and participation in all socio-cultural, economic, and political pursuits, services, and organizations. The later denoted not only voting, but also service in all the elective and appointive public offices in the land including the highest, with early and special emphasis given to service in judicial roles in the newly created court system.

At the same time, an attempt was made to set social processes in motion in conjunction with the formal legal moves. These processes were designed to spur the mobility and iconoclastic self-assertion of women and youth, and thus to undermine the mainstays of traditional obligations, obedience, and dependence not only in public life, but also in the private realms of family and home. First, the Communist Party in both cases created not only komsomol units, but also special sections for work among women. Both units were instructed to create new associational foci for the respective groups and to use these foci for political agitation and recruitment. Toward the end of the first post-revolutionary decade, women's sections in European Russia were formally abolished; they were specifically developed and augmented in the Chinese and Central Asian milieus at that time. Second, communist cadres were assigned the task of personally encouraging women to sue for divorce from undesirable husbands or to leave oppressive familial situations, and of personally supervising and assisting them toward these ends in court. And third, the entire party and state apparatus was instructed not only to organize mass meetings and demonstrations of women and youth repeatedly and on a vast scale, but to encourage at these meetings massive and dramatic public violations of traditional taboos. These violations included the mass unveiling of Moslem women in Central Asia, the casting out of ritualized female attire and footwear in China, and the breaking of rules concerning female separation and relative seclusion in both cases, accompanied (especially in China) by attacks on the ideals of filial piety and (in both cases) by public denunciation of male and patriarchal authority and of local traditional elites.

Significantly enough, the period of high tide in specifically female mobilization in Central Asia (*ca.* 1926–28) was officially named by Moscow the period of "cultural revolution" *(khudzhum)*, of "all-out attack" and "storm" against the symbols and institutions of the old order.

EMPHASES AND AIMS OF LEGAL ENGINEERING: SOME DIVERGENCIES BETWEEN CENTRAL ASIAN AND CHINESE MODELS

What was especially remarkable about these deliberately induced trends was that, while in both cases the emphases and aims of legal engineering remained officially the same, by and large, a subtle and fairly sudden shift occurred in actual practice. Broadly speaking, in Central Asia the end of the first post-revolutionary decade was marked by a deliberate *deceleration* of female and youth-oriented mobilization (late 1920s), and in China by a forceful *acceleration* of such mobilization (late 1950s). In China, of course, the decade that followed was ushered in by the Great Leap Forward which, after some periods of retreat and hesitation, grew quite dramatically into the Great Proletarian Cultural Revolution.

To be sure, in neither of the two cases are there absolutely coherent, consistently articulated, tightly monolithic policies and views. Neither can one speak about a clear-cut congruence between official attitudes and actions either before or after a shift in emphasis. In each evolving pattern one can easily point to deviant cases. But there seems little doubt about the predominant orientations and trends. In the sphere of legally or extralegally inspired social mobilization, especially by way of manipulating sexual and generational tensions, some salient differences between the two models became pronounced almost overnight. It is useful to review them briefly through the prism of several broad analytical categories.

In drawing essential dichotomies pertaining to the judicial process, it is customary to distinguish between two processual types: the *due process* model and the *crime control* model.[10] However, these two models seem more inherently suitable for analysing what one might call managerial legal systems than revolutionary ones.

A *managerial* system is most often associated with the relatively routine administration of a relatively stable, explicitly articulated, and basically legitimated set of norms, rules, and institutions. A *revolutionary* system, on the contrary, tends to be associated with deliberately engineered and radical social transformation, having a consciously induced discontinuity, and a relatively fluid, heavily politicized and basically unlegitimated set of norms, practices, and sanctions. The first is characterised by a high (though not evenly distributed) degree of autonomy from political interference by the regime. Its primary (though not exclusive) emphasis is on containing tensions, reconciling conflicts, and maintaining a maximum of order. The second is characterised by a very low degree of autonomy within the political-administrative framework of the state. Its primary (though not exclusive) emphasis is on inducing tensions, manipulating conflicts for political purposes, and promoting a maximum of disorganization in the established antecedent social order. While some parallels can indeed be drawn between some organizational forms and procedural arrangements of these two systems (thus reducing the sharpness of the dichotomy between them), the differences in

---

[10] The normative and organizational underpinnings of these two models are too well known to require elaboration here. For a recent attempt to test this dichotomy (in comparing Chinese and American legal systems), *see, e.g.,* R. Pfeffer, *Crime and Punishment: China and the United States,* 21 WORLD POLITICS 152–81 (Oct. 1968). While Pfeffer (like Herbert Packer and Jerome Skolnick, among others) explicitly deals only with the criminal process in the context of his analysis, it is clear that the emphases he distinguishes would easily find their equivalents in the realm of family law.

their basic aims, emphases, and assigned functions seem great enough to be
seen as differences in quality and not just in degree.

With this in mind, three basic Soviet strategies of revolutionary social
change in Central Asia may be distinguished—strategies that evolved in the
course of attempts to engineer a normative and behavioral revolution in a
Moslem traditional milieu: revolutionary legalism, administrative assault, and
systematic social engineering.[11] While these approaches were differentially
related to judicial processes as such—in form as well as in degree—they shared
at least one crucial characteristic: neither due process nor crime control per se
figured prominently in their calculations. The primary considerations in all
of them were social mobilization, cultural change, economic performance,
and political control, and these were pursued irrespective of whether the
imperatives of due process or crime control were duly served.

The three strategies of planned social change, which we propose to view
as direct approaches to social engineering (a number of indirect approaches
can also be deduced from Soviet experience), may be conceived as three main
steps in a learning process on the part of the Soviet revolutionary elites in
Central Asia, a process with what were at first rudimentary, though by no
means negligible, feedback mechanisms. Needless to say, ideal types and
analytical constructs, and not rigorously delimited historical stages, are being
dealt with here. There was much overlapping among the three approaches
and only imperfect correspondence to chronology. But in the use made of
Moslem women and in the overall attack against traditional customs, values,
and relationships, there was clearly a trial-and-error progression from
"legalism" (*ca.* 1924–28), to "assault" (*ca.* 1927–29), to "systematic social
engineering" (*ca.* 1928–).

Revolutionary legalism as a strategy of social change emphasized reliance
on a newly superimposed judicial system for the routinization of revolutionary
norms in traditional society. It reflected expectations that the new judicial
system would set in motion a full-fledged revolutionary process by supplanting
traditional adjudicative institutions and by vigorously championing and applying the principle of equality of the sexes and generations before the law. The
emancipation of women and youth was viewed, at this point, as primarily a
juridical problem to be solved by a stress on strict legalistic consistency. It is
in this sense that revolutionary legalism may be characterized as an ethical
and political attitude that holds moral and politically requisite conduct to be
a matter of rule following, and moral as well as instrumental relationships to
consist of duties and rights determined by rules that are imposed and enforced
by revolutionary elites.[12]

---

[11] *See* notes 1 and 2.

[12] This is a paraphrase of Judith Shklar's formulation. *See* J. SHKLAR, LEGALISM 1
(1964).

Administrative assault as a revolutionary strategy reflected, on the one hand, a wave of revolutionary self-confidence, enthusiasm, and zeal and, on the other hand, a radical impatience with the potentially slow, long-term implantation and routinization of new behavioral norms by way of legal and other mediating institutions. It involved a preference to engage Moslem traditional society head on, to "storm" it (hence the party's reference to the decreed offensive as *khudzhum*—a Turko-Arabic term denoting all-out attack, storm). It called for reliance on administratively inspired mass action; that is, direct popular action in response to direct command from above, action embodying extra-judicial mechanisms and pressures, and the mass realization of explicit and implicit new judicial norms outside of formal judicial channels. Such action, involving primarily massive, public, and dramatic violations of traditional taboos pertaining especially to women (beginning with induced mass unveiling in the streets), was expected to have a shock effect on traditional mores and institutions. In the process of such widespread and simultaneous combustion on political cue, prevailing "feudal-patriarchal" attitudes, customs, and relationships were expected to be short-circuited, ushering in a "cultural revolution" and causing the walls of tradition to crumble virtually overnight.

The strategic emphasis in systematic social engineering reflected a realistic appreciation both of the narrowness and limitations of revolutionary legalism, and of the pitfalls and illusions implicit in administrative assault upon a Moslem traditional milieu. It called for systematic evaluation, exploitation, and coordination of diverse courses of action: legal, organizational, cultural, and economic. It involved an aggressive search, on the one hand, for means to optimize the conditions of insurgence, modernization, and development, and, on the other hand, for ways to minimize the dangers implicit in this process for the incumbent regime. It thus engendered a pragmatic commitment to relatively patient, specifically focused, and systematic social action, wherein at least as much time and effort would be devoted to the building of bridges to Moslem traditional society and to the creation of an infrastructure of alternative institutions and opportunities for the meaningful exercise of rights and roles, as to actual and direct confrontation with the traditional system. It is perhaps most useful to visualise this strategic approach as a quest for optimal balance between the imperatives of modernization and of control.

By early 1929, only two and one-half years after the inception of the "cultural revolution" in Central Asia, the communist party felt obliged to bring the "storming" activities on behalf of female emancipation and the massive and overt forms of the cultural revolution itself to an abrupt halt. The retrenchment pattern included the following components: (1) emphasis on specialized cadre-formation, stressing selective recruitment of indigenous personnel and its training in protected cultural islands, rather than general social (including female) mobilization; (2) temporary exemption of some especially sensitive Central Asian districts from the sanctions of the new legal code; (3) tailoring of some provisions in the code to bring them into closer accord with local mores; (4) scaling down sanctions for some "customary crimes"; (5) formal or informal abandonment of the retroactive application of criminal sanctions in most cases involving "crimes based on feudal-patriarchal residues" in family relations; (6) withdrawal of official encouragement from female-initiated divorces, designed to halt the divorce wave altogether; (7) preservation, where necessary, of segregated facilities for Moslem women; (8) prohibition of massive and dramatic violations of traditional taboos, and especially of administered female unveiling in public; (9) shelving, indefinitely, all official proposals for outlawing female veiling and seclusion in Moslem societies under Soviet rule; and (10) planning a new social infrastructure stressing actually felt needs rather than political agitation, and intended to allow a gradual, but comprehensive and coordinated approach to social reconstruction.

In this connection, the party's Central Asian Department for Work among Women *(zhenotdel)* was instructed to commence or accelerate—in cooperation with appropriate industrial, agricultural, labor, trade, health, education, and welfare agencies of the state—the organization of "Councils of Women's Delegates," as well as of especially tailored clubs, stores, producers' and consumers' cooperatives, vocational centers, literacy and hygiene circles, and mother-and-child medical units catering exclusively to girls and women, and to use such new associational foci as forums for long-term political recruitment. Many of these new associational forms had legal aid centers built into their organizational framework. But such centers were to be used for substantive juridical consultation and not for incitement to precipitous acts. They were to serve as foci for the gradual dissemination of new norms regarding specific duties and rights, as well as foci for the redress of individual grievances. By clear implication, both the legal aid centers and the new people's courts were to avoid rigorous litigational entanglements in the sphere of family relations that might provoke widespread revulsion in local communities or that might adversely affect the population's economic performance.

Thus, within only a few years of the beginning of their experimental approaches to social engineering in Central Asia, Soviet authorities found it necessary to reverse their emphasis from direct, precipitate legalistic and administrative pressures for the sake of drastic social transformation, to circumspect, long-term social rebuilding for the sake, in part, of meaningful legal change and administrative reorganization. In effect, the same decade (1928–38) that saw a vast intensification of pressures for economic production, as well as for political conformity (including terror, and purges of "enemies of the people"), was also marked by growing caution and retreat in matters affecting family relations.

While a number of factors were involved in this reversal, and some of them surely had to do with self-generated limitations in the engineering agencies themselves, one set of factors unquestionably stands out as crucial: the extraordinarily tenacious resistance of a Moslem traditional milieu to direct revolutionary manipulation. I have described the modalities of this response elsewhere.[13] While some aspects of this response (such as a wave of female-initiated divorces, and growing political recruitment of girls and women, especially child-brides, orphans, widows, and divorcees, into communist ranks) were clearly desirable from the Soviet point of view, others were not. The behavior of native law administrators and political personnel, for example, was marked by widespread circumlocution and sabotage. Partly for this reason, women, upon abandoning the traditional fold, found all too few opportunities to translate their newly won rights into meaningful roles. In fact, no significant tie-in existed between legal action conferring legal rights and extra-legal initiative (including requisite socioeconomic supportive structures) permitting the utilization of these rights in real roles and opportunities. As a result all too many women—without skills or means for self-support—came to be a heavy economic burden to the regime itself or drifted into prostitution. At the same time (1927–28), while the fragmentation of families and households was very badly affecting Central Asia's agricultural production, Moslem men responded with an explosion of hostility and violence unequaled in intensity and scope until then (at least since the October Revolution and the Civil War).

In effect, the specter of massive and dramatic emancipatory activities in public seemed to drive traditionalist males—"poor" as well as "rich"—and the sacred Moslem intelligentsia and clan notables closer together, for all of them felt challenged as Moslems, as heads of kin groups, and as males. This meant that, instead of sharpening the class struggle, as the communists had hoped, precipitate Soviet initiatives tended to mitigate that struggle. Instead of leading to the alienation of substantial segments of society from the traditional way of life, sudden and massive female mobilization tended to lead to widespread and intense alienation from the Soviet system and its works, accompanied by cleavages running along primarily sexual and ethnic lines. Instead of helping to induce conflicts that would be socially, culturally, politically, and economically productive from the Soviet point of view, precipitate female mobilization was activating conflicts that were highly destructive. Faced with the unanticipated consequences of its actions and with the full panoply of implications of massive judicial enforcement and administrative repression on a large scale, the Soviet regime was moved to reduce tensions at their source. It is in this context that both revolutionary legalism and administrative assault came to be de-emphasized in favor of more cautious, gradual, systematic social engineering, involving a stress on organizational and economic development rather than on a voluntaristic mass movement.

---

[13] *See* G. Massell, *supra* note 1, especially 202–219 (in the article in LAW AND SOCIETY).

Paradoxically, even though China has been studied far more intensively and comprehensively than Soviet Central Asia, it appears that we know rather less about some of its crucial developmental trends (which is hardly encouraging, since our knowledge of Central Asia is severely limited). There is an especially sharp asymmetry in the extent to which we know the most important dimensions of the judicial process in action here. We know a great deal about the evolution of the communist regime's stated ideals, perceived imperatives, organizational arrangements, and specific moves in the field of law; we know relatively little about actual organizational performance and human behavior at the operational level; that is, about the modes of application, enforcement, reception, and adjustment of new legal rules in society. In Communist China, then, one of the perennial problems of social science is especially magnified, because we know far more about actions than about interaction.

It would seem that, partly due to conscious emulation, the Maoist regime at first attempted to transpose quite literally many features of the Soviet judicial model to Chinese soil. This could not have been an easy operation, since the Soviet patterns were themselves undergoing rapid modification. What Mao could borrow in the late 1920s was very different from that which he confronted in Soviet reality in the 1950s. Broadly speaking, it seems reasonable to visualise Mao's regime as initially (at least until 1957) following what we have described as a strategy of revolutionary legalism in Central Asia. This was reflected in a relatively heavy stress on formal, significantly differentiated judicial institutions and on juridical enforcement of elaborate emancipatory legislation in the sphere of family relations. Moreover, what we witness here in 1957–59 (concurrently with the inception of the Great Leap Forward) is strikingly reminiscent of what we have depicted as a period of administrative assault in Central Asia (1927–29).

But it is what followed that is of greatest interest here. The decade between 1959 and 1969 is replete with violently fluctuating crosscurrents. For a brief period in the early 1960s, following the disasters of the Great Leap Forward, it is possible to discern definite signs of caution, consolidation, and retrenchment. Most tellingly, perhaps, both judicial and extrajudicial pressures for female and youth-oriented mobilization, and even direct attacks on the family itself, showed signs of subsiding. For that matter, in ways strongly suggestive of Soviet moves in Central Asia after 1929, Chinese women were at least tacitly encouraged to gravitate back into the fold of family and home. In short, one can speak of this period as one of a complex quest for a modernization-and-control balance, such as we have witnessed at the inception of systematic social engineering in the Central Asian context. Yet here, it would seem, many of the parallels end. As if picking up some of the threads of the Great Leap Forward, the Great Proletarian Cultural Revolution of the second half of the 1960s moved China quite decisively onto a different path.

As we know, the break from the Soviet model was as dramatic as it was defiant. While some lip service continued to be paid to familial stability, a broad spectrum of extrajudicial mechanisms was brought to bear in further-ance of social mobilization that was as violent in intensity as it was vast in scale. In the realm of family relations (and of sexual and generational roles), a number of desiderata were forcefully brought to the fore. Young women and men, in particular, were expected to proceed separately, if need be, to assigned locales and tasks, irrespective of marital and familial bonds. Marital unions were expected to shed all vestiges of traditional style and custom, and marital relationships were to be heavily politicized. Marriages were to be deferred as long as possible, to assure the longest possible period of productive labor (especially on the part of girls) and optimal accessibility and maneuverability of the labor force. Most strikingly, perhaps, the attack on traditional values, customs, and institutions, and the attack on all bureaucratic (including communist) authority, were explicitly or implicitly equated with an assault on parental, and especially patriarchal, authority.

It is in this context that the rise of the Red Guards and the guided surge of the young generation (including children) against the relics of the old (includ-ing communist) order may be seen as part of a larger pattern harking back to the Great Leap Forward in China and to the "all out assault" of *khudzhum* in Central Asia. In the process, formal judicial institutions that had been grafted, in part, in emulation of the Soviet model, were openly denigrated, relegated to distinctly secondary roles, or altogether submerged in the framework, function, and activities of new collectivistic political agencies springing up side by side with (or in replacement of) the established political-administrative apparatus. Just as formal legal rules, codes, and procedures were shorn of much of their stature and relevance, so were courts, judges, prosecutors, and lawyers by and large deprived of the modicum of differentiated functions they possessed, at least formally, in the 1950s. In the field of law, as in other fields, Mao's Cultural Revolution marked a full-blown return to the rule of "revolutionary conscience" and "revolutionary masses," as exemplified in part by the period of Militant (and Military) Communism and Civil War in Russia.

Toward a Comparative Perspective in Revolutionary Manipulation of Family Relations: A Preliminary Balance Sheet

How is one to explain the growing divergencies between the two models following a decade of fairly parallel evolution? We have suggested that the Soviet pattern of retrenchment in Central Asia, involving a significant retreat from both revolutionary legalism and administrative assault, owed much to Moscow's reevaluation of the risks involved in an "all-out assault" on a traditional value and kinship system. If this is correct, why should Maoist China have been seemingly more inclined and able to take risks on this account than Stalinist Russia?

Determinants of Revolutionary Retrenchment: a Soviet Perspective

It would seem that the different departures may be accounted for by different perceptions of a major crisis: the crisis of insurgency by an incumbent. As I have pointed out elsewhere,[14] the action schemes that evolved under communist auspices were analogous to insurgency—albeit insurgency generated and controlled by the incumbent and, therefore, governed both by the requirements of social revolution and by the imperatives of incumbency itself. Basically, this process had twin purposes: that of inducing a psychological and organizational revolution at the nerve-centers of a relatively intact social order, and that of consolidating and legitimizing the incumbent's power. In Soviet Central Asia, it turned out to be of fundamental importance that the imperatives of insurgency could not be reconciled in every respect with the imperatives of incumbency, since both sets of imperatives were generated and needed to be weighed by one and the same party—the incumbent revolutionary Soviet regime.

In this connection, it is obvious that the use of judicial and extrajudicial mechanisms among the Communist Party's approaches to revolutionary change, and their massive and dramatic concentration on sexual and generational equality, constituted a fundamental challenge to the structure and life-style of local communities. Indeed, they constituted powerful heretical models. At the same time, both of the Communist Party's approaches to revolutionary change may be said to have required the introduction of a specialized tension-management system into a traditional milieu, a system combining tension-inducing and tension-controlling purposes. Specifically, the strategic objectives had to be: to induce (positive) tensions that would fundamentally undermine the traditional order (the target system), and, at the same time, to control those (negative) consequences of induced tensions that threatened to affect the stability of the Soviet regime (the sponsor system) and the safety of its developmental objectives. In other words, the impact of "legalism" and "assault" as heretical models depended to a large extent on their viability as regulative mechanisms. As it turned out, it was far from easy to attain the requisite symmetry between these functions. Revolutionary instruments that were themselves not easily controllable and were themselves seeking legitimation in a traditional world, could not very well control tensions and ensure order in that world while they were enforcing with all the power at their command the very quintessence of illegitimacy: heresy.

---

[14] This part summarizes and adapts here an argument developed in greater detail in G. Massell, *supra* note 1, at 193–98 (in the article in LAW AND SOCIETY).

It is in this sense that we speak of Soviet perceptions of a crisis induced by Soviet insurgent moves at the grassroots of Moslem traditional societies. What was supposed to be a controlled revolutionary process threatened to get out of hand. Specifically, the conclusion seems to have been reached that a revolution in family relations could not be managed concurrently with large-scale political, organizational, and economic change. While it was clear that congruence between these two processes was extremely important for success in all of them, it was equally clear that some of the consequences of the family revolution constituted an immediate, direct threat to the broader goals of change. In effect, it would seem that Soviet authority could not successfully legitimate itself and pursue its developmental objectives while it was destroying some of the most sensitive social bases on which legitimacy had to rest.

In the case of China, too, we can speak of a crisis coming to the fore toward the end of the first decade of communist rule.[15] At least we can speak of a major turning point and critical stage in Chinese revolutionary development as perceived by the supreme Maoist command. The analysis that follows is a tentative and roughly schematic reconstruction of the main forces at work. However, while it might be relatively easy to infer a number of long-term trends and short-term precipitants in this case, it is as yet enormously difficult to trace their interaction and to judge their relative weights. What does appear to be both necessary and feasible here is to distinguish analytically between compelling and enabling factors in China's move toward its own revolutionary model.

Determinants of Revolutionary Acceleration :
Compelling Factors—a Chinese Perspective

As had been apparent since the late 1920s, the attitudes and moves of the Chinese Communist Party were subject to a number of local determinants. Most obviously, the need to function as a territorial guerrilla movement engaged in protracted partisan warfare in a rural hinterland imposed on the Chinese communists some elements of political structure and style that differed significantly from the Soviet model. But it was only in the latter half of the 1950s that the Chinese regime found itself compelled—and able—to differentiate sharply and openly between its own and Russia's system. The main operative factors may be listed briefly.

The crisis of the primal model. Clearly, the developments in the Soviet Union in the period between 1953 and 1956 posed an immediate challenge to Peking's leadership. Stalin's disappearance from the scene and the iconoclastic politics of his successors, served not only as a point of departure for some liberalization

---

[15] *Cf.* H. Schurmann, *Peking's Recognition of Crisis,* in Modern China 89–104 (A. Feuerwerker ed. 1964).

of the Soviet system, but as a watershed for generalized questioning and doubt throughout the Soviet bloc.[16] Precisely because of Russia's heretofore pre-eminent role in this bloc, Moscow's questioning of some specific features of a Stalinist system tended to encourage a general reassessment, both of the aims and means of communist systems and of relationships between individual communist movements and regimes. To reveal the imperfection or even perniciousness of some aspects of Soviet rule meant to detract from the established legitimacy and automatic superiority of the primal model.

The crisis of personalistic leadership. The most burning issue generated by Moscow's de-Stalinization campaign pertained, of course, to the nature, role, and legitimacy of supreme leadership in a communist system. Precisely because Maoist leadership had replicated so many Stalinist characteristics in the course of several decades, the denigration of the reality and symbols of Stalin's political charisma could not but be perceived as a direct threat in Peking. The "cult of personality" was, after all, not merely a particular attribute developed around a particular man or group of men in equivalent positions; it was, most importantly, a principle defining the relationship between leaders and masses. To tamper with this principle meant to confront some extremely painful readjustments, especially in China. If there was any doubt about the possible ramifications, it was surely dispelled by the Hundred Flowers experience in 1957, when the principles of both totalitarianism as a system and authoritarian personalism as a leadership-style were challenged the moment the reins of coerced conformity were slackened.[17]

The crisis of national-revolutionary identity. Precisely because China's revolutionary movement had evolved and triumphed in the context of a struggle for national liberation from foreign occupiers, and because so much of its following had been rallied to the cause by appeals to national unity and pride, the question of Chinese group identity had to come up sooner or later. It is possible to say, with the benefit of hindsight, that after decades of fairly self-effacing Chinese recognition of Soviet primacy, the events of 1953–56 served as catalysts for tough-minded national self-assertion and for a resolute cutting of bonds that seemed shackles of perennial deference and dependence. Of course, the fact that, by 1953, the Chinese Communist Party had behind it half a decade of successful consolidation in power and had stood its ground in an important military confrontation (with the United States in Korea), had much to do with the new spirit of self-confident reappraisal in Peking and

---

[16] For an excellent review and analysis of the politics of the Soviet bloc, *see* Z. BRZEZINSKI, THE SOVIET BLOC: UNITY AND CONFLICT (rev. ed. 1967); *Cf.* D. ZAGORIA, THE SINO-SOVIET CONFLICT (1962).

[17] *See, e.g.,* T. H. E. CH'EN, THOUGHT REFORM OF THE CHINESE INTELLECTUALS (1960); R. LIFTON, THOUGHT REFORM AND THE PSYCHOLOGY OF TOTALISM (1961); THE HUNDRED FLOWERS CAMPAIGN AND THE CHINESE INTELLECTUALS (R. MacFarquhar ed. 1960).

with a willingness to experiment in accordance with indigenous sovereign judgment.

The crisis of socioeconomic dynamism. It would seem that there was an intimate and catalytic interaction between the resurgent will for nativistic self-assertion and the experience of the consequences of such an act. The greater the self-generated pressure for autonomous initiative in all spheres, the more disillusioning and bitter was the experience of Soviet reluctance to part with (or crude unwillingness to abandon) earlier prerogatives, and the sharper was the recognition of imperatives and dilemmas inherent in China's proceeding on its own. Most importantly, to go it alone meant to forego Moscow's organizational, technical, and economic assistance. While the earlier momentum had been sufficient to win politically in China and militarily in Korea, it might have seemed inadequate for dealing with the age-old problem affecting China's political imagination: the matter of overcoming the nation's evident impotence to generate the kind of self-sustaining social dynamism, political unity, and economic growth that would strengthen the state's performance and legitimacy at home, and its power and status abroad.[18] Thus, just as the quest for identity went hand in hand with the quest for potency, so did the quest for performance go hand in hand with the quest for total social mobilization and national integration.

The Macedonian gambit—a Sino-Soviet variant. If these factors carried an impact due to long festering issues immanent in both Chinese and Soviet development, there also seems to have been a purely reactive element at play. This element probably did much to sustain the pressures originating elsewhere and to endow them with an emotional style. I have in mind: (a) a general compulsion, in a highly competitive situation, to reject (in an act of vengeance and defiant self-assertion) precisely those things that a feared and hated rival values and takes for his own; and (b) a specific Chinese compulsion, born in cultural ambivalence regarding inferiority-superiority relationships in the outer world, to reject all that is foreign precisely because it is foreign. It seems to have been crucial here that Russia was thrust fairly suddenly from a recent role of brother and friend to a traditional category of stranger and foe.

All these factors affected the operation of the sociopolitical system as a whole and did not relate directly to the judicial process and family relations. Yet these factors also served to raise and sharpen immeasurably the issues of legal rule, patriarchal authority, and sexual and generational roles. Resurgent Chinese "nativism," accompanying the sharpening differentiation between Chinese and Soviet communism, found one of its expressions in the rejection

---

[18] *See, e.g.,* B. Schwartz, In Search of Wealth and Power: A Biography of Yen Fu (1964).

of a variant of Western legalistic forms embodied (no matter how superficially) in the Soviet model.[19]

Determinants of Revolutionary Acceleration :
Enabling Factors—a Sino-Soviet Perspective

It is never easy to distinguish in real situations between elements of necessity and will, or between elements of capacity and disposition. Thus, while singling out here enabling vis-à-vis compelling factors, I am fully aware that in these (as in other) social and political contexts, such factors always overlap. No attempt is made here to pinpoint all pertinent factors. Rather, I focus only on those that seem to be both of primary significance and of direct relevance to the matter at hand: the capacity of the Maoist regime to accelerate revolutionary manipulations of sexual and generational roles and overall family relations as part of accelerated social mobilization, and of a large-scale attempt, in effect, to institutionalize permanent revolution. These factors may be grouped in three broad categories pertaining to the nature of revolutionary agents, targets, and modes of action.

Profile of revolutionary agents : background and legitimacy of incumbents as insurgents. There were some obvious and decisive differences in the makeup of Chinese and Soviet communist cadres, including the leaders themselves, and it seems safe to assume that these differences had much to do with the course that was ultimately followed in each case.

In actual recruitment or experiential reference point, the core of the Chinese communist movement was heavily weighted in favor of rural and military elements with a sprinkling of radical intellectuals. This further minimized the significance of law in the commitments of a movement that was ideologically biased against legalism in the first place and that was not notable for the presence of lawyers (or of legally trained people) in its ranks.[20] In the Soviet case, on the other hand, there was a relatively heavy representation of elements socialized in urban and industrial milieus, and in the ranks of the intelligentsia. Both Lenin and a number of his collaborators had been exposed to legal training or legalistic procedures, and their social environment (tsarist Russian) stressed heavily formalized, legalistic, bureaucratic structures.

This was compounded in Central Asia. Here, the flow of revolutionary pressures was almost exclusively from urban to rural locales, because both the centers of Soviet (and Russian) power and the arenas of indigenous revolutionary activity were primarily in the cities. Moreover, as the confrontation of

---

[19] The literature on the modalities of China's response to Western institutions is enormous. *See, e.g.,* J. FAIRBANK & S. TENG, CHINA'S RESPONSE TO THE WEST . . . (1954).

[20] *See, e.g.,* J. LEWIS, LEADERSHIP IN COMMUNIST CHINA (1963); B. SCHWARTZ, CHINESE COMMUNISM AND THE RISE OF MAO (1951); R. NORTH, KUOMINTANG AND CHINESE COMMUNIST ELITES (1952).

Soviet elites with Moslem traditional communities unfolded, Moscow was persuaded by its cadres in the field to permit a relatively heavy involvement of Russian lawyers (and even of law-oriented ethnographers and anthropologists) in the formulation of approaches to local communities and cultures. At the same time, many among Moscow's leading indigenous allies, while formally members of the communist party, were not necessarily committed to the objectives of a full-scale, sudden, and violent revolutionary overturn. If anything, they showed themselves more interested in gradual and selective secular reform, and in the preservation, for the foreseeable future, of some customs and structures of Moslem traditional societies. Some of them came from families of merchants, civil servants, teachers, and Islamic legal scholars. For that matter, some of the most highly placed of Central Asia's political (including Soviet) leaders came to the communist movement primarily to reform Islamic education and law, and, in the process, to delimit the role of religious, communal, and tribal elites in the life-style of local ethnic groups.[21]

The triumph of Chinese communists in the late 1940s was the triumph of a heavily militarized guerrilla movement, coming to the fore after a full generation of ceaseless battle in a rural hinterland. It was also the triumph of a movement that was ethnically indigenous, that fought and thrived among the peasantry, and that played a leading role in China's anti-colonial struggle. What we have here, then, is a remarkable confluence of elements forming some essential underpinnings of mass-based political legitimacy. Moreover, these elements were intimately fused and interdependent. The imagery and imperatives of social revolution and reform, of membership in a mass movement, of militarized mass struggle, of a war of the countryside against the cities, and of national liberation from foreign occupiers—all these elements were inextricably intertwined and mutually supportive, and could thus aid immeasurably in the legitimation of communist insurgents as incumbents.[22] In turn, just as successful mass-based insurgency eased the new incumbent's tasks in establishing legitimate authority, so did it provide both precedents and relatively broad leeway for the incumbent's engagement in large-scale

---

[21] For references to the background and commitments of Central Asia's reformist intelligentsia, *see* especially R. PIPES, THE FORMATION OF THE SOVIET UNION (1964); S. ZENKOVSKY, PAN-TURKISM AND ISLAM IN RUSSIA (1960); B. HAYIT, TURKESTAN IM XX JAHRHUNDERT (Turkestan in the twentieth century) (1956); E. ALLWORTH, UZBEK LITERARY POLITICS (1964); CENTRAL ASIA: A CENTURY OF RUSSIAN RULE (E. Allworth ed. 1967); A. BENNIGSEN & C. LEMERCIER-QUELQUEJAY, ISLAM IN THE SOVIET UNION (1967); T. WINNER, THE ORAL ART AND LITERATURE OF THE KAZAKHS OF RUSSIAN CENTRAL ASIA (1958); H. D'ENCAUSSE, RÉFORME ET RÉVOLUTION CHEZ LES MUSULMANS DE L'EMPIRE RUSSE (Reform and revolution among the Muslims of the Russian empire) (1966).

[22] *See, e.g.,* C. JOHNSON, PEASANT NATIONALISM AND COMMUNIST POWER (1963).

revolutionary experiments once the mechanisms of power were acquired and consolidated.

The case of Soviet Central Asia differed sharply in a number of crucial aspects. The main revolutionary impulse came from sources outside the region and under the auspices of ethnically or culturally alien groups. The triumph of the Soviet regime in Central Asia was the relatively quick triumph of an army (most of it Russian), not of a movement; it came in the process of Moscow's military reconquest of Tsarist imperial patrimony; it represented to a large extent the acquisition (or re-acquisition) of power in a handful of heavily Russian or European cities, and the imposition of military and administrative controls in the region from above. Far from participating in a Soviet-sponsored movement, the rural masses either remained aloof during the Soviet takeover or violently resisted the arrival of Soviet forces. There were relatively few exceptions to this rule. Needless to say, just as the conquest of power in this case was in no way a result of indigenous, mass-based insurgency, so were the regime's subsequent attempts to induce a revolutionary process deprived of at least one crucial component of effective command—legitimacy.

Brute force, centralized and authoritarian organization, and monopolistic control of the administrative apparatus could go a long way to secure Soviet rule in the area and even to carry out a number of drastic moves in the local environment (such as the annihilation of the traditional elites, destruction of formalized traditional structures, and collectivisation of agriculture).[23] But the means at the incumbent's disposal were relatively useless for the purposes of insurgency at the nerve-centers of local societies and cultures (solidarities based on kinship, custom, and religion) and, concomitantly, for the direct revolutionary manipulation of one of the most carefully institutionalized and sanctified, and hence heavily sensitized, realms of Moslem society—sexual and generational roles and family relations.[24]

Profile of revolutionary targets: sociocultural underpinnings of political community. In some respects, the targets of revolutionary action were alike. In both cases the milieu was overwhelmingly rural, and the societies may be said to have been "traditional." Moreover, there were significant resemblances in some essential features of kinship structure (extended families and clans), dominant authority (patriarchal), and status systems (differentiating

---

[23] *See* especially A. PARK, BOLSHEVISM IN TURKESTAN, 1917–1927 (1957); G. WHEELER THE MODERN HISTORY OF SOVIET CENTRAL ASIA (1964); O. CAROE, SOVIET EMPIRE: THE TURKS OF CENTRAL ASIA AND STALINISM (1967); M. RYWKIN, RUSSIA IN CENTRAL ASIA (1963).

[24] *See* G. Massell, *supra* note 1; *cf.* S. Dunn & E. Dunn, *Soviet Regime and Native Culture in Central Asia and Kazakhstan: The Major Peoples,* 8 CURRENT ANTHROPOLOGY 147–84 (June 1967).

sharply on the basis of age and sex).[25] But there were also highly significant differences, and they played a very important role in determining the susceptibility (or lability)[26] of local societies to direct revolutionary manipulation.

Chinese cleavages were primarily regional or sectional in nature. They never contradicted the conception of the Chinese sociocultural universe as a single nation-state with a relatively high degree of ethnic homogeneity and administrative, as well as legal, uniformity. Central Asia, on the contrary, while inhabited by a primarily Turkic and Moslem population, had a highly complex pattern of social and cultural pluralism.[27] Here the uneven distribution of Islamic influences, the fairly sharp dichotomies in the life-styles of sedentary and nomadic communities (and of village and tribal milieus), as well as the absence of meaningful historical precedents for supracommunal structures, meant that cleavages ran primarily along ethno-cultural, sectarian, and tribal lines. When accompanied by perennial fragmentation into warring princely-theocratic principalities (such as Khiva, Bukhara, and Kokand), these divisions made the emergence (and even the very idea) of a single nation and nation-state in the area quite problematic.

Concomitantly, the legal realm represented a heterogeneous and multi-layered universe. In addition to a division into two major categories of law (*shariat*—codified Moslem law, and *adat*—local customary law), Central Asia was crisscrossed by a variegated patchwork of religious, tribal, and communal tribunals, usages, and rules. The resolution of disputes might be entrusted to local Moslem clergymen, tribal leaders, or clan and village notables; conflict resolution could be formal or highly informal, public or private. The prevailing legal norms, forms, and practices depended to a large extent on the particular communal organization, ethnic group, and cultural milieu, as well as on the personal charisma of the particular judicial mediator. Thus, the very act of manipulating such a universe through a unified judicial mechanism involved far greater problems than in China.

---

[25] For some general studies of Chinese society and culture, *see, e.g.,* K. LATOURETTE, THE CHINESE, THEIR HISTORY AND CULTURE (rev. ed. 1964); M. FRIED, FABRIC OF CHINESE SOCIETY (1953); M. FREEDMAN, CHINESE LINEAGE AND SOCIETY (1966); CHINA: ITS PEOPLE, ITS SOCIETY, ITS CULTURE (C. Hu, *et al.* eds. 1960); J. FAIRBANK, THE UNITED STATES AND CHINA (1958).

[26] Harry Eckstein's term in discussing the social bases of political stability and instability. *See* H. ECKSTEIN, AUTHORITY RELATIONS AND GOVERNMENTAL PERFORMANCE: A THEORETICAL FRAMEWORK especially pt. 5 (1968).

[27] *See, e.g.,* L. KRADER, PEOPLES OF CENTRAL ASIA (1963); A. HUDSON, KAZAKH SOCIAL STRUCTURE (1938); E. BACON, CENTRAL ASIANS UNDER RUSSIAN RULE: A STUDY IN CULTURE CHANGE (1966); V. Masal'skii, *Turkestanskii Kray* (Turkestan territory), in 19 ROSSIIA (Semenov-Tianshanskii ed. 1913); V. BARTOL'D, ISTORIIA KUL'TURNOI ZHIZNI TURKESTANA (History of Turkestan culture) (1927).

It is a safe assumption that Central Asian societies were relatively more intact as traditional systems and ways of life than was the case in China at the time of initial revolutionary experimentation. They were more intact in the sense that they were subjected to the processes of urbanization, industrialization, and large-scale commerce to a far lesser extent than China. There were no Central Asian counterparts to China's great ports, which served as contact points with the West. While the Russian conquest of Central Asia in the latter half of the nineteenth century did set in motion some secularizing and disorienting processes, the nature of Tsarist imperial occupation was such as to severely limit the regime's direct contact with, and manipulative intervention at, the grassroots of rural communities.[28] The Central Asian traditional universe, then, was relatively more intact: its primordial kin and custom-based solidarities had eroded to a lesser extent; the influence of its traditional elites was less affected; and the formation of its reformist and revolutionary counter-elites was slower, more recent and delimited, and far narrower in scope than in China. By the same token, its traditional family patterns, including sexual and generational roles, were less drastically affected by shifts in the social, economic, and political environment than in China.[29] All in all, the traditional value and belief systems of Central Asians seem to have been far less affected by doubt, alienation, and fragmentation, and hence were less susceptible and vulnerable to revolutionary initiatives than were those of the Chinese.[30]

Yet another and more directly relevant perspective helps to emphasize the differences in the two milieus. Central Asian societies were classic cases of what may be called *non-instrumental legalism*. By this I mean that they were examples of societies in which legal norms and related social arrangements are regarded as fruits of divine revelation or primordial and sanctified custom, and therefore comprehensive, perfect, and final. In such societies, supracommunal agencies (for example, those of a modern state) do sometimes play a regulative role in particular problems at particular moments in social life. However, as a rule, they are collectively not expected to play (by way of political manipulations in general and legal engineering in particular) a systematic and sustained interventionist and transforming role in the life of the family and local community. For that matter, not only the instrumental role of law, but the very notion of law as an ongoing invention and as subject to autonomous legislative action by secular authorities in the realm of all, including the most

---

[28] For an account of Tsarist policies in Central Asia, *see* especially R. PIERCE, RUSSIAN CENTRAL ASIA: 1867–1917 (1960); S. BECKER, RUSSIA'S PROTECTORATES IN CENTRAL ASIA: BUKHARA AND KHIVA, 1865–1924 (1968).

[29] For a highly incisive study of the evolution of Chinese family patterns, *see* M. LEVY, THE FAMILY REVOLUTION IN MODERN CHINA (1949). For a comparative cross-cultural study, *see* W. GOODE, WORLD REVOLUTION AND FAMILY PATTERNS (1963).

[30] *See, e.g.,* D. BARNETT, CHINA ON THE EVE OF COMMUNIST TAKEOVER (1963).

intimate interpersonal relationships, is regarded as heretical by definition and as a contradiction in terms.[31]

It would seem that this characteristic was crucial in differentiating between China and Central Asia as milieus subject to social engineering through law. To be sure, in some respects, the Chinese process of adjudication was oral, private, and informal, and it could be regarded in many ways as rooted in immemorial custom. But a powerful countervailing force was also at play here. The history of the Chinese state is, after all, a history of fairly continuous attempts to promulgate and enforce legal rules from a single administrative and political center. It is also a history, beginning in the late nineteenth century, of growing preoccupation with positive law as a deliberate instrument of government policy in adapting the social order (including family relations) to the requirements of a centralized nation-stage—a state faced with unprecedented challenges from abroad and attempting through legislation to weaken clan-oriented and communocentric loyalties, to permeate and integrate society more efficiently, and to augment the power potentials of the country as a whole.[32] Even if these attempts were only partly successful, the very precedent of creative and centrally promulgated legislation was of unquestionable value in legitimizing later communist initiatives in the same realm.

On all counts, then, both as insurgents and as incumbents, the Chinese communists could gain access to traditional communities, could lay claim to supracommunal loyalties, and could permeate established social structures for the purposes of mobilization and command to a far greater extent than was possible for the Soviet regime in Central Asia.

Patterns of revolutionary action: the interaction of susceptibilities and techniques. We know that the decision of the Maoist command to accelerate revolutionary transformation involved, among other things, the use of variants of precisely those approaches that had been largely abandoned in Soviet Central Asia after only a few years. It also involved the utilization of mobilizational means that, by definition, could never be tried in Central Asia at all. An attempt to explain reasons for this dichotomy should shed some light on the perceptions of two sets of communist elites regarding the revolutionary options open to them in different circumstances and milieus.

Perhaps most obviously, the Chinese model involved an increasingly heavy stress on voluntarism as a mobilizational technique and a concomitant

---

[31] *See, e.g.,* R. LEVY, THE SOCIAL STRUCTURE OF ISLAM (1962); *Cf.* M. HALPERN, THE POLITICS OF SOCIAL CHANGE IN THE MIDDLE EAST AND NORTH AFRICA especially chs. 1–2, 7–8 (1963); E. ROSENTHAL, POLITICAL THOUGHT IN MEDIEVAL ISLAM (1958); SOUTH ASIAN POLITICS AND RELIGION especially pt. 1 (D. Smith ed. 1966).

[32] The most comprehensive recent evaluation of legal policy and the judicial process in China, especially pertaining to family law, may be found in the proceedings of the Conference on the Role of Law in Modernizing Nations: Chinese Family Law and Social Change, *supra* note 4.

424   GREGORY J. MASSELL

de-emphasis of bureaucratic structures and systematized regulations and procedures. The distrust of formalized organizational frameworks went hand in hand with a growing emphasis on guided mass persuasion, conversion, consensus, and heightened inner and outer struggle—in effect, on perennial instability in selected aspects of life as a precondition for permanent revolution. It clearly involved a fear that psychological, social, and organizational stabilization might impose undesirable constraints on the revolutionary process, halt the fragmentation of the old order, serve as a brake on economic dynamism, unduly consolidate the position, security, and autonomy of the new bureaucratic stratum, delimit the access of supreme leadership to the masses, and thus not only sap revolutionary momentum, but also threaten the legitimacy and incumbency of the Maoist command.[33]

Such a disposition could be based on quite tenable assumptions. The stress on voluntaristic mass participation and ritualized mass consensus could tap at least two important indigenous dispositions: the ancient Chinese emphasis on harmony and manipulation through negotiation and persuasion;[34] and the recent Chinese experience of large-scale guerrilla war. While the former source could serve as an important cultural underpinning for desirable action, the latter could provide a specific political one. It was surely crucial that the disintegration in Chinese traditional structures and institutions (between the beginning of the first and the end of the second world wars) took place in conjunction, not only with the quickening pace of urbanization and industrialization, but also with the emergence of a well-organized (in effect, highly "developed") insurgent force.

Given such a movement and force, men as well as women, and young as well as old, who were either displaced or alienated from traditional institutions (including the family) could find a new mode of mass participation outside the existing order. In effect, the emergence of such a guerrilla force (one that stressed social reform as well as anti-colonial war, and combined morally and ethnically universalistic criteria with a national rather than a regional base)

[33] For a discussion of the patterns of, and the motives underlying, China's "cultural revolution," see, e.g., E. Vogel, Voluntarism and Social Control, in SOVIET AND CHINESE COMMUNISM, supra note 6, at 168–84; F. HOUN, TO CHANGE A NATION: PROPAGANDA AND INDOCTRINATION IN COMMUNIST CHINA (1965); F. YU, MASS PERSUASION IN COMMUNIST CHINA (1964); J. TOWNSEND, POLITICAL PARTICIPATION IN COMMUNIST CHINA (1967); R. SOLOMON, THE CHINESE POLITICAL CULTURE AND PROBLEMS OF MODERNIZATION (1964); D. BARNETT, CADRES, BUREAUCRACY AND POWER IN COMMUNIST CHINA (1967); R. LIFTON, THOUGHT REFORM AND THE PSYCHOLOGY OF TOTALISM (1961); F. SCHURMANN, IDEOLOGY AND ORGANIZATION IN COMMUNIST CHINA (1966); B. SCHWARTZ, COMMUNISM AND CHINA: IDEOLOGY IN FLUX (1968).

[34] See, e.g., D. BODDE, CHINA'S CULTURAL TRADITION (1957); H. CREEL, CHINESE THOUGHT FROM CONFUCIUS TO MAO TSE-TUNG (1953); SOURCES OF THE CHINESE TRADITION (W. de Bary, et al. eds. 1960); CONFUCIANISM IN ACTION (D. Nivisen, et al. eds. 1953).

provided an arena for political recruitment and participation at a suprafamilial and supracommunal level and on a massive scale. Thus, the Chinese model for transformation could rely on an element that was largely absent from the Central Asian scene—the precedent of significantly voluntaristic, emotionally charged mass participation at levels transcending parochial solidarities and locales.

This bears directly on a second major consideration. The Chinese coupled their attack on bureaucratic organization and residues of the old order with an unleashing of the young generation against the old, of women against traditional male authority, of spontaneous self-assertion against the hierarchy of an authoritarian kinship system. By equating the imperatives and aims of the two sets of pressures, the Chinese communists could probably count on requisite native susceptibilities to a far greater extent than the Soviets could in Central Asia. While this is a highly complex and problematic issue, it is probably justified to say that, on the whole, China's psycho-cultural milieu was more susceptible to generational and sexual conflict than Central Asia's—at least at the time of the experiment and under the auspices available to manage this conflict.

We know that, basing themselves in part on the pronounced father-son crisis in Russia's recent history and in part on orthodox Leninist organizational imperatives pertaining especially to youth, Soviet agencies automatically proceeded to replicate in Central Asia, not only party, but also komsomol organizations. It was explicitly expected that, through this medium, requisite native political cadres would be mobilized and, at the same time, the induced or exploited generational tensions would help to accelerate the dissolution of what was understood to be a "feudal-patriarchal" system, one based on a father's coercive—and therefore often resented—authority in the family. As one communist organizer put it, native social organizations were bound to collapse the moment they lost the young generation, "the marrow of their bones." And that would happen when the young men turned against their elders, and sons against their fathers.[35]

As it turned out, organizational work with Moslem youth had to mean almost exclusively work with male youth, since Moslem girls were largely unavailable for political participation. At the same time, throughout the 1920s the political performance of Central Asian komsomol units was found to be one of the most consistently lagging sectors in the entire spectrum of Soviet efforts in the region. For that matter, Moscow found these units to be the least reliable, from an ideological and political standpoint, of all the units comprising the komsomol network of the Soviet Union. While the reasons for this were necessarily complex, it would appear that at least one of them had to do with the status of young males in Islamic societies. In these societies,

---

[35] *See* G. Massell, *supra* note 2, at 61 ff.

while the father's authority was indeed dominant as a rule, it was not necessarily arbitrary, overwhelming, and therefore invariably resented. Most important in relation to that authority, sons comprised a stratum that, no matter what its socioeconomic background, tended to be the most highly prized and favored one, and hence the most indulged, in the extended, patriarchal Moslem family.

At the same time, unlike China, both a low density population and the survival of significant residues of tribal organization and communal landholding patterns tended to mitigate tensions based on primogeniture and on progressive fragmentation of inherited property, including land. On all these counts, then, it turned out to be a far from simple matter to elicit grievances of young Moslem males and to turn them against patriarchal authority and the kinship system.

On the other hand, while the deliberate manipulation of familial sexual roles in Central Asia did expose what appeared to be the greatest vulnerability of Moslem societies, it also engendered their most determined efforts to resist. What the Soviet regime lacked here was not only the legitimate authority, but also the institutional capacity to follow through and to shoulder the attendant responsibilities.[36]

It would appear that the Chinese communists could count on far greater leeway in this respect—both in terms of the "inputs" and the "outputs" of the situation. On the one hand, a relatively high degree of legitimation in and of itself permitted a rather broad range of social experimentation. But, perhaps more important, the encouragement of mass radicalism and collective violence, accompanied by collective acts of symbolic parricide, seems to have been able to tap a vein of congruent dispositions not readily apparent in relatively intact Moslem traditional societies.[37]

On the other hand, the highly charged outputs of the situation could, to some extent, be channeled and controlled, and this type of mobilization could indeed be sustained over time, in that there existed in China an element conspicuously absent from the Central Asian scene. I have in mind the

---

[36] *See* G. Massell, *supra* note 1, at 202–23 (in the article in LAW AND SOCIETY); and *supra* note 2, at 65 ff.

[37] I owe the term "symbolic parricide" to L. FEUER, THE CONFLICT OF GENERATIONS: THE CHARACTER AND SIGNIFICANCE OF STUDENT MOVEMENTS (1969). For some highly suggestive insights on the possible relationship of authority patterns, characteristic psycho-cultural dispositions, and communist political action in China, *see, e.g.,* R. LIFTON, REVOLUTIONARY IMMORTALITY: MAO TSE-TUNG AND THE CHINESE CULTURAL REVOLUTION (1968); L. PYE, THE SPIRIT OF CHINESE POLITICS (1968). *Cf.* R. H. Solomon, *Communication Patterns and the Chinese Revolution,* THE CHINA QUARTERLY No. 32, at 88–110 (Oct.–Dec. 1967); R. H. Solomon, *Mao's Effort to Reintegrate the Chinese Polity : Problems of Authority and Conflict in Chinese Social Processes,* in CHINESE COMMUNIST POLITICS IN ACTION 271–351 (E. Barnett ed. 1969). See also R. H. Solomon, MAO'S REVOLUTION AND THE CHINESE POLITICAL CULTURE (1971).

opportunity for young men and women disposed or compelled to break familial loyalties and ties to transfer emotional allegiance to a patriarchal, genuinely charismatic, ethnically akin figure of a supreme leader: Mao. No comparable figure had emerged in Central Asia, despite strenuous Soviet attempts to promote the largely distant, impersonal, and ethnically alien images of Lenin and Stalin for this purpose. Moreover, if there were some opportunities for Central Asian youth to identify with such a figure, they were systematically undermined by the Soviet regime itself as, one after another, the most brilliant and authoritative of Central Asia's emerging native communist leaders were politically constrained, publicly disgraced, and physically annihilated.

It seems reasonable to assume that in China the direct manipulation of generational roles and family relations for the sake of social mobilization was sustained, in part, because of the regime's concurrent willingness and ability to fan nationalist xenophobia in the country at large. The ancient Chinese vision of the outer world, the successive traumas and humiliations of confrontation with powerful and overbearing expansionist states (including Russia), and the more recent role of the communist party in waging an anti-colonial war with Japan (as well as against the United States in Korea)—all these reservoirs of actual or latent passion could be tapped as extra propellants of revolutionary fervor and action in other spheres.

Nothing of this sort was even remotely possible in Soviet Central Asia. For one thing, to encourage nationalism here would have meant to encourage ethnic, national, or racial loyalties that were heterogeneous and conflicting (Uzbek, Turkmen, Kazakh, Kirghiz, Tadzhik), or potentially homogeneous but relatively amorphous (Turkic). The former option would have had a divisive rather than a unifying effect; the latter was ruled out by definition, since it involved a threat that had concerned Moscow from the very beginning of Soviet rule—the threat of a Pan-Turkic or Pan-Islamic movement within Soviet frontiers.

For another thing, and more specifically, for the Soviet regime to arouse nationalist xenophobia in Central Asia was, *ipso facto,* to turn virtually the entire local population against Soviet rule. The reason for this was obviously a function of the peculiar circumstances under which a sense of national identity had taken hold in this area; beginning in the eighteenth century, most indigenous Central Asian revolts—including responses to military invasion and occupation, and economic exploitation, as well as cultural and political domination—were revolts expressly against Russians. No amount of political legerdemain could disguise the fact that today's effective power-wielders in the region were the kinsmen of yesterday's imperial Russian occupiers, and that some of the control arrangements of the former were very much akin to those of the latter. In short, for the Soviets to place local nationalist (or ethnic or racial) passions in the service of politics and social mobilization was to court unmitigated disaster.

428 GREGORY J. MASSELL

Summary and Conclusion

This analytical overview suggests that legal engineering of family relations is very much contingent on a host of more broadly conceived imperatives and capabilities. Legal revolution in the service of sponsored social mobilization and fundamental transformation cannot be analyzed except in intimate correlation with such factors as the makeup and legitimacy of the sponsor, the condition and orientations of the target, and the "fit" between a society's dispositions and a revolutionary's commitments, techniques, and alternative institutional arrangements. Even the monopolistic, centralized, coordinated, and morally unconstrained force of a totalitarian revolutionary cannot automatically overcome the constraints imposed by such a correlation.

This should not merely lead us to question the utility of law (and especially family law) as an autonomous instrument of rapid, administered social change. Nor should we merely conclude that totalitarian incumbents bent upon drastic social change find little use for law. To be sure, after initial experiments with what we have called revolutionary legalism, both the Soviet and the Chinese incumbents de-emphasized the use of formal legal institutions for revolutionary purposes. Yet they did so for very different reasons, and they drew significantly differing conclusions from their particular experiences. It is this dimension of the problem that seems especially important in the context of our analysis.

The Soviet communists retreated from revolutionary legalism in Central Asia, because they found this approach, on the whole, *too destabilizing,* both with respect to other developmental objectives and to the legitimation and institutionalization of the incumbent regime.[38] In effect, they found that consistent enforcement of new rules governing sexual and generational roles and family relations called for nothing short of massive repression. At the same time, it turned out that the Soviet regime could least of all afford the consequences of such repression; coercive force—applied by this particular incumbent, in this milieu, and in this realm of human relationships—tended to raise progressively the magnitude of societal resistance and civil violence. More than that, it tended to fuse and trigger popular resentments stemming from the entire spectrum of Soviet sponsored actions in the Moslem traditional milieu.[39] Hence, there was a reversal in Soviet emphasis, from precipitate legal change (especially in the realm of family relations) for the sake of rapid social transformation, to long-term social rebuilding (including the construc-

---

[38] *See* G. Massell, *supra* note 1, at 223–27.

[39] For a highly suggestive theoretical treatment of the general conditions of several forms of civil strife, *see* T. Gurr, *A Causal Model of Civil Strife: A Comparative Analysis Using New Indices,* 62 AM. POL. SCI. REV. 1104–1124 (1968); although Gurr's analysis is cast in a very different perspective from mine, its conclusions seem very relevant here and are strongly supported by my own findings.

tion of a complex infrastructure of social service, educational, associational, expressive, and economic facilities) for the sake, in part, of meaningful legal change. It is this latter emphasis that we have characterized as an attempt at systematic social engineering, wherein a modicum of stability was to be purchased at the price of revolutionary purity and of a lower rate of change.

The Chinese communists seem to have shifted their emphasis away from revolutionary legalism, because they found this approach *not destabilizing enough,* in the sense that it seemed neither broad enough in scope nor swift and intense enough in its impact on established solidarities and customs. To be sure, while we do not know enough about the mode and magnitude of popular responses to Maoist pressures in this realm, we know that both resistance and evasion were among the outcomes. Yet, basing ourselves on what followed, we can speculate that noncompliance either was not dangerously widespread and disfunctional, or was not *perceived* by the regime to be a problem that was serious enough to cause the postponement and modification of revolutionary plans. In effect, the Maoist command accelerated social mobilization, shifting to a variant of what we have characterized in the Central Asian milieu as administrative assault. It is not absolutely crucial at this point to know whether the Chinese leadership could objectively afford such a shift.[40] What is perhaps more relevant here is that there were a number of things that could permit them to believe that they could move by and large in this fashion for the foreseeable future, regardless of repercussions.

Paradoxically, the Soviet regime felt both disposed and compelled to utilize a legalistic approach to social engineering, but was not quite able to do so, certainly not in the short term. It was even less able—and indeed, found it disastrous—to utilize variants of mass action as extrajudicial propellants of social mobilization. On the contrary, Peking (at least under Mao) was capable of relying on a legalistic approach to a far greater extent than Moscow, but apparently felt neither disposed nor compelled to do so. Moreover, it seemed confident enough to turn to sustained and violent mass action, without undue concern for institutionalizing a formal organizational framework and extralegal supportive arrangements.

In reviewing the possible reasons for this dichotomy, it is perhaps best to start from what might be the simplest ones.

Peking could very well have felt compelled to accelerate social mobilization because of the enormity of physical and administrative problems facing any regime merely in feeding and controlling the Chinese population. Here there were really no significantly developed (in the economic and administrative sense) components of the system that were well-endowed and strong enough to serve as anchoring points for the country as a whole—while means were

---

[40] We know as yet too little about the costs and benefits of particular revolutionary approaches to be able to evaluate this at this point.

found to integrate and strengthen the remaining less developed parts. Also the region as a whole was both physically and politically exposed to actual or potential (or imagined) internal and external pressures in the 1950s, when those who had made the revolution faced the task of consolidating it.

Moscow, on the other hand, could easily feel more sanguine about decelerating social mobilization in Central Asia. Here it had to deal with a population that was minuscule in comparison with China's and with a ratio of land and natural resources to population that was very favorable indeed. In addition, within the Soviet Union as a whole, Central Asia's relative underdevelopment could easily be balanced by European Russia—a large central core that was well endowed and relatively developed and that contained the numerically dominant ethnic group. One part could "carry" the other, as it were, as well as control it.[41] Moreover, Central Asia probably was the Soviet Union's most isolated and least threatened component, since literally all of its neighbors (Turkey, Iran, Afghanistan, India and China) were in the 1920s in a state of internal weakness, turmoil, or disintegration. It may be said, then, that Moscow could afford to wait; Peking could not.[42]

There were also more subtle factors at work. The Chinese regime could very well feel both compelled and able to engage its population politically, emotionally, and morally. Shared ethnicity and culture, shared experience of physical and emotional hardships, and the regime's relatively long period of legitimation as a revolutionary and anti-colonial movement, facilitated a high degree of affective interaction between the elite and the masses. A Maoist guerrilla in power might feel it as his obligation and his right to come to grips with the hearts and minds of his own kinsmen.

The conditions of interaction between Soviet elites and Central Asia's masses could not have been more different. This was not merely a matter of less time and fewer opportunities for the regime's legitimation in the area. Nor was it solely because the totalitarian incumbent appeared to members of a traditional society, not only as a deeply threatening revolutionary force, but also as an alien force—that is, as an ethnically distinct group. Perhaps most important, the bolsheviks (including many of Lenin's closest collaborators) in the commanding core of the Soviet apparatus (which was overwhelmingly European and Slavic in composition) never regarded the conquered Asian territories as more than useful appendages of the "proletarian" and "revolutionary" Russian center. Neither did they regard the Asian masses, and even their new secular intelligentsia (including indigenous communist

---

[41] For an analysis of Central Asia's position in the Soviet economic system, see, e.g., A. NOVE & J. NEWTH, THE SOVIET MIDDLE EAST . . . (1967); V. CONOLLY, BEYOND THE URALS . . . (1967); C. K. WILBER, THE SOVIET MODEL AND UNDERDEVELOPED COUNTRIES (1969).

[42] For some representative studies of trends in Chinese economy, see, e.g., A. ECKSTEIN, COMMUNIST CHINA'S ECONOMIC GROWTH AND FOREIGN TRADE (1966).

leadership), as particularly trustworthy. In too many cases, the distrust verged on barely concealed contempt. This was crucial. In a very fundamental sense, dominant segments of the incumbent regime lacked the moral incentives to become intimately involved with the beliefs, values, and relationships of Central Asian peoples. At the same time, those who had or might have had such incentives, that is, the native reformist or radical intelligentsia, were systematically constrained, undermined, or liquidated in successive purges.

What is perhaps the subtlest and most immediately relevant factor in this case concerns the issue of sanctions. For a variety of reasons that should be apparent at this point, Moscow could attempt to impose new legal rules in Moslem family relations only by means of draconically enforced criminal sanctions. In other words, the only hope of attaining a sudden and dramatic breakthrough in Moslem behavioral patterns and status systems lay in the persistent imposition of coercive controls from the outside, at the cost of equally persistent internal irritation, hostility, and friction.

The Maoist regime, on the other hand, had very different (and a broader spectrum of) options at its disposal. Most important, the regime's relatively high degree of legitimation, as well as the psycho-cultural profile of Chinese society, freed the communist regime to a significant extent from the necessity and obligation to rely on formal legal institutions and criminal sanctions to inculcate new behavioral norms. In fact, what called for massive coercive pressures from the outside in Central Asia could, in the Chinese context, seem to require primarily voluntaristic mass persuasion from the inside, with correspondingly fewer costs in internal friction and greater benefits in collective consensus and cooperation. Thus what involved maximum risks in Central Asia could seem to involve relatively small risks in China.

This asymmetry in risks is underscored by different patterns and degrees of interdependence in the two sociocultural systems. Traditional Islamic society is not only a highly integrated system, but one wherein the pattern of family relations (including especially sexual and generational roles) is inextricably intertwined with both religious and ego-oriented sensibilities.[43] The most critically important (and hence most sensitive) dimensions in the interdependence of its component parts (norms, relationships, statuses, and roles) concern women.

Hence, an assault on this realm of the system was not merely an attack on sacred against secular aspects of life, or on consummatory against instru-

---

[43] For analysis and requisite citations, *see, e.g.,* M. BERGER, THE ARAB WORLD TODAY (1964); W. SMITH, ISLAM IN MODERN HISTORY (1957); R. LEVY, THE SOCIAL STRUCTURE OF ISLAM (1962); UNITY AND VARIETY IN MUSLIM CIVILIZATION (G. von Grünebaum ed. 1955); H. GIBB & H. BOWEN, ISLAMIC SOCIETY IN THE EIGHTEENTH CENTURY (1950). *Cf.* M. Halpern, "Patterns of Continuity and Change, Collaboration and Conflict in Traditional Islamic Society," paper for MESA Annual Meeting, Nov. 1968, Houston, Texas.

mental values. The manipulation of familial-sexual and generational roles, to the extent that it had to involve women, was an assault on the role that was the most distinctly ascribed rather than achieved one in the entire system and that was functionally highly diffuse rather than specific. It was diffuse in the sense that its functions tended to be critically interdependent with more (and more emotionally charged) roles, values, and meanings than was probably true in any other case. In other words, an attack on female positions in a Moslem milieu meant an attack on a highly interlocking set of roles with a very wide spectrum. A significant departure in one of its components seemed to imply the collapse of the entire system. For, in this context (in what David Riesman calls a "typical example of a male-vanity culture"), men's roles may be said to have been to an extraordinary extent defined by apposition to female roles; maleness seems to have been, in effect, negatively defined with respect to the very concept of woman. Thus, to drastically alter this concept threatened to dissolve the boundaries defining maleness itself, and hence not just a man's superordinate position vis-à-vis women, but in effect his self-image, self-definition, self-esteem, and ego-identity. A sharp shift in female status (as woman, daughter, wife, or mother) threatened to affect critically the nexus of authority relations in the most intimate circles of a man's life. This, it would seem, is the ultimate implication of the concept of 'ird in Islam—the extraordinary degree of interlocking and interdependence between male and family honor on the one hand, and the role and concept of woman on the other in Moslem imagination.[44]

While I would hesitate to speak about Chinese society on this account with equal certainty, it is reasonable to assume that there was, here, no comparable degree of mutual sensitivity of the system's component parts—at least not in precisely this dimension and not at the time of full-blown Maoist social experimentation. If one were to pinpoint this system's most important axes of strategic interdependence, one would probably place the father-son relationship ahead of the male-female relationship on the scale of intense, emotionally charged, critically interdependent roles.[45] But, while the manipu-

---

[44] See G. Massell, supra note 2, at 63–66. Some anthropological investigations in Islamic societies other than Central Asia's seem to support such an assessment. See, e.g., H. MINER & G. DE VOS, OASIS AND CASBAH: ALGERIAN CULTURE AND PERSONALITY IN CHANGE (1960); HONOUR AND SHAME: THE VALUES OF MEDITERRANEAN SOCIETY (J. Peristiany ed. 1965), especially essays by Bourdieu and Abou-Zeid. For a very interesting case study including an excellent bibliography, see D. GORDON, WOMEN OF ALGERIA: AN ESSAY ON CHANGE (1968). Cf. W. GOODE, supra note 29, at especially ch. 3; J. BERQUE, THE ARABS: THEIR HISTORY AND FUTURE especially ch. 9 (1964).

[45] I consider the sensitivity of these roles only in the context of the family as a target of deliberate revolutionary manipulation. We are dealing here, then, primarily with intrafamilial relationships. No attempt is made to correlate these dimensions of human interaction with extrafamilial ones; for example, with relationships between families or large-scale kin-oriented solidarities and factions. Such inter-familial relationships have

lation of generational roles (and especially father-son relationships) in China might have been more explosive than in Central Asia, there was at least one element here that departed significantly from the Islamic model, and thus considerably mitigated the potential dangers.

It seems warranted to suggest that, just as Moslem religious civilization was formally more rigorously (and rigidly) articulated than China's socio-ethical order,[46] the basic orientations and commitments prescribed in Islam were more inclusive in scope. Concomitantly, traditional Islamic society could be characterized as more unitary than the Chinese one, at least in the sense that it involved a greater degree of interdependence between social roles and statuses on the one hand and religious sensibilities (including the view of the world and the self) on the other.[47] Thus, the manipulation of authority relations in China (especially in the 1950s and 1960s) seems to have involved less intense perceptions of a fundamental threat in society than was clearly the case in the Moslem traditional milieu.

Finally, though Chinese social mobilization through the manipulation of sexual and generational tensions was potentially explosive, there were elements in the pattern of communist action that could, in and of themselves, mitigate the implicit dangers.

As we pointed out above, the acuteness of perception of a fundamental threat in society could be attenuated in China, in part, because of the presence of an element that was conspicuously absent from the Central Asian scene.

---

always been characterized by conflicts or latent tensions with important implications for the performance of the political system as a whole. It should be fruitful to explore the linkages between these two major dimensions of social interaction and their cumulative effect on the lability of the Chinese milieu to engineered social revolution. Arthur J. Lerman has explored some aspects of the interaction between kin-oriented factions in "Taiwanese Local Politics," Ph.D. Dissertation, Department of Politics, Princeton University. *Cf.* D. DeGlopper, The Origins and Resolution of Conflict in Traditional Chinese Society, 1965 (unpublished M.A. Thesis, University of London). I am indebted to Mr. Lerman for reviewing the implications of this problem with me. For some direct or indirect considerations of the father-son relationship in the context of Maoist politics, see note 37 *supra.*

[46] For a classic study of China's socio-ethical order, *see* M. WEBER, THE RELIGION OF CHINA (1964). *Cf.* E. HUGHES & K. HUGHES, RELIGION IN CHINA (1950); W. SOOTHILL, THE THREE RELIGIONS OF CHINA (1929); J. DE GROOT, THE RELIGIOUS SYSTEM OF CHINA (3 vols. 1892, 1894, 1897).

[47] For some discussions of Chinese society along lines that are relevant here (although they do not necessarily, or fully, support my interpretations in this matter), *see* M. LEVY, *supra* note 29; W. GOODE, *supra* note 29, especially ch. 6; C. YANG, CHINESE COMMUNIST SOCIETY: THE FAMILY AND THE VILLAGE (1965); M. FRIED, *supra* note 25; M. FREEDMAN, *supra* note 25; O. LANG, CHINESE FAMILY AND SOCIETY (1946); Y. LIN, THE GOLDEN WING: A SOCIOLOGICAL STUDY OF CHINESE FAMILISM (1948); M. Freedman, *The Family in China, Past and Present,* in MODERN CHINA 27–40 (A. Feuerwerker ed. 1964); and M. Freedman, ed., FAMILY AND KINSHIP IN CHINESE SOCIETY (1970).

When faced with the erosion of traditional kinship loyalties and ties, men and women, and fathers as well as sons, could more easily withstand and transcend the drastic shift in authority relations through an opportunity to transfer emotional allegiance to a highly potent parental/patriarchal surrogate and charismatic figure: Mao.

As we also pointed out earlier, social mobilization could be both accelerated and sustained in China, in part because of the Maoist regime's concurrent will and capacity to fan nationalist xenophobia in the country at large (something that was unthinkable in Central Asia under Soviet Russian rule). We may now restate this proposition in a slightly different and more immediately relevant perspective.

In Central Asia, the immediacy and violence of popular response were directly correlated to Soviet attempts to focus legal and extrajudicial means on the most sacred realms of social life, the most sensitized traditional Moslem taboos. In China, too, we can speak of sharp infringements on primordial sensibilities. But here, it seems, an important countervailing force played a major part in the over-all scheme of action. The manipulation of some sacred and nonrational elements of social life was feasible precisely because it was executed in conjunction with the deliberate mobilization of loyalties based on another set of potent nonrational sensibilities, those pertaining to nationality, ethnicity, and race. Because, in China, there was a remarkable congruence between loyalty axes based on race, ethnicity, and nationality, the Maoist command could successfully evoke a sense of group identity and make it into a powerful focus of passionate human sentiments.[48] In the maelstrom of such sentiments, animosities or frictions engendered by judicial or extrajudicial manipulation of family relations could be at least temporarily submerged or defused.

In short, in manipulating sexual and generational roles for revolutionary purposes, Maoist forces in China have so far been able to accomplish what Soviet forces in Central Asia were quite unable to do: to introduce a specialized tension management system into the traditional milieu, wherein tension-inducing devices (as heretical models) would serve to undermine the traditional order, while tension-controlling means (as regulative mechanisms) would mitigate the negative consequences of induced tensions.[49]

---

[48] For a discussion of the background of such sentiments in China and for requisite citations, see, e.g., H. Isaacs, *Group Identity and Political Change,* in COLOR AND RACE especially 89–93 (J. Franklin ed. 1968). For a comparative cross-cultural perspective, consult the entire volume.

[49] For a very useful discussion, from a somewhat different perspective, of the relationship between social mobilization and political destabilization, see S. Huntington, *Political Development and Political Decay,* 17 WORLD POLITICS 386–430 (April 1965), as well as his POLITICAL ORDER IS CHANGING SOCIETIES (1968). For an excellent theoretical treatment of the social bases of political stability in terms that are very relevant here, see H. ECKSTEIN, *supra* note 26.

This is not to say that these conditions can be replicated and perpetuated in China indefinitely. Shifts in leadership, as well as in social structure and economic imperatives, may quickly bring to the fore new priorities, possibilities, and needs. One may already point to some signs of caution, attempted stabilization, and possible retrenchment. For one thing, massive, volatile, and aggressive expressions of youthful contempt for organized authority in general, and patriarchal authority in particular, as well as overt attacks on the ideal of filial piety, are being reined in. Similarly, overly easy divorces have come to be discouraged. All the same, persuasive evidence still points to a remarkable persistence of a mobilizational and revolutionary impetus in Communist China. Such persistence, against enormous odds, tells us much about the extraordinary potentialities of revolutionary action in circumstances where a high degree of "fit" exists between revolutionary agents and clients, and between innate susceptibilities and particular techniques.[50] In effect, it makes of Communist China something of a classic case, wherein new behavioral norms could be applied in the most sensitive realms of social life over an extended period of time, by and large without the systematic mediation of formalized legal rules, institutions, and procedures.

---

[50] In pointing to such a fit, I do not wish to suggest anything indicative of capabilities for unilateral and unilinear action in the Chinese case—or anything approaching a perfectly easy and complete congruence between revolutionary actors and clients. As Stanley Lubman has rightly pointed out in his comments on this paper, it would be folly to minimize the persistent tensions inside Chinese communist ranks (due not only to competing personalities but also to competing operational models) as well as the continuing tensions between regime and society (due to the strength of particularistic ties and societal resistance to particular communist actions). Indeed, I have attempted to juxtapose two courses of revolutionary transformation, and to marshall relevant factors in comparative perspective, in order to identify crucial elements in each case—in a way that would make it possible to speak about particular conditions and capabilities in relative terms. It is in this sense that I have emphasized the characteristic elements in the Chinese case as indicative of a high—perhaps extraordinarily high—degree of fit between the forces and targets of revolutionary change at a particular point in time.

For an exceptionally fruitful conceptualization of resistance-capacities of a milieu facing revolutionary or other manipulative pressures—in effect, for a paradigm of internal-war potential in society—*see* H. Eckstein, *On the Etiology of Internal Wars,* 4 HISTORY AND THEORY No. 2, at 133–63 (1965).

Marriage Law and Policy
in the People's Republic of China*

MARINUS J. MEIJER

THE KIANGSI LEGISLATION

Land Reform and Marriage Reform

Wherever the Chinese communists established themselves they promulgated a marriage law and a land reform law. This happened in the Chinese Soviet Republic in 1931, and the same combination is seen in 1950 after the establishment of the People's Republic. In the time between these two great moments, the period of the "Border Areas,"[1] more or less the same synchronization can be found, though the measures show more restraint.

There is obviously a relationship between these two laws. Land reform naturally was aimed at changing the structure of landholding. It took land from the rich and gave it to the poor. Actually, however, it did more than that; it changed the structure of landed property on the basis of village population (or combination of villages—the *hsiang*); that is, on an individual basis according to the number of persons in the household.[2] Each person became the owner of land. Land was no longer the family heirloom, inherited

---

* After this article was first written the author's book has appeared. M. J. MEIJER, MARRIAGE LAW AND POLICY IN THE CHINESE PEOPLE'S REPUBLIC (Hong Kong: Hong Kong University Press, 1971.) 369 pp.

[1] Border Areas were autonomous areas under Communist influence. The first was the Autonomous Area of Shensi, Kansu and Ninghsia, established in 1937, with Yen-an as the capital. Several others were established during the war; they were in fact guerrilla areas. In these areas Mao Tse-tung's concept of New Democracy was put into practice, and coalition governments under Communist influence were established. The land reform movement was mitigated to a movement for the reduction of land rent, and in the marriage reform ostensibly the spirit of the Civil Code was followed. There were, however, significant deviations from the Code.

[2] K. HATANO, CHŪGOKU KYŌSANTŌ-SHI (History of the Chinese communist party) Pt. I, 582 (1951) gives the text of the first draft of the Land Reform Law of 1931, Part I. The principle is found in Article 1.

from the ancestors and destined to be transferred to the next generation and to be administered in the interim by the father as head of the family. Henceforth it was property received during land reform, even if it had originally been one's own property.[3]

Land reform also provided the basis for the marriage law, because it gave the woman property rights to land. It was therefore made possible for her to divorce her husband without losing her economic independence. The ownership of land gave her equality with her husband during marriage. The fact that even children were allotted land and that a wife at the time of divorce could take her children with her, if she wished, provided her with a strong position vis-à-vis her husband. For all such reasons the land reform had a profound influence upon the legal relations within the family and was effective in the further weakening of tradition.

The Feudal Family

In the material published during the Kiangsi Republic there is evidence of strong efforts to get women to support the land reform as a means of emancipating them from the bonds of the traditional family.[4] Obtaining the support of the "masses of women" was part of a policy designed to awaken their political consciousness and to break their acquiescence to the traditional forms of life.

The simultaneous introduction of marriage legislation was intended to give the *coup de grâce* to the old family. The first article of the marriage Regulations of the Chinese Soviet Republic, promulgated on December 1, 1931, reads:

> The principle of freedom of marriage between man and woman is established and the entire feudal system of marriage arranged by persons other than the parties themselves, forced upon the parties and contracted by purchase and sale is abolished. The practice of taking a "foster daughter-in-law" is forbidden.[5]

---

[3] Supreme Court, Central and South China Branch, May 7, 1951. *Chung-hua jen-min kung-ho-kuo min-fa tzu liao hui-pien* (Collection of materials on the civil law of the People's Republic of China) published by the Jen-min ta-hsüeh (People's University) 354 (Peking, 1954) [hereinafter cited as COLLECTION].

[4] For instance in the *Plan for Work among Women,* Special Committee for Northern Kiangsi of the Central Committee of the C.C.P., March 3, 1931 (*Ch'en Cheng Papers* reel 10, no. 6, at 34). "The most important of the Women's movement is to mobilize the broad masses of toiling women to join the revolution. Only the land reform, only the Soviet Government can liquidate the feudal forces and liberate the women."

[5] For the complete text of the law, *see* the translation by Bela Kun in FUNDAMENTAL LAWS OF THE CHINESE SOVIET REPUBLIC (Martin Lawrence Ltd. 1934); the translation in Japanese by Fukushima Masao & Miyazaka Hiroshi in CHŪKA SOBIETO KYŌWAKOKU, CHŪGOKU KAIHŌKU, KONYINHŌ SHIRYŌ (Material on marriage laws of the Chinese Soviet Republic and the Chinese Liberated Areas) 27 (1966); and the translation by M. Meijer, *Early Communist Marriage Legislation in China,* 6 CONTEMPORARY CHINA 87–98 (1962–64).

This article embodies a declaration of war on the traditional family as it still existed in large parts of the countryside. It attacks not only the old forms of marriage, but the whole family system—the so-called feudal family.

The use of the word "feudal" requires further explanation. It implies that China was living in the feudal period, the third of the five societies that every human society has to pass through in its progress—primitive, slave, feudal, capitalist, and socialist or communist society. The productive process in a society is characteristic of the particular stage through which it is passing. In feudal society the means of production, primarily land, are in the hands of the nobility or landlords. The great mass of people are serfs or tenants who are in a dependent position so that they are not free to leave the land and are sold together with the land. They own their own implements and have an interest in the landlord's affairs in so far as they are allowed to till part of the domain for their own use or to retain part of the yield for their own maintenance. The superstructure of culture established on this economic substructure serves to confirm the position of the landlord in every respect. Law, religion, and social institutions all fulfill their role in the affirmation of this system of exploitation. The structure of the family also reflects the basic social relations. The husband-wife relationship can be compared with that of the lord and his subject, and the relations between a father and his children to those between a landlord and his tenants. The children were bound to the family as the tenant was bound to the soil; the father had the right to dispose of his children as he pleased. He could sell them, pawn them, and even kill them with impunity. The official criminal law supported him in his position. The Confucian teachings of *Li* and *I* were meant to keep the children and the wife in their places. This was the way Marxist doctrine viewed the traditional family.[6]

Since the last century changes had taken place in the structure of a part of Chinese society. Capitalism had entered upon the scene, and the process of its development was accelerated by the advent of Western imperialism. Consequently, Chinese society could be characterized as semi-feudal and semi-bourgeois, a typical dualistic phenomenon in a period of transition from one society into another.

The basic premise of this reasoning is wrong, since economic circumstances do not correspond to this representation. The majority of Chinese farmers were not tenants but free small holders of land. The superstructure of society, if that term has to be employed, was radically different from the picture that was drawn. The Chinese *"patria potestas"* had definite limitations; for instance, a father could not disinherit a son. In extreme cases a wayward child, who by his conduct could involve the whole family in sincere difficulties,

[6] The clearest exposition of this view is perhaps found in N. NIIDA, CHŪGOKU HŌSEISHI KENKYŪ; DOREINŌDOHŌ KAZOKU SONRAKUHŌ (Studies in Chinese legal history; law of slave and serf, and family and village law) 97–146, 329–65 (1962).

would be put to death by the clan council, but such an act sprang rather from motives of fear of becoming embroiled in official investigations than from an alleged "right of life and death." Killing, pawning, or selling a wife were crimes,[7] although pawning and selling (which had a provisional character) were more or less condoned, when the choice was that of starvation because of extreme poverty.[8] Infanticide was an offense as well, although it was often practiced on newly born girls.[9] There too, however, the main reason was poverty.

The position of the father was indeed strong and supported by deeply ingrained concepts of morality. The children owed their father obedience. However, the counterpart of paternal privileges was the duty to rear the children and the responsibility for their behavior. The children were not at all without rights. The fact that they were born within a family entitled them to be reared from the family property and family income.[10] Nobody can seriously maintain that marriage in China was in general a transaction by which the parents of the bridegroom bought the woman from her parents. The costly marriage presents represented the guarantee of the parents of the bride and the groom to abide by the betrothal contract and at most had an element of compensation for the cost of rearing the bride, who went over into the family of the groom.[11]

The cost to be borne by the bride's parents for the marriage rites were not negligible. Marrying one's sons in traditional China was a duty of the parents toward the ancestors, to ensure the continuation of "incense and fire," the ancestral cult.[12] Much more important considerations than financial gain were involved, like ensuring the care of the spirit after death and being cared for in old age.

The so-called seven reasons for divorce, representing the unilateral right of the husband to send his wife packing, were as Shiga points out largely an empty phrase.[13] In practice they were seldom invoked by the common people. The legal position of the wife indeed was comparatively weak, at least as long as the husband was alive. It was very strong, however, when she became a widow.

---

[7] G. BOULAIS, MANUEL DE CODE CHINOIS (Manual of Chinese statutes) 565 (1924). The husband was only excused if he killed his wife in a fit of fury when he caught her in the act of adultery. *Id.*, 265, 530, 546, 569, 584, 685.

[8] *Id.*, 265.

[9] *Id.*, 569, 571.

[10] S. SHIGA, CHŪGOKU KAZOKUHŌ NO GENRI (Basic principles of Chinese family law) ch. 2, §3; ch. 4, §2 (Sobunsha 1967).

[11] M. YOUNG, A CHINESE VILLAGE 108 (1945); H. FEI, PEASANT LIFE IN CHINA 53 (1939); S. KULP, COUNTRY LIFE IN SOUTH CHINA 174 (1925); F. HSÜ, UNDER THE ANCESTORS' SHADOW 87 (1949).

[12] F. HSÜ, *supra* note 11, at ch. 4.

[13] S. SHIGA, *supra* note 10, at 476.

Although the Communist regimes were very well acquainted with the real situation, they deliberately represented the traditional family as the embodiment of all evil. It is interesting to see how, every now and then, the propaganda clashed with the more realistic view that was generally held. There are, for example, references to "completely" and "incompletely" feudal marital relations.[14] The reasons for the distaste of the communists for the tradition family are twofold: economic and political. The traditional family was an obstacle to economic progress. It kept women in a subordinate position and hampered their participation in economic life. It belonged to an obsolete system of production; the women were in a position of "semi-slavery." The purpose of Communist policy is to make all women participate in public industry in a position of equality with men. The traditional family had to be destroyed because it was a remnant of feudal society. Politically the traditional family was an obstacle to the complete socialization of man. The old family with its tradition of common life narrowed the sense of duty of the individual and his loyalties down to the small circle of his own family. It created tensions between family solidarity and the demands of the Party, which were to represent the interests of the whole society. These sound and logical arguments from the Party's point of view are behind the misrepresentation of the traditional family.

The New Marriage System

So much for the concept of the "feudal marriage system." The alternative provided by the Regulations of 1931 and its revised version, the Marriage Law of 1934,[15] was a free marriage and, consequently, a free family on the basis of monogamy. The Regulations had twenty-three articles. The first articles were devoted to general principles. The next six dealt with the conditions for marriage. And the remainder regulated divorce and its consequences, except for the last three, which provided for the status of illegitimate children, the introduction of penal sanction for contraventions of the Regulations, and immediate enforcement of the Regulations.

Conditions for marriage. The conditions for a valid marriage were:

1. Age: twenty years for the man and eighteen for the woman (art. 3).
2. Consent of both parties and absence of any coercion (art. 4).

---

[14] Ch'en Shao-yü, Introduction to the 1950 Draft of the Marriage Law, in COLLECTION 277. Ch'en Shao-yü (alias Wang Ming) in 1950 was chairman of the Legal Committee, a committee for the drafting and interpreting of laws under the Central People's Government Administration Council. He introduced the draft of the marriage law into the Government Council on April 14, 1950. Wherever he is quoted in this paper, the quotation refers to this introduction.

[15] M. Meijer, *supra* note 5, at 89–91.

3. No consanguinity between the parties is allowed within five "generations"; that is, the eighth Roman degree (art. 5).

4. The parties should not suffer from certain contagious or mental diseases (arts. 6 and 7).

5. Registration and prohibition of marriage presents (art. 8).

The age of twenty for a man to marry has been mentioned as desirable in several traditional Chinese sources,[16] but commonly the parents would arrange marriage for their sons at an earlier age. It seems doubtful, however, that the legislator would let the traditional argument weigh very heavily. The consideration would be that at twenty a man could make up his mind, as could a woman at eighteen. To make up one's mind in this context meant to be free from parental domination and to be able to appreciate the teachings of the Party to select one's partner on the basis of "love." Counterrevolutionary partners can hardly be loved. The other element was hygienic.

The freedom of marriage expressed in Article 1 has been made a condition for a valid marriage. The prohibition of coercion found its sanction in Article 22. It referred mainly to parental interference, but anybody's interference could be covered by it. The article made love between the parties the only basis for marriage. Calculations of a financial character should be excluded, and this was emphasized by the prohibition of marriage presents in any form by Article 8. The fact that this prohibition was contained in the Article that required registration and not in that dealing with coercion probably meant that the registrar was to investigate whether presents had been given or not, and should refuse to register traditionally arranged marriages when they obviously impaired the freedom of choice.

The strict exogamy required by Article 5 seems a bow to traditional notions *(t'ung shing pu hun)*.[17] In fact, however, it was much more severe than the traditional prohibition and also excluded the marriage between so-called *piao* cousins and with relatives on the maternal side, which had been traditionally permitted.[18] One wonders whether this reverence for tradition was indeed so strong. Ch'en Shao-yü in his commentary on the draft of the law of 1950, which maintained the prohibition in mitigated form, also shows a remarkable respect for the intuition of the people for what is good for them. Curiously enough this intuition was considered in need of correction in 1934. The traditional concept of exogamy was related to the problem of succession. When a man was without male offspring, he had to choose a successor within

---

[16] CH'EN KU-YÜAN, CHUNG-KUO HUN-YIN SHIH (History of Chinese marriage) 129 (1936).

[17] S. SHIGA, *supra* note 10, at 28.

[18] *"Piao"* cousins are cross cousins, sons or daughters of father's sisters or the brothers and sisters of the mother. CHENG CHING-I, FA-LÜ TA TZU-SHU (Dictionary of law) 970 (1936).

the clan according to strict rules. Such a successor was legally presumed to become his son and, of course, could not marry his presumptive sister. Thus the rule of exogamy was meant to avoid confusion of ranks within the clan. There were also superstitious fears of intra-clan marriage. Respect for such notions on the part of the legislator can be safely considered unlikely. A more logical explanation for maintenance of this traditional prohibition seems to be provided by the distaste of the regime for the selection of a marriage partner within the circle of paternal or maternal relatives on the grounds of class consciousness and by the desire to avoid the collusion of clans through marital affiliations. This makes more sense than the ostensive explanation of respect for intuition or tradition.

The Family Code of the USSR of 1926, which in some respects served as a model for the Regulations, only prohibits marriage between relatives in the direct line of descent and between brothers and sisters, whether of the full or the half blood.[19] It would be difficult to see why the Chinese legislator would harbor such exaggerated notions of the evil effects of marriage between consanguineous partners.

The origin of these prohibitions should probably be sought in the legislation of the USSR and should be considered sound countermeasures against excesses, which were sometimes caused by the traditional duty of continuation of the line.

The function of registration in this system is a difficult problem. The fact that registration is not a condition for a valid marriage is expressly provided in the Marriage Law of 1934, Article 9: "In all cases of a man and a woman co-habiting, whether they have registered the marriage, they shall be considered to have contracted a marriage."[20] This means the recognition of *de facto* marriage as a fundamental principle. This principle was most probably also inherent in the Regulations of 1931. The Law of 1934 seems to clarify rather than correct the 1931 Regulations. The material available on the application of the law and the Regulations for this period, however, does not warrant any further comment.

Married life. The Regulations were silent on the subject of married life. The matrimonial property regime was not a subject that came within the sphere of regulation. The point of view seems to be that for an ordered society it would be necessary to regulate the conditions for marriage, but that the internal relationship between husband and wife should be left for the parties themselves to arrange. The obligations arising out of marriage were only regulated upon dissolution, hence the great emphasis on divorce and its consequences. The family was completely ignored in the marriage legislation of the Kiangsi Republic, and it may be validly argued that the regime then considered the

---

[19] R. Schlesinger, The Family in the USSR 155 (Art. 6) (1949).

[20] M. Meijer, *supra* note 5, at 89–91.

possibility of a society in which the family would occupy an insignificant position and would gradually wither away, leaving the State *in loco parentis* as far as the rearing and education of the children were concerned. These considerations were also the basis of the Family Code of 1926 in the USSR, although there the regulation of relations between husband and wife was definitely felt to be a task of the legislator.[21]

Divorce

Freedom of divorce was felt to be a corollary of the freedom to marry and was especially provided for in Article 10. The only required formality was registration, but it was nowhere stated that for this purpose the parties were required to go together to the *hsiang* or the municipal soviet to attend to the matter. However, it was made clear in several documents that the freedom of divorce should not be taken as absolute and be an excuse for morally loose behavior. If such misbehavior occurred, the party would investigate the matter.[22]

There were no conditions for divorce. It could be brought about by mutual consent or by the expression of the desire to do so by either of the parties, and it would have immediate effect (Article 10). The function of registration (Article 11) was not clear here either. The term to express the compulsory character is *hsü*, the same as for the registration of marriage, and it appears that this term itself does not convey the idea of a *conditio sine qua non*. However, it would be out of character for the regime to assume *de facto* divorce, since that would completely undermine the position of the woman, and the strengthening of the woman's position was one of the main tenets of marriage legislation. In later developments in the Border Areas and during the People's Republic there has never been any doubt regarding the constitutive effect of the registration of divorce.[23] There is no reason to suppose that a different view prevailed during the Kiangsi period.

Consequences of Divorce

The consequences of divorce were treated in chapters four and five. Chapter five dealt with the obligations of the husband after divorce. The general principle was that each took his own property and settled the debts he

---

[21] R. SCHLESINGER, *supra* note 19, at 155.

[22] And others referred to in the *Plan for Work Among Women, supra* note 4.

[23] As long as the divorce is not registered, a second marriage constitutes bigamy. This is made clear in a publication entitled "On Our Marriage Regulations" in the Border Area of Shansi, Ch'ahar, and Hopei in 1949. The publication is qualified as a directive and probably emanates from the Area Administrative Council. The passage that divorce definitely must be registered occurs in the third section, "Problems of Enforcement." HSIEN-HSING FA HUEI-CHI (Collection of laws in force) 231 (Administrative Council of the Chin-Ch'a-Ch'o Area 1945).

or she had contracted (Article 17). If the parties had managed the property conjointly for over a year and had made a profit, that profit would be equally divided between them, and if there were children the division should be per capita (Article 17). If the joint management had resulted in a deficit, however, the husband would take the responsibility (Article 18). The husband should provide his former wife with dwelling space in his house, if she so desired, and should sell her a part of it (Article 19). He had to support her or till the land for her until she married again (Article 20).

These arrangements showed a distinct preferential treatment of women. In fact they almost seemed to be an encouragement to divorce, at least if they were literally applied. I have not been able, however, to find any documents or other material on the application of these provisions.

The wording of Article 17 *(Nan nü ko tzu ti t'ien-ti, ts'ai-ch'an, chai-wu, ko tzu ch'u-li)* suggests that the matrimonial property regime envisaged by the Regulations may have been one of separation of property in principle with freedom of parties to make arrangements such as common management. This was also the arrangement made in the Family Code of the USSR,[24] and it was invariably so in the various Border Areas.[25] Only in the Marriage Law of 1950 is a different arrangement made, which will be discussed later.

The fourth chapter (Articles 11–16) dealt with the care and custody of the children after divorce. This is a matter which in the course of time has passed through many changes and experiments. In these Regulations the children were in principle entrusted to the man, being the economically stronger party. Only if the woman expressed the desire to rear them, could she have custody although infants would naturally be entrusted to her (Articles 11 and 12). Land obtained by the children during land reform would be retained by the children wherever they went (Article 13). When a woman had the custody of the children, the man was to pay two-thirds of their upkeep until they were sixteen (Article 14). If the woman married again, the new husband could if he wished take over the care of the children under her custody, and the father would be discharged from his obligation for partial support. The intentions of the new husband in this regard should be registered at the *hsiang* or municipal soviet (Articles 15 and 16).

In 1934 the arrangement was changed in that, as a rule, the woman would receive the custody of the children (Marriage Law, Article 16).[26] This to a certain extent reflects a changed attitude toward women in general. They were credited with more independence at that time, and the possibility of parasitism of the divorced woman was also lessened by the provision that the

---

[24] R. SCHLESINGER, *supra* note 19, at 156 (Art. 10).

[25] The publication "On our Marriage Regulations," *supra* note 23, refers to this. HSIEN-HSING FA HUEI-CHI 228.

[26] M. Meijer, *supra* note 5, at 90.

man had to support her only if she lacked the capacity to work and could not support herself, and the man was excused if he lacked that capacity (Article 15).

During the Border Area period the rules pertaining to custody of children were frequently changed. Sometimes the rule was made that children under four years of age would be taken care of by their mother.[27] At other times this age limit was raised to seven. In other areas the matter was made dependent on the preference of the child.[28] And, last, if the parents could not arrive at an agreement in this respect, the court would decide in the interest of the child.[29]

Illegitimacy

The Regulations of 1931 deal in Article 21 with the question of children born before the registration of their parents' wedding. It does not refer to the important problem of illegitimacy in general and therefore the article is somewhat awkward. If the parents were subsequently to marry, the simple procedure of legitimation would suffice to solve the problem. There would then be no reason to restrict the father's responsibility to two-thirds of the costs of rearing and education, unless the parents were divorced. Apparently there was some hesitation in the mind of the legislator to state clearly that illegitimate children enjoyed the same status as children born in wedlock. This must actually be the meaning of the article, which should be read as "when the parents, whether legitimate or illegitimate, are not living together in matrimony the children that can be proven to be generated by the man shall be supported by him to the extent of two-thirds of the expenditure of their rearing until they are sixteen years old." This anomaly was corrected in the Law of 1934 which states that "children born out of wedlock shall enjoy all the rights granted to legitimate children in this Marriage Law. To maltreat or abandon such children is forbidden."[30]

This provision goes much further than the comparatively mild attitude toward illegitimate children in traditional China.[31] It is a result of the distaste for illegitimacy in Communist doctrine and reflects the small value attached to the family at the time.

Criminal Law

The introduction of the criminal law into the Marriage Law in Article 22 is a permanent feature of the legislation on marriage in Communist-dominated

---

[27] M. Meijer, *supra* note 5, at 100, for Article 21 of the Chin-chi-Lu-yü Border Area marriage regulations of 1943.

[28] M. Meijer, *supra* note 5, at 94–95, for Article 12 of the Shen-Kan-Ning Border Area marriage regulations of 1944.

[29] M. Meijer, *supra* note 5, at 91, for Article 19 of the Chin-Ch'a-Chi Border Area marriage regulations of 1943.

[30] *Ibid.*

[31] S. SHIGA, *supra* note 10, at 247, 249.

areas of China. It is found in most of the Border Area regulations and in the
law of 1950. As far as I know this is a special Chinese feature of the Marriage
Law. In the various states of the USSR the criminal codes contain specific
provisions against what are called the "traditional offenses" such as purchase
of a bride, marrying before the marriageable age, and abduction with a view
to marriage. But I do not know of any marriage law in the USSR that contains
such a provision. The result in China is criminal conviction on the grounds of
contravention of a law belonging to private law—a confusion of public and
private law. For although the article maintains the fiction that there is a
criminal law, in fact, such a law does not exist. Except for an abortive effort
in 1957, when a draft of a criminal code was made but never promulgated,
the People's Republic of China has no general criminal law. Therefore, if
there were convictions on bigamy, for instance, the Article to be invoked in
1931 would be Article 1 of the Marriage Regulation. This reflects traditional
disregard of the difference between private and public law. It seems that all
written law is public.

Enforcement

An equally permanent featuie is the immediate enforcement of the Marriage
Regulations after the date of promulgation. The Marriage Law of 1950 also
contains such a provision in Article 27. Ch'en Shao-yü defended the need for
this provision by pointing to the ardent desire of the masses of women that the
law be immediately enforced.[32] The actual reason seems to be that since the
Marriage Regulations as well as the Marriage Law of 1950 were promulgated
as part of a series of laws and regulations aimed at the transformation of
society, it was as undesirable to provide for a period of transition as it was in
the case, for instance, of the Land Reform Law.

Review

Reviewing the 1931 Regulations, we may say that it was mainly a women's
law. Its avowed purpose was to "liberate the masses of women from the
shackles of the feudal family"[33] and, in fact, from the shackles of any family.
Provided she abided by the provisions of Articles 3–8, the woman could marry
when and whom she pleased, and divorce her husband, who would rear the
children, pay common debts, and provide her with a pension as long as she
did not marry again. She was even assured a roof over her head. One wonders
how far these exaggerated Regulations were accepted by the people and to
what extent they were simply meant to be propaganda "to activate the

---

[32] COLLECTION 297.

[33] *Plan for Work among Women, supra* note 4; C. BRANDT, *et al.,* A DOCUMENTARY
HISTORY OF CHINESE COMMUNISM 13 (1952); Mao Tse-tung, *Report to the Executive
Committee,* 1934, in K. HATANO, *supra* note 2, at pt. 4, 195.

emotions of the young women and to consolidate their revolutionary determination."[34] However, the extreme paucity of material on the application of
these regulations makes it impossible to give an opinion on this matter. The
revisions made in 1934, which clarify some of the points of the Regulations
and moderate others, may serve as indications that an effort was made to
enforce the Regulations and that in the course of enforcement it was felt that
some alterations had to be made.

THE BORDER AREA LEGISLATION

The legislation on marriage of the Kiangsi Republic contained many of the
principles that found their way into the Marriage Law of the People's Republic
of China of 1950. Even the wording in some provisions is almost identical. In
essence, however, the Marriage Regulations of 1931 and the Marriage Law of
1950 were entirely different statutes. The intervening period, the period of the
Japanese War, when the communists worked together with the Nationalist
Government, was a period of compromise. The Marriage Regulations that
were promulgated in the various areas under Communist influence around
and within the areas occupied by the Japanese army show a certain restraint.
One of the effects was that land reform was abandoned or at least restricted in
those areas, which caused mitigation of all other social reform. Another factor
may have been that in the USSR the attitude toward the family and its
regulation had appreciably changed to have its influence in China.[35] It would
not be feasible to trace the development of the legislation on marriage during
this period in this paper. No less than nine sets of regulations have been found,
and there were probably more. A common feature of all is that the concept of
feudalism is absent from the texts, as well as the terms "freedom of marriage"
and "freedom of divorce." However, in the commentaries which exist on some
of them, these terms are freely used. Some of these regulations devoted
considerable attention to the institution of betrothal,[36] and all of them
required the registration of marriage as well as divorce. But the interesting
characteristic of some of them is that they veer in the direction of family law.
They insist on the equality of husband and wife,[37] a concept that is entirely
absent in the texts of the Kiangsi statutes, although undoubtedly the ideal was
one of those aspired to.[38] Since equality of husband and wife referred to the

---

[34] *Plan for Work among Women, supra* note 4.

[35] The change is described by R. SCHLESINGER, *supra* note 19, at 235.

[36] M. Meijer, *supra* note 5, at 93, for Article 6 of the Shen-Kan-Ning Border Area
marriage regulations of 1944; and at 96, 98, for Articles 7–9 of the Chin-Chi-Lu-Yü
Border Area marriage regulations of 1943.

[37] This is more apparent in the documents explaining or elaborating on the regulations; among others, "On Our Marriage Regulations," *supra* note 23, *passim.*

[38] K. HATANO, *supra* note 2, at Pt. 4, 195 (1951).

situation during marriage, it was probably felt not to belong to the field covered by the Regulations of 1931. Another remarkable trait is found in the Chin-Ch'a-Chi Regulations of 1941, which contain some provisions on the relations between husband and wife.[39] The spouses retained their premarital property (Article 15); they had the exclusive right to manage it and to enjoy the income from their individual labor during marriage (Article 16). Any debts they incurred were their own. They could agree to common management of property, but then debts were also common (Article 19), and increases of property were common property (Article 17). Another important innovation was that henceforth divorce had to be requested and was dependent on a decision of the authorities.[40] It was no more simply a question of registration, as suggested by the articles of the Kiangsi statutes. A distinction was often made between *ex parte* application and divorce by mutual consent. In the former case some regulations required a judicial decision.[41] All these features show a remarkable improvement from legislation that seemed to suffer from propagandistic influences to a serious effort to deal with reality, although the reasons for the change may be partly due to frustration. The influence of the Border Area legislation on the final law of 1950, at any rate, is considerable.

THE MARRIAGE LAW OF 1950

General Characterization

When the final victory had been won, Communist measures to transform society were again introduced with full orchestration. Land reform, democratic reform movement, and a marriage law were among the first. On May 1, 1950, the Marriage Law was promulgated and the Land Reform Law followed on June 2.[42] The Land Reform Law was accompanied by "Decisions Concerning the Differentiation of Class Status in the Countryside" (August 4, 1950), which determined the position of any individual on an economic basis called his *ch'eng-fen* (in other words, his class background).[43] This background could be mitigated or aggravated in its effects by the individual's personal record, his *shen-fen*. In every judicial decision, whether of divorce or punishment, we

---

[39] Fukushima Masao & Miyazaka Hiroshi, *supra* note 5, at 68.

[40] M. Meijer, *supra* note 5, at 94, for Articles 10–11 of the Shen-Kan-Ning Border Area marriage regulations of 1944; at 96, for Articles 7–8, 13, 15 of the Chin-Ch'a-Chi Border Area marriage regulations of 1943.

[41] *Ibid.*

[42] A. BLAUSTEIN, FUNDAMENTAL LEGAL DOCUMENTS OF COMMUNIST CHINA 276 ff. (1962).

[43] *Id.*, 291.

find the definition of the class status of the persons concerned behind their names.[44]

The new Marriage Law has twenty-seven articles divided into eight chapters: I. General Principles (1–2); II. Conclusion of Marriage (3–6); III. Rights and duties of Husband and Wife (7–12); IV. Relations between Parents and Children (13–16); V. Divorce (17–19); VI. Maintenance and Education of Children after Divorce (20–22); VII. Property and Maintenance after Divorce (23–35); VIII. Additional Provisions (26–27).

One glance at the table of contents is sufficient to bring out differences with the Marriage Regulation of 1931. The greater part of the law is concerned with the family. Marriage is the foundation of the family, and the law not only provides for the conditions necessary to conclude and dissolve marriage, but it takes an active interest in the family that results from marriage. It intends to be a family as well as a marriage law.

When we look at the terminology of the law, we find that the term "feudal" has returned, and furthermore the terms "equality of the sexes," "equality of rights of husband and wife," and "equal status within the family" occur, combined with those of "respect," "love," "duty to support," "duty to assist," and even the term "inheritance" *(chi-ch'eng)*.

The Article that is most illustrative of the new spirit is Article 8 which reads: "Husband and wife are duty bound to love, respect, assist, and support each other; they shall unite in harmony, while working and producing, rearing and educating the children, and struggling jointly for the happiness of the family and the establishment of a new society."

Although the Article reads as a propagandistic speech, it clearly sums up the principles of the family that the regime wished to establish, and it is an elaboration of the "New-Democratic marriage system" that is established in Article 1 "based on the free choice of the partners, monogamy, equal rights for both sexes and the protection of the lawful interests of women and children." In fact, Article 8 states the purpose of the law. The spouses will form a family in the service of communism, a social cell with positive content.

This development followed the example of the USSR under Stalin[45] without merely being an imitation. In the Chinese context the anti-feudal element was still deemed indispensable, and still the law is called a marriage law and not a family law.

The fact that the law is still defined as a marriage law is very important. If the family relations are subsumed under marital relations, it would logically follow that if the marriage were dissolved, the existence of the family would be

---

[44] *See, e.g.,* Yün-nan jih-pao (K'un-ming), Jan. 25, 1953: The plaintiff, Ting Hua, was a rich peasant and the defendant, Li Min, was a middle peasant; both were seasoned "revolutionary workers."

[45] R. SCHLESINGER, *supra* note 19, at 295 ff.

terminated as well. In traditional China, the notion was prevalent that the relationship between father and children, especially sons, was a natural or even celestial union[46] *(t'ien-ho)*, and that between husband and wife was man made *(jen-ho)*. The father had infused his fluidum *(ch'i)* into his son, and after the father's death the son would continue his personality.[47] The family as a unit would survive after the death or divorce of the mother under the management of the father. The patrilineal family was perennial and would be continued artificially by means of legal fiction through the adoption of a successor, if there were no sons left. This, of course, was considered "feudal," and this type of family was exactly what the new law wished to abolish.

The insistence on the title of marriage law evokes the spirit of the Regulation of 1931; namely, that notwithstanding all the provisions that recognize the family as a unit, the true purpose of the law is to establish the position of women on an equal footing with men and that in fact this is the only purpose of the law. The recognition of the family is only of the milieu in which this equality may be achieved under present circumstances, but this does not reflect a positive attitude toward the family in the future. As long as the family exists it is preferable that it should fulfill a function in the establishment of socialism. As to its desirability in the future, the attitude remains at best ambivalent. This attitude is revealed in the publications on the family during the first fifteen years of the enforcement of the law. There is no negation of the family, but there are distinct shades in the attitude of support for it. At times, the harmonious family is extolled; at other times the family is hardly mentioned, and voices to abolish it are permitted a hearing.[48]

However, whatever the ultimate purpose of the policy toward the family may be, we now have to consider the actual contents and the way of enforcement of the law. The standard translation of the text is found in the Appendix to this paper.

General Principles

The first paragraph of Article 1 is reminiscent of the 1931 Regulations, but there are significant changes. The reasons for rejection of the old marriage system are given; that is, the meddling and compulsion *(pao-pan ch'iang-po)* of the parents, the superiority of the male, and the so-called disregard of the lawful interests of the wife and children. The New-Democratic system is characterized by freedom of marriage for men and women, the principle of one husband and one wife, the equality of rights of men and women, and the protection of the lawful interests of the wife and children.

---

[46] S. SHIGA, *supra* note 10, at 475.

[47] *Id.*, 124 ff.

[48] Chung-kuo ch'ing-nien (Chinese youth) (Peking), Oct. 28, 1958; and Jen-min jih-pao (People's daily) (Peking), Dec. 10, 1958, criticize this view.

Article 2 gives a list of forbidden feudal acts: bigamy, concubinage, the taking in of a foster daughter-in-law, interference with the freedom of marriage of a widow, and the exaction of money or goods by any person on account of marital problems (of another person). Such acts are forbidden and sanctioned by Article 26 "according to Law."

Thus among the general principles of the law the anti-feudal aspect is predominant. In the first three years of its application, it almost seemed as if the main function of the law were the destruction of the "feudal" family. Cases where husbands killed their wives, and foster parents their foster daughters-in-law; where widows forced their daughters into undesired marriages and drove them to suicide; and where a widow was killed because she wished to marry again and not continue living in the husband's family to honor his memory by preserving chastity were publicized. All these cases were staged with great publicity and the attendance of hundreds of people. They were called model cases. A staggering number of suicides were published to give an impression of the misery of women under the traditional system.[49] All the tricks of propaganda were employed to create the impression that the traditional family was an institution of the most barbaric savagery. This way of applying the Marriage Law as a criminal law coincided with the application of the land reform as a huge punitive expedition against former landlords. The bad characters in the marriage cases were often persons of landlord origin, who had sneaked into the new organizations and abused their new power.[50] Cases of a socio-pathological character were represented as characteristic of the old family system in order to discredit it. The theory of marriage by purchase and sale, although the text of the law does not refer to it, again appears and is often adduced by the courts.

During this same period of violence, however, tendencies are discernible that apply the positive side of the law as well. Such will be shown when we deal with the problems of divorce. There were in fact two distinct trends: one

---

[49] COLLECTION 293; Jen-min jih-pao (Peking), Feb. 25, 1953, in outline for the implementation of the marriage law.

[50] *E.g.*, a murder case found in HUN-YIN WEN-T'I TS'AN-K'AO TZU-LIAO HUI-PIEN (Collection of reference material on problems relating to marriage) 12 (1950). A revolutionary cadre became involved with a widow of one of the members of an influential clan in the village where he performed his function. The clan did not agree to this marriage and in collusion with the woman's own clan conspired and killed the woman. The head of the clan had posed as a revolutionary hero and used his power with the police and the militia to waylay and abduct the woman, after which she was murdered. A second example: A woman who was betrothed by her mother to a butcher fell in love with a member of the New Democratic Youth Corps. They had sexual intercourse, which was discovered. The man was cautioned by the Corps not to marry the woman. The woman was brought to the police station by her mother. The police jeered at her, and she went home and committed suicide. The man tried to commit suicide, but failed. Jen-min jih-pao (Peking), Sept. 17, 1950.

seeking to destroy the feudal marriage system granted every request to dissolve a marriage on that ground; the other trend attempted to preserve a marriage that did not smack of traditional relations and had a chance to develop in the desired way.

The first tendency, however, met with probably unforeseen difficulties in the economic field. These were difficulties that were due to the lack of intelligent personnel and to conflicting aspects of the policy. In this period, freedom of marriage and divorce, the latter at least for anti-feudal motives, were complementing each other. But since the woman had received land under land reform, divorce became a matter of utmost economic importance. For if a woman chose another husband, this meant not only the loss of the marriage presents, which still might be overcome, but also loss of the land she owned; that was a much more serious matter since it undermined the economic basis of the family. Therefore, the problem of divorce raised much more serious problems than merely the disruption of the marital life. It could mean a change in the economic status of the husband and a serious loss of social prestige. The cadres who had been in charge of land reform had often settled down in the district where this reform had been carried out. They were prepared for that task, and once the redistribution of land was carried out, they may have felt they performed a splendid piece of work. If they were capable and honest people, they may have felt that they carried out an operation which had its cruel side, but which at least left poor farmers better off than they had been before. Now, however, they were confronted with an altogether different set of problems with which they were not at all acquainted and which threatened to undo their work as economic reorganizers for reasons that were utterly beyond their grasp. No wonder they tended to ignore these women who upset their work by ruining the farmer's household economy. On the other hand, the women themselves were being awakened with the reform of their feudal husbands, and if they did not want to be reformed, a divorce from them was a revolutionary task. However, when they arrived at the proper quarters with their requests for divorce, they spoke at best to deaf ears and sometimes they were made to look ridiculous. The tensions thus created within the family may very well have been the cause of an irate husband killing the wife who desired to divorce him, while the cadre looked the other way, or of a woman who had finally decided to divorce her husband, but who took her own life out of sheer frustration and loss of face.[51] The Marriage Law seems to have become very unpopular at that time, and people called it a "divorce law." Cases of violence and suicide continued to increase, bringing about concern in the highest quarters.[52] Several attempts were made in the first place to

---

[51] The second case mentioned in note 50 is suggestive of this behavior.

[52] The attitude of the cadres toward women was severely criticized by the Ch'ang-chiang jih-pao (Nanking), July 5, 1950, in a report of the provincial government and the C.C.P. provincial headquarters of Hunan. Another report from that province is

educate the cadres. Thereafter, investigation teams were sent through the provinces, and as a last measure a grandiose movement was organized in 1953 called the "Movement for the Implementation of the Marriage Law."[53] It should be noted, however, that this movement was not launched before the land reform had been carried out in most of the provinces, and the period of initial violence had somewhat subsided. It may be said that at that time, the economic aspect of the feudal element in Chinese society had been basically eliminated.

This movement brought forth a last wave of anti-feudal divorces. The law was henceforth more strictly interpreted, owing to a kind of catechism which was issued by the Legal Committee in 1953.[54]

The time had come for making preparations for the first five-year plan, and cooperation with the USSR was proceeding smoothly. In the field of law, the Chinese looked up to the USSR for guidance. It is quite possible that this influence also resulted in a more sedate and legalistic approach to the question of marriage. At the end of 1953 and in 1954 we witness an interesting debate as to whether feudalism had been or had not been overcome in China.[55] The more liberal-minded scholars assumed that feudalism had been largely eliminated and that feudal thought was no longer a danger. The trend of thought that was of concern at present was primarily bourgeois thought. Capitalistic or bourgeois thought was a less formidable enemy and more apt to be corrected by education. The following years, therefore, are characterized more by a policy of education in the field of marital problems and less by violent mass manifestations in model cases. The trend persists in 1955–57, and comes to an end in 1958. In that year the mass movement of the Great Leap Forward

---

found in Ch'ang-chiang jih-pao (Nanking), Aug. 30, 1951. The first directive from the Central Government is of Sept. 26, 1951, Investigation into the Circumstances of the Application of the Marriage Law, given in COLLECTION 301–03.

[53] The directive of September 26, 1951, *supra* note 52, brought a collection of other directives in its wake from the New Democratic Women's League, the Ministry of the Interior, the Supreme Court, and the Ministry of Justice. Subsequently, investigation teams were sent out from October until December. A summarizing report from those teams appeared in the Jen-min jih-pao (People's daily) in the middle of 1952. This was followed by the directive of February 1, 1953 in which the Government Administration Council ordered the Movement for the Implementation of the Marriage Law. In that movement 3,470,000 cadres were mobilized, 20 million copies of propaganda pamphlets were distributed, and 2,726 formal examinations of cadres were held.

[54] This catechism contained eighteen questions and answers. It appears in COLLECTION 309–14.

[55] The debate was started off by the fact that "frivolous" divorce was so frequent, especially among the industrial workers who could not be accused of a "feudal" mentality. The Kuang-ming Daily and the Worker's Daily of the years 1956 and 1957 are full of stories of such divorces. The People's Daily still held on to the thesis that feudal thought was the main enemy. In fact, the difference of point of view seems to result from the fact as to whether the countryside or the cities were the focal point.

required all attention to and questions of marriage to be relegated to an insignificant place. After the introduction of the communes in the countryside, the question of the desirability of the family came to the fore. There were voices which stated that when the communes took care of the old people in "happy homes" and of the children in creches, the family would become superfluous.[56] The official point of view remained, however, that the family was still necessary. The marriage and family policy comes to the fore again in the socialist education campaign of the early sixties, only to become obscure once more with the advent of the cultural revolution. In the period last mentioned the voices of radicals were again heard who doubted the necessity of maintaining the family as an institution.

These various attitudes toward marital problems are reflected in legal publications and decisions in the different periods. Consequently, an article or a decision must always be viewed as a manifestation of a particular period, and it is doubtful whether an opinion voiced in one period is still valid a few years later. This narrow connection between the general policy and the application of the Marriage Law poses its problems and imposes the need for extreme caution in explaining the law. It is not an easy task to describe what a "New-Democratic marriage system" means in 1968. It is too early to draw definite conclusions, and one should keep in mind the period of 1950-53, when the general impression prevailed that the Marriage Law was a "divorce law" (although in reality the divorce rate seems to have been comparatively moderate even then, as compared to other countries that had gone through a war).

Conditions for Marriage

The conditions for marriage correspond to some extent to those of the Regulations of 1931, but there are notable differences.

The first article of Chapter II deals with free will. With the exception of members of the armed forces, one is free in the choice of a partner. Army men have to ask the permission of their superiors. Party members are free, but should consult the "organization."[57] In 1957 there was some criticism voiced on abuse of their position by Party superiors by preventing young members from marrying women of their choice.

The fact that a marriage had not been free before the promulgation of the marriage law was in itself no reason to request a divorce, unless the sentiments between the spouses had deteriorated or the husband had comported himself in a feudal or very bourgeois way such as committing bigamy or adultery.

Interference by anybody in the marriage of another person is forbidden. In 1951 a young man in Chungking was sentenced to two months in jail,

---

[56] Chung-kuo ch'ing-nien (Chinese youth) (Peking), Oct. 28, 1958.
[57] *Id.*, May 16, 1956 and April 1, 1957.

because he had assisted a schoolmate in finding a marriage partner and the girl had been raped by the prospective candidate.[58] The prohibition also extends, of course, to the traditional go-between. Yet the latter institution has survived it seems to a remarkable extent, owing to the fact that many Chinese youths are shy and still consider marriage a very important matter.[59]

The age limit is the same as in 1931, but the Legal Committee decided in 1953 that the computation could be in full years *(nien-t'ou)*, which may result in one year's difference with the computation from date of birth. This was done "in consideration of the actual circumstances in former times."[60] Whether this way of computation is still allowed seems questionable, since it is not mentioned in a handbook for registrars which appeared in 1963.[61] There, on the contrary, we find a warning to the registrars that the age limit is the lowest possible age to marry and that for the physical well-being as well as for the education of the nuptial parties, it would be preferable to postpone the marriage until the man is twenty-five and the woman at least twenty.[62] Later reports from China have reported that in the cities considerable persuasion is applied to postpone marriage until the age of thirty for men and twenty-five for women. However, if the parties definitely wish to marry when they are twenty and eighteen, they cannot be stopped. How far this basic provision is honored in the breach is difficult to surmise. We still find reports in 1958 that indicate people married at an earlier age than twenty and eighteen, and that cadres assisted in the ceremonies.[63]

An obvious difference with the 1931 Regulations occurs in the prohibition of marriage between collateral relatives. Article 5 follows the pattern of the Family Code of the USSR,[64] but adds that with regard to the marriage of collateral relatives by blood within the fifth generation (the standard translations state wrongly the "fifth degree") custom will be followed. This is in fact a very elastic provision. The handbook for registrars referred to above severely interdicts a marriage between lineal relatives and brothers and sisters, but it further reads, "well, if it is the custom not to marry within the fifth generation, then by all means follow the custom." And if it is the custom to marry *piao* cousins, the same advice is given.[65] I have only seen one case where

---

[58] Ch'ungking Ta kung pao (Ch'ungking), Dec. 7, 1951.

[59] Ho-pei jih-pao (Pao-ting), Feb. 8, 1957. The paper put in a good word for go-betweens who abided by the Marriage Law.

[60] COLLECTION 311, Question 8.

[61] Nei-wu Pu Min-cheng Szu (Ministry of the Interior, Division of Civil Affairs), TS'EN-YANG TSO HAO HUN-YIN TENG-CHI KUNG-TSO (How to make a good marriage registration work) 18–20 (1963) [hereinafter cited as REGISTRATION WORK].

[62] *Id.*

[63] Chung-kuo ch'ing-nien (Chinese youth) (Peking), Jan. 1, 1958.

[64] R. SCHLESINGER, *supra* note 19, at 155 (Art. 6).

[65] REGISTRATION WORK 11.

marriage between full cousins was refused *(t'ang hsiung-ti chieh-mei)*.[66] Moreover customs are liable to change with circumstances, and circumstances have changed considerably, so that I doubt whether after the anti-feudal period the provision is still of much value. Another question is, however, whether the custom is still alive in the countryside.

Registration

The registration of marriage and its function still constitute an important problem. As Bilinsky points out, registration in the USSR had been primarily instituted as an alternative for the church ceremony and had no constitutive force.[67] This attitude had changed by 1936, but what the attitude in China is, is not very clear. Ch'en Shao-yü in his commentary on the draft justifies registration as an expression of the concern the government feels for the important matter of marriage, which means nothing.[68] The People's Court of Southern Anhwei decided in 1951 that: "In general the relations between husband and wife cannot be decided according to the rigid standard of whether the marriage has been registered or not or whether a certificate of marriage has been issued or not."[69] This opinion was confirmed by the Supreme Court and the next year, once again, by the Branch Court of the Supreme Court for Southwestern China.[70] This means that dependent on whether the other conditions of the law had been fulfilled, *de facto* marriage was recognized at the time. A different opinion was severely attacked in the People's Daily in 1952.[71] The Legal Committee has given as its opinion that up to 1953 the neglect of registering the marriage was excusable, but that after that time "it is not as it should be" *(shih pu ying-kai ti)*.[72] An article on "Bigamy and Adultery" in the legal magazine *Fa Hsüeh* in 1957 recognizes as a valid marriage "any marriage concluded not in contravention of the provisions of the Marriage Law but where only the procedure of registration has not been fulfilled."[73] Among Japanese scholars this matter has been the subject of much controversy. Niida Noboru sees it "at present" (1961) as a measure to prevent feudal marriage (in which he believes). On the other hand, he states that it is a measure to establish beyond doubt the legal position of the woman in the

---

[66] WANG NAI-TS'UNG, HUN-YIN-FA CHIAI-SHIH WEN-TA (Interpretative questions and answer on the Marriage Law) (1951). This is a collection of cases taken from provincial newspapers.

[67] A. BILINSKY, DAS SOVIETISCHE EHERECHT (The Soviet Marriage Law) 13 (1961).

[68] COLLECTION 272.

[69] *Id.*, 342.

[70] *Id.*, 351.

[71] Jen-min jih-pao (Peking), Jan. 17, 1952.

[72] COLLECTION 312.

[73] Tung Ching-chih, *T'an ch'ung-hun yü t'ung-chien* (On bigamy and adultery), FA HSÜEH No. 4, at 36 (1957).

eventuality of divorce. "Without obligatory registration the provisions of the Marriage Law would have no backbone and the ideals of the law could not be realized." "Simple recognition of *de facto* marriage would probably entail all sorts of judicial snags, even assuming there was a basis for *de facto* marriage in China" (which there is not). However, the regime did not wish to promulgate a law and simply force people to accept it, thus trying to avoid the mistakes of the National Government. Still, according to Niida, the reference in this connection is not clear. The regime does not simply abide by external form, it wishes to recognize marriage as a social fact. Therefore, the attitude of the government is dualistic. The idea is that through education and persuasion the people should be brought to register voluntarily.[74] Personally, I believe, despite Niida's opinions, that registration has no connection with the validity of a marriage at all, for any registered marriage that is faulty in some other respect could be nullified. In principle *de facto* marriage is recognized, provided the other conditions have been fulfilled and the spouses are cohabiting and behave for all the world as husband and wife. Considering the tendency to protect the position of women, it would seem unreasonable to deny her the position of a *de facto* wife and the rights accruing from that status at divorce. The function of registration is that of a ceremony, an alternative for the old marriage rites and an act of allegiance toward the regime. By registration, a person accepts the government sanction of his marriage and shows his loyalty by voluntarily accepting its checks. As to checking the fulfillment of the conditions, the registration official nowadays is often the bookkeeper of the commune.[75] There is very little that is secret in a Chinese village. In the beginning there may have been some need for investigation, but now that the regime is so firmly established, it would hardly seem necessary. There is only some sense in a checking system in the cities, but there it is much more difficult. I believe that registration is much more of a psychological matter—"now we are married"—and a political manifestation, than an effective instrument of control. Incidentally, the cases where registration is refused these days seem to be almost negligible.

Betrothal and Marriage Presents

Traditionally betrothal *(ting-hun)* was a most important institution involving ceremonies and the handing over of marriage presents. The Kiangsi legislation is silent on betrothal, and the Marriage Law of 1950 does not mention it either. This does not mean, however, that betrothal was forbidden, but that it did not have any legal effect. A betrothed person who married one other than his or her fiancée was not punishable in any way. Besides that,

---

[74] N. NIIDA, CHŪKA JINMIN KYŌWAKOKU KONINHŌ (Marriage law of the People's Republic of China) 38, reprinted from SHIN HIKAKU KONINHŌ (a comparison of laws relating to marriage and divorce) (1961).

[75] Registration work 8.

Madame Shih Liang, the Minister of Justice in 1950, stated: "love between man and woman will not be protected by procedures like betrothal and it is not necessary that the law provides a legal procedure for it. . . ."[76] Still it remains widely practiced in China, and the *Workers' Daily* in 1957 commented on the institution. It stated that from a moral point of view, a person should not "talk love" to a girl already betrothed, except when the betrothal had been arranged for the girl by the parents, when as an anti-feudal manifestation such talk might have its merits. However, the paper concludes that even if concluded by the free will of the parties, betrothal "shall not be propagated."[77] It probably reminded the paper too much of feudal times. In 1964 it was stated that betrothal could be terminated by simple oral communication from one party to the other.[78]

Narrowly related to the problem of betrothal was that of the foster daughter-in-law *(t'ung-yang-hsi)*. This institution was mostly practiced by poor people in order to avoid expensive marriage presents and ritual.[79] A girl was taken into the house of her future parents-in-law at an early age and reared there. The many stories of cruel treatment by the future mother-in-law run parallel to those of young women and their hardships after marriage. In all Communist statutes in China this practice has been forbidden as the most blatant manifestation of feudal trade in children. It was undoubtedly a cruel institution, although when one remembers that it was sometimes an alternative to infanticide or starvation, it appears in a less damning light. Nor should it be forgotten that often the foster mother-in-law was the girl's aunt.[80] The cruelty stories were an important ingredient of the anti-feudal menu of the early fifties. We also read that in 1953 in Fukien 1300 of these girls were "liberated."[81] The question is, however, what happened to them? We find no examples of foster parents being punished for taking in such a girl, except in cases of cruel treatment, nor of parents who had given their daughters as *t'ung-yang-hsi*. The Legal Committee stated in 1953 that a *t'ung-yang-hsi* who was yet unmarried at the time of the promulgation of the Marriage Law could not be prevented from choosing a husband of her own free will.[82] That this fact was not appreciated by the family who had reared the girl stands to reason, and some of the murder cases may be attributable to the liberation of the *t'ung-yang-hsi*. The Legal Committee also forbade the foster family from lodg-

---

[76] Ta kung pao (Peking), June 16, 1953.

[77] Kung-jen jih-pao (Peking), April 25, 1957.

[78] HUN-YIN-FA WEN-TA (Questions and answers on the Marriage Law) 18 (Anhwei Provincial Court and Judicial Bureau, 1964) [hereinafter cited as QUESTIONS AND ANSWERS].

[79] H. FEI, *supra* note 11, at 51 ff.

[80] *Id.*

[81] Fu-kien jih-pao (Fuchou), March 10, 1952.

[82] COLLECTION 310, Question 4.

ing claims for the rearing of the girl or for return of the marriage presents, which probably made things worse. The prohibition was, however, a logical consequence of the freedom, which otherwise might have become illusory.[83]

By virtue of Article 13 the original parents were bound to take the girl back, provided they were still alive. Otherwise the prohibition of the institution had little value for the existing foster daughters-in-law.

The marriage presents formerly given at the time of betrothal were, contrary to the Regulations of 1931, not specifically forbidden by the Law of 1950, but a prohibition could be construed from Article 2, containing the prohibition of money or gifts in connection with marriage or rather "dependent on problems in marital relations." In fact, the official attitude toward marriage presents had to some extent been modified, and gifts provided by the future bridegroom to his bride as a token of affection were not forbidden; even goods provided by his family directly to the bride or her family, such as furniture for the house, were acceptable.[84] Only when presents were a condition for the marriage, could they be confiscated. In practice the interpretation was often faulty as appears from an article in *Fa Hsüeh* in 1957,[85] where the "divergent views" of legal cadre in this respect were ridiculed. It seems, however, that the cases of dispute over marriage presents arose when demands for their return were made; namely when the intended marriage did not take place; and it was especially then that comrades made rather erratic decisions. There is a booklet entitled "Questions and Answers on the Marriage Law," compiled by the Anhwei Provincial Court and Judicial Bureau in 1964. This booklet says that in "feudal times" there had been bad customs in connection with marriage presents. "In extreme cases" the presents "and the trousseau" formed a condition of the marriage. That is all. The text further criticizes expensive marriage ceremonies in the style of the old feudal landlords. Nowadays, the nuptial parties should be happy with a cup of tea and invest the money in the building of socialism.[86]

Consequences of Marriage

Relations between husband and wife. Article 7 defines the married couple as "companions" *(p'an-lü)* living together with equal status in the family. In the literature appearing in the early sixties the tendency can be discerned to read companions as "comrades," stressing the ideological consonance.[87] The term

---

[83] Jen-min jih-pao (Peking), June 28, 1950, Question 3.

[84] *Id.*

[85] Lu Yü-ch'i & Wei Huan-hua, *Kuan-yü tang-ch'ien hun-yin k'ai-li ti hsing-chieh chi ch'u-li yüan-ts'e ti t'an-t'ao* (Investigation into the nature of marriage presents at the present time), FA HSÜEH No. 5, at 32–36 (1957).

[86] QUESTIONS AND ANSWERS 19–20.

[87] This happens in several articles in Women in China and Chinese Youth throught 1962 and 1963.

"living together" is different from the living together of Article 9 of the Law of 1934. The term then used was cohabitation *(t'ung chü)* ; now it is *kung-t'ung sheng-huo*. The use of this term is significant, inasmuch as it evokes the image of the traditional saying "common dwelling and common use of property" *(t'ung chü, kung ts'ai),* applicable to the family.[88] The parallel is imperfect, but the family unit meant in this chapter of the law is of a much more coherent character than the types of family that have been suggested by previous statutes. It should also be noted that Article 8 places the family in the service of the establishment of socialism, an ideal which transcends generations, since in traditional times the formation of a new family by marriage meant the forging of a new link in the chain of generations. The new family is intended to be a nucleus of communism in which the communist character of society prevails, a matrix for the new communist generation, a small communist community, and a training ground of the new society where all citizens will live together in common property relations and where everyone as a member of the "big household" will have a right to be fed and educated from the common fund and will contribute his labor to the common weal. Although one should not stretch the parallel with traditional concepts nor exaggerate the similarities, the idea of the family as a mirror of the great society in the service of past and future generations is not entirely alien to the Chinese mind; what formerly was *kung ts'ai,* now definitely becomes *kung yu,* common ownership between husband and wife. I shall return to this aspect in connection with inheritance.

The free choice of occupation (Article 9) is an illustration of the equality of the married parties. It is everyone's duty to perform labor, and the labor of the wife in the household is considered of as great value as that of the husband in whatever occupation he is engaged. The social activities, of course, include Party activities. In some cases divorce was granted a wife from a husband who opposed the political activities of his wife, but a wife who objected to her husband's social activities could not be divorced, but should be educated.[89]

The new family is endowed with property, and for the first time we find the introduction of family property. Both parties, the husband and the wife, have the right of ownership (this is the meaning of the word "possession" in the standard translation) and management of the family property. The Legal Committee in 1953 prescribed that family property included:

---

[88] S. SHIGA, *supra* note 10, at 68 ff.

[89] The wife out of jealousy opposed her husband's free social contacts in the labor unions. P'ANG T'UN-CHIH, HUN-YIN-FA CHI-PEN CHIH-SHIH (Basic knowledge on the marriage law) 60 (1954). This small book contains many interpretative replies from the Shanghai Municipal Court shortly after the fall of the city. It was intended for overseas Chinese.

1. All property owned by the spouses before marriage.
2. All property acquired during the period of life in common, meaning:
   a. Property acquired by labor.
   b. Property inherited by either of the spouses during this time.
   c. Property belonging to the children (like land obtained in the land reform).
3. Property acquired as a gift by either of the spouses during marriage.[90]

This does not leave anything outside family property, except perhaps the trousseau of the woman.

There must be a considerable amount of material on this subject in the records of the numerous mediation committees, but we shall have to wait until it is released before we can have a clearer picture of the way this system works in practice. There is no scarcity of literature on the Marriage Law, but it is hardly the sort of publicity we would most like to have. The impression is gained that we are still confronted only with some sort of public law. What is published is only important for the State. Exactly where the rights of the individuals lie is often difficult to find out.

The Supreme Court stated in 1950 that when the spouses really led a life according to Articles 7 and 8, and were living a common life, it was natural that their rights would be equal. "If one of the spouses only wishes to squander (the property) to such an extent that conflicts arise, then the Law of the State shall protect the progressive party and to the backward party education shall be applied so that he or she shall adopt a serious attitude towards the management of the common property."[91]

The principle that comes to us in Chapter III of the Marriage Law is mainly that of equality of the husband and the wife, a principle that is also found in the provision of Article 11 allowing the wife to retain her own name, and in Article 12 giving the spouses the right to inherit from each other. To the latter provision I shall return later.

Parents and children. The duty to rear and educate the children of Article 13 is circumscribed by the booklet "Questions and Answers on the Marriage Law" (1964): ". . . that the parents strengthen the education of the children so that they become of good moral character and members of the society with high socialist consciousness. . . . The children should be taught to be loyal to their parents and to the socialist enterprise, they should love the Party, love the leadership, love labor, and love common production."[92] This preaching of a communist morality is very typical of the propaganda for the Marriage Law since 1953. The technique has been refined in the course of the years.

---

[90] COLLECTION 312, Question 12.

[91] Jen-min jih-pao (Peking), May 29, 1950.

[92] QUESTIONS AND ANSWERS 92–31.

One could speak of a communist *"Li chi,"* the teaching of *Li,* if we take *Li* in the broad sense of moral consciousness of the people. It is almost a kind of rarified Confucianism. The "study" of the Marriage Law that was propagated in this period is not a study of law, but of principles of communist morality by which the duties to society are emphasized rather than the rights of individuals. Love seems to be taught by law. Its counterpart is "struggle." The parents should also educate the children "in the fierce class struggle of the present society."[93] They should approach their task from the side of thought, virtue, and knowledge.

The same applies to the children's duty of supporting their parents in their old age. This duty stems from "respecting love on the basis of the fact that the parents have toiled for society, the collectivity and their children."[94] The inheritance from the parents "is their tradition of unselfish labor." The fact that the Party and the State nowadays support the old is no excuse for the children to neglect this duty, for the Party and the State have the duty to accelerate by all possible means the establishment of socialism; the fulfillment of the children's duty means supplementing this task of the authorities and is indirectly a contribution to this end.

The duty of the husband to assist his wife in establishing good relations with her parents-in-law is also mentioned in connection with this article, and there are many stories of progressive wives curing their parents-in-law of backward feudal thoughts and of other commendable activities on her part. One even cured her mother-in-law of insanity.[95]

Article 13 also mentions that it is applicable to foster children, which introduces the subject of adoption. Though it has not been mentioned in any law, there is no doubt that adoption has always been condoned by the Communist legislator, if only for socioeconomic reasons. Adoption in traditional China has been distinguished by two very different varieties. One is the adoption of a successor, which was a duty toward the ancestors to continue the line of generation. The child to be adopted in this capacity had to be male and had to be chosen according to the system of rank within the clan. If the man had died without leaving male posterity, the widow had to adopt a successor for him. The adopted child was bound to serve offerings to the spirit of the deceased adopter and to continue his personality, exercise his rights, and fulfill his duties, including paying his debts. Quite a different kind was also practiced in traditional China; namely, the adoption out of charity. The adopted child could be anybody's, and it could be male as well as female in that case. Such an adopted child had no right to participate in the division of the family property and was not a member of the clan into which he was

---

[93] CHOU CHIA-CH'ING, HUN-YIN-FA CHIANG-HUA (Discussions on the marriage law) 80 (1964). This is a small book intended for young people about to marry.

[94] QUESTIONS AND ANSWERS 31.

[95] Chung-kuo ch'ing-nien (Chinese youth) (Peking), Dec. 16, 1964.

adopted, but remained a member of his original clan and fulfilled the rites of mourning toward its members. He could be given the name of the adopter, but this did not make him a member of the latter's clan. Still there were provisions that under certain circumstances the adopted child could receive a certain part of the inheritance of his adoptive father.[96] The adoption out of charity thus created relations of inequality among the members of the household.

The Civil Code of the Nationalist Government, which did not recognize the ancestral cult, did away with the distinction of traditional law, and only one kind of adoption was recognized.[97] Yet in the countryside and in many of the established families in the cities as well, the old custom survived.[98]

The Marriage Law followed the pattern of the Civil Code. The institution of a successor to continue the cult was abolished, and one general type of adoption was accepted. The Supreme Court decided at some time before 1954 that an agreement between the former parents of the child and the adopting parents did not have to be in wiiting.[99] Annulment could be demanded by the parents of the child when the adoptive parents ill-treated or abandoned it, but poverty of the adoptive parents could not be grounds for this action.[100] In such matters the interest of the child should be the decisive factor for the court that had to handle such disputes. The contact between the child and its original parents should be the subject of a reasonable arrangement between them and the adopting parents.

The position of an adopted child was to be in every respect the same as that of a child born from the parents themselves. However, on account of the theory that the blood relationship between parents and children is one that cannot be altered in any way (*cf.* Divorce), the duty of supporting the physical parents remained, and the child apparently had two sets of parents whom he had to support. But his right of inheritance was limited to that from his adopting parents (*cf.* Inheritance).

The position of illegitimate children who "too are the revolutionaries of the future" and are not to be blamed for the mistakes of their parents is equalized with those of children born in wedlock. They have the same right to be reared and educated by their physical parents as children born in lawful wedlock and naturally, therefore, the same duties.

---

[96] S. Shiga, *supra* note 10, at 575 ff.

[97] M. van der Valk, An Outline of Modern Chinese Family Law 134 ff. (1939). This book deals with the section, Family, of the Civil Code of the National Government.

[98] Chung-hua jen-min kung-ho-kuo min-fa ts'an-k'ao tzu-liao (Reference material on the civil law of the Chinese People's Republic) 624 (1957) [hereinafter cited as Reference Material]. This is actually a second edition of Collection. Collection 359.

[99] Collection 359. At other times such a document was required, but the most recent development seems to be that it is unnecessary. Questions and Answers 31.

[100] Collection 408.

Divorce

The Articles 17 and 18 of Chapter V deal with divorce, while Chapter VI (Articles 20–22) and VII (Articles 23–25) describe its consequence for the spouses and children.

From the Border Area legislation stems the difference in procedure between divorce by mutual consent and by *ex parte* application.[101] According to the law (Article 17) the divorce by mutual consent is a comparatively simple affair to be registered at the government of the *ch'ü* (*ch'ü* is a subdistrict in the country or a ward in the cities; the order is roughly *hsiang*—village or combination of villages, nowadays generally synonymous with commune—*ch'ü*, and *hsien* district.) The official charged with registration was to verify that both parties were desirous of the divorce, that the appropriate measures had been taken for the care of the children, and that there was an equitable division of the family property. When these conditions had been satisfactorily complied with, he had to issue a certificate of divorce forthwith.

The procedure in the case of *ex parte* application was more complicated. The parties had to address their request to the *ch'ü* government, which tried by mediation to bring the parties together again. When this failed, it referred the matter to the district court, which tried to mediate again, and in the case of a negative result would grant the divorce and issue a certificate.

We shall pass over the inadequacies that occurred in the first years of the application of the law. The performance of the *ch'ü* governments in general, however, gave the Central Committee for the Movement on the Implementation of the Marriage Law in 1953 cause to propose that divorce by mutual consent should also be taken to the district court and be mediated.[102] In 1955, however, an Ordinance *(pan-fa)* on Registration provided that the arrangement of the law should be followed and the agency of first instance was to be the People's Council of the Sub-district or Ward.[103] During the period of the introduction of the rural communes, the administrative system was thoroughly affected. The *ch'ü* disappeared and were incorporated into huge communes, which subsequently were again divided into smaller units. The handbook for registrars, referred to earlier, which appeared in 1963, gives "a new interpretation of the spirit of the law" by the Ministry of the Interior. Henceforth, the Council of the Commune *(kung-she kuan-li wei-yuan-hui)* under the authorization of the District People's Council was to perform the task. In cases of divorce by mutual consent, the Commune Council is capable of handling the case, but it first applies mediation and "persuasive education."

---

[101] First introduced in the 1939 Marriage Regulations of the Shen-Kan-Ning Border Area. M. Meijer, *supra* note 5, at 91.

[102] COLLECTION 402.

[103] REFERENCE MATERIAL 581; M. van der Valk, *The Registration of Marriage in the CPR*, 16 MONUMENTA SERICA 347–59 (1957).

If you think that the parties give any indication that a possibility of resumption of marital ties exists, you must persuade them most strongly to make up their quarrel and not to divorce. If after serious reflection they are still determined to obtain a divorce, then you should assist them to solve satisfactorily the problems of the family property and the care of the children. When this has been adequately dealt with, you must according to the requirements of the Marriage Law permit them to divorce and issue a certificate to that effect.[104]

In cases of *ex parte* application, the same agency is approached. After mediating with negative result, the facts and findings of the preliminary procedure are referred to the Hsien People's Council. Mediation is done from the class point of view. The Hsien Council inspects these documents and may either refer the case back to the Commune, or if the preliminary investigation has been satisfactory, it may refer the matter to the Hsien Court, which starts mediating again. If in matters of registration of divorce the bookkeeper of the commune is also the functionary charged with this duty, he must be a versatile person whose class point of view is well developed.

The way of applying the Articles on divorce has varied in various periods. During the first years the tendency prevailed to grant divorce for any application that had an anti-feudal taste. Many cadres obtained a divorce from wives who "reeked after the countryside" and married educated women to add culture to their status—a decidedly bourgeois trend which was often criticized. Yet even in this period the rate of divorce seems to have been comparatively low (if the figures are correct, about 3.2 million in four years).[105] At the same time, there was a tendency to restrain divorce for other than feudal reasons, a tendency which became more and more pronounced after 1953, although the degree of severity of the courts seems to have been uneven.

With regard to reasons for divorce, the following may be mentioned: concubinage, bigamy, and adultery. The existing concubines could claim their right to be liberated. Concubinage was a "by-product of the feudal marriage system." However, there were some problems. The husband was frequently married to a wife whom he did not love, and, therefore, it was not easy to decide who finally had to be his partner. There was no prohibition against keeping a concubine taken before the promulgation of the Marriage Law, so in many cases the composition of the family remained the same, except that the concubine now became a full wife. Engaging in concubinary relations after the promulgation of the marriage law was equal to committing bigamy.[106]

---

[104] REGISTRATION WORK 26.

[105] Jen-min jih-pao (Peking), April 13, 1957. Ku Chou, *On the Principles Followed in Matters of Divorce Since the Promulgation of the Marriage Law,* CHENG-FA YEN-CHIU No. 5 (1956). The figure of 3.2 million is an approximation. For 1950 the figure of 993,000 is given. For 1953, the year of the great movement, 1.1 million; the figure for 1952 is missing, but should be about one million. For the following years the figure constantly declines: 1954—710,000; 1955—610,000; 1956—510,000.

[106] COLLECTION 339.

Adultery has often been considered a criminal offense, but since about 1956 the criminal aspect seems to be de-emphasized. The booklet "Questions and Answers on the Marriage Law" (1964) contains the following passage:

Question: Someone has asked: When either the man or the woman commit adultery, can the other party institute proceedings of divorce?

Reply: Husband and wife both have the duty to be loyal in love; if one party commits adultery, this means disloyal behavior toward marital love and violation of the Marriage Law. However, it does not mean that divorce has to follow. If either the husband or the wife have practiced such faulty behavior, the correct way to behave for the other party is to assist that party to recognize his mistake, to reform him (her) self resolutely and to treat marital love as something precious, to make henceforth a good job of marital relations. One should not so easily take recourse to divorce.[107]

Impotence is among the physical reasons for divorce, if it is medically declared to be incurable. This should not be confused with childlessness, which is not a reason for divorce. Venereal disease is a cause for divorce, but the same source as quoted above states that "of course the law does not force people to divorce. It is always possible to separate and assist each other to have the disease cured."[108] Incurable mental disease may be a reason. Deafness and muteness may be a reason for divorce, when life becomes unbearable for the other party. Blindness comes under the same category.[109]

Difference in education between the married parties is not considered a reason to divorce. The other party should be patient and educate his wife or her husband.

Unfavorable economic circumstances can never be a reason even if it is the husband's own fault.[110] Conviction for an offense is not grounds either; only counterrevolutionary crimes seem to furnish a reason for divorce.[111] The Ministry of Justice said in 1950 that it was not even necessary to hear the criminal; the Public Security officials could consult him on the question of property arrangements, if this were feasible.

Absence for a long time without any correspondence could be a ground for divorce, and a period could be fixed and made public to call upon the party who had disappeared; after that the divorce could be granted.[112]

The pregnancy of the woman prohibited the man from requesting divorce from her (Article 18). The question was raised in 1958 whether this Article 18 also applied when the woman was pregnant from adultery. The opinions were divided, but the last reply was that the Article did not apply.[113]

---

[107] QUESTIONS AND ANSWERS 43.
[108] Id., 42.
[109] COLLECTION 350.
[110] Kung-jen jih-pao (Peking), Jan. 12, 1957.
[111] COLLECTION 344.
[112] Id., 352.
[113] C. Tung, supra note 73, at 66; Y. T'ao & H. Wei, supra note 85, at 36.

In general, one may say that divorce policy is a means of proletarian character building. The Legal Committee stated in 1953 that "even though the mediation of the *ch'ü* or court was not successful, if the facts prove that both sides have not reached the stage where it becomes impossible to continue living together, divorce can still be refused."[114] In a *Fa Hsüeh* article an author proclaimed as his opinion that the parties were not to judge the possibility of continuing to live together. Such a decision could only be reached with the assistance of the people; that is, the court.[115]

Consequences of Divorce

Care of the children. The relationship between parents and children, being one of the blood, cannot be changed by divorce. This is the principle of Article 20. Ch'en Shao-yü in his commentary on the draft of the Marriage Law states that formerly the fight over the custody of children was a dispute over property rights. He discerned a tendency nowadays toward the idea that the party who had received the custody of the children was also the only party responsible for them.[116]

The fundamental principle of Article 20 means that the relationship between parents and children is not based on marriage but on blood. The relationship between a divorced parent and his child is the same as that of a natural parent and his illegitimate child. Basically there is no difference between the father and the mother of the child in this respect.

As far as awarding the custody of the children is concerned, the present law takes the position that the parents should attempt to reach an agreement. If they fail to reach such agreement, the court shall decide, based on the interest of the children. The interpretation of "interest" is made on the basis of the ideological correctness of the parents.[117] Only infants are invariably given to their mother, who nurses them. This is for purely physical reasons. Thus, if the mother has no milk, the provision (Article 20, last paragraph) does not apply.

The matter of support of the child is also dependent on the agreement of the parents or, failing such agreement, on the court's decision. If an agreement has been reached or a decision rendered, the child does not have to abide by it, but may ask for more. (Article 21, paragraph 3) This provision has probably mostly a propaganda value and refers to the situation when the circumstances of either parent have changed for the better.[118]

---

[114] COLLECTION 313, Question 14.

[115] Liu Yün, *On the Correct Understanding and Handling of Divorce at Present,* FA HSÜEH No. 3, at 55, (1958).

[116] COLLECTION 291.

[117] *Id.,* 362; Ku Chou, *supra* note 105. C. CHOU, *supra* note 93, at 99.

[118] COLLECTION 292.

Though the law does not state this, the parent who is awarded the custody of the child is to be the child's legal representative,[119] which may be of importance in cases of inheritance. Yet, from the principle that both parents retain the duty of rearing and educating the child, it would follow that the parent who has not been awarded custody still has a say in the child's education. The law does not provide for legal guardians of such children.

After studying these provisions on the maintenance of the children, the impression is that in fact the law only provides that the parents in equal measure are responsible for the children and that the child's ideological education must be assured as much as possible. As a curious phenomenon it may be mentioned that in the beginning it was often difficult to obtain payment of alimony from the divorced father for his wife and children. The employers were sometimes unwilling to deduct the amount from the laborer's wages, for fear that it would dampen his productive enthusiasm. Nowadays this device seems to be generally adopted.

Property arrangement between the divorcing parties. Divorce is accompanied by a division of the family property, which then apparently ceases to exist. The woman recovers, according to Article 23, such property as belonged to her before her marriage. The division of the rest of the family property takes place according to agreement between the parties. If no agreement can be reached, the court decides considering the following three points: (1) the concrete circumstances of the family property; (2) the interest of the women and children; and (3) the interest of production.

The text of the law seems to suggest that the interest of the husband is not considered. This, however, is not quite true, but there is a bias in favor of the wife, unless this conflicts with the third consideration.

Family debts shall be paid out of the property jointly acquired during marriage. If such property is nonexistent or insufficient, the debt shall be paid by the party responsible (Article 24).

The meaning of the articles is not too clear. The only principle that emerges is a preferential treatment for the woman whenever possible. Unfortunately, there are no cases that have come to our knowledge in which a clear picture has been drawn as to how the procedure is actually carried out. The divorce certificates are, as far as I have seen, extremely simple documents stating: "feeling has deteriorated" or "broken down," the parties agree to divorce; the court has taken cognizance of that fact and allows them to divorce; the children will be awarded to the woman; and the man agrees to pay alimony or the expenses for the rearing and education of the children. In one case (1964) he agreed to transfer the furniture of the home to the wife and children as their property, and it was stipulated that in case the woman should marry again the house would revert to the property of the man and the children.

---

[119] Ch'ün-chung jih-pao (Si-an), May 21, 1951.

In 1953 the Legal Committee stated:

... in general the economic condition of the woman in our country is not equal to that of the man, and therefore the man should in economic respects bear a somewhat heavier responsibility. When the economic circumstances of the woman are indeed more affluent than those of the man, she may also bear more of the costs of rearing and educating the children and she may also pay back the debts contracted during life together.[120]

In the beginning these Articles (23 and 24) may have been very important, for at that time the woman still could possess land, and the Articles may be explained as motivated by the desire that she should retain that land after divorce as much as possible without servitudes. Nowadays, the importance of Articles 23 and 24 seems to be reduced to matters relating to house, furniture, savings, and articles of consumption. The "Questions and Answers on the Marriage Law" of 1964 stress that at the time of the division of the family property after divorce "we must not partially only consider the interest of the woman and make compromises in an unprincipled way, the woman cannot, on account of the fact that her economic position is still somewhat lower than that of the man, make unreasonable demands." It is further stated that, "when we analyze the family property at divorce we must consider the principle of benefit for the development of production and we cannot in a mechanical way divide houses, trees, furniture, and tools for production belonging to members of the commune, as this would affect production itself."[121]

Article 25 deals with the question of alimony. Only when one party has not remarried and has difficulties in supporting himself or herself shall the other party render assistance. "The woman should be educated into earning her own living."[122] The way such assistance should be rendered is left to the agreement of the parties or the decision of the court. The assistance is not dependent on the reason of the divorce.[123] An adulterous woman should be supported as well. The support is a matter of an altogether different nature than the divorce itself, and alimony is only a means to protect those who are weak in an economic respect.

In general we may say of this section of the law that the principle is expressed that the woman and the children, because their economic position is considered weak, should be properly looked after, inasmuch as such is compatible with the interest of production; the way of achieving this is left to the parties, theoretically under the supervision of the judicial organs.

---

[120] COLLECTION 313. This principle still obtained in 1964. QUESTIONS AND ANSWERS 60.

[121] COLLECTION 295.

[122] QUESTIONS AND ANSWERS 58.

[123] *Id.*, 356.

Inheritance

Although the law only states that husband and wife and parents and children shall be each other's heirs (Articles 11 and 14), the matter of inheritance is one of the most interesting of the Marriage Law. First of all, the introduction of the subject itself sets this law apart from all of its predecessors; second, when dealing with this subject, it is possible to form some idea of the concept of the family in actual life and of the purposes of the policy in a concrete way. Moreover, there is considerable material on this subject, although it all dates from the period when the influence of the law in the USSR was still strong.[124]

According to the law there are only three categories of heirs: spouses, parents, and children. The Supreme Court has put these three groups of heirs in the first category for purposes of inheritance. It added another person to this category, namely, the person who had been supported for over a year by the decedent, thus continuing the idea of the family as a unit of mutual support.[125] In case the parents were still capable of work, they should, according to the Court, inherit after the spouse and the children. Behind the group of parents, children, spouses, and supported persons comes the group of brothers and sisters of the decedent.

In this important opinion given by the Court in 1965, it is stated that division in group one should be carried out in equal parts, but this was a guideline for internal use only—other considerations could influence the division. Differences in economic circumstances, considerations of the actual state of the family property, and reflections on the interest of production, all play a role in the actual division of the property. From these considerations one could conclude that the right to inherit only gives a certain status to the prospective heir. He is "in," but it is not specified what his share will be.

We shall consider the practical position of this group of heirs on the basis of the facts furnished by the courts and other material.

The Spouse. The spouse is co-owner of the family property; in case there are no other heirs, she inherits all.[126] If there are two or more "wives," former concubines, they share the inheritance in equal parts.[127] This simple situation, however, may seldom represent reality. Assuming that there are children, one might suppose that, as in the event of divorce, the woman first should take out of the estate the goods she personally owned before her marriage, that the debts would be settled out of the estate in so far as they were common

---

[124] SHIH HUAI-PI, LÜEH-LUN WO KUO CHI-CH'ENG CHIH-TU TI CHI-KE CHI-PEN WEN-T'I (A discussion of several basic problems of the system of inheritance in our country) (1957). Sections of this book can be found in COLLECTION 407–22, and in REFERENCE MATERIAL 585–636. For further material, *see* M. van der Valk, *China,* 5 LAW IN EASTERN EUROPE 297–364 (1961).

[125] REFERENCE MATERIAL 588.

[126] *Id.,* 594.

[127] *Id.,* 601.

debts, and that she would partake to an equal degree with the children in the division of the remainder. Of course, in traditional China the widow would manage the whole estate in the case of minor children, or a good portion of the property would be set aside for her as land to take care of her old age *(yang-lao-t'ien)*,[128] but that naturally was feudal. A decision was rendered, although it is not clear in what year, that the widow should inherit together with the children in equal parts. But whether "equal parts" refers to the whole family property or whether she was allowed to take out her separate property first was not stated. An argument that she may do so may be deduced from an investigation into court practice by the Research Bureau of the Standing Committee of the National People's Congress. The question posed there concerned what the widow could take with her when she married again. The courts applied three principles:

1.   The childless widow could take with her "part or the whole" of the property she had inherited in her husband's family. This depended on the "concrete circumstances."

2.   If the widow had children, she should leave part of the property she inherited and part of her own property behind in the husband's family for the rearing and education of the children. If she took the children with her, she could take both inherited and separate property.

3.   A widowed daughter-in-law could take her inherited as well as her separate property, but if the late husband's parents were poor, she might take "little or nothing" out of the inherited property, although her personal property was hers.[129] This is probably a case of "concrete circumstances."

The parents. The idea of the Supreme Court to allow the parents to inherit in the same category as the spouse and the children of the decedent, if they had no capacity to work, and in a lower category, if they possessed such capacity, hails from the USSR.[130] But if one reads the practice of the courts as reported by the Research Bureau quoted above, it appears that the courts do not make such a distinction, and they allow the parents to inherit in the first category. This is also the idea of a jurist, Shih Huai-pi, who wrote a thesis on the question of inheritance.[131] The courts, however, adopted another important criterion; namely, whether the parents had been living together with the deceased son, in which case they always granted the parents the power to inherit with the spouse and children. "Not to do so would not be in conformity with the customs of the masses."[132]

---

[128] S. SHIGA, *supra* note 10, at 415 ff.

[129] REFERENCE MATERIAL 594–95.

[130] *Id.,* 588; *cf.* also, J. HAZARD & J. SHAPIRO, THE SOVIET LEGAL SYSTEM 252 (1962).

[131] SHIH HUAI-PI, *supra* note 124, at 26.

[132] REFERENCE MATERIAL 602, 604.

The court practice to let the parents inherit equally with the spouse and children was subject to criticism by the Research Bureau, because the married daughters and sons usually lived apart from the parents, and because the inheritance of the spouse and the children should not be influenced by the existence of a parent. Furthermore, such an arrangement would place property in the hands of old people, which was not stimulating for production. Still another argument was that at the death of the parent, the property would be dispersed into other branches of the family. The Bureau advocated that the spouse with children should inherit all and the parent nothing, but the childless spouse should share with the parent.[133]

Children. Only in one case was a child denied the right to inherit; that is, when the relations between him and the parent had been bad owing to differences in political opinions.[134]

When land was still a commodity that could be owned by an individual, the right to inherit by married daughters was subject to acrimonious disputes. The Legal Committee had decided that claims from married daughters should be evaluated according to the following criteria:

1.   Whether the reason for claiming her portion was due to objective impediments to making the claims at the time of the opening of the inheritance. If a voluntary waiver could be construed, the claim should not be honored.

2.   The concrete circumstances and whether it would be difficult to make a redivision of the property.

3.   The evaluation of the concrete circumstances of the lives of the daughter and other heirs.[135]

Later other criteria were added; for instance, her portion would depend on her relative contribution through labor to the family property[136] and the time that had elapsed since the division of the property had taken place. The tendency was to ignore long overdue claims "in order to avoid confusion in society" and instead grant a certain sum by way of support *(chao-ku)* to the daughter, if she really needed it.

Adopted children took the same place as real children. The old successor to the cult *(szu-tzu)* was in many cases recognized by the courts as an adopted child, since it was still a living custom among the masses and had its use in the support of the old people.[137] In one case, the court even acquiesced in the recognition of a posthumously instituted successor; it was willing to construe the case as one of adoption by the widow and of voluntary waiver of her

---

[133] *Id.,* 611.

[134] *Id.,* 601.

[135] COLLECTION 407.

[136] *Id.,* 417.

[137] REFERENCE MATERIAL 624.

inheritance rights by the daughter of the decedent.[138] In practice there was a good amount of wrangling over an inheritance between daughters and nephews of the deceased, since the latter still felt they had a right to become the heirs of the sonless uncle.[139]

There was a tendency to deny the (widowed) daughters-in-law inheritance from their parents-in-law, but if she had been living with them and had supported them in their old age, she was considered qualified.[140] A similar attitude was taken toward the son-in-law who had married into his wife's family *(chui-fu* or *chao-fu)*, although in his case he was allowed a compensation for having contributed to the family property by his labor rather than an inheritance.[141] Nor do adopted children as a rule inherit from their natural parents, but only from their adoptive ones. Only in cases of need could they be supported *(chao-ku)* from the estate of their natural parents.[142] It has been pointed out that the adopted child retains the duty to take care of his own parents, so that the construction of rights of inheritance as a sort of compensation for the support rendered to the decedent would not apply. But the notion of the family as a unit of mutual support and mutual rights of inheritance could still be maintained, and this would exclude persons who had not been working members of the social cell.

Brothers and sisters. In the absence of nearer relatives the practice is to allow brother and sisters to inherit from each other, provided there had been relations of support. This would probably refer to the case where the brothers and sisters had continued to live together in a family of a type known as *"Fuku-go-kei no ka"* by Shiga.[143]

Distant relatives. Even distant relatives are not excluded from the inheritance, provided there had been relations of mutual aid and support between them and the decedent. This probably refers mostly to nephews who were traditionally bound to pay the funeral expenses for uncles to whom they naturally would succeed. But that act alone did not entitle them to inherit, since they could be compensated from the estate.[144]

Escheat. The policy seems to have been to avoid escheat as much as possible. Shih Huai-pi devoted interesting meditations on the subject,[145] but it seems doubtful whether they were ever put in practice. A more appropriate agency to inherit than the State would seem to be the commune, and in practice it seems that people who have been supported by the commune under the principle

---

[138] COLLECTION 409.

[139] REFERENCE MATERIAL 605.

[140] *Id.,* 609; COLLECTION 414, 416.

[141] COLLECTION 418.

[142] *Id.,* 410.

[143] S. SHIGA, *supra* note 10, at 235 ff.

[144] REFERENCE MATERIAL 603.

[145] SHIH HUAI-PI, *supra* note 124, at 49.

of the "five guarantees"[146] would also have the commune as their heir. Sometimes fierce disputes developed between other heirs (whether heirs at law or those by will) and the commune. Shih Huai-pi, whose book dates from the time of the cooperatives before the institution of the communes, states that in disputes between heirs and cooperatives in the provinces of Hu-pei, Ho-pei, and Ho-nan the principle was adopted that if the decedent had been supported by the cooperative for a long time[147] and the funeral expenses had been borne by it, the estate would go to the cooperative; persons who had assisted the decedent during his illness would be compensated. If there were heirs at law, they would inherit, but they should compensate the cooperative for its expenses, and the contributions of the decedent to the commune were not reclaimable.[148]

Review. From the material it seems clear that the heirs are in the first place the members of the family, which is seen as a unit of common work and mutual support, a unit of "rearing the young and supporting the old" as Shih Huai-pi is fond of observing. As Shih's opinion is colored by his socialist ideals, he is probably more representative of the trend after 1958 than are the other sources. The family is a working community in the service of socialism and should fulfill a socialist task of working and producing, and its members should enjoy the benefits gained in the process. According to Shih, inheritance laws should be based on the following principles:

1. Protection of the property rights of the citizens.

2. Consolidation of the citizen's family—the inheritance law should be beneficial to the unity within the citizen's family. In order to achieve the latter objective it is not only necessary to determine exactly the circle of heirs and to include his linear and collateral relatives, but also to practice the principle of equal division between heirs of the same category. However, it is also necessary to consider the relationship of mutual support and maintenance of the old and the young that existed between the decedent and the heir, and the circumstances under which the heirs are living. It is necessary that the division of the estate should take place in the spirit of mutual assistance. If this cannot be achieved by agreement, the courts shall render a decision based on that principle, under which a solution will be found by means of common property, compromise, and mutual compensation.

3. The principle of equality of the sexes.

---

[146] The Five Guarantees refer to five categories of people who will be supported by the cooperative (or commune). They are: the aged, the weak, the orphaned, the widows, and the disabled. *Cf.* A. BLAUSTEIN, *supra* note 42, at 436, for Article 53 of the Model Regulations for Advanced Agricultural Cooperatives.

[147] *Id.,* 46.

[148] *Id.,* 46.

4. The principle of combining relations of blood, marriage, and those of social mutual assistance and love. This principle is related to the freedom of making a will. As long as the will does not interfere with the relationship of support existing between the decedent and the heirs at law, the freedom of making a will can be recognized.[149]

Shih Huai-pi was a legal scholar who was under strong influence of the USSR (1958). Some of his ideas, for instance, to include the supported person among the heirs, stem from there and do not reflect Chinese court practice, although his wide interpretation of the notion of support or care *(chao-ku)* may perhaps be linked with traditional tendencies. His book was written at a time when the compilation of a civil code for the CPR was considered.

In the newer literature on the Marriage Law the question of inheritance receives little attention. The "Discussions on the Marriage Law," *(Hun-yin-fa chiang-hua)*, a publication of the Chinese Youth Publishing Company of 1964, written by Chou Chia-ts'ing, hardly mentions the subject. The earlier quoted "Questions and Answers on the Marriage Law" only stated that the article brings out the equality of husband and wife and that since they have the duty of mutual assistance, mutual inheritance is a logical corollary.[150] It is perhaps possible that as the objects to be inherited become of lesser importance, the notion of inheritance itself is paid less attention. Particularly in the most recent years, it would seem that litigation regarding rights of inheritance would indicate bourgeois flaws and reflect an undesirable attitude.

Yet, in view of the fact that in the newer literature, the justification of the institution of inheritance is considered as a corollary of the duty of support, it seems safe to assume that the family is still regarded as an institution of which the main duty is to rear the young and support the old, and that in this way it contributes to the building of socialism. It relieves the State of that duty for which it is not yet sufficiently equipped. The institution of inheritance serves to insure that the possessions of the deceased member of the family go to his spouse and linear relatives, not as a concession to tradition, but as a means of keeping the family as a unit of persons between whom the duty of support exists. This consideration is also the basis of decisions to allow other relatives with whom the decedent had lived to inherit from him as a stimulus to the principle of mutual assistance. This principle is considered a valuable asset to society.

GENERAL REVIEW AND CONCLUSIONS

Perhaps there has never been written so much about any marriage law in the world as that of the People's Republic of China. Thousands of newspaper articles and millions of propaganda pamphlets have been devoted to it. Some

---

[149] *Id.*, 6–24.
[150] QUESTIONS AND ANSWERS.

three million cadres were mobilized to implement the law in 1953. To conclude that nowadays the Chinese on the mainland are an extremely legalistically minded people, however, would be erroneous. By far the greater part of the propaganda material was not directed at making the people aware of their rights, but at their political and moral education. The law undoubtedly provides women with rights which they did not enjoy under the traditional system. It places the women on an equal footing with the men, and it establishes safeguards for her economic position, which although still lower than that of the man, is not a handicap to her full development as an economically independent member of society. As long as the State or social organizations are not able to obviate the difficulties resulting from this inferior position, the man must continue to shoulder that burden, pay alimony to his wife when she is divorced, and contribute to the expenses of rearing and educating the children. In the final analysis the man in performing this duty is assisting the State in the establishment of socialism.

The family is seen as an institution which bears the duty of relieving the State of the task of rearing the young and supporting the old. It is a unit of which the members are pledged to assist each other. This mutual assistance is a valuable asset from the point of view of the State. The traditional feeling of family solidarity, which was so strong in China, must now serve a different cause. The family, however, should not replace society. There is the propagation of the idea that the "small family" should not absorb all the energy of its members, particularly the women, but that they must perform their duties therein as part of their obligations toward the "Big Family"; that is, society.

The duties of the citizen are reflected in the duties of the members of the family toward each other. In this respect, the family is a preparatory school for society and one's conduct within the family is held characteristic of one's behavior in society and, therefore, a matter of great interest to the State.

Thus, the Marriage Law in the first place gives rules for proper behavior, and as such it is studied and propagated. The rights that are accorded to the woman are provided so that she can develop as a full working member of society, devoting her talents in an unhampered way to the building of socialism. Any interference with these rights by parents or husband is not only an infringement on the woman's individual rights, but is also in direct conflict with the State's policy and detrimental to the development of society. The background of the safeguards of the interests of women and children is the furtherance of the political aims of the regime. The law, therefore, has a didactic purpose, which is clearly revealed in the decisions of the judiciary and the conciliation committees.

The study of the Marriage Law is a study, not of law, but of communist morality. Love, on which marriage and family are based, is communist love. Divorce should be primarily on ideological grounds and have an educative slant. The principle of behavior within the family is mutual help in thought struggle and education in the "fierce class struggle." It is a new sort of education in moral values with its technique reminiscent of the old Confucian teachings of *Li;* it is the establishment of a new morality among the people.

If we accept this propaganda, we run the risk of judging present day Chinese society as traditional society had been judged, on the basis of the study of *Li*, the Confucian rules of proper behavior. It would amount to accepting the Classic of Filial Piety as a yardstick for the behavior of the common people in pre-revolutionary days, and ignoring their daily customs and rules by which they ordinarily abided in their life. For the assessment of the legal life of traditional China it is not advisable to ignore the notions of morality that were then alive, and therefore it is not advisable either to ignore the moral and political values which the regime now tries to inculcate. However, it is a different matter to accept them as standards.

The turbulent times in China and the fact that the real situation, the way the people live and their present notions of what their rights are, is largely concealed, make it extremely difficult to assess the real application of the Marriage Law and to form a clear idea of the way in which its provisions are being applied. There is no doubt still, as referred to in the report of the Research Bureau on inheritance, a good deal of confusion among those who are in charge of the application of the law. However, when we read divorce decrees, they are comparatively simple documents, stating, for instance, that Mr. *X* and Mrs. *Y* have divorced because their sentiments did not allow them to continue living together, and indicating some clear and uncomplicated rules about the expenses of rearing the children and often about the occupation of the house, if it was private property. In one case, the house was allotted to the woman. It was provided, however, that if she married again, the house would again revert to the man's side and be common property between himself and the children. (The husband was an Overseas Chinese.) Both parties were perfectly satisfied with this arrangement.

Such documents are, however, seldom seen. And the scarcity of such material makes it impossible to assess the impact of the law. Judicial work, as it is called, is considered of great importance by the regime, and it would seem possible that at some time in the future more material may be released which would shed light on the actual application of the law with respect to property rights, division of family property, and inheritance. Until such time, one should reserve one's judgment on the impact of the law in this respect.

APPENDIX

THE MARRIAGE LAW OF THE PEOPLE'S REPUBLIC OF CHINA

CHAPTER I
GENERAL PRINCIPLES

Article 1

The feudal marriage system which is based on arbitrary and compulsory arrangements and the superiority of man over woman and ignores the children's interests shall be abolished.

The New-Democratic marriage system, which is based on the free choice of partners, on monogamy, on equal rights for both sexes, and on the protection of the lawful interests of women and children, shall be put into effect.

Article 2

Bigamy, concubinage, child betrothal, interference with the re-marriage of widows, and the exaction of money or gifts in connection with marriages, shall be prohibited.

CHAPTER II
THE MARRIAGE CONTRACT

Article 3

Marriage shall be based upon the complete willingness of the two parties. Neither party shall use compulsion and no third party shall be allowed to interfere.

Article 4

A marriage can be contracted only after the man has reached 20 years of age and the woman 18 years of age.

Article 5

No man or woman shall be allowed to marry in any of the following instances:

a) Where the man and woman are lineal relatives by blood or where the man and woman are brother and sister born of the same parents or where the man and woman are half-brother and half-sister. The question of prohibiting marriage between collateral relatives by blood (up to the fifth degree of relationship) is to be determined by custom.

b) Where one party, because of certain physical defects, is sexually impotent.

c) Where one party is suffering from venereal disease, mental disorder, leprosy or any other disease which is regarded by medical science as rendering a person unfit for marriage.

Article 6

In order to contract a marriage, both the man and the woman shall register in person with the people's government of the district or hsiang in which they reside. If the marriage is found to be in conformity with the provisions of this Law, the local people's government shall, without delay, issue marriage certificates.

If the marriage is not found to be in conformity with the provisions of this Law, registration shall not be granted.

CHAPTER III
RIGHTS AND DUTIES OF HUSBAND AND WIFE

Article 7

Husband and wife are companions living together and shall enjoy equal status in the home.

Article 8

Husband and wife are in duty bound to love, respect, assist and look after each other, to live in harmony, to engage in productive work, to care for the children and to strive jointly for the welfare of the family and for the building up of the new society.

Article 9

Both husband and wife shall have the right to free choice of occupation and free participation in work or in social activities.

Article 10

Both husband and wife shall have equal rights in the possession and management of family property.

Article 11

Both husband and wife shall have the right to use his or her own family name.

Article 12

Both husband and wife shall have the right to inherit each other's property.

CHAPTER IV
RELATIONS BETWEEN PARENTS AND CHILDREN

Article 13

Parents have the duty to rear and to educate their children; the children have the duty to support and to assist their parents. Neither the parents nor the children shall maltreat or desert one another.

The foregoing provisional so applies to foster-parents and foster-children. Infanticide by drowning and similar criminal acts are strictly prohibited.

Article 14

Parents and children shall have the right to inherit one another's property.

Article 15

Children born out of wedlock shall enjoy the same rights as children born in lawful wedlock. No person shall be allowed to harm them or discriminate against them.

Where the paternity of a child born out of wedlock is legally established by the mother of the child or by other witnesses or by other material evidence, the identified father must bear the whole or part of the cost of maintenance and education of the child until the age of 18.

With the consent of the mother, the natural father may have custody of the child.

With regard to the maintenance of a child born out of wedlock, in case its mother marries, the provisions of Article 22 shall apply.

Article 16

Husband or wife shall not maltreat or discriminate against children born of a previous marriage.

CHAPTER V

DIVORCE

Article 17

Divorce shall be granted when husband and wife both desire it. In the event of either the husband or the wife alone insisting upon divorce, it may be granted only when mediation by the district people's government and the judicial organ has failed to bring about a reconciliation.

In cases where divorce is desired by both husband and wife, both parties shall register with the district people's government in order to obtain divorce certificates. The district people's government, after establishing that divorce is desired by both parties and that appropriate measures have been taken for the care of children and property, shall issue the divorce certificates without delay.

When only one party insists on divorce, the district people's government may try to effect a reconciliation. If such mediation fails, it shall, without delay, refer the case to the county or municipal people's court for decision. The district people's government shall not attempt to prevent or to obstruct either party from appealing to the county or municipal people's court. In dealing with a divorce case, the county or municipal people's court must, in the first instance, try to bring about a reconciliation between the parties. In case such mediation fails, the court shall render a verdict without delay.

In the case where, after divorce, both husband and wife desire the resumption of marital relations, they shall apply to the district people's government for a registration of re-marriage. The district people's government shall accept such a registration and issue certificates of re-marriage.

Article 18

The husband shall not apply for a divorce when his wife is with child. He may apply for divorce only one year after the birth of the child. In the case of a woman applying for divorce, this restriction does not apply.

Article 19

The consent of a member of the revolutionary army on active service who maintains correspondence with his or her family must first be obtained before his or her spouse can apply for divorce.

Divorce may be granted to the spouse of a member of the revolutionary army who does not correspond with his or her family for a subsequent period of two years from the date of the promulgation of this Law. Divorce may also be granted to the spouse of a member of the revolutionary army who had not maintained correspondence with his or her family for over two years before the promulgation of this Law and who fails to correspond with his or her family for a further period of one year subsequent to the promulgation of the present Law.

CHAPTER VI

MAINTENANCE AND EDUCATION OF CHILDREN AFTER DIVORCE

Article 20

The blood ties between parents and children do not end with the divorce of the parents. No matter whether the father or the mother acts as guardian of the children, they still remain the children of both parties.

After divorce, both parents still have the duty to support and educate the children.

After divorce the guiding principle is to allow the mother to have custody of a baby still being breast-fed. After the weaning of the child, if a dispute arises between the two parties over the guardianship and an agreement cannot be reached, the people's court shall render a decision in accordance with the interests of the child.

Article 21

If, after divorce, the mother is given custody of a child, the father shall be responsible for the whole or part of the necessary cost of the maintenance and education of the child. Both parties shall reach an agreement regarding the amount and the duration of such maintenance and education. In the case where the two parties fail to reach an agreement, the people's court shall render a decision.

Payment may be made in cash, in kind or by tilling land allocated to the child.

Such agreement reached between parents or a decision rendered by the people's court in connection with the maintenance and education of a child shall not prevent the child from requesting either parent to increase the amount decided upon by agreement or by judicial decision.

Article 22

In the case where a divorced woman re-marries and her husband is willing to pay the whole or part of the cost of maintaining and educating the child or children by her former husband, the father of the child or children is entitled to have the cost of maintenance and education reduced or to be exempted from bearing such cost in accordance with the circumstances.

CHAPTER VII

PROPERTY AND MAINTENANCE AFTER DIVORCE

Article 23

In case of divorce, the wife shall retain such property as belonged to her before her marriage. The disposal of other family properties shall be subject to agreement between the two parties. In cases where agreement cannot be reached, the people's court shall render a decision after taking into consideration the actual state of the family property, the interests of the wife and the child or children, and the principle of benefiting the development of production.

In cases where the property allocated to the wife and her child or children is sufficient for the maintenance and education of the child or children, the husband may be exempted from bearing further maintenance and education costs.

Article 24

After divorce, debts incurred during the period of their married life together shall be paid out of the property jointly acquired by husband and wife during this period. In cases where no such property has been acquired or in cases where such property is insufficient to pay off such debts, the husband shall be held responsible for paying these debts. Debts incurred separately by the husband or wife shall be paid off by the party responsible.

Article 25

After divorce, if one party has not re-married and has maintenance difficulties, the other party shall render assistance. Both parties shall work out an agreement with regard to the method and duration of such assistance; in case an agreement cannot be reached, the people's court shall render a decision.

CHAPTER VIII
BY-LAWS

Article 26

Persons violating this Law shall be punished in accordance with law. In cases where interference with the freedom of marriage has caused death or injury the person guilty of such interference shall bear responsibility for the crime befoi e the law.

Article 27

This Law shall come into force from the date of its promulgation. In regions inhabited by national minorities, the people's government (or the Military and Administrative Committee) of the Greater Administrative Area or the provincial people's government may enact certain modifications or supplementary articles in conformity with the actual conditions prevailing among national minorities in regard to marriage. But such measures must be submitted to the Government Administration Council for ratification before enforcement.

PART V
COMPARATIVE DEVELOPMENTS

Remarks on Family Law Change in Post-Revolutionary Indonesia

DANIEL S. LEV

In these brief comments I want to discuss some sources of change in Indonesian family law since 1945. The principal tendencies of such change are not unique to Indonesia, and some of my points can, I think, be applied equally well to other countries in Asia and Africa. What is unique, as must be, are the pace and specific issues of change.

As we have been mainly concerned with China and Taiwan in this volume, it is probably worthwhile to point out some distinctions relevant to legal change between those countries and countries like Indonesia. In the first place, modern Indonesia is culturally more heterogeneous than China and has not had so long and relatively consistent a history. The shared experience of most Indonesian ethnic groups has been limited to colonialism and, now, the turbulent history of the independent state. Second, ethnic, religious, and geopolitical diversity has made it exceedingly difficult for Indonesia to establish the kind of powerful, centralized bureaucratic state common to both ancient and modern Chinese history. As effective power does not exist at the center, in Jakarta, formal legal development in independent Indonesia has therefore been haphazard. Apart from inability to enforce legislation consistently, religious cum political conflict has indeed made legislative bodies impotent to enact new statutes in so delicate a matter as family law. The result so far has been that the primary institutional focus of family law change is by default in the judiciary, which, though politically weak, has been able to bring new trends of legal thought to bear on these matters.

These new trends derive largely from ideological concerns of Indonesian leaders and can be summed up under the headings "integration" and, as a sub-theme, "modernization." Anxiety to achieve some workable unification of the country has had both institutional and substantive legal consequences. Soon after the revolution the national judicial system was established through-

out Indonesia at the expense of local customary *(adat)* courts, thus extending
everywhere an institutional transmission belt for new national legal ideas.
At about the same time, the Supreme Court started to send down signals of a
distinctly uniformizing kind. During the colonial period the Dutch had
developed local *adat* law jurisprudence to a remarkable degree and had also
evolved an intricate system of conflicts rules to accommodate inter-ethnic and
inter-communal transactions. These began to give way fairly early after
independence in the jurisprudence of the Supreme Court, though not without
some tension that reflected the binding power of older law myths—particularly
that of "to each culture group its own law." The older judicial base of *adat*
law having disappeared, the first instance national courts *(pengadilan negeri)*
now serve something of a particularizing function and as a buffer between
local and national law views, but they are restricted by the national judicial
hierarchy and, moreover, by ideological influences on the national educated
elite of which judges are part.

These influences have helped to determine the content of such new family
jurisprudence as there is. "Modernization," in addition to justifying the idea
of change itself, has permitted both international ideological trends and
national elite aspirations to have effect. These are not always separable, but
the Indonesian elite has tended to be conscious of international, especially
European, views. The argument of "international standard" is occasionally
used as a lever to support the further emancipation of women, as well as to
justify, say, the retention of colonial commercial law. But, if in the latter case
the argument is essentially one of efficiency, at least on the surface, and can be
sustained without further ideological qualm, what is at stake in the former
matter is equality, which is far more complicated ideologically.

The issues on which the Supreme Court has laid down new rules have to
do primarily with inheritance, the only area of family law over which secular
courts have fairly complete jurisdiction; matrimonial law is governed, for the
majority Moslems, by Islamic law and courts. The thrust of Supreme Court
decisions has been to strengthen the inheritance rights of women, widows in
Java and elsewhere, and daughters as well. In 1960 the Court ruled, in a case
originating from the partrilineal Batak area of north Sumatra, that everywhere
in Indonesia women now have a right, not fully defined, to inherit property.
The decision aroused considerable protest among Batak groups, who regarded
the ruling as a challenge to the integrity of Batak social structure—in which
view they were quite right. The ruling stuck, however, partly no doubt
because court decisions represent an apparently lesser force than statutes.

But this is not the only reason. In addition, there is some social support for
the views indicated in this decision and similar ones that have followed. Local
elites in various parts of the country have long since begun to ignore parts of
the old *adat*. This is not to say that they reject tradition altogether, but merely
that certain practices no longer suit them for any number of reasons. In the

past, and still now, those who sought release from traditional ties might achieve it through religious conversion. Islam and, more recently, Christianity served to redefine one's community and personal law. Now, in the independent state, national political and legal institutions serve a similar function for those anxious to break away from local traditions. Thus, in the inheritance case mentioned above, it is important both that a woman sued for a share of an estate and that a jurisdiction existed that might be favorable to her challenge against the customary order.

Although most of the Supreme Court's innovative decisions have been related to *adat* law, where no statutory imperatives impede the judiciary, personal law provisions of the civil code have also received some attention. The civil code, originating in the colony, applies only to Europeans and those assimilated in greater or lesser degree into European law status. For example, Chinese are subject to most common civil code personal law rules, except for adoption, for which special provision was made in 1917 to accommodate the assumption that Chinese custom prohibited adoption of female children. In 1963 an Indonesian Chinese couple requested the first instance court of Jakarta to validate their adoption of a girl from an orphanage in Hong Kong. Not long before, the court would have had to reject the request as contrary to statutory provision. But earlier in 1963, during a period of considerable ideological activity in which President Sukarno had pressed symbols of "revolutionary change," the Chairman of the Supreme Court had declared the civil code to be no more than a "guide" to the customary law of those to whom the code had formerly applied. Taking advantage of this new condition, the first instance judge undertook to examine through expert testimony whether the old rules of adoption were still socially valid for Indonesian Chinese. The witnesses agreed that Chinese patrilinealism was on the wane in Indonesia and that, though the civil code rules were otherwise still adequate for Chinese needs, there should no longer be any objection to the adoption of daughters. The judge decided accordingly with some outspoken dicta on the equality of sexes intended by recent developments in Indonesian society and law.

It is tempting to suggest that all these decisions, under both the *adat* law and the civil code, are meshing closely with social change—urbanization, emancipation of women, and so on—to push Indonesia's remaining unilineal kinship societies irrevocably toward bilateralism. There is no question that some bilateral characteristics are becoming more evident among such ethnic groups as the Minangkabau and Batak, but for the time being that is all that can be said. What needs to be emphasized here is that many national leaders, including law professionals, are quite explicitly committed to the assumptions of bilateralism and believe that societies in the archipelago that are not already bilateral should be made so. This idea was in fact adopted in the ineffective eight year plan of 1961, where new national legislation on inheritance was proposed that was based on a strict bilateral model.

Why should this be so? There are several reasons, none of which can receive the attention it deserves here. In the first place, there is enough evidence of direct or indirect government encouragement of bilateralism in many new states to suggest that it is closely related to the modern conception of the state and its functions and problems. The point here is obvious: governments of modern and "modernizing" states want a direct line of communications with their citizens, and this is more easily achieved if loyalties to intermediary structures like clans and extended families are broken down. If this is correct, unilineal societies are, if not doomed, at least in for some very heavy atomizing pressure. Similarly, within bilateral societies one can expect increasing official encouragement of nuclear families, whose development may be further stimulated by urbanization and, in some cases, by economic pressures.

In addition, in Indonesia—which in this case is also comparable to several other new states—the dominant ethnic group, the Javanese, are bilateral, and there is a powerful tendency for its culture to spread outwards toward numerically smaller groups via the political system and bureaucracy which it dominates, even as elites of other ethnic groups tend to emulate Javanese social patterns. The inheritance decisions of the Supreme Court are not surprising when seen in this light of both Javanese and cosmopolitan cultures in Indonesia.

So far as any open debate over family structure has developed at all in Indonesia, it has been within the world of Indonesian Islam. The debate is between those who insist upon the sacred validity of the basically patrilineal family law rules of Islamic law, and those who, in an ongoing attempt to gain greater acceptance of the *sjariah* by liberalizing it, claim those rules to be no more than Arabic custom which the Prophet had intended to change in a bilateral direction. The leading proponent of this latter view, Professor Hazairin, has not won great support by any means, but he has at least kept debate over the law alive. Other Islamic scholars press for liberalization of the Islamic law in various respects in which Indonesian Islam, partly because of its continuous conflict with essentially non- and anti-Islamic forces, has remained highly conservative. But despite some challenge, for example, Islamic law leaders in Indonesia continue to insist upon the exclusive use of the Sjafi'i rules rather than drawing upon all four schools of Sunni law.

It will be apparent from the above discussion that more is happening under the surface of family law development than has appeared in the form of new statutes and regulatory processes. It is likely that the judiciary will continue for a time to bear the burden of formal law change, because political and ideological conflict limits legislative possibilities. Only recently, in fact, have attempts been made to pass new legislation on marriage. The reluctance of Islamic groups prevented a unified marriage statute from being presented to

Parliament, and the separate statutes for Moslems, Christians, and Balinese Hindus that were offered (along with a basic common statute) did not provide for all that much innovation. Even so the bills have stalled in Parliament, mainly as a result of Islamic anxiety about reform challenges.[1] Indeed, the generally defensive posture of Islam in Indonesia works against reform of such institutions as polygamy, not because polygamy is all that common, but because agreeing to its abolition might appear to be a surrender of Islamic principles. It should be mentioned, however, that in the past efforts have been made to reduce the very high ra'e of divorce among Moslems by creating local marriage counseling bodies with the support of the Ministry of Religion.

One final point deserves attention. Such change as there has been in Indonesian family law since the revolution has been inspired mainly by noneconomic considerations. 'Unification,' 'modernization,' concern over the position of women, and a certain degree of pressure by local elites who have moved or are moving into a national level of social awareness and interaction have been behind new court decisions and attempts to transform family law. All these are of course important, and they are common elements in the development of personal law everywhere in recent centuries. What seems to be missing, not only in Indonesia but in many other new states—Communist countries are one obvious exception—is economic inspiration. An economic rationale for changes in inheritance law, for example, is not readily apparent. There may of course be economic effects of tendencies now prevailing in family law evolution, but they cannot easily be predicted. The basic problem here is that economic policy in some of the new states is not at all clear, even to those making it. The difficulties of economic planning without a large measure of administrative control are formidable. But until that control is established, if it is, and economic policy and planning become more consistent than they now are, the relationship between family law policy and economic change is likely to be tenuous at best.

---

[1] In January 1974, after a prolonged and exceedingly tense debate, a new marriage law was finally promulgated. Islamic groups were able to prevent any radical challenge to Islamic principles from being incorporated into the statute, and the analysis in the text still stands.

Remarks on Family Law and Social Change in India*

MARC GALANTER

At the conference, it was mentioned that in a contemporary Chinese university a faculty member's divorce might well come under discussion at a faculty meeting. In India, by way of contrast, a faculty promotion may very possibly be disputed in the courts. Any Indian university, especially in the north, is likely to have several lawsuits going among members of the faculty. The readiness of Indians to take their disputes to governmental tribunals suggests that they have become, in Professor Rheinstein's term, "juridicalized" to a high degree—much more so, it appears, than is the case in China. Indians seem to have more need or willingness to resort to courts to intervene in disputes and forward their interests. In the absence of comparative data on litigation, we may take as a rough measure of this propensity the lawyer/ population ratio which is much higher than is found in Southeast and Eastern Asia. A comparison of India's 183 lawyers per million population with 70 in Japan, 58 in Taiwan, 35 in Malaysia/Singapore, and 17 in Indonesia provides some idea of the prevalence of lawyers in India. With few exceptions, they all function as "barristers" (even though there is no formal distinction of solicitors and barristers). Lawyers and clients concur in visualizing the lawyer as a man whose principal function is to argue in court. The Indian lawyer is literally to be found at the court and, typically, it is only when the client is ready to litigate that he goes to the court to engage a lawyer.[1]

---

* I am indebted to Professor Harold Levy of the University of Maryland for insight-ful comments on these remarks.

[1] On Indian lawyers and their milieu, see 3 *Law & Society Review* No. 2–3 (1968–69), devoted to The Legal Profession in India. The figures on lawyer/population ratios are from my introduction to that collection. [Because of the general nature of these remarks, footnotes are confined to direct citation. A general bibliographical note appears at the end.]

In Myron Cohen's description of the ad hoc Ch'ing councils, I was struck by the definiteness of their mandate and by the clarity and thrust of their work. Indians, too, traditionally took (and take) matters to nongovernmental tribunals—they might be caste or village tribunals or other kinds—but it is my impression that the outcome was typically much more ambiguous. It was very difficult to obtain a decision that had any finality and, if you got it, the tribunal would not necessarily exert itself to enforce its decision. Why the outcome of Indian tribunals, as compared to the Chinese, has this diffuse character can only be conjectured. I suspect it has something to do with the extreme fragmentation of Indian society, the breakdown into many, many small caste groups, cross-cut by village, sect, guild, and other groupings, each of which constitutes its own tribunals. This fragmentation is given ideological support by the traditional Indian notion that every group—caste, village, guild, or whatever—should be relatively autonomous, both in making its own rules and in applying these rules to itself. What happened, I conjecture, is that the groups became so small that they became unable in many cases to control powerful persons and factions within themselves. They were unable to invoke fixed legal principles, apply them to the case, and make their decision stick. The decisions that they were capable of making were often little more than reflections of the current power position of the parties.

When the British administration provided an opportunity to take disputes to the Government's courts, this diffuseness and indefiniteness of the unofficial tribunals led Indians to use the courts to a much greater extent than in other Asian areas where the British provided similar judicial institutions. The courts offered "more bang for your buck": a clear "all or none" decision; the matter settled with finality; and, best of all enforcement by outside authority. It was possible to have an outcome with real impact and independent of local opinion and local configurations of power.

In resorting to the courts, Indians subjected themselves to the rules that prevailed in these courts, and these rules typically were at some variance with the attitudes and understandings of the locality. This gap between the norms of the courts and those of the population occurred, not only in the general criminal, civil and commercial law, where indigenous law was replaced by that of British origin or inspiration, but also in the area of family law and religious endowments where the British attempted to administer Hindu and Muslim law. The British retained the system of personal law in matters of family law (marriage, divorce, adoption, guardianship, and so on), inheritance and succession, caste, and religious endowments. In these fields, each community had its own laws, but they were applied in the government's courts (unlike, e.g. the Ottoman millet system)—and in a spirit far removed from that in indigenous tribunals. It was an established rule that custom—it could be the custom of a locality, caste, or even of a family—overrode the written law. However, custom was difficult to prove, and the attempt of the courts to deal with all Indians as if their affairs were habitually regulated by the texts undoubtedly had the result of imposing on many Hindus rules which were at variance with their customary law. Again, the administration of Hindu law by a hierarchy of courts staffed by judges trained in the common law and interpreting the texts according to common law techniques introduced considerable changes in Hindu law. But such inadvertent change aside, the British were reluctant to institute any large scale innovations in the personal law of the Hindus.

Legislative innovation during the British period can roughly be divided into three stages. First, the British somewhat hesitantly introduced some reforms that seemed demanded by basic humanitarianism; female infanticide, immolation of widows, and slavery were all abolished in the first half of the nineteenth century. Second, there was occasional legislation protecting converts and regarding wills, remarriage of widows, and civil marriage. These measures were only permissive, designed to provide an escape for those who wished to avoid the stringencies of Hindu law; they did not alter the law for those who were prepared to adhere to it. Only in the last few decades of British rule did the legislature undertake to alter Hindu law as it applied to everyone. This third stage saw restraints on child marriage, slight changes in the rules of inheritance to favor women, the improvement of the position of widows, and the Gains of Learning Act—which provided that the fruits of an education financed by joint family funds accrued to the individual and not to the family. These pre-independence reforms marked the successful assertion of legislative power over the Hindu law and modified it in important respects, but they left its basic structure unchanged.

Until nearly the end of British rule proposals that the legislature codify and reform the entire system of Hindu law, which was conceded to be a most confusing and uncertain body of law, were rejected on the ground that the legislature had no mandate to undertake such drastic changes. By the time the Constitution was drafted the idea of a complete overhaul of Hindu law was accepted by a large section of "advanced" opinion and was on the agenda for legislative attention. One of the Constitution's Directive Principles of State Policy was that the legislature enact "a uniform civil code," thereby abolishing the system of separate personal laws. There has not been any serious effort in this direction, and it is unlikely that there will be in the near future since a uniform code could be adopted only by abolishing the separate Muslim law, a move that would be fiercely resented by many Indian Muslims. Until now the Indian legislatures have steered clear of tampering with Muslim law, and it seems likely that they will continue to pursue the course of prudence.

In spite of the infeasibility of a uniform civil code—or as a step toward it—Parliament has felt free to introduce wholesale changes in Hindu law. The earliest proposals for a Hindu code were merely to record and systematize the existing law, incorporating some needed amendments. But by the time the matter came before the Parliament of independent India, it was clear that the code would not merely declare the law but would radically alter it. The early proposals had sought to justify themselves as incorporating the best or earliest of *sastric* law and as purging Hindu law of impurities introduced by British administration. But after independence the sponsors of Hindu law reform clearly abandoned *sastra* as their standard in favor of modernity, equality, and freedom. The revamping of Hindu personal law was regarded, not as an exercise in restoration, but, in Dr. Ambedkar's phrase, as a piece of legal "slum-clearance."

In 1955–56 the long heralded reforms became law in a series of enactments known collectively as the Hindu Code. The institution of marriage was radically altered: polygamy was abolished; caste and *gotra* restrictions on partners were abolished; divorce was introduced (for the higher castes—the lower always had customary nonjudicial divorces). The position of women was vastly improved by giving them equal rights of succession and increased control over property, thus eliminating their economic dependence within the family. The preference for males was eliminated; male and female lines were equated. The Mitakshara joint family was curtailed by treating interests in it as separate for purposes of inheritance. Adoption was liberalized: the adoption of and by females was introduced. Rights of guardianship (and liability for maintenance) were extended to women.

Before discussing the impact of these changes, let me make a few general observations about the implications of this large-scale reform. First, for the first time the classical texts and commentaries have been entirely supplanted as the source of Hindu family law. Hindu social arrangements are for the first time moved entirely within the ambit of legislative regulation. Previous enactments introduced specific modifications into the framework of *sastric* law. But now the whole field is pre-empted by the legislature, and there is every indication that it will remain there. For purposes of Hindu law, appeal to the whole *sastric* tradition has been dispensed with.

Second, the passage of the Code marks the acceptance of the Indian Parliament as a kind of central legislative body to the Hindus in matters of family and social life. The older notion that government had no mandate or competence to redesign Hindu society has been discarded. For the first time the bulk of the world's Hindus live under a single central authority with both the desire and the techniques to enforce changes in their social arrangements. Throughout the history of Hinduism, no across the board reform was possible because of the absence of centralized governmental or ecclesiastical institutions. Reformers might gain acceptance as a sect, but there was no way for them to win the power to enforce changes for others. Now it is possible to have changes enforced among all Hindus by a powerful central authority.

Third, the Code subjects the Hindus to a degree of uniformity unprecedented in Hindu legal history. Regional differences, the schools of commentators, differences according to *varna,* customs of locality, caste, and family, distinctions of sex—all have fallen by the wayside. Some narrow scope is allowed for custom, but for the first time a single set of rules is applicable to Hindus of every caste, sect, and region. This both reflects and presages an unprecedented degree of unification and integration of the Hindus. It marks an important step in the consolidation of a single Hindu community.

Fourth, it may fairly be said that the Code represents a kind of "Westernization" and secularization. *Sastric* notions of *varna,* indissoluble marriage, preference for males, inheritance by those who can confer spiritual benefit, etc., are discarded and replaced by emphases on individual rights, equality of women, the nuclear family, and so forth. Considerations of unseen benefit are replaced by notions of worldly welfare. Very few rules remain with a specifically religious foundation.

Finally, the Code represents the use of law by an elite to procure a legal regime congenial to its interests and sentiments. As in other areas of law, the family law reforms are not a response to the felt needs of the generality of the law's clientele nor an accommodation of conflicting interests. Rather they are an expression of the aspirations of those 'advanced' power holders who hope to use the educational and coercive powers of the law to improve the unenlightened.

In this area of the law, as in many others, the Indian legal system is vastly overcommitted. There is a great disparity between the new regulations on the one hand and the resources (including the will) for inducing compliance on the other. In a multi-level system where commitments outrun resources, a gap between theory and practice is a normal and typical condition. As in other areas, a high value is put on the symbolic outputs of the law, and there is a broad tolerance of the discrepancy between the law on the books and social practice.[2] The educated urban elite have their desired uniformity, modernity, and individualism, while the rural and traditional populace are left to accommodate themselves to the new dispensation. It is difficult as yet to discern just what the impact of the Code on prevailing social patterns will be. For example, in the exogamous villages of the Gangetic plain, the Code's provision for equal inheritance by daughters might mean that over time the village property would be owned largely by women residing outside the village. And the brother-sister relationship, in many places the closest and most unshakable of family bonds, would be exposed to rivalry and conflict now that sisters inherit equally with their brothers.

It is too early to discern the patterns of accommodation, but there is no reason to expect that social relations will automatically align themselves to

---

[2] For an example of this discrepancy from another field, *see* M. Galanter, *The Abolition of Disabilities—Untouchability and the Law,* in J. Michael Mahar, ed., THE UNTOUCHABLES IN CONTEMPORARY INDIA, Tucson: University of Arizona Press, 1972.

correspond to the law's dispensation. The sheer lack of penetration of the law in a diverse, stratified society limits its impact. One very early study reported that immediate impact to be very small: changes had not been communicated to potential beneficiaries, "benefits" were not perceived as such, and the resources needed to pursue them were not available.[3] Where the changes are known, I gather that a variety of arrangements (deeds of gift, testamentary provisions) are devised to make property arrangements that are regarded as suitable. We may anticipate then that ignorance, indifference, and avoidance will cushion any drastic effects.

Rather than expecting that the population will passively conform to this new dispensation, we may expect that they will actively manipulate it to serve their own ambitions and concerns. The new law and its procedures will be used to carry on disputes and to pattern relationships in ways that depart from the intention of the law makers.[4] The active use of government law by Indians need not be thought of as an abandonment of "tradition," for this "modern" law may be used to pursue traditional ambitions and uphold traditional values. The official law becomes entwined with indigenous norms at the same time that it modifies present social practice. For example, the criminal law has been thoroughly domesticated and has become very much a part of the life and lore of the village. The emerging patterns of accommodation in the family law area are not yet clear and badly need to be researched.

[3] M. Luschinsky, *The Impact of Some Recent Indian Government Legislation on the Women of an Indian Village,* 3 ASIAN SURVEY 573–83 (1963).

[4] *See* J. Derrett, *Aspects of Matrimonial Causes in Modern Hindu Law,* REVUE DU SUD-EST ASIATIQUE 203–41 (1964).

Hindu Family Law and Social Change

HAROLD LEWIS LEVY

This brief effort is limited to intra-Indian comparison, vastly oversimplified at that. The focus is on: (1) classical Brahmanism of antiquity, and (2) Reform Hinduism, Nationalism, Liberalism, and Socialism in the legislative history of the "Hindu Code" of family law, 1921–56. While emphasis is placed upon these outlooks as strategies for using law to cause social change, law is also examined as a result, as well as a cause, of social change.

Brahmanical legal theory is justifiably noted for its emphasis upon law as a means for maintaining social stability, for example, maintaining caste and family continuity by discouraging inter-caste marriages, providing apt rules of succession to property, and so on. What may be overlooked are its conception of the specific kinds of social change to be attained (a conception at least as visionary as that of the boldest modern revolutionary), and its marked degree of success in the attainment.

Brahmanical strategy aimed at achieving complex coordination and gradual moral-religious assimilation of numberless groups (some barely, if at all, "Hinduized") that are scattered over an enormous territorial expanse without political unification, with great disparities in level of civilization, and with staggeringly diverse family regulations. In this strategy the social stability that law helped to maintain was seen as a necessary condition of a very gradual, but cumulatively revolutionary, moral-religious transformation. The intended transformation was a movement toward a complex psychic and organizational terminus. All Hindu individuals would be moved toward a single psychic standard, the attainment of internalized equipoise; and in each separate region Hindus collectively would be moved toward a single organizational standard, the attainment of a fourfold *varna,* or caste, hierarchy. Hindus also would be moved toward a great multiplicity of psychic standards as members of a caste and of one of the myriad sub-caste groupings. The basic caste division of labor required differentiation of types of mentality and character to suit the differentiation of tasks. A complete division of labor required very great, further internal organizational-psychic differentiation of each caste. Also, it was important not to disturb ancient customary habits of regional and other groups. Diffusion throughout of a universal psychic standard and a universal organizational standard would go hand in hand with diffraction into diverse psychic standards along the lines of correspondingly diverse ritual-occupational, regional, and customary groupings.

Hindu family law was intended to be an aid in moral-religious education over countless generations—and regenerations (involving all species); it was designed to make individuals fit to function well in this complex Hindu world and to make them fit ultimately to transcend it. The education would tame the desire for individual material gain and would develop other psychic forces. These would bring about the attainment of both the habitual doing of duty and the equipoise, requisite to the intended psychic-organizational transformation, and to the final social transformation—the termination of all change by holy surrender to nonmaterial oneness with eternal Brahman. In regard to social change, Hindu family law had cosmological as well as characterological significance.

Whatever its cosmological efficacy may have been, the characterological strategy was a striking social success, as its critics have attested for centuries. This fostered and reflected the social success of the prestigious Brahman sub-castes that supplied moral educators, priests and jurists. Evidence of the precise actual function of family law in this Hindu socialization process is scarce. It seems to show that Hindu family law supported moral habituation, not only by sanctioning conditions of social stability, but also by more directly encouraging higher-norm achievement. For example, jurists acted authoritatively to determine the ritual rank of Hindu sub-castes and thereby could sanction the adherence of a sub-caste to higher, more prestigious, family law norms. Legal sanction followed and legitimated this social change but also preceded the social change by operating as an incentive for it. Also, consistent with the strategic imperatives of coordinated diversity and gradual upward assimilation, classical jurisprudence permitted legitimation of valid customary deviations from these norms and explicitly required certain deviations by lower-caste groups. Much of actual practice was expected, whether permitted or required, to deviate from the highest family law norms, which were known to be those of a minority composed of Brahman and other higher-caste groups. Orthodox Hinduism was quite comfortable with a multiplicity of family law standards.

Beginning under British Indian rule in 1921, the legislative pressure for a Hindu Code reflected the political influence and activism of primarily middle-class, western-educated, higher-caste Hindu groups, above all of the lawyers. Lawyers formed most of the leadership of both the constitutional and the extra-constitutional forms of public life and were increasingly perceived as a primarily reformist-modernist force. Also, some women of this Hindu stratum formed their own organizations, participated in both forms of public life, and were increasingly regarded in the different strategies of British officialdom and Indian constitutionalist and extra-constitutionalist leaders as a major force for future Indian political, economic, and social development. At the same time, women were increasingly regarded by reformers as the prime victims of Hindu family law.

In the 1920s, 1930s, and 1940s leading British officials and Indian liberals agreed that economic individualism, by generally liberating the individual desire to accumulate unlimited material possessions (from its traditional subordination to social duty) would greatly advance Indian political, economic, and social development. The Liberal strategy was to provide appropriate individual legal rights as a partially self-enforcing incentive to the initiative and enterprise necessary to make Hindus, and India, fit to function well in the complex modern world. Hindus would undergo social transformation into individual citizens with the kind of psychic equipoise and sense of their own rights that are requisite to a regime of political liberty and economic prosperity. Together with an emphasis upon fairness to the individual producer, something of this conception influenced legislation (Hindu Gains of Learning Act, 1930) that freed the rising professional classes from the legal duty to return earnings to the joint family pool. The social impact of this measure remains qualified by the partially surviving sense of family duty among Hindu professionals, which moves some to return a portion of their earnings to the family. Together with a firm emphasis upon sex equality, the Liberal conception also formed the basis of a recommendation, made in 1947 by the Government-appointed Hindu Law Committee, that the entire Hindu joint family property system be abolished. The argument for women's rights and especially for their economic independence turned out to supply the minor premise for this recommendation, which signified wholesale reform of the family structure. This egalitarian principle required that new and unrestrained family property rights proposed for daughters also be proposed for sons and, therefore, required the recommendation to abolish the joint family property system's restraints upon sons' existing property rights. In legal theory, this was a proposal to liberate the whole (propertied) younger Hindu generation from restraints upon economic individualism.

The Indian Nationalist strategy, of using legal means to consolidate national consciousness and the Hindu community, animated the quest by the Hindu Law Committee and others for a uniform Hindu family law—a single set of unvarying, universally applicable family law norms. The strategy of Reform Hindus to purify Hinduism by purging Hindu family law of harsh and demeaning features in regard to women and lower castes and/or the intentions of Liberal Democrats to facilitate full citizenship for women and lower castes are reflected in that Committee's work and in somewhat effective legislation (Hindu Women's Rights to Property Act, 1937, as amended 1938) considerably improving the inheritance rights of widows; in an ineffective measure (Child Marriage Restraint Act, 1929) discouraging child brides and child widowhood; and in an infrequently used Act (Hindu Marriages Validity Act, 1949) validating inter-caste marriages. Both Nationalist and Reform Hindu concern for conserving the best of Hinduness, or Indianness, motivated some of the effort to find and show that these legal changes were sanctioned by the letter and/or spirit of ancient Hindu texts.

These legal initiatives were proposed or taken, not only to transform much of Indian social life, but also to legitimate or accelerate social change that was already taking place. Those Hindus who sought universally to apply these new family law norms constituted a group—if a small one—which seemed already prepared to enjoy the benefit of their application. Many reformers and conservatives believed that Hindu social institutions, particularly the joint family, were in the process of widespread disintegration under the impact of new individualistic-hedonistic ideas and alternatives. The desired uniformity of law was expected to spread, crystallize, and intensify a national consciousness that was already in existence.

To the extent that at least the Nationalist and Liberal elements of this new dominant Hindu minority did share a common strategy, it aimed at achieving a gradual, primarily permissive diffusion of a single, national set of family law norms sanctioned by national legislation. (Space does not permit consideration of other important strategic combinations.) In regard to social change, Hindu family law was expected to have some religious importance and to have an enduring political, social, and economic importance of the first magnitude.

In the 1950s, while the specific slate of family law reforms remained largely the same (and thus could continue to attract the support of those who pressed them in earlier decades), the strategic horizon was altered by the addition of a layer of socialism, reflecting a new but still very mixed balance of post-independence political forces. The boldness of the socialist vision and especially its new stress on collectivism and duty have a limited, but nevertheless interesting, comparability to classical Brahmanism. After a period of psychic polarization and of widespread social disorganization and instability, but of firm political management, psychic-social reorganization on a new, uniform foundation would be possible. Purged by socialist legislation and moral propaganda of exploitative inequalities and oppressive restraints, the revitalized family collectivity and family law would in their way radically subordinate liberated individualism and unliberated parochialism to an overriding sense of socialist identification with and duty to the larger Indian collectivity. Thus made fit to live in the new socialist world, socialist man would have the kind of material and psychic equipoise that is requisite to the final social transformation, the termination of all social struggle by secular surrender to fraternal oneness with the entire human species, itself at one with inevitable history. In regard to social change, Hindu family law re-acquired something like cosmological, as well as new characterological, significance under Socialist strategy.

With certain exceptions (including a compromise on the subject of joint family property), in legal theory the Hindu Code, enacted as a series of separate Acts (Hindu Marriage Act, 1955; Hindu Succession Act, 1956; Hindu Adoption and Maintenance Act, 1956; Hindu Minority and Guardianship Act, 1956), placed the sexes on a par and removed caste distinctions and barriers. Its social success thus far has been modest, scattered, and uneven (in part reflecting the variety of local traditions) whether measured by the intentions of reform Hinduism, nationalism, liberalism, or socialism. For example, the provision of inheritance rights for daughters has been widely circumvented, although this may lessen when this generation of daughters is deceased and their surviving sons claim shares. (The possibility of unintended consequences is indicated by those observers who claim that the higher-caste divorces permitted by the Code are sometimes coercive and at the expense of wives who might have had better legal protection as the senior wife in a polygamous marriage.) It appears that proponents of modern strategies of social change, which are in principle hostile to multiple family law norms, must learn to live with multiplicity and complexity.

Bibliography

Aldous, Joan. *Urbanization, the Extended Family, and Kinship Ties in West Africa.* SOCIAL FORCES 41 (Oct. 1961): 6–11.

ALLEN, C. LAW IN THE MAKING. 7th ed. Oxford: The Clarendon Press, 1964.

ALLWORTH, E. UZBEK LITERARY POLITICS. New York: Humanities Press, 1964.

ALLWORTH, E., ed. CENTRAL ASIA: A CENTURY OF RUSSIAN RULE. New York: Columbia University Press, 1967.

ALMOND, G., and POWELL, G. COMPARATIVE POLITICS: A DEVELOPMENTAL APPROACH. Boston: Little, Brown, 1966.

Antimov, B., and Pergament, A. *Nužny li izmenenija v porjadke rastorženija braka?* (Are amendments in the divorce ordinance needed?). SOCIALISTICESKAJA ZAKONNOST (The socialist rule of law). No. 9 (1954): 24–37.

AOYAMA, M. KINDAI KAZOKUHŌ NO KENKYŪ (近代家族法の研究) (Study of modern family law). Tokyo: 2d ed. 1967.

BACON, E. CENTRAL ASIANS UNDER RUSSIAN RULE: A STUDY IN CULTURE CHANGE. Ithaca, N.Y.: Cornell University Press, 1966.

BAHRO, H. DAS KINDSCHAFTSRECHT IN DER UNION DER SOZIALISTISCHEN SOWJETREPUBLIKEN. Frankfurt a. M. Alfred Metzner Verlag, 1966.

BARBER, B. SOCIAL STRATIFICATION. New York: Harcourt Brace & Co., 1957.

BARCLAY, G. COLONIAL DEVELOPMENT AND POPULATION IN TAIWAN. Princeton, N.J.: Princeton University Press. 1954.

Baric, L. *Levels of Change in Yugoslav Kinship.* In SOCIAL ORGANIZATION, essays presented to Raymond Firth.
edited by M. Freedman. London: F. Cass, 1967.

BARNETT, A. DOAK CADRES, BUREAUCRACY AND POWER IN COMMUNIST CHINA. New York: Columbia University Press, 1967.

BARNETT, A. DOAK CHINA ON THE EVE OF COMMUNIST TAKEOVER. New York: Praeger, 1963.

BARTOL'D, V. ISTORIIA KUL'TURNOI ZHIZNI TURKESTANA (History of Turkestan culture). Leningrad: 1927.

Batkis. *Die Sexualrevolution in Russland.* In BEITRÄGE ZUM SEXUALPROBLEM, edited by F. A. Theilhaber. Vol. 4. Berlin, 1925.

BAUER, W. CHINAS VERGANGENHEIT ALS TRAUMA UND VORBILD. Stuttgart: Kohlhammer, 1968.

BEBEL, A. DIE FRAU UND DER SOZIALISMUS. 34th rev. ed. Stuttgart, Dietz Verlag, 1903.

BECKER, S. RUSSIA'S PROTECTORATES IN CENTRAL ASIA: BUKHARA AND KHIVA, 1865–1924. Cambridge: Harvard University Press, 1968.

Befu, H. *Patrilineal Descent and Personal Kindred.* AMERICAN ANTHROPOLOGIST. 65 (1963): 1328–1341.

BENNIGSEN, A., and LEMERCIER-QUELQUEJAY, C. ISLAM IN THE SOVIET UNION. New York: Praeger, 1967.

BENNIS, W., *et al.,* eds. THE PLANNING OF CHANGE. Rev. ed. New York: Holt, Rinehart and Winston, 1968.

BERGER, M. THE ARAB WORLD TODAY. Garden City, N.Y.: Doubleday, 1964.

BERGER, M. EQUALITY BY STATUTE. Rev. ed. Garden City, N.Y.: Doubleday, 1967.

BERGMANN, A., and FERID, M., eds. INTERNATIONALES EHE UND KINDSCHAFTSRECHT. Volume 5. Looseleaf collection. 3d ed. Frankfurt a. M., 1965.

BERMAN, H. JUSTICE IN THE USSR. Cambridge: Harvard University Press, 1963.

BERQUE, J. THE ARABS: THEIR HISTORY AND FUTURE. New York: Praeger, 1964.

BIEHL, M. DIE CHINESISCHE VOLKSKOMMUNE IM "GROSSEN SPRUNG" UND DANACH. Hamburg: Verlag Weltarchiu 9, 1965.

BILINSKY, A. DAS SOWJETISCHE EHERECHT. Herrenalb (Schwarzwald); Verlag fur internationale Kulteraustausch 1961.

BLAUSTEIN, A., ed. FUNDAMENTAL LEGAL DOCUMENTS OF COMMUNIST CHINA. South Hackensack, N.J.: Fred B. Rothman & Co., 1962.

BODDE, D. CHINA'S CULTURAL TRADITION. New York: Rinehart, 1957.

Bohannan, P. *The Differing Realms of the Law.* AMERICAN ANTHROPOLOGIST 67 (Dec. 1965): 1508–1511.

Bogue, D. *International Migration.* In THE STUDY OF POPULATION, AN INVENTORY AND APPRAISAL, edited by P. Hauser and O. Duncan. Chicago: University of Chicago Press, 1959.

BOULAIS, G. MANUEL DU CODE CHINOIS. Shanghai: Imprimerie de la Mission Catholique, 1924 Reprint. Taipei: Ch'eng-wen Publishing Co., 1966.

BOULDING, K. THE IMPACT OF THE SOCIAL SCIENCES. New Brunswick, N.J.: Rutgers University Press, 1966.

BRANDENBURGSKIJ, J. KURS PO SEMEJNO-BRACNOMU PRAVU (Lectures on family and marriage law). Moscow: 1928.

BRANDT, C., *et al.* A DOCUMENTARY HISTORY OF CHINESE COMMUNISM. Cambridge: Harvard University Press, 1952.

BROMLEY, P. FAMILY LAW. 2d ed. Toronto: Butterworth & Co., 1962.

BRUSIIN, O. ZUM EHESCHEIDUNGSPROBLEM. Helsinki: Akademische Buchhandlung, 1959.

BREZEZINSKI, Z. THE SOVIET BLOC: UNITY AND CONFLICT. Rev. ed. Cambridge: Harvard University Press, 1967.

BUCK, J. LAND UTILIZATION IN CHINA. Nanking: University of Nanking, 1937.

Bünger, K. *Das Ehegesetz der Volksrepublik.* RABELS ZEITSCHRIFT FÜR AUSLANDISCHES UND INTERNATIONALES PRIVATRECHT 16 (1951): Berlin und Tübingen: 112–120.

Bünger, K. *Die Rezeption des europaischen Rechts in China.* In BEITRAGE ZUR RECHTS-FORSCHUNG, edited by E. Wolff. Special printing of RABELS ZEITSCHRIFT FÜR AUSLANDISCHES UND INTERNATIONALES PRIVATRECHT, 1950.

BÜNGER, K. ZIVIL UND HANDELSGESETZBUCH VON CHINA. ed. in Germany, 1934.

BURCKHARDT, W. METHODE UND SYSTEME DES RECHTS. Zürich: 1936.

BURGESS, E., and LOCKE, H. THE FAMILY. New York: American Book Co., 1945.

Buxbaum, David C. *Chinese Family Law in a Common Law Setting.* JOURNAL OF ASIAN STUDIES 25 (1966): pp. 621–644.

Buxbaum, David C. *Horizontal and Vertical Influences Upon The Substantive Criminal Law in China.* OST EUROPA RECHT 1 (1964).

Buxbaum, David C. *Introduction.* JOURNAL OF ASIAN & AFRICAN STUDIES. 2 (1967): 1–8.

Buxbaum, David C. *Preliminary Trends in the Development of . . . Criminal Law.* INTERNATIONAL AND COMPARATIVE LAW QUARTERLY, Jan. 1962, pp. 1–30.

Buxbaum, David C. *Preliminary Trends in the Development of the Legal Institutions of Communist China and the Nature of the Criminal Law.* INTERNATIONAL AND COMPARATIVE LAW QUARTERLY, Jan. 1962. Reprinted in GOVERNMENT OF COMMUNIST CHINA, edited by G. Jan. San Francisco: Chandler Publishing Co., 1966.

Buxbaum, David C. *Review of* LAW AND SOCIETY IN TRADITIONAL CHINA, *by T. Ch'ü.* JOURNAL OF ASIAN STUDIES 21 (1962): 372–373.

BUXBAUM, DAVID C., ed. FAMILY LAW AND CUSTOMARY LAW IN ASIA. The Hague: Martinus Nijhoff, 1968.

CAROE, O. SOVIET EMPIRE: THE TURKS OF CENTRAL ASIA AND STALINISM. 2nd ed. New York: St. Martin's Press, 1967.

CHANG, CHI 張籍. CHANG SZU-YEH CHI 張司業集 (Collection of Imperial Tutor Chang [Chi]). Ch'angsha: Shang-wu ch'ien yin, 1938.

CH'ANG, CH'Ü (棠璩). HUA-YANG KUO-CHIH (華陽國志) (Gazetteer of Hua-yang). Taipei: Shih-chieh shu-chü ed. 1962.

Chang, H. *Taiwan sheng ti yang-nü wen-t'i* (台灣省的養女問題) (Problems of women in the Province of Taiwan). TAIWAN WEN-HSIEN (台灣文獻). (Sept. 1963).

Ch'ang-chiang jih-pao (長江日報). Daily newspaper "Yangtze Daily" (Nanking), July 5, 1950; Aug. 30, 1951.

CHAO FENG-CH'IEH 趙風喈. MIN-FA CH'IN-SHU LUN 民法親屬論 (Discussions of family law in the civil code) 1945. Taipei: kuo-li-pien-yi-kuan 國立編譯舘. (National Compilation Committee), 1955.

CHARCEV, A. BRAK I SEM'JA V SSSR (Marriage and the family in the USSR). Moscow, 1964.

Chartschew, A. *Ehe und Familie in der Sowjetunion.* NEUE JUSTIZ 19 (1965): 256–258.

CHAVANNES, E. MÉMOIRES HISTORIQUES. Paris: Adrien-Maisonneuve, 1895–1905.

Che-chiang jih-pao (浙江日報) The Che Kiang [Provincial] (浙江) Daily, Che Kiang: March 11, 1952.

Chen, C. *The Foster Daughter-in-law System in Formosa.* AMERICAN JOURNAL OF COMPARATIVE LAW 6 (1957): 302–314.

Ch'en Ch'eng Papers (陳誠), reel 10, no. 6. Stanford: filmed by The Hoover Institute.

CH'EN, HUNG-MOU (陳宏謀). HSÜN SU I KUEI (訓俗遺規) (Bequeathed teachings about social life). In WU CHUNG I KUEI (五種遺規), 1822.

CH'EN, KU-YÜAN (陳顧遠). CHUNG-KUO HUN-YIN-SHIH (中國婚姻史) (History of Chinese marriage). Taipei: Taiwan shang-wu yin-shua-kuan, 1966.

CH'EN, KU-YÜAN (陳顧遠). CHUNG-KUO HUN-YIN SHIH (中國婚姻史) (History of Chinese marriage). Shanghai: Commercial Press, 1936.

CH'EN, KU-YÜAN (陳顧遠). HUN-YIN FA SHIH (婚姻法史) (History of Chinese marriage laws).

CH'EN, KU-YÜAN (陳顧遠). CHUNG-KUO KU-TAI HUN-YIN SHIH 中國古代婚姻史 (A history of marriage in traditional times in China). Reprint. Shanghai: Commercial Press, 1925.

CH'EN MENG-LEI (陳夢雷). KU-CHIN T'U-SHU CHI-CH'ENG (古今圖書集成) (A comprehensive collection of ancient and modern illustrations and documents). Shanghai: T''u-shu chi-ch'eng chü, 1884.

CHEN, S. (陳壽). SAN-KUO-CHIH (三國志) (History of the Three Kingdoms). I-wen yin-shu-kuan (藝文印書館) ed., n.d. (See also: Peking: Ku-chi ch'u-pan-she, 1957.)

CH'EN, T. Y. 陳東原. Chung-kuo fu-nü sheng-ho shih (中國婦女生活史) (History of the livelihood of women in China). Shanghai: Commercial Press, 1937.

CHEN, T. THE CHINESE COMMUNIST REGIME. Documents and Commentary. New York, Washington, London: Frederick A. Praeger, 1967.

Ch'en T. H. E. *Elementary Education in Communist China.* CHINA QUARTERLY, April–June 1962, pp. 98–122.

CH'EN, T. H. E. THOUGHT REFORM OF THE CHINESE INTELLECTUALS. Hong Kong: Hong Kong University Press. 1960.

Cheng, Ching-i (鄭競毅). Fa-lü ta tz'u-shu (法律大辭書) (Dictionary of law). Shanghai: Commercial Press, 1936.

[Cheng, Chung (鄭衆)]. *Chou-li: Cheng Ssu-nung chieh-chu* (周禮: 鄭司農解註) (Interpretive commentary by Minister of Agriculture Cheng to the Rites of Chou). In YU-HAN SHAN-FANG CHI-I-SHU 玉函山房輯佚書 (Collected [fragments of] lost books in the Yü-han mountain dwelling), by Ma Kuo-han (馬國翰). IN CHUNG-KUO SSU-HSIANG MING-CHU (中國思想名著). Taipei: Shih-chieh shu-kuan, 1959.

CH'IEN, T. H. 錢大昕. HUN-YI 昏義 (Marriage ceremonies). n.d.

CHI FU T'UNG-CHIH (畿輔通志) (History of Chi Fu Province), 1884.

CH'IH-HSI HSIEN-CHIH (赤溪縣志) (History of Ch'ih-hsi district), 1920.

CHIKUSA, TATSUO (千種達雄). MANSHŪ KAZOKU-SEIDO NO KANSHŪ (滿洲家族制度の慣習) (Customs of the Manchurian family system). 3 vols. Tokyo: Ichirūsha, vol. 1, 1964; vol. 2, 1965; vol. 3, 1967.

CHIN, AI-LI S. MODERN CHINESE FICTION AND FAMILY RELATIONS. Cambridge, Mass., Center for International Studies, Massachusetts Institute of Technology, 1966.

CH'IN CHOU-CHIH (欽州志). (History of Ch'in Province), 1834.

CHINESE CIVIL CODE, 1930.

CHINA YEAR BOOK. Shanghai: Commercial Press, 1935–36.

CH'ING HSIEN-HSING HSING-LÜ 清現行刑律 (Existing criminal laws of the Ch'ing dynasty). Peking: 1908.

CH'ING MING CHI (清明集). See MING-KUNG SHU P'AN CH'ING-MING-CHI.

CH'ING TING TA-CH'ING HUI-TIEN SHIH-LI 欽定大清會典事例 (Supplement to collected institutes of the great Ch'ing dynasty). Peking, 1908.

CHIN-KU CH'I-KUAN 今古奇觀 (Traditional and modern strange and wonderful sights). Shanghai Yatung, 1949.

CHIN-SHU 晉書 (The annals of the Chin dynasty). Reprint. Shanghai: Commercial Press, 1934.

CHIU-T'ANG-SHU 舊唐書 (The old annals of T'ang dynasty). In Pai Na Pen erh-shih-ssu shih (百衲本二十四史册), n.d.

CHOU, CHIA-CH'ING 周家清. HUN-YIN-FA CHIANG-HUA 婚姻法講話 (Discussions on the marriage law) Peking: Chinese Youth Publishing Company, 1964.

CHOU, MI 周密. CH'I-TUNG YEH-YÜ 齊東野語 (Unfounded talk). In SSU-LING SHU-HUA-CHI 思陵書畫記, n.d.

CHOU-LI 周禮 (Rites of Chou). In SHIH-SAN CHING CHU-SU ed.

CH'Ü CHIANG HSIEN-CHIH 曲江縣志 (History of Ch'ü Chiang district), 1875.

CHŪGOKU NŌSON KANKŌ CHŌSA IINKAI 中國農村慣行調查委員會 (Committee on Chinese rural customs and practice). CHŪGOKU NŌSON KANKŌ CHŌSA 中國農村慣行調查 (Research data on Chinese rural customs and practices). Tokyo: Iwanami shoten, 1952–58.

CHŪKAMINKOKU SHŪKAN CHŌSAROKU 中華民國習慣調錄查 (A record of investigation of customs in the Republic of China). Tokyo: 1943.

CH'UN CH'IU 春秋 (Spring and autumn annals). In CHUNG-KUO KU-TIEN MING-CHU PA-CHUNG 中國古典名著八種 (The Chinese Classics) Reprint: Shanghai Commercial Press, 1937.

CHUNG-HUA JEN-MIN KUNG-HO-KUO MIN-FA CHI-PEN WEN-T'I 中華人民共和國民法基本問題 (Fundamental questions of civil law in the People's Republic of China). Composed by a collective authorship of the Civil Law Department, Central School for Juristic Cadres. Peking: 1958.

CHUNG-HUA JEN-MIN KUNG-HO-KUO MIN-FA TS'AN-K'AO TZU-LIAO 中華人民共和國民法參考資料 (Reference material on the civil law of the Chinese People's Republic). Jen-min ta-hsüeh (人民大學) People's University, Peking: 1957.

Chung-hua jen-min kung-ho-kuo min-fa tzu-liao hui-pien 中華人民共和國民法資料彙編 (Collection of materials on the civil law of the People's Republic of China). Peking: Jen-min ta-hsüeh (人民大學) People's University, 1954.

CHUNG-HUA MIN-KUO SSU-FA HSING-CHENG-PU 中華民國司法行政部 (Ministry of Justice, Republic of China). MIN-SHANG-SHIH HSI-KUAN TIAO-CH'A PAO-KAO-LU 民商事習慣調查報告錄 (Report of inquiry into civil and commercial customs). 1930. Reprint. Taipei: Ku-t'ing shu-wu, 1969.

CHUNG HUA TA TZ'U TIEN 中華大辭典. Shanghai: Chung hua shu chü, 1916.

Chungking ta kung pao 重慶大公報 (Ch'ungking). Dec. 7, 1951. Daily newspaper.

Chung-kuo ch'ing-nien 中國青年 (Chinese youth) (Peking) Jan. 1, 1958; Oct. 28, 1958; Feb. 1, 1964; Dec. 16, 1964.

CHUNG-KUO MIN-SHIH HSI-KUAN TA-CH'ÜAN 中國民事習慣大全 (Compendium of Chinese civil customs). Reprint. Taipei: Wen-hsing shu-tien, 1962.

CHUNG-WEN TA TZ'U-TIEN 中文大辭典. Encyclopedic dictionary of the Chinese language. Compiled by CHUNG-KUO WEN-HUA YEN-CHIU-SO 中國文化研究所. Taipei: 1968.

CH'Ü, T. LAW AND SOCIETY IN TRADITIONAL CHINA. Paris: Mouton & Co., 1961.

CHU, V. TA TA, TAN TAN, DIE WIRKLICHKEIT ROT-CHINAS. German ed. Dusseldorf, Wien, Econ Verlag, 1964.

CIVIL CODE, 1931.

Cohen, J. *Chinese Mediation on the Eve of Modernization.* JOURNAL OF ASIAN & AFRICAN STUDIES 2 (1967): 54–76.

Cohen, Myron L. *A Case Study of Chinese Family Development and Economy.* JOURNAL OF ASIAN & AFRICAN STUDIES 3 (1968): 161–180.

Cohen, Myron L. *Chinese Family Development and Economy in Yen-liao, Taiwan.* Ph.D. dissertation, Columbia University, 1967.

Cohen, Myron L. *Variations in Complexity among Chinese Family Groups : The Impact of Modernization.* In TRANSACTIONS OF THE NEW YORK ACADEMY OF SCIENCES. Series 2. Vol. 29, 1967.

CONOLLY, V. BEYOND THE URALS . . . London: Oxford University Press, 1967.

CONSTITUTION OF THE PEOPLE'S REPUBLIC OF CHINA of 1954. English ed. Peking: 1954.

CORBETT, P. THE ROMAN LAW OF MARRIAGE. Oxford: The Clarendon Press, 1930.

CREEL, H. CHINESE THOUGHT FROM CONFUCIUS TO MAO TSE-TUNG. Chicago: University of Chicago Press, 1953.

CRIMINAL CODE, 1935.

Cruppi, M. *Le Divorce Pendant la Révolution.* Thesis, Paris, 1909.

DAVID, R., and DEVRIES, H. THE FRENCH LEGAL SYSTEM. AN INTRODUCTION TO CIVIL LAW SYSTEMS. New York: Oceana Publications, 1958.

DAVID, R., and HAZARD, J. DROIT SOVIÉTIQUE. Paris: Pichon et Durand-auzias, 1954.

DAVIES, J. A REPORT OF CASES AND MATTERS IN LAW RESOLVED AND ADJUDGED IN THE KINGS COURTS IN IRELAND. [1604–1612]. Dublin: Printed for Sarah Cotter, 1762.

Davydov, V. *Obsuždeni proektov Gk i Gpk Mozdavskoj SSR* (Discussion of the draft of the private law code and the civil procedure law of the Mold SSR). SOVETSKOE GOSUNDARSTVO I PRAVO (Soviet state and law) No. 6 (1963): 134–135.

DE BARY, W., *et al.,* eds. SOURCES OF THE CHINESE TRADITION. New York: Columbia University Press, 1960.

DeGlopper, D. *The Origins and Resolution of Conflict in Traditional Chinese Society.* Unpublished, M.A. thesis, University of London, 1965.

DE GROOT, J. THE RELIGIOUS SYSTEM OF CHINA 3 vols. 1892, 1894, and 1897. Reprinted in six volumes; New York: Paragon Book Reprint Corp., 1966.

DEKRETY ULASTI SOVETSKOJ (Decrees of the Soviet Authority). Moscow, Vol. 1 (1957); Vol. 3 (1964).

D'ENCAUSSE, H. RÉFORME ET RÉVOLUTION CHEZ LES MUSULMANS DE L'EMPIRE RUSSE 1867–1924. Paris: A. Colin, 1966.

DEPARTMENT OF CIVIL AFFAIRS. TAIWAN PROVINCIAL GOVERNMENT. MONTHLY BULLETIN OF POPULATION REGISTRATION STATISTICS OF TAIWAN. 2 (Feb. 1967): Table 6.

Darrett, J. *Aspects of Matrimonial Causes in Modern Hindu Law.* REVUE DU SUD-EST ASIATIQUE (1964): 203–41.

DICEY, A. V., A DIGEST OF THE LAW OF ENGLAND WITH REFERENCE TO THE CONFLICT OF LAWS. 7th ed. London: Stevens and Sons, Ltd., 1958.

DORE, R. CITY LIFE IN JAPAN. Berkeley: University of California Press, 1958.

DROBNIG, U. IDEOLOGIE, RECHT UND WIRKLICHKEIT DER FAMILIE IN DER D D R. Jahrbuch für Ostrecht, vol. 8, no. 2. 1967, 157–184.

Dror, Y. *Law and Social Change*. TULANE LAW REVIEW Vol. 33 (1959): 787–802.

DUBS, H. HISTORY OF THE FORMER HAN DYNASTY. 3 Vols. Baltimore: Waverly Press, Inc., 1938–1955.

Dull, Jack L. *A Historical Introduction to the Apocryphal (ch'an-wei)* 讖緯 *Texts of the Han Dynasty*. Ph.D. dissertation. University of Washington, 1966.

Dunn, E., and Dunn, S. *Soviet Regime and Native Culture in Central Asia and Kazakhstan: The Major Peoples*. CURRENT ANTHROPOLOGY vol. 8. no. 3 (June 1967): 147–84.

EBERHARD, W. SOCIAL MOBILITY IN TRADITIONAL CHINA. Leiden: E. J. Brill, 1962.

ECKSTEIN, A. COMMUNIST CHINA'S ECONOMIC GROWTH AND FOREIGN TRADE. New York: McGraw-Hill, 1966.

ECKSTEIN, H. AUTHORITY RELATIONS AND GOVERNMENTAL PERFORMANCE: A THEORETICAL FRAMEWORK. Center of International Studies, Princeton University. September, 1968.

Eckstein, H. *On the Etiology of International Wars*. HISTORY AND THEORY. Vol. IV, no. 2 (1965): 133–63.

Egurskaja, E. *Normy zakonov o brake i seme nuždjutsja k izmenenii* (The statutory provisions on marriage and family are in need of change). SOCIALISTICESKAJA ZAKONNOST (The socialist rule of law) No. 1 (1965): 31–33.

Engels, Friedrich. *Der Ursprung der Familie, des Privateigentums und des Staates*. In BUCHEREI DES MARXISMUS-LENINISMUS. Vol. 2. East Berlin: Dietz: 1953.

ESCARRA, J. CHINESE LAW: CONCEPTION AND EVOLUTION, LEGISLATIVE AND JUDICIAL INSTITUTIONS, SCIENCE AND TEACHING. Translated by G. Browne (for Works Progress Administration, W.P. 2799, University of Washington, Seattle; Peking 1936). Cambridge: Harvard Law School, 1961.

FAIRBANK, J. THE UNITED STATES AND CHINA. Cambridge: Harvard University Press, 1958.

FAIRBANK, J. and TENG, S. CHINA'S RESPONSE TO THE WEST. Cambridge: Harvard University Press, 1954.

Family Law Code of 1918.

Family Law Code of 1927.

Family Law Code of 1968.

FAN, HUNG 范鋐. LIU-YÜ YEN-I 六諭衍義 (Lectures on the Six Edicts) ca. 1660. Reprinted Japan, 1721.

FAN, YEH 范曄. HOU-HAN-SHU 後漢書 (Annals of the latter Han dynasty). Peking: Chung-hua shu chü ed., 1965.

FANG HSUAN-LING 房玄齡. CHIN-SHU 晉書 (History of the Chin Dynasty). I-wen yin-shu-kuan, n.d.

FEI, HSIAO T'UNG, PEASANT LIFE IN CHINA. London: Routledge and K. Paul, 1939.

FENG, H. THE CHINESE KINSHIP SYSTEM. Cambridge: Harvard University Press, London: Routledge and K. Paul Press, 1948.

FEUER, L. THE CONFLICT OF GENERATIONS: THE CHARACTER AND SIGNIFICANCE OF STUDENT MOVEMENTS. New York: Basic Books, 1969.

Florkowski, E. *Das sowjetische Ehescheidungsrecht*. Thesis, Göttingen, 1967.

FORKE, A. LUN-HENG. New York: Paragon Book Gallery, 2d ed., 1962.

FOSTER, G. TRADITIONAL CULTURES AND THE IMPACT OF TECHNOLOGICAL CHANGE. New York: Harper, 1962.

Fox, T., and Miller, S. *Economic, Political and Social Determinants of Mobility*. ACTA SOCIOLOGICA 9 (1965): 76–93.

FREEDMAN, M. CHINESE FAMILY AND MARRIAGE IN SINGAPORE. London: H. M. Stationery Office (Cd. Res. Stud. No. 20), 1957.

FREEDMAN, M. CHINESE LINEAGE AND SOCIETY. New York: Humanities Press, 1966.

Freedman, M. *The Family in China, Past and Present*. In MODERN CHINA, Edited by A. Feuerweker. Englewood Cliffs, N.J.: Prentice-Hall, 1964.

FREEDMAN, M. LINEAGE ORGANIZATION IN SOUTHEASTERN CHINA. [London] University of London: The Athlone Press, 1958.

Freund, H. *Das Zivilrecht in der Sowjetunion*. In ZIVILGESTEZE DER GEGENWART, edited by K. Heinsheimer. Vol. 6. Mannheim, Berlin, Leipzig: J. Bensheimer, 1927.

FRIED, M. FABRIC OF CHINESE SOCIETY. New York: Octagon Press, 1953.

Fried, M. *Some Political Aspects of Clanship in a Modern Chinese City*. In POLITICAL ANTHROPOLOGY, edited by M. Swartz, *et al*. Chicago: Aldine, 1966.

Friedman, L., and Ladinsky, J. *Law as an Instrument of Incremental Social Change*. Paper read at the Annual Meeting of the American Political Science Association, Sept. 8, 1967, at Chicago, Illinois.

Fu, S. *The New Marriage Law of Communist China*. In CONTEMPORARY CHINA, edited by E. Stuart Kirby. Vol. 1. Hong Kong: Hong Kong University Press, 1955.

FU, T. 符定一 LIEN-MIEN TZU-TIEN 聯綿字典 (A dictionary of binominal expressions). Peking: Ching-hua yin-shu-chü, 1943.

Fu tai-hui pang-chu ch'un-chung i-feng i-su 婦代會幫助群衆移風移俗 (The Women's Association assists the masses in changing their customs). CHUNG-KUO FU-NÜ 中國婦女 (Chinese women). Jan. 1, 1966.

Fu-kien jih-pao 福建日報 (Fukien Daily) (Fuchow), March 10, 1952.

FUKIEN T'UNG-CHIH 福建通志 (History of Fukien Province). 1834.

FUKUSHIMA, MASSO 福島正男, and MIYAZAKI, HIROSHI 宮崎宏, trans. CHUKA SOBIETO KYŌWAKOKU, CHŪGOKU KAIHOKU, KONYINHO SHIRYO 中華リビエワト共和國, 中國解放區婚姻法資料 (Material on marriage laws of the Chinese Soviet Republic and the Chinese Liberated Areas.) Socialist Law Research Society and the Society for Research into the Circumstances of Chinese Rural Villages, Tokyo, 1965.

Galanter, Marc. *The Abolition of Disabilities: "Untouchability" and the Law*. ECONOMIC AND POLITICAL WEEKLY. (Bombay) Annual number (Jan. 1969): 131–170.

Gale, E., *et al*. "Discourses on Salt and Iron." JNCBRAS 65 (1934): 73–110.

GALLIN, BERNARD. HSIN HSING, TAIWAN: A CHINESE VILLAGE IN CHANGE. Berkeley: University of California Press, 1966.

Gallin, Bernard. *Mediation in Changing Chinese Society in Rural Taiwan*. JOURNAL OF ASIAN & AFRICAN STUDIES 2 (1967): 77–90.

Gallin, Bernard. *Political Factionalism and Its Impact on Chinese Village Social Organization in Taiwan*. In LOCAL LEVEL POLITICS, edited by M. Swartz. Chicago: Aldine Publications, 1968.

GEIGER, H. THE FAMILY IN SOVIET RUSSIA. Cambridge: Harvard University Press, 1968.

GIBB, H., and BOWEN, H. ISLAMIC SOCIETY IN THE EIGHTEENTH CENTURY. London: Oxford University Press, 1950.

GIDULJANOV, P. KODEKS ZAKONOV O BRAKE, SEMJE I OPEKI S POSTATEJNYMI KOMMENTARIJAMI (Code of laws on marriage, family and guardianship with commentary). Leningrad: 1927.

Giebel. *Ehescheidungen in der Sowjetunion.* DAS STANDESAMT. Frankfurt/Main Verlag für Standesamitswesen: 1968, p. 32.

GIERKE, O. DEUTSCHES PRIVATRECHT. Leipzig: Duncker and Humboldt, 1895.

GLUCKMAN, M. THE JUDICIAL PROCESS AMONG THE BAROTSE OF NORTHERN RHODESIA. Chicago: Free Press, 1955.

GLUCKMAN, M. POLITICS, LAW, AND RITUAL IN TRIBAL SOCIETY. Chicago: Aldine Publishing, 1965.

GOODE, W. READINGS ON THE FAMILY AND SOCIETY. Englewood Cliffs, N.J.: Prentice Hall, 1964.

Goode, W. *Family and Mobility.* In CLASS, STATUS AND POWER, SOCIAL STRATIFICATION IN COMPARATIVE PERSPECTIVE, edited by R. Bendix and S. Lipset. 2d ed., New York: Free Press, 1966.

GOODE, W. WORLD REVOLUTION AND FAMILY PATTERNS. New York: Free Press of Glencoe, 1963.

GORDON, D. WOMEN OF ALGERIA: AN ESSAY ON CHANGE. Distributed for the Center for Middle Eastern Studies of Harvard University by the Harvard University Press (Harvard Middle East monograph, no. 19), 1968.

GOTHEIN, E. DER CHRISTLICH-SOCIALE STAAT DER JESUITEN IN PARAGUAY. Leipzig: Duncker and Humbolt, 1883.

Gould, H. *Lucknow Richshawallas: The Social Organization of an Occupational Category.* International Journal of Comparative SOCIOLOGY 6 (March 1965): 37-45.

GRAVESON, R. H. STATUS IN THE COMMON LAW. [London] University of London: Athlone Press, 1953.

Gruschin, B. *Slušaetsja delo o razvode . . . o tak nazyvaemych "legkomyslennich brakach"* (Discussion of the divorce problem . . . Concerning the so-called "lightly considered marriages"). MOLODAJA GWARDIJA No. 6/7 (Moscow 1964). Extracts in German in OST-PROBLEME 16 (1964): 600-608.

GRZYBOWSKI, K. SOVIET LEGAL INSTITUTIONS. Ann Arbor: University of Michigan Press, 1962.

GSOVSKI, V. SOVIET CIVIL LAW. Ann Arbor: University of Michigan Law School, 1948-49.

Gudoshnikov, L. U.S. JOINT PUBLICATION RESEARCH SERVICE. No. 1. 1968, 9.

Guins, G. SOVIET LAW AND SOVIET SOCIETY. The Hague: Nijhoff, 1954.

Gurr, T. *A Causal Model of Civil Strife: A Comparative Analysis Using New Indices.* AMERICAN POLITICAL SCIENCE REVIEW LXII, 4 (December, 1968), 1104-24.

Halpern, M. *Patterns of Continuity and Change, Collaboration and Conflict in Traditional Islamic Society.* Paper read at the Annual Meeting of the Middle East Studies Association, Nov. 1968, at Houston, Texas.

HALPERN, M. THE POLITICS OF SOCIAL CHANGE IN THE MIDDLE EAST AND NORTH AFRICA. Princeton, N.J.: Princeton University, 1963.

Han-fei-tzu 韓非子 (Book of Han Fei-tzu), Shanghai: Commercial Press, 1929.

Hastrich, A. *Zum Eheguterrecht der RSFSR.* OSTEUROPARECHT (1961): 258-265.

HATANO, K. 波多野乾一 CHŪGOKU KYŌSANTŌ-SHI 中國共產黨史 (History of the Chinese Communist Party). Jiji-tsu shin-sha 時事通信社, Tokyo: 1951.

Hayashi, E. 林惠海. Chūgoku nōka no kintō bunsan sōzoku *no kenkyū* 中國農家の均等分產相續の研究 (A study of the inheritance of equal shares in Chinese peasant households). In GENDAI SHAKAIGAKU NO SHOMONDAI 現代社會學の諸問題 (Problems of modern sociology) by TOKYO DAIGAKU SHAKAIGAKKAI 東京大學社會學會 (Sociology circle, Tokyo University). Tokyo: Kobundo, 1949.

HAYIT, B. TURKESTAN IM XX JAHRHUNDERT. Darmstadt: C. W. Leske, 1956.

Hazard, J. *Le Droit soviétique et le dépérissement de l'état.* TRAVAUX ET CONFÉRENCES 8 Bruxelles: Université Libre (1960):

HAZARD, J. LAW AND SOCIAL CHANGE IN THE USSR. Toronto: Carswell Co., 1953.

HAZARD, J., and SHAPIRO, I. THE SOVIET LEGAL SYSTEM. Part III. New York: Oceana, 1962.

Henderson, Dan F. *Promulgation of Tokugawa Statues.* In TRADITIONAL AND MODERN LEGAL INSTITUTIONS IN ASIA AND AFRICA, edited by D. Buxbaum. Leiden: E.J. Brill, 1967.

Henderson, Dan F. *Promulgation of Tokugawa Statues.* JOURNAL OF ASIAN & AFRICAN STUDIES 2 (1967): 9–25.

HIGASHIGAWA, T. 東川德治 SHINA HŌSEISHI KENKYŪ 支那法制史研究 (A study on legal history in China). 1926.

HIGHTOWER, J. HAN SHIH WAI CHUAN, HAN YING'S ILLUSTRATIONS OF THE DIDACTIC APPLICATION OF THE CLASSICS OF SONGS. Harvard-Yenching Institute Monograph Series, Vol. XI, 1952.

HO, P. 何炳棣. STUDIES ON THE POPULATION OF CHINA, 1368–1953. Cambridge: Harvard University Press, 1956.

HOANG, P. NOTIONS TECHNIQUES SUR LA PROPRIÉTÉ EN CHINE (Technical comments on property in China). Shanghai: Imprimerie de la mission catholique, 1898.

Ho-pei jih-pao 河北日報 (Hopei Daily) (Pao-ting), Feb. 28, 1957.

Horkheimer, M. *Die Zukunft der Ehe.* In KRISE DER EHE? 13 Contributions by F. Hermann, among others. Munchen: Piper, 1966. pp. 217 et seq.

HOUN, F. TO CHANGE A NATION: PROPAGANDA AND INDOCTRINATION IN COMMUNIST CHINA. New York: Free Press of Glencoe, 1965.

Hsiao, K. *Legalism and Autocracy in Traditional China.* TSING HUA JOURNAL OF CHINESE STUDIES. Taipei: (1960).

HSIAO, K. RURAL CHINA, IMPERIAL CONTROL IN NINETEENTH CENTURY. Seattle: University of Washington Press, 1960.

HSIEN-HSING FA HUEI-CHI 現行法彙集 (Collection of laws in force). Administrative Council of the Chin-ch'a-chi Area, 1945.

Hsin Chung-kuo ti hun-yin chih-tu 新中國的婚姻制度 (Marriage institutions of New China). CHUNG-KUO HSIN-WEN 中國新聞. March 10, 1966.

Hsin-min wan-pao 新民晚報 (Shanghai), March 7, 1964; Jan. 13, 1966.

HSIN-T'ANG-SHU 新唐書 (The new history of the T'ang dynasty). Shanghai: Commercial Press, 1933.

Hsin-wen jih-pao 新聞日報 (Shanghai Daily News), (Shanghai). Dec. 21, 1952.

HSING-AN HUI-LAN 刑案滙覽 (Conspectus of penal cases). 1852.

HSU, F. AMERICANS AND CHINESE. New York: Schuman, 1953.

HSU, F. *The Myth of Chinese Family Size.* AMERICAN JOURNAL OF SOCIOLOGY 48 (1943): 555–62.

HSU, F. UNDER THE ANCESTORS' SHADOW London: Routledge and Kegan Paul, 1949.

Hsu, S. 許慎. Wu-ching i-i su-cheng 五經異議疏證 (Variant interpretations of the Five Classics with critical comments). In HUANG-CH'ING CHING-CHIEH 皇清經解 (Classical exigetics of the Ch'ing dynasty), edited by Juan Yuan. 1829.

HSÜ TZU-CHIH T'UNG-CHIEN CH'ANG-PIEN 續資治通鑑長編 (An extended or [extensive] compilation continuing the Tzu-chih Tung-chien). By Pi Yuan. Shanghai: Chung-hua shu-chu, 1928.

HU, C. 胡長清. CHUNG-KUO MIN-FA CHI-CH'ENG LUN 中國民法繼承論 (Inheritance under China's civil code). Taipei: Shang-wu yin-shu kuan, 1964.

HU, C. ET AL., eds. CHINA: ITS PEOPLE, ITS SOCIETY, ITS CULTURE. New Haven: Hraf Press, 1960.

HU, W. 胡文楷. LI-TAI FU-NÜ CHU-TSO K'AO 歷代婦女著作考 (An examination of the writings of women through the ages). Shanghai: Commercial Press, 1957.

HUAN, K'UAN 桓寬. YEN-T'IEH-LUN 鹽鐵論 (Discourses on salt and iron). Kuo-hsüeh chi-pen ts'ung-shu ed., 國學基本叢書. Taipei: Shang-wu yin-shu kuan, 1965.

HUANG, C. 黃靜嘉. JIH-CHÜ SHIH-CH'I CHIH TAIWAN CHIH-MIN-TI FA-CHIH YÜ CHIH-MIN T'UNG-CHIH 日據時期之台灣殖民地法制與殖民統治 (Colonial legal institutions and control in Taiwan during the Japanese period). 1960.

HUANG, KAN 黃幹. MIEN-CHAI HSIEN-SHENG HUANG WEN-SU-KUNG WEN-CHI 勉齋先生黃文肅公文集 (The complete works of Huang Kan). Southern Sung ed. Possession of Seikadō Bunko, Tokyo.

HUDSON, A. KAZAKH SOCIAL STRUCTURE. London: Oxford University Press, 1938.

HUGHES, E., and HUGHES, K. RELIGION IN CHINA. New York: Hutchinson's University Library, 1950.

HULSEWÉ, A. REMNANTS OF HAN LAW. (Sinica Leidensia, editat, Institutum Sinologium Lugduno Batavum, IX), Leiden: E. J. Brill, 1950.

HU-NAN SHENG-LI CH'ENG-AN 湖南省例成案 (Precedents and leading cases of Hu-nan Province). 1820.

Hung, P'ien-shou. *Meaning and Execution of Marriage Registration*. In *Hsin-wen jih-pao* 新聞日報 (Shanghai Daily News). (Shanghai). Dec. 21, 1952.

Huntington, S. *Political Development and Political Decay*. WORLD POLITICS Vol. XVII (April, 1965): 386–430.

HUNTINGTON, S. POLITICAL ORDER IN CHANGING SOCIETIES. New Haven: Yale University Press, 1968.

HUN-YIN WEN-T'I TS'AN-K'AO TZU-LIAO HUI-PIEN 婚姻問題參考資料彙編 (Collection of reference material on problems relating to marriage). Peking: Hsin-hua shu-kuan ed., 1950.

HUN-YIN-FA WEN-TA 婚姻法問答 (Questions and Answers on the Marriage Law). Anhwei Provincial Court and Judicial Bureau. Hofei, 1964.

IBRAGIMOV, U. OB OSMOVNYEH POLOŽENIJACH PROEKTA BRACNO-SEMEJNOGO KODEKSA UZBEKSKOJ SSR (Basic principles of the draft of the marriage and family code of the Uzbek SSR). Izvestija of the Uzbek SSR, Academy of Sciences, Social Sciences Series, no. 5. Tashkent: 1959.

IOFFE, O. S. SOVETSKOE GRAZDANSKOE PRAVO (Soviet civil law). Vol. III. Leningrad: 1965.

Isaacs, H. *Group Identity and Political Change*. In COLOR AND RACE, edited by J. Franklin. Boston: Houghton, Mifflin, 1968.

JAMIESON, G. CHINESE FAMILY AND COMMERCIAL LAW. Shanghai: Kelly and Walsh, 1921.

JAPANESE CIVIL CODE

Jen-min jih-pao 人民日報 (People's daily) (Peking), May 29, 1950; June 28, 1950; Sept. 17, 1950; Sept. 29, 1951; Sept. 30, 1951; Jan. 17, 1952; Feb. 25, 1953; March 20, 1953; April 13, 1957; Dec. 10, 1958; Jan. 24, 1964; June 20, 1964.

JERNIGAN, T. CHINA IN LAW AND COMMERCE. New York: Macmillan, 1905.

JOHNSON, C. PEASANT NATIONALISM AND COMMUNIST POWER. Stanford, Calif.: Stanford University Press, 1963.

Johnson, E. *The Stem Family and Its Extension in Present Day Japan.* AMERICAN ANTHROPOLOGIST 66 (1964): 839–851.

JOINT PUBLICATION RESEARCH SERVICE. Translation no. 4879.

Kahl, J. *Some Social Concomitants of Industrialization and Urbanization.* HUMAN ORGANIZATION 18 (1959): 53–74.

Kasjukov, I., and Mendeleev, A. *Nužen li talant sem'janinu?* (Must one be talented for family life?). NEDELJA No. 12 (Moscow, 1967). Extracts in German in OST-PROBLEME 19 (1967): 447–450.

KASSOF, A., ed. PROSPECTS FOR SOVIET SOCIETY. New York: Praeger, 1968.

Kauschansky, D. Das europaische Eherecht. In NIEMEYERS ZEITSCHRIFT FÜR INTER-NATIONALES RECHT, edited by T. Niemeyer. 40 (1929): 67 et seq.

KISH, L. SURVEY SAMPLING. New York: J. Wiley, 1965.

KLIBANSKI, H. DIE GESETZGEBUNG DER BOLSCHEWIKI (The Legislation of the Bolsheviks). Leipzig and Berlin: 1920.

KOBLER, A. DER CHRISTLICHE KOMMUNISMUS IN DEN REDUKTIONEN VON PARAGUAY. 1877.

Kodeks zakonov o brake, sem'e i opeke—su RSFSR. 1926. SU 1926, No. 82, St 612.

Korbe, H. *Zum Problem der Scheidung aus beiderseitigem Einverständnis.* NEUE JUSTIZ 4 (1950): 339–340.

KRADER, L. PEOPLES OF CENTRAL ASIA. Bloomington: Indiana University, 1963.

Ku, Chou 古周. *On the Principles Followed in Matters of Divorce Since the Promulgation of the Marriage Law.* CHENG-FA YEN-CHIU (政法研究) Peking. No. 5 (1956).

Ku, H. 顧樓三. *Pu Hou-Han-shu i-wen-chi* 補後漢書藝文志 (A supplementary treatise on literature of the history of the later Han dynasty). In ERH-SHIH-WU SHIH PU-PIEN 二十五史補編 (Supplements to the Twenty-five Histories). Vol. 2. Shanghai: K'ai-ming shu-tien ed.

KUAN HSIEN HSIEN-CHIH 冠縣縣志 (History of Kuan Hsien district), 1934.

KULP, D. H. COUNTRY LIFE IN SOUTH CHINA. New York: Teachers College, Columbia University, 1925.

KUN, BELA, trans. FUNDAMENTAL LAWS OF THE CHINESE SOVIET REPUBLIC. London: Martin Lawrence, Ltd., 1934.

Kung-jen jih-pao 工人日報 (Workers Daily) (Peking), Jan. 12, 1957; 25, 1957.

Kung-min jih-pao 公明日報 (Peking), Feb. 3, 1953.

KUNG-YANG CHUAN 公羊傳 (Kung-yang commentary). With commentary by Ho Hsiu 何休.

KUO, W. 郭衞. TA-LI-YÜAN P'AN-CHÜEH-LI CH'ÜAN-SHU 大理院判決例全書 (Complete records of the decisions and precedents of the Supreme Court). Shanghai: Hui-wen-t'ang, 1932.

Kutschinsky, B. *Law and Education: Some Aspects of Scandinavian Studies into "The General Sense of Justice."* ACTA SOCIOLOGICA 10 (1967): 21–41.

KUWAHARA, J. 桑原隲藏 SHINA HŌSEISHI RONSŌ 支那法制史論叢 (Essays on Chinese legal history). Tokyo: Kobundo, 1935.

KU-WEN-YÜAN 古文宛 (Anthology of ancient literature). Ssu-pu ts'ung-k'an ed. 四部叢刊 (See also, Taipei: Taiwan wu-yin shu-kuan, 1968).

LANG, O. CHINESE FAMILY AND SOCIETY. New Haven: Yale University Press, 1946.

LANG, O. CHINESE FAMILY AND SOCIETY. New Haven: Yale University Press, 1949.

LANSING, J. AND MUELLER, E. THE GEOGRAPHIC MOBILITY OF LABOR. Ann Arbor: Survey Research Center, University of Michigan, 1967.

LASSALLE, FERDINAND. AUSGEWAHLTE TEXTE. Edited by T. Ramm. Stuttgart: Koehler, 1962.

LATOURETTE, K. THE CHINESE, THEIR HISTORY AND CULTURE. Rev. ed. New York Macmillan, 1964.

LAW AND SOCIETY REVIEW (Nov. 1968).

LEC, S. NEUE UNFRISIERTE GEDANKEN. Munchen: Hanser, 1964.

LEGGE, J. LI-KI New Hyde Park: University Books reprint, 1967.

LEHMANN, H. DEUTSCHES FAMILIENRECHT. 2d. ed. Berlin: De Gruyter, 1948.

LENIN, V. WERKE. East Berlin: Dietz, 1959.

LENSKI, G. POWER AND PRIVILEGE. New York: McGraw-Hill, 1966.

LEVY, M. Jr. THE FAMILY REVOLUTION IN MODERN CHINA. Cambridge: Harvard University Press, 1949.

Levy, M. Jr. MODERNIZATION AND THE STRUCTURE OF SOCIETIES. Princeton, N.J. Princeton University Press, 1966.

Levy, M. Jr. *Aspects of the Analysis of Family Structure*. In ASPECTS OF THE ANALYSIS OF FAMILY STRUCTURE, edited by A. Coale *et al*. Princeton, N.J.: Princeton University Press, 1965.

LEVY, R. THE SOCIAL STRUCTURE OF ISLAM. Cambridge [England]: Cambridge University Press, 1962.

LEWIS, J. LEADERSHIP IN COMMUNIST CHINA. Ithaca, N.Y.: Cornell University Press, 1963.

LI CHI 禮記 (Book of rites or Record of the rules of propriety). Shanghai: Chung-hua shu-chü ed, 1927.

LI, F. 李昉. T'AI-P'ING YÜ-LAN 太平御覽 ([Encyclopedia for] imperial perusal of the T'ai-p'ing era). Hsin-shing shu-chü ed., 1959.

LI, YEN-SHOU 李延壽 NAN SHIH 南史 (History of southern dynasties). Taipei: Tu-che shu-tien, 1959.

LI, YÜ 李漁. TZU-CHIH HSIN-SHU 資治新書; 1663. (Guide to governing, new text).

Lien-ho-pao 聯合報 (Taipei), Dec. 4, 1963.

LIFTON, R. REVOLUTIONARY IMMORTALITY: MAO TSE-TUNG AND THE CHINESE CULTURAL REVOLUTION. New York: Random House, 1968.

LOFTON, R. THOUGHT REFORM AND THE PSYCHOLOGY OF TOTALISM. New York: Norton, 1961.

LIN, Y. THE GOLDEN WING: A SOCIOLOGICAL STUDY OF CHINESE FAMILISM. New York: Oxford University Press, 1948.

Lippit, Victor D. *Development of Transportation in Communist China*. CHINA QUARTERLY, July–Sept. 1966, pp. 101–19.

Literaturnaja Gazeta (Moscow), Dec. 25, 1965.

LI, Tz'U-MING 李慈銘. YUEH-MAN-T'ANG JIH-CHI 越縵堂日記 (Diary of Li Tz'u-ming). Shanghai: Commercial Press, 1936.

LIU, A. 劉安. HUAI-NAN-TZU 淮南子. I-wen yin-shu kuan ed., 1953. (See also Shanghai: Commercial Press, 1953).

LIU CHI 劉基. CH'ENG-YI-PO WEN-CHI 誠意伯文集 (Collected works of Liu Chi). Taipei: Taiwan Shang-wu, 1968.

LIU, H. W. THE TRADITIONAL CHINESE CLAN RULES. Locust Valley, N.Y.: J. J. Augustin, 1959.

Liu, S. and Lou, C. 劉掞藜, 婁景斐 *Han-tai chih hun-yin ch'i-hsiang* 漢代之婚姻奇象 (Strange phenomena regarding marriage in the Han dynasty). KUO-LI WU-HAN TA-HSÜEH WEN-CHE CHI-K'AN 國立武漢大學文哲季刊 (National Wuhan University literature and philosophy quarterly) 1 (no. 1) (1930): 257–280.

Liu, Shao-ch'i. In EXTRACTS FROM CHINA MAINLAND MAGAZINES No. 149 (Dec. 1, 1958). Hong Kong: American Consulate General.

Liu Yün-hsiang 劉云祥. Kuan-yü cheng-ch'ueh jen-shih yü ch'u-li tang-ch'ien ti li-hun wen-t'i (關於正確認識與處理當前的離婚問題). *On the Correct Understanding and Handling of Divorce Problems at Present.* FA HSÜEH 法學, no. 3 (1958).

Loeber, D. *Eherecht in der Sowjetunion.* Thesis, Marburg, 1950.

LOEBER, D. OSTEUROPA. 1952. no. 3, p. 169–176.

Loeber, D. *Die sowjetsche Rechtsreform von 1958:* Osteuropa 9 (1959): 355–359.

Lu Yü-chi and Wei, Huan-hua. *Kwan-yü tang-ch'ien hun-yin k'ai-li ti hsing-chieh chi ch'u-li yüan-ts'e ti t'an-t'ao* (Investigation into the nature of marriage presents at the present time.) FA HSÜEH 法學, No. 5 (1957).

Lubman, S. *Mao and Mediation.* CALIFORNIA LAW REVIEW 55 No. 5 (1967): 1284–1359.

Luschinsky, Mildred S. *The Impact of Some Recent Indian Government Legislation on the Women of an Indian Village.* ASIAN SURVEY 3: 573–83.

Luther, G. Verlöbnis. In RECHTSVERG LEICHENDES HANDWÖRTERBUCH, edited by F. Schlegelberger. Berlin: Franz Valten 1929–1939 vol. 7, p. 193–216 (1939).

MA KUO-HAN 馬國翰. YU-HAN SHAN-FANG CHI-I-SHU 玉函山房輯佚書 (Collected [fragments of] lost books in Yü-han mountain dwelling). In CHUNG-KUO SSU-HSIANG MING-CHU (中國思想名著). Taipei: Shih-Chieh Shu-chu, 1959.

MACFARQUHAR, R., ed. THE HUNDRED FLOWERS CAMPAIGN AND THE CHINESE INTELLECTUALS. New York: Praeger, 1960.

MACKENROTH, G. BEVÖLKERUNGSLEHRE. Berlin: Springer, 1953.

MAGIDSON, J. DAS SOWJETISCHE EHERECHT UNTER BESONDERER BERÜCKSICHTIGUNG DES EHEAUFLÖSUNGSRECHTS. In LEIPZIGER RECHTSWISSENSCHAFTLICHE STUDIEN H. 62 (1931), Leipzig: Weicher, 1931, pp. 1 et seq.

MAKI, K. 牧健. NIPPON HOSEI SHI 日本法制史 (Japanese legal history). Tokyo: Kōbundō, 1937.

MAKINO, T. 牧野巽. SHINA KAZOKU KENKYŪ 支那家族研究 (A study of the Chinese family). Tokyo: Seikatsusha, 1944.

MANNHEIM, K. MAN AND SOCIETY IN AN AGE OF RECONSTRUCTION. STUDIES IN MODERN SOCIAL STRUCTURE. London: K. Paul, Trench, Trubner & Co., Ltd., 1940.

MANTETSU CHŌSA SHIRYŌ 滿鐵調查資料 (Research report of the Southern Manchurian Railway Company). Report no. 165, 1934.

Mao, Tse-tung. *Report on an Investigation of the Peasant Movement in Hunan* (March 1927). In QUOTATIONS FROM CHAIRMAN MAO TSE-TUNG. Peking: Foreign Languages Press, 1966.

MAO-MING HSIEN-CHIH 茂名縣志 (History of Mao-ming district), 1888.

MARRIS, P. FAMILY AND SOCIAL CHANGE IN AN AFRICAN CITY. A STUDY OF REHOUSING IN LAGOS. London: Routledge & K. Paul, 1961.

Marsh, R. *The Taiwanese of Taipei.* JOURNAL OF ASIAN STUDIES 27 (1968): 572–75.

MARX, KARL and ENGELS, FRIEDRICH. AUSGEWÄHLTE SCHRIFTEN IN 2 BÄNDEN. East Berlin: 1955.

Marx, Karl and Engels, Friedrich. *Kommunistisches Manifest* (1848). In KARL MARX and FRIEDRICH ENGELS. WERKE. Vol. 4. East Berlin: 1957.

MARX, KARL and ENGELS, FRIEDRICH. WERKE. East Berlin: 1957.

Masal 'skii, V. *Turkestanskii Kray* (Turkestan territory). In ROSSIA, edited by Semenov-Tianshanskii, Vol. 19. St. Petersburg, 1913.

Massell, Gregory J. *Law as an Instrument of Revolutionary Change in a Traditional Milieu : The Case of Soviet Central Asia.* LAW AND SOCIETY REVIEW, II 2, (Feb. 1968): 179–228.

Massell, Gregory J. *The Vulnerability of Islamic Society to Revolutionary Social Engineering : Soviet Central Asia.* Paper read at the Plenary Session of the Annual Meeting of the Middle East Studies Association, November 15, 1968, at Austin, Texas.

Meijer, Marinus J., trans. *Early Communist Marriage Legislation in China.* In CONTEMPORARY CHINA, edited by E. Stuart Kirby. Vol. 6 (1962–64): 84–102. Hong Kong: Hong Kong University Press, 1968.

MEIJER, MARINUS J. THE INTRODUCTION OF MODERN CRIMINAL LAW IN CHINA. Sinica Indonesiana, no. 2; Batavia, 1950.

Meijer, Marinus J. *Specific Problems of Translation : Family Law,* Unpublished manuscript presented at the conference on Chinese Communist Law, Bermuda, May 27–30, 1967.

MEIJER, MARINUS J. MARRIAGE LAW AND POLICY IN THE CHINESE PEOPLE'S REPUBLIC. Hong Kong: Hong Kong University Press, 1971.

Merson, B. *Husbands with More than One Wife.* LADIES HOME JOURNAL 84 (June 1967).

MINER, H. and DeVos, G. OASIS AND CASBAH: ALGERIAN CULTURE AND PERSONALITY IN CHANGE. Ann Arbor: University of Michigan Press, 1960.

MING-KUNG SHU-P'AN CH'ING-MING-CHI 名公書判清明集 (Illustrious compilation of the decisions of famous judges). Southern Sung ed. Reprint. Tokyo: Seikadō Bunko, 1964.

Moore, W. *Change in Occupational Structures.* In SOCIAL STRUCTURE AND MOBILITY IN ECONOMIC DEVELOPMENT, edited by N. Smelser and S. Lipset. Chicago: Aldine Publishing Co., 1966.

MOORE, W. SOCIAL CHANGE. Englewood Cliffs, N.J.: Prentice-Hall, 1963.

Morioka, K. *Life Cycle Patterns in Japan, China, and the United States.* JOURNAL OF MARRIAGE AND THE FAMILY 29 (1967): 595–606.

Morohashi, T. 諸橋轍次 DAIKANWA JITEN 大漢和辭典 (Great Chinese and Japanese dictionary). Tokyo: Tai shukan shoten, 1955–59.

MÜLLER-FREIENFELS, W. EHE UND RECHT. Tubingen: Mohr, 1962.

Müller-Freienfels, W. *Legal Unification of Family Law*. AMERICAN JOURNAL OF COMPARATIVE LAW 16 (1968): pp. 175–218.

Müller-Freienfels, W. *Zur Revolutionären Familiengesetzgebung, insbesondere zum Ehegesetz der Volksrepublic China* vol 1. 5. 1950. In JUS PRIVATUM GENTIUM *(Festschrift für Max Rheinstein)*. Vol. 2. Tubingen: Mohr, 1969, pp. 843–908.

Murdock, G. *Cognatic Forms of Social Organization*. In SOCIAL STRUCTURES IN SOUTHEAST ASIA, edited by G. Murdock. Chicago: Quadrangle Books, 1960.

MURDOCK, G. SOCIAL STRUCTURE, paperback ed. New York: Free Press, 1965.

NAKATA, K. 中田薫. HŌSEI SHI RONSHŪ 法制史論集 (Collected essays on legal history). Vol. 1, 1926.

Nakata, K. 中田薫. *Tōsō-jidai no kazoku kyōsansei* 唐宋時代の家族共産制 (Communal Property Family in T'ang and Sung Times). HŌSEISHI RONSHŪ 法制史論集 (Collected essays on legal history), by K. NAKATA. Vol. 3. Tokyo: Iwanami Shoten, 1943.

Nan-fang jih-pao 南方日報 (Canton), Feb. 13, 1952.

Nathan, H. *Gedanken zum sozialistischen Güterrecht*. NEUE JUSTIZ 12 (1958): 120–126.

Nei-wu Pu Min-cheng Szu 內務部民政司 (Ministry of Interior, Division of Civil Affairs) compl. TSEN-YANG TSO HAO HUN-YIN TENG-CHI KUNG TSO 怎樣做好婚姻登記工作 (How to do good marriage registration work). Peking, 1963.

New York Times. Feb. 14, 1968, pp. 51, 55.

New York Times. Aug. 28, 1968 (Weekly Review).

NIIDA, N. 仁井田陞 CHUGOKU HOSEISHI KENKYU; DOREINODOHO KAZOKU SONRAKUHO 中國法制史研究；奴隸農奴法家族村落法 (Studies in Chinese legal history; law of slave and serf, and Family and village law). Tokyo: Toyo Bunka kenkyujo (東洋文化研究所), 1962.

Niida, N. *Chūgoku no jinmin minshushgi kakumei to kazoku* 中國の人民民主主義革命と家族 (People's democratic revolution and family law in China). KAZOKUMONDAI TO KAZOKUHŌ 家族問題と家族法 (Family problems and family law), edited by A. Nakagawa *et al*. Vol. 1. Tokyo: 1958.

NIIDA, N. 仁井田陞. CHŪGOKU NO NOSON KAZOKU 中國の農村家族 (The Chinese rural family). Tokyo: Tokyo University Press, 1952.

Niida, N. *Chūka Jinmin Kyōwakoku Koninhō* 中華人民共和國婚姻法 (Marriage law of the People's Republic of China). In SHIN HIKAKU KONINHŌ 新比較婚姻法 (A new comparison of laws relating to marriage), edited by K. Miyazaki. Vol. 1. Tokyo: 1961.

NIIDA, N. CHŪKA JINMIN KYŌWAKOKU KONINHŌ 中華人民共和國婚姻法 (Marriage law of the People's Republic of China). Reprint from HSIN IKAKU KONYINHŌ 新比較婚姻法 (New comparative Marriage Law). ed. F. Tsuda, Tokyo: 1960.

Niida, N. *Kyū chūgku shakai no nakama-shugi to kazoku* 舊中國社會の人中間主義と家族 (The family and notion of fellowship in old China). In CHŪGOKU HŌSEISHI KENKYŪ; DOREINŌDOHŌ KAZOKU SONRAKUHŌ (Studies in Chinese legal history; law of slave and serf, and family and village law), by N. NIIDA. Tokyo: Toyo Bunka Kenkyūjo, 1962.

Niida, N. *Min Shin Jidai no Hitouri Oyobi Hitojichi Bunsho no Kenkyū* 明清時代の人賣及び人質之書の研究 (Research on documents re the sale and pawning of people in the Ch'ing and Ming dynasties). SHIGAKU ZASSHI 史學雜誌 (Journal of historical studies) 46: No. 6.

Niida, N. *Seimeishū kokonmon no kenkyū* 清明集戶婚門の研究 (A study of the section on household and marriage in the illustrious compilation). Tōhō GAKUHō 東方 學報 (Journal of Oriental Studies) 4.

NIIDA, N. SHINA MIBUNHōSHI 支那身分法史 (Historical Survey of Social Status in Chinese Law). Tokyo: Zayuho Kankokai, 1942.

Niida, N. *Shūkyō ni kankeinaki koninhō; chūgoku koninhō no kihonmondai* 宗敎に關係 なき婚姻法; 中國婚姻法の基本問題 (Law of marriage without any religious influence; fundamental problems of the new Chinese marriage law). HIKAKUHō KENKYū 比較法研究 (Comparative law journal) 18. Tokyo: April 1959.

Niida, N. *Sōdai no kasanhō ni okeru joshi no chii* 宋代の家產法に於ける女子の地位 (The position of women in the family property law of the Sung). In CHUGOKU HOSEISHI KENKYU; DOREINōDōHō KAZOKU SONRAKUHō 中國法制史研究; 奴隷農奴 法家族村落法 (Studies in Chinese legal history; law of slave and serf, and family and village law), by N. Niida. Tokyo: Toyo Bunka kenkyūjo, 1962.

Niida, N. TōRYO SHūI 唐令拾遺 (Remnants of the T'ang statues). Tok,o: Tohobunka Gakuin, 1933. Reprint. Tokyo: Tokyo University Press, 1964.

NIIDA, N. Tōsō Hōritsu monjo no KENKYū 唐宋法律文書の研究 (Research on the legal documents of the T'ang and Sung dynasties). Tokyo: Tohobunka Gakuin, 1937.

NIMKOFF, M., ed. COMPARATIVE FAMILY SYSTEMS. Boston: Houghton Mifflin, 1965.

Nimkoff, M. and Middleton, R. *Types of Family and Types of Economy.* AMERICAN JOURNAL OF SOCIOLOGY 66 (1960): 215–25.

NIVISEN, D. *et al.* eds. CONFUCIANISM IN ACTION. Stanford, Calif.: Stanford University Press, 1953.

NIZSALOVSKY, E. ORDER OF THE FAMILY. Budapest: Akadémiai Kiadó, 1968.

NORTH, R. KUOMINTANG AND CHINESE COMMUNIST ELITES. Stanford, Calif.: Stanford University Press, 1952.

NOVE, A., AND NEWTH, J. THE SOVIET MIDDLE EAST. . . . New York: Praeger, 1967.

OGBURN, W. AND NIMKOFF, M. TECHNOLOGY AND THE CHANGING FAMILY. Boston: Houghton Mifflin, 1955.

Ottenberg, S. *Local Government and the Law in Southern Nigeria.* In TRADITIONAL AND MODERN LEGAL INSTITUTIONS IN ASIA AND AFRICA, edited by D. Buxbaum. Leiden: E.J. Brill, 1967.

ŌYAMA, H. 大山彦一. CHūGOKUJIN NO KAZOKU SEIDO NO KENKYū 中國人の家族制度 の研究 (Study of the family institutions of the Chinese). Kyoto: Seki Shoin, 1952.

PAN KU 班固. HAN SHU 漢書 (History of the [former] Han dynasty). Peking: Chung-hua shu-chü ed., 1962.

P'ANG T'UN-CHIH 龐敦志. HUN-YIN-FA CHI-PEN CHIH-SHIH 婚姻法基本知識 (Basic knowledge on the marriage law). Hua-ch'iao t'u-shu-she (華僑圖書社) Kowloon: 1950.

Pao, C. *Indoctrination of the People's Liberation Army.* In SURVEY OF CHINA MAINLAND PRESS. No. 4176. Hong Kong: American Consulate General, May 13, 1968.

PARK, A. BOLSHEVISM IN TURKESTAN. 1917–1927. New York: Columbia University Press, 1957.

Parsons, T. *An Analytical Approach to the Theory of Social Stratification.* In ESSAYS IN SOCIOLOGICAL THEORY, edited by T. Parsons. Rev. ed. Chicago: Free Press, 1954.

Parsons, T. *The Kinship System of the Contemporary United States*. In Essays in Sociological Theory, edited by T. Parsons. rev. ed. Chicago: Free Press, 1954.

Pei-ching kung-jen jih-pao (Peking Daily Workers Newspaper). (Peking), April 14, 1966.

Pennell, W. *Review of* The Peasant and the Communes *(1962) by Henry Y. Lethbridge*. Current Scene Developments in Mainland China. No. 9 (1963).

Pergament, A. *O kodifikacii respublikanskogo zakonodal'stva o brake, sem'e i opeke* On the codification of the Republic legislation on marriage, family and guardianship). In Naucnaja sessija posvjascennaja voprosam kodifikacii sovetskogo respublikanskogo zakonodatel'stva (Scientific conference on problems of Soviet Republic legislation). Moscow, 1957. pp. 72–94.

Pergament, A. *Pravovoe polozenie vnebracnych detej dolžno byt'izmeneno* (The legal status of illegitimate children shall be changed). Sovetskoe gosundarstvo v pravo (Soviet state and law) 9 (1956): 65–72.

Pergament, A. *Das Sowjetische Familienrecht*. In Die Sowjetunion Heute. Bonn: 4, 1959. ed. of June 1, 1959, p. 14 and ed. of June 10, p. 14.

Peristiany, J., ed. Honour and Shame: The Values of Mediterranean Society. Chicago: University of Chicago Press, 1965.

Pfeffer, R. *Crime and Punishment : China and the United States*. World Politics, XXI, 1, (Oct. 1968): 152–81.

Pierce, R. Russian Central Asia: 1867–1917. Berkeley: University of California Press, 1960.

Pipes, R. The Formation of the Soviet Union. Cambridge: Harvard University Press, 1964.

Plato. The Republic. Edited by B. Jowett. Oxford: Oxford University Press, 1937.

P'o-ch'u chiu hsi-su, ch'uang-li hsin feng-shang 破除舊習俗，創立新風尙 (Destroy old customs and establish new trends). In *Chung-kuo ch'ing-nien* 中國青年 (Chinese youth). (Peking), Feb. 1, 1964.

Po-shing hsien-chih 博興縣志 (History of Po-hsing district). 1840.

Postanovlenie No. 13 Plenuma Verchovnogo Suda SSR ot 29. 12. 1965g. "O primenerii sudami Ukaza Prezidiuma Verchovnogo Soveta SSSR ot 10. 12. 1965g. O nekotorom izmenii porjadka rassmotrenija v sudach del o rastorženii braka" (Directive no 13 of the Plenary Supreme Court of the USSR of December 29, 1965: "On the judicial application of the decree of the Praesidium of the Supreme Soviet of the USSR of December 10, 1965, on several amendments of the procedural system in divorce matters"). Sowjetskaja justizja (Soviet justice) No. 3 (1966): 32.

Postanovlenie Plenuma Verchovnogo Suda SSSR No. 12/8/Y at 16. 9. 1949g. "O sudebnoj praktike po delem o restorzenii braka" (Directives of the Plenary Supreme Court of the USSR No. 12/8/Y of September 16, 1949: "On the judicial practice in matters of divorce"). In Kodeks zakonow o brake, semje i opjekje (Code of laws on marriage, family and guardianship). Official ed. Moscow: 1961.

Pravda (Moscow), June 28, 1968.

Proceedings of the Conference on the Role of Law in Modernizing Nations : Chinese Family Law and Social Change. August 1968, at the University of Washington Law School, Seattle, Washington.

P'u-chou chih 濮州志 (History of P'u-chou Province), 1908.

Pye, L. The Spirit of Chinese Politics. Cambridge: Massachusetts Institute of Technology Press, 1968.

QUOTATIONS FROM CHAIRMAN MAO TSE-TUNG. Peking: Foreign Languages Press, 1966.

Rabinovic, N. *Semejnoe pravo* (Family Law). In SOROK LET SOVETSKOGO PRAVA, 1917–57 (Forty years of Soviet law, 1917–57), edited by M. D. Sargorodskij. Vol. II, p. 263–300, Moscow: 1957.

Raiser, T. *Sozialistisches Familienrecht zum neuen Familiengesetzbuch. Der "Dor"* JURISTENZEITUNG 21 (1966) p. 423–428.

Rheinstein, M. *How to Review a Festschrift.* AMERICAN JOURNAL OF COMPARATIVE LAW 11 (1962): p. 632–634.

Rheinstein, M. *The Law of Family and Succession.* In CIVIL LAW IN THE MODERN WORLD, edited by A. Yiannopolus, Baton Rouge: Louisiana State University Press, 1965.

RHEINSTEIN, M., ed. MAX WEBER ON LAW IN ECONOMY AND SOCIETY. Cambridge: Harvard University Press, 1966.

RINJI TAIWAN KYŪKAN CHŌSAKAI 臨時台灣舊慣調查會 (Temporary committee on research of customs and practices on Taiwan). TAIWAN SHIHŌ 台灣私法 (Taiwan private law), 1910.

RINJI TAIWAN KYŪKAN CHŌSAKAI 臨時台灣舊慣調查會 (The Temporary Commission for the Investigation of Old Laws and Customs in Formosa). TAIWAN SHIHŌ 台灣私法 (The private laws of Taiwan). Vol. 2, 1910.

RINJI TAIWAN KYŪKAN CHŌSAKAI. TAIWAN SHIHŌ FUROKU SANKŌSHO 台灣私法附錄 參考書 (Reference materials appended to the private laws of Taiwan), 1910–1911.

ROSE, A. *The Use of Law to Induce Social Change.* TRANSACTIONS OF THE THIRD WORLD CONGRESS OF SOCIOLOGY. Vol. VI, (1956) 52–63.

ROSENTHAL, E. POLITICAL THOUGHT IN MEDIEVAL ISLAM. Cambridge [England]: Cambridge University Press, 1958.

RYWKIN, M. RUSSIA IN CENTRAL ASIA. New York: Macmillan, 1963.

SALMON, J. S. JURISPRUDENCE. 11th ed. London: Sweet and Maxwell, Ltd., 1957.

SCHLESINGER, R. THE FAMILY IN THE USSR. CHANGING ATTITUDES IN SOVIET RUSSIA, London: Manheim, 1949.

SCHMIDT, F. DER CHRISTLICH-SOCIALE STAAT DER JESUITEN IN PARAGUAY, 1913.

Schneider, D., and Homans, G. *Kinships Terminology and the American Kinship System.* AMERICAN ANTHROPOLOGIST. 57 (1955).

SCHUR, E. LAW AND SOCIETY: A SOCIOLOGICAL VIEW. New York: Random House, 1968.

SCHURMANN, F. IDEOLOGY AND ORGANIZATION IN COMMUNIST CHINA. Berkeley: University of California Press, 1966.

Shurmann, H. *Peking's Recognition of Crisis.* In MODERN CHINA, edited by A. Feuerwerke. Englewood Cliffs, N.J.: Prentice Hall, 1964.

SCHWARTZ, B. CHINESE COMMUNISM AND THE RISE OF MAO. Cambridge: Harvard University Press, 1951.

SCHWARTZ, B. COMMUNISM AND CHINA: IDEOLOGY IN FLUX. Cambridge: Harvard University Press, 1968.

SCHWARTZ, B. IN SEARCH OF WEALTH AND POWER: A BIOGRAPHY OF YEN FU. Cambridge: Harvard University Press, 1964.

Schwind. *Probleme des oesterreichischen Eherechts* EHE UND FAMILIE IM PRIVATEN UND ÖFFENTLICHEN RECHT, ZEITSCHRIFT FÜR DAS GESAMTE FAMILIENRECHT 3 (1956): 11–15.

SEPP, A. REISSBESCHREIBUNG, 1697.

Shanghai chieh-fang jih-pao (Shanghai Liberation Daily), July 20, 1952.

SHIGA, SHŪZŌ 滋賀秀三. CHŪGOKU KAZOKU HŌ NO GENRI 中國家族法の原理 (Basic principles underlying Chinese family law). Tokyo: Sobunsha (倉文社), 1967.

SHIGA, SHŪZŌ 滋賀秀三. CHŪGOKU KAZOKUHŌ HOKŌ 中國家族法補考 (Supplementary studies on Chinese family law). KOKKA GAKKAI ZASSHI 國家學會雜誌 (Journal of the association of political and social sciences, the University of Tokyo) 67, nos. 5, 9, and 11; 68, No. 7 (1953–55).

Shiga, Shūzō 滋賀秀三. CHŪGOKU KAZOKUHŌRON 中國家族法論 (Theory of Chinese family law). Tokyo: Kombundo, 1950.

SHIH, HUAI-PI. LUEH-LUN WO KUO CHI-CH'EN CHIH-TU TI CHI-KE CHI-PEN WEN-T'I 略論我國繼承制度的幾個基本問題 (A discussion of several basic problems of the system of inheritance in our country). Peking: 1957.

SHKLAR, J. LEGALISM. Cambridge: Harvard University Press, 1964.

Siu, Kia-pei. *La Réforme du Droit du Mariage en Chine Communiste.* REVUE INTERNATIONALE DE DROIT COMPARÉ 8 (1956): pp. 577–578.

SJOBERG, G. THE PREINDUSTRIAL CITY PAST AND PRESENT. New York: Free Press of Glencoe, 1960.

Skinner, G. *Marketing and Social Structure in Rural China, Part I. Journal of* ASIAN STUDIES 24 (1964): 3–43.

SMELSER, N. and LIPSET, S., eds. SOCIAL STRUCTURE AND MOBILITY IN ECONOMIC DEVELOPMENT. Chicago: Aldine Pub. Co., 1966.

SMITH, D., ed. SOUTH ASIAN POLITICS AND RELIGION. Princeton, N.J.: Princeton University Press, 1966.

SMITH, W. ISLAM IN MODERN HISTORY. Princeton, N.J.: Princeton University Press, 1957.

Solien de Gonzales, N. *Family Organization in Five Types of Migratory Wage Labor.* AMERICAN ANTHROPOLOGIST 63 (1961): 1264–81.

SOLOMON, R. THE CHINESE POLITICAL CULTURE AND PROBLEMS OF MODERNIZATION. Cambridge: Massachusetts Institute of Technology, 1964.

Solomon, R. H. *Communication Patterns and the Chinese Revolution.* CHINA QUARTERLY, No. 32 Oct.–Dec. 1967, pp. 88–110.

Solomon, R. H. *Mao's Effort to Reintegrate the Chinese Policy-Problems Of Authority and Conflict in Chinese Local Processes.* In CHINESE COMMUNIST POLITICS IN ACTION, edited by A. D. Barnett: Seattle: University of Washington Press, 1969.

Soloweitschik, G. *Das Eherecht der Russischen Sozialistischen Föderativen Sowjetrepublik unter besonderer Berücksichtigung seiner Stelling im internationalen Privatrecht.* Thesis, Leipzig, 1931.

SOOTHILL, W. THE THREE RELIGIONS OF CHINA. London: Oxford University Press, 1929.

SSU-MA, CH'IEN 司馬遷. SHIH CHI 史記 (Records of the historian). Peking: Chung-hua-shu-chü, 1959 ed.

Stahnke, A. *The Background and Evolution of Party Policy on the Drafting of Legal Codes in Communist China.* AMERICAN JOURNAL OF COMPARATIVE LAW 15 (1967): pp. 506 et seq.

Statute on the Amendment and Supplementation of the Text of the Constitution of the USSR. VEDOMOST; VERCHOVNOGO SOVETA, SSSR (Bulletin of the Supreme Soviet of the USSR) No. 8 (Feb. 25, 1947).

STAUNTON, G. TA TSING LEU LEE: BEING THE FUNDAMENTAL LAWS AND A SELECTION FROM THE SUPPLEMENTARY STATUTES OF THE PENAL CODE OF CHINA. London: T. Cadwell, 1810.

STEELE, J. THE I-LI OR BOOK OF ETIQUETTE AND CEREMONIAL. Taipei: Ch'eng-wen Publishing Company, 1966 (1917).

STONE, J. THE PROVINCE AND FUNCTION OF LAW. Cambridge: Harvard University Press, 1950.

SURVEY OF CHINA MAINLAND MAGAZINES No. 566 (Apr. 6, 1967).

SURVEY OF CHINA MAINLAND PRESS (American Consulate General, Hong Kong) 4153/9 (April 4, 1968).

Sverdlov, G. *Das Eherecht der Union des Sozialistischen Sowjetrepubliken* in LESKE AND LOEWENFELD. DAS EHERECHT DER EUROPAISCHEN UND DER AUSSEREUROPAISCHEN STAATEN. Vol. I, pp. 561–616. Koln: Heymanns, 1965.

Sverdlov, G. *Die Entwieklung des Sowjetischen Familienrechts seit der Oktober revolution.* NEUE JUSTIZ 11 (1957): 683–687.

Sverdlov, G. *O Razvode* (Concerning Divorce) SOVETSKOE GOSUNDARSTVO I PRAVO (Soviet state and law) No. 12 (1958): 48–58.

SVERDLOV, G. OCHRANA INTERESOV DETEJ V SOVETSKOM SEMENJOM I GRAZDANSKOM PRAVE (The protection of the interests of children in the Soviet family and civil law). Moscow: 1955.

SVERDLOV, G. SOVETSKOE SEMEJNOE PRAVO (Soviet family law). Moscow: Gosjurizdat, 1958.

SWANN, N. PAN CHAO: FOREMOST WOMAN SCHOLAR OF CHINA. New York: The Century Co., 1932.

SWOD SAKONOV GRAZDANSKICH (Civil code).

TA-CH'ING MIN-LÜ TS'AO-AN 大清民律草案 (Draft of the civil code of the Great Ch'ing dynasty), in Chung-hua liu-fa chüan-shu (中華六法全書). Shanghai: Fa-cheng shüeh-she, 1912.

TA-CH'ING HUI-TIEN SHIH-LI 大清會典事例 (Established precedents and collected institutes of the great Ch'ing dynasty). Reprint of 1899 ed. Taipei: Chi-wen ch'u-pan-she, 1963.

Ta kung pao 大公報 (Peking), June 16, 1953.

TA-CH'ING LÜ-LI TSENG-HSIU T'UNG-TSUAN CHI-CH'ENG 大清律例增修統纂集成 (Revised comprehensive edition of the statutes and established precedents of the Great Ch'ing dynasty). Shanghai: Wen-jui-kou-chung-pan shih-yin. ed., 1878.

TA-CH'ING T'UNG-LI 大清通禮 (Rites and regulations of the Great Ch'ing dynasty), 1824.

TAI, Y. 戴炎輝. CHUNG-KUO CH'IN-SHU FA 中國親屬法 (Chinese family law). 1962. 4th ed. Taipei: 1965.

TAI, Y. 戴炎輝. CHUNG-KUO FA-CHIH SHIH 中國法制史 (A legal history of China). Taipei: 1966.

TAI, Y. *Kinsei Shina oyobi Taiwan no kazoku kyōsansei* 近世支那及び台灣の家族共產制 (Family Communal property in China and on Taiwan in recent times). HŌGAKU KYŌKAI ZASSHI 法學協會雜誌 (Journal of the jurisprudence association, the University of Tokyo) 52 Nos. 10 and 11 (1934).

TAI, Y. In 台灣省通志稿 TAIWAN SHENG T'UNG-CHIH KAO (Draft history of Taiwan Province), 1954.

TAI, YEN-HUI, T'ANG-LÜ T'UNG-LUN 唐律通論 (Comprehensive discussions of the T'ang code), 1964.

TAIWAN KANSHŪ KIJI 台灣慣習記事 (Records of customs in Taiwan), 1901–07.

TAIWAN KANSHŪ KENKYŪKAI 台灣慣習研究會 (Research Society of Customs in Taiwan). TAIWAN KANSHŪ KIJI 台灣慣習記事 (Reports on customs in Taiwan). 1904.

TAIWAN NUNG-CHIA CHI-CHANG PAO-KAO 台灣農家記帳報告 (Report on rural household in Taiwan). 1965.

T'AIWAN SHENG HSING-CHENG CHANG-KUAN T'UNG-CHI-SHIH (台灣省行政長官統計室) TAIWAN WU-SHIH-I NIEN LAI T'UNG-CHI T'I-YAO 台灣省五十一年來統計提要 (Fifty-one year summary of Taiwan statistics). Taipei: Taiwan-sheng yin-shua chih-yeh ed., 1946.

TAKIKAWA, K. 瀧川龜太郎. SHIKI KAICHŪ KŌSHŌ 史記會注考證 (Historical memories). Reprint, 1934.

Ta-kung pao 大公報 (T'ien-chin), Feb. 2, 1953.

T'AO, H. 陶希聖. HUN-YIN YÜ CHIA-TSU 婚姻與家族 (Marriage and family) Shanghai: Commercial Press, 1934.

Teng, Ying-chao. *La Loi sur le Mariage de la République Populaire* (On the marriage law of the People's Republic of China), in "Rapport sur la Loi sur le Mariage de la République Populaire de Chine" given in Kalgan: May 14, 1950. Quoted in English in *The New Marriage Law of Communist China*, by S. Fu. In CONTEMPORARY CHINA, edited by E. Stuart Kirby. Vol. 1. Hong Kong: Hong Kong University Press, 1955.

Thibault-Laurent, G. *La Première Introduction du Divorce en France sous la Révolution et l'Empire*. Thesis, Montpellier, 1938.

Tilly, C. and Brown, C. *On Uprooting, Kinship and the Auspices of Migration*. INTERNATIONAL JOURNAL OF COMPARATIVE SOCIOLOGY 8 (Sept. 1967), 139–64.

TJAN, T. S. PO HU T'UNG: THE COMPREHENSIVE DISCUSSIONS IN WHITE TIGER HALL. (Sinica Leidensia, editit, Institutum Sinologium Lugdano Batavum, vol. VI), Leiden: E. J. Brill, 1949.

TOWNSEND, J. POLITICAL PARTICIPATION IN COMMUNIST CHINA. Berkeley: University of California Press, 1967.

TREADGOLD, D. ed. SOVIET AND CHINESE COMMUNISM: SIMILARITIES AND DIFFERENCES. Seattle: University of Washington Press, 1967.

Tscherwenkow, W. *Narodnite komuni v. kitaj* (The people's communes in China). In *Rabotnitschesko delo* (Sofia), Jan. 15, 1959. Slightly abridged and reprinted in OST-PROBLEME 11 (1959): pp. 84–86.

Tso, CH'IU-MING 左丘明. TSO-CHUAN 左傳 (Tso commentary) in Chung-kuo ku-tien ming-chu pa chung (中國古典名著八種). Peking: Wen-hsing shu-tien ed., 1966.

Ts'UI PAO 崔豹. KU-CHIN CHU 古今注 (Notes on the traditional and modern). Shanghai: Commercial Press, 1937 ed.

Ts'ui, Y. C. and Lin, T. L. A STUDY OF RURAL LABOR MOBILITY IN RELATION TO INDUSTRIALIZATION AND URBANIZATION IN TAIWAN. Economic Digest Series, No. 16, 1964.

T'U-CHI FUKIEN LIEN-CHIANG LU-HUO FEI-FANG WEN-CHIEN HUI PIEN 突擊福建連江 鹵攫匪文件彙編 (Compilation of Communist documents captured in the surprise attack on Lien-chiang [district] in Fukien). Taipei: 1964.

Tung, C. 董家遵. *Han-T'ang-shih "ch'i-ch'u" yen-chiu* 漢唐時 [七出] 研究 (Research on the "seven grounds of divorce" in Han and T'ang times). WEN-SHIH HUI-K'AN 文史滙刊 (Journal of literature and history) 1 (March 1, 1935): 285-95.

Tung, C. 董家遵. *Ts'ung Han tao Sung kua-fu tsai-chia hsi-su k'ao* 從漢到宋寡婦再嫁習俗考 (Research on the custom of remarriage of widows from the Han to the Sung dynasties). WEN-SHIH HSÜEH YEN-CHIU-SO YÜEH-K'AN 文史學研究所月刊 (Monthly bulletin of the Research Institute of the Study of Literature and History) 3 (1934): 193-213.

Tung, Ching-chih 董敬之. *T'an ch'ung-hun yü t'ung-chien* 談重婚與通姦 (On bigamy and adultery). FA HSÜEH 法學 No. 4, Peking (1957).

TUNG P'EI 董沛. JU-TUNG P'AN-YÜ 汝東判語. 1883. (Decisions composed in the eastern area of the Ju River).

T'UNG-AN HSIEN-CHIH 同安縣志 (History of T'ung-an district). Chuan-shou ch'ien-yin-pen ed., 1929.

TU, Y. 杜佑. T'UNG-TIEN 通典 (Comprehensive encyclopedia) Kuo-hsüeh chi-pen ts'ung-shu, ed. In the Hsin-hsing shu-chü reprint.

TZ'U HAI 辭海. Shanghai: Chung hua shu chü, 1939.

TZ'U YÜAN 辭源. Shanghai: Shang wu yin shu kuan, 1915.

UCHIDA, T. 內田智雄. CHŪGOKU NŌSON NO BUNKE SEIDO 中國農村の分家制度 (The institution of the division of the household in Chinese rural communities). Tokyo: Iwanami shoten, 1956.

UCHIDA, T. 內田智雄. CHŪGOKU NŌSON NO KAZOKU TO SHINKŌ 中國農村の家族と信仰 (Family and belief in China's rural communities). Tokyo: Kōbundō, 1948.

UNION RESEARCH SERVICE. Vol. 27.

UNITED NATIONS. COMPARATIVE ANALYSIS OF ADOPTION LAWS (st/soa/30), June 27, 1956.

van der Valk, M. CHINA. In LAW IN EASTERN EUROPE, edited by Z. Szirmai, Leiden: Sijthoff, 1961.

VAN DER VALK, M. CONSERVATISM IN MODERN CHINESE FAMILY LAW. Leyden: E. J. Brill, 1956.

VAN DER VALK, M. AN OUTLINE OF MODERN CHINESE FAMILY LAW. Monumenta Serica Monograph, No. 2. Peking: 1939.

van der Valk, M. *The Registration of Marriage in Communist China.* MONUMENTA SERICA. Journal of Oriental Studies 16 (1957): 347 et seq.

Vogel, E. *Voluntarism and Social Control.* In SOVIET AND CHINESE COMMUNISM: SIMILARITIES AND DIFFERENCES, edited by D. Treadgold. Seattle: University of Washington Press, 1967.

VON GRUNEBAUM, G. ed. UNITY AND VARIETY IN MUSLIM CIVILIZATION. Chicago: University of Chicago Press, 1955.

WANG, F. 王符. CH'IEN-FU-LUN 潛夫論 (Discourses by a man in hiding). Ts'ung-shu chi-ch'ing, ed., 1937.

WANG, H. 王先謙 ed. HAN-SHU PU-CHU 漢書補注 (The history of the Han dynasty with supplementary annotations). I-wen yin-shu-kuan ed., n.d.

WANG, H. 王先謙 ed. HOU HAN-SHU CHI-CHIEH 後漢書集解 (The history of the later Han dynasty with collected explications). I-wen yin-shu-kuan ed., n.d.

WANG, HUI 王煇. CH'I-CH'U YI 七出議 (Discussions of the seven conditions for divorcing a wife).

WANG, NAI-TS'UNG 王廼聰. HUN-YIN-FA CHIAI-SHIH WEN-TA 婚姻法解釋問答 (Interpretative questions and answers on the Marriage Law). Wen-hua kung-ying-sh'e (文化供應社), 1951.

WARNER, W.; MEEKER, M.; and ELLS, K. SOCIAL CLASS IN AMERICA. A MANUAL OF PROCEDURE FOR THE MEASUREMENT OF SOCIAL STATUS. Chicago: Science Research Associates, 1949.

WATSON, B. RECORDS OF THE GRAND HISTORIAN, TRANSLATED FROM THE Shih-chi of SSU-MA CHIEN. New York: Columbia University Press, 1961.

WEBER, M. THE RELIGION OF CHINA. Garden City, N.Y.: Free Press of Glencoe, 1964.

Wei Wen-ti 魏文帝. *Tien-lun* 典論 (Discourse on institutes). In CH'ÜAN SHANG-KU SAN-TAI CH'IN-HAN SAN-KUO LIU-CH'AO WEN. CH'ÜAN SAN-KUO WEN 全上古三代秦漢三國六朝文. 全三國文 (Complete [collection of] literature from antiquity, the Three Dynasties, the Ch'in and Han dynasties, the Three Kingdoms, and the Six Dynasties. Complete [collection of] literature from the Three Kingdoms). Shih-chieh shu-chü, ed.

WESTERMARCK, E. A SHORT HISTORY OF MARRIAGE. New York: Macmillan Co., 1926.

WHEELER, G. THE MODERN HISTORY OF SOVIET CENTRAL ASIA. New York: Praeger, 1964.

WILBER, C. K. THE SOVIET MODEL AND UNDER-DEVELOPED COUNTRIES. Chapel Hill, N.C.: University of North Carolina Press, 1969.

WILENSKY, H. and LEBEAUX, C. INDUSTRIAL SOCIETY AND SOCIAL WELFARE; THE IMPACT OF INDUSTRIALIZATION ON THE SUPPLY AND ORGANIZATION OF SOCIAL WELFARE SERVICES IN THE UNITED STATES. New York: Russell Sage Foundation, 1958.

WILHELM, H. GESELLSCHAFT UND STAAT IN CHINA. ACH VORTAGE. Peking: H. Vetch, 1944.

WINNER, T. THE ORAL ART AND LITERATURE OF THE KAZAKHS OF RUSSIAN CENTRAL ASIA. Durham, N.C.: Duke University Press, 1958.

Wirth, L. *Urbanism as a Way of Life.* In CITIES AND SOCIETY, THE REVISED READER *in Urban Sociology.* Edited by P. Hatt and A. Reiss, Jr. Chicago: Free Press of Glencoe, 1957.

Witke, R. *Mao Tse-tung, Women and Suicide in the May Fourth Era.* CHINA QUARTERLY, No. 31 (July–Sept. 1967): 128–147.

Wolfe, A. *Childhood Association, Sexual Attraction and the Incest Taboo.* AMERICAN ANTHROPOLOGIST 68 (Aug. 1966): 883–898.

Woodsworth, K. *Family Law and Resolution of Domestic Disputes in The People's Republic of China.* MCGILL LAW JOURNAL 13 (1967): 169–177.

Wylie, T. *A Standard System of Tibetan Transcription.* HARVARD JOURNAL OF ASIATIC STUDIES 22 (1959): 261–267.

Wyschinski, A. *Uber einige Fragen der Theorie des Staates und des Rechts.* In 36. BEIHEFT ZUR "SOWJETWISSENSCHAFT." East Berlin: Kultur and Fostschritt, 1953, pp. 109–128.

YANG, H. 楊鴻烈. CHUNG-KUO FA-LÜ SZU-HSIANG SHIH 中國法律思想史 (History of Chinese legal philosophy). Reprint. Taipei: Taiwan Shang-wu yin-shu-kuan, 1964.

YANG, C. CHINESE COMMUNIST SOCIETY: THE FAMILY AND THE VILLAGE. Boston: Massachusetts Institute of Technology Press, 1965.

YANG, M. A CHINESE VILLAGE; TAITOU, SHANTUNG PROVINCE. New York: Columbia University Press, 1945.

YANG, S. 楊樹達. HAN-TAI HUN-SANG LI-SU K'AO 漢代婚喪禮俗考 (An examination of the marriage and mourning ritual customs of the Han dynasty). Shanghai: Commercial Press, 1933.

Yang-ch'eng wan-pao 羊城晚報 (Yang-ch'eng evening paper), Apr. 16, 1964.

Yao, C. 姚振宗. *Hou-Han I-wen-chih* 後漢藝文志 (Treatise on literature of the history of the Later Han dynasty). In ERH-SHIH-WU SHIH PU-PIEN 二十五史補編 (Supplements to the Twenty-five Histories) Vol. 2, 1936–37.

YING-KE HSIANG-T'U CHIH 鶯歌鄉土誌 (Local records of the rural area of Ying-ke). Taipei: 1934. [In Japanese]

YOUNG, M. A CHINESE VILLAGE. New York: Columbia University Press 1954.

Yozo, W. and Rheinstein, M. *The Family and the Law: The Individualistic Premise and Modern Japanese Family Law*. In LAW IN JAPAN: THE LEGAL ORDER IN A CHANGING SOCIETY. Edited by A. von Mehren, Cambridge: Harvard University Press, 1963.

YU, F. MASS PERSUASION IN COMMUNIST CHINA. New York: Praeger, 1964.

YÜAN SHIH SHIH FAN 袁氏世範. In Chih-pu-tsu-chai ts'ung-shu (知不足齋叢書) (Teachings of Master Yüan Ts'ai 袁采 about social life).

YUAN SHIH 元史 (History of the Yuan dynasty). Taipei: Kuo-fang yen-chiu yuan, chung-hua ta-tien-pien ho-tso, 1966–1967.

YUAN TIEN CHANG 元典章. (Full title: Ta-yuan sheng-cheng Kuo-ch'ao tien chang 大元聖政國朝典章 [Law and precedents under Yuan dynasty] reprint. Taipei: Wen-hai ch'u-pan, 1964.

Yun-nan jih-pao 雲南日報 (Yunan Daily, K'un-ming), Jan. 25, 1953.

ZAGORIA, D. THE SINO-SOVIET CONFLICT. Princeton, N.J.: Princeton University Press, 1962.

Zelditch, M. Jr. *Cross Cultural Analysis of Family Structure*. In HANDBOOK OF MARRIAGE AND THE FAMILY, edited by H. Christensen. Chicago: Rand McNally, 1964.

ZENKOVSKY, S. PAN-TURKISM AND ISLAM IN RUSSIA. Cambridge: Harvard University Press, 1960.

Zetkin, C. Ausgewählte Reden und Schriften. 3 vol. Berlin: Dietz, 1957–1960.

Zetkin, C. *Erinnerungen an Lenin*. East Berlin: Dietz, 1957.

ZIMMERMAN, C. and FRAMPTON, M. *Theories of Fredric Le Play*. In KINSHIP AND FAMILY ORGANIZATION, edited by Bernard Farber. New York: J. Wiley and Sons, 1966, pp. 14–23.

Glossary

A

Ai-ti 哀帝
Anhwei 安徽
Aoyama 青山
A-shao 阿邵

B

bunchi haitō 分知配當
bunchi haitō no yōshi 分知配當之養子
bushi kaikyū 武士階級

C

cā-bô-kàn 媘媒姆
Ch'ahar 察哈爾
chang 丈
Chang Ao 張敖
Ch'ang-chiang jih-pao 長江日報
Chang Erh 張耳
Chang Fu 張負
Chang Po 張博
Ch'ang-she so pu-yüan 常赦所不原
Chang Shih-chih 張釋之
ch'ang-sun t'ien 長孫田
Chang Szu-yeh chi 張司業集
Chang-ti 章帝
chan-ts'ui 斬衰
Ch'ang-yen 昌言
chang-yu 長幼
chao-chui 招贅
Chao Feng-chieh 趙風嗜
chao-fu 招夫

chao-hsü 招壻
chao-ju ch'ü-ch'u 招入娶出
chao-ku 照顧
Chao-ti 昭帝
chao-t'ing li-hun 詔聽離婚
Che-chiang jih-pao 浙江日報
che-hsiu-ch'ien 遮羞錢
Ch'en An-chieh lun Ch'en An-kuo tao-mai
  t'ien-ti shih 陳安節論陳安國盜賣田地事
Ch'en Ch'eng 陳誠
Cheng 鄭
ch'eng 承
Cheng Ch'eng-kung 鄭成功
ch'eng-chi 承繼
ch'eng-chi-jen 承繼人
Cheng Ch'ung 鄭崇
Cheng Chung 鄭衆
Ch'eng-chung 城中
Cheng-fa yen-chiu 政法研究
ch'eng-fen 成分
Cheng Hsing 鄭興
ch'eng-shou 承受
ch'eng-t'iao 承祧
Ch'eng-yi-po wen-chi 誠意伯文集
Ch'en Ho 陳賀
Ch'en-hou 陳后
Ch'en Hui-hsiang su Kuo Liu-ch'ao san
  shu-t'ien 陳會鄉訴郭六朝散贖田
Ch'en Hsi-tien Shuai Wen-hsien cheng-
  t'ien 陳希點帥文先爭田
Ch'en Hung-mou 陳宏謀
Chen Ku-yüan 陳顧遠
Ch'en P'ing 陳平

Chen P'ing chuan 陳平傳
Ch'en Shao-yü 陳韶禹
Ch'en Sheng 陳省
Chen-shun chuan 貞順傳
Chen-tsung 眞宗
Ch'en Tung-yuan 陳東原
Ch'en Wu 陳午
chi 繼
ch'i 氣
ch'i 氣
ch'i 棄
Ch'i 齊
chia 家
chia 甲
chia-ch'an 家產
chia-ch'an chün-fen 家產均分
chia-chang 家長
chia-ch'eng 家乘
chia-ch'ü 嫁娶
chia-chuang 嫁粧
chia-chuang feng-shang jen-hsin 嫁粧風尚人心
chia-mai tzu 嫁賣字
chia-miao 家廟
Chiang-hsi 江西
Chiang Hsing-ko ch'ung-hui chen-chu-shan 蔣興哥重會珍珠衫
ch'iang-p'o 强廹
Chiang Shih 姜詩
Chiang shih chuan 姜詩傳
Chiang Te 蔣德
Chiang-tu wang 江都王
chiao 醮
Ch'iao Ch'i-ming 喬啓明
chiao-chüeh 醮爵
chiao-kung 交工
chiao nü 醮女
chia-p'u 家譜
chia-ts'ai ti-hsiung fen-cheng chia-ch'an shih 家財弟兄分爭家產事
chi-ch'eng 繼承
Ch'i-ch'ieh ou-li ku-fu fu-mu t'iao 妻妾毆罵故夫父母條
ch'i chih 妻姪
ch'i ch'in 妻親
ch'i-ch'in 期親
chi-chiu p'ien 急就篇
chi-chu 輯註
ch'i-chuo 碛桌
Ch'i-ch'u yi 七出議
ch'ieh 妾

Chieh-ti 桀帝
chien 柬
ch'ien 遣
chien-cheng 諫錚
Ch'ien-fu lun 潛夫論
Chien-lin ch'ü so chien-lin nü t'iao 監臨娶所監臨女條
Ch'ien Ta-hsin 錢大昕
chien-t'iao 兼祧
chien-t'iao-jen 兼祧人
Ch'ien-yen-t'ang wen-chi 潛研堂文集
Chi-fu t'ung-chih 畿輔通志
chigyō 知行
ch'ih 斥
chih fu wei hun 指腹爲婚
Ch'ih-hsi hsien-chih 赤溪縣志
chih-p'ai 支派
chih-yüan 至元
Chikusa Tatsuo 千種達雄
Chi-mu chiang yang-lao-t'ien i-chu yü ch'in-sheng-nü 繼母將養老田遺囑與親生女
Chin 金
ch'in 寢
ch'in 香
Ch'in 秦
Ch'in Chia 秦嘉
Ch'in-chou chih 欽州志
ching 景
ch'ing-ch'i 請期
Ching Fang 京房
Ch'ing hsien-hsing-lü 清現行律
Ch'ing-kang hsien 青岡縣
Ch'ing-lü chi-chieh 清律集解
Ch'ing-lü chi-chu 清律輯註
Ch'ing lü-li 清律例
Ch'ing-lü pen-chu 清律本注
Ch'ing-ming-chi 清明集
Ch'ing-ming-chieh 清明節
Ch'ing-p'ing-shan-t'ang hua-pen 清平山堂話本
Ching-ti 景帝
Ch'ing-yüan t'iao 慶元條
Ch'ing-yüan t'iao-fa shih-lei 慶元條法事類
Chin Kuan-yen 金廣延
Chin-ku ch'i-kuan 今古奇觀
Chin-ling hsüeh-pao 金陵學報
Chin-lü 金律
Chin Shang 金賞
Ch'in Shih-huang-ti 秦始皇帝

Chin Shu 晉書
ch'in-shu 親屬
Ch'in-ting ta-Ch'ing hui-tien shih-li 欽定
　大清會典事例
ch'in-ying 親迎
Ch'i-shan 旗山
Ch'i-shih-erh ti-tzu chieh 七十二弟子解
Chi-t'ai-hou 紀太后
Chi Tso-ch'a teng ch'eng-tz'u p'an 季作
　乂等呈詞判
Ch'i-tung yeh-yü 齊東野語
chi-tzu 繼子
ch'i wai-sheng 妻外甥
Ch'i wu ch'i-ch'u t'iao 妻無七出條
Ch'i yi fu-chia p'in erh p'i-li 妻以夫家貧
　而仳離
cho-chi 酌給
Chou Chia-ch'ing 周家清
Chou Chia-ts'ing 周家清
ch'ou ch'ien 抽籤
ch'ou ch'ou 仇讎
Chou -li 周禮
Chou-li Cheng Ssu-nung chieh-chu 周禮
　鄭司農解注
Chou-ti 紂帝
Cho Wen-chün 卓文君
Chow Mi 周密
ch'ü 區
ch'u 出
ch'ü 去
chu 逐
chüan-chü 捐據
Chuang-kung 莊公
chuang-lien 粧奩
Ch'üan-T'ang-wen 全唐文
Chü-chiang hsien-chih 曲江縣志
Ch'u-ch'i chih tzu wei mu su 出妻之子為
　母疏
Chu chih lun-so i-chu-ch'ien 諸姪論索遺
　囑錢
Ch'u ch'in-shu ch'i-ch'ieh t'iao 娶親屬妻
　妾條
Ch'ü ch'i pu ch'ü t'ung-hsing 娶妻不娶
　同姓
Ch'u ch'i t'iao 出妻條
chüeh-mai ch'i 絕賣契
chüeh-wei 爵位
ch'u-fan 觸犯
ch'u-fu 出婦
Chu-fu Yen 主父偃
chu-hun-jen 主婚人

Ch'ü-li 曲禮
Chu Mai-ch'en 朱買臣
Ch'un-ch'iu 春秋
Ch'ün-chung jih-pao 群衆日報
chung chang-sun 衆張孫
Chung-ch'ang T'ung 仲長統
chung-chih 終止
Chung Chin 鍾瑾
Chung-hua ta tz'u-tien 中華大辭典
chung-jen 中人
Chungking 重慶
Chungking Ta-kung-pao 重慶大公報
Chung-kuo ching-chi nien-ch'ien 中國經
　濟年鑑
Chung-kuo ch'ing-nien 中國青年
Chung-kuo fu nü 中國婦女
Chung-kuo hsin-wen 中國新聞
Chung-shan-wang 中山王
chung-tzu 衆子
Chung-wen ta tz'u-tien 中文大辭典
chung-yüan-chieh 中元節
Ch'ün-hsiung chieh-sha shih 群兇劫殺事
Chu Po 朱博
Ch'ü-sang chia-ch'ü t'iao fu-li 居喪嫁娶
　條附例
Chu-se fan chien 諸色犯姦
Ch'ü t'ao-wang fu-nü t'iao 娶逃亡婦女條

D

Dai kan-wa jiten 大漢和辭典
dai kazoku 大家族
dōzoku 同族

E

Erh-tsui chü-fa yi chung lun t'iao 二罪俱
　發以重論條
erh-yüeh hsi 二月戲

F

fa-ch'ien 發遣
Fa-hsüeh 法學
fa-li 法理
Fa-lü ta tz'u-shu 法律大辭書
Fan 范
fang 房
fang 放
Fang Hsüan-ling 房玄齡
Fan-liu ying-p'ei t'iao 犯流應配條
Fan Yeh 范曄

Fa-shih lei 法事類
fên-chia 分家
fen-chia-tan 分家單
Feng shun 馮順
Feng-t'ien 奉天
Feng Yen 馮衍
Feng Yen chuan 馮衍傳
fen-hsing t'ung-ch'i 分形同氣
Fen-k'ao 分考
Fu 傅
fu ch'ien-chai tzu tang huan, tzu ch'ien-chai fu pu chih 父欠債子當還, 子欠債父不知
fu-chih ling 服制令
fu-ch'i i-t'i 夫妻一體
Fu-fu ti-erh 夫婦第二
fūfu yōshi 夫婦養子
Fukien 福建
Fukien jih-pao 福建日報
Fukien t'ung-chih 福建通志
fuku-gō-kei no ka 複合型の家
Fukushima Masao 福島正男
fu-mai tzu-tuan 父賣子斷
fu-ma tu-we, 駙馬都尉
fu-nü-hui 婦女會
Fu-nü lien-ho hui 婦女聯合會
fusai-ittai 夫妻一體
fushi ittai 夫子一體
Fu tai hui pang-chu ch'ün-chung yi feng-su 婦代會幫助群衆移風俗
Fu Ting-i 符定一
futsū hō 普通法
fu-tzu i-t'i 父子一體
Fu wang 夫亡

G

gōyū 合有

H

Hai-ch'eng hsien 海城縣
haike 廢家
Hailar 海拉爾
Han 漢
han-hsi 漢席
Han Kuang 韓光
Han-shih wai-chuan 韓詩外傳
Han-shu 漢書
Han-tan 邯鄲
hao-shih huai-shih 好事壞事
Harbin 哈爾賓

Hatano Kenichi 波多野乾一
Hayakawa Tamotsu 早川保
Hayashi E. 林惠海
Heh-lung-chiang 黑龍江
Higashigawa 東川
Miyazaki Hiroshi 宮崎弘
Ho-ch'ü jen-ch'i t'iao 和娶人妻條
Ho Kuang 霍光
ho-li 和離
Ho-nan 河南
honke 本家
Ho-pei 河北
Ho-pei jih-pao 河北日報
Ho-ti 和帝
hou 後
Hou-Chou 後周
Hou-chou chih 後周敕
Hou-Han-shu 後漢書
Hou Kung-pu 侯工部
hsia-fang 下方
hsia-hu 下戶
hsiang-fu-tzu 降服子
Hsiang-kung 襄公
hsiao 孝
Hsiao Kung-ch'üan 蕭公權
Hsiao-shun fu-mu 孝順父母
hsiao-t'ai-t'ai 小太太
hsiao tsung 小宗
Hsiao-yu lieh-chuan 孝友烈傳
hsia-ting 下定
Hsieh Hsüan 薛宣
Hsien-hsing fa huei-chi 現行法彙集
Hsien p'an hei yüan-shih 憲判黑冤事
Hsien-ti 獻帝
Hsien-wang 憲王
hsing 刑
Hsing-fa chih 刑法志
Hsin-min wan-pao 新民晚報
Hsin-wen jih-pao 新聞日報
hsiu 休
hsiu-ch'i 休妻
hsiu-ch'i 休棄
Hsiu-ch'i li-yi mai-hsiu-ch'i 休棄離異買休妻
hsiu-shu 休書
hsü 須
Hsüan-ti 宣帝
Hsüan-tung 宣統
Hsü Chia 許嘉
Hsü Ching 許敬
Hsü-hou 許后

Hsü Kuang-han 許廣漢
Hsü sheng 許升
Hsü Yen 徐彥
Hsü Yen-shou 許延壽
Hsün Shu 荀淑
Hsün Shuang 荀爽
Hsün-su i-kuei 訓俗遺規
Hsün Ts'ai 荀采
Hsün tzu-sun wen 訓子孫文
hu 戶
hua-chiao 花轎
Huai-nan-tzu 淮南子
Huai-yang 淮陽
Huan-chia t'an-mien yi-shang ch'in t'iao 皇家袒免以上親條
Huan-ch'ing ching-chieh 皇清經解
Huang Ching-chia 黃靜嘉
Huang-fu Kuei 皇甫規
Huang Kan 黃幹
Huang Pa 黃霸
Huang Shan-ku wen-chi 黃山谷文集
Huang-t'ai-tzu fei t'iao 皇太子妃條
Huang Yün 黃允
Huan K'uan 桓寬
Huan-ti 桓帝
hu-chang 戶長
hu-chi 戶籍
Hu-hun 戶婚
Hu-hun-lü 戶婚律
Hu-hun men 戶婚門
Hu-ling 戶令
hui 會
hui-hsiang 回鄉
hui-kee (huo-chi) 夥計
Hui-ti 惠帝
Hui Tung 惠棟
hu-lü 戶律
Hun-chia chieh wei-fa t'iao 婚嫁皆違法條
hung-ch'u-ch'ü 閧出去
Hung Kua 洪适
hung-pao 紅包
Hun-li 婚禮
hun-shu 婚書
Hun-yi 昏義
Hun-yin-fa chiai-shih wen-ta 婚姻法解釋問答
Hun-yin-fa chiang-hua 婚姻法講話
Hun-yin fa chi ch'i yu-kuan wen-chien 婚姻法及其有關文件
Hun-yin-fa chi-pen chih-shih 婚姻法基本知識

Hun-yin wen-t'i ts'an-k'ao tzu-liao hui-pien 婚姻問題參考資料彙編
Hun-yin yü chia-tsu 婚姻與家族
Hu-pei 湖北
Hu-pu 戶部
Hu Wen-k'ai 胡文楷
Hu-yi 戶役

I

i 揖
i 儀
i-ch'i 一氣
i-chih liang-pu chüeh 一支兩不絕
i-chih san-pu chüeh 一支三不絕
i-chü 異居
i-chu 遺囑
ie 家
ie o sōzoku-suru 家を相續する
ie o tsugu 家を繼ぐ
ie o yuzuru 家を讓る
i-k'ou tai-pi-jen 依口代筆人
I-li 儀禮
I-li chiu-shu 儀禮舊書
inkyo 隱居
iseki 遺跡
iseki sōzoku no yōshi 遺跡相續の養子
i-tzu 義子
Iwanami shoten 岩波書店

J

jen-ho 人和
jen-k'ou 人口
Jen-min jih-pao 人民日報
jen-min kung-she 人民公社
Jen Pao 任寶
Jen Wu-ta 任武達
Jen Yen 任延
Jinji kishū 人事奇習
Jinruigakkai zasshi 人類學會雜誌
Juan Yüan 阮元
jun'yōshi 順養子
ju-p'u-yin 入僕銀；乳哺銀
Ju Tun 汝敦
Ju tung p'an-yü 汝東判語

K

kachō 家長
kai-chang 蓋章
kai-chia tzu 改嫁字

Kaiping 蓋平
Kajo jō 嫁女條
Kajo kisai jō 嫁女棄妻條
kamei sōzoku 家名相續
kamyo 家廟
kan-ch'u-ch'ü 趕出去
Kandai ni okeru kazoku no ōkisa 漢代に
　おける家族の大まさ
Kansu 甘肅
Kantō-chō no hōtei ni arawaretru shina
　no minji kanshū ihō 關東廳の法廷に現
　れたる支那の民事慣習彙報
Kaohsiung 高雄
Kaohsiung Hsien 高雄縣
Kao-tsu 高祖
kasan bunkatsu 家產分割
kaso 家祖
katoku sōzoku 家督相續
katoku sozōku no yōshi 家督相續の養子
kazoku kyōsan sei 家族共產制
Kazoku mondai to kazokuhō 家族問題と
　家族法
k'e-hsiung 客兄
keifu 系譜
keihō 刑法
Keiji oyobi shokanbun ruishū 刑事及び
　諸官文類集
Keishi-ryō 繼嗣令
Keishi sōzoku-hō 繼嗣相續法
kei zaisan sōzoku-hō 繼財產相續法
Kiangsi 江西
Kiangsu 江蘇
Kirin 吉林
Kokon-ryō 戶婚令
kōminka-undō 皇民化運動
k'o-nü 客女
Koryō 戶令
Kou Pin 苟賓
Ku-chin chu 古今注
Ku-chin hsiao-shuo 古今小說
Ku-chin t'u-shu chi-ch'eng 古今圖書集成
kua-hang 掛領
K'uai-chi 會稽
K'uai-chi tien-lu 會稽典錄
K'uai-tsui Li Ts'ui-lien chi 快嘴李翠蓮記
K'uai T'ung 蒯通
K'uai-t'ung chuan 蒯通傳
Kuan-cheng 官政
Kuan-hsien hsien-chih 冠縣縣志
kuan-nei hou 關內侯
Kuan-tung-t'ing 關東廳

kuan-yüan hsi-yin 官員襲廕
Kuang-ming jih-pao 光明日報
Kuang-te 廣德
Kuang-wu-ti 光武帝
ku-chiu-chih 姑舅姪
Kuei-chieh 鬼節
kuei-tzu 櫃子
Ku Huai-san 顧檁三
kung-ch'in 公親
Kung-fan-tsui tsao-yi wei shou t'iao 共犯
　罪造意爲首條
Kung-jen jih-pao 工人日報
kung-k'ai 公開
K'ung Kuang 孔光
Kung-ming jih-pao 公明日報
kung-she kuan-li wei-yüan-hui 公社管理
　委員會
Kung-sun Tsan 公孫瓚
kung-ts'ai 共財
kung-t'ung sheng-huo 共同生活
K'ung-tzu chia-yü 孔子家語
Kung-yang chuan 公羊傳
Kung-yang chuan, Ho Hsiu chu 公羊傳,
　何休注
kung-yu 共有
K'un-ming 昆明
kuo-chi 過繼
kuo-chi tan 過繼單
kuo-fang-tzu 過房子
kuo-tzu-tan 過子單
Kuo wei 郭衛
kuo-yü 國語
Kuwahara J. 桑原隲藏
Ku-wen-yüan 古文宛
Ku-yung 谷永
kyōsan 共產
kyōyū 共有
kyōzai 共財
Kyūkan mondō 舊慣問答

L

Lan-hsi hsien 蘭西縣
li 禮
li 里
li 離
li huo li-chih 離或離之
Liang 梁
Liang chi 梁冀
Liang-huang-wang 梁荒王
Liang Hung 梁鴻
liang i chih 兩姨姪

Liang Shu-yü 梁叔魚
li-chang 里長
Li Ch'ang-ling 李昌齡
Li-chi K'ung-su 禮記孔疏
Li-ching wen-ta 禮經問答
Li Chuang fu-jen 黎莊夫人
Li Ch'ung 李充
Li Ch'ung chuan 李充傳
Lieh-nü chuan 烈女傳
Lien-chiang 連江
lien-chü 奩具
Lien-t'ien t'ing fu-chia wei-chu 奩田聽夫
　家為主
li-fu 離婦
li-hui 立會
li-hui-jen 立會人
li-hun 離婚
li-i 離異
Li-kang 里港
Li Ku 李固
Li-lei 離類
lin 鄰
Lin 林
lin-chang 鄰長
ling 令
ling-kuo 另過
Ling-ti 靈帝
li-ping 禮餅
li-ping shih shen-ma hsien 禮餅是什
　麼餡
Li-pu 禮部
Li-shih 隸釋
Li ti-tzu wei-fa t'iao fu-li 立嫡子違法條
　附例
Li Tzu-ch'in 李子勤
Li Tz'u-ming 李慈銘
Liu 劉
Liu Ch'ang (pao) 劉昌 (寶)
Liu Chi 劉基
Liu Ch'i 劉琦
Liu Chien 劉建
Liu Chih-yüan 劉智遠
Liu Chün-liang 劉君良
Liu Hsiang 劉向
Liu Hsing 劉興
Liu Hsün 劉勳
Liu K'uan 劉寬
Liu Li 劉立
liu-li 六禮
Liu Piao 劉表
Liu Shan-li 劉柀藜

Liu-Sung 劉宋
Liu Ting-kuo 劉定國
Liu Tsung 劉宗
Liu Tz'u-ch'ang 劉次昌
Liu Yen 劉延
Liu Yün 劉雲
Liu-yü yen-i 六諭衍義
Li-wang 立王
Li-wang 厲王
Li Ying 李膺
li-yüan 離緣
Lo Kung 羅貢
Lo Ping nü shih Lai-an su chu-mu to-
　ch'ü so po t'ien ch'an 羅柄女使來安訴
　主母奪去所撥田產
Lo-shan-lu 樂善錄
Lou Ching-p'ei 婁景斐
lü 律
luan hun-yin chih li 亂婚姻之禮
luan-ming 亂命
Lueh-mai ch'i-ch'in pei-yu t'iao 略賣期親
　卑幼條
Lü-hou 呂后
Lü Jung 呂榮
Lukang 鹿港
lü-ling 律令
Lung-tu 龍肚
Lung-yü ho-t'u 龍魚河圖
Lun-heng 論衡
Lü P'ing 呂平
Lu Yü ch'i 陸予奇

M

Ma-hou 馬后
Makino Tatsumi 牧野巽
Manchoukuo 滿洲國
Mantetsu chosa shiryō 滿鐵調查資料
Mao-ming hsien-chih 茂名縣志
Ma Yüan 馬援
Ma Yung 馬融
mei-jen 媒人
Meiji 明治
Mei-nung 美濃
meiseki sōzoku no yōshi 名跡相續の養子
mei-shih 媒氏
Meng-ch'i pi-t'an 夢溪筆談
miao 廟
min-cheng chu-li 民政助理
min-cheng-k'e 民政課
Ming 明
ming-hun 冥婚

Ming-li 名例
Ming-ling 明令
ming-ling-tzu 螟蛉子
Ming-lü 明律
Ming-ti 明帝
Mokumō jō 目盲條
Morohashi Tetsuji 諸橋轍次
mou 畝
mu-chu 木主
muko iseki 壻遺跡
muko yōshi 壻養子
Mu-tzu 牧子

N

na-cheng 納徵
na-chi 納吉
Nakata Kaoru 中田薫
Nan-fang jih-pao 南方日報
Nan-nü ko-tzu ti t'ien-ti, ts'ai-ch'an, chai-wu ko-tzu ch'u-li 男女各自的田地，財產，債務各自處理
Nan shih 南史
Nan-Sung 南宋
Nan-tzu 楠梓
na-ts'ai 納采
nei-ch'in 內親
nei-nan wai-nü 內男外女
Nei-tse su 內則疏
nien-keng 年庚
nien-t'ou 年頭
Niida Noboru 仁井田陞
Ninghsia 寧夏
Nü-chi 女記
Nü-chieh 女誡
Nü ho ch'eng-fen 女合承分
nü-hsü 女壻
nu-pei 奴婢

O

ōbunjō 應分條
Ou-hou 歐侯
Ōyama H. 大山彦一

P

pai 拜
P'ai-an ching-ch'i 拍案驚奇
Pai chü-yi (Po chü-i) 白居易
Pai-hu-t'ung 白虎通
pai-pai 拜拜
pai-t'ang 拜堂

Pai-t'u-chi 白兔記
Pan chao 班昭
p'an-chieh-fa 判解法
pan-fa 辦法
pang-mang 幫忙
P'ang T'un-chih 龐敦志
pan-lü 伴侶
p'an t'ou t'ieh 盤頭帖
p'an-yü 判語
pao 胞
pao-chang 保長
pao-chia 保甲
Pao Hsüan 鮑宣
pao-pan 包辦
Pao Yung 鮑永
Pao Yung chuan 鮑永傳
pa-tzu 八字
Pei-ching kung-jen jih-pao 北京工人日報
pei-fen 輩分
P'ei-wen yün-fu 佩文韻府
pen-chi 本籍
Pen-ming 本命
Pen-ming-chieh 本命解
piao 表
piao-chih 表姪
piao-hsiung-ti tzu-mei 表兄弟姊妹
pieh k'ai sheng-mien ti hun-li 別開生面的婚禮
Pien-ching 汴京
Pien-kuan 編管
pi-mi chieh-hun hsiao-yi 秘密結婚小儀
p'in 聘
p'in-chin 聘金
p'in-li 聘禮
P'ing-ti 平帝
p'in-ts'ai 聘財
p'i-p'a-chi 琵琶記
Pi-shu 逼書
p'o-ch'u chiu hsi-su ch'uang-li hsin feng-shang 破除舊習俗創立新風尚
Po chü-i 白居易
po-fu 伯父
Po-hsing hsien-chih 博興縣志
Po-hu t'ung-i 白虎通義
po-kung 伯公
Po-kung hui 伯公會
po-mu 伯母
P'u-chou chih 濮州志
pu-ch'ü 部曲
pu-fu 補服
p'u-fu 僕婦

R

Rikonsho no tegata 離婚書の手形
Ryōshūge 令集解

S

San-fu chüeh-lu 三輔決錄
San-kuo-chih 三國志
sang-fu 喪服
San-nien shan-tzu 三年上字
san-pu-ch'u 三不出
San-ts'ung 三從
sehō seroku 世俸世祿
senyū jō 先由條
Shang-fang Chin 尚方禁
Shanghai chieh-fang jih-pao 上海解放日報
Shang-kuan An 上官安
Shang-kuan-hou 上官后
Shang-wen 上汶
shan-liang feng-su 善良風俗
Shansi 山西
Shantung 山東
Shan-yin 山陰
shen 神
Shen Ch'in-han 沈欽韓
shen-fen 身分
sheng-fu 盛服
Sheng-t'ing-hui 聖亭會
Shen K'uo 沈括
shen-niang 嬸娘
Shensi 陝西
Shen-tsung 神宗
Shen-yang 瀋陽
Shichishutsujō 七出條
Shiga Shūzō 滋賀秀三
shigo yōshi 死後養子
Shih 施
Shih-chi 史記
Shih-ching 詩經
Shih Huai-pi 史懷璧
Shih Liang 史良
shih pu ying-kai ti 是不應該的
Shih Tan 史丹
Shina kinsei no gikyoku shōsetsu ni mietaru shiho 支那近世の戲曲小說に見えたる私法
shishi 嗣子
shō 庄
shōgorō-shu 蕉梧樓主
Shōwa 昭和
Shuang-ch'eng 雙城
Shuang-yüan 雙園

shu-fu 叔父
shu-hui kai-chia tzu 贖回改嫁字
Shui-hu chuan 水滸傳
shu-jen 庶人
Shūkanroku 習慣錄
Shu-kuan pei-feng 書館悲逢
Shu-lin 樹林
Shun-ti 順帝
Shuo-lin 說林
shu-shen-tzu 贖身字
shu-shu 叔叔
shu-sun 庶孫
shu-tzu 庶子
Si-an 西安
Sōbunsha 創文社
Sōdai no kasanhō ni okeru joshi no chii 宋代の家產法における女子の地位
Soochow 蘇州
sōshu-teki kyōyū 總手的共有
ssu 嗣
ssu 寺
ssu-chih 私志
ssu-fu 嗣父
Ssu-ma ch'ien 司馬遷
Ssu-ma Hsiang-ju 司馬相如
ssu-tzu 嗣子
sui ch'e 隨車
sui mu chia chih tzu t'u-mou ch'in-tzu chih yeh 隨母嫁之子圖謀親子之業
sui-shih fu-la 歲時伏臘
Sung 宋
sung han-i 送寒衣
Sung-hou 宋后
Sung hsing-t'ung 宋刑統
Sung Hung 宋弘
Sungshan 松山
sung-ting 送定
szu-ma 總麻
szu-tzu 嗣子

T

ta-chiao 大轎
Ta-Ch'ing Hui-tien 大清會典
Ta-Ch'ing hui-tien shih-li 大清會典事例
Ta-Ch'ing lü-li 大清律例
Ta-Ch'ing min-lü ts'ao-an 大清民律草案
Ta-Ch'ing t'ung-li 大清通禮
Ta-chung-hsiang-fu 大中祥符
Taichung 台中
Taika 大化
Tai Liang 戴良

Tainan 台南

Taipei wen-hsien 台北文獻

tai-pi-jen 代筆人

T'ai-p'ing yü-lan 太平御覽

Taishō 大正

Tai-wang 戴王

Taiwan sheng pao-hu yang-nü hui 台灣省
保護養女會

Taiwan sheng ti yang-nü wen-t'i 台灣省
的養女問題

Taiwan wen-hsien 台灣文獻

Takikawa Kametaro 瀧川龜太郎

Ta-li-yüan 大理院

Ta-li-yüan p'an-chüeh-li ch'üan-shu 大理
院判決例全書

tan 單

T'ang 唐

t'ang 堂

tang-chia 當家

t'ang hsiung-ti chieh-mei 堂兄弟姐妹

T'ang hu-ling 唐戶令

T'ang-shan 唐山

ta-niang 大娘

tan-kuo 單過

T'an Nien-ts'ao 譚念草

Tan-shui 淡水

t'an-t'ing 探聽

T'an yu-chi 譚友吉

T'ao Hsi-sheng 陶希聖

tao-mai 盜賣

tao-mai 盜買

Ta-Tai-li 大戴禮

Ta-Tai Li-chi 大戴禮記

T'a tso te wan-ch'üan ho-ch'ing ho-li
他做得完全合情合理

ta-tsung 大宗

ta-tui 大隊

te 德

Te-an hsien 德安縣

Teng Hsiang 鄧香

t'en-shou (Hakka) 膽手

t'iao 條

t'iao-ling 條令

ti-chang-ts'eng-sun 嫡長曾孫

ti-chang-tzu 嫡長子

ti chang-tzu hsiung-ti 嫡長子兄弟

ti-ch'u chang-sun 嫡出長孫

T'ien 田

T'ien Fen 田蚡

t'ien-ho 天和

Tien-hsüeh hui 塾學會

Tien-lun 典論

t'i-hun 締婚

ting 定

t'ing 廳

ting-hun 訂婚

ting-p'in 定聘

Tōkei teki ni mita Nisshi kazoku hōsei
ho hikaku 統計的に見た日支家族構成の
比較

Tokugawa 德川

Tōrei shūi 唐令拾遺

Tōryō shūi 唐令拾遺

tōshu 當主

Tou 竇

Tou Mu 竇穆

Tou-sung 鬥訟

Tou-sung lü 鬥訟律

t'ou-tui 頭對

Tou Yüan 竇元

tsa-chi 雜記

Tsa-chu tsa-lun 雜著雜論

Tsa-lei 雜類

tsai-ts'ung-i 再從姨

Ts'ai yung 蔡邕

Tsa-men 雜門

Tsang Erh 臧兒

Ts'ang hsien-chih 滄縣志

Ts'ao Chih 曹植

Ts'ao Feng-sheng 曹豐生

Ts'ao Pao 曹褒

Ts'ao Ts'ao 曹操

tse-li 則例

Tseng Ts'an 曾參

Tse-tao lü 賊盜律

Tsitsihar 齊齊哈爾

Tso-chuan 左傳

tso-k'e 做客

Tso-ying 左營

tsu 族

tsu chang 族長

tsu-ch'i 族戚

Ts'ui Pao 崔豹

Tsu-kuo 祖國

Tsuma no sofubo o naguru jō 毆妻祖父
母條

tsung 宗

tsung-ch'in 宗親

tsung-fa 宗法

tsung-p'u 宗譜

tsung-t'iao 宗祧

tsung-tsu 宗族

tsung-tzu 宗子
tsu ni 祖禰
tsun-pei 尊輩
tsu-shu 族叔
tsu-ti 族弟
tsu-t'ien 族田
Tuan-yü 斷獄
tu-hsing 獨行
T'u-liu-jen yu fan-tsui t'iao 徒流人又犯
   罪條
t'ung 銅
T'ung-an hsien-chih 同安縣志
t'ung-ch'i 同氣
Tung Chia-tsun 董家遵
Tung Cho 董卓
t'ung-chü 同居
Tung Chung-shu 董仲舒
Tung-fang Shuo 東方朔
Tung-hsien pi-lu 東軒筆錄
t'ung hsin 同心
t'ung-hsing 同姓
t'ung-hsing-hui 同姓會
t'ung-hsing pu-hun 同姓不婚
Tung-kuan Han-chi 東官漢記
Tung P'ei 董沛
t'ung-shan-t'ang 同善堂
T'ung-tien 通典
t'ung-tsu 同族
t'ung-tsung 同宗
t'ung yang-hsi 童養媳
Tung Yen 董偃
Tun-huang 敦煌
Tu Yu 杜佑
tz'u-ch'an 祠產
Tzu-chih hsin-shu 資治新書
Tzu-chi tsou tao p'o-chia ch'ü 自己走到
   婆家去
Tz'u Hai 辭海
tz'u-t'ang 祠堂
Tz'u Yüan 辭源

U

Uchida T. 內田智雄

W

wai-ch'in 外親
wai-sheng 外甥
Wang 王
Wang Chi 王吉
Wang Chi chuan 王吉傳

Wang Chin 王禁
Wang Chün 王俊
Wang Ch'ung 王沖
Wang Ch'ung 王充
Wang Chung-wen kung chi 王忠文公集
Wang Chung-wu 王仲武
Wang Fu 王符
Wang Hsien 王咸
Wang Hsien-ch'ien 王先謙
Wang Hui 王褘
Wang Keng-te 王更得
Wang Mang 王莽
Wang Nai-ts'ung 王廼聰
Wang Sung 王宋
Wang Tsun 王尊
wang-yeh-miao 王爺廟
Wang Yen 王琰
Wan-hua 萬華
Wei 魏
Wei-cheng chiu-yao 爲政九要
Wei Ch'ing 衞青
Wei Huan-hua 魏煥華
Wei-lü wei hun-li cheng-t'iao 違律爲婚離
   正條
Wei-nan wen-chi 渭南文集
wei-p'ai 位牌
Wei Shu-tzu jih-lu 魏叔子日錄
Wei Tzu-hao 衞子豪
Wei Wen-ti 魏文帝
wen-ming 問名
Wen-shih hui-k'an 文史滙刊
wen-ta 問答
Wu-ching i-i su-cheng 五經異議疏證
wu-ssu 無嗣
Wu-tai 五代
Wu-ti 武帝
Wu-ti pen-chi 武帝本紀
wu-tzu 無子

Y

Yang Ch'iao 楊喬
yang-ch'in 養親
Yang Hung-lieh 楊鴻烈
yang-lao 養老
yang-lao-ti 養老地
yang-lao-t'ien 養老田
yang-nü 養女
yang-shan 養贍
Yang shu-ta 楊樹達
yang-tzu 養子
Yao 姚

Yao Chen-tsung 姚振宗
yao-t'iao 窈窕
Yeh Szu 葉四
yeh wei-fen erh ssu li-ch'i tao-mai 業未分而私立契盜賣
Yen 燕
yen 雁
yen-chi 延吉
Yen K'o-chün 嚴可均
Yen Shih-ku 顏師古
Yen-t'ieh-lun 鹽鐵論
Yen-wang 燕王
yi ch'eng-hun erh fu li-hsiang pien-kuan che t'ing-li 已成婚而夫離鄉編管者聽離
Yi-chüeh 義絕
Yi-chüeh li-chih 義絕離之
Yi-chüeh li-chi t'iao 義絕離之條
yi-hsiang 移鄉
Ying-fen t'iao 應分條
Ying Shun 應順
yin-yüeh ti-san 音樂第三
yi-t'ai-t'ai 姨太太
yi-tui-yin 一對銀

Yōrōryō 養老令
yōshi 養子
Yüan 元
yüan-ch'eng 元城
Yüan-ch'ü hsüan 元典選
Yüan-feng 元豐
Yüan hsing-fa chih 元刑法志
Yüan Hung 袁弘
Yüan-tien-chang 元典章
Yüan Ts'ai 袁采
yüan-tzu 院子
Yüan Wei 袁隗
yüeh-fu 樂府
Yü li-tzu 郁離子
Yung-cheng 雍正
Yünnan 雲南
Yün-nan jih-pao 雲南日報
Yu-ssu chüeh-ch'iu teng-ti 有司决囚等第

Z

zekke 絶家

Index

Contributors

DAVID C. BUXBAUM, formerly Professor, School of Law, University of Washington, Seattle, is presently in private practice in New York City

TATSUO CHIKUSA is retired from Seikei University, Tokyo, where he was Professor of Law

MYRON L. COHEN is Professor of Anthropology, Columbia University, New York

JACK DULL is Director of the East and Inner Asia Language and Area Center, Institute for Comparative and Foreign Area Studies, University of Washington, Seattle

MARC GALANTER is Professor of Law at the State University of New York at Buffalo, and serves as editor of the *Law and Society Review*

BERNARD GALLIN is Professor of Anthropology, Michigan State University, East Lansing

MELVYN C. GOLDSTEIN is Associate Professor of Anthropology, Case Western Reserve University, Cleveland, Ohio

DANIEL S. LEV is Professor of Political Science, University of Washington, Seattle

HAROLD LEVY is Assistant Professor of Political Science at the University of Maryland, Baltimore

GREGORY J. MASSELL is Professor of Political Science, Hunter College, New York

MARINUS J. MEIJER, who served for many years in Asia with the Netherlands diplomatic corps, is a member of the Ministry of Foreign Affairs at The Hague

W. MÜLLER-FREIENFELS is Director, Institut für ausländisches und internationales Privatrecht, University of Freiburg

WILLIAM L. PARISH is Professor of Sociology, University of Chicago

SHŪZŌ SHIGA is Professor of Law, University of Tokyo

TAI YEN-HUI is Professor of Law, National Taiwan University, Taipei, and President, Judicial Yuan, Taiwan